TABLE OF
CONTENTS

UNIT 1

READING FOR
STRUCTURE
THEME *The Brain: Memory, Learning, and Substance Use*

Garry Gay/Getty Images

CHAPTER 4: UNDERSTANDING IMPLIED MAIN IDEAS   244
THEME: Group Behavior

UNIT 3

READING FOR
STUDY
THEME *Education and Responsibility*

Dan Tero/iStockphoto.com

UNIT 4

READING FOR
CRITICALLY
THEME *Crime, Medicine, and Ethics*

Purestock/Alamy

PREFACE

Mindscapes's metacognitive approach helps students bridge the distance between reading and understanding. With *Mindscapes* as their guide, students become active, mindful readers and develop practical study skills that help them to improve their performance in all of their college courses.

WHAT ARE MINDSCAPES?

In this text, "mindscapes" are mindful thinking processes and strategies that students learn to apply when they approach new reading material.

Reading for comprehension requires thinking, yet many college students don't know how to read and think purposefully when approaching new material. To help students develop purposeful college reading strategies, reading study skills, vocabulary skills, and strategies for interpreting graphics are integrated into each chapter in a way that relates to the topic being discussed.

Students who are unfamiliar with the mental landscape necessary for success in reading critically for college report a number of frustrations: **an inability to focus or remember, an uncertainty about what's important, and a lack of knowledge about how to study efficiently.**

> ### LEARNING READING SKILLS IN WAY THAT THE BRAIN LEARNS BEST . . .
> #### addresses students' inability to focus or remember.

Mindscapes helps students use skills and strategies to process information the way their brains can best absorb and memorize it.

- **Learning and memory process.** Information about how we learn permeates the text, in both the instruction and the readings selected, and informs the selection and ordering of specific skills and strategies. Chapter 1 explains how the brain remembers and processes memories to help students understand. Once students know how their brain learns information, they can use this knowledge to their advantage across the college curricula, applying effective reading strategies to any reading and learning situation. Unit 1's theme for readings is "The Brain: Memory, Learning, and Substance Use." Students learn how the brain processes information and how they can work in harmony with the brain's natural tendencies to learn more effectively.

- **REVISED! Thematic readings build prior knowledge and help students make connections.** As students build knowledge on a topic, they become more comfortable and are able to focus more on the reading skills they are trying to master. Thematic chapters allow students to build knowledge on a topic and then use what they know to focus their attention and remember what they read, all the while building essential background knowledge for core college courses. The second edition has many new readings to facilitate building core knowledge necessary for comprehension of college material.

- **Pre- and Post-Assessments and Quick Tips.** A Pre- and Post-Assessment in each chapter help students and instructors identify students' strengths and weaknesses in applying the skills and strategies. These features allow instructors to establish benchmarks for their students and then later determine what areas may still need further attention. Answers are in the Instructor's Edition. Quick Tips summarize key ideas and concrete strategies relevant to the chapter topic.

"I love how this text builds background knowledge."

—Cynthia Crable, Allegany College of Maryland

IDENTIFYING UNDERLYING STRUCTURE TO UNLOCK THE MYSTERY OF AN UNKNOWN TOPIC AND COMPLEX READINGS . . .
addresses students' uncertainty about what's important.

The approach to building reading skills is based on the latest research in brain-based learning, which shows that readers without adequate background knowledge of a subject maximize their learning power when they use text structure to "unpack the text" as a means to learn new information. *Mindscapes* teaches students to use a reading's underlying structure to make sense of it, even if they have no prior knowledge of the subject. *Mindscapes* presents the recognition of text structure as a foundational skill, providing a framework onto which upper-level developmental readers can apply new knowledge about a subject, and understand and remember it more effectively. Throughout the text, information is presented in a carefully crafted sequence that builds upon students' growing academic knowledge base and awareness of text recognition—and allows them to gradually expand their portfolio of skills and strategies.

- **Topic and pattern identification first.** Students begin using text structure to their advantage right from the start in Chapter 1, when they practice previewing readings and identifying key topics. In Chapter 2, they expand their skills, learning how to recognize and use overall patterns of organization to absorb and retain new information.

- **Vocabulary focus keeps students engaged.** Comprehension improves when students understand the words, and it can be derailed when they don't. That's why vocabulary strategies are included in each chapter, rather than in one separate chapter. Understanding individual words is also integral to comprehending a passage and zeroing in on main and supporting ideas, so *Mindscapes* emphasizes recursive vocabulary strategies throughout the book. Readings are accompanied by guiding questions and vocabulary exercises, helping students learn to seek and identify important words and ideas and build a college-level vocabulary.

"I want my students to be better readers. I want them to have a clearer understanding of reading comprehension skills and I want them to have had a great deal of practice when they finish with my course. In addition, I want them to be able to use these skills in their other college classes. Using this book, I think I could accomplish my goals."

—Yvonne Frye, Community College of Denver

> ## PREPARING STUDENTS FOR THE RIGORS OF ACADEMIC READING . . .
> ### addresses students' lack of knowledge about how to study efficiently.

Many students come to college underprepared for the rigor required to succeed in reading their textbooks. Academic reading requires an efficient and effective process to find important information. *Mindscapes*'s recursive, integrated, and in-depth strategies develop the skills and mindset for college success through integrating primary features:

- **REVISED! Reading study strategies.** Every chapter focuses on specific reading study strategies— like previewing, paraphrasing, and note taking—that help students become more efficient critical readers building upon yet extending beyond just reading comprehension. They also enhance students' ability to learn what is important, and improve their performance on college tests and assignments in all of their courses. General study skills—like goal setting, time management, and study environments—are now available in an Introduction to be used at the instructor's discretion.

- **NEW! Discipline-specific vocabulary.** Each chapter targets key word parts and fundamental vocabulary and key terms for a range of college-level disciplines linked to each chapter's theme and focus. The Increase Your Discipline-Specific Vocabulary feature will help students build the knowledge they will use throughout their college coursework.

- **NEW! Additional skill and strategy practice.** Based on reviewer feedback, each chapter now offers extra practice so instructors can customize instruction for students who would benefit from extra review. In addition, these practice opportunities at the end of each chapter can be used to assess students' progress.

- **REVISED! Authentic full-length textbook chapter practice opportunities.** Every instructor knows that the purpose of a reading course is to prepare students to interact critically with content-area textbooks. The Textbook Applications after each unit allow students to test-drive their newly honed skills and strategies with authentic and rigorous chapters. A full-length textbook chapter in its original design provides students with background knowledge and vital practice in applying their new skills and strategies directly to college course content. The high-interest material is drawn from texts in health science, history, education, and law, related to the unit themes. These chapters can be used for individual work for portfolio assessment, tests, or interactive collaborative learning opportunities. The successful navigation of these representative cross-discipline chapters assure developing college readers and their instructors that newly learned skills and strategies transfer to college coursework—the ultimate goal of reading instruction.

"We chose Mindscapes because it covered the basics of reading without talking down to students and offers college level readings that are similar to the kinds of reading they do in their other classes."
—Victoria Williams, St. Cloud State University

"Mindscapes can be used to enhance the achievement of student learning outcomes in my course, and is well-organized with engaging readings and clear explanations. Being able to use Aplia as a supplement to the text is the 'icing on the cake'!"
—Audrey Morris, Riverside City College

FOSTERING CRITICAL THINKING STRATEGIES . . .
develops college-level readers.

Critical thinking is the bedrock of a successful college student's thought process. Critical thinking differentiates the college-level thinker who can look deeper into a question, situation, or reading. To learn to formulate sound opinions, make connections within and between classes, logically assess different viewpoints, and draw on background knowledge develops the college-level reader. The more students learn, the more aware they become of their thinking, and the more critically they can evaluate ideas. *Mindscapes* helps students sharpen these skills.

- **Modeling critical thinking with practice opportunities.** Guided Thinking It Through activities model the thought process involved in applying a particular skill. These activities invite students to "think aloud" with the author in a step-by-step, nonthreatening context, discover what is important in a reading, and then apply the strategies and skills that enable students to focus on what matters most. Each Thinking It Through is followed by On Your Own, a similar activity that students complete alone or in small groups, challenging students to practice applying the targeted strategies and skills. Students are guided in building skills incrementally, gradually taking more responsibility as they increase confidence and ability.

- **REVISED! Strategies for understanding graphics.** Every chapter includes a short feature helping students critically read and decode the various graphic types they are certain to encounter in their future college readings. These explanations provide practical insights into how to focus on key points and relationships between ideas in a variety of graphic types, like line graphs, bar graphs, maps, cartoons, print advertisements, and tables. As a result, students learn to derive full value from visuals that so often support narrative discussions in college textbooks. Each new strategy is practiced in context in the Application readings at the end of each chapter.

- **REVISED! Application readings with diverse questions that target all components of critical reading.** These diverse, high-interest selections allow students to see the positive results of using their new skills and theme-based knowledge. Each chapter has two substantive Application readings from a variety of disciplines and sources (but coherent in theme), each with an introduction, guiding questions, and diverse activities to keep students engaged:
  - **Comprehension Check** asks students to use their reading skills to derive meaning from the reading.
  - **NEW! Reading Graphics** supplies a topical graphic for students to read and apply to the Application reading.
  - **NEW! Developing Your College-Level Vocabulary** has students interact with vocabulary from the reading to enhance retention of words they will be expected to know in future college courses.
  - **NEW! Thematic Connections** provides writing opportunities where students can demonstrate critical thinking by making connections to their own experiences and opinions on reading topics and chapter themes.

"We teachers learn that we should model what we're teaching and then provide guided practice and then independent practice. . . . I think these exercises do what best practices tells us to do."

—Justina Sapna, Delaware Technical Community College

"The reasons I choose to use Mindscapes are because much of the materials listed in the book help me to prepare lessons which bridges critical thinking skills into the daily lessons for the students. . . . In the end, the students learn from the book, coupled with the online activities and activities which I plan, which makes for a great recipe for "Students' Success" in college reading."

—Asha Dey, South Mountain Community College

NEW TO THIS EDITION

Every chapter includes the following revisions:

- Revised: Pre- and Post-Assessment Comprehension Check questions emphasize reading comprehension and vocabulary comprehension.
- Revised: Understanding Graphics have been shortened to help students critically read and decode the various graphic types they are certain to encounter in their future college readings. Ample practice to apply these new skills follows in the Application reading exercises.
- NEW! Increase Your Discipline-Specific Vocabulary exposes students to word parts and key terms associated with the disciplines of that chapter's theme. This focus on key affixes and terminology will enhance students' journeys throughout the college disciplines.
- NEW! Additional Skill and Strategy Practice gives students more practice with each chapter skill.
- NEW! Application reading post-reading activities now all include Comprehension Checks, Reading Graphics, Developing College-Level Vocabulary, and Thematic Connections to embrace all the critical reading skills in which a student should be participating when reading for college.

Chapter-by-chapter revisions include the following:

Chapter 1

- Revised: Emphasis on differences between surveying and previewing as reading study strategies; more coverage and practice on creating guide questions to identify topic
- NEW! More coverage on how to use context clues with practice

Chapter 2

- Revised: More instructive figures to demonstrate patterns visually
- NEW! More individual practice for the types of patterns: On Your Own: Patterns That List; On Your Own: Patterns That Explain; On Your Own: Patterns That Analyze; On Your Own: Mixed Patterns; and On Your Own: Identifying an Overall Pattern of Organization in a Longer Reading

- Revised: New reading selections in Thinking It Through: Finding Relationships Between Ideas and On Your Own: Finding Relationships Between Ideas
- NEW! Application 1, Is There a Link Between Creativity and Addiction?
- NEW! Post-Assessment Reading, New Tests Show if You Are a Shopaholic

NEW! Unit 1 Textbook Application: "Chapter 3: Caring for Your Mind" from *An Invitation to Health* by Dianne Hales

Chapter 3

- Revised: Simplified Quick Tips boxes
- Revised: Greater emphasis placed on the thesis when discussing explicit main idea in whole reading
- Revised: New examples for paragraphs showing location of main idea
- New and expanded practice for finding explicit main ideas
- NEW! Application 1, The Internet—Meeting Online and After by David Knox and Caroline Schacht and Application 2, Culture, Gender, and Identity

Chapter 4

- NEW! Pre-Assessment reading: Milgram's Experiment on Obedience to Authority
- Revised: More clarity added to the methods of determining implied main idea
- New and expanded practice for finding implied main ideas
- Replaced several reading selections in On Your Own: Finding Implied Main Ideas in Paragraphs; new reading selections in Thinking It Through: Finding the Implied Main Idea of a Longer Reading; On Your Own: Finding the Implied Main Idea of a Whole Reading; and On Your Own: More Practice with Finding Implied Main Ideas of a Whole Reading

NEW! Unit 2 Textbook Application: "Chapter 27: The Limits of Liberalism: The 1970s" from *HIST* by Kevin M. Schultz

Chapter 5

- Revised: More coverage on text marking and annotating
- NEW! Thinking It Through: Marking Text in a Paragraph and On Your Own: Marking Text in Paragraphs
- Revised: New reading selection for Thinking It Through: Marking and Annotating a Longer Text
- NEW! Understanding Graphics focusing on reading complex tables

Chapter 6

- NEW! Reading Study Strategy featured: Using Textbook Features
- Revised: Increased coverage of taking notes from reading explaining the double-column and Cornell methods

- Revised: New reading selection for Thinking It Through: Creating an Outline
- NEW! Understanding Graphics focusing on reading and understanding maps
- NEW! Application 2, World Population Hits 7 Billion

Chapter 7

- NEW! Sections on how to read online sources, using appropriate online sources in research, and questions to ask when evaluating online sources
- NEW! Understanding Graphics focusing on distinguishing fact from opinion in visuals
- NEW! Thinking It Through: Mapping an Argument; Thinking It Through: Mapping an Argument and Recognizing Support; On Your Own: Mapping an Argument; and On Your Own: Mapping an Argument and Recognizing Support

Chapter 8

- NEW! Pre-Assessment reading: Designer Babies: Ethical? Inevitable?
- Revised: Reading Study Strategy now featuring the critical thinking strategies of Bloom's taxonomy and question–answer relationships, previously in Chapter 5
- Revised: Connection between deductive and inductive reasoning and argument clarified
- Revised: Differences between logical fallacies and propaganda made more evident with clearer examples
- NEW! Application 1, Cash to Doctors Can Ruin Patients' Trust
- NEW! Thinking It Through: Evaluating an Argument

"I am very pleased to find several additions to the text, including active learning strategies, text marking, text annotating, and text note-taking strategies. These are left out of many developmental reading texts but are essential to development of students' improved comprehension and ongoing academic success. . . . The readings for the Applications exercises in each chapter are very current and relevant to the students' generation."

—Laura C. Padgett, Lees-McRae College

SUPPLEMENTS

For Students

APLIA FOR *MINDSCAPES*

Aplia for Developmental Reading is an online learning solution that improves comprehension and outcomes by increasing student effort and engagement. Students stay on top of coursework with regularly scheduled graded practice. The Grade It Now feature provides students with detailed, immediate explanations for every answer. Grades are automatically recorded in the instructor's Aplia grade book. Updated for the second edition, Aplia assignments match the language, style, and structure of this text, allowing students to seamlessly apply chapter concepts. Find out more at www.aplia.com /developmentalenglish.

For Instructors

INSTRUCTOR'S MANUAL AND TEST BANK

Streamline and maximize the effectiveness of your course preparation with the Instructor's Manual and Test Bank. The revised Instructor's Manual contains new group exercises, teaching tips, and sample syllabi to help you organize and teach your class. The Test Bank offers a variety of testing questions that not only test students' comprehension but also gives them practice using the skills they have learned in the book. Quizzes for each chapter and a midterm and final exam are included in the Test Bank.

INSTRUCTOR COMPANION SITE

The Instructor Companion Web site features helpful teaching tools, including an electronic version of the Instructor's Manual and Test Bank. The Web site also features sample syllabi, activity worksheets, and PowerPoint slides to use during lectures.

ACKNOWLEDGMENTS

I am indebted to the many professionals with whom I have worked to develop this second edition. Thanks for all you have done to make this a smooth and rewarding process.

- Annie Todd, Director of Developmental Studies
- Shani Fisher, Executive Editor, Developmental Reading
- Corinna Dibble, Content Project Manager
- Marita Sermolins, Development Editor. I am beyond grateful for your help and professionalism always.

Also, many thanks to those who took the time to review this manuscript and provide such thought-provoking and creative suggestions:

- Barbara Cox, Redlands Community College
- Cynthia Crable, Allegany College of Maryland
- Asha Dey, South Mountain Community College
- Marie Eckstrom, Rio Hondo Community College
- Beth Holmberg, Frederick Community College
- Cari Kenner, St. Cloud State University
- Linda Mininger, Harrisburg Area Community College
- Audrey Morris, Riverside City College
- Christine Pruitt, Harding University

- Betty Raper, Pulaski Technical College
- Justina Sapna, Delaware Technical Community College
- Alexa Schumacher, Glendale College
- Nancy Walker, University of La Verne
- Victoria Williams, St. Cloud State University

Also, many thanks to the following people:

- My students at St. Louis Community College at Meramec over the past thirteen years
- My colleagues at St. Louis Community College at Meramec
- For my family, as always

FOREWORD TO STUDENTS:
THE *MINDSCAPES* APPROACH

Put a check mark after each statement that could apply to you.

- I often read an assignment for school, and then cannot remember what I've read. _____
- I read and think I understand a passage, but figuring out the main point is challenging. _____
- I read assigned material for my college classes, but have trouble identifying what to study. _____
- It's hard to determine what information is important and what is not. _____

These are very common problems for college students. *Mindscapes: Critical Reading Skills and Strategies* will help you improve your reading so you can increase your success in college-level courses. This book is titled *Mindscapes* because the readings, skills, and strategies discussed compel you to think about what you already know about a particular topic. You can become a better reader if you connect what an author has written to your experience and background knowledge.

Reading involves using both skills and strategies to aid comprehension. A *skill* is an ability that is developed through practice. Skills, when learned, become automatic and require little thought in their application. A *strategy* is a plan or method used to achieve a specific result. Strategies are battle plans for learning that let you use a series of skills to your best advantage. Strategies require you to think about what you should do to address a particular problem or challenge. They provide a framework to help you determine *why and when* to use a particular skill. Knowing which strategy to use in which situation requires metacognition. *Metacognition,* simply defined, is thinking about your thought processes. Being aware of how much you already know about a topic is using metacognition to your advantage. Being aware of when a reading is not making sense allows you to use strategies to fix the problem.

If you do not have prior knowledge related to a subject, then looking at *how* a text is written can help you make sense of your reading. This is why you will begin to look at the structure of a reading in Unit 1. When information is more organized, you will remember it more accurately. What better way to organize information in your mind to learn it than to use the same pattern as the author did in writing the information?

You will also build your knowledge from the *Mindscapes* readings, drawn from popular subjects common in college courses. By learning about related topics in each chapter, you will build background knowledge and develop college-level vocabulary. This will make future college work easier for you, as background knowledge, understanding of vocabulary, and comprehension of a reading are closely linked. In addition, you will apply what you learn to actual college textbook chapters from popular introductory courses.

As you interact with *Mindscapes,* you will learn how to work with your brain to process information more effectively. You will learn how to overcome the problems commonly encountered in reading at the college level—and what you read will begin to make better sense. A smart student can use the *Mindscapes* approach to become a more effective, efficient, and successful learner.

INTRODUCTION: FUNDAMENTAL STUDY STRATEGIES FOR COLLEGE SUCCESS

Are you a first-semester college student? Have you been away from academia for a few years or many years? Do you have trouble juggling the demands of school and life? Are you determined to put your best foot forward this semester? Everyone has his or her own struggles when it comes to successfully navigating the demands of college courses. It is worthwhile to plan effectively and efficiently for these demands by preparing yourself mentally for the pressures of the college experience from the outset. There are some fundamental skills you must have to approach your college experience prepared to be successful. Throughout this textbook, you will learn multiple skills and strategies to improve your reading skills. However, being successful in college requires a mindset of applying helpful skills and strategies from the outset that you can apply to all your college courses.

This introduction will help prepare the optimum mindset for your success. In this introduction, you will enrich yourself as a learner by developing your insight into these topics that will apply to your success in all college courses and help you navigate the college experience:

- Familiarizing yourself with college resources and starting the semester off correctly
- Increasing your motivation
- Setting achievable goals
- Managing your time
- Knowing your learning style
- Capitalizing on your knowledge of multiple intelligences
- Taking tests

HOW TO PREPARE FOR YOUR COURSES

A strong start to a semester or academic quarter's work sets the tone for the duration of your classes. You should research many fundamental resources and take several basic steps to set this positive tone for your success. Here are some tips for starting off well and in a positive frame of mind. As you complete these steps, put a checkmark in the appropriate box:

☐ Be prepared as a college student.

    ☐ Familiarize yourself with Blackboard or other college web systems.

    ☐ Set up your school e-mail account.

    ☐ Get parking passes and school identification card or library card.

☐ Make sure you have the typical school supplies for the first class.

   ☐ For each of your classes, get the books as soon as possible. If this is an issue, talk directly with your instructors.

   ☐ A weekly or monthly planner

   ☐ Writing materials

   ☐ Flash drive

☐ Read and understand the syllabus.

   ☐ Know your instructor's name.

   ☐ Know your instructor's office hours, e-mail address, and office location.

   ☐ Read and understand class assessments and assignments.

☐ Be aware of college resources.

   ☐ Library

   ☐ Tutoring center

   ☐ Access office (for students with documented disabilities)

   ☐ Assessment center

   ☐ Advising and counseling

   ☐ Academic support programs

   ☐ Career counseling or assessment

   ☐ Financial aid office

☐ Schedule study time.

   ☐ Set your work and personal schedule in advance.

☐ Ask questions—college staff is there to help you succeed.

Now that you have prepared for your college experience, focus on creating your best mindset for success with the following topics.

MOTIVATION AND GOAL SETTING

To become a successful college student, you need to begin on the right path to success. This path requires that you be organized, focused, and knowledgeable about not only how people learn but how *you* learn best. How to become the best learner that you can be means you need to be aware of your strengths and weaknesses; you need to improve your strengths and minimize your weaknesses for maximum success. The first step is to work on your attention and learning skills.

Are you a study whiz, or do you struggle with study skills? To find out your strengths and weaknesses, answer this self-report questionnaire.

Self-Assessment of Study Skills for Attention and Learning

Complete the following assessment by checking the box that best suits your view of your skills in each area.

SKILL/STRATEGY	I'M GREAT AT THIS	I'M OKAY AT THIS	I NEED SOME HELP	I NEED A LOT OF HELP
1. I am able to concentrate well on a reading for study.				
2. I manage my time effectively.				
3. I have a study system.				
4. I can set useful goals and achieve them.				
5. I have good organizational skills.				
6. I know what to do before, during, and after studying.				
7. I work effectively to study academic subjects.				
8. I know how to schedule my time.				
9. I set specific goals for success.				
10. I use what I know about my learning styles to succeed in classes.				

If you checked "I need some help" or "I need a lot of help" in any area, you'll get extra help in this introduction, so pay extra attention. Think about retaking this quiz *after* you complete this textbook and compare your responses. You will see how much progress you have made!

Before you can apply any study strategy to become the best learner you can be, you must be motivated to succeed. **Motivation** is the impetus, or reason, to push you to succeed in any task, especially college learning. There are two types of motivation: external, or extrinsic, and internal, or intrinsic.

External motivation, motivation from outside sources, comes from the "threat" or "encouragement" of outside influences that compel your effort as a student. External motivators can be parents or other people, an employment situation that requires you to upgrade your skills, or the promise of a better salary with some further schooling. These external motivators can be helpful in pushing you to do your best at college or even attend college in the first place. Sometimes external motivation can be positively received, such as support and encouragement from an instructor; sometimes external motivation can be negatively received, like the threat of losing your job without further education. In either case, external motivation can be put to good use and encourage you to be productive and expend the effort necessary to be a successful student. However, external motivation alone is not enough.

Internal motivation, motivation from within you to succeed, is necessary for any long-term success. Regardless of external reasons or motivators to attend college and achieve academic goals, *you must want to succeed*. College requires great self-discipline, effort, time, resilience, and focus. Without an internal motivation to succeed, it will be a struggle to maintain your focus and sustain your drive.

SETTING ACHIEVABLE GOALS

To continue to be internally motivated, you need to set achievable goals. For some people, setting goals is something automatic and natural. For others, actually writing down goals seems forced and awkward. Regardless of which category you fall into, there's little doubt that thinking about and actually *writing down* long-term, intermediate, and short-term goals is effective. If you do not know specifically what you want to accomplish, then it is hard to accomplish those goals. Also, when the going gets rough, referring to these goals can boost morale and reposition you on your path to be successful.

Maybe you find it easy to set an intention, or a mental plan about something you mean to do, like to do quality work or get good grades. But having intentions may not be enough. The next step is to actually take those intentions and convert them into goals. Here's the difference. An intention is "I intend to get a B in English 101 this semester" or "I plan to pass my classes." A goal, in contrast, is written down and provides some strategies to realize the intention, or to make it happen. A goal is "I will get a B in English 101 this semester by completing all the readings *prior* to the class for which they are assigned" or "I will observe the study strategy of spaced practice for test review by starting to study *at least* five days before each test" or "I will make use of the writing and learning facilities at my college immediately if I have difficulty in the class." Intentions are vague, while goals are concrete and very specific.

The brain likes information to be organized so that the information can be easily digested. Similarly, as a student, you want to be organized and always be aware of where you are going and exactly what you need to accomplish to get there. This type of focus on outcomes and routes for achieving these outcomes often separates an okay student from an outstanding student. It's easy for time to slip away; and without a concrete and realistic plan, you'll end up with little to show for that time. Better to have some concrete and realistic ideas of where you want to be by the end of the day, week, month, and year and have a step-by-step plan of how to get where you want to be!

Long-term goals are life goals that help you see where you are now in relation to where you want to end up in the future. Examples of long-term goals are to use your sociology degree to obtain a position in a social service agency working with disadvantaged children, and to make enough money at that job to afford to live in a decent apartment in the city of your choice. Long-term goals are important because they help you deal with the pressures, burdens, and sacrifices you make today. Think of long-term goals as the "light at the end of the tunnel" when you are staying up late to get that reading assignment done for the next day. Of course, if you plan your time correctly and gauge the length and difficulty of your assignments accurately, this won't happen too often!

Intermediate goals are goals that span two to five years. An example of an intermediate goal is an action plan to attain an associate of arts degree within two and a half years and then transfer to a four-year college to earn a bachelor's degree in sociology. To make this a concrete goal rather than just an intention, you need to plan out your course of study with an advisor at your college so you know exactly what courses you will need to complete during which semester. In addition, you want to make sure that the courses for the associate's degree transfer smoothly to the program of study at the four-year college or university to which you intend to transfer.

Short-term goals (which are sometimes called *objectives*) are the goals you set for yourself to accomplish day-to-day activities that lead you to your intermediate and long-term goals. An example of this is wanting to outline your psychology textbook chapter by Thursday so you are prepared when the information is presented by your instructor in class on Friday morning. Short-term goals can also be the goals you set for the semester. For example, you might intend to earn at least a C in each of your classes this semester, as that would put you in good standing academically. In addition, you might intend to note specific strategies for troubleshooting problems to ensure that you reach this goal. The table that follows features long-term, intermediate, and short-term goals. Notice how the long-term and intermediate goals become more specific and concrete as they move to short-term goals. Also, notice the words associated with each type of goal.

LONG-TERM GOAL	INTERMEDIATE GOAL	SHORT-TERM GOALS
I want to be a medical technologist and earn a good living.	I want to achieve an associate's degree in science with a certificate in medical technology.	I will attend each class. I will review my notes before each class. I will complete all reading prior to the class for which it is assigned. I will sit near the front of the class to focus my attention. I will ask questions to clarify any misunderstandings during the class period.

TIME MANAGEMENT

To be a successful college student, you *must* have efficient time-management strategies. Effective **time management** means using time wisely and efficiently to be productive. If you are taking several courses and work at a job, or if you have family and other obligations, time management can make the difference between success in college and underachievement. You need to use every spare moment in order to learn new information and study. The brain absorbs information through repetition, and studying requires repetition. Here are some basic steps for effective time management:

1. Purchase a planner with both daily to-do pages as well as monthly planning pages.

2. Insert all assignments and tests into your monthly plan.

3. Insert all work and social obligations into your monthly plan.

4. Each day, set short-term goals in your to-do pages, with things you need to achieve that day. If you don't get to something that day, be sure to transfer it to your next day's to-do list.

5. Make note of the chunks of time in your schedule and use them to your advantage.

6. Take advantage of the breaks in between classes or appointments and bring along notes or vocabulary flash cards from which to study.

7. Use the 10 minutes before or in between classes to scan your notes to refresh your memory and prepare your brain for new learning.

8. Keep up with day-to-day assignments and reading, so you have a grasp of the material prior to the class in which it will be discussed.

9. Plan ahead for tests, essays, and projects. Start the assignment early by breaking it into smaller chunks, so you'll have time to complete it and make necessary revisions. Overestimate the time you'll need for assignments so you're not caught at the last moment.

10. Make sure to build some relaxation time into your schedule *after* study periods with brief rewards between study periods, like getting a snack or watching an episode of your favorite television show.

LEARNING STYLES

Making the most of your motivation, goals, and time also requires that you know how you learn best. Researchers have investigated how people learn best and have categorized the results into specific **learning styles**. You can benefit from understanding more about your own learning preferences. The more awareness you have, the better student you can become.

VARK

A useful learning style inventory is **VARK**, a 16-item questionnaire that provides a profile of your learning preferences. The name of this profile is an **acronym**, or word where each letter stands for another word:

V = visual

A = aural or auditory

R = read/write

K = kinesthetic, or hands-on

If you learn in accord with your learning preference, you are more likely to be motivated; if you are motivated, you are more likely to be successful. It is what you do *with* your knowledge of your learning preference that will make you successful.

Most people learn predominantly with one of the four VARK learning styles, but some people have a secondary type that works well for them, too. Which of the following learning styles sounds most like you?

Learning style inventories, such as VARK, are available online or through the advising or academic center at your institution.

TYPE OF INTELLIGENCE	LEARNING ACTIVITIES THAT WORK WELL
Visual A preference for visual displays	• Examining maps, charts, graphs, and other visuals • Viewing PowerPoint presentations • Writing notes and rereading
Aural or auditory (hearing) A preference for hearing information	• Taping class lectures to relisten • Downloading podcasts for the course • Listening to radio programs about the topic • Reciting material out loud
Read/Write A preference for reading and writing	• Viewing information displayed in words, like lists • Viewing PowerPoint presentations • Reading written directions, explanations, books, and handouts • Writing summaries and rewrite notes
Kinesthetic A preference for hands-on or "real" applications of information	• Participating in simulations, movies, experiments, labs, and other hands-on situations • Attending events and demonstrations, such as science centers, museums, art galleries • Walking or otherwise moving around when studying • Participating in group activities for study and learning

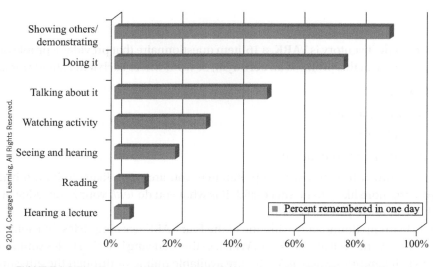

FIGURE I.1 The Percent of Information Remembered in One Day with Types of Learning

Multimodal learners are people who use two or more learning styles on a regular basis. If you are a multimodal learner, try the strategies related to your preferred modes of learning. Be aware of which work best, and design your own best study plan based on what works for you with different types of subject areas. For example, science may be clearer with visual study strategies such as creating diagrams or flow charts. Sociology, on the other hand, may make more sense when you write down the main points. Experiment with the strategy and make it work for you.

With a partner, consider Figure I.1, which shows the relationships between different types of learning and how long information is remembered with that learning method. What conclusions can you draw about how students learn most effectively? How might the information in the bar graph relate to learning styles?

Multiple Intelligences

Howard Gardner is credited with determining that there are numerous ways that individuals are "smart." These ways are referred to as **multiple intelligences** (Figure I.2). Some of us are intelligent in several different ways; not all people have the same "academic" abilities, but this is just one of many ways to be intelligent. This research is revolutionary because it is now accepted that intelligence is not just academic in nature. It can take many forms.

Gardner established that there are eight main ways of learning that correspond to the different types of intelligence. Table I.1 explains the differences and shows how these types of intelligence could apply to the academic topic of "global education."

Multiple intelligences inventories may be available through the advising or academic center at your institution. It is well worth your while working on your awareness of how *you* learn best.

To learn to your capacity, all your study and reading skills need to work together for optimum advantage. Studying in a good setting will help you make the most of what you have learned. Setting up a good study environment is not hard but it takes some consideration.

FIGURE I.2 Multiple intelligences

TABLE I.1 Gardner's Multiple Intelligences and Their Application to Global Education

WHAT ARE YOUR STRENGTHS?	TYPE OF INTELLIGENCE	APPLYING YOUR INTELLIGENCE TO YOUR STUDYING
Words	Verbal/Linguistic intelligence	Read about the topic.
Numbers or logic	Logical/Mathematical intelligence	Look at and learn statistics about the topic.
Pictures	Visual/Spatial intelligence	Read and learn graphic material.
Music	Musical/Rhythmic intelligence	Associate different learning theories with music particular to that culture.
Self-reflection	Intrapersonal intelligence	Reflect on your own learning's strengths and weaknesses.
Physical experience	Bodily/Kinesthetic intelligence	Visit schools and/or interact with people with different learning backgrounds.
Social experience	Interpersonal intelligence	Interview others to hear their experiences or interact with others from a different learning background.
Experience in the natural world	Naturalist intelligence	Observe learning in nature: i.e., animal learning and how it relates to human learning and memory.

HOW TO TAKE TESTS IN COLLEGE

Taking successful notes in your courses and using those notes to study will help you to be successful at taking college tests (see Chapters 5 and 6 for more on marking and note taking). Being aware of the types of tests that you might encounter will enable you to be better prepared and not get overwhelmed with anxiety, while putting all the knowledge you learned from studying your notes to good use.

Objective Tests

Objective tests are common in college. There are three types of objective tests: multiple choice, true/false, and matching terms with definitions.

QUICK TIPS GENERAL TIPS FOR TAKING OBJECTIVE TESTS

 Read through the test first.

 Plan your time and aim to move quickly, skipping (and marking) questions you can't answer easily. You can come back to those after you have done the majority of the work (and solidified the majority of points).

Sometimes, the answers to questions you do not know are suggested in other questions later in the test.

MULTIPLE-CHOICE TEST QUESTIONS

Multiple-choice test questions can be intimidating, but remember that you usually have four answers to choose from (a, b, c, or d). Your first strategy is to eliminate possible answers that you know are incorrect to increase your odds of choosing the right answer. Try rephrasing the questions in your own words, as this may help you eliminate answers that you know are incorrect. Answers that are absolute, such as those that contain the words *always* and *never,* are usually incorrect; few things in life are absolute. Usually, an answer contains qualifiers, words such as *sometimes, often,* or *usually.* Also, longer answers are often correct, as it takes more words to explain a difficult concept completely. Similarly, answers with "all of the above" or "none of the above" deserve careful consideration because they are often correct. Remember: If you first eliminate answers that you know are incorrect, you increase your odds of guessing correctly. On an interesting note, students who change their first answer after second-guessing themselves tend to have been correct the first time! It's a good rule of thumb, then, to change your answer only if you are sure the new one is correct. When in doubt, go with your first instinct.

TRUE/FALSE TEST QUESTIONS

Here, of course, you have a 50 percent chance of guessing correctly. There are usually more true than false items. (One reason for this is that instructors may make up tests that concern explaining a key term or concept in the material. It is, frankly, easier to use the true statement than to create a clever statement that is false). If part of a statement is true and the rest is false, the entire answer must be considered false. Again, qualifiers such as *sometimes, often,* or *usually* are often correct, or true.

MATCHING TEST QUESTIONS

Start with the easiest matches and cross them out. Look for other questions that contain the key words that are in the matching question with which you are struggling, and use your knowledge of vocabulary context clues to help you decide. Sometimes there are more possible answers than terms with which they can be matched. Be careful to go with your first instinct. If you can use a term more than once, do not be afraid to do so.

Essay Exams

Essay exams are often used to elicit your understanding of and opinion about an issue or reading. You will use your knowledge of evaluating a reading in order to write a good essay response. When you write a response to an essay question, make sure your writing is coherent (makes sense) and logical and that all of its parts fit together. It is very important to make an outline of all the key points you wish to make, including your examples as secondary support, *before* you write. A good guideline is to spend at least half as much time *planning* your essay as you do writing it, to consider what you will say and how you will say it. A poorly planned essay usually lacks organization. It is important to recognize the organizational pattern (see Chapter 2) when you read an essay and equally important to use an organizational pattern when you write an essay. When you have completed drafting your essay, read it over carefully several times. Make any revisions you believe are necessary, and then proofread your work to locate and correct spelling, punctuation, and grammatical errors.

There are three major parts to taking an essay exam: preparing for the exam, taking the exam, and submitting the exam.

Preparing for the Exam

1. Look over your notes for the class.

2. Refine your own notes on the reading.

3. Anticipate questions that might be asked; look at discussion questions following the readings for ideas on what might be asked.

4. Prepare notes on possible questions and draft or outline your answers.

Taking the Exam

1. Read the questions carefully before responding.

2. Underline important parts of the questions so you make sure to address each part in your answer.

3. Make a detailed outline of what you are going to say, including all examples.

4. Plan your time carefully according to the point value of the question.

5. Provide at least three supporting points for your analysis or argument.

6. If you are not sure how to structure your essay, turn the question you are answering into a thesis statement by providing your opinion on the topic.

Submitting the Exam

1. Read your essay over to make sure the structure is clear and to catch any mistakes in spelling, punctuation, and grammar.

2. Double-check that you have included your name and the question to which you are responding!

TYPES OF ESSAY QUESTIONS

In Chapter 8, you will learn about question–answer relationships. This technique—learning how to identify exactly what you are being asked to write about—is helpful in writing essays or even short-answer questions. Most essay questions require that you have a firm grasp of the readings on which the essays are based. In addition, you will need to add your opinion or ideas in interpreting the readings.

Here are 10 common words used in formulating essay questions, along with a brief explanation of what you should do in responding to the question. If you understand the question, you will be able to use the appropriate pattern of organization in your response.

1. **Summarize:** Provide main points only.

2. **Outline:** Provide main points only.

3. **Compare/contrast:** What are the similarities and/or differences?

4. **Trace:** What is the sequence of events in time order?

5. **Explain:** Why? State your point and provide explanatory examples or reasons.

6. **Evaluate (or critique):** What are the arguments for or against and what are the strengths and/or weaknesses of each?

7. **Interpret:** What does the idea mean? How does it fit in with other, related information?

8. **Describe:** What are the important characteristics?

9. **Classify:** In what category does the subject belong? Explain why.

10. **Define:** What does the concept or key term mean? Provide examples of the idea.

Overcoming Test Anxiety

Everyone at one time or another suffers from test anxiety. Most of the time, you get nervous for the following reasons:

1. You are not feeling well.

2. You are not prepared.

3. The test is really important, like a final exam or a placement test.

Let's face it: Testing is a part of school and it's a part of life. Testing is here to stay, so you need to use strategies to reduce anxiety in order to do your best.

Before the Test

1. If you have a documented learning disability, make sure to research testing accommodations at your school early and completely.

2. Get a good night's sleep.

3. Review information just before you go to sleep as there is some evidence that your mind processes this information while you sleep.

4. Eat a good breakfast.

5. Wear loose clothing.

6. Do not cram—used spaced practice and overlearn material.

7. Review major points right before the test—short-term memory can hold information for a brief amount of time, so there are limits to this tactic.

8. Use acronyms and rhymes to learn complicated information.

During the Test

1. Breathe deeply, tense and untense muscles, and think of a calm, pleasant scene to reduce stress and anxiety.

2. Read the entire test over.

3. Answer questions to which you know the answer (take care if you are using a scantron test answer sheet to mark your answers in the correct space).

4. Do not change answers unless you are positive the new answer is correct.

5. Note the time allotted for the test. For essay tests you should plan to prepare your answer for at least half the allotted time.

6. Spend the most time on questions that are worth the most points.

7. Put difficult questions into your own words (paraphrase them).

8. Determine exactly what you are being asked to do.

9. Always read over your test answers or essays.

After the Test

1. Review your notes again to catch missing points only to the extent that it may help you learn the information for another test.

2. Do not obsess over the test once it's done. Learn from your mistakes. Look over the questions on which you lost points. Read the instructor's comments, and see the instructor for further explanation if you have questions.

3. Take a deep breath, and move on to the next assignment.

If you apply these strategies consistently, your anxiety should diminish and your performance on tests should improve. If this isn't the case, talk with your instructor, advisor, or counselor about alternative measures.

This fundamental study-skill introduction has provided tools to begin the semester from your strongest vantage point. Remember, persistence and effort are required for success; if you need assistance, make sure to use the resources at your disposal and ask for help.

READING FOR
STRUCTURE

THEME *The Brain: Memory, Learning, and Substance Use*

UNIT
1

Garry Gay/Getty Images

Understanding ACTIVE READING

🔆 Why Do You Need to Know This?

If you were asked *how* to read a passage for school, would you say, "Just read it"? Many students are unaware that there are effective methods of reading and learning for college success. Reading actually starts with some investigating *before* you start reading a passage from top to bottom. In this chapter, you are introduced to strategies that work *with* your brain to learn new information through reading. The skills of surveying, previewing, recognizing topic, and looking for the organization of a whole reading work with your brain to process new information. One consistent finding in memory research is that the brain requires organized information to learn. The skills you'll learn

IN THIS CHAPTER, YOU WILL LEARN

- Active learning and metacognition techniques
- About memory and how the brain processes information
- Reading strategies
- To identify topic
- To understand graphics: applying topic and questioning to a graph

READING STUDY STRATEGIES

- Surveying and previewing a reading

VOCABULARY STRATEGIES

- Using context clues
- Increasing your discipline-specific vocabulary: college orientation and communication

VLADGRIN/Shutterstock.com

VLADGRIN/Shutterstock.com

> " THAT IS WHAT LEARNING IS. YOU SUDDENLY UNDERSTAND SOMETHING YOU'VE UNDERSTOOD ALL YOUR LIFE, BUT IN A NEW WAY. "
>
> DORIS LESSING British Writer and Nobel Prize winner (1919–)

in this chapter will empower you to "encode" or submit information to your brain in an organized form that your brain can digest. In using the same organizational construct, your brain retrieves information as well. Prereading techniques and identifying topic allow you to see the organization the writer intends and work with your brain to help you understand the major points in a reading.

To be an efficient reader and learner, you need to know something about how your brain processes information. The theme of this first chapter is about how the brain learns and remembers. Through these readings, you will learn how to work in harmony rather than in conflict with your brain's natural tendencies. This will make you a better learner and will increase your chances for success in college-level reading and studying. How do you approach a reading to maximize your chances of learning and doing well in college courses?

✓ CHECK YOUR PRIOR KNOWLEDGE

Jot down some facts you know about memory and how the brain works. Do not edit your list—just brainstorm!

_____

_____

_____

_____

_____

_____

_____

_____

_____

_____

_____

_____

_____

♣ PRE-ASSESSMENT

ONLINE SCIENCE MAGAZINE

This assessment will help you understand your strengths and weaknesses in the skills and strategies discussed in this chapter. Don't worry if you do not know what all the terms mean. The purpose of this Pre-Assessment is to find out how much you already know about the reading skills and strategies introduced in this chapter. First, think about what you already know about memory problems. Next, think about your purpose for reading this Pre-Assessment. You need to read carefully enough to answer 10 multiple-choice questions following the reading.

5 Things You Must Never Forget
by Greg Soltis

1   Whether it is a name, date, or directions, there always seems to be something new to remember. Yet you probably feel like there's just not enough room in those little brain cells of yours to cram the latest tidbit. And unfortunately you have no external hard drive. But don't despair. Several recent studies reveal how memory works and what you can do to improve it.

1. The Aided Memory

2   Don't want to forget what you learned today? Sleep on it. Naps, ideally 90 minutes long, help you register the happenings and how-to's learned during the day. Then when you catch your z's at night, your brain creates memories of the day's events.

3   But overload your brain with long-term memories and you may struggle to remember recent events.

4   Scientists once thought that memory improved when new neurons were created in the hippocampus, the region of the brain that forms memories. Instead, a better memory may be possible in brains with less new neurons developing in the hippocampus.

5   Recent studies also found that migraines, music, habits, zinc, and thinking like a child each improved individual memory.

2. The Jaded Memory

6   Doctored photos can skew how you perceive the past, according to a recent study using images of well-known demonstrations. The first was the well-known picture of a man blocking a row of tanks in Tiananmen Square in 1989 with a crowd of spectators added to the original. And the second photograph showed a 2003 anti-war protest in Rome, with both riot police and a masked protester added to the picture. Those who viewed the altered images recalled more violence and damage than actually occurred, compared to those who saw the original snapshots. People who looked at these altered images also felt less inclined to participate in future demonstrations than those who viewed the original photographs.

7   These results should not come as a big surprise. Participants of previous studies also thought their imagined images were real.

8   Other detriments to achieving total recall could include catching a cold, smoking a joint, playing football, and being a guy, research shows.

3. The Aged Memory

9   Partially due to the decline in hippocampus function with age, the elderly suffer from a loss of <u>episodic memory</u>. This impairs their ability to recall more vivid memories—what was seen, heard, or felt during a previous event. And because we use the same parts of the brain to imagine and to remember, older adults may not only become forgetful but also struggle to picture hypothetical situations. But some seniors have staved off memory decline by maintaining active social lives and simply believing that they still have a good memory.

10   Interestingly, the risk factors for dementia—obesity, hypertension, and high choles-terol—coincide with those for cardio-vascular disease. Scientists found that having only one of these three risk factors doubles the chance of getting dementia. And suffering from all three risk factors makes dementia six times as likely. Controlling for these three factors can save both the heart and brain. But the factors of genes and age cannot be denied.

11   The elderly may improve their memory in a few weeks by eating well, exercising, and keeping mentally sharp. To prevent drops in blood glucose, seniors should eat five meals daily. These should be high in whole grains, antioxidants, and omega-3 fats. And the golden years should consist of brisk daily walks, stretches, relaxation exercises, brainteasers or other mental stimulants. Consistent mental exercise has been shown to cut the risk of dementia in half.

4. The Educated Memory

12   Educated individuals often have more knowledge at their disposal. Studies show that the more you know, the easier it is to learn about related topics. And the degree-holding older crowd outperforms its less educated counterpart on mental-status tests.

13   But the ability to remember what was learned seems to decline at a faster rate. Granted, the more one knows, the more one has to forget. But don't expect the springs of your education to feed the fountain of youth against memory loss.

14   Those with a higher working-memory capacity sacrifice this advantage when sweating bullets during pressure-filled situations. For example, worrying about potential mistakes on an exam squanders brain activity that could otherwise be devoted to recalling a syn-onym for "fastidious" or calculating the surface area of a sphere.

5. The Devastated Memory

15   Poignant events have a more lasting impact compared to lackluster experiences that usually don't stay in the brain's long-term storage unit. And our recollection of events that triggered a bad memory are more likely to be accurate than memories from more uplift-ing times in our lives. This is because these trying times compel the brain to focus on a specific detail.

16   Trying to forget a bad memory is possible, but will likely require many attempts. If suc-cessful, your brain will first negate the sensory aspects of the memory before removing the actual memory.

(Continued)

17   And don't forget that from an evolutionary standpoint, it makes sense that traumatic times have a long shelf life. The survival of a species is enhanced by its ability to remember threatening situations and then avoiding them when they happen again.

COMPREHENSION CHECK

Circle the best answer to the following questions.

Reading Comprehension

1   **What is the topic of this reading?**

A. Five things you must never forget

B. Memory

C. Memory problems and improvement

D. Jaded memories

2   **What would be a good guide question to ask about the first subheading, "The Aided Memory"?**

A. What is the aided memory?

B. Where is the aided memory?

C. When do we use aided memory?

D. Why is there an aided memory?

3   **In subsection 4, "The Educated Memory," what is the topic?**

A. Good memory

B. Learning

C. Good and bad memory

D. Education and memory

4   **According to subsection 5, "The Devastated Memory," which type of events are most likely to be remembered inaccurately?**

A. Bad events

B. Confusing events

C. Events related to learning

D. Happy events

5   **What is the topic of subsection 5, "The Devastated Memory"?**

A. Good memory

B. Learning

C. Traumatic or bad memory

D. Poignant memory

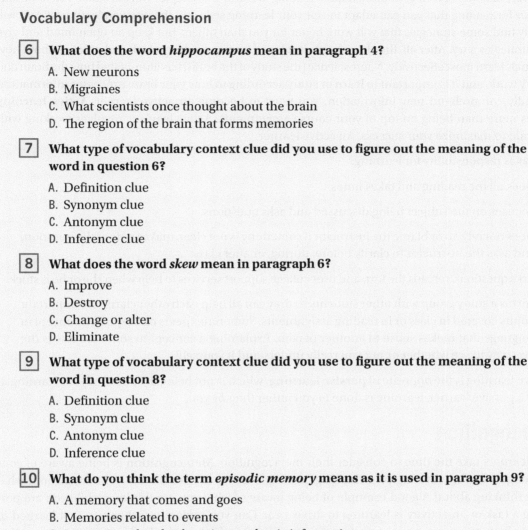

Vocabulary Comprehension

6 **What does the word *hippocampus* mean in paragraph 4?**

A. New neurons

B. Migraines

C. What scientists once thought about the brain

D. The region of the brain that forms memories

7 **What type of vocabulary context clue did you use to figure out the meaning of the word in question 6?**

A. Definition clue

B. Synonym clue

C. Antonym clue

D. Inference clue

8 **What does the word *skew* mean in paragraph 6?**

A. Improve

B. Destroy

C. Change or alter

D. Eliminate

9 **What type of vocabulary context clue did you use to figure out the meaning of the word in question 8?**

A. Definition clue

B. Synonym clue

C. Antonym clue

D. Inference clue

10 **What do you think the term *episodic memory* means as it is used in paragraph 9?**

A. A memory that comes and goes

B. Memories related to events

C. Memories related to learning academic information

D. Memory that older adults use

HOW YOU LEARN

To become a successful college student, you need to begin on the right path to success. This path requires that you be organized, focused, and knowledgeable about not only how people learn but how *you* learn best. How to become the best learner that you can be means you need to be aware of your strengths and weaknesses; you need to improve your strengths and minimize your weaknesses for maximum success. The first step is to work on your attention and learning skills.

The vast majority of college courses require reading to learn. This chapter will introduce you to various strategies for reading that you can adapt to suit your learning style and the way you learn best. You will probably find some strategies that will work better for you than others, but keep an open mind and give all the strategies a try. After all, they have been developed from years of research and practice about how individuals learn most effectively. Neuroscience (the study of the brain) has illuminated how the brain and memory work, and it is important to learn or study according to how your brain processes information.

To fully comprehend new information, you need to become an active learner. **Active learning** involves more than being on top of your course assignments. Active learning involves working with your brain to maximize your success. An active learner

- Takes responsibility for learning.

- Does all the reading and takes notes.

- Focuses on the subject being discussed and asks questions.

- Does not rely on or blame the instructor if something is not clear, makes note of the question, and asks the instructor to clarify before, during, or after class.

- Asks questions, rereads the text, and uses college support services to help when she or he is stuck.

- Forms a study group with other students so they can all help each other clarify the important points covered in class or in reading assignments. Sometimes peers can explain a concept in language that makes sense to another person. Explaining a concept to someone else is the best way to see whether or not you really understand it yourself!

Active learning is the opposite of **passive learning,** which is not being in control of your learning. If you are a passive learner, learning is done *to* you rather than *by* you.

Metacognition

Active learners take the time to consider their metacognition. **Metacognition** is being aware of your own thoughts and monitoring your thinking. In simple terms, metacognition is thinking about what you are thinking about! A good example of being aware of what you are thinking while you are performing a task or an activity is learning to drive a car. Can you remember when you first learned to drive? At first, every activity you performed—putting your foot on the brake, turning the steering wheel, negotiating a left turn after coming to a full stop—required concentration and focus. You were hyperaware of what you were doing while you were doing it. Now, after years of practice, you perform these tasks easily and automatically. Similarly, when you first use a reading strategy or practice a reading skill, you must *mindfully* concentrate on each separate step of the process. So although using the reading strategies you'll learn in this textbook will feel like hard work at the beginning, the process will eventually come to you naturally. Like an experienced driver, you will find the application of these strategies comes without conscious thought; it becomes automatic.

Memory and How the Brain Processes Information

But how do processes become automatic to you? How does your brain remember? There has been a lot of research on how people learn and remember. Researchers agree that memory is comprised of three processes in the brain: the sensory memory, the working—or short-term—memory, and the long-term memory. Each part of this system plays a crucial role in learning. And the more you know about the way memory works, the more you can learn *with* your brain rather than *against* it. The reading strategies you will learn will make a lot more sense, too.

Imagine your brain as a computer. First, information must be put into the device for the central processing unit to accept and manipulate the information. The central processing unit, or your computer terminal, must **encode** or organize this new information in order for it to be stored and **retrieved,** or accessed again from the hard drive storage. All of these systems rely on the others to make information useable and retrievable. If there is a glitch in any of these systems, the whole system is compromised. In short, if you do not "save" the information and store it correctly, it will be lost. Your brain works in much the same way as your computer (Figure 1.1). Look closely at the three parts of memory processes: sensory, working or short-term, and long-term memory.

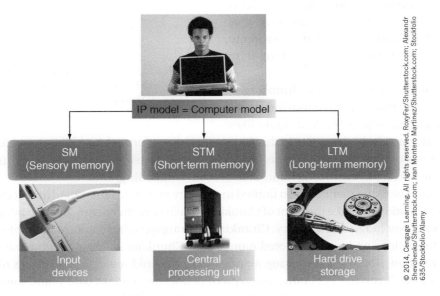

FIGURE 1.1 Memory as a Computer

SENSORY MEMORY

Your brain receives information through your five senses (sight, hearing, taste, touch, smell), hence the name *sensory memory*. This part of your memory system holds information for a brief period of time during which you decide to accept or reject the incoming stimuli. For example, if you are at a party and are engaged in an interesting conversation with someone you like, you may not hear your name being called from across the room. However, if you are distracted, bored, or not paying full attention, you will hear your name being called from across the room. If you are consciously aware of the incoming stimuli, if you accepted this incoming information, then it is moved to your working memory to be further processed. If you did not hear the incoming information within a few seconds, it never registered at all.

WORKING (SHORT-TERM) MEMORY

If incoming sensory information is perceived, or accepted, it is now in your working memory. Your working memory is, essentially, your mind: what you are thinking about at any given time. The working memory is where you start the process of learning information, or studying. Your working memory can only store about seven to nine pieces of information at one time. If you try to cram more information into this limited system, something you were thinking about or studying will get "bumped" from your thoughts. Unfortunately, not only is the working memory limited in capacity, but it can also only hold information for a limited time without forgetting before it transfers it to the long-term memory.

"I'm having trouble with my short term memory...
I'm here because of my short term memory...
I'd like to talk to you about my short term memory..."

To prevent the working memory from forgetting, the information you are studying needs to be as organized as possible. Your brain likes organized information because it is in this format that new information can be stored for later recall. (It is for this reason that this book begins by inviting you to consider "structure" as a primary reading strategy.) The process of organizing information is called **encoding.**

Because your working memory is so limited in capacity and in the amount of time it can remember, encoded information can take the form of chunking, which is further organizing the information to be processed into your long-term memory. **Chunking** is arranging related information into categories so the new information can be remembered more easily. Chunking involves creating meaningful clusters of information. Because the working memory can only hold seven to nine pieces of information at any given time, if you tried to cram a tenth piece of information into your brain, something would be bumped. But if you condensed the seven to nine pieces of information into one, you could free up space in your working memory to remember more things. Imagine you are learning about commas in your English class, and you need to memorize all the coordinating conjunctions: *for, and, nor, but, or, yet, so.* You can make an acronym, a word created by using the first letter of a group of words, of the coordinating conjunctions to help you remember them: FANBOYS. By using an acronym, you have chunked the information into one unit that is organized and therefore easier to remember. And because this information is organized, you brain has an easier time remembering it and committing it to long-term memory.

LONG-TERM MEMORY

Unlike your short-term memory, your long-term memory has an unlimited capacity. In other words, if it were possible to study 24 hours a day for the rest of your life, you would never run out of storage space for your learned information. In fact, the more you learn, the more you are capable of remembering because the connections between your prior knowledge and new knowledge are strengthened. In short, the more electrical signals that are sent between cells in the brain, the stronger the connections grow. Your brain's organization of memories is continually changing, so the more you learn about a subject, the more elaborate the connections become between related information stored in your long-term memory. This related information is called **schema** (singular: **schemata**). The important point for you to understand is that you need to associate new information you are learning to

information you have already learned that is related to that topic. You need to think about what you know about a subject before trying to learn more about that topic in order to help remember the new information later (see Figure 1.2). This mental activity is known as accessing **background** or **prior knowledge,** like you did in the beginning of this chapter in the "Check Your Prior Knowledge" activity.

FIGURE 1.2 Memory Flow Chart

FORGETTING

Forgetting information is a frustrating experience for all students. There are a few reasons why you may forget information that you have studied. Here are the main reasons for recall problems:

- Your new information was not organized effectively enough to be stored and retrieved.

- You did not repeat this information often enough to retain it.

- There may be a problem with retrieving the information.

If these problems with forgetting seem familiar to you, here are some basic points to reduce the likelihood of forgetting.

- Overlearn. Study more than you think you need to.

- Distribute your learning over a longer period of time instead of trying to learn a lot in a small space of time. (This is known as cramming.)

- Review information regularly after you have learned it in order to improve retrieval of the information, or recall.

- Space your studying. **Spaced practice** means that you study in "chunks." Fifty- to 60-minute chunks are optimal for concentrating and absorbing information. After this, take a 10- to 15-minute break during which you think about or do something else. Work on the most challenging subject first. Usually, the most concentration-intensive work is reading.

QUICK TIPS — MEMORY AND STUDY STRATEGIES FOR COLLEGE SUCCESS

College classes are cumulative: Today's information builds on yesterday's and provides the basis for tomorrow's.

Before strategies prime your brain to learn information most effectively, taking into account the limits and processes of the working memory.	**During strategies** allow you to focus on understanding and organizing information most effectively.	**After strategies** focus on working with your brain's memory system to learn and recall important information.
■ Set up a good environment for study. ■ Set a purpose for your task. ■ Think about what you already know to prime your brain.	■ Use active learning to stay focused. ■ Use metacognition to assess your learning and concentration. ■ Use organization to improve encoding.	■ Use spaced practice to aid in retrieval. ■ Avoid cramming. ■ Overlearn material.

READING STRATEGIES

Now that you understand how your brain learns best, you can apply that to some broad reading strategies. A **holistic reading strategy** puts before-, during-, and after-reading strategies into a unified system. Reading strategies make your learning more effective because they prime the brain for the receipt of new information and provide a method to organize new information so it can be learned. Most important, these strategies improve your comprehension of the new information, increase your concentration, and promote active learning and metacognitive awareness. As you practice using a reading strategy, be aware of what works for you and what does not work for you.

SQ3R and SQ4R

The most famous and widely used strategy for before, during, and after reading is SQ3R, which is an acronym that stands for

> **S**urvey
>
> **Q**uestion
>
> **R**ead
>
> **R**ecite
>
> **R**eview

SQ4R is a variation on this, adding *Reflect* to the end of the list. These strategies are best for reading textbook material or long passages with subheadings. *Surveying* a reading involves scanning important headings and information before reading. *Questioning* refers to posing guide questions based on the topic or headings to focus your reading. You will practice these skills later in this chapter. *Recite* refers to repeating the answers to the questions in your mind or aloud (or even in writing) to reinforce learning. (Whichever method you choose—reciting out loud, in your mind, or in writing—will depend on your learning style, as you learned earlier in the introduction to this book, so choose which is best for you.) *Review* compels the reader to go through the process of repeating or reciting the answers on a regular basis to learn, such as during a spaced-practice learning system. *Reflect* refers to thinking about the information and critically evaluating it, as well as relating it to your prior knowledge and other information previously learned.

PQ4R

PQ4R is a variation of SQ3R and SQ4R. The acronym PQ4R stands for

> **P**review
>
> **Q**uestion
>
> **R**ead
>
> **R**eflect
>
> **R**ecite
>
> **R**eview

The foundation of this reading strategy is to help learners organize new information to make it meaningful, and therefore easier to learn and retain. Because this strategy focuses on previewing, a more focused pre-reading review of a passage, rather than surveying, it is best for reading essays and articles that are shorter and that may or may not contain subheadings.

KWL

KWL is a basic strategy that allows you to make the connection between what you already know about a topic, the goals you have for reading and learning the passage, and new information that you have learned.

K = **K**now as in: What do you **know** about the topic?

W = **W**hat as in: **What** do you want to learn?

L = **L**earned as in: What have you **learned**?

WHAT DO I KNOW?	WHAT DO I WANT TO KNOW?	WHAT HAVE I LEARNED?

To employ this strategy, divide a piece of paper into three columns and jot down information related to each of the three parts of this strategy, like this:

With KWL, you are setting up the brain to learn new information, but the main focus is on connecting prior knowledge and setting learning goals. This strategy also compels you to generate ideas about what you want to learn from a reading, putting you in control of what your purpose for reading is. It emphasizes making connections between your list of what you wanted to learn and what you actually learned. You can monitor your improvement over time as your statements about what you want to learn and the contents of the reading become more closely linked. Ultimately, the result will be improved comprehension of material. Table 1.1 summarizes the three reading strategies.

On Your Own APPLYING READING STRATEGIES

Reading strategies work when they are practiced. Apply one or more of these holistic strategies to a chapter or reading assigned for this class or another class you are currently taking. Your instructor may ask you to submit your work for feedback.

Whichever reading strategy you ultimately choose and employ for college reading, rest assured that each of these is effective, worth your time, and has been developed in accord with our knowledge about how the brain learns. While the application of these strategies may be cumbersome at first, remember the awkwardness of first learning to drive an automobile! Keep in mind how automatic that process is now and how efficient you are with the process. Also, keep in mind that you can adapt these strategies to maximize their effectiveness for you.

TABLE 1.1 Reading Strategies

SQ3R	SQ4R	PQ4R	EXPLANATION
SURVEY Quickly scan the reading, taking note of titles, subheadings, boldfaced words, graphics, and photographs to get an overview of the reading section.	**SURVEY** Quickly scan the reading, taking note of titles, subheadings, boldfaced words, graphics, and photographs to get an overview of the reading section.	**PREVIEW** Read the title, the first paragraph in its entirety, the first sentence of each body paragraph, and the conclusion in its entirety to get an overview of the reading section.	Surveying or previewing a reading beforehand allows your brain to see the structure of the reading. You can identify the topic of the reading as well as predict the most important points. Also, you get a glimpse at how the author organizes ideas, so you can do the same.
QUESTION Turn headings and subheadings into questions to focus your reading, and concentrate on the answers to these questions (who, what, where, when, why, how).	**QUESTION** Turn headings and subheadings into questions to focus your reading, and concentrate on the answers to these questions (who, what, where, when, why, how).	**QUESTION** After previewing, create a question, or questions, to answer for the reading as a whole and/or for each paragraph or section. Turn subheadings into questions, or determine the topic, and then use it to formulate a question in order to focus your reading (who, what, where, when, why, how).	Creating questions forces you to actively focus your reading to find answers to those questions.
READ Read to find the answers to the questions you posed.	**READ** Read to find the answers to the questions you posed.	**READ** Read to find the answers to the questions you posed.	Focusing your reading to find answers to the questions you posed reduces the likelihood of losing concentration and increases the likelihood of understanding what you are reading.

(Continued)

TABLE 1.1 Reading Strategies (Continued)

SQ3R	SQ4R	PQ4R	EXPLANATION
RECITE Repeat aloud, in your head, or in writing the answers to your questions, as well as any notations you have taken while reading.	**RECITE** Repeat aloud, in your head, or in writing the answers to your questions, as well as any notations you have taken while reading.	**REFLECT** Connect what you have read and the answers to the questions that you have posed to (a) what you already know; (b) the connections between parts of the reading: how do the questions and answers relate to each other? (c) applications to the "real world."	*Recitation* is repeating information in order to begin the process of encoding it and storing it in the long-term memory. In PQ4R, thinking about your prior knowledge primes the brain for storage of new information before the act of processing (repeating) it.
REVIEW Practice repeating the new information to learn it. Apply the spaced-practice technique.	**REVIEW** Practice repeating the new information to learn it. Apply the spaced-practice technique.	**RECITE** Repeat aloud, in your head, or in writing the answers to your questions, as well as any notations you have taken while reading.	Review further develops the process of learning the information through the repetition of thinking about it, storing it in the long-term memory, *and practicing retrieving the new information*. In PQ4R, once you relate prior knowledge to the reading, the process of learning begins.
	REFLECT Think about the information, critically evaluate it, and relate it to your prior knowledge and other information learned to which it relates.	**REVIEW** Repeatedly review the material by asking yourself questions and saying, thinking, or writing the answers. Only refer to your notes if you have to!	SQ4R ends with analysis, synthesis, and evaluation of materials (critical in college-level comprehension). PQ4R ends with the repetition necessary to process new information into the long-term memory and retrieve it accurately.

YOUR PURPOSE FOR READING

No matter what reading strategy you use, to read and learn effectively, you need to have a clear understanding of why you are reading an assigned passage and what *your* learning goals are for reading. Different purposes for reading influence different rates or speeds in reading as well as different degrees of concentration. For example, if you are reading a complex passage to learn the information for a test, you need to slow down your reading to concentrate on the key points. Your purpose is to learn and understand the information thoroughly. If, however, you are reading a magazine for pleasure, and your purpose is to gain an overview of the content, you can speed up your reading to accomplish this. Also, if you know a lot about a subject and have a good deal of prior knowledge, then you may not have to read slowly because your knowledge base is already significant. If you have little prior knowledge about a subject, you will have to adapt your reading in order to slow down to concentrate, understand, and learn the new information.

READING STUDY STRATEGIES

SURVEYING AND PREVIEWING A READING

Two important prereading strategies help you be an active reader These strategies function to provide an overview of a reading to prime your brain to learn the new information. **Surveying,** or quickly scanning a reading, helps you consider what you already know about the topic, connects your prior knowledge to the reading, and primes your brain for learning new information. **Previewing,** or skimming, the reading more closely helps you to determine important features of the passage, like its structure. Both techniques involve very rapid reading (about 1,000 words per minute). Regular reading, whether for study or pleasure, varies from between 150 and 300 words per minute, depending on the reading task and reader's familiarity with the topic.

Surveying a Reading

When you first encounter a text, you should survey it by looking it over and making a mental note of the title, boldfaced words, subheadings, and graphics. <u>You survey when you are preparing to read a longer reading, like a textbook chapter.</u> You prime your brain to accept this information by first seeing the overall structure.

Surveying a reading involves quickly scanning the reading and considering what you already know about the topic of the reading so your brain will be ready to learn new information. To survey a reading, do the following:

1. Read the title and ask yourself, *What is this reading about?*

2. Ask yourself, *What do I already know about this topic?* Jot down some main points (or discuss what you know with a partner). This step is important because you are activating your prior knowledge to prepare your memory to accept new information about the topic. So don't skip this part!

3. Predict what you think the reading will cover.

4. Flip through the reading and read headings and captions. Look at the diagrams or pictures.

5. Turn the title and headings into questions to hone in on content and organization.

6. Scan for words you don't know and circle them.

7. Repeat step 3. What do you *now* think the reading will cover?

These steps will provide you with a general overview of the structure of the chapter and help set up your brain to process the information.

QUESTIONING: CREATING GUIDE QUESTIONS

One of the steps of surveying is to turn the title and headings into questions to help you focus on what the reading is about. Questioning focuses your attention and guides your reading, so you actively look for information. You read to find a specific answer to your question, which aids your comprehension. And, the answers to your guide questions form a solid basis for a study guide from which you can review the information.

Use the six journalist questions to design your questions: who, what, where, when, why, or how. Decide which of the six prompts best elicits the key points of the section. Don't worry if your questions seem awkward at first; they will improve as you practice. You can create guide questions in two main ways:

- **Creating questions from headings.** If a reading has textual clues, like headings, you can easily create guide questions. A **heading** is a major section in larger or bold print. A **subheading** is a smaller section within a major section. A subheading can be recognized by distinct print or size, too, but is smaller in size or fainter in color than a major heading.

- **Creating questions from topic.** If a reading does not have headings or subheadings, you can ask yourself, *Who or what is the passage about?* The answer to this question is the topic of the passage. (You will learn about topic later in this chapter.) Once you have determined the word or phrase that answers your question, use your answer to formulate your own question, using one of the journalist questions. This technique is like using headings, but instead of having the author's words to form a question, you create your own word or phrase to form your guide question.

Thinking It Through FORMULATING GOOD GUIDE QUESTIONS

Look at the subheading in this section: "Questioning: Creating Guide Questions." What would be reasonable questions to ask yourself while you read this subsection? You could ask:

- What is questioning?
- How does questioning work?
- Who should use questioning?
- Where is questioning used?
- When is questioning used?
- Why use questioning?

Which question would yield the best results? In this case, "Why use questioning?" would be the best to pull out the important points. If you asked yourself this question, you would find the key points are (1) questioning focuses your attention and guides your reading, (2) questioning is an active learning strategy that improves concentration and comprehension, and (3) the answers to self-generated questions form a basis to review new information.

"Who should use questioning?" would be a less effective question to ask because the passage doesn't address the answer specifically, although you could make an educated guess that every active reader should use this strategy. The other questions would be okay, but not as focused as asking why. How do you know which of the six prompts to use with any given heading? The answer is simple: Practice. If you preview or survey a reading you will develop the skill of predicting what the author's train of thought or organizational pattern will be.

On Your Own SURVEYING A READING

Look at one of the four Textbook Applications included at the end of each unit. Apply surveying strategies, making sure to turn the headings and subheadings of the chapter into questions. Write your questions in the text next to the headings so you can use them later when you are assigned to read and prepare this chapter. Discuss your answers with a partner or with your class as a whole.

Previewing a Reading

Previewing is a more in-depth technique for looking at the structure of an essay, article, or reading of a few pages or less. While you may survey a textbook chapter in its entirety, you preview only a section of the chapter at a time. Whereas surveying is flipping through pages and noting important features, previewing is actually *reading* significant parts of the passage.

The basic steps of previewing include looking at the introduction, the first sentence of body paragraphs, and the concluding paragraph. By quickly previewing the reading, you are looking at how the author arranges information and locating the author's main point. This technique allows you to see the bones, or "skeleton," of a reading passage, which is also the structure. Here are the steps to preview a reading:

1. Read the title.
2. Read the first paragraph.
3. Read the first sentence of each of the middle paragraphs.
4. Read the entire concluding paragraph.

If there are headings, turn them into questions to guide your reading. If there are no headings, turn the topic of the section into a question to guide your reading. Consider the following questions.

1. Why read the title?
2. Why read the first paragraph? What might be in it?

3. Why read the first sentences of each body paragraph? What might be significant about the first sentences?

4. Why read the concluding paragraph? What might be in it?

5. Why bother to preview a reading beforehand?

   It is important to read the first paragraph when previewing because it may contain the author's key points. Similarly, the author's key points may be stated in the concluding paragraph. Both the introduction and conclusion are important for you to understand the overall point of the reading. The first sentences of each body paragraph are likely to include the major point about that paragraph, so they also are important to understanding the overall structure of the reading. Previewing as a whole is important because it activates your prior knowledge, primes your brain for receiving new information, and allows you to make predictions about what the passage will be about and what important points the author will discuss. Table 1.2 examines the differences between surveying and previewing a reading.

TABLE 1.2 THE DIFFERENCES BETWEEN SURVEYING AND PREVIEWING A READING

	SURVEYING	PREVIEWING
PURPOSE	To gain an overview before you begin to read a textbook chapter or long passage	To begin to understand the structure and topic of an essay, article, or section of a textbook chapter before you begin to read
GOAL	To provide a general overview of topic and structure to plan your reading task in a long passage	To provide more precise information on topic, structure, and main idea of a short passage or section of a long passage
STEPS	1. Read the title and ask yourself, *What is the reading about?* 2. Ask yourself, *What do I already know about this topic?* 3. Predict what you think the reading will cover. 4. Flip through the reading and read headings and captions, and look at the diagrams and illustrations. 5. Turn the title and headings into questions to hone in on content and organization. 6. Scan for words you don't know and circle them. 7. Repeat step 3. What do you *now think* the reading will cover?	1. Read the title. 2. Read the first paragraph. 3. Read the first sentence of each of the middle paragraphs. 4. Read the entire concluding paragraph.

IDENTIFYING TOPIC

To analyze a reading, you need to recognize *who* or *what* the passage is about. A topic is not a sentence. Instead, it is a word or phrase, and it should be as specific as you can make it. The more specific you can make your statement of topic, the easier it will be to determine the author's most important point about the topic, or the author's main idea. (This point will become clearer to you in Unit 2.)

You know you can create questions from headings or from the topic if there are no headings. Well-considered statements of topic yield good guide questions. For example, stating the topic of the reading in the Pre-Assessment on page 4 as memory is certainly what the passage discusses, but it is too general. From this word alone, you don't know if the reading is about memory and childhood, memory and the brain, memory and traumatic events, or memory and something else. When you establish a very specific topic, you narrow down the contents of the reading into a format that leads to finding the important points of the reading. With this in mind, stating the topic of the Pre-Assessment as memory problems and improvement is far more focused and specific. You can then take this phrase and pose this question: What are memory problems, and how can they be improved? This question will guide your reading to focus on finding the answer. See how much better your grasp of the key points will be if you really focus your topic and, as a result, your guide question? Now you would be ready to read the article and pull out the key points that answer this specific and focused question. To identify the topic, follow these steps:

1. Look for a title, subtitle, headings, or subheadings that provide clues.

2. Look for bold or italicized words—this visual clue often indicates a definition or another important point and frequently reveals the topic of the passage.

3. Look for a word or words in the reading that occurs over and over again. This is a clue that indicates what the author is discussing.

Thinking It Through IDENTIFYING TOPIC

Preview and then read the following reading written in *UC Irvine Today*—a press release blog from the University of California–Irvine. Afterward, read the explanations that follow for determining the topic of the whole reading and each paragraph and posing good guide questions based on the topic.

Study Finds How Brain Remembers Single Events
Brief experiences activate neurons, genes as effectively as repetitive activities

1   Single events account for many of our most vivid memories—a marriage proposal, a wedding toast, a baby's birth. Until a recent UC Irvine discovery, however, scientists knew little about what happens inside the brain that allows you to remember such events.

(Continued)

2   In a study with rats, neuroscientist John Guzowski and colleagues found that a single brief experience was as effective at activating neurons and genes associated with memory as more repetitive activities.

3   Knowing how the brain remembers one-time events can help scientists design better therapies for diseases such as Alzheimer's in which the ability to form such memories is impaired.

4   "Most experiences in life are encounters defined by places, people, things and times. They are specific, and they happen once," says Guzowski, UCI neurobiology and behavior assistant professor. "This type of memory is what makes each person unique."

5   It is well known that a brain structure called the hippocampus is critical to memory and learning, but many questions exist about how brief experiences trigger the physical changes necessary for memory. In his study, Guzowski set out to learn how neurons in the hippocampus react to single events—particularly in the CA3 region, which is thought to be most critical for single-event memory.

Amygdala

Hippocampus

Cerebellum

Diagram of the Brain

SOURCE: How the Brain Remembers (sidebar). by Editors, Issues and Controversies, 26 January 1996. FACTS.com. Facts On File News Services.

1. Who or what is the whole passage about? _____
    The title gives you a strong clue: "Study Finds How Brain Remembers Single Events."
    ■ Answer: *brain and single event memory* (or something similar, such as *the brain and remembering single events,* or even *how the brain remembers single events*).
    ■ What is a good guide question to ask about this reading? *How does the brain remember single events?*

2. Who or what is paragraph 1 about? _____
    After reading paragraph 1, you can see the words *brain, memories, remembers,* and the word *events* is repeated.
    ■ Answer: *brain and remembering,* or *memory and events.*
    ■ What is a good guide question to ask about this paragraph? *How does the brain remember events?*

3. Who or what is paragraph 2 about?_____

When you read paragraph 2, you *see experience, memory, events,* as well as words referring to the brain, like *neuroscientist, neurons,* and *genes.*

- Answer: *experiences or events and memory, the brain and experiences/events and memory,* or *memory and brain.*
- What is a good guide question to ask about this paragraph? *How do brain networks remember experiences or events?*

4. Who or what is paragraph 3 about? _____

Again, you see the paragraph is about memory and the brain—not surprising. You also see the words *one-time events, therapies, diseases,* and *Alzheimer's.*

- Answer: *memory, the brain and remembering events, events and memory and diseases or therapies.*
- What is a good guide question to ask about this paragraph? *How does knowing how the brain remembers events help therapies or treat disease?*

5. Who or what is paragraph 4 about? _____

When you read for useful clues, you see the words *experiences* and *memory.*

- Answer: *experiences and memory.*
- What is a good guide question to ask about this paragraph? *How do experiences affect memory?*

6. Who or what is paragraph 5 about? _____

When you read for useful clues you see the words *hippocampus/brain, brief experiences,* and *memory.*

- Answer: *brief experiences, the hippocampus, and memory.*
- What is a good guide question to ask about this paragraph? *How does the hippocampus affect the memory of brief experiences?*

Notice that each of these paragraphs is about memory. If you just said "memory" as the topic for each paragraph, you would have trouble creating a guide question to focus on pulling out main points. When you narrow the topic into memory and something else, the focus of the paragraph is clearer, as are the questions you can create to guide your reading.

QUICK TIPS IDENTIFYING TOPIC

☑ *Topic* is who or what a passage is about.

☑ Topic can be found in the title, boldfaced words, or words repeated in a passage.

☑ Try to narrow the topic down to two parts: "_____ and _____." This will make your self-generated guide question more effective and finding the key points easier.

☑ Remember: A *topic is a word or a phrase,* not a sentence!

On Your Own IDENTIFYING TOPIC AND POSING GUIDE QUESTIONS

Refer to the Pre-Assessment "5 Things You Must Never Forget" on page 4. Answer the following questions by applying your skills of recognizing topic and posing guide questions. Fill in the chart, noting the topic of the paragraph and posing a good guide question about the topic. The first example is completed for you. Discuss your answers with a partner.

1.   Who or what is the reading about? _____

_____

PARAGRAPH	TOPIC	GUIDE QUESTION
Paragraph 1	How memory works/how to remember	Why is it hard to remember?
Paragraph 2		
Paragraph 4		
Paragraph 6		
Paragraph 9		
Paragraph 10		
Paragraph 11		
Paragraph 12		
Paragraph 15		
Paragraph 16		

APPLYING TOPIC AND QUESTIONING TO A GRAPH

Just as you determine topic and pose questions based on written text, you can apply these same strategies to reading graphics. A **graphic** is a visual representation of information that an author includes to illustrate an important point. Textbooks frequently contain various visual aids, like charts, tables, graphs, illustrations, figures, diagrams, cartoons, and photographs. Even though the information is graphic rather than textual, you begin to read it the same way you would any other reading.

A **graph** shows the relationship between two or more variables. Sometimes, as in a line graph or bar graph, there are two *axes* that indicate components being compared: the *x* or horizontal axis and the *y* or vertical axis. The axes are usually labeled to help you identify what each represents. Figure 1.3 is made up of two axes. The vertical information shows the percentage of recall on the *y* axis. The horizontal information provides the amount of time that has passed since the learning session on the *x* axis. It is important to look at these labels and the title to help determine the topic of the graph. Next, consider the curved line that shows the point of the graph: how much learned information you forget as time goes on. What does this say about how much we *really* learn without repeated practice to learn the new information?

FIGURE 1.3 Ebbinghaus's Curve of Forgetting

Reading graphics can best be accomplished by following a process, just like reading texts. Try answering these questions about Figure 1.3.

1. Determine the topic or subject. Who or what is the graphic about? *The graphic is about learning and forgetting.*

2. Determine a question to pose about the topic. *What is important about learning and forgetting?*

3. Look at the structure of the graphic: What are the parts? *The parts concern the amount remembered as compared with the amount of time elapsed.*

4. Answer your question: What is important about learning and forgetting? *The author of the graphic is communicating to the reader that as time passes, the "curve" of forgetting becomes steep.*

5. What is suggested by the graph? *The suggestion is that we need to review information as soon as possible, or we will forget what we heard in a class or learned.*

VOCABULARY STRATEGY

USING CONTEXT CLUES

What do you do when you encounter words in a reading that you don't know? College texts are full of mysterious words whose meanings elude many readers, and every academic discipline has its own vocabulary (for more on discipline-specific vocabulary, see the vocabulary sections of each chapter). However, there is a way to unlock the meaning of an unknown word without having to resort to a dictionary each time. As you know, your working memory has a small capacity. Because of this finite capacity, it is important for you to maintain concentration. Resorting to the dictionary, while sometimes necessary, is apt to "bump" your flow of concentration. So you need to explore other options for figuring out unknown words. One way is to use context clues.

Context clues are always your first strategy when unlocking the meaning of an unknown word or term, just like surveying and previewing are your first strategies for unlocking the topic of a reading. A vocabulary **context clue** is the surrounding information in the text that allows a reader to deduce, or figure out, the meaning of an unknown word (see Table 1.3). The surrounding information may be within the sentence that contains the unknown word, or in sentences around the sentence containing the unknown word. There are four types of context clues.

1. **Definition clue.** A definition clue is given when an author *directly* defines a word for you in a phrase or sentence. This type of clue is helpful for readers because the information you need—what the unknown word means—is readily available and obvious because it is directly stated. Many disciplines in college 100-level classes have textbooks full of definition clues, as these introductory courses are geared to build up your awareness of the language of a discipline. Definition clues often feature the unknown word in bold print or italics so it stands out. Sometimes, words or phrases like *means, is defined as,* or *is* follows the boldfaced word or the word you do not know. Definition clues can also be recognized through punctuation, such as a colon (:) or a dash (—) followed by the definition.

2. **Synonym clue.** A synonym is a word that means the same as another word—in this case, the word with which you aren't familiar. A synonym for the unknown word can appear next to it, offset by commas or with the word *or,* clarifying that the words are synonyms. Synonym clues are much like definition clues, but instead of being a direct definition or longer phrase, a synonym clue is usually only a word or two in length. Synonyms for an unknown word may not just be within that same sentence, however. A synonym for an unknown word can be in a sentence before, after, or even a few sentences before or after.

3. **Antonym clue.** An antonym is a word that means the opposite of another word—in this case, the word with which you aren't familiar. An antonym context clue is also called a **contrast clue.** Antonym clues are often (but not always) recognizable by certain transition or signal words that signify contrast. Common contrast transition words and phrases are: *instead of, on the other hand, rather than, but, however,* and *conversely.* An antonym for the unknown word can appear next to it and is usually only a word or two in length. An antonym for an unknown word may not just be within that same sentence, however; it can be in a sentence before, after, or even a few sentences before or after.

TABLE 1.3 Signal Words That Indicate Context Clues

TYPE OF CONTEXT CLUE	SIGNAL WORDS OR PUNCTUATION	EXAMPLES WITH DEFINITIONS UNDERLINED
Definition Clue A definition (phrase) of a term, often in boldface or italics	• is, is defined as, means • : (colon) followed by definition • — (dash) followed by definition • , (comma) followed by definition • **boldface** • *italics*	**Long-term memory** is <u>the part of the mind that holds all memories from past experience in a network of organized ideas.</u> **Mnemonic devices**—<u>memory aids that facilitate learning information</u>—are useful for studying and learning.
Synonym Clue A word that means the same thing as the one you don't know	• A word that means the same within commas • A word later in the sentence (or surrounding sentences) that means the same • The word *or* that follows with a synonym of the unknown word	**Repressing** memories can lead to inaccurate recall. This <u>blocking of your recollections</u> may mean that you may not remember the event. **Retrieval** or <u>recall</u> is a vital part of the memory and learning system.
Antonym Clue A word or phrase that means the opposite of the unknown word	• unlike • instead • but • however • on the other hand • rather • conversely	An instructor may give **tacit** praise for study skills <u>instead of telling you directly</u> how impressed he is with your organization. <u>Rather than tell the truth</u> about not completing the assignment, the student was **mendacious** and created an excuse.
Inference Clue An educated guess based on information and reasonable deduction from the sentence or surrounding sentences	• A list of examples or a specific example that clarifies the word • Descriptive details that clarify the word • A list of items that clarifies the word	I remembered that **encoding** was needed to make my study <u>information organized</u> and <u>easily processed</u> by the brain. Short-term memory capacity is so **precarious** that I forced myself to <u>stare at the page</u> and <u>block out everything else.</u> My long-term memory was **abysmal**. <u>I forgot the date I moved here, the details leading up to the move, and the process itself.</u>

4. **Inference clue.** An inference is an "educated" or reasonable guess. An inference context clue is a clue in the surrounding sentence or sentences that provides a strong hint as to the meaning of the unknown word; but unlike a definition clue, the word is not directly defined. Also, an inference clue differs from synonym and antonym clues because a word or phrase meaning the same or the opposite of the unknown word is not provided in the surrounding sentence or sentences. Instead, the author provides clues in the form of examples or just common sense.

To determine which type of context clue is available in a reading, you need to use all your powers of metacognition. You need to think about what you're thinking about and analyze *how* you will figure out the meaning of the unknown word. To do this, always begin from the top and eliminate possible types of clues. Ask yourself, *Is this a definition?* If not, ask, *Is this a synonym clue?* If not, look for an antonym clue. If you have eliminated each of these three possibilities, and you can still figure out the meaning of the unknown word, you most likely have used an inference clue.

Thinking It Through USING CONTEXT CLUES

Here is an example of a passage that incorporates all four types of context clues. Read the passage and see if you can spot a definition clue, a synonym clue, an antonym clue, and an inference clue.

A vocabulary <u>context clue</u> is the surrounding information in the text that allows the reader to <u>deduce</u>, or figure out, the meaning of an unknown word. Rather than make the meaning of a word <u>obscure</u>, context clues help the reader to clarify the meaning of an unknown word. Context clues <u>elucidate</u> what an author is communicating by making clear his or her point in the sentence. Effective context clues are not meant to make writing <u>verbose</u> with long strings of unnecessary words that cloud the author's meaning. Context clues should streamline the information into a comprehensible and a digestible form.

- **A definition clue** is used to help you understand the definition of the phrase *context clue* in the first sentence. The definition of *context clue* is the rest of the sentence. The clue is the word *is*, which alerts the reader that a direct definition follows to explain the word or phrase.

- **Synonym clue.** Also in the first sentence, a clue is given for the meaning of the word *deduce*. See how a comma is used and another phrase is provided—*figure out*—which means "to deduce." Also, a synonym clue is provided to help you figure out the meaning of the word *elucidate*. Later in the sentence, the phrase "making clear" means the same as *elucidate*.

- **Antonym clue.** The word *obscure* is clarified with a contrast clue to help you figure out the word's meaning. In the second sentence, the signal word *rather* alerts you to a contrast thought pattern. The antonym of *obscure* is *clarify*. To clarify something, then, is the opposite of to make something obscure or difficult to understand.

- **Inference clue.** The author of this passage does not come right out and tell you what the word *verbose* means with a definition or synonym clue. Nor does the author use a word that means the opposite of *verbose*. In this case, the rest of the sentence helps you make an inference, or reasonable guess, as to what the word *verbose* might mean. The clue is contained in the following phrase: *with long strings of unnecessary words that cloud the author's meaning.* The clue words here are *unnecessary* and *cloud.* What do you think *verbose* means? The last sentence also provides an inference clue, offering that context clues should *streamline the information . . . into a digestible form* rather than be verbose. With this additional information, you can infer what the word *verbose* means or, at the very least, realize that the word carries negative connotations! The actual meaning is "using too many words or being wordy."

Go back to Table 1.3 and review the signal or transition words and clues for using context to unlock the meaning of unknown words.

On Your Own USING CONTEXT CLUES

Making new words part of your vocabulary is important. You need to learn new words in order to use them and improve your speaking, writing, and reading ability. Here are some tips for learning new vocabulary by using context clues.

- Use context clues as your <u>fundamental</u> strategy for <u>decoding</u>, or figuring out, an unknown word in general or any discipline-specific word you encounter. Using context clues is always your go-to strategy.

- Use this word <u>deliberately</u>, or with conscious intention, and insert it into your conversations in and out of class.

- Make sure to use your new word often to <u>instill</u> it into your long-term memory.

- Make up a sentence you understand, so you can use the word correctly and <u>eruditely</u>.

- Vary the part of speech of the word as you use it—if you learned a noun, use it as an adjective, an adverb, or a verb if possible. This will <u>augment</u> your <u>facility</u> with new vocabulary.

- Repeat the word many times. <u>Recapitulation</u> is the key to memorization. On the other hand, if you believe you will learn new vocabulary with one, isolated effort, you will be disappointed.

- Study new words every day to <u>incorporate</u> them firmly into your vocabulary.

- New words are <u>ubiquitous</u>. This means that new opportunities for expanding your vocabulary are all around you. Notice and ask questions about words used by academic and nonacademic people in all areas of your life: peers, coworkers, teachers, on television, encountered when reading, etc. If these people know a word and use it correctly and you do not, make a point of learning that word.

(Continued)

Define each of the underlined words in the list on the previous page. Next, indicate the type of context clue you used to figure out the unknown word. Then, use the new word in a sentence that you made up, clearly showing the word's meaning.

WORD FROM THE LIST	MEANING OF THE WORD	CONTEXT CLUE USED	NEW SENTENCE USING WORD
1. Fundamental			
2. Decoding			
3. Deliberately			
4. Instill			
5. Eruditely			
6. Augment			
7. Facility			
8. Recapitulation			
9. Incorporate			
10. Ubiquitous			

On Your Own BE AWARE OF NEW VOCABULARY

For a week, listen to your co-workers, boss, instructors, friends, and family. Notice words on TV, on billboards, in magazines—everywhere. Observe what you read for school or for leisure. Use your daily life to look for words to add to your vocabulary. Write five new words below along with the context in which you heard or read them. Then write each word's definition and the type of context clue you used to understand each new word. Share these new words in class discussion or in small groups.

NEW WORD	CONTEXT	MEANING

INCREASE YOUR DISCIPLINE-SPECIFIC VOCABULARY

COLLEGE ORIENTATION AND COMMUNICATION

As a college student, you will be taking many different courses in different disciplines. Each chapter will introduce you to core vocabulary for specific disciplines. It is helpful to familiarize yourself with common prefixes, suffixes, and root words that occur in readings for these different subjects (Table 1.4). You will learn more about prefixes, suffixes, and root words more generally in Chapters 2 and 3.

TABLE 1.4 Vocabulary Associated with College Orientation and Communication

WORD PART	MEANING	VOCABULARY
audio	hear	audiotape, auditory, audience, applaud, audition
dict	to speak	contradict, dictator, dictionary, diction, jurisdiction, predict, addiction, verdict
inter	between	interview, Internet, interact, intermediate, internship, interpersonal, introvert
pro	forward, before, for	procrastinate, proclaim, profuse, propensity, proponent, improvise, produce, pronoun
re	back, again	recede, receive, recreation, resilient, irreversible, revert, retain, referee, revise
scrib, script	to write	scribe, inscription, prescription, scribble, script, describe, subscription, transcript
spect, spec, spic	to look	inspect, spectator, speculate, spectacular, conspicuous, aspect, retrospect, specific
trans	across	transform, transaction, transcribe, translate, transport, transient, transparent
vis, vid	see	visual, envision, invisible, visionary, video, visa, visit, visor, evident, provision
voc	to call	vocabulary, vocal, invoke, provoke, advocate, revoke, vocation

To communicate effectively, it is also important that you use words correctly. Table 1.5 presents a list of commonly misused words. With a partner or as part of class discussion, identify some of these words and how you have seen them misused.

TABLE 1.5 Commonly Misused Words

accept / except	*accept*: to receive; *except*: to take or leave out
advice / advise	*advice*: guidance; *advise*: to recommend or to offer guidance
affect / effect	*affect*: to influence; *effect*: result
a lot / alot /allot	*a lot* (two words): many.; *alot* (one word): not the correct form; *allot*: to divide or portion out
allusion / illusion	*allusion*: an indirect reference; *illusion*: a false perception of reality
are / hour / our	*are* is a plural verb or helping verb; *hour* refers to a period of 60 minutes; *our* is a possessive pronoun.
bazaar / bizarre	*bazaar*: a market; *bizarre*: weird or strange
capital / capitol	*capital*: the governmental central city; an uppercase letter; money or property. *Capital* as an adjective also can mean "punishable by death," as in capital punishment; *Capitol* is capitalized if used to refer to the congressional headquarters (the Capitol building).
council / counsel	*council*: a group that consults or advises; *counsel*: to advise
desert / dessert	*desert*: as a noun, an arid geographic area; as a verb, to leave or abandon; *dessert*: a sweet dish
farther / further	*farther*: at a distance; *further*: additional
imply / infer	*imply*: to suggest without stating directly; *infer*: to draw a conclusion
its / it's	*its*: of or belonging to it; *it's*: the contraction for "it is"
lose / loose	*lose*: to misplace or not win; *loose*: not form-fitting
principal / principle	*principal* (adjective): most important; (noun): a person who has authority; *principle*: a law or truth
than / then	*than*: a comparison; *then*: time
their / there / they're	*their*: possessive form of *they*; *there*: indicates location; *they're*: the contraction for "they are"
to / too / two	*to*: toward; *too*: also; *two*: a number
who / which / that / whom	*who*: a possessive pronoun, used for people; *which*: a pronoun, not used to refer to persons; *that*: refers to things or a group or class of people; *whom*: used as an object to refer to a person or people
whose / who's	*whose*: a possessive case of *who*; *who's* the contraction for "who is"
your / you're	*your*: a possessive that means "belonging to you"; *you're*: the contraction of "you are"

APPLICATIONS

These applications will develop your skills of surveying, previewing, recognizing topic, using context clues for vocabulary comprehension, and understanding graphics. Follow the directions for each application, and then answer the Comprehension Check questions. Each application serves to release more responsibility to the reader as these techniques become more automatic.

APPLICATION   College Success Textbook

This reading comes from a chapter called "Developing Your Memory," in *FOCUS on Community College Success* by Constance Staley. Survey the reading first; then read the whole section. As you read, answer the questions in the margin. These questions prompt you to identify the topic of each subsection and to pose guide questions for the subsections. Remember to use the journalist questions to create your guide questions: who, what, where, when, why, or how. Also, in the margins you will practice figuring out the meanings of words and key terms from context clues. At the end of the reading, you will determine the topic of a graphic and pose questions to focus your analysis of the graphic.

1. What is the topic of this reading? _____

2. Based on the title, what is a good question to ask to guide your reading? _____
   _____

3. Can you answer your guide question based on the title? What is the answer? _____
   _____

4. How many major sections are included in this reading? _____
   _____
   _____

The Three R's of Remembering:
Record, Retain, Retrieve
by Constance Staley

1   Improving your memory is easier if you understand how it works. Memory consists of three parts:

- your sensory memory
- your working memory (called short-term memory by some psychologists)
- your long-term memory

These three parts of the memorization process are connected to these three memory tasks, the "Three R's of Remembering":

- recording
- retaining
- retrieving

We'll compare the three R's of remembering to the process involved when taking pictures with a digital camera: record, retain, retrieve.

Your Sensory Memory: Focus

What is the topic of this section?

Guide question:

Based on the information in this section, how would you define sensory memory?

2 Before we discuss the first R of remembering—namely, *Record*—we have to talk first about focus. Before you even push the button to snap a picture, you have to focus on your subject. Most digital cameras today focus on things automatically, and unlike older cameras, you don't have to turn the focus knob until the image is clear. But you do need to decide what to focus *on*. What do you want to take a picture of? Where will you point the camera? When it comes to your college classes and the role your memory plays in your success, remember that focus doesn't come automatically. It requires <u>consciously</u> deciding where to direct your attention.

3 Imagine this: You're on your way to class. You walk through a crowded street corner and get brushed by people on all sides. Then you cross a busy intersection a little too slowly and get honked at by a speeding car. Finally, you see a billboard you've never noticed before: "I love you, Whitney. Will you marry me? Carl." *How romantic*, you think to yourself.

4 Three major sensations just passed through your *sensory memory* in this scenario, in this case, your <u>*haptic*</u> memory (touch, the crowd), your <u>*echoic*</u> memory (sounds, the car horn), and your <u>*iconic*</u> *memory* (sight, the billboard), all parts of your sensory memory. You have a different channel for each of these three senses. Most experts believe that your sensory memory retains an exact copy of what you've seen or heard—pure and unanalyzed—for less than a second. Some of these images, or icons, will be transferred to your working memory.

5 To help you to focus, consider the following suggestions:

1. **Slow down; you move too fast.** Imagine trying to take a photo of something on the way to class if you were running. Everything would be a blur; trying to take a picture would be useless. Focus requires your full attention aimed at one thing at a time. Turn down the music, turn off the television, shut down the six windows open on your browser, and focus.

Guide question:

2. **Deal with it.** If something is driving you to distraction, maybe you need to take care of it first so that you *can* focus.

Guide question:

3. **Notice where you go.** Wandering thoughts are normal. When *your* attention wanders off, where does it go? Knowing

Guide question:

(Continued)

your mental habits helps you to recognize the pattern and work on changing it.

4. **Watch for signals.** As a college student, you'll probably take many different courses from different departments in your college and be exposed to <u>literally</u> thousands of facts. Not even a memory expert could master them all at once. You must be selective about focus. You're most likely to learn the subject material presented by your instructor and through your course readings. Your textbooks will guide you as you read by using bold fonts, different colors, charts, tables, and headings. Think of them as <u>animated</u> .jpegs on the page, calling out, "Hey, look at me!" In class, watch the instructor's body language; listen to her <u>inflection</u>; notice what gets written on the board or which PowerPoint slides stay on the screen longer than others. Keep those handouts handy. Plenty of subtle signals exist, but you have to pay attention to them.

Guide question:

5. **Get help if you need to.** If you have been diagnosed with ADHD, your brain is wired somewhat differently, affecting your memory and your ability to concentrate. If you've not been diagnosed with a learning disability, but your attention appears to be extremely challenging to harness and you're not sure why, get help from a counselor or learning specialist on campus.

Guide question:

Your Working Memory: Record

6   After you've focused your camera on your subject, you're ready to take a picture, right? But with a digital camera, you don't just click and walk away. You actually click and then review the picture on the small viewing screen to decide whether you want to save it or delete it.

What is the topic of this section?

Guide question:

7   Similarly, *recording* sensory impressions involves an evaluation process that takes place in your short-term or *working memory*. Your working memory is like a review screen, where you review recently <u>acquired</u> sensory impressions. In fact, your working memory is often involved in the focus process. In our example of you walking to class, which of these three specific sensations you just experienced are you likely to remember: the crowd, the car, or the billboard? To stay true to the camera <u>analogy</u>, which one would you take a picture of? It depends, right? You may remember the billboard because you plan to show it to someone else later, or the crowd because you hate crowded places, or the

Based on the information in this section, how would you define working memory?

car horn because it scared you. Your working memory records something because it holds personal meaning for you.

8   The problem with working memory is that the length of time it can hold information is limited. You probably don't remember what you ate for dinner last Monday, do you? You'd have to reconstruct the memory based on other clues. Where was I? What was I doing? Who was I with?

9   The other problem with working memory is that it has limited capacity. It fills up quickly and then dumps what it doesn't need. If that weren't the case, our working memories would be cluttered with useless information. If you look up a number in the campus directory, you can usually remember it long enough to walk over to the phone, right? A few minutes after you've dialed, however, the number is gone. Current estimates are that you can keep something in working memory for one to two minutes, giving your brain a chance to do a quick review, selecting what to save and what to delete. Look at these letters and then close your eyes and try to repeat them back in order.

SAJANISMOELIHHEGNR

10   Can't do it? This task is <u>virtually</u> impossible because the string contains eighteen letters. Researchers believe that working memory can recall only seven pieces of information, plus or minus two. (There's a reason why telephone numbers are prechunked for us.) Chunking these eighteen letters into five units helps considerably. Now look at the letters again and try to recall all eighteen.

SAJA NISM OELI HHEG NR

If we rearrange the letters into recognizable units, it becomes even easier, right?

AN IS MAJOR ENGLISH HE

And if the words are rearranged to make perfect sense, the task becomes simple.

HE IS AN ENGLISH MAJOR

11   The principle of chunking is also used to move information from your working memory to your long-term memory bank, and it's used in memorization techniques described later in this chapter.

Your Long-Term Memory: Retain and Retrieve

12   Let's go back to our camera analogy. Once your camera's memory card gets full, you probably transfer the photos to your computer, or you print them out and put them in photo albums or

What is the topic of this section?
Guide question:

(Continued)

FIGURE 1.4 Your Memory as a Digital Camera

picture frames. However, before you do that, you generally review the photos, decide how to arrange them, where to put them, whether to print them, and so forth. In other words, you make the photos memorable by putting them into some kind of order or context.

13   Just as you must transfer photos from your camera's memory stick to a more permanent location with more storage room, you must transfer information from short-term, or working, memory to long-term memory. You *retain* the information by transferring it, and this transfer takes place if you review and use information in a way that makes it memorable. It is this review process that we use when we study for a test. You transfer information to long-term memory by putting the information into a context that has meaning for you, linking new information to old information, creating stories or using particular memory techniques, or organizing material so that it makes sense. You can frame material you're learning by putting a mental border around it, just as you put pictures into frames. Sometimes you need to frame information to keep it <u>distinct</u> and separate from other information.

14   Your long-term memory is the computer in which you store new knowledge until you need to use it. However, while the memories in long-term memory aren't easily disturbed, they can be challenging to retrieve. Ideally, you'd like your memories to be readily available when you want to retrieve them, just like the pictures or digital images that you have transferred to your computer or put in a photo album (Figure 1.4). You can click on them to view them again, arrange them into a slideshow and publish them on the web, send them to your friends as e-mail attachments, or just review them yourself to recapture the earlier experience. If you just dump your photos onto your hard drive, or print them out and then put them into a box, with no organization or labeling system, how easy will it be to find a specific photo? Difficult,

What is the topic of Figure 1.4?

What is a good guide question to ask about this figure?

Looking at Figure 1.4, what is a good guide question to ask about the 3R's of remembering?

Can you answer your guide question? What is the answer?

Based on the information in this section, how would you define long-term memory?

right? Retrieving information from your long-term memory can be equally challenging if you haven't organized your information, or created mental labels that will help you retrieve them later. Good recall often depends on having a good storage system. The remainder of this chapter will be about how to *retain* information by transferring it from working memory into long-term memory and how to *retrieve* information when you need to.

SOURCE: From STALEY, *FOCUS on Community College Success*, 1E. © 2010 Cengage Learning.

COMPREHENSION CHECK

1 Imagine you are explaining the concepts of sensory memory, working memory, and long-term memory to a 10-year-old child. Using simple and clear language, write a paragraph explaining each concept. _____

_____

_____

_____

_____

2 The author provides five tips to help you focus. Which of these tips do you already use? Which of these tips are you prepared to try?

_____

_____

3 In the section on sensory memory, the author uses these terms: *haptic memory, echoic memory*, and *iconic memory*. Imagine you have just arrived in your first class of the semester. What might you experience on these three levels of sensory memory? Provide a concrete or specific example of probable haptic, echoic, and iconic memory.

_____

_____

4 For each of the following events, indicate which type of memory is at work: sensory memory, working memory, long-term memory, or a combination of these types of memories.

- You are taking notes from a reading for sociology. _____

_____

- As a child, you eat your first pumpkin pie at Grandma's house on Thanksgiving. From this point on, pumpkin pie always makes you think of Grandma. _____

_____

- You are at work and someone mentions that it will be Columbus Day in a few days. You immediately think, "In 1492, Columbus sailed the ocean blue." _____

_____

(Continued)

- You are writing an essay but decide to check your Facebook page. When you return to your essay a few minutes later, you have completely lost your train of thought. _____ _____

- You are fast asleep. Your teenage sister walks in to the house at around midnight, slamming the door and you jolt out of bed. _____ _____

READING GRAPHICS

Look at Figure 1.5 on memory loss versus memory recall. Analyze the graph by answering these questions.

FIGURE 1.5 Memorization Recall

1. Determine the topic or subject. Who or what is the graphic about? _____

2. Determine a question to pose about the topic. _____

3. Look at the structure of the graphic. What are the parts? _____ _____ _____

4. Answer your question. _____ _____ _____

5. What is suggested by the graph? _____
_____
_____

6. How does the information in the graphic relate to the information about memory in the
reading? _____
_____
_____

7. How does Figure 1.5 increase your understanding of memory and learning as it relates to
Figure 1.3 on page 25? Answers will vary. _____
_____
_____
_____

DEVELOPING YOUR COLLEGE-LEVEL VOCABULARY

Use each of these words from the reading in a sentence using the type of context clue provided in brackets. The first example is completed for you.

Example: Consciously (paragraph 2) [synonym] **Every student needs to consciously,
or mindfully, use active reading strategies until they become automatic.**

1. Haptic (memory) (paragraph 4) [synonym] _____
_____
_____

2. Echoic (memory) (paragraph 4) [definition] _____
_____
_____

3. Iconic (memory) (paragraph 4) [synonym] _____
_____
_____

4. Literally (paragraph 5) [inference] _____
_____
_____

5. Animated (paragraph 5) [synonym] _____
_____
_____

(Continued)

6. Inflection (paragraph 5) [definition] _____
   _____
   _____

7. Acquired (paragraph 7) [antonym] _____
   _____
   _____

8. Analogy (paragraph 7) [definition] _____
   _____
   _____

9. Virtually (paragraph 10) [synonym] _____
   _____
   _____

10. Distinct (paragraph 13) [antonym] _____
    _____
    _____

THEMATIC CONNECTIONS

1. Write a paragraph about how understanding how your memory functions to process and retain information will help you as a college student.

2. How does the information in this reading relate to the Pre-Assessment and/or the readings throughout this chapter?

3. What information in this reading relates to information you have learned in your other classes? How can you use this information to help you to succeed in your college classes?

APPLICATION ②

College Success Textbook

This is a section of a chapter on memory from a college success text called *The Confident Student* by Carol Kanar. Survey this reading first, and then read it all the way through, answering the questions in the margin as you read. After you read, respond to the questions that follow the reading.

1. What is the topic of the reading as a whole? _____

2. What is a good question to ask to guide your reading? _____
   _____

3. How many major sections are included in this reading? _____
   _____

Increase Your Memory Power
by Carol Kanar

1   The strategies that follow have worked for many students. Perhaps you already use some of them, or maybe you'll discover a new technique to try.

- **Decide to remember.** Resist passivity. Become an active learner by making a conscious, deliberate decision to remember. Follow through on this decision. This is the most important step you can take. Unless you *decide* to remember, none of the other techniques will work.

  Guide question:

- **Try relaxed review.** Don't wait until the last minute before a test to do your reviewing. Review regularly and do it in a relaxed way. When you are tense, you cannot concentrate. Try the chair-seat relaxation technique described next.

  Guide question:

  1. Start off in a positive frame of mind. Believe that you can and will remember.
  2. Sit in a straight-backed chair with your feet together, flat on the floor.
  3. Close your eyes; grasp the chair seat with both hands.
  4. Pull up on the chair seat as hard as you can.
  5. While you are pulling up with your hands, press your feet firmly to the floor.
  6. Hold that position and count slowly to ten. Feel how tense all the muscles of your body are becoming.

(Continued)

7. Now relax completely, letting your arms hang loosely at your sides. Settle down into the chair and feel how calm you've become.

8. With your eyes still closed, visualize yourself being successful. Experience how success feels.

9. Slowly open your eyes and, in this calm state, begin to review your study material.

10. If you feel yourself becoming tense again, repeat steps 1–9. This relaxation technique is a variation of anxiety-reduction techniques used by professionals in fields such as psychology, medicine, education, and sports.

Guide question:

- **Combine review with a physical activity.** Each sense that you use while reviewing provides another pathway for information to reach your brain. Recite, whether silently or aloud, while riding a bicycle, while doing aerobics or calisthenics (floor exercises like sit-ups and jumping jacks), and while walking and running. Feel good about yourself for keeping fit and for exercising your mind. This technique works well for anyone but is especially good for student athletes.

Guide question:

What are *mnemonics*?

Context clue you used:

- **Use mnemonics.** *Mnemonics* are tricks, games, or rhymes that aid memory. You learned some as a child—for example, "In 1492, Columbus sailed the ocean blue." Also, you may have learned the rhyme that begins with; "Thirty days hath September" to help you remember the number of days in each month. Here is one that you probably haven't heard: "Tyranny nixed in '76." This rhyme recalls the year the Declaration of Independence was signed.

Guide question:

What is an *acronym*?

Context clue you used:

- **Use acronyms.** An *acronym* is a word formed by the first letters of other words. You probably know many others such as ASAP, a business acronym that means *as soon as possible*, and HUD, a government acronym that stands for the Department of Housing and Urban Development. An acronym may help you remember the steps in a process. Choose a key word that will help you remember each step. Then, using the first letter of each key word, create your acronym.

Guide question:

What is *association*?

Context clue you used:

- **Associate to remember.** *Association* is the process of connecting new information that you want to remember to something that you already know. An association is often personal. For example, a student who wanted to remember the particles of the atom—proton, electron, and neutron—associated the names of the particles with the names of her brothers—Paul,

Eric, and Norman. Her brothers' names and the particle names begin with the same letters, and they form the acronym *PEN*.

To help yourself remember the three stages of memory, you could associate the mind with a computer and associate memory's three stages (reception, retention, and recollection) with three computer processes (input, storage, and output). If your instructor asks you to describe the three stages of memory, think of how a computer works, and you should be able to recall the three stages.

- **Visualize.** Form an image, or picture, in your mind of something that you want to remember. Visualization is an especially good way to link names with places or parts with locations. In geography, visualize places on a map. In physical science, draw an idealized continent that could stand for any continent and fill in climate zones. When reviewing this information or recalling it during a test, picture the continent and visualize the zones. In anatomy, label the bones on a drawing of a human skeleton. When reviewing or recalling, close your eyes and see the skeleton with your labels.

  Guide question:

- **Use an organizational technique.** Organize information in a meaningful pattern that shows how each item relates to the others. List steps in a process. Outline complex material. Make charts, diagrams, and information maps that show the relationship of parts to a whole or one part to another. Table 1.6 is a comparison chart showing the memory functions and stages discussed in this chapter. The chart condenses the information into one page that you can use for quick reference. Read the chart across the rows *and* down the columns. As you can see, the stages and functions are related: Your sensory, short-term, and long-term memory functions process information throughout the three stages.

  Guide question:

- **Sleep on it.** Reviewing before sleep helps you retain information. Because you are relaxed, your concentration is focused. The information stays in your mind while you are sleeping, and interference from conflicting sounds, images, or ideas is minimal. When you wake, try to recall what you reviewed the night before. Chances are good that you will remember.

  Guide question:

- **Remember key words.** Sometimes you have to remember a series of connected ideas and explanations, such as the chair-seat relaxation technique described early in this chapter. To recall items stated in phrases or sentences, select one or more

  Guide question:

(Continued)

Guide question:

key words in each item that sum up the phrase or sentence. Recalling key words will help you recall the whole item.

- **Memorize.** Some educators have reservations about memorization. They say memorization is not learning because it is usually done out of context. Students may not be able to recall items memorized in a certain order if the instructor puts them in a different order on a test. Critics also say that memorization is an inefficient technique and that memorized items are difficult to recall. Yet memorization does work. What is 9 times 9? You probably know the answer.

Memorization can be a useful technique for recalling certain kinds of information, especially if it is combined with another memory strategy and is not the only technique you know how to use. Of course, you cannot expect to remember anything that you do not understand. First, make sure you comprehend any new information well enough to link it to knowledge you have already acquired. Memorization works best on information such as the spelling and definition of words, math and chemical formulas, poetry, and facts that belong in a certain order, such as historical events, life cycles, or food chains.

SOURCE: From KANAR, *The Confident Student*, 5E. © 2004 Cengage Learning.

TABLE 1.6 Functions and Stages of Memory

	STAGES OF MEMORY		
FUNCTIONS OF MEMORY	RECEPTION: GETTING INFORMATION	RETENTION: STORING INFORMATION	RECOLLECTION: RECALLING INFORMATION
Sensory Memory	Registers perceptions	Quickly lost without selective attention	Automatic from second to second
Short-Term Memory	Focuses on facts and details	Quickly lost unless recited or reviewed	Possible for short time only until information is lost
Long-Term Memory	Forms general ideas, images, and meanings	Integrates information transferred from short-term memory for storage	Possible for long periods of time or for a lifetime

From KANAR. *The Confident Student*, 5E. © 2004 Cengage Learning.

COMPREHENSION CHECK

1. Write the name of the learning technique most appropriate to each situation listed. Choose from the following techniques: association, memorization, mnemonics, visualization, and acronyms.

- An _____ may help you remember the steps in a process or sequence, such as the order of the planets.
- _____ works best on information such as the spelling and definition of words, math and chemical formulas, poetry, and facts that belong in a certain order, such as historical events, life cycles, or food chains.
- If you need to learn dates in history, such as "In 1492, Columbus sailed the ocean blue," you use _____.
- _____ is an especially good way to link names with places or parts with locations.

2. In a brief paragraph in your own words, summarize the most important information in this section, making sure to include the topic and to follow the organization of this section.

_____

_____

_____

_____

_____

_____

_____

_____

_____

_____

_____

_____

_____

READING GRAPHICS

1. What is Table 1.6 about? _____

_____

2. What is a guide question to pose about the title of Table 1.6? _____

3. What questions could you pose about the headings of each of the four columns in Table 1.6?

_____

_____

(Continued)

4. Look back at Table 1.6, and then refer to Figure 1.1, "Memory as a Computer," on page 9. Create your own graphic based on information from both Table 1.6 and Figure 1.1, and share it with your class. Be creative. For some examples of different types of graphics, look at Chapter 6.

DEVELOPING YOUR COLLEGE-LEVEL VOCABULARY

Use the following key terms from the reading in a complete sentence using clear context clues. Do not just copy the definition of the word. Next, create examples of each of these techniques for learning information for one of your courses. Create an acronym, an example of association, and an example of a mnemonic device.

1. Acronym: _____
   _____
   _____

2. Association: _____
   _____
   _____

3. Mnemonic: _____
   _____
   _____

THEMATIC CONNECTIONS

1. Which of the suggestions in this reading do you already use? Which of the suggestions are you going to try?

2. How do these suggestions to study and remember relate to how your brain processes information as discussed earlier in this chapter and in Application 1?

WRAPPING IT UP

In the following study outline, fill in the definitions and a brief explanation of the key terms in the "Your Notes" column. Use the strategy of spaced practice review these key terms on a regular basis. Use this study guide to review this chapter's key topics.

KEY TERM	YOUR NOTES
Active learning	
Metacognition	
Schema/Prior knowledge	
Surveying	
Previewing	
Guide questions	
Topic	
Context clues	

GROUP ACTIVITY: PANEL DISCUSSION

Use a search engine such as Google or Yahoo to find further information about one of the following topics. Present your findings to the class. It may be useful (and more interesting) to present what you find out in a panel discussion in which teams become "experts" on their research question.

1. Teaching for learning
2. Memory improvement
3. Drugs and memory

4. Sleep, memory, and mood

5. Student success and study skills

REFLECTIVE JOURNAL QUESTIONS

1. What is the most interesting information you've learned in this chapter?

2. What is the most useful information you've learned in this chapter?

3. What have you learned in this chapter that might improve your life as a student or as a citizen?

THEMATIC CONNECTIONS

Respond to one of the following questions. Prepare notes for class discussion or write a response to submit to your instructor. Be sure to proofread your work.

1. What do you believe is the most significant piece of information regarding memory and learning covered in this chapter? What are some ways you could use this information to improve your learning?

2. Several readings in this chapter concern brain research and its relationship to memory. Based on these readings, what do you think scientists ought to work on next?

3. What are the qualities needed for an individual to improve memory and learning? Choose three qualities (behaviors, techniques, or attitudes) that characterize a successful student. Support your answer with specific examples.

ADDITIONAL SKILL AND STRATEGY PRACTICE

Surveying

Survey an assigned reading from a textbook for another class and answer the following questions:

1. What is the topic of the chapter?

2. How many major subsections does the chapter contain?

3. How many visual aids are in the chapter? What is their function?

4. What type of learning support does the chapter offer? Put a check mark beside the following that apply:

   - A list of objectives at the beginning of the chapter

   - Questions to consider after each subsection

   - Review questions at the end of the chapter

   - A chapter summary at the end

   - A glossary of key terms at the end and/or in the margins.

5. Create a list of guide questions you will use as you read the chapter based on the headings and subheadings.

Previewing

Preview a subsection of a chapter you are assigned in another class following your survey of that chapter or preview a shorter essay or assignment. Answer the following questions:

1. What is the topic?
2. What do you already know about the topic?
3. What is a good question to pose as you read based on the title/heading or topic?
4. Based on previewing the introduction, first sentence of each body paragraph and conclusion, what do you think is the author's most important point about the topic?
5. Based on previewing the selection, what do you think the author's pattern of organization might be? The most common are compare and contrast, cause and effect, time order, and listing.
6. Now read the entire section or essay and confirm if your answers to questions 4 and 5 are correct.

Topic and Posing Guide Questions

Review the Post-Assessment, "The Spotless Mind," on the next page. Read each paragraph and fill in the chart. Write the topic of the paragraph and an effective guide question you create from the statement of topic.

PARAGRAPH	TOPIC	GUIDE QUESTION
Paragraph 1		
Paragraph 2		
Paragraph 3		
Paragraph 4		
Paragraph 5		

POST-ASSESSMENT   SCIENCE MAGAZINE

Preview the following article from *Popular Science* and then read it all the way through. Then go to the end of the article and answer the questions. This assessment will help you determine your strengths and weaknesses in understanding, learning, and applying the skills and strategies discussed in this chapter.

The Spotless Mind
by Michael Rosenwald

1   Clinical psychologist Alain Brunet of McGill University in Montreal doesn't usually torture his patients. But lately he has been pressing those with post-traumatic stress disorder, or PTSD, to relive emotionally scarring incidents. For some it's rape, others battlefield trauma. When his patients get particularly upset—crying, shaking, blood pressure rising—he gives them a 25-year-old hypertension drug called propranolol. The idea, though, is not to lower their blood pressure. Brunet's goal is much more profound: to wipe away the trauma of bad memories.

2   Propranolol, it turns out, blocks the effects of stress hormones, which the body creates during traumatic "fight or flight" situations. These hormones serve a critical function—namely, they help us survive life-threatening scenarios by sharpening our senses. But they can also permanently scorch traumatic sights, sounds and smells into the brain, creating a biochemical warehouse in which bad memories can live forever. For the estimated 1.9 million Americans suffering from PTSD, recalling a traumatic event can elicit the same panic response as the event itself.

3   Harvard University psychiatrist Roger Pitman has already published study results showing that patients given propranolol shortly after a traumatic event are significantly less emotional when recalling the experience. Now he and Brunet are taking the idea even further, attempting to deaden bad memories years after traumatic experiences. Their efforts build on groundbreaking research by Karim Nader, another McGill scientist, whose 2000 studies in rats showed that memories don't become completely fixed in the brain, as was previously thought. Instead, when memories are recalled, they temporarily transfer back to short-term storage, where they can be more easily "edited."

4   Brunet's hope is that the drug will subdue the patient's stress response and soften his or her perception of the traumatic memory [see illustration], thereby helping the patient create a new memory of the event—one without all the emotional baggage. So the next time the patient recalls the trauma, the memory of it will no longer cause panic.

5   In the past few months, Brunet has treated about 20 patients with the new method. "So far, we're encouraged by what we've found," he says. The implications of his work are tantalizing, if a tad unnerving: People could essentially pop a pill to lighten up the darkest moments of their lives.

Kevin Hand

How It Works

1. Trauma triggers the amygdala to release stress hormones, which enhance memory formation in the brain.

2. Memories of the trauma are first stored in the hippocampus. Then a chemical reaction encodes them into neurons in the cerebral cortex, cementing them into long-term storage.

3. When a victim recalls the trauma, the memory transfers back to the hippocampus, where it can trigger the release of more stress hormones.

4. Propranolol blocks the effects of the hormones and softens the victim's perception of the trauma. The brain re-stores the newly edited memory.

SOURCE: The Spotless Mind by Michael Rosenwald from *Popular Science*, May 2006. Reprinted by permission.

COMPREHENSION CHECK

Circle the best answer to the following questions.

Reading Comprehension

1 **What is the article about (topic or subject)?**
   A. Bad (traumatic) memories and drug therapy
   B. How memory works
   C. Spotless minds
   D. Drug therapy

(Continued)

2 In finding the topic of this article, which of the clues for determining topic did you use?

A. The title
B. Boldfaced words
C. Words repeated throughout the passage
D. A combination of a and b

3 What is the overall point of this article?

A. Scientists have explored different uses for routine drugs.
B. Memory of traumatic events is seared into the brain.
C. Scientists have discovered routine drugs can reduce bad memory.
D. There are many questions left about PTSD (post traumatic stress disorder).

4 What is the topic of the graphic?

A. How memory works
B. Stress and memory
C. The brain
D. Stress hormones, the brain, and drugs

5 Based on the topic, what is a good question to ask about the graphic of the brain and the neurons?

A. How does memory work?
B. How does the brain work?
C. What is important about the brain?
D. How do stress hormones and drugs work in the brain?

6 What is the topic of the second subsection, "How It Works"?

A. Memory
B. How stress affects the brain
C. How the brain works
D. Traumatic memory and the brain

Vocabulary Comprehension

7 Use context clues to figure out the meaning of the underlined word in the following sentence from the article.

For the estimated 1.9 million Americans suffering from PTSD, recalling a traumatic event can elicit the same panic response as the event itself.

A. Subdue
B. Suppress
C. Draw out
D. Stop

8 **Use context clues to figure out the meaning of the underlined word in the following sentence from the article.**

The implications of his work are tantalizing, if a tad unnerving: People could essentially pop a pill to lighten up the darkest moments of their lives.

A. Tempting

B. Unethical

C. Upsetting

D. Surprising

9 **What is a synonym for the word unnerving in the example sentence in question 8?**

A. Worrisome

B. Hopeful

C. Confusing

D. Promising

10 **Why does the author of the article say in the example sentence in question 8 that the implications of the research are both "tantalizing" and also "unnerving"? What is "unnerving" about these implications?**

A. Something may go wrong with the experiment.

B. The drugs may not work on those who do not have PTSD.

C. We are being seduced by Pitman's experiments without all the facts.

D. The ability to wipe out bad memories, while good in some ways, presents ethical problems and concerns.

Understanding
PATTERNS OF ORGANIZATION AND SUPPORTING DETAILS

✳ Why Do You Need to Know This?

If you were going on a road trip to an unfamiliar spot, wouldn't you look at key intersections on a map first? Similarly, to understand a college-level text, you need to see the structure or key intersections in a reading first. In this chapter, you will develop the skills of looking for the structure of a reading by identifying patterns of organization and supporting details. If you can see *how* an author links sentences and paragraphs with an organizational pattern to make a larger point, you begin to understand all the author's thoughts. And from Chapter 1, you learned that you can better support your memory by finding structure and organization.

IN THIS CHAPTER, YOU WILL LEARN

- To identify patterns of organization
- To recognize transition words
- To identify supporting details
- To identify the relationships between ideas in sentences
- To understand graphics: identifying patterns of organization and supporting details

READING STUDY STRATEGIES

- Paraphrasing to aid comprehension

VOCABULARY STRATEGIES

- Identifying prefixes and suffixes as clues to unlocking the meaning of words
- Increasing your discipline-specific vocabulary: psychology

CamiloTorres/iStockphoto.com

"THERE ARE NO SECRETS TO SUCCESS. IT IS THE RESULT OF PREPARATION, HARD WORK, AND LEARNING FROM FAILURE."

COLIN POWELL U.S. General (1937–)

In this chapter, you will explore a theme prevalent in our society: substances and stressors.

Everyone knows that excessive use of substances is bad—but do you know *how* it affects learning, memory, and the brain? Here, you will learn more about how your brain works, both in dealing with habits both good and bad and in dealing with reading texts. *Do you find it easier to remember something from a reading when you notice a pattern?*

✔ CHECK YOUR PRIOR KNOWLEDGE

Jot down some facts you know about how the brain copes with stress and substances. Do not edit your list—just brainstorm!

_____

_____

_____

_____

_____

_____

_____

_____

_____

_____

_____

PRE-ASSESSMENT

Read the passage and then answer the questions that follow. Don't worry if you do not know what all the terms mean. The purpose of this Pre-Assessment is to find out how much you already know about the reading skills and strategies introduced in this chapter.

Alcohol Stunts Neuron Generation
by Carolyn Seydel

1   It's no secret that guzzling alcohol kills brain cells. Now, research shows that, in rats, a 4-day bender also cuts the production of new brain cells by half. Adding insult to injury, the scientists found that cells born during the binge die sooner too.

2   Though it was long believed that the adult brain can't generate new neurons, that idea was proven wrong several years ago. One region where new brain cells arise is the hippocampus, a key learning and memory center. Given that alcoholics often struggle with learning and memory, Kim Nixon and Fulton Crews of the University of North Carolina, Chapel Hill, examined the effects of bingeing on the generation of new brain cells in the hippocampus.

3   Using a catheter, the pair piped alcohol into the stomachs of male rats; a control group received an equal volume of sugar water, matched for calories. The drunken animals maintained a blood alcohol level of 0.35 percent for 4 days, comparable to that of chronic alcoholics. The researchers also gave both groups daily injections of a chemical that stains new cells. Examining the brains of half the rats immediately after the binge, Nixon and Crews found about 2,500 new brain cells in the teetotalers, but only 57 percent as many in the drinkers. A month later, when they studied the remaining rats, they found that while the control group had lost about half the estimated number of cells they'd produced, nearly all the new cells in the alcoholic group had died. Next, Nixon plans to determine whether alcohol prevents neuron birth for months on end.

4   "It raises more questions than it answers, which I think good findings should do," says neuropharmacologist Judson Chandler of the Medical University of South Carolina in Charleston. Chandler notes that the big puzzle is whether the deficit of new neurons in the rats' hippocampus can be linked to the learning and memory problems seen in human alcoholics.

SOURCE: From ScienceNOW article "Alcohol Stunts Neuron Generation," by Carolyn Seydel, 20 November 2001: 4. Reprinted with permission from AAAS.

COMPREHENSION CHECK

Circle the best answer to the following questions.

Reading Comprehension

1 **What is the topic of this article?**

A. Studies and rats

B. Alcohol and the brain

C. Rat brains

D. Humans and alcohol

2 **What is the author's overall pattern of organization?**

A. Sequence or process order

B. Definition and example

C. Comparison and contrast

D. Cause and effect

3 **What is the pattern of organization in this sentence from paragraph 2?**

Given that alcoholics often struggle with learning and memory, Kim Nixon and Fulton Crews of the University of North Carolina, Chapel Hill, examined the effects of bingeing on the generation of new brain cells in the hippocampus.

A. Comparison and contrast

B. Sequence or process order

C. Simple listing

D. Cause and effect

4 **What is the function of paragraph 3?**

A. To contradict paragraph 2

B. To clarify and explain paragraph 2

C. To demonstrate the irrelevance of paragraph 2

D. There is no function of paragraph 3

5 **Some paragraphs use more than one pattern of organization to explain ideas. What are the two main patterns of organization of paragraph 3?**

A. Cause and effect and simple listing

B. Sequence or process order and comparison and contrast

C. Comparison and contrast and simple listing

D. Simple listing and definition

(Continued)

6 **What do you think is the author's most important point?**

A. Rats' brains are adversely affected by alcohol.

B. Studies on rats' brains affected by alcohol demonstrate severe neuron degeneration, which may offer insight into the brain dysfunction of human alcoholics.

C. Humans should not drink alcohol.

D. Rats are treated unfairly in science.

7 **Why did the scientist conduct this study?**

A. To see how humans differ from rats

B. To understand rat brains and alcohol

C. To set a standard to experiment on human brains

D. To answer some questions about the effects of alcohol on brain function, which might help humans

Vocabulary Comprehension

8 **In paragraph 2, the author uses both the word *generate* (sentence 1) and *generation* (sentence 3). The two words share the same root *gen*, but have different suffixes. What parts of speech do these suffixes indicate?**

A. Adjective and adverb

B. Verb and noun

C. Adjective and noun

D. Verb and adverb

9 **What is the meaning of the underlined word in this sentence from paragraph 4?**

Chandler notes that the big puzzle is whether the <u>deficit</u> of new neurons in the rats' hippocampus can be linked to the learning and memory problems seen in human alcoholics.

A. Growth

B. Confusion

C. Complexity

D. Lack

10 **The word *deficit* has a prefix, *de-*. What do you think the prefix *de-* generally means?**

A. To take away from

B. To add to

C. To go before

D. To follow after

RECOGNIZING PATTERNS OF ORGANIZATION

In this chapter, you will build on the skills of surveying, previewing, and identifying topic by zeroing in on structure by recognizing patterns of organization. You learned that the brain requires organization to learn most effectively; by recognizing the structure of a reading passage, you will be able to recognize the organization that the author intends. In turn, you can use the pattern of organization to see the relationship between key ideas and to move the information from your working memory to your long-term memory and then retrieve and learn it most effectively.

Organizational patterns are important for a reader to recognize because they reveal how an author arranges the information in the passage, which allows you, the reader, to understand the "skeleton" of the piece of writing—the bones that support the "flesh" of the reading. To continue with this metaphor, the "skeleton" is how the author arranges ideas as a whole—the pattern of organization the author has used (Figure 2.1). The "flesh" is all the details that the author includes to elaborate on and explain more about his or her topic. You want to see the skeleton of the reading, so you can understand and remember what the author is trying to communicate about the topic. If you do not have much background knowledge about the topic of the reading, the pattern of organization will help you because if you can follow the author's train of thought more effectively, you will have less difficulty comprehending the reading and you can focus on the key points. Figure 2.2 summarizes the benefits of recognizing organizational patterns.

This "skeleton" is known by several names: *organizational patterns, patterns of organization, author's writing patterns, rhetorical modes,* and *writing structure,* depending on the class in which the topic is discussed. In reading classes, *patterns of organization* is the most common name.

Patterns of organization, like a topic, can apply to a whole reading (its structure), a subsection of a reading, or a paragraph. Patterns of organization can also help you see the relationships between

Organizational techniques used for a whole reading, or section of a reading, or a paragraph

▼ support

▼ Details about the Topic (supported by the structure)

FIGURE 2.1 Applications of Patterns of Organization and Topic

Comprehension

Learning

Writing

Benefits of Patterns of Organization

Predicting Test Questions

Retrieval

Notetaking

FIGURE 2.2 Learning How to Recognize Patterns of Organization in a Reading Will Help You in Many Ways

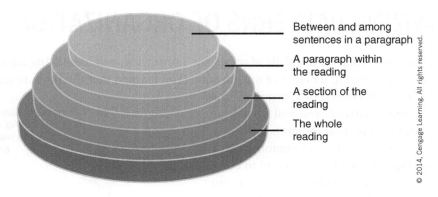

Between and among sentences in a paragraph

A paragraph within the reading

A section of the reading

The whole reading

FIGURE 2.3 Four Ways You Can See a Pattern of Organization

ideas in sentences. There are four ways you can see a pattern of organization, from the larger to the smaller perspective, as you can see in Figure 2.3. Think of the bottom layer (the whole reading) as the most general, overall pattern. The top layer (between and among sentences) is the most detailed, or specific pattern.

Patterns of organization function to provide a structure to a reading, a subsection, a paragraph, or the interrelationship between ideas and sentences in a paragraph. Patterns of organization also help you determine the main details in a passage that support the main point. These main details within a reading are called **supporting details** because they support the author's most important point about the topic. These supporting details are arranged in the reading according to the pattern of organization. Stop and think about how logical this is: An author writes a passage about the causes of stress—this is the topic. What would be the main points the author would logically discuss? The author would discuss a series of causes or reasons that lead to stress. These causes or reasons are the major points that support the topic—the supporting details.

The Role of Transition Words

What do you already know about transition words? You are already familiar with all the transition words used in college writing. They are not complicated words. You may not have considered before, however, how important they are to notice. For example, you look at transition words in order to figure out context clues for vocabulary, as you learned in Chapter 1—you look at the words that surround the unknown word. Many of the words to watch out for when you use context clues are also the clues used in organizational patterns. For example, consider these transition words for antonym or contrast context clues: *unlike, instead, but, however, on the other hand, rather,* and *conversely.* Remember how helpful these words are to finding out the meaning of a word you don't know? Transitions play the same role in helping you to understand the pattern of organization in a reading.

Transitions are words or phrases writers use to introduce a pattern of organization in the writing and between ideas within the writing. The prefix *trans-* means "across." When you make a *transi*tion from high school to college, you bridge the gap between the two levels. *Trans*ition words, then, link ideas in a logical progression from one idea to the other. These words will look familiar to you <u>because</u> they are used frequently in writing to make the ideas flow together and to indicate important points. Transition words or phrases are <u>also</u> called signal words or phrases <u>because</u> they signal how the author is arranging ideas. Later, you will find lists of transition words for each type of pattern of organization.

<u>First</u>, transition words function to show the relationships within a sentence, a paragraph, a subsection, or an entire reading. Transition words <u>also</u> introduce supporting details. <u>In addition</u>, these words help ideas flow more smoothly in writing. <u>Furthermore</u>, transition words improve understanding between connected thoughts and provide and indicate a logical organization between the ideas in a reading. <u>In short</u>, they function to "lubricate" the parts of a reading to make them work smoothly together. <u>As a result</u>, your understanding of these ideas proceeds smoothly in your mind while you are reading.

Supporting Details

In the paragraphs about transition words and phrases, several main points were made, signaled by transition words and phrases. You could ask the question "What is the role of transition words?" and this would be your list of answers:

1. They show the relationships within a sentence, within a paragraph, or within a whole reading.

2. They introduce supporting details.

3. They help ideas flow more smoothly in writing.

4. They improve understanding between connected thoughts and indicate a logical organization between the ideas in a reading.

5. They facilitate the comprehension of these ideas to connect more smoothly in your mind while reading.

Points 1 through 5 are **supporting details** that back up the overall point of the paragraph about the topic—the role of transition words. Did you notice the underlined words in the above paragraphs? These are transition words that introduce the supporting details. Go back to these passages and notice how these words in the paragraphs help to make the ideas easier to follow. You would still be able to understand the two paragraphs without the transition words, but they make the ideas flow better, don't they? If so, the transition words are accomplishing their job. Their job, then, is to make the connections between supporting details flow smoothly.

MAJOR AND MINOR DETAILS

Supporting details can be classified as either major details or minor details. **Major details** are the main points to support the overall point in the reading. **Minor details** are more specific points that support the major points, usually by providing examples of the major details. (You will learn more about details in Unit 3.) Read the paragraph on the next page and underline the transition words as you read.

Combating Stress

There are several ways to minimize stress in your life. First, make exercise a regular habit at least three times per week. Exercise releases endorphins that improve mood. Exercise also improves vascular health and overall fitness. Another good preventative measure is taking stock of the internal stressors you can control. Use meditation techniques when overwhelmed and make sure to get sufficient rest to alleviate internal negative talk. Last, make sure to take time out of your busy schedule to do things that you enjoy. When stress builds up, time with family or friends can help reduce its effects. Similarly, regularly pursuing hobbies and other pleasurable interests serves to diminish the buildup of everyday stresses and strains.

Which of the sentences are major details? Which of the sentences are minor details? There are three major details, each indicated by a transition (*first, another,* and *last*). The first major detail is followed by two minor details that back it up. The second major detail is followed by one minor detail that supports it. The third major detail is followed by two minor details that provide examples. This is how the paragraph would look if the major and minor details were separated.

TOPIC	COMBATING STRESS
Main Point	There are several ways to minimize stress in your life.
1st Major Detail	<u>First</u>, make exercise a regular habit at least three times per week.
1st Minor Detail	Exercise releases endorphins that improve mood.
2nd Minor Detail	Exercise <u>also</u> improves vascular health and overall fitness.
2nd Major Detail	<u>Another</u> good preventative measure is taking stock of the internal stressors you can control.
Minor Detail	Use meditation techniques when overwhelmed and make sure to get sufficient rest to alleviate internal negative talk.
3rd Major Detail	<u>Last</u>, make sure to take time out of your busy schedule to do things that you enjoy.
1st Minor Detail	When stress builds up, time with family or friends can help reduce its effects.
2nd Minor Detail	<u>Similarly</u>, regularly pursuing hobbies and other pleasurable interests serves to diminish the buildup of everyday stresses and strains.

See how the minor details function to provide further information about the major details? The major details, in turn, provide support for the topic of the paragraph (Figure 2.4). Supporting details provide information to support the overall topic (Figure 2.5).

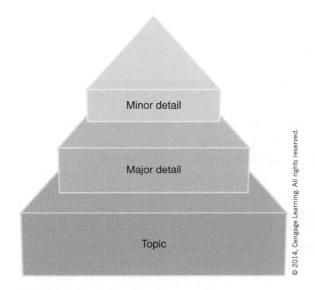

FIGURE 2.4 Relationships Between Ideas

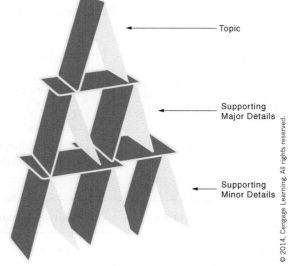

FIGURE 2.5 Support Details Work to Support the Topic

Categories of Organizational Patterns

There are three main categories of organizational patterns as shown in Table 2.1: patterns that list, patterns that explain, and patterns that analyze.

TABLE 2.1 Categories of Organizational Patterns

PATTERNS THAT LIST	PATTERNS THAT EXPLAIN	PATTERNS THAT ANALYZE
Random order list • Simple listing **Specific order list** • Order of importance • Chronological order • Sequence or process order • Spatial (or place) order	• Example/illustration or clarification • Definition and example • Description	• Division/classification • Cause and/or effect • Problem and/or solution • Compare and/or contrast

PATTERNS THAT LIST

Patterns that list include simple listing (or just list), order of importance, chronological order, sequence or process order, and spatial or place order. All of these patterns, except for simple listing, include items that must be in a certain order to convey the meaning that the author intends. In Table 2.2, review the transition words that indicate patterns that list.

TABLE 2.2 Transitions That Indicate Patterns That List

PATTERN OF ORGANIZATION	TRANSITIONS
Random Order	
Simple listing	Also, another, in addition, first, second, third, for example; punctuation (bullets, dashes); numbers (1, 2, 3); letters (a, b, c)
Specific Order	
Order of importance	Most important, finally, primarily
Chronological order	First, second, third, next, then, after, later, dates, after, afterward
Sequence or process order	First, second, next, then, after, later, finally, initially, follows, followed by, the first stage, stages, steps, the final step
Spatial (or place) order	To the left, to the right, above, below, next to, around, opposite, ahead, north, south, east, west, continuing from, near, beside, further, originate, endpoint

Simple Listing

Simple listing means that the items the author lists can be arranged in any order and still make sense. Every piece of writing is a list of something, whether causes, effects, similarities, differences, or steps in a process. So be careful not to oversimplify and see everything as a simple list. Always eliminate the other patterns of organization before you choose simple listing as the organizational pattern. Simple listing should always be your last choice, after you have eliminated all the other possibilities.

> **Example:** Memory tricks, <u>such as</u> mnemonic devices, word association, and visualization are used for studying information and learning it.

Note that these three memory tricks can be in any order and still make sense because the order does not change the meaning of the sentence. The signal phrase *such as* indicates a list of examples.

Next you'll read a passage from the National Institute on Alcohol Abuse and Alcoholism Web site targeted to parents. Read the passage, paying attention to the transition words that signal a supporting detail. Then, look at the visual that reflects how the ideas connect with one another.

Tips for Talking with Your Teen

Developing open, trusting communication between you and your child is essential to helping him or her avoid alcohol use. If your child feels comfortable talking openly with you, you'll have a greater chance of guiding him or her toward healthy decision-making. Some ways to begin:

- Encourage conversation. Encourage your child to talk about whatever interests him or her. Listen without interruption and give your child a chance to teach you something new. Your active listening to your child's enthusiasms paves the way for conversations about topics that concern you.
- Ask open-ended questions. Encourage your teen to tell you how he or she thinks and feels about the issue you're discussing. Avoid questions that have a simple "yes" or "no" answer.
- Control your emotions. If you hear something you don't like, try not to respond with anger. Instead, take a few deep breaths and acknowledge your feelings in a constructive way.
- Make every conversation a "win-win" experience. Don't lecture or try to "score points" on your teen by showing how he or she is wrong. If you show respect for your child's viewpoint, he or she will be more likely to listen to and respect yours.

SOURCE: From Make a Difference: Talk to Your Child About Alcohol, NIAAA website (National Institute on Alcohol Abuse and Alcoholism) NIH Publication No. 06-4314 Revised 2006, http://www.collegedrinkingprevention.gov/OtherAlcoholInformation/makeDifference.aspx#TeensWorld

There are four tips for talking with your teen about alcohol use. These tips are indicated by bullet points. Ask yourself: Do these four techniques have to be in a specific order to make sense? These tips are in a random order—the tips could be rearranged and the meaning and intent of the passage would remain uncompromised. The pattern of organization, then, is simple listing.

Order of Importance

Order of importance (or emphatic order) means the items in the list need to be in a specific order to convey the author's point. Usually, the last point is the most important reason for, or an example of, the author's main point.

Example: To remember learned information accurately, use memory tricks such as mnemonic devices, word association, visualization, and, <u>most importantly</u>, repetition.

The three memory tricks of using mnemonic devices, word association, and visualization can be in any order and still make sense, but the last item—repetition—is put at the end of the sentence because it is the most important point.

Here is a passage in order of importance from the National Institute on Alcohol Abuse and Alcoholism Web site on alcohol poisoning.

What Can Happen to Someone with Alcohol Poisoning That Goes Untreated?

- Victim chokes on his or her own vomit.
- Breathing slows, becomes irregular, or stops.
- Heart beats irregularly or stops.
- Hypothermia (low body temperature).
- Hypoglycemia (too little blood sugar) leads to seizures.
- Untreated severe dehydration from vomiting can cause seizures, permanent brain damage, or death.

Even if the victim lives, an alcohol overdose can lead to irreversible brain damage. Rapid binge drinking (which often happens on a bet or a dare) is especially dangerous because the victim can ingest a fatal dose before becoming unconscious.

Don't be afraid to seek medical help for a friend who has had too much to drink. Don't worry that your friend may become angry or embarrassed—remember, you cared enough to help. Always be safe, not sorry.

SOURCE: From Make a Difference: Talk to Your Child About Alcohol, NIAAA website (National Institute on Alcohol Abuse and Alcoholism) NIH Publication No. 06-4314 Revised 2006, http://www.collegedrinkingprevention.gov/OtherAlcoholInformation/factsAboutAlcoholPoisoning.aspx

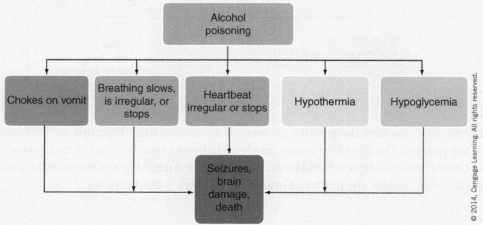

When you read the six bulleted points, which are the major supporting details, you can see that the worst outcome is placed last. In the visual, the first five points could be in another order and still make sense. For example, you could rank irregular heartbeat as worse than hypothermia. However, it is clear that seizures, permanent brain damage, or death are the most horrific possibilities. This outcome is the worst case scenario and, thus, is put last to make a point or emphasize the severity.

Chronological Order

Chronological order (or time order) shows how something unfolds over time. The items in the list need to be in this order to make sense, such as events in history that occur over time.

> **Example:** <u>First</u>, take thorough notes during class. <u>Then</u>, review class notes <u>immediately</u> after class. <u>Afterwards</u>, as soon as you have a chance, rewrite your notes to aid in learning the main points.

Notice how you are advised to review notes first, right <u>after class</u>, and <u>then</u> to rewrite the notes <u>later in the day</u>. These events must occur in this order because you cannot review and rewrite your notes until you have actually taken the notes.

Here is a passage on the topic of heroin withdrawal. What is the timeline for withdrawal?

Heroin Withdrawal

When addicted individuals stop using cocaine, they often become depressed.…. This initial crash may last one to three days after cutting down or stopping the heavy use of cocaine. . . . Symptoms usually reach a peak in <u>two to four days</u>, although depression, anxiety, irritability, lack of pleasure in usual activities, and low-level cravings may continue for <u>weeks</u>. . . . <u>For many weeks after</u> stopping, individuals may feel an intense craving for the drug.

SOURCE: From HALES, *An Invitation to Health*, 15E. © 2013 Cengage Learning.

In this passage, the withdrawal symptoms are in an order according to time. Similarly, the information in the visual has to be in that order to make sense: it is a progression of symptoms. There are four major supporting details, characterized by the timeline and associated symptoms.

Sequence or Process Order

Sequence or **process order**, like chronological order, indicates that certain steps need to be followed in a specific order for the result to make sense, such as the steps in a recipe or stages of growth or development. The difference between chronological order and sequence or process order is the subject matter. In sequence or process order, the author uses stages or steps rather than a clear timeline in hours, weeks, or days.

> **Example:** <u>Initially</u>, information goes into the sensory memory and, if accepted, information <u>then</u> is processed in the short-term memory. <u>Next</u>, information is stored in the long-term memory and can be learned if <u>followed by</u> repetitive study.

In this example, the steps or parts of the memory system are a process or must be in sequence to make sense. Following is a brief reading about the stages or steps in a process to relieve stress through relaxation. Like chronological or time order, the progression needs to be in a certain order. Unlike time order, specific references to time are not included. Instead, the process is emphasized.

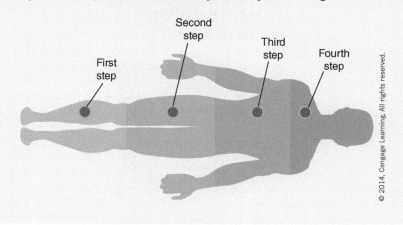

Relaxation is a powerful technique for reducing stress. To relax your body, lie on your back, breathe deeply and do the following exercise. <u>First</u>, tighten your toes and calves as tightly as you can, hold for ten seconds and relax. <u>Second</u>, tighten your thighs and hands, hold for ten seconds and relax. <u>Third</u>, tighten your core, hold for ten seconds and relax. <u>Fourth</u>, tighten your shoulders and face, hold for ten seconds and relax. When you've completed this exercise, your body will feel light and tension free.

Spatial or Place Order

Spatial or **place order** shows an organized format for describing or making points about something, usually a three-dimensional space, such as a place. Descriptions may be organized from front to back, left to right, north to south, or bottom to top. This organization allows the points to be made in a coherent, structured fashion.

Example: <u>Continuing from</u> the brain stem at the back of the brain's structure and <u>near</u> the base of the spinal cord is the amygdala.

The organization of the information leads the reader to visualize the structure of the brain, from the brain stem at the back, moving upward.

Here is a map from BBC News showing the flow of opium and heroin to the United Kingdom.

Flow of Heroin to UK

United Nations Office On Drugs and Crime (UNODC)

Heroin Trafficking into the United Kingdom

Here is a passage that illustrates the spatial order conveyed in the map.

The majority of the opium consumed in Western Europe and the world follows a typical trade route from origination to consumption. Most opiates <u>originate</u> in Afghanistan and make their way to Pakistan to the <u>south</u>. Then the drugs move to Iran to the <u>west</u>. Moved <u>farther west</u>, the drugs reach Turkey. At this point, the drugs are exported west over Europe and into the United Kingdom. In the United Kingdom the opiates are consumed or <u>further</u> shipped for distribution worldwide.

Notice how geographical connections are vital to the explanation of the map of the trade route. There are five major supporting details, arranged in order, according to the main geographical steps in the movement of opium from Afghanistan to the United Kingdom: Afghanistan to Pakistan to Iran to Turkey to the United Kingdom.

QUICK TIPS WHEN IS A LIST A LIST?

When you encounter a list of something, ask yourself, Do the items in the list need to be in a certain order to make sense? (See Figure 2.6.) If so, the pattern is order of importance, chronological order, sequence or process order, or spatial order. If not, the pattern is simple listing.

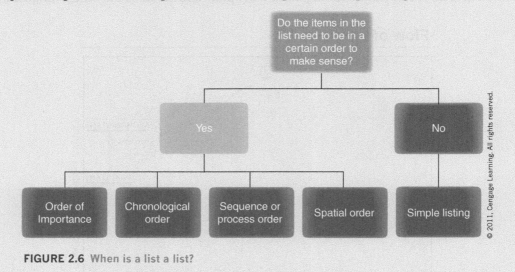

FIGURE 2.6 When is a list a list?

On Your Own PATTERNS THAT LIST

Identify the type of listing pattern used in each of the following paragraphs.

1.   Students often suffer from stress, especially during exams. However, there are several easy tips to alleviate the pressure and help. One useful tip is to learn and practice relaxation tips. Also be aware of the triggers for stress that alert you to taking action. If you can know yourself well enough to see the approaching stress response, you may be able to head off a full-blown stress meltdown. Furthermore, practice imagining a stressful situation when you are not stressed to strengthen your coping mechanisms and contemplate a stress-reducing solution.

2. Neurons
    Your brain contains about 100 billion neurons—nerve cells that work nonstop to send and receive messages. Within a neuron, messages travel from the cell body down the axon to the axon terminal in the form of electrical impulses. From there, the message is sent to other neurons with the help of neurotransmitters.

—National Institute on Drug Abuse http://teens.drugabuse.gov/facts/facts_brain1.php

3.　　Heroin is becoming more popular with teens and young adults than it has been in years. The use of this drug consists of the risk of drowsiness, slowed breathing, increased tolerance for the drug, physical dependence, psychological craving, and, worst of all, death.

4.　　After the initial effects, abusers usually will be drowsy for several hours. Mental function is clouded by heroin's effect on the central nervous system. Cardiac function slows. Breathing is also severely slowed, sometimes to the point of death. Heroin overdose is a particular risk on the street, where the amount and purity of the drug cannot be accurately known.

—National Institute on Drug Abuse http://www.drugabuse.gov/publications/research-reports/
heroin-abuse-addiction/what-are-immediate-short-term-effects-heroin-use

5.　How Widespread Is Heroin Abuse?

According to the Monitoring the Future survey, there was little change between 2008 and 2009 in the proportion of 8th- and 12th-grade students reporting lifetime, past-year, and past-month use of heroin. There also were no significant changes in past-year and past-month use among 10th-graders; however, lifetime use increased significantly among this age group, from 1.2 percent to 1.5 percent. Survey measures indicate that injection use rose significantly among this population at the same time.

HEROIN USE BY STUDENTS, 2009: MONITORING THE FUTURE SURVEY			
	8TH GRADE	10TH GRADE	12TH GRADE
Lifetime	1.3%	1.5%	1.2%
Past Year	0.7	0.9	0.7
Past Month	0.4	0.4	0.4

—National Institute on Drug Abuse http://www.drugabuse.gov/publications/infofacts/heroin

PATTERNS THAT EXPLAIN

Patterns that explain include example/illustration or clarification, definition and example, and description. These patterns allow an author to make a point, and then elaborate on or further explain that point to make sure the reader understands. These patterns are common in textbook readings because often a concept is introduced or a definition is stated, and then the next paragraph provides additional clarification of the concept or definition. In Table 2.3, review the signal words that indicate patterns that explain.

Example/Illustration

Example/illustration or **clarification** occurs when an author makes a point—usually a complex point—and uses the rest of the paragraph to make sure the reader sees the importance of the point.

TABLE 2.3 Transitions That Indicate Patterns That Explain

PATTERN OF ORGANIZATION	TRANSITIONS AND TEXTUAL CLUES
Example/Illustration or Clarification	For example, to illustrate, to clarify, for instance, in other words, that is to say, to put it another way
Definition and Example	Punctuation following a boldfaced term (dash, comma, colon, parentheses), italics of term, is defined as, is known as, means, is
Description	Adjectives that describe (nice, colorful, misty, gloomy) to support the dominant impression (feeling) about the topic or describe or characterize and create a visual image.

This organizational pattern is used most often in longer passages where an author makes a point in a paragraph, and then uses the following paragraph(s) to elaborate on and clarify the first point.

> **Example**: Spaced practice aids in learning. <u>For example</u>, imagine pockets of time during your day that could be used for study. You may find 10 minutes between classes to review vocabulary, or you may use the bus ride to or from school to preview a chapter.

The point about spaced practice is made, and then examples of using this time are provided. Here is another example of an example/illustration or clarification pattern of organization.

> Data from national and state surveys suggest that inhalant abuse is most common among 7th- through 9th-graders. <u>For example</u>, in the Monitoring the Future Study, an annual NIDA-supported survey of the nation's secondary school students, 8th-graders regularly report the highest rate of current, past-year, and lifetime inhalant abuse compared to 10th- and 12th-graders.

In this excerpt, the author states the point about the age group responsible for most inhalant use, and then gives a specific example to clarify and illustrate the concept. Notice how the phrase *for example* signals that an illustration or clarification of a previous point will be made. There is one major detail to back up the overall point about inhalant use among teenagers. This major detail is the findings reported in the NIDA study.

Definition and Example

Definition (and **example**) is commonly used in concept-dense text, or writing with many complicated ideas. This pattern is useful for stating a concept or the meaning of a word and then providing examples to further explain the concept. The key term itself is often in special print, such as boldface, italics, or color. Definition patterns of organization always contain a definition vocabulary context clue.

> **Example:** To **preview** a reading is to assess the topic, structure, and overall point of a reading before reading the passage through in its entirety. For example, instead of reading from the first paragraph to the end, the reader previews the reading to determine important information first.

The term or concept *preview* is defined, and then an explanation of what previewing consists of is provided. Look at another excerpt.

> **Claustrophobia:** This is a phobia in which an individual has an irrational fear of enclosed spaces. While all phobias are considered "irrational"—meaning that there is no specific reason for the development of the fear—claustrophobia is quite common. The word derives from the Greek *phobis* and the Latin *claudere*, meaning to shut.

Notice in the reading how the term to be defined (*claustrophobia*) is in bold print followed by a colon (:). This definition is then followed by additional information to explain the term. In the visual, the definition is indicated as the main piece of information on the left; the supporting details are leading from it on the right. There are two supporting details to back up the definition.

Description

Description is used when an author describes a person, place, or thing. With this pattern, the author uses sensory details to paint a mental picture for the reader of the subject to create a dominant impression. A sensory detail is a description that relates to one of the five senses: smell, sight, hearing, taste, touch. A dominant impression, the emotional mood or feeling of the passage, is created through the use of sensory details. If there are many adjectives (words that describe a person, place, or thing) that describe the topic of the passage, this would indicate description.

> **Example:** Every year, after the lottery, Mr. Summers began talking again about a new box, but every year the subject was allowed to fade off without anything being done. The black box grew <u>shabbier</u> each year: by now it was <u>no longer completely black</u> but <u>splintered badly</u> along one side to show the original wood color, and in some places <u>faded or stained</u>.
>
> —from "The Lottery" from *The Lottery* by Shirley Jackson. Copyright © 1948, 1949 by Shirley Jackson. Copyright renewed 1976, 1977 by Laurence Hyman, Barry Hyman, Mrs. Sarah Webster and Mrs. Joanne Schnurer. Reprinted by permission of Farrar, Straus and Giroux, LLC and Penguin Books Ltd.

In this passage, the author describes an object: a black box. She creates a visual image in the reader's mind of the object. Notice the descriptive words that detail the box's appearance. The dominant impression you get of the box is that it's shabby and old and has been in use for a long time, generations perhaps. Two supporting details back up the dominant impression of the shabbiness of the box. These supporting details are that the box is splintered badly and that it is faded or stained.

Here is another descriptive passage. Notice all the adjectives and descriptive phrases in the passage that make the description of the drug vivid.

> **PCP** is a <u>white crystalline powder</u> that is readily soluble in water or alcohol. It has a distinctive <u>bitter chemical taste</u>. PCP can be mixed easily with dyes and is often sold on the illicit drug market in a variety of <u>tablet, capsule, and colored powder forms</u> that are normally <u>snorted, smoked, or orally ingested</u>. For smoking, PCP is often applied to a leafy material such as mint, parsley, oregano, or marijuana.
>
> —National Institute on Drug Abuse http://www.drugabuse.gov/publications/infofacts/ hallucinogens-lsd-peyote-psilocybin-pcp

On Your Own PATTERNS THAT EXPLAIN

Identify the type of patterns that explain in each of the following paragraphs.

1.   Prescription drug abuse is the use of a medication without a prescription, in a way other than as prescribed, or for the experience or feelings elicited. According to several national surveys, prescription medications, such as those used to treat pain, attention deficit disorders, and anxiety, are being abused at a rate second only to marijuana among illicit drug users. The consequences of this abuse have been steadily worsening, reflected in increased treatment admissions, emergency room visits, and overdose deaths.

> —National Institute on Drug Abuse http://www.drugabuse.gov/publications/research-reports/ prescription-drugs/what-prescription-drug-abuse

2.   Those who see marijuana as a harmless or even beneficial substance criticize studies as providing an inaccurate or incomplete picture of marijuana's effects. They argue, for example, that the same dopamine receptors activated by marijuana and heroin are also activated by sex and chocolate—and that few people would call for the criminalization of those pleasures. Moreover, the correlation between early marijuana use and later use of "hard drugs" could be due more to the people with whom marijuana users become involved than to any property of the drug itself.

—From BERNSTEIN/PENNER/CLARKE-STEWART/ROY, *Psychology*, 7E. © 2006 Cengage Learning.

3.   Peyote: The top of the peyote cactus, also referred to as the crown, consists of disc-shaped buttons that are cut from the roots and dried. These buttons are generally chewed or soaked in water to produce an intoxicating liquid.

—National Institute on Drug Abuse http://www.drugabuse.gov/publications/infofacts/hallucinogens-lsd-peyote-psilocybin-pcp

Herman Eisenbeiss/Photo Researchers/Getty Images

PATTERNS THAT ANALYZE

Patterns that analyze are division/classification, cause and effect, problem and solution, and comparison and contrast. Analysis is the act of looking at the parts of an entity and where they fit in to understand the big picture. Each of these patterns shows the relationship between two or more distinct features. In Table 2.4, review the signal words that indicate patterns that analyze.

TABLE 2.4 Transitions That Indicate Patterns That Analyze

PATTERN OF ORGANIZATION	TRANSITIONS
Division/Classification	Two (or more) types, groups, classified as, classes, category, kinds of, types of, characterized by
Cause	Is caused by, causes, for the reason, because, due to, being that, in that, inasmuch as, since, that is why
Effect	The effect is, consequently, as a result, results in, leads to, thus, as a consequence, hence, so, accordingly, therefore, for this reason
Problem and Solution	The problem is, can be solved by, the solution is
Comparison	Likewise, like, similar to, similarly, in the same way, equally, by the same token, in a like manner, comparable, in common
Contrast	However, but, in contrast, on the other hand, conversely, although, nevertheless, yet, while, whereas, still, though, otherwise, if not, neither . . . nor, some people, others

Division and Classification

Division/classification patterns simplify a difficult concept by breaking down the complex idea into manageable parts or categories. This type of pattern is common in college 100-level classes. Because introductory classes function largely to introduce you to the vocabulary of the discipline, patterns that provide terminology and put concepts into categories are common. Because classification involves introduction to the vocabulary of a discipline, this pattern also tends to contain definition clues. However, this pattern is different from definition and example patterns because the supporting details are specifically there to show the different categories or to divide a concept into different groups or types. Consider this passage where the author classifies, or divides, intermediate memory into two types.

> **Example:**   There are <u>two types</u> of intermediate memory processing: short-term and working memory.

Here is a passage that classifies phobias into different types. Notice that it begins with a definition of *phobia,* but it then goes on to classify phobias as one of two different types.

Types of Anxiety Disorders

Phobia

   An intense, irrational fear of an object or situation that is not likely to be danger-ous <u>is called</u> a **phobia.** People who experience phobias usually realize that their fears are groundless, but that's not enough to make the anxiety go away. The continuing discomfort and avoidance of the object or event may greatly interfere with daily life.

Thousands of phobias have been described. . . . Phobias can be <u>classified</u> into specific, social, and agoraphobia <u>subtypes.</u>

SOURCE: From BERNSTEIN/PENNER/CLARKE-STEWART/ROY, *Psychology*, 7E. © 2006 Cengage Learning.

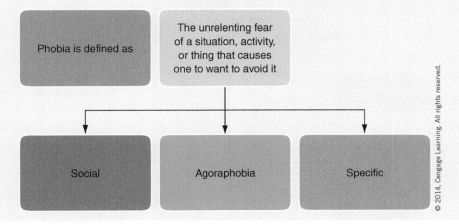

Three supporting details back up the overall topic: What is a phobia? The three major details are the categories of phobias: specific, social, and agoraphobia. Notice how the word *phobia* is defined first. Definitions are often within classification patterns. This pattern is different from the definition pattern because the supporting details are specifically there to show the different categories of phobias.

Cause and Effect

Cause and effect patterns show causes of a situation or phenomenon, or the effects or results of a situation or phenomenon to show the relationship between ideas. Some passages may show both causes and effects.

> **Example**: The human capacity for denial is boundless, and the <u>effects</u> of refusing to see the truth are overpowering.

The author provides a cause (self-denial) and the effect (being overpowered). A passage may explain both causes and effect, or one or the other.

Usually the focus of a passage is on either causes or effects. Notice the difference between the two in the following passages. The first passage explores the effects or consequences of college drinking, while the second example explores the causes of college drinking to excess.

A Snapshot of Annual High-Risk College Drinking Consequences

The <u>consequences</u> of excessive and underage drinking <u>affect</u> virtually all college campuses, college communities, and college students, whether they choose to drink or not.

■ **Death:** 1,700 college students between the ages of 18 and 24 die each year from alcohol-related unintentional injuries, including motor vehicle crashes.

(Continued)

■ **Injury:** 599,000 students between the ages of 18 and 24 are unintentionally injured under the influence of alcohol.

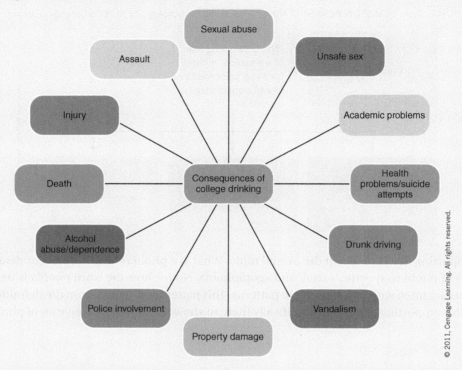

■ **Assault:** More than 696,000 students between the ages of 18 and 24 are assaulted by another student who has been drinking.
■ **Sexual Abuse:** More than 97,000 students between the ages of 18 and 24 are victims of alcohol-related sexual assault or date rape.
■ **Unsafe Sex:** 400,000 students between the ages of 18 and 24 had unprotected sex and more than 100,000 students between the ages of 18 and 24 report having been too intoxicated to know if they consented to having sex.
■ **Academic Problems:** About 25 percent of college students report academic consequences of their drinking including missing class, falling behind, doing poorly on exams or papers, and receiving lower grades overall.
■ **Health Problems/Suicide Attempts:** More than 150,000 students develop an alcohol-related health problem and between 1.2 and 1.5 percent of students indicate that they tried to commit suicide within the past year due to drinking or drug use.
■ **Drunk Driving:** 2.1 million students between the ages of 18 and 24 drove under the influence of alcohol last year.
■ **Vandalism:** About 11 percent of college student drinkers report that they have damaged property while under the influence of alcohol.
■ **Property Damage:** More than 25 percent of administrators from schools with relatively low drinking levels and over 50 percent from schools with high drinking

levels say their campuses have a "moderate" or "major" problem with alcohol-related property damage.

- **Police Involvement:** About 5 percent of 4-year college students are involved with the police or campus security as a result of their drinking and an estimated 110,000 students between the ages of 18 and 24 are arrested for an alcohol-related violation such as public drunkenness or driving under the influence.
- **Alcohol Abuse and Dependence:** 31 percent of college students met criteria for a diagnosis of alcohol abuse and 6 percent for a diagnosis of alcohol dependence in the past 12 months, according to questionnaire-based self-reports about their drinking.

It is very clear from the visual depiction of the passage that there are 12 major supporting details that back up the topic of consequences of college drinking. The supporting details are all effects of alcohol use. In the next excerpt, notice how the passage and graphic explore the *causes* of widespread college drinking.

Student Body as a Whole: The key to affecting the behavior of the general student population is to address the factors that encourage high-risk drinking. They include:

- Widespread availability of alcoholic beverages to underage and intoxicated students;

- Aggressive social and commercial promotion of alcohol;

- Large amounts of unstructured student time;

- Inconsistent publicity and enforcement of laws and campus policies; and

- Student perceptions of heavy alcohol use as the norm.

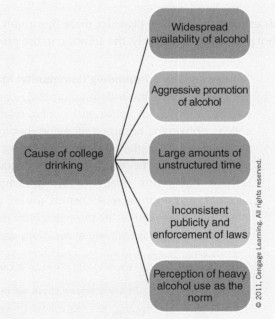

From 3-in-1 framework, from "College Drinking—Changing the Culture, NIAAA website (National Institute on Alcohol Abuse and Alcoholism) http://www.collegedrinkingprevention.gov/StatsSummaries/3inone.aspx

In this passage, there are five causes or influences that result in high-risk college drinking; these five factors lead to or promote the outcome of excessive drinking behaviors.

A specific type of cause and effect pattern is **problem and solution.** This subtype focuses on problems that lead to solutions, or a particular problem that has one or more solutions. Consider the passage on the next page.

What Should I Do If I Suspect Someone Has Alcohol Poisoning?

- Know the danger signals.
- Do not wait for all symptoms to be present.
- Be aware that a person who has passed out may die.
- If there is any suspicion of an alcohol overdose, call 911 for help. Don't try to guess the level of drunkenness.

From from College drinking—changing the culture, NIAAA website (National Institute on Alcohol Abuse and Alcoholism) http://www.collegedrinkingprevention.gov/OtherAlcoholInformation/factsAboutAlcoholPoisoning.aspx#WhatHappens

In this example, the author provides three tips about what a person should do if someone might have alcohol poisoning. Ultimately, the solution to the problem is to call for help.

College and the Surrounding Community: Mutually reinforcing interventions between the college and surrounding community can change the broader environment and help reduce alcohol abuse and alcohol-related <u>problems</u> over the long term. When college drinking is reframed as a community as well as a college <u>problem</u>, campus and community leaders are more likely to come together to address it comprehensively. The joint activities that typically result help produce policy and enforcement reforms that, in turn, affect the total drinking environment. Campus and community alliances also improve relationships overall and enable key groups such as student affairs offices, residence life directors, local police, retail alcohol outlets, and the court system to work cooperatively in resolving issues involving students.

—From "College Drinking—Changing the Culture, NIAAA website (National Institute on Alcohol Abuse and Alcoholism) http://www.collegedrinkingprevention.gov/StatsSummaries/3inone.aspx

In this next example, the problem is college drinking. What is the solution for effecting change? In this example, the problem is college drinking, and the solution to the problem is to combine both campus and community resources to effect change by improving community and campus relationships in the areas of student affairs, residency policy, police policy, enforcement at retail alcohol outlets, and within the court system.

Comparison and Contrast

Comparison and **contrast** show similarities and/or differences between two or more concepts or entities. The paragraph or passage usually emphasizes similarities (comparisons) or differences (contrasts). The following passage contrasts methamphetamine and cocaine.

Methamphetamine is structurally similar to amphetamine and the neurotransmitter dopamine, but it is quite different from cocaine. Although these stimulants have similar behavioral and physiological effects, there are some major differences in the basic mechanisms of how they work. In contrast to cocaine, which is quickly removed and almost completely metabolized in the body, methamphetamine has a much longer duration of action and a larger percentage of the drug remains unchanged in the body. This results in methamphetamine being present in the brain longer, which ultimately leads to prolonged stimulant effects. And although both methamphetamine and cocaine increase levels of the brain chemical dopamine, animal studies reveal much higher levels of dopamine following administration of methamphetamine due to the different mechanisms of action within nerve cells in response to these drugs. Cocaine prolongs dopamine actions in the brain by blocking dopamine re-uptake. While at low doses, methamphetamine blocks dopamine re-uptake, methamphetamine also increases the release of dopamine, leading to much higher concentrations in the synapse, which can be toxic to nerve terminals.

Methamphetamine vs. Cocaine	
Stimulant	Stimulant and local anesthetic
Man-made	Plant-derived
Smoking produces a long-lasting high	Smoking produces a brief high
50% of the drug is removed from the body in 12 hours	50% of the drug is removed from the body in 1 hour
Increases dopamine release and blocks dopamine re-uptake	Blocks dopamine re-uptake
Limited medical use	Limited use as a local anesthetic in some surgical procedures

National Institute on Drug Abuse/ National Institutes of Health

In the previous passage, methamphetamine and cocaine are contrasted in terms of several criteria. Notice the transition or signal words that indicate points of comparison and contrast: *similar to, different from, similar, differences, in contrast, although,* and *both.* While there are some points of comparison made between the two drugs, the major focus of the passage is the differences between methamphetamine and cocaine. Notice also that the heading for the chart uses the abbreviation *vs.,* which is short for *versus,* indicating contrast.

In the following example about hypnotherapists, the author shows similarities or commonalities between these health care professionals. This example shows comparison.

Although hypnotherapists, <u>like</u> other health care practitioners, have their own style, expect some <u>common</u> elements:

- A typical session lasts from 30 to 60 minutes.
- The number of sessions can range from one to several.
- You generally bring yourself out of hypnosis at the end of a session.
- You can usually resume your daily activities immediately after a session.

SOURCE: From Hypnosis: An altered state of consciousness, from MayoClinic.com. Special to CNN.com
http://www-cgi.cnn.com/HEALTH/library/SA/00084.html

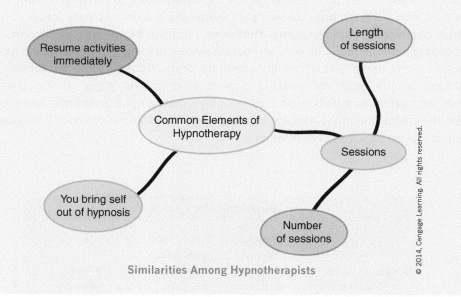

Similarities Among Hypnotherapists

In this passage and in the accompanying chart, the four major supporting details are clearly stated to support the topic of how hypnotherapists have these characteristics in common.

On Your Own PATTERNS THAT ANALYZE

Identify the type of pattern that analyzes in each of the following paragraphs. Choose classification, cause and effect, problem and solution, or compare and contrast.

1.   The question of marijuana's long-term effects on memory and reasoning is also difficult to resolve, partly because studies of academic achievement scores and marijuana use tend to be correlational in nature. Cause and effect cannot easily be determined in such studies. Does marijuana use lead to poor academic performance, or does poor academic performance lead to increased marijuana use? Both possibilities are credible. The same can be said of the correlation between marijuana and mental disorder. Heavy use of marijuana could be a reaction to, or an early symptom of, mental disorder, not necessarily its cause.

—From BERNSTEIN/PENNER/CLARKE-STEWART/ROY, Psychology, 7E. © 2006 Cengage Learning.

2.   Hallucinogenic compounds found in some plants and mushrooms (or their extracts) have been used—mostly during religious rituals—for centuries. Almost all hallucinogens contain nitrogen and are classified as alkaloids. Many hallucinogens have chemical structures similar to those of natural neurotransmitters (e.g., acetylcholine-, serotonin-, or catecholamine-like).

—National Institute on Drug Abuse, http://www.drugabuse.gov/publications/infofacts/
hallucinogens-lsd-peyote-psilocybin-pcp.

3.   Those who would decriminalize the use of marijuana argue that when marijuana was declared illegal in the United States in the 1930s, there was no evidence that it was any more harmful than alcohol or tobacco. Scientific evidence supports that claim, but more by illuminating the dangers of alcohol and tobacco than by declaring marijuana safe. In fact, although marijuana is less dangerous than, say, cocaine or heroin, it is by no means harmless.

—From BERNSTEIN/PENNER/CLARKE-STEWART/ROY, Psychology, 7E. © 2006 Cengage Learning.

4.   Marijuana easily reaches a developing fetus and should not be used by pregnant women; it suppresses some immune functions in humans; and marijuana smoke is as irritating to lungs as tobacco smoke. Further, because possession of marijuana is still a crime almost everywhere in the United States, as well as in many other countries throughout the world, it would be foolish to flaunt existing laws without regard for the legal consequences.

—From BERNSTEIN/PENNER/CLARKE-STEWART/ROY, Psychology, 7E. © 2006 Cengage Learning.

QUICK TIPS STEPS TO DETERMINING ORGANIZATIONAL PATTERN

To determine organizational pattern or structure, follow these steps.

1. When determining the structural pattern of a reading, ask yourself, What is the author trying to do, list, explain, or analyze?

2. If your answer to question 1 is list, does the reading list
   - items in a random order so that the details would make sense in any order?
   - items arranged according to importance?
   - events organized by time?
   - steps in a process?
   - items arranged according to space?

3. If your answer to question 1 is that the passage is explaining something, is a
   - general point made with examples to make it clearer?
   - definition given along with examples?
   - description of a topic presented using adjectives?

4. If your answer to question 1 is that the passage is analyzing something, does it
   - break a big concept into different parts, classifications, or categories?
   - show causes or effects?
   - outline a problem and its solution?
   - show comparison and/or contrast?

Thinking It Through MIXED PATTERNS

Sometimes an author uses more than one pattern of organization to express his or her points about the topic. Also, an author may use transition words that indicate more than one type of pattern within a reading. This can be confusing to readers because they do not know which pattern is the main pattern. The truth is there is a way to determine the main pattern, even if another one is also used to convey information within the paragraph. The rule of thumb is that the main pattern of organization is the one that is reflected in the author's most important point about the topic. (In Chapters 3 and 4, you will learn more strategies and skills to improve your ability to zero in on predominant patterns as mirrored in the main point.)

This passage explores different types of inhalants. Can you determine more than one possible pattern of organization in this passage? Which pattern is the predominant or main pattern of organization?

What Are They?

Inhalants <u>are</u> breathable chemical vapors that produce psychoactive (mind-altering) effects. A variety of products common in the home and in the workplace contain substances that can be inhaled. <u>Examples</u> are some paints, glues, gasoline, and cleaning fluids. Many people do not think of these products as drugs because they were never meant to be used to achieve an intoxicating effect.

Although inhalants differ in their effects, they generally fall into the following <u>categories</u>:

Volatile solvents, liquids that vaporize at room temperature, present in:

- certain industrial or household products, such as paint thinner, nail polish remover, degreaser, dry-cleaning fluid, gasoline, and contact cement
- some art or office supplies, such as correction fluid, felt-tip marker fluid, and electronic contact cleaner

Aerosols, sprays that contain propellants and solvents, including:

- spray paint, hair spray, deodorant spray, vegetable oil sprays, and fabric protector spray

Gases, that may be in household or commercial products, or used as medical anesthetics, such as in:

- butane lighters, propane tanks, whipped cream dispensers, and refrigerant gases
- anesthesia, including ether, chloroform, halothane, and nitrous oxide

—National Institute on Drug Abuse (NIDA)

Which two main patterns of organization are reflected in this reading?_____
_____
Which pattern is the predominant pattern? _____
Explain your reasoning. _____
_____

In this passage, the author begins with a definition of inhalants: *Inhalants are breathable chemical vapors that produce psychoactive (mind-altering) effects.* The author then continues with examples of different types of inhalants. So far, a definition and example pattern seems predominant. However, the passage then divides, or classifies, inhalants into three categories or types: volatile solvents, aerosols, and gases. What is the main pattern of organization, given both the characteristics of definition and example as well as classification? To answer this question, consider what the author's primary purpose is in writing this passage. If you think the author's primary purpose is to classify different types of inhalants, you are correct. The primary pattern of organization, then, is classification.

On Your Own MIXED PATTERNS

Read the following paragraph from a psychology textbook, and identify the two patterns of organization within it. Underline the transition words and phrases that indicate a pattern of organization. Be prepared to explain your answer.

> We obviously need more definitive evidence about marijuana's short- and long-term effects, and it should be based on well-controlled experiments with large and representative samples of participants. Still, evaluating the meaning of even the best possible evidence will be difficult. The issues in the marijuana debate involve questions of degree and relative risk. For example, is the risk of marijuana dependence greater than that of alcohol dependence? And what about individual differences? Some people are at much greater risk than others for negative consequences from marijuana use. So far, however, we have not determined what personal characteristics account for these differences. Nor do we know why some people use marijuana only occasionally, whereas others use it so often and in such quantities that it seriously disrupts their ability to function. The physical and psychological factors underlying these differences have yet to be identified.
>
> —From BERNSTEIN/PENNER/CLARKE-STEWART/ROY, *Psychology*, 7E. © 2006 Cengage Learning.

1. What are the two primary patterns of organization? _____
    _____

2. Which do you think is the primary pattern and why? _____
    _____

On Your Own IDENTIFYING THE MAIN PATTERN OF ORGANIZATION

Here are 10 practice exercises—some are textual and some are visual. For each, determine the topic and the main pattern of organization. Underline transition words or clues within the passage that help you decide on the main pattern. Then, list the major details that explain the topic. Be prepared to defend your answers.

1. **Where Do Hallucinogens Come From?**

    Some hallucinogens can be found in plants. Mescaline comes from a cactus called peyote. And certain mushrooms, also known as magic mushrooms, are hallucinogens. But many hallucinogens are chemicals that don't occur in nature. Some examples are:
    - LSD, also called acid
    - MDA, an amphetamine

- MDMA, an amphetamine, called ecstasy
- PCP (phencyclidine), often called angel dust

— National Institute on Drug Abuse (NIDA)

Topic: _____

Pattern: _____

Supporting details: _____

_____

2. Convert the following visual into written text. Use transition words in your paragraph, clearly indicating what pattern of organization is suggested by the information in the visual.

Symptoms of Post-Traumatic Stress Disorder

Your explanation of the visual: _____

_____

_____

_____

3. **Opiates Act on Many Places in the Brain and Nervous System**

The limbic system controls emotions. Opiates change the limbic system to produce increased feelings of pleasure, relaxation and contentment. (red)

The brainstem controls things your body does automatically, like breathing or coughing. Opiates can act on the brainstem to stop coughing or slow breathing. (blue)

The spinal cord transmits pain signals from the body. By acting here, opiates block pain messages and allow people to bear even serious injuries. (yellow)

—National Institute on Drug Abuse (NIDA)

(Continued)

Topic: _____
Pattern: _____
_____
Supporting details: _____
_____

4. What Is Drug Addiction?

Addiction is defined as a chronic, relapsing brain disease that is characterized by compulsive drug seeking and use, despite harmful consequences. It is considered a brain disease because drugs change the brain—they change its structure and how it works. These brain changes can be long lasting, and can lead to the harmful behaviors seen in people who abuse drugs.

—National Institute on Drug Abuse (NIDA)

Topic: _____
Pattern: _____
_____
Supporting details: _____
_____

5. Convert the following visual into written text. Use transition words in your paragraph, clearly indicating what pattern of organization is suggested by the information in the visual.

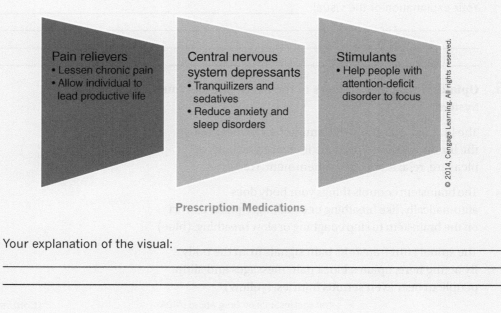

Pain relievers
• Lessen chronic pain
• Allow individual to lead productive life

Central nervous system depressants
• Tranquilizers and sedatives
• Reduce anxiety and sleep disorders

Stimulants
• Help people with attention-deficit disorder to focus

Prescription Medications

Your explanation of the visual: _____
_____
_____

6.   MDMA was developed in Germany in the early 1900s as a parent compound to be used to synthesize other pharmaceuticals. During the 1970s, in the United States, some psychiatrists began using MDMA as a psychotherapeutic tool, despite the fact that the drug had never undergone formal clinical trials nor received approval from the U.S. Food and Drug Administration (FDA) for use in humans. In fact, it was only in late 2000 that the FDA approved the first small clinical trial for MDMA that will determine if the drug can be used safely with 2 sessions of ongoing psychotherapy under carefully monitored conditions to treat post-traumatic stress disorder. Nevertheless, the drug gained a small following among psychiatrists in the late 1970s and early 1980s, with some even calling it "penicillin for the soul" because it was perceived to enhance communication in patient sessions and reportedly allowed users to achieve insights about their problems. It was also during this time that MDMA first started becoming available on the street. In 1985, the U.S. Drug Enforcement Administration (DEA) banned the drug, placing it on its list of Schedule 1 drugs, corresponding to those substances with no proven therapeutic value.

—National Institute on Drug Abuse (NIDA)

Topic: _____

Pattern: _____

Supporting details: _____

_____

7.   **The brain continues to develop into adulthood and undergoes dramatic changes during adolescence.**

One of the brain areas still maturing during adolescence is the prefrontal cortex—the part of the brain that enables us to assess situations, make sound decisions, and keep our emotions and desires under control. The fact that this critical part of an adolescent's brain is still a work-in-progress puts them at increased risk for poor decisions (such as trying drugs or continued abuse). Thus, introducing drugs while the brain is still developing may have profound and long-lasting consequences.

—National Institute on Drug Abuse (NIDA)

Topic: _____

Pattern: _____

Supporting details: _____

_____

8.   Convert the following visual into written text. Use transition words in your paragraph, clearly indicating what pattern of organization is suggested by the information in the visual.

(Continued)

Your explanation of the visual: _____

_____

9. **How Science Has Revolutionized the Understanding of Drug Addiction**

Throughout much of the last century, scientists studying drug abuse labored in the shadows of powerful myths and misconceptions about the nature of addiction. When science began to study addictive behavior in the 1930's people addicted to drugs were thought to be morally flawed and lacking in willpower. Those views shaped society's responses to drug abuse, treating it as a moral failing rather than a health problem, which led to an emphasis on punitive rather than preventative and therapeutic actions. Today, thanks to science, our views and our responses to drug abuse have changed dramatically. Groundbreaking discoveries about the brain have revolutionized our understanding of drug addiction, enabling us to respond effectively to the problem.

—National Institute on Drug Abuse (NIDA)

Topic: _____

Pattern: _____

Supporting details: _____

_____

_____

_____

10. Convert the visual to the right into written text. Use transition words in your paragraph, clearly indicating what pattern of organization is suggested by the information in the visual.

Your explanation of the visual:

_____

_____

_____

_____

_____

_____

Adrenaline elevates heart rate and blood pressure

Cortisol elevates blood sugar in body and brain

Body's alarm system

Understanding the Natural Stress Response

Thinking It Through IDENTIFYING AN OVERALL PATTERN OF ORGANIZATION IN A LONGER READING

Now that you have had practice looking for patterns in shorter passages, apply what you have learned to a longer college-level reading. This reading passage is from a communications textbook. To understand the overall pattern of organization of the reading, take the following steps: preview the reading, determine the topic, and determine the pattern of organization based on the topic.

1.   Who or what is the reading about? What is the topic? _____

2.   With that topic in mind, and the overview of the structure you have gleaned from previewing, what is the pattern of organization?_____

3.   How has the author organized information about this topic? Do they list, explain, or analyze? What specific pattern is used in this passage? _____

Next, turn your topic into a question. Read the passage to verify if your idea about topic and pattern was correct and to answer the question you created. Finally, read the explanation that follows the reading and compare it with your reasoning.

Gambling on Campus

1   Problem gambling has become more common among American adults than alcohol dependence. According to recent national surveys, levels of gambling, frequent gambling, and problem gambling increase during the teen years (even though underage gambling is illegal in most states), reach the highest point in the 20s and 30s, and decline after age 70. Men, who are more than twice as likely to be frequent gamblers as women, reach their highest gambling rates in their late teens. Whites are much more likely to report any gambling in the past year than blacks or Asians, but both African Americans and Native Americans report higher levels of frequent gambling.

2   Gambling also is becoming a more serious and widespread problem on college campuses. Many college students buy lottery or scratch tickets, bet on sporting events, or go to casinos. About half of those who gamble at least once a month experience significant problems related to their gambling, including poor academic performance, heavy alcohol consumption, illicit drug use, unprotected sex, and other risky behaviors. An estimated 3 to 6 percent of college students engage in "pathological gambling," which is characterized by "persistent and recurrent maladaptive gambling behavior."

3   Researchers identified key indicators associated with "pathological" gambling: gambling more than once a month, gambling more than two hours a month, and wagering more than 10 percent of monthly income. A combination of parental gambling problems, gambling frequency, and psychological distress also is associated with college gambling.

(Continued)

4   College students who gamble say they do so for fun or excitement, to socialize, to win money, or to "just have something to do"—reasons similar to those of adults who gamble. Simply having access to casino machines, ongoing card games, or Internet gambling sites increases the likelihood that students will gamble.

5   Although most people who gamble limit the time and money they spend, some cross the line and lose control of their gambling "habit." The term *problem gambling* refers to all individuals with gambling-related problems, including mild or occasional ones.

6   Researchers now view problem or pathological gambling as an addiction that runs in families. Individuals predisposed to gambling because of their family history are more likely to develop a problem if they are regularly exposed to gambling. Alcoholism and drug abuse often occur along with gambling, leading to chaotic lives and greater health risks.

SOURCE: From HALES, *An Invitation to Health*, 15E. © 2013 Cengage Learning.

Who or what is the reading about? What is the topic? *The title tells us that this passage is about gambling on campus. Also, the words gambling and college as well as students and problem are repeated numerous times throughout the passage. Try to narrow it down as you think the information through. So the topic is gambling on campus or problem gambling and college students.*

How has the author organized information about this topic?

a. Is it a list? *No, there are no strings of processes, steps, or information.*

b. Does the passage explain? *This is possible; the author seem to be providing information about the problems associated with gambling on campus.*

c. Does the passage analyze? *Is the author looking at parts and how they fit into the whole? Yes. The author considers the problem of gambling, specifically on college campuses.*

The author's chosen structure is to analyze the problem of gambling on college campuses. You could ask the question "What is problem gambling on college campuses?"

The pattern of this passage is problem and solution, as the author investigates the problems experienced by college gamblers. The author does not provide solutions for this problem in this passage, however; so, this is a problem passage.

Now, as you read the passage in its entirety, your brain is "primed" for the information that will be presented; your comprehension will be improved as a result of taking the time to see this skeleton first. Supporting points will make more sense because you understand what the author is trying to do.

Not only is it useful to determine the pattern of organization of a whole reading during the previewing stage, but it is also helpful to determine the structure of major sections and even paragraphs. While the overall structure of this passage is problem and solution, the author may also use different organizational patterns in paragraphs within the passage.

On Your Own ## IDENTIFYING AN OVERALL PATTERN
OF ORGANIZATION IN A LONGER READING

Read the following passage and answer the questions about the overall topic and pattern of organization. As you read, circle the words that indicate the pattern of organization used in this passage.

Teens and Drugged Driving

1   According to the Centers for Disease Control and Prevention, vehicle accidents are the leading cause of death among young people aged 16 to 19.[9] It is generally accepted that because teens are the least experienced drivers as a group, they have a higher risk of being involved in an accident compared with more experienced drivers. When this lack of experience is combined with the use of marijuana or other substances that impact cognitive and motor abilities, the results can be tragic.

2   Results from NIDA's Monitoring the Future survey indicate that in 2007, more than 12 percent of high school seniors admitted to driving under the influence of marijuana in the 2 weeks prior to the survey.

3   The 2007 State of Maryland Adolescent Survey indicates that 11.1 percent of the State's licensed adolescent drivers reported driving under the influence of marijuana on three or more occasions, and 10 percent reported driving while using a drug other than marijuana (not including alcohol).

SOURCE: NIDA, What Is Drugged Driving? http://www.drugabuse.gov/publications/infofacts/drugged-driving.

1. Who or what is the reading about? What is the topic? _____
_____

2. How has the author organized the information about this topic? _____

QUICK TIPS PATTERNS OF ORGANIZATION FACTS

☑ There is an overall topic, structure, and point to a reading in its entirety.

☑ There is an overall topic, structure, and point to each subsection in a textbook chapter.

☑ There is an overall topic, structure, and point to each paragraph.

☑ When in doubt or if there seems to be two or more possible patterns in a section of text, go with the one that seems to be predominant.

RELATIONSHIPS BETWEEN IDEAS

Now that you have developed skills to see the "skeleton" or "big picture" or the patterns of organization in a reading, you will learn to see the relationships between ideas, or the "small picture," between sentences, and within a paragraph or section of a reading. The skills of seeing both the big picture and small picture are vital to understanding what you read. Developing these skills will make pinpointing the author's most important point, or main idea, far less perplexing.

Relationships between ideas can be defined as an author's arrangement of supporting details in a reading, often indicated by transition words or phrases that clarify, reflect, and support the most important point. Sometimes the author does not use transition words, but there is still a relationship between the ideas. In this case, you need to infer or make an educated guess about the relationships by applying what you already know. Just as the main pattern of organization of a reading dominates the different patterns used within subsections of paragraphs of a longer reading, so within a paragraph there are often mixed patterns, yet there is a dominant pattern that overarches the entire paragraph. Similarly, just as a good reader finds evidence of an overall pattern of organization in a reading, a good reader also notes relationships between ideas in a passage (Figure 2.7). Both approaches involve

- Identifying transitions that provide clues to the author's structure or pattern of organization.

- Determining a predominant pattern even though there may be other patterns in use.

- Making reasonable inferences, or educated guesses, about how the author is presenting information.

FIGURE 2.7 Determining an author's thought pattern is useful not only for understanding a whole reading or parts of a reading, but also for understanding how ideas connect between sentences.

Consider this passage:

> The United States has just experienced the greatest economic crisis since the Great Depression. People are likely to experience high stress levels and high unemployment rates this year.

What is the relationship between ideas in these two sentences?

a. Sentence 1 restates the ideas found in sentence 2.

b. Sentence 2 states the result of sentence 1.

c. Sentence 2 gives an example of the point made in sentence 1.

d. Sentence 2 describes the statement made in sentence 1.

Sentence 1 states that there has been an economic crisis of large proportion. Sentence 2 states that stress levels and unemployment will be high. Notice that there are no transition words to clarify the relationship between the ideas in the two sentences.

The answer to the question is *b*. The relationship between ideas is that sentence 2 *follows from* or is the *result of* sentence 1. In these sentences, there are no transitions to connect the ideas, but you could guess that words like *because of this, as a result,* or *for this reason* would fit at the beginning of the second sentence. Despite the absence of transitions, the ideas are very much connected: the connection is one of cause and effect. The first sentence states the cause and the second sentence states the effect. Understanding the relationships between ideas allows you, the reader, to connect and make sense of an author's ideas.

Thinking It Through FINDING RELATIONSHIPS BETWEEN IDEAS

Here is an abstract, or brief summary of main points, from an article on adolescents and gambling. Complete the following steps to become familiar with the reading.

1. Preview the paragraph. _____

2. Determine the topic. _____

3. Determine the pattern of organization. _____

4. Read the paragraph. _____

5. Underline transitions or key words that show the relationship between ideas.

6. Answer the questions following the passage about the relationship between ideas in the paragraph.

Gender Differences Among Adolescents with Gambling-Related Problems
By Stephen Ellenbogen, Jeffrey Derevensky, and R. Gupta

Abstract

[1]Data from five recent studies using self-reports were merged to explore gender differences in the characteristics of adolescent problem gambling, including comorbidity with other youth problems. [2]The sample consisted of 2,750 male and 2,563 female participants. [3]Male problem gamblers were more likely than females to report signs of psychological difficulties while females were more likely to note behavioural problems as a consequence of their gambling problems. [4]Males and females with severe gambling problems had remarkably similar prevalence rates

(Continued)

of depression, substance use and weekly gambling. [5]In the non-problem gambling group, depression was more likely to afflict females <u>whereas</u> substance use and frequent gambling were more prevalent among males.

SOURCE: Abstract from: http://www.ncbi.nlm.nih.gov/pubmed/17265189 Ellenbogen S, Derevensky J, Gupta R., Gender differences among adolescents with gambling-related problems.

The topic of this abstract is gender differences among adolescents with gambling-related problems. The title provides the clue as well as repeated words in the passage.

The pattern of organization is compare and contrast. The authors show similarities and differences between males and females with regard to gambling-related problems.

Now, consider the relationship between ideas among the sentences. Can you follow the author's reasoning and train of thought? How would you explain how each sentence's ideas connect to the next?

1. **What is the relationship between sentences 1 and 2?** *In the first sentence, the authors establish their topic and the subjects of the study. They expand on the problems related to gambling by using the language "comorbidity with other youth problems." What do you think comorbidity means, using prefix clues to determine a logical definition? If co- means "with" and morbidity refers to disease, comorbidity in this context means "a related disease or state that can occur alongside gambling." In sentence 2, the authors provide the numbers of participants or subjects in the study. The authors set up the contrast between the genders.*

2. **What is the relationship between sentences 2 and 3?** *Sentence 3, building on sentence 2, clearly contrasts males and females by clarifying the differences in how each attributes or categorizes the consequences of problem gambling. Note the transition words that indicate contrast.*

3. **What is the relationship between sentences 3 and 4?** *While sentence 3 provides a clear contrast between the genders, sentence 4 shows similarity. Both males and females with severe gambling problems encountered similar rates of comorbidity.*

4. **What is the relationship between sentences 4 and 5?** *Sentence 5 functions to contrast those with severe gambling problems with those adolescents described as "non-problem" gamblers. Sentence 5 also functions to contrast male and female "non-problem" gamblers.*

5. What are the major supporting details in this paragraph?

	PROBLEM GAMBLERS' REPORTED CONSEQUENCES	SEVERE PROBLEM GAMBLERS' REPORTED CONSEQUENCES	NON-PROBLEM GAMBLERS' REPORTED CONSEQUENCES
Male	Psychological difficulties	Depression, substance use, and weekly gambling	Substance use and frequent gambling
Female	Behavioral problems	Depression, substance use, and weekly gambling	Depression

- Male problem gamblers were more likely <u>than</u> females to report signs of psycho-logical difficulties, <u>while</u> females were more likely to note behavioral problems as a <u>consequence</u> of their gambling problems.
- Males and females with severe gambling problems had remarkably <u>similar</u> preva-lence rates of depression, substance use, and weekly gambling.
- In the non-problem gambling group, depression was more likely to afflict females, <u>whereas</u> substance use and frequent gambling were more prevalent among males.

On Your Own FINDING RELATIONSHIPS BETWEEN IDEAS

Read this passage from a college psychology textbook. Then answer the questions to uncover the relationships between the ideas.

What is the topic? _____

   In Canada, it is legal to grow and use marijuana for medicinal purposes, and despite fed-eral laws to the contrary, the same is true in ten U.S. states. Although the American Medical Association has recently rejected the idea of medical uses for marijuana, scientists are intent on objectively studying its potential value in the treatment of certain diseases, as well as its dangers (or lack thereof). Their work is being encouraged by bodies such as the National Insti-tute of Medicine, and drug companies are working to develop new cannabis-based medicines. The United Nations, too, has recommended that governments worldwide sponsor additional work on the medical uses of marijuana. Ultimately, the most reasonable conclusions about marijuana use must await the outcome of this research.

—From BERNSTEIN/PENNER/CLARKE-STEWART/ROY, Psychology, 7E. © 2006 Cengage Learning.

1. What is the relationship between sentences 1 and 2? _____
   _____
   _____
   _____
   _____
   _____

2. What is the relationship between sentences 2 and 3? _____
   _____
   _____

3. What is the relationship between sentences 3 and 4? _____
   _____
   _____

(Continued)

4. What is the relationship between sentences 4 and 5? _____

_____

_____

5. What are the major supporting details?

- _____

    _____

    _____

- _____

    _____

    _____

- _____

    _____

    _____

- _____

    _____

    _____

    _____

✛ UNDERSTANDING GRAPHICS

IDENTIFYING PATTERNS AND SUPPORTING DETAILS IN A GRAPH

Understanding patterns of organization, supporting details, and the relationship between ideas are vital to understanding graphics. After all, a graphic is made up of parts, and those parts suggest an overall point. In some graphics, the author tells what the overall point is. In most graphics, there is a title or topic and many supporting details (as in Figure 2.8), but the author doesn't come right out and tell the point of the graphic. You have to figure out the point by seeing the relationship between ideas.

Preview this line graph using the same steps as you would for a reading. Then try to answer the questions before reading the answers.

*Difference between this estimate and the 2010 estimate is statistically significant at the .05 level.

SOURCE: Figure 3.3 Binge Alcohol Use among Adults Aged 18 to 22, by College Enrollment: 2002-2010 from http://www.samhsa.gov/data/NSDUH/2k10NSDUH/2k10Results.pdf, page 32

FIGURE 2.8 Binge Alcohol Use among Adults Aged 18 to 22, by College Enrollment: 2002–2010

1. **What is the topic?** *The topic is percent in the past month of binge alcohol use among adults, aged 18–22, by college enrollment, 2002–2010.*

2. **What is the pattern of organization?** *This graph shows the differences between full-time college students and non-full-time college students over an eight year span. The patterns are comparison and contrast, as well as sequence.*

3. **What are the parts and how do they relate to one another?**

The red line indicates full-time college students' binge alcohol use percent and the blue line refers to non-full-time college students' binge alcohol use percent. Over the span of eight years between 2002 and 2010, full-time college students' binging percentage is greater than that of non-full-time college students.' The highest activity year for full-time college students' binge alcohol use was 2006, and lowest activity in 2008. The highest percentage among non-full-time students in this age bracket was in 2004; the lowest percentage in 2010.

4. **What is the overall point of the graphic?** *Full-time students between 18 and 22 report higher rates of binge alcohol use than non-full-time students. One assumption could be that full-time college enrollment promotes binge alcohol use.*

READING STUDY STRATEGIES

PARAPHRASE TO AID COMPREHENSION

Paraphrasing is vital to your success in college reading and writing because it is a skill that proves you understand what you read. To paraphrase something you've read is to put an author's ideas into your own words. Paraphrasing doesn't mean repeating the author's words exactly; it means putting the author's ideas into your own words, yet maintaining the same ideas. In order to paraphrase effectively, you need to focus on both the overall pattern of organization and the relationships between ideas within the paragraph. Paraphrasing is effective for three main reasons.

1. **Paraphrasing proves you comprehended what you read.** Paraphrasing makes you sure you understand what the author has written. It is good to keep in mind that if you cannot put an author's ideas into your own words, then you should think about whether or not you *really* understand what the author has written. If not, reread the passage, paying careful attention to context clues to make sure you can figure out the meanings of unfamiliar words. Remember to monitor your comprehension as you read. Monitoring your comprehension is using metacognition—thinking about what you are thinking.

2. **Paraphrasing helps you understand subtle relationships between ideas in sentences.** If you rewrite a passage in your own words, you can more clearly see how the author arranges ideas and how these ideas fit together to express the author's thoughts.

3. **Paraphrasing helps you remember and learn the new information about which you are reading.** Because the brain requires both organized material and the repetition of the material to learn it, paraphrasing material is an effective study strategy.

A good paraphrase represents an author's thoughts clearly and completely. A poor paraphrase is not clear or represents incomplete ideas. Keep in mind that when you paraphrase, you are restating all the author's ideas in your own words. As a result, your paraphrase would be almost as long as the original reading. Paraphrasing as a study technique, then, is usually only helpful with shorter passages. Imagine you had to paraphrase this paragraph:

Prescription Drug Abuse on Campus

One of every five teenagers and adults—about 50 million Americans—have used a prescription drug for a nonmedical purpose. Nonmedical use of any prescription medication is highest among young adults between the ages of 18 and 25, compared with other age groups, and opioid painkillers . . . are the most widely misused.

SOURCE: From HALES, *An Invitation to Health*, 15E. © 2013 Cengage Learning.

Which of the following is the better paraphrase?

> Most nonmedical use of prescription drugs is by the 18–25 age group in America, with 1 in 5 Americans admitting to using these drugs without a doctor's order. Opioid painkillers are the most widely misused.

> According to the passage on prescription drug abuse on campus, by Dianne Hales from *An Invitation to Health*, one-fifth of the American population, 50 million adults and teenagers, have used prescription drugs without a medical need. Young adults between 18 and 25 are the largest group to use prescription medicine for nonmedical reasons, opioid painkillers being the most popular.

Both examples are retellings of the important ideas in the passage, but the second example is better. See how the second paraphrase is the same length as the original but worded more simply? While both paraphrases repeat the author's main ideas, the second example arranges the author's ideas in the same order as the original. Also, it references the author and the reading passage, which is important.

In the first paraphrase, some of the wording is the same as the original—exact phrasing is not acceptable in paraphrasing as the goal is to put someone else's ideas into your own words. In addition, this paraphrase does not represent all the ideas in the passage.

When paraphrasing, you reword ideas. Also, you focus on all the supporting details in the original passage, expressing them in your own words. Later, as you become better at paraphrasing, you can put the author's ideas into your own words *in your head* instead of writing it down.

If you are using a paraphrase of an author's work in an essay or in any other work in class, make sure to give credit to the author of the original because the ideas are the author's, not your own. Claiming ideas that are not your own is called *plagiarism,* which is an ethical infraction that is treated seriously in college and can result in expulsion. To use a paraphrase of another's ideas, you should directly state the source of your ideas in your paraphrase. Alternatively, your instructors may outline footnote and endnote formats that you can also use to reference other people's ideas within a paper you write.

TABLE 2.5 Comparison of Paraphrases

GOOD PARAPHRASE	POOR PARAPHRASE
• Is the same length as the original	• Is much shorter or longer than the original
• Uses key terms	• Does not use key terms
• References the author and title	• Does not reference the author and title
• Cuts out unnecessary information	• Includes unnecessary information
• Puts ideas into new wording that communicates the same point	• Consistently uses the same wording as the original (therefore doesn't paraphrase)
• Includes all the major and minor supporting details	• Excludes some major and minor details

QUICK TIPS HOW TO PARAPHRASE

To paraphrase a reading, follow these steps.

1. Read the original passage.

2. Without looking back at the original, try to formulate your rewording of the ideas.

3. Write down your paraphrase.

4. Go back and reread the original, checking to make sure the basic idea is the same.

Thinking It Through PARAPHRASING A READING

In this exercise, you'll read more from the article that discusses prescription drug use. Determine the topic and pattern of this whole passage. Determining topic and pattern can help you paraphrase the important ideas.

Topic: _____

Pattern of organization:_____

If you said the topic is prescription drug use on campus, you are correct. You can see repeated words clarifying the topic of the passage circled.

If you said that the pattern of organization is problem or cause, you are correct. What is the problem?_____

The problem is clearly prescription drugs abused on campus. The author outlines this epidemic and provides details of this drug abuse.

Now, read the paragraphs in the left column and then read the paraphrase of these paragraphs in the right column. The first paragraph discussed earlier is included.

Prescription Drug Abuse on Campus

1   One of every five teenagers and adults—about 50 million Americans—have used a prescription drug for a nonmedical purpose. Nonmedical use of any prescription medication is highest among young adults between the ages of 18 and 25, compared with other age groups, and opioid painkillers . . . are the most widely misused.

According to the passage on prescription drug abuse on campus, by Dianne Hales from *An Invitation to Health,* one-fifth of the American population, 50 million adults and teenagers, have used prescription drugs without a medical need. Young adults between 18 and 25 are the largest group to use prescription medicine for nonmedical reasons, opioid painkillers being the most popular.

2   The abuse of (prescription) medications on college campuses has
increased in the last 15 years. As
many as one in five college students
misuses or abuses a prescription
medication every year. Young adults
(between ages 18 and 25) have
the highest rates of prescription
painkiller abuse of any age group in
the country. Only marijuana use is
more widespread on campus.

3   College men have higher rates of
prescription drug abuse than women.
White and Hispanic undergraduates are significantly more likely to
abuse medications than are African
American and Asian students. Many
students taking prescription drugs
for medical purposes report being
approached by classmates seeking
drugs. Undergraduates who misuse
or abuse prescription medications
are much more likely to report heavy
binge drinking and use of illicit drugs.
College women who do so are at
greater risk for sexual victimization
and assault.

SOURCE: From HALES, *An Invitation to Health*,
15E. © 2013 Cengage Learning.

In the last 15 years, prescription drug abuse on college
campuses has grown. Each
year one-fifth of the college
student population is likely to
have abused prescription drugs.
The most common abusers of
prescription drugs are 18- to
25-year-olds. Marijuana is the
only drug that is used more
widely on college campuses.

The highest abuse of pre-
scription drugs is among college
men. Asian and African American students are less likely to
abuse prescription drugs than
White or Hispanic college students. Reports show that those
actually prescribed drugs are
often approached by others
wanting to acquire these drugs.
The use or abuse of prescription drugs coincides with heavy
drinking and the use of other
illegal substances. Furthermore,
prescription drug abuse is
linked with sexual victimization
and assault for undergraduate
females.

On Your Own PARAPHRASING A READING

In your own words, paraphrase three paragraphs of a related passage from Dianne Hale's book about prescription stimulant abuse. Write your paraphrase next to the original paragraph in the column provided. Then discuss your rewording of the paragraphs with a partner. Remember to make your paraphrase as clear as you can without using the author's original words. Follow the steps outlined in the Quick Tips.

(Continued)

Prescription Stimulants

1   The most widely abused prescription drugs are stimulant medications such as Ritalin. Students often view illicit stimulant use as physically harmless and morally acceptable. Many think that stimulants can help them focus, concentrate, and study longer. Yet users of these drugs actually have lower GPAs than nonusers, and there is little evidence that stimulants provide any boost.

2   In various studies, 5 to 35 percent of college-age individuals have reported nonprescribed use of stimulants, and 16 to 29 percent of students prescribed stimulants for ADHD reported being asked to give, sell, or trade their medications.

3   Students who are white, are traditional college age (under 24), belong to fraternities or sororities, have lower grade-point averages, and report some symptoms of ADHD are most likely to misuse or pass on stimulants to others. Most illicit users obtain the drugs from friends or peers for free or at a cost of $1 to $5. In a study of 1,550 undergraduates at a large southern university, about four in ten reported illicit stimulant use. These users, along with students with ADHD, reported significantly greater drug use than others.

4   Although proper medical use of this agent appears safe, misuse or abuse of any stimulant medication can be dangerous, even deadly. When taken in high doses, either orally or nasally, the risk of addiction

Paraphrase:

increases. Physical side effects include cardiorespiratory complications, increased blood pressure, and headache. High doses can trigger panic attacks, aggressive behavior, and suicidal or homicidal impulses. Overdoses can kill.

SOURCE: From HALES, *An Invitation to Health*, 15E. © 2013 Cengage Learning.

Paraphrasing is a skill that you will develop through practice. It helps you fully understand the readings you encounter, often very complex, in college-level texts. It also helps move the new information into your long-term memory through repetition—aloud, silently, or in writing. With practice, the skill of paraphrasing will become more automatic. Until that point, it is a good idea to write down your paraphrase of a particularly difficult passage.

VOCABULARY STRATEGY

IDENTIFYING PREFIXES AND SUFFIXES

Just as you can determine the structure of a reading, you can also identify the structure of a word. Looking at word structure clues requires breaking the word that you don't know into parts. Your first strategy when figuring out words with which you are not familiar is to look at clues in surrounding information—context clues, as you learned in Chapter 1. Another strategy is to pay attention to the parts of the unknown word that may give you clues to understanding its meaning. You do not necessarily have to memorize lists of word parts to use this strategy. In fact, your very best chance at expanding your reading and speaking (and writing) vocabulary is to read! Most people who read for about a half hour each day for a year increase their vocabulary by over one thousand words.*

Word parts are called **affixes.** There are three parts of words you should be aware of:

- prefixes, which are at the beginning of words

- suffixes, which are at the end of words

- roots, which are in the middle of words

Not all words have all three of these parts. You'll learn more about root words in Chapter 3. In this chapter, you will learn to recognize the beginning and ends of words—prefixes and suffixes.

---

*Anderson, R. C., & Nagy, W. E. (1991). Word meanings. In R. Barr, M. L. Kamil, P. B. Mosenthal, & P. D. Pearson (Eds.), *Handbook of Reading Research* (Vol. 2, pp. 690–724). Hillsdale, NJ: Erlbaum.

Prefixes

Prefixes are the parts of words that come at the beginning of a word (see Table 2.6 for the most common prefixes). When you encounter a word you do not recognize, look at surrounding words and sentences. Think about context clues and transitions that might help you make an educated guess. Next, look at the beginning of the word. Brainstorm other words that have the same beginning or prefix. For example, let's say you do not know the word *prefix* and it was in this sentence:

> The prefix is found at the beginning of a word.

There is a context clue—an inference clue—here that *prefix* is somehow associated with *beginning*. To clarify the guess, think about other words you know that contain *pre: predict, presume, premeditate, prevent, prescribe*. What do all these words have in common? They all have to do with something coming before, such as <u>predict</u>, which means to state or make known in advance. *Presume* means to assume or take for granted.

> I presume you want me to meet you at the usual time.

Premeditate means to plan before doing something.

> Because he planned the crime in advance, he was charged with premeditated murder.

Prevent means to keep something from happening.

> I wish I could prevent anything bad from happening to my friend in Iraq.

Prescribe means to set down a rule or to order a medicine or other treatment.

> The doctor said, "I'll prescribe a medicine that will help clear up your cough."

Prefix, then, must mean a part of a word that is at the beginning or comes *before* other parts of a word.

TABLE 2.6 10 Common English Prefixes

Here is a list of common prefixes used in English. Can you think of other words that contain each prefix? Write your additions in the chart.

PREFIX	MEANING	EXAMPLE	WHAT OTHER WORDS DO YOU KNOW THAT USE THIS PREFIX?
a-, ab-, il-, im-, in-, ir-, non-, un-	not	asymptomatic, abnormal, illicit, impossible, inaccurate, irreplaceable, nonentity, unstructured	
com-, con-,	with	combine, conform	
de-	opposite, away from	departure	
em-, en-	cause to	empower, encourage	
ex-	out	export	

TABLE 2.6 10 Common English Prefixes (Continued)

PREFIX	MEANING	EXAMPLE	WHAT OTHER WORDS DO YOU KNOW THAT USE THIS PREFIX?
inter-	between	interview	
mis-	wrongly	misidentify	
pre-	before	prescribe	
re-	again	review	
sub-	under	submarine	
trans-	across	translate	

Many disciplines use numerical prefixes that originated with Greek or Latin languages. Table 2.7 shows a list of must-know numerical prefixes.

TABLE 2.7 Numerical Prefixes

PREFIX	MEANING	EXAMPLE	WHAT OTHER WORDS DO YOU KNOW THAT USE THIS PREFIX?
uno/uni/mono	one	uniform—one type monocle—one lens	
bi/di/duo	two	bisect—divided into two parts dual—two	
tri	three	tricycle—three wheels	
quad	four	quadrangle—four-sided shape	
quint	five	quintuplets—five babies at birth	
dec	ten	decade—ten years	
cent	hundred	centipede—one-hundred-legged	
milli	thousand	millennium—one thousand years	
poly	many	polygamy—the practice of having many spouses	

On Your Own USING PREFIXES TO ALTER THE MEANING OF A WORD

Using one of the prefixes in Table 2.6 that negates a word (means "not or opposite"), convert the following words to their opposite. Use a dictionary to define the word. The first example is completed for you.

advantage: *disadvantage: something that puts one in an unfavorable position or condition.*

1. moral: _____

_____

2. finished: _____

_____

3. partisan: _____

_____

4. theist: _____

_____

5. cipher: _____

_____

6. literate: _____

_____

Suffixes

Suffixes are the parts of words that come at the end of a word. (Table 2.8 lists the most common suffixes.) Suffixes are useful to notice because they can indicate the part of speech of a word, like whether it is an adjective, noun, adverb, or verb. Look at these examples.

- *Beautiful: -ful* indicates an adjective form.

- *Beautifully: -ly* indicates that the word describes how an action was done, so *beautifully* is an adverb.

Notice how you can convert the following words to another part of speech using a different suffix.

- *Biology* (noun) can be converted to an adjective, a word that modifies a noun, using the suffix *-al: biological.*

- *Happy* (adjective) can be converted to a noun by adding the suffix *-ness: happiness.* By adding *-ly, happy* can be converted to an adverb: *happily.*

- *Intention* (noun) can be converted to an adverb by adding the suffix *-ally: intentionally.*

TABLE 2.8 10 Common English Suffixes

SUFFIX	MEANING	EXAMPLE	WHAT OTHER WORDS DO YOU KNOW THAT USE THIS SUFFIX?
-able, -ible	can be done	consumable, digestible	
-er, -or	one who	teacher, advisor	
-est	comparative	fairest	
-ful	full of	beautiful	
-ing	verb form, present participle	conversing	
-ion	act, process	contribution	
-ly	characteristic of	cheerfully	
-ment	action or process	compliment	
-ness	state of, condition of	helpfulness	
-ous	possessing the qualities of	gracious	

Not all words can be converted to all four parts of speech, but some can. For example:

to comprehend (infinitive verb)
comprehension (*-ion* indicates noun)
comprehensible, comprehensive (adjective)
comprehensively (adverb)

On Your Own **USING SUFFIXES TO ALTER THE PART OF SPEECH OF A WORD**

Convert the following words to alternative parts of speech using suffixes. Convert each word to an adjective, a noun, an adverb, and a verb

	ADJECTIVE	NOUN	ADVERB	VERB
1. attract				
2. abuse				
3. suggest				
4. create				
5. predict				

INCREASE YOUR DISCIPLINE-SPECIFIC VOCABULARY

PSYCHOLOGY

Many students take a general psychology course. Words originating with roots based in psychology are also commonly found in other academic textbooks and courses. Learning common affixes that pertain to psychology can give you a boost in recognizing and defining other academic terms. How many word parts in Table 2.9 have you heard before?

TABLE 2.9 Vocabulary Associated with Psychology

WORD PARTS	MEANING	VOCABULARY
cogni, gnos	to know	cognitive, diagnosis, incognito, metacognition, prognosis, recognition, ignorance, precognition
fid	faith	confident, fidelity, infidel, affidavit, confide
hetero	different, mixed, unlike	heterogeneous, heterosexual, heterozygous
homo	alike, same	homogeneous, homosexual, homo sapiens
hyper	too far	hyperactive, hyperbole, hypertension
hypno, dorm	sleep	hypnosis, hypnotic, dormitory, dormant,
ology	the study of	psychology, biology, anthropology, sociology
phil	to love	philosophy, bibliophile, philanthropy
phob	fear	acrophobia, claustrophobia, xenophobia
psyche	mind	psychology, psychopath, psychotic, psychiatry

Key Terms—Psychology

- **Control group:** the subjects in a scientific study that are not exposed to the specific variable being studied in order to isolate the results of the experimental group.

- **Variable:** the factor that can be changed or altered in an experiment.

- **Placebo:** a substance that has no active properties used in experiments by control group.

- **Empirical:** observable or tangible information—used in experiments.

- **Cognition:** thought, awareness, or consciousness.

- **Ego:** Sigmund Freud (1836–1939), the "father of psychoanalysis", categorized the mind into three components: the ego is the conscious mind; the superego is the "parental" part of the personality, dictating moral or appropriate behavior; and the id is the shadow side of the personality residing in the unconscious.

- **Neurosis:** a term invented by Freud refers to an emotional disorder characterized by anxiety.

- **Psychosis:** the state of not knowing the difference between what's real and illusion.

- **Insanity:** a legal medical term used to describe incompetence to stand trial; inability to understand trial proceedings, a danger to oneself or others, or psychosis during a crime.

- **Affect:** a term used to describe observable mood or presentation of a person.

APPLICATIONS

APPLICATION ①

This is an interview from a popular science magazine with a neuroscientist (a scientist that studies the brain) named David Linden. Preview the reading using the steps you learned in Chapter 1. Then, determine the topic and pattern of organization of the whole reading.

Read the interview, noticing the questions that are posed in the headings. As you read, underline and note the transitions that signal the pattern of organization of each paragraph. Also, you will apply your skills of recognizing prefixes and suffixes. After you read, complete the questions that follow.

Is There a Link Between Creativity and Addiction?
by David Biello

What is the topic of the reading?

What question will you read to answer?

1   A drink of alcohol, any kind; "rails" of white powder; a pill **prescribed** by a pediatrician to assist with attention deficit disorder. Whatever the poison, addiction can take a powerful toll. Nor is it limited to drugs—food, sex and even death-defying stunts can exert the same pull.

What pattern of organization is suggested by the title?

2   But it seems to be a particular breed of person who succumbs to addiction, most recently **exemplified** by the late singer Amy Winehouse. She joins the "27 Club" of rock stars who died, via addictive behavior, too young—Kurt Cobain, Jimi Hendrix, Janis Joplin and Jim Morrison. Nor is it limited to the rock-and-roll lifestyle—Thomas de Quincey invented the modern **addiction** memoir with his *Confessions of an English Opium-Eater* in 1821. In fact, the list of addicts often overlaps with the giants of culture.

What does the prefix *pre-* mean in *prescribed*?

What does the prefix *ex-* mean in *exemplified*?

What part of speech does the suffix *-ion* indicate as in *addiction*?

3   So is there a link between creativity and addiction? To find out, *Scientific American* spoke with neuroscientist David Linden of Johns Hopkins University School of Medicine and author of *The Compass of Pleasure: How Our Brains Make Fatty Foods, Orgasm, Exercise, Marijuana, Generosity, Vodka, Learning and Gambling Feel So Good.*

What pattern of organization is suggested by the heading?

Is there a link between creativity and addiction?

4   No. I think the link is not between creativity and addiction **per se**. There is a link between addiction and things which are a prerequisite for creativity. . . . We know that 40 percent of a predisposition to addiction is genetically determined, via studies on heritability in families and twins. There's no single addiction gene. We don't even know all the genes involved in **conferring**

What do you think the expression *per se* means? What kind of context clue did you use?

What does the prefix *-con* mean in *conferring*?

Which pattern does the transition phrase *on the contrary* indicate?

What does the prefix *re-* mean in *receptors*?

What part of speech does the suffix *-ive* indicate in the word *compulsive*?

What pattern of organization is suggested by the heading?

What part of speech does the suffix *-ing* indicate in the word *associating*?

What pattern of organization is suggested by the heading?

What part of speech does the suffix *-al* indicate in the word *behavioral*?

addiction risk. But the ones we do know have to do with the signaling of the neurotransmitter dopamine for pleasure and reward.

5   You don't become addicted because you feel pleasure strongly. On the contrary, addicts seem to want it more but like it less. They feel pleasures more weakly and are more likely to try more to achieve more. This blunted dopamine hypothesis is supported by brain-imaging studies and biochemistry tests in rats and monkeys. It also holds for addictions to food, sex and gambling.

6   Genetic variants make for a low-functioning dopamine system, specifically D2 **receptors**. If you carry those variants, you are more likely to be more risk-taking, novelty-seeking and compulsive. None of which are explicitly creative, but they are things that get to creativity. So novelty-seeking might be a spur to creativity. Risk-taking might lead you to go more out on a limb. If you're **compulsive**, you might be more motivated to get your art, science idea or novel out into the world. These traits that come from having low dopamine function have an upside. These traits can contribute to people having great success in the world, like business leaders.

7   Genetics is 40 percent, it's not 100 percent—it's not the whole show. It's possible to carry the variants and not be an addict, and it's possible to not carry the variants and still be an addict.

Is there a link between addiction and other human attributes we might value?

8   There have been some studies in Scandinavia **associating** personality traits with the genetics of D2 receptors. If you carry these variants that turn down dopamine, you become more socially desirable. There is something charismatic about risk-takers.

Does curing the addiction eliminate the creativity?

9   Usually not. When you cure the addiction, you're not changing your genes. People are in recovery for life. . . . There is always a tremendous risk of relapse. Successful recovering addicts adopt **behavioral** strategies that allow you to resist or reduce cravings.

10   If you develop a full-blown addiction to a drug, the indications in rats are that it changes the brain forever. You can get it back a little but never entirely.

(Continued)

Is there a specific time that is more vulnerable?

11   There is nothing magic about that age [27]. Brain maturation ends at about age 20. In the early 20s, you have your adult brain. In the late 20s, it's the same.

12   Generally speaking, 27 is an age where you can have achieved a lot and be at a place that is very **enabling**. The one thing that we really know about relapse and addiction is that it is stress-triggered. Anyone dealing with an addict knows that relapse doesn't happen when things are going great.

13   Stress is a biological phenomenon. We know the **intermediate** steps. You argue or you're fighting off an infection and your body releases stress hormones, which bind to receptors in the brain pleasure circuitry that ultimately result in cravings. We know how stress causes craving…. The two biggest factors are genetics and stress.

What pattern of organization is suggested by the heading?

What does the prefix en- mean in enabling?

What does the prefix inter- mean in intermediate?

COMPREHENSION CHECK

1   What is the main point of the essay? _____

_____

2   Look back at the reading and fill in the chart. Determine the topic and pattern of organization of each paragraph indicated. Then, paraphrase each paragraph.

PARAGRAPH	TOPIC	PATTERN OF ORGANIZATION	PARAPHRASE
1			

PARAGRAPH	TOPIC	PATTERN OF ORGANIZATION	PARAPHRASE
2			
4			
5			
6			

(Continued)

PARAGRAPH	TOPIC	PATTERN OF ORGANIZATION	PARAPHRASE
7			
8			
9			
10			
11			
12			
13			

READING GRAPHICS

Look carefully at Figure 2.9. Then answer the questions that follow it.

Blood Alcohol Concentration	0.01–0.06	0.06–0.10	0.11–0.20	0.21–0.29	0.30–0.39	> 0.40
• **Changes in Feelings and Personality**	• Relaxation, sense of well-being, loss of inhibition, lowered alertness, joyous	• Reflexes, impaired reasoning, depth perception, distance acuity, peripheral vision, glare recovery	• Over-expression, emotional swings, angry or sad, boisterous	• Stupor, lose understanding, impaired sensation	• Severe depression, unconsciousness, death possible	• Unconsciousness, death
• **Physical and Mental Impairments**	• Thought, judgment, coordination, concentration	• Blunted feelings, disinhibition, extroversion, impaired sexual pleasure	• Over-expression, emotional swings, angry or sad, boisterous	• Severe motor impairment, loss of consciousness, memory blackout	• Bladder function, breathing, heart rate	• Breathing, heart rate

Based on Virginia Tech, Alcohol Effects (http://www.alchohol.vt.edu /Students/alchoholEffects/index.html).

FIGURE 2.9 Progressive Effects of Alcohol

1. What is the topic? _____

2. What is the pattern of organization? _____

3. What are the parts and how do they relate to one another (supporting details)? _____
   _____
   _____

4. What is the overall point of the graphic? _____
   _____
   _____

5. At what level or levels of impairment listed in the chart might an individual feel more "creative" or more comfortable performing? _____
   _____

DEVELOPING YOUR COLLEGE-LEVEL VOCABULARY

In the reading, many words with the prefixes *pre-* and *re-* are used. Fill in the following charts by either manipulating the prefix of a word to change the meaning of the word or, in the case of the second chart, changing the part of speech of the word by altering its suffix.

(Continued)

WORD	PARAGRAPH	MEANING	CHANGE PREFIX	NEW MEANING
Prescribed	1	To write beforehand		
Prerequisite	4	Required before		
Recovery	9	To get better again		
Resist	9	To do without again		
Reduce	9	To make smaller		

WORD	PARAGRAPH	PART OF SPEECH	CHANGE SUFFIX	NEW PART OF SPEECH
Predisposition	4	Noun		
Reward	4	Noun		
Relapse	9	Noun		
Releases	13	Verb		
Result	14	Noun		

THEMATIC CONNECTIONS

1. Why do you think so many famous performers died at the age of 27? Contrast or compare your views with those of David Linden, the neuroscientist who is interviewed in this reading.

2. Do you know someone whom you would characterize as an addict? What types of traits does this person manifest? What are good aspects of his or her personality as well as bad?

3. Has your view of addiction changed since reading this interview? Why or why not?

4. If addiction is often linked with genetics and is exacerbated by stress, how can an addict reduce stress in his or her life effectively? What type of treatment would you recommend given the stress-linked research findings?

5. What do you think it takes to be a creative person? What character traits do you think are necessary for creative success? Write a paragraph listing and explaining these traits following an "order of importance" pattern of organization.

APPLICATION ②

This article is from the National Institute on Health—NIDA (National Institute on Drug Abuse). Preview the article as outlined in Chapter 1. Examine the relationships between ideas, and apply vocabulary word part clues you have learned by responding to questions in the margins. As you read, underline transition words to identify the relationships between ideas. At the end of the reading, apply your graphics skills and answer the Comprehension Check questions.

Drugs and the Brain

Introducing the Human Brain

1   The human brain is the most complex organ in the body. This three-pound mass of gray and white matter sits at the center of all human activity—you need it to drive a car, to enjoy a meal, to breathe, to create an artistic masterpiece, and to enjoy everyday activities. In brief, the brain regulates your basic body functions; **enables** you to interpret and respond to everything you experience; and shapes your thoughts, emotions, and behavior.

2   The brain is made up of many parts that all work together as a team. Different parts of the brain are responsible for coordinating and performing specific functions. Drugs can alter important brain areas that are necessary for life-sustaining functions and can drive the compulsive drug abuse that marks addiction. Brain areas affected by drug abuse:

- **The brain stem** controls basic functions critical to life, such as heart rate, breathing, and sleeping.
- **The limbic system** contains the brain's reward circuit—it links together a number of brain structures that control and regulate our ability to feel pleasure. Feeling pleasure motivates us to **repeat** behaviors such as eating—actions that are critical to our existence. The limbic system is activated when we perform these activities—and also by drugs of abuse. In addition, the limbic system is responsible for our perception of other emotions, both positive and negative, which explains the mood-altering properties of many drugs.

What is the overall topic of this reading?
What is the overall pattern of organization?
What is the pattern of organization of this section?

What are the major supporting details?

What does the prefix *en*-mean in *enables*?

What does the prefix *re*- mean in *repeat*?

(Continued)

What part of speech does
the suffix *-ions* indicate in
functions?

What is the topic of this section?

What is the pattern of organization
of this section?

What are the major supporting
details?

What part of speech does the
suffix in *neurotransmitters*
indicate?

What does the prefix *inter-*
mean in *interacting*?

What does the prefix *trans-*
mean in *transporters*?

What is the topic of this
section?

What is the pattern of
organization of this section?

- **The cerebral cortex** is divided into areas that control specific **functions**. Different areas process information from our senses, enabling us to see, feel, hear, and taste. The front part of the cortex, the frontal cortex or forebrain, is the thinking center of the brain; it powers our ability to think, plan, solve problems, and make decisions.

How Does the Brain Communicate?

3   The brain is a communications center consisting of billions of neurons, or nerve cells. Networks of neurons pass messages back and forth to different structures within the brain, the spinal column, and the peripheral nervous system. These nerve networks coordinate and regulate everything we feel, think, and do.

- **Neuron to Neuron** Each nerve cell in the brain sends and receives messages in the form of electrical impulses. Once a cell receives and processes a message, it sends it on to other neurons.
- **Neurotransmitters—The Brain's Chemical Messengers** The messages are carried between neurons by chemicals called **neurotransmitters**. (They transmit messages between neurons.)
- **Receptors—The Brain's Chemical Receiver**s The neurotransmitter attaches to a specialized site on the receiving cell called a receptor. A neurotransmitter and its receptor operate like a "key and lock," an exquisitely specific mechanism that ensures that each receptor will forward the appropriate message only after **interacting** with the right kind of neurotransmitter.
- **Transporters—The Brain's Chemical Recyclers** Located on the cell that releases the neurotransmitter, transporters recycle these neurotransmitters (i.e., bringing them back into the cell that released them), thereby shutting off the signal between neurons.

How Do Drugs Work in the Brain?

4   Drugs are chemicals. They work in the brain by tapping into the brain's communication system and interfering with the way nerve cells normally send, receive, and process information (Figure 2.10). Some drugs, such as marijuana and heroin, can activate neurons because their chemical structure mimics that of a natural neurotransmitter. This similarity in structure

Here's how people communicate.   Here's how brain cells communicate.

Transmitter   Receptor   Neurotransmitter   Receptor

Concept courtesy: B.K. Madras

National Institute on Drug Abuse/ National Institutes of Health

FIGURE 2.10 To send a message, a brain cell releases a chemical (neurotransmitter) into the space separating two cells called the synapse. The neurotransmitter crosses the synapse and attaches to proteins (receptors) on the receiving brain cell. This causes changes in the receiving brain cell and the message is delivered.

What is the topic of Figure 2.10?

What is the pattern of organization?

What is the relationship between ideas?

"fools" receptors and allows the drugs to lock onto and activate the nerve cells. Although these drugs mimic brain chemicals, they don't activate nerve cells in the same way as a natural neurotransmitter, and they lead to **abnormal** messages being transmitted through the network.

What does the prefix *ab*- mean in *abnormal*?

5   Other drugs, such as amphetamine or cocaine, can cause the nerve cells to release abnormally large amounts of natural neurotransmitters or prevent the normal recycling of these brain chemicals. This disruption produces a greatly amplified message, ultimately disrupting communication channels. The difference in effect can be described as the difference between someone whispering into your ear and someone shouting into a microphone.

How Do Drugs Work in the Brain to Produce Pleasure?

6   All drugs of abuse directly or indirectly target the brain's reward system by flooding the circuit with dopamine. Dopamine is a neurotransmitter present in regions of the brain that regulate movement, emotion, cognition, motivation, and feelings of pleasure. The overstimulation of this system, which rewards our natural behaviors, produces the euphoric effects sought by people who abuse drugs and teaches them to repeat the behavior.

What is the topic of this section?

What is the pattern of organization of this section?

How Does Stimulation of the Brain's Pleasure Circuit Teach Us to Keep Taking Drugs?

7   Our brains are wired to ensure that we will repeat life-sustaining activities by associating those activities with pleasure or reward. Whenever this reward circuit is activated, the brain notes that something important is happening that needs to be

What is the topic of this section?

What is the pattern of organization of this section?

(Continued)

remembered, and teaches us to do it again and again, without thinking about it. Because drugs of abuse stimulate the same circuit, we learn to abuse drugs in the same way (Figure 2.11).

SOURCE: "Drugs and the Brain" National Institute on Health, NIDA (National Institute on Drug Abuse), http://www.drugabuse.gov/Scienceofaddiction/brain.html.

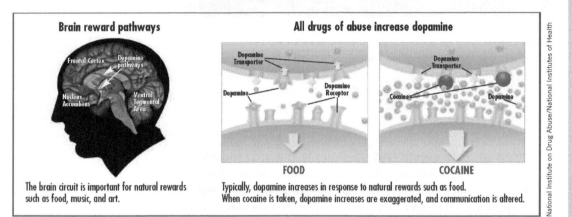

FIGURE 2.11 All drugs of abuse target the brain's pleasure center.

COMPREHENSION CHECK

1 What is the function of these areas of the brain: the brain stem, the limbic system, and cerebral cortex? _____
_____
_____
_____
_____

2 How are those areas affected by drug abuse? (Draw conclusions based on information in paragraph 2.) _____
_____
_____
_____
_____

3 What are the four steps in the brain's communication system? Draw a diagram to represent this process. _____
_____

4 Paraphrase the section "How do drugs work in the brain?" _____
_____

_____
_____
_____
_____
_____
_____

READING GRAPHICS

Study Figure 2.11 and answer the following questions.

1. What is the topic? _____

2. What is the pattern of organization? _____
_____

3. What are the parts and how do they relate to one another? _____
_____
_____
_____
_____

4. What is the overall point of the figure? _____
_____

5. What might be a connection between Figure 2.11 and the discussion about addiction and creativity in Application 1? _____
_____
_____

DEVELOPING YOUR COLLEGE-LEVEL VOCABULARY

Review the prefixes used in this reading. Then fill out this chart, recalling from memory the meaning of the prefix and creating words using that same prefix.

PREFIX	PARAGRAPH	MEANING	OTHER WORD
en-	1		
re-	2		
inter-	3		
trans-	3		
ab-	4		

(Continued)

THEMATIC CONNECTIONS

1. Why do you think that drug use and abuse are so common in our culture?

2. Research other cultures and their use of substances for recreation or ritual.

3. Choose one drug mentioned in this chapter and outline the brain circuit reaction (the four steps in the brain's communication system).

WRAPPING IT UP

In the following study outline, fill in the definitions and a brief explanation of the key terms in the "Your Notes" column. Use the strategy of spaced practice to review these key terms on a regular basis. Use this study guide to review this chapter's key topics.

KEY TERM OR CONCEPT	YOUR NOTES
Transitions	
Supporting details	
Major detail	
Minor detail	
Patterns of organization	
Simple listing	
Order of importance	
Chronological order	
Sequence or process order	
Spatial order	
Example/illustration or clarification	
Definition and example	
Description	
Division/classification	
Cause and effect	
Problem and solution	
Compare and contrast	
Mixed patterns	
Relationships between ideas	
Paraphrasing	

GROUP ACTIVITY: RESEARCH PRESENTATION

Use a search engine to find additional information about one of the following topics on the Internet. Present your findings to the class for group discussion. Follow this format for outlining your findings.

1. What was the topic of the site/research?
2. What were the key points?
3. What was the overall message?
4. What did you find most interesting?
5. How does this information relate to the other readings in the chapter?

Possible topics for further reading.

1. Creativity and personality
2. Brain development in adolescents
3. National trends in substance abuse prevention or use
4. Stress management techniques and causes and effects of stress
5. The history of illegal substances

REFLECTIVE JOURNAL QUESTIONS

1. Find a passage or subsection of about a half page in length from a text you are using in another course. Paraphrase this section using the strategies you learned in this chapter.
2. Find an example of three different types of patterns of organization from a text you are using for another course. How can recognizing each pattern help you improve your study strategies in that course?

THEMATIC CONNECTIONS

Respond to one of the following questions. Prepare notes for class discussion or write a response to submit to your instructor.

1. What do you believe is the most significant reason people choose to overuse substances? What do you think accounts for such trends in our community?
2. Readings in this chapter are concerned with brain research and its relationship to addiction. Based on these readings, what do you think scientists ought to work on next?
3. What are the qualities needed for an individual to overcome excessive use of a substance? Choose three qualities (behaviors, techniques, or attitudes) that characterize a successful recovery from addiction. Support your answer with specific examples.

ADDITIONAL SKILL AND STRATEGY PRACTICE

A. Patterns of Organization

This is an excerpt from an introductory psychology textbook. You will apply what you have learned about recognizing patterns of organization and transition words.

Is Marijuana Dangerous?
by Douglas A. Bernstein, Louis A. Penner, Alison Clarke-Stewart, and Edward J. Roy

1   A large-scale study of U.S. teenagers indicated a dramatic rise in their use of marijuana from 1991 to 1996. Usage almost tripled among eighth-graders (from 4 to 11 percent) and more than doubled among tenth-graders (from 9 to 20 percent). During this same period, the number of students who believed that there is a "great risk" associated with using marijuana declined in about the same proportions though that decline has now leveled off. Regular marijuana use has remained steady at about 21 percent among U.S. high school students but has increased somewhat among college students. In one study, for example, the percentage of college students reporting marijuana use in the previous month was 17 percent in 2001, compared with 13 percent in 1993. Overall, it appears that about 3.1 million people in the United States have used marijuana on a daily or almost daily basis over a 12-month period. In response to these trends, U.S. government officials have condemned marijuana use as "dangerous, illegal, and wrong." Concern about the drug has also been voiced in many other countries.

What is the topic?

What is the pattern of organization? Go back and underline transition words that indicate the pattern.

2   At the same time, the medical community has been engaged in serious discussion about whether marijuana should be used for medicinal purposes, and in the United States and around the world many individuals and organizations continue to argue for the decriminalization of marijuana use. Those who support legalization of marijuana cite its medical benefits. Some doctors claim to have successfully used marijuana in the treatment of problems such as asthma, glaucoma, epilepsy, chronic pain, and nausea from cancer chemotherapy. There is also evidence that marijuana can affect the immune system in ways that help fight some types of cancer. But some argue that medical legalization of marijuana is premature, because its medicinal value has not been clearly established (Bennet, 1994). They point out, too, that—even though patients may prefer marijuana-based drugs—other medications may be equally effective and less dangerous.

What is the topic?

What is the pattern of organization in this paragraph?

What is the topic?

What is the pattern of organization?

What Am I Being Asked to Believe or Accept?

3   Those who see marijuana as dangerous usually assert four beliefs: (1) that marijuana is addictive; (2) that it leads to the use of "hard drugs," such as heroin; (3) that marijuana intoxication endangers the user and other individuals; and (4) that long-term marijuana use leads to undesirable behavioral changes, disruption of brain functions, and other adverse effects on health.

What Evidence Is Available to Support the Assertion?

What is the topic?

What is the pattern of organization? Go back and underline transition words that indicate the pattern.

4   Without a doubt, some people do use marijuana to such an extent that it disrupts their lives. According to the criteria normally used to define alcohol abuse, these people are dependent on marijuana—at least psychologically. The question of physical dependence (addiction) is less clear, inasmuch as withdrawal from chronic marijuana use has long been thought not to produce any severe physical symptoms. However, some evidence of a mild withdrawal syndrome has been reported in rats. In humans, withdrawal from marijuana may be accompanied by increases in anxiety, depression, and aggressiveness. Other research has found that marijuana interacts with the same dopamine and opiate receptors as does heroin, implying that marijuana could be a "gateway drug" to the use of more addictive drugs.

What is the topic?

What is the pattern of organization? Go back and underline transition words that indicate the pattern.

5   Regardless of whether marijuana is addicting or leads to "harder drugs," it can create a number of problems. It disrupts memory formation, making it difficult to carry out complex tasks. And despite the fact that people may feel more creative while using marijuana, the drug appears to actually reduce creativity. Because marijuana affects muscle coordination, driving while under its influence is quite hazardous. Compounding the danger is the fact that motor impairment continues long after the obvious effects of the drug have worn off. In one study, for example, pilots had difficulty landing a simulated aircraft even a full day after smoking one marijuana cigarette. As for marijuana's effects on intellectual and cognitive performance, long-term use can lead to lasting impairments in reasoning and memory. One study found that adults who frequently used marijuana scored lower on a twelfth-grade academic achievement test than did nonusers with the same IQs. Among long-term users, impairments in memory and attention can persist for years after their drug use has stopped. Heavy use of marijuana in teenagers has also been associated with the later appearance of anxiety, depression, and other mental disorders as severe as schizophrenia.

SOURCE: From BERNSTEIN/PENNER/CLARKE-STEWART/ROY, Psychology, 7E. © 2006 Cengage Learning.

❀ POST-ASSESSMENT

SCIENCE MAGAZINE

Preview the following article and then read it all the way through. Then go to the end of the article and answer the questions. This assessment will help you determine your strengths and weaknesses in understanding, learning, and applying the skills and strategies discussed in this chapter.

New Test Shows If You Are a Shopaholic
by Jeanna Bryner

1   A new shopaholic test could tell if you should leave your credit card at home when heading out to the mall.

2   The test makes it clear that there's shopping and then there's over-the-top purchasing that can wreak havoc on a person's life. People who become preoccupied with buying stuff and repeatedly spend money on items, regardless of need, are commonly referred to as shopaholics. Scientists call it compulsive buying.

3   The new test was administered along with a survey that revealed that nearly 9 percent of a sample of 550 university staff members, mostly women, would be considered compulsive buyers. Past studies had put the incidence of compulsive buying somewhere between 2 percent and 8 percent 15 years ago, and more recently, at nearly 6 percent, the researchers say. Other research has found men are just as addicted to shopping as women.

4   The new test includes six statements, for which individuals answer on a 7-point scale from strongly disagree to strongly agree:

- My closet has unopened shopping bags in it.

- Others might consider me a "shopaholic."

- Much of my life centers around buying things.

- I buy things I don't need.

- I buy things I did not plan to buy.

- I consider myself an impulse purchaser.

Respondents who score 25 or higher would be considered compulsive buyers.

5   "We are living in a consumption-oriented society and have been spending ourselves into serious difficulty," researcher Kent Monroe, a marketing professor at the University of Illinois at Urbana-Champaign, told *LiveScience*. "Compulsive buying is an addiction that can be harmful to the individual, families, relationships. It is not just something that only afflicts low-income people."

6   Wondering where your score lies? "An individual could respond to the six items to check whether they may have these tendencies," Monroe said. "However, as with any attempt at self-diagnosing, it should be carefully done and honestly responded to."

(Continued)

7   Monroe and his colleagues found that compulsive buying was linked to materialism, reduced self-esteem, depression, anxiety and stress. Compulsive shoppers had positive feelings associated with buying, and they also tended to hide purchases, return items, have more family arguments about purchases and have more maxed-out credit cards.

8   Previous scales for identifying problem buyers are lacking because they depend in large part on the consequences of shopping, such as financial difficulties and family strain over money matters, the researchers note. But for compulsive shoppers with higher incomes, money matters could be non-existent.

9   A dwindling bank account is just one of the upshots of shopping 'til you drop. Others include family conflicts, stress, depression and loss of self-esteem.

10   The shopaholic test is just part of the answer.

11   "There needs to be more research not only identifying people who have a tendency to buy compulsively, but also on developing education and self-help programs for people who are buying things they do not need or use," Monroe said. "It can lead to a waste of resources and to deterioration in families and relationships."

12   The research is detailed in the December issue of the *Journal of Consumer Research*. Financial support for the research was provided by the J. M. Jones endowment fund at the University of Illinois.

SOURCE: New Test Shows If You Are a Shopaholic, Jeanna Bryner, September 22, 2008, from http://www.livescience.com/2875-test-shows-shopaholic.html

COMPREHENSION CHECK

Circle the best answer to the following questions.

Reading Comprehension

1   **What is the topic of this article?**

   A. Shopping
   B. Compulsive shopping
   C. Bargain shopping
   D. Testing before shopping

2   **What is the relationship between ideas in the following sentence?**

   Compulsive buying is an addiction that can be harmful to the individual, families, relationships.

   A. Comparison and contrast
   B. Sequence or process order
   C. Definition and example
   D. Cause and effect

3 **What is the pattern of organization of paragraph 2?**

A. Cause and effect
B. Definition and example
C. Simple listing
D. Chronological order

4 **In the following sentence, what is the relationship between ideas?**

Past studies had put the incidence of compulsive buying somewhere between 2 percent and 8 percent 15 years ago, and more recently, at nearly 6 percent, the researchers say.

A. Comparison and contrast
B. Cause and effect
C. Definition
D. Sequence or process order

5 **What transition word in the following sentence indicates the relationship between ideas?**

Previous scales for identifying problem buyers are lacking because they depend in large part on the consequences of shopping, such as financial difficulties and family strain over money matters, the researchers note.

A. *Previous*
B. *Because*
C. *Consequences*
D. *Both B and C*

6 **Considering the relationship between ideas, what is the important point of paragraph 5?**

A. Compulsive spending is a growing trend among richer people
B. There is an income difference between appropriate buyers and compulsive buyers.
C. Compulsive buying reflects our consumer-oriented society and has many negative consequences.
D. People ought to shop less.

7 **Considering the relationship between ideas in the paragraph, what is the important point of paragraph 6?**

A. The problem is that over-spending can be harmful.
B. Self-tests are especially dangerous when abused.
C. Self-tests may reveal important information but only if done honestly.
D. The problem is that people tend to lie on tests.

8 **What is the important point of the reading?**

A. Our consumer society produces compulsive buyers and the repercussions can be devastating.

(Continued)

B. Many people tend to overspend.

C. More and more higher income people are shopaholics.

D. Compulsive shopping is being recognized by others.

Vocabulary Comprehension

9 **In the following sentence, what does the prefix *com-* mean in the word *compulsive*?**

The new test was administered along with a survey that revealed that nearly 9 percent of a sample of 550 university staff members, mostly women, would be considered compulsive buyers.

A. Negative

B. Before

C. With

D. After

10 **In the following sentence, what do the two underlined prefixes mean?**

"It can lead to a waste of resources and to deterioration in families and relationships."

A. Before and after

B. Before and not

C. Again and away from

D. Not and not

TEXTBOOK APPLICATION

Chapter 3: Caring for Your Mind from *An Invitation to Health*, 15th Edition, by Dianne Hales

This chapter is from a health textbook about ensuring mental health. This chapter concerns the brain, gender and age differences in the brain, mental health and mental illness, risk factors for college students regarding mental health, symptoms of major depression, major anxiety disorders, suicide prevention, and therapy for mental health problems. You can see from the long list of varied topics in this chapter that the author draws on psychology, health science, as well as student success strategies to approach this important chapter information.

You now have a foundation in applying reading strategies and assessing text structure and supporting points from your study of Chapters 1 and 2. You also have some skills in identifying important words from context and from prefixes and suffixes. You now need to practice transferring these skills to real college textbook chapters. This is your goal as a successful college student. This may seem a daunting task, but you will find the content of this chapter to be interesting and not as hard as you may think. The trick is to look at the sections in the text and to use what you have learned.

Apply what you have learned about surveying and previewing a reading, identifying topic and patterns of organization, paraphrasing, and recognizing the relationships between ideas. Also apply your knowledge about recognizing patterns of organization and the relationship between ideas to visual aids in this chapter. In addition, use your knowledge of vocabulary context clues and prefixes as well as suffixes to increase your comprehension.

There are six major subsections in this chapter. The main patterns of organization used are definition and example, and cause and effect. There are also sections that use a sequence or process order and some that focus on comparison and/or contrast.

1. Survey the chapter, paying special attention to the "Interim Summary" sections.

2. Take one section at a time, turning the headings into questions. For the outline on the next page, convert the headings into question format. The first three are completed for you.

3. Read each section first, looking for the answers to the questions you created from the headings.

4. As you read, write down major points that answer the question posed by your guide question.

5. Circle any vocabulary that is unfamiliar and use context clues or prefix and suffix clues to help you make a guess as to the word's meaning.

A. **The Brain: The Last Frontier**

   1. Inside the Brain

   2. Communication Within the Brain

   3. Sex Differences in the Brain

   4. The Teenage and Twenty-Something Brain

B. **Understanding Mental Health**

   1. What Is a Mental Disorder?

   2. Who Develops Mental Disorders?

   3. The Mind-Body Connection

     a. Disease Risks

     b. Personality and Health

C. **Mental Health on Campus**

   1. Students at Risk

   2. The Toll on Students

D. **Depressive Disorders**

   1. Depression in Children and Teens

   2. Depression in Students

   3. Gender and Depression

     a. Female Depression

     b. Male Depression

   4. Dysthymic Disorder

   5. Minor Depression

   6. Major Depression

E. **Anxiety Disorders**

   1. Phobias

   2. Panic Attacks and Panic Disorder

   3. Generalized Anxiety Disorder

   4. Obsessive-Compulsive Disorder

F. **Attention Disorders**

G. **Autism and Autism Spectrum Disorders**

Why/how is the brain the last frontier?

What is inside the brain?

How does communication within the brain work?

H. Schizophrenia

I. Suicide

1. Suicide in the Young

2. Suicide on Campus

3. Factors that Lead to Suicide

    a. Mental Disorders

    b. Substance Abuse

    c. Hopelessness

    d. Combat Stress

    e. Family History

    f. Physical Illness

    g. Brain Chemistry

    h. Access to Guns

    i. Other Factors

J. Overcoming Problems of the Mind

1. Getting Help for a Psychological
    Problem

2. Where to Turn for Help

    a. Types of Therapists

    b. Choosing a Therapist

3. Types of Therapy

    a. Psychodynamic Psychotherapy

    b. Cognitive-Behavioral Therapy

    c. Interpersonal Therapy

4. Other Treatment Options

    a. Psychiatric Drugs

    b. Alternative Mind-Mood Products

After you read and take notes, answer the Review Questions at the end of the chapter on page 000. Your notes should be a helpful guide to answering these questions. Prepare for a quiz on this subject matter. Following the quiz, your instructor will help you assess the strengths and weaknesses in your understanding of this textbook chapter.

INCREASE YOUR DISCIPLINE-SPECIFIC VOCABULARY

HEALTH SCIENCE

Key Terms

The terms listed are used on the page indicated. Define each of these terms.

KEY TERM	DEFINITION
antidepressant, p. 143	
anxiety disorders, p. 154	
Asperger syndrome, p. 158	
attention-deficit/hyperactivity disorder (ADHD), p. 156	
axon, p. 142	
axon terminal, p. 142	
behavioral therapy, p. 165	
bipolar disorder, p. 153	
certified social worker or licensed clinical social worker (LCSW), p. 163	
cognitive therapy, p. 165	
dendrites, p. 142	
dysthymia, p. 151	
generalized anxiety disorder(GAD), p. 154	
glia, p. 142	
interpersonal therapy (IPT), p. 165	

KEY TERM	DEFINITION
major depression, p. 151	
marriage and family therapist, p. 163	
mental disorder, p. 145	
neuron, p. 142	
neuropsychiatry, p. 141	
neurotransmitters, p. 142	
nucleus, p. 142	
obsessive-compulsive disorder(OCD), p. 154	
panic attack, p. 154	
panic disorder, p. 155	
phobia, p. 154	
psychiatric drugs, p. 165	
psychiatric nurse, p. 163	
psychiatrist, p. 163	
psychodynamic, p. 164	
psychologist, p. 163	
receptors, p. 143	
reuptake, p. 143	
schizophrenia, p. 158	
synapse, p. 143	

3

After studying the material in this chapter, you should be able to

- List the key structures of the brain and describe the role of neurons in communication within the brain.

- Discuss gender- and age-based differences in the brain.

- Explain the differences between mental health and mental illnesses and list some effects of mental illness on physical health.

- Identify risk factors in college students for mental health problems.

- List the symptoms of major depression and discuss the pros and cons of using antidepressants.

- Describe the major anxiety disorders, including symptoms and treatments.

- Discuss some of the factors that may lead to suicide, as well as strategies for prevention.

- List the criteria for considering therapy for a mental health problem.

For years, Travis put on his "happy face" around his friends and family. Popular and athletic in high school, he never let anyone know how desperately unhappy he actually felt. "Whatever I was doing during the day, nothing was on my mind more than wanting to die," he recalls. On a perfectly ordinary day in his senior year, Travis tried to kill himself with an overdose of pills. Rushed to a hospital, Travis recovered, resumed his studies, and

Caring for Your Mind

entered college. By the middle of his freshman year, he was struggling once more with feelings of hopelessness. This time he realized what was happening and sought help from a therapist. "I thought college was supposed to be the happiest time of your life," he said. "What went wrong?"

This is a question many young people might ask. Although youth can seem a golden time, when body and mind glow with potential, the process of becoming an adult is a challenging one in every culture and country. Psychological health can make the difference between facing this challenge with optimism and confidence or feeling overwhelmed by expectations and responsibilities.

This isn't always easy. At some point in life almost half of Americans develop an emotional disorder. Young adulthood—the years from the late teens to the midtwenties—is a time when many serious disorders, including bipolar illness (manic depression) and schizophrenia, often develop. The saddest fact is not that so many feel so bad, but that so few realize they can feel better. Only a

third of those with a mental disorder receive any treatment at all. Yet 80 to 90 percent of those treated for psychological problems recover, most within a few months.

By learning about psychological disorders covered in this chapter, you may be able to recognize early warning signals in yourself or your loved ones so you can deal with potential difficulties or seek professional help for more serious problems.

The Brain: The Last Frontier

The brain has intrigued scientists for centuries, but only recently have its explorers made dramatic progress in unraveling its mysteries. Leaders in **neuropsychiatry**—the field that brings together the study of the brain and the mind—remind us that 95 percent of what is known about brain anatomy, chemistry, and physiology has been learned in the last 25 years. These discoveries have reshaped our understanding of the

neuropsychiatry The study of the brain and mind.

organ that is central to our identity and well-being and have fostered great hope for more effective therapies for the more than 1,000 disorders—psychiatric and neurologic—that affect the brain and nervous system.

Inside the Brain

The human brain, the most complex organ in the body, controls the central nervous system (CNS) and regulates virtually all our activities, including involuntary, or "lower," actions like heart rate, respiration, and digestion, and conscious, or "higher," mental activity like thought, reason, and abstraction. More than one hundred billion **neurons**, or nerve cells, within the brain are capable of electrical and chemical communication with tens of thousands of other nerve cells. (The basic anatomy of the brain is shown in Figure 3.1.)

The neurons are the basic working units of the brain. Like snowflakes, no two are exactly the same. Each consists of a cell body containing the **nucleus**; a long fiber called the **axon**, which can range from less than an inch to several feet in length; an **axon terminal**, or ending; and multiple branching fibers called **dendrites** (Figure 3.2). The **glia** serve as the scaffolding for the brain, separate the brain from the bloodstream, assist in the growth of neurons, speed up the transmission of nerve impulses, and engulf and digest damaged neurons.

Until quite recently scientists believed no new neurons or synapses formed in the brain after birth. This theory has been soundly disproved. The brain and spinal cord contain stem cells, which turn into thousands of new neurons a day. The process of creating new brain cells and synapses occurs most rapidly in childhood but continues throughout life, even into old age. Whenever you learn and change, you establish new neural networks.

Anatomically, the brain consists of three parts: the forebrain, midbrain, and hindbrain. The forebrain includes the several

neuron A nerve cell; the basic working unit of the brain, which transmits information from the senses to the brain and from the brain to specific body parts; each neuron consists of a cell body, an axon terminal, and dendrites.

nucleus The central part of a cell, contained in the cell body of a neuron.

axon The long fiber that conducts impulses from the neuron's nucleus to its dendrites.

axon terminal The ending of an axon, from which impulses are transmitted to a dendrite of another neuron.

dendrites Branching fibers of a neuron that receive impulses from axon terminals of other neurons and conduct these impulses toward the nucleus.

glia Support cells for neurons in the brain and spinal cord that separate the brain from the bloodstream, assist in the growth of neurons, speed transmission of nerve impulses, and eliminate damaged neurons.

Figure 3.1 **The Brain**
The three major parts of the brain are the cerebrum, cerebellum, and brainstem (medulla). The cerebrum is divided into two hemispheres—the left, which regulates the right side of the body, and the right, which regulates the left side of the body. The cerebellum plays the major role in coordinating movement, balance, and posture. The brainstem contains centers that control breathing, blood pressure, heart rate, and other physiological functions.

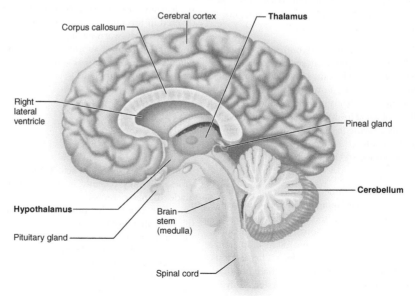

Figure 3.2 **Brain Messaging: Anatomy of a Neuron**

This figure shows how nerve impulses are transmitted from one neuron to another within the brain.

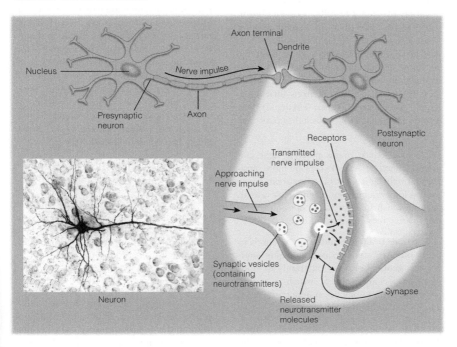

lobes of the cerebral cortex that control higher functions, while the mid- and hindbrain are more involved with unconscious, autonomic functions. The normal adult human brain typically weighs about three pounds.

Communication within the Brain

Neurons "talk" with each other by means of electrical and chemical processes (see Figure 3.2). An electric charge, or impulse, travels along an axon to the terminal, where packets of chemicals called **neurotransmitters** are stored. When released, these messengers flow out of the axon terminal and cross a **synapse**, a specialized site at which the axon terminal of one neuron comes extremely close to a dendrite from another neuron.

On the surface of the dendrite are **receptors**, protein molecules designed to bind with neurotransmitters. It takes only about a tenthousandth of a second for a neurotransmitter

and a receptor to come together. Neurotransmitters that do not connect with receptors may remain in the synapse until they are reabsorbed by the cell that produced them—a process called **reuptake**—or broken down by enzymes.

A malfunction in the release of a neurotransmitter, in its reuptake or elimination, or in the receptors or secondary messengers may result in abnormalities in thinking, feeling, or behavior. Some of the most promising and exciting research in neuropsychiatry is focusing on correcting such malfunctions.

The neurotransmitter serotonin and its receptors have been shown to affect mood, sleep, behavior, appetite, memory, learning, sexuality, and aggression and to play a role in several mental disorders. The discovery of a possible link between low levels of serotonin and some cases of major depression has led to the development of more precisely targeted **antidepressant** medications that boost serotonin to normal levels. (See "Psychiatric Drugs" later in the chapter.)

neurotransmitters Chemicals released by neurons that stimulate or inhibit the action of other neurons.

synapse A specialized site at which electrical impulses are transmitted from the axon terminal of one neuron to a dendrite of another.

receptors Molecules on the surface of neurons on which neurotransmitters bind after their release from other neurons.

reuptake Reabsorption by the originating cell of neurotransmitters that have not connected with receptors and have been left in synapses.

antidepressant A drug used primarily to treat symptoms of depression.

Sex Differences in the Brain

From birth, male and female brains differ in a variety of ways. Overall, a woman's brain, like her body, is 10 to 15 percent smaller than a man's, yet the regions dedicated to higher cognitive functions such as language are more densely packed with neurons—and women use more of them. When a male puts his mind to work, neurons turn on in highly specific areas. When females set their minds on similar tasks, cells light up all over the brain.

Male and female brains perceive light and sound differently. A man's eyes are more sensitive to bright light and retain their ability to see well at long distances longer in life. A woman hears a much broader range of sounds, and her hearing remains sharper longer.

The female brain responds more intensely to emotion. According to neuroimaging studies, the genders respond differently to emotions, especially sadness, which activates, or turns on, neurons in an area eight times larger in women than men.

Neither gender's brain is "better." Intelligence per se appears equal in both. The greatest gender differences appear both at the top and bottom of the intelligence scales. Nevertheless, more than half the time, regardless of the type of test, most women and men perform more or less equally—even though they may well take different routes to arrive at the same answers.

Cognitive skills show greater variability both among women and among men than between the genders. The best evaluation may have come from essayist Samuel Johnson. When asked whether women or men are more intelligent, he responded, "Which man? Which woman?"

The Teenage and Twenty-Something Brain

If you are under the age of 25, your brain is a work in progress. As neuroimaging techniques such as PET scans (positron-emission tomography) and fMRIs (functional magnetic resonance imaging) have revealed, the brain continues to develop throughout the first quarter-century of life.

The number of synapses surges in the "tween" years before adolescence, followed, by a "pruning" of nonessential connections. In a sense, each individual determines which synapses stay and which are deleted. If you started to play the piano as a child and continue as an adolescent, for instance, you retain the synapses involved in this skill. If you don't practice regularly, your brain will prune the unused synapses, and your piano-playing ability will diminish. Inadequate pruning of synapses may contribute to mental disorders such as schizophrenia, which usually first occur in late adolescence.

Brain areas responsible for tasks such as organizing, controlling impulses, planning, and strategizing do not fully develop until the midtwenties. Brain chemicals such as dopamine that help distinguish between what is worthy of attention and what is mere distraction also do not reach optimal levels until then.

The brains of teens and young adults function differently than those of older individuals. In dealing with daily life, they rely more on the amygdala, a small almond-shaped region in the medial and temporal lobes that processes emotions and memories. This is one reason why any setback—a poor grade or a friend's snub—can feel like a major crisis. As individuals age, the frontal cortex, which governs reason and forethought, plays a greater role and helps put challenges into perspective.

A young, "maturing" brain does not necessarily lead to poor judgments and risky behaviors. However, if you are under 25, you should be aware that your brain may not always grasp the long-term consequences of your actions, set realistic priorities, or restrain potentially harmful impulses. You can learn to center yourself, seek the counsel of others, and not fly off the handle. Be cautious of drugs and alcohol, which are especially toxic to the developing brain and increase the risk of acts you may later regret.[1]

Understanding Mental Health

Mentally healthy individuals value themselves, perceive reality as it is, accept their limitations and possibilities, carry out their responsibilities, establish and maintain close relationships, pursue work that suits their talent and training, and feel a sense of fulfillment that makes the efforts of daily living worthwhile (Figure 3.3).

The state of mental health around the world is far from ideal. Psychiatric illness and substance abuse cause more premature deaths than any other factor, according to a recent report by the World Health Organization (WHO). These conditions also account for about a third of years lost to disability among people older than 14. The most common psychiatric conditions worldwide are depression, alcohol dependence and abuse, bipolar disorder, schizophrenia, Alzheimer's and other forms of dementia, panic disorder, and drug dependence and abuse.

Across the globe, depression is the leading cause of years of health lost to disease in both men and women. The worldwide rate of depression among women is 50 percent higher than in men, and women and girls have higher rates of anxiety disorders, migraine, and Alzheimer's disease. Men's rates of alcohol and substance abuse are nearly seven times higher than women's.

Preventive steps can help maintain and enhance your psychological health, just as similar actions boost physical health. (See Making Change Happen, p. 84.)

Despite public education campaigns, the level of prejudice and discrimination against people with a serious mental illness has changed little over the last ten years. More people now attribute problems like depression and substance abuse to neurobiological causes—and are more likely to favor providing treatment. Yet even these individuals are no less likely to stigmatize patients with mental illness.[2]

What Is a Mental Disorder?

While laypeople may speak of "nervous breakdowns" or "insanity," these are not scientific terms. The U.S. government's official definition states that a serious mental illness is "a diagnosable mental, behavioral, or emotional disorder that interferes with one or more major activities in life, like dressing, eating, or working."

Figure 3.3 **The Mentally Healthy Individual**
Mental well-being is a combination of many factors.

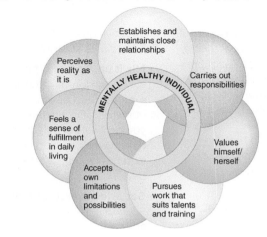

The mental health profession's standard for diagnosing a mental disorder is the pattern of symptoms, or diagnostic criteria, spelled out for the almost 300 disorders in the American Psychiatric Association's *Diagnostic and Statistical Manual*, 4th edition (DSM-IV). Psychiatrists define a **mental disorder** as a clinically significant behavioral or psychological syndrome or pattern that is associated with present distress (a painful symptom) or disability (impairment in one or more important areas of functioning) or with a significantly increased risk of suffering death, pain, disability, or an important loss of freedom.[3]

Who Develops Mental Disorders?

In the course of their lifetime, almost half of all Americans experience a diagnosable psychological problem. The most common mental disorders are substance abuse (discussed in Chapters 11 and 12), mood disorders such as depression and bipolar disorder, and anxiety disorders such as phobias and panic disorder.

Unlike most disabling physical diseases, mental illness starts early in life. Anxiety disorders often begin in late childhood, mood disorders in late adolescence, and substance abuse in the early twenties. Researchers describe such problems as "the chronic diseases of the young," striking when men and women are in their prime.

mental disorder Behavioral or psychological syndrome associated with distress or disability or with a significantly increased risk of suffering death, pain, disability, or loss of freedom.

The Exercise Prescription

Imagine a drug so powerful it can alter brain chemistry, so versatile it can help prevent or treat many common mental disorders, so safe that moderate doses cause few, if any, side effects, and so inexpensive that anyone can afford it. This wonder drug, proved in years of research, is exercise.

Chapter 8 provides detailed information on improving your fitness. To make a difference in the way you look and feel, follow these simple guidelines:

- **Work in short bouts.** Three 10-minute intervals of exercise can be just as effective as exercising for 30 minutes straight.

- **Mix it up.** Combine moderate and vigorous intensity exercises to meet the guidelines. For instance, you can walk briskly two days a week and jog at a faster pace on the other days.

- **Set aside exercise times.** Schedule exercise in advance so you can plan your day around it.

- **Find exercise buddies.** Recruit roommates, friends, family, coworkers. You'll have more fun on your way to getting fit.

The prevalence of mental disorders increases from early adulthood (ages 18 to 29) to the next-oldest age group (ages 30 to 44) and then declines. Women have higher rates of depressive and anxiety disorders; men have higher rates of substance abuse and impulse disorders.

About 6 percent of Americans have a "severe" mental disorder, one that significantly limits their ability to work or carry out daily activities or that has led to a suicide attempt or psychosis (a gross impairment of a person's perception of reality). On average, they are unable to function for nearly three months of the year.

The Mind-Body Connection

According to a growing number of studies, mental attitude may be just as important a risk factor for certain diseases as age, race, gender, education, habits, and health history. Positive states like happiness and optimism have been linked with longer lifespans as well as lower risk of cardiovascular and lung disease, stroke, diabetes, colds, and upper respiratory infections.

Gratitude, in particular, has proven health benefits. (See "Health in Action: Count Your Blessings," p. 63.)

In addition to its head-to-toe physical benefits, discussed in Chapter 8, exercise may be, as one therapist puts it, the single most effective way to lift a person's spirits and to restore feelings of potency about all aspects of life. People who exercise regularly report a more cheerful mood, higher self-esteem, and less stress. Their sleep and appetite also tend to improve. In clinical studies, exercise has proved effective as a treatment for depression and anxiety disorders. But remember: Although exercise can help prevent and ease problems for many people, it's no substitute for professional treatment of serious psychiatric disorders.

Disease Risks Mental disorders, on the other hand, can undermine physical well-being. Anxiety can lead to intensified asthmatic reactions, skin conditions, and digestive disorders. Stress can play a role in hypertension, heart attacks, sudden cardiac death, and immune disorders in the young as well as in older individuals. People who suffer from migraine headaches are at increased risk of depression, anxiety, and neurological disorders.

The brain and the heart—and the health of each—are linked in complex ways. Heart disease increases the likelihood of depression, and depression increases the likelihood of heart disease. For people with heart disease, depression can be fatal. It may contribute to sudden cardiac death and increase all causes of cardiac mortality.

Large-scale, longitudinal studies have found complex links between depression and diabetes. Individuals who are depressed are at much higher risk of developing diabetes, and those with diabetes are much more likely to become depressed. Preventing diabetes, which affects about 10 percent of Americans, may prevent depression—and preventing depression, which affects about 7 percent of adults over age 18, could prevent diabetes.[4]

Major depression is associated with lower bone density in young men and in adolescent girls. A history of depression increases the risk of physical problems such as headache and shoulder and neck pain in women as they reach middle age.

MENTAL HEALTH PROBLEMS ON CAMPUS

Students reporting the following feelings at any time with the last 12 months:

____ Exhausted (not from physical activity)	**80 percent**
____ Very sad	**61 percent**
____ Overwhelmingly anxious	**48 percent**
____ Hopeless	**46 percent**
____ So depressed it was difficult to function	**31 percent**

Students reporting a diagnosis of a mental disorder by a professional in the last 12 months.

____ Anxiety	**10 percent**
____ Depression	**10 percent**
____ Both anxiety and depression	**6 percent**
____ Panic attacks	**5 percent**
____ Attention disorder	**4 percent**
____ Insomnia	**4 percent**

HOW DO YOU COMPARE?

Check any of the feelings or diagnoses that apply to you. To tune into your current moods, track your feelings over a three-day period. Several times a day, jot down a few words about how you're feeling: blue, worried, excited, frustrated, happy, content. Think of it as taking your emotional temperature. Record your reflections on your feelings in your online journal.

From HALES, *An Invitation to Health,* 15E. © 2013 Cengage Learning.

Personality and Health Various personality types and behaviors have also been linked to certain illnesses. Aggressive, impatient, Type A people may be more prone to heart disease, high blood pressure, high cholesterol levels, and increased stomach acid secretion than more relaxed Type B people.

Individuals with a Type C personality—hard-working, highly responsible, quiet, courteous—tend to suppress negative emotions (especially anger), avoid conflicts, never retaliate, and rarely pursue their own desires. These behavioral and emotional characteristics are frequently seen in patients with cancer and may be associated with a suppressed immunity in patients with AIDS.

The Type D (for distressed) personality, characterized by tendencies both to experience negative emotions and to inhibit these emotions while avoiding contact with others, has emerged as an independent risk factor for heart disease, a poor prognosis if cardiovascular problems develop, and increased mortality.

Mental Health on Campus

Young people in their late teens and early twenties are at risk of mental health problems simply because of their age. In three of four cases, the first episodes of mental and substance abuse disorders occur before age 24.5 Nearly half of all young adults have suffered some form of a psychological disorder. The rates of such problems are lower among students than among those not enrolled in higher education, but undergraduates are far from immune.

Among entering freshmen, self-reported emotional health is at the lowest point in the last quarter-century. The percentage of students describing their mental state as above average or in the top 10 percent dropped to 52 percent, with much fewer women (46 percent) than men (59 percent) rating their mental health highly.[6]

In the American College Health Association National College Health Assessment, almost half (46 percent) of the more than 95,000

Count Your Blessings

As discussed in Chapter 2, gratitude has proven as effective in brightening mood and boosting energy as the standard, well-studied techniques used in psychotherapy. Below are some simple steps to cultivating and expressing gratitude. See "The Grateful Thread" in *Labs for IPC* for more suggestions:

- Every day write down ten new things for which you are grateful. You can start with this list and keep adding to it: your bed, your cell phone and every person whose efforts led to its development, every road you take, loyalty, your toothbrush, your toes, the sky, ice cream, etc.

- Record the ways you express gratitude. How do you feel when doing so?

- Create a daily practice of appreciation. This may be as simple as saying a few words of thanks before each meal (if only to yourself) or writing down your feelings of gratitude.

- Make a list of ten people to whom you owe a debt of gratitude. Write a one- to two-page letter to each of them, stating your appreciation of what he or she has contributed to you and your well-being. These people could include schoolteachers, music or dance instructors, coaches, doctors, neighbors, and, of course, family members. It is not important that you send the letters. What is important is that you focus deeply on the contribution of each person and allow feelings of gratitude to come as they may.

undergraduates surveyed reported feeling that things were hopeless within the last 12 months. About 61 percent felt very sad at least once, while 48 percent reported overwhelming anxiety and 31 percent reported being so depressed that it was difficult for them to function.7 (See table in "How Do You Compare?: Mental Health Problems on Campus.)

According to the American College Counseling Association (ACCA), which surveyed 28,000 students from 66 colleges and universities, more students are seeking counseling—and with more serious problems than in the past. Here are some of the survey findings:[8]

- Forty-four percent of students treated—up from 16 percent in 2000—suffer from a severe psychological disorder, such as depression, anxiety, attention disorders, alcohol or drug abuse, or eating disorders.

- About one in four undergraduates (24 percent) takes a psychiatric medication, up from 17 percent a decade ago.

- A quarter (25 percent) of students have seriously considered suicide prior to college, after starting college, or both; 21 percent have engaged in "nonsuicidal self-injury."

- Five percent have intentionally harmed another person. (See Chapter 18 for a discussion of violence on campus.)

Students at Risk

Why are so many students feeling so distressed? Many arrive on campus with a history of psychological problems. Medications for common disorders such as depression and attention disorder have made it possible for young people who might otherwise not have been able to function in a college setting to pursue higher education. Some are dealing with ongoing issues such as bulimia, self-cutting, and childhood sexual abuse. Others become depressed in college or begin abusing alcohol or drugs.

Among the strongest factors that put college students at risk for mental problems is a romantic breakup or loss. In the survey, about one in eight individuals reported a breakup in the previous year. Their odds of having a psychiatric disorder are significantly higher than those who hadn't been through a breakup.

Some psychiatric symptoms increase the risk of developing other disorders. College women who reported symptoms of depression, for example, are at higher risk for alcohol problems.

The few studies that have looked into ethnic differences in psychological health have yielded conflicting or inconclusive results: Some found no differences; others suggested higher rates of depression among Indian, Korean, and South Asian students.[9] Various ethnic groups report less of a sense of belonging and a lack of mentoring and peer support. A recent survey of Latino/a college students found that they did not differ from other students in overall mental health, but showed subtle signs of low-level psychological problems, such as a past history of depression and feeling "worried" or "sad."

The Toll on Students

Psychological and emotional problems can affect every aspect of a student's life, including physical health, overall satisfaction, and relationships. Students who struggle with symptoms of anxiety or depression, which can interfere with concentration, study habits, classroom participation, and testing, commonly report struggling with academics.

In the ACHA's national assessment, 18 percent of students reported that anxiety had impaired their ability to learn and earn higher grades; 12 percent said that depression had affected their academic performance.10 Some estimate that 5 percent of undergraduates may not complete their degrees because of psychological problems.

The impact of mental health problems extends beyond an individual student to roommates, friends, classmates, family, and instructors. Suicides or suicide attempts affect all members of the campus community, who may experience profound sadness and grief. (See the discussion of suicide later in this chapter.)

Many schools are setting up programs, such as depression screening days, to identify students at risk and refer them for follow-up and, when needed, professional treatment. Others have set up peer-counseling networks and are using social networking to raise awareness of problems like depression. However, there is only limited evidence that interventions like these might prevent a psychological disorder or lead to earlier recognition and treatment.[11]

Why don't distressed students seek professional care? Many feel they don't need help. Others worry about the stigma of admitting there's something wrong or of seeing a therapist. Although they are as likely to suffer psychological problems as others, African American students are much less likely to seek help. Their families' negative views about seeking help are a common deterrent.

Without help, many students' problems remain unresolved. When researchers assessed students' mental health and then checked back in two years later, more than a third of those surveyed had a mental health problem.

Depressive Disorders

 Depression, the world's most common mental ailment, affects more than 13 million adults in the United States every year and costs billions of dollars for treatment and lost productivity and lives. In a Centers for Disease Control and Prevention (CDC) survey of more than 235,000 people, 9 percent met the criteria for clinical depression, including 3 percent who could be diagnosed with major depression.[12] The prevalence of major depression increased with age, from about 3 percent among those ages 18 to 24 to almost 5 percent among persons ages 45 to 64. It declined to less than 2 percent among those older than age 65.

Those most likely to have major depression include:

- women
- racial and ethnic minorities
- those without a high school education
- divorced or never-married individuals
- the jobless
- those without health insurance[13]

Depression in Children and Teens

 An estimated 5 to 10 percent of American teenagers suffer from a serious depressive disorder; girls are twice as susceptible as boys. Prior to puberty, girls and boys are equally likely to develop depression.

The risks of depression in the young are high. Four in ten depressed adolescents think about killing themselves; two in ten actually try to do so. Every year an estimated 11 to 13 in every 100,000 teens take their own lives, twice as many as the number who die from all natural causes combined.

No one knows the reason for this steady surge in sadness, but experts point to the breakdown of families, the pressures of the information age, and increased isolation. A family history of depression greatly increases a young person's vulnerability. A mother's anxiety and depression during early childhood can increase the risk that adolescents will develop symptoms of anxiety and depression. Racial and ethnic factors also contribute. Among Asian American college students, for instance, perfectionism has been linked to depressive symptoms.

Teens who spend many hours watching television are at higher risk of depression as adults. However, the strongest predictor of depression is cigarette smoking. Depressed teens may smoke because they think smoking will make them feel better, but nicotine alters brain chemistry and actually worsens symptoms of depression.

Treatment with antidepressants and cognitive behavioral therapy helps most adolescents recover from major depression, but the risk of relapse is high, especially in girls. In one recent study, nearly half of adolescents developed a second episode of major depression.[14]

Depression in Students

An estimated 15 to 40 percent of college-age men and women (18- to 24-year-olds) may develop depression. Among the most vulnerable students are those being treated for mental disorders. (See the Self Survey: "Recognizing Depression," p. 83.)

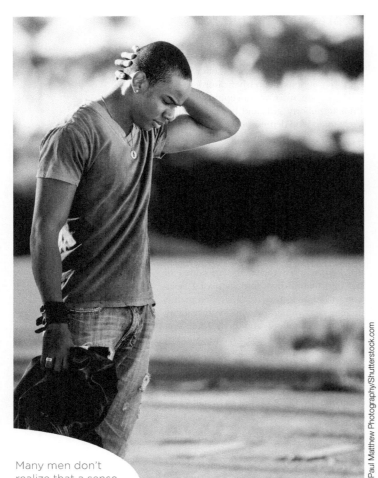

Many men don't realize that a sense of hopelessness, worthlessness, helplessness, or feeling dead inside can be a symptom of depression.

© Paul Matthew Photography/Shutterstock.com

Researchers at the University of Michigan have identified three key contributors to depression in college students: stress, substance abuse, and sleep loss.

As they adjust to campus life, undergraduates face the ongoing stress of forging a new identity and finding a place for themselves in various social hierarchies. This triggers the release of the so-called stress hormones (discussed in Chapter 4), which can change brain activity. Drugs and alcohol, widely used on campus, also affect the brain in ways that make stress even harder to manage.

Too little sleep adds another ingredient to this dangerous brew. Computers, the Internet, around-the-clock television, and the college tradition of pulling all-nighters can conspire to sabotage rest and increase vulnerability to depression.

Gender and Depression

Female Depression Depression is twice as common in women as men. However, this gender gap decreases or disappears in studies of men and women in similar socioeconomic situations, such as college students, civil servants, and the Amish community. Women may not necessarily be more likely to develop depression, this research suggests, but may have an underlying predisposition that puts them at greater risk under various social stressors.[15]

Brain chemistry and sex hormones may play a role. Women produce less of certain metabolites of serotonin, a messenger chemical that helps regulate mood. Their brains also register sadness much more intensely than men's, and they are more sensitive to changes in light and temperature. Women are at least four times more likely than men to develop seasonal affective disorder (SAD) and to become depressed in the dark winter months.

Some women also seem more sensitive to their own hormones or to the changes in them that occur at puberty, during the menstrual cycle, after childbirth, or during perimenopause and menopause. Primary ovarian insufficiency, a condition that causes menopause-like symptoms and that can develop as early as the teens or twenties, greatly increases a woman's risk of depression.[16] Pregnancy, contrary to what many people assume, does not "protect" a woman from depression, and women who discontinue treatment when they become pregnant are at risk of a relapse. Women and their psychiatrists must carefully weigh the risks and benefits of psychiatric medications during pregnancy.

Childhood abuse also contributes to female vulnerability. In epidemiological studies, 60 percent of women diagnosed with depression—compared with 39 percent of men—were abused as children. In adulthood, relationships may protect women from depression, while a lack of social support increases vulnerability to depression. Women with at least one "confiding relationship," as researchers put it, are physically and psychologically more resilient.

Male Depression More than 6 million men in the United States—1 in every 14—suffer from this insidious disorder, many without recognizing what's wrong. Experts describe male depression as an "under" disease: underdiscussed, underrecognized, underdiagnosed, and undertreated.

Depression "looks" different in men than women. Rather than becoming sad, men may be irritable or tremendously fatigued. They feel a sense of being dead inside, of worthlessness, hopelessness, helplessness, of losing their life force. Physical symptoms, such as headaches, pain, and insomnia, are common, as are attempts to "self-medicate" with alcohol or drugs.

Genes may make some men more vulnerable, but chronic stress of any sort plays a major role in male depression, possibly by raising levels of the stress hormone cortisol and lowering testosterone. Men also are more likely than women to become depressed following divorce, job loss, or a career setback. Whatever its roots, depression alters brain chemistry in potentially deadly ways. Four times as many men as women kill themselves; depressed men are two to four times more likely to take their own lives than depressed women.

Dysthymic Disorder

Dysthymia is a depressive disorder characterized by a chronically depressed mood. Symptoms include feelings of inadequacy, hopelessness, and guilt; low self-esteem; low energy; fatigue; indecisiveness; and an inability to enjoy pleasurable activities.

Minor Depression

Minor depression is a common disorder that is often unrecognized and untreated, affecting about 7.5 percent of Americans during their lifetime. Its symptoms are the same as those of major depression, but less severe and fewer in number. They include either a depressed mood most of the day, nearly every day, or diminished interest or pleasure in daily activities.

Psychotherapy is remarkably effective for mild depression. In more serious cases, antidepressant medication can lead to dramatic improvement in 40 to 80 percent of

Your Strategies for Prevention

How to Help Someone Who Is Depressed

- **Express your concern, but don't nag.** You might say: "I'm concerned about you. You are struggling right now. We need to find some help."

- **Don't be distracted by behaviors like drinking or gambling, which can disguise depression in men.**

- **Encourage the individual to remain in treatment until symptoms begin to lift (which takes several weeks).**

- **Provide emotional support.** Listen carefully. Offer hope and reassurance that with time and treatment, things will get better.

- **Do not ignore remarks about suicide.** Report them to his or her doctor or, in an emergency, call 911.

depressed patients. Exercise also works. Several studies have shown that exercise effectively lifts mild to moderate depression.

Major Depression

The simplest definition of **major depression** is sadness that does not end. The incidence of major depression has soared over the last two decades, especially among young adults. Major depression can destroy a person's joy for living. Food, friends, sex, or any form of pleasure no longer appeals. It is impossible to concentrate on work and responsibilities. Unable to escape a sense of utter hopelessness, depressed individuals may fight back tears throughout the day and toss and turn through long, empty nights. Thoughts of death or suicide may push into their minds.

The characteristic symptoms of major depression include:

- **Feeling depressed,** sad, empty, discouraged, tearful.

- **Loss of interest** or pleasure in once-enjoyable activities.

- **Eating more or less** than usual and either gaining or losing weight.

dysthymia Frequent, prolonged mild depression.

major depression Sadness that does not end; ongoing feelings of utter helplessness.

- **Having trouble sleeping** or sleeping much more than usual.
- **Feeling slowed down** or restless and unable to sit still.
- **Lack of energy**.
- **Feeling helpless,** hopeless, worthless, inadequate.
- **Difficulty concentrating**, forgetfulness.
- **Difficulty thinking clearly** or making decisions.
- **Persistent thoughts of death** or suicide.
- **Withdrawal from others**, lack of interest in sex.
- **Physical symptoms** (headaches, digestive problems, aches and pains).

As many as half of major depressive episodes are not recognized because the symptoms are "masked." Rather than feeling sad or depressed, individuals may experience low energy, insomnia, difficulty concentrating, and physical symptoms.

Treating Depression

The most recent guidelines for treating depression, developed by the American Psychiatric Association, call for an individualized approach tailored to each patient's symptoms. Specific treatments might include medication, healthy behaviors, exercise (proven to reduce depressive symptoms, especially in older adults and those with chronic medical problems), and psychotherapy.[17]

The rate of depression treatment, particularly with antidepressants, has increased in the last decade. Medication has become the most common approach, while fewer patients receive psychotherapy than in the past, possibly because of limited insurance

---

❶ CONSUMER ALERT

The Pros and Cons of Antidepressants

Millions of individuals have benefited from the category of antidepressant drugs called selective serotonin reuptake inhibitors (SSRIs). However, like all drugs, they can cause side effects that range from temporary physical symptoms, such as stomach upset and headaches, to more persistent problems, such as sexual dysfunction. The most serious—and controversial—risk is suicide.

Facts to Know

- The FDA has issued a "black box" warning about the risk of suicidal thoughts, hostility, and aggression in both children and young adults. The danger is greatest just after pill use begins.
- This risk of suicide while taking an antidepressant is about 1 in 3,000; the risk of a serious attempt is 1 in 1,000.
- Recent reviews of antidepressant use have found that the risk of suicide for both children and adults was *higher* in the month *before* starting treatment, dropped sharply in the month after it began, and tapered off in the following months.

Steps to Take

- If you are younger than age 20, be aware of the increased suicide risk with the use of SSRIs. Talk these over carefully with a psychiatrist. Discuss alternative treatments, such as psychotherapy.
- For individuals older than age 20, the benefits of antidepressants have proved to outweigh their risks in most cases. Adults treated with SSRIs are 40+percent less likely to commit suicide than depressed individuals who do not receive this therapy.
- In patients initially treated with antidepressants, two approaches based on mindfulness (discussed in Chapter 4)—mindfulness-based cognitive therapy and mindfulness meditation—have proven as effective as continuing drug therapy in preventing a return of depression symptoms.[19]
- Whatever your age, arrange for careful monitoring and follow-up with a psychiatrist when you start taking an antidepressant. Familiarize yourself with possible side effects, and seek help immediately if you begin to think about taking your own life.

coverage. A combination of psychotherapy and medication is considered the most effective approach for most patients.[18]

Psychotherapy helps individuals pinpoint the life problems that contribute to their depression, identify negative or distorted thinking patterns, explore behaviors that contribute to depression, and regain a sense of control and pleasure in life. Two specific psychotherapies—cognitive-behavioral therapy and interpersonal therapy (described later in this chapter)—have proved as helpful as antidepressant drugs, although they take longer than medication to achieve results.

Antidepressants have proven most effective in individuals with severe depression, with minimal or nonexistent benefits for those with mild or moderate symptoms. (See "Consumer Alert: The Pros and Cons of Antidepressants.")

For individuals who cannot take antidepressant medications because of medical problems, or who do not improve with psychotherapy or drugs, *electroconvulsive* therapy (ECT)—the administration of a controlled electrical current through electrodes attached to the scalp—remains the safest and most effective treatment. About 70 to 90 percent of depressed individuals improve after ECT. Newer options include transcranial magnetic stimulation, which uses highly focused, pulsed magnetic fields to stimulate brain regions linked with depression, and vagus nerve stimulation, which delivers electrical stimulation to a major nerve linking the brain to internal organs.

Even without treatment, depression generally lifts after six to nine months. However, in more than 80 percent of people, it recurs, with each episode lasting longer and becoming more severe and difficult to treat.

"All the while the depression goes untreated, it is causing ongoing damage that shrivels important regions of the brain," says John Greden, M.D., director of the University of Michigan Depression Center. "The exciting news is that, as brain scans show, treatment turns the destructive process around and stops depression in its tracks."[20]

Bipolar Disorder

Bipolar disorder, known as manic depression in the past, consists of mood swings that may take individuals from manic states of feeling euphoric and energetic to depressive states of utter despair. In episodes of full mania, they may become so impulsive and out of touch with reality that they endanger their careers, relationships, health, or even survival. Psychiatrists view bipolar symptoms on a spectrum that includes depression and states of acute irritability and distress.[21]

One percent of the population—about 2 million American adults—suffer from this serious but treatable disorder. Men tend to develop bipolar disorder earlier in life (between ages 16 and 25), but women have higher rates overall. About 50 percent of patients with bipolar illness have a family history of the disorder.

The characteristic symptoms of bipolar disorder include:

- **Mood swings** (from happy to miserable, optimistic to despairing, and so on).
- **Changes in thinking** (thoughts speeding through one's mind, unrealistic self-confidence, difficulty concentrating, delusions, hallucinations).
- **Changes in behavior** (sudden immersion in plans and projects, talking very rapidly and much more than usual, excessive spending, impaired judgment, impulsive sexual involvement).
- **Changes in physical condition** (less need for sleep, increased energy, fewer health complaints than usual).

During manic periods, individuals may make grandiose plans or take dangerous risks. But they often plunge from this highest of highs to a horrible, low depressive episode, in which they may feel sad, hopeless, and helpless and develop other symptoms of major depression.

Professional therapy is essential in treating bipolar disorders. An estimated 25 to 50 percent of bipolar patients attempt suicide at least once. About 1 percent take their own lives every year.[22] Mood-stabilizing medications are the keystone of treatment, although psychotherapy plays a critical role in helping individuals understand their illness and rebuild their lives. Most individuals continue taking medication indefinitely after remission of their symptoms because the risk of recurrence is high.

bipolar disorder Severe depression alternating with periods of manic activity and elation.

Systematic desensitization is one behavioral approach to treating a fear of snakes and other phobias.

anxiety disorders A group of psychological disorders involving episodes of apprehension, tension, or uneasiness, stemming from the anticipation of danger and sometimes accompanied by physical symptoms, which cause significant distress and impairment to an individual.

phobia An anxiety disorder marked by an inordinate fear of an object, a class of objects, or a situation, resulting in extreme avoidance behaviors.

panic attack A short episode characterized by physical sensations of light-headedness, dizziness, hyperventilation, and numbness of extremities, accompanied by an inexplicable terror, usually of a physical disaster such as death.

Anxiety Disorders

Anxiety disorders are as common as depression but are often undetected and untreated.[23] They may involve inordinate fears of certain objects or situations (**phobias**), episodes of sudden, inexplicable terror (**panic attacks**), chronic distress (**generalized anxiety disorder**, or **GAD**), or persistent, disturbing thoughts and behaviors (**obsessive–compulsive disorder**, or **OCD**). These disorders can increase the risk of developing depression. Over a lifetime, as many as one in four Americans may experience an anxiety disorder. More than 40 percent are never correctly diagnosed and treated. Yet most individuals who do get treatment, even for severe and disabling problems, improve dramatically.

Phobias

Phobias—the most prevalent type of anxiety disorder—are out-of-the-ordinary, irrational, intense, persistent fears of certain objects or situations. About 2 million Americans develop such acute terror that they go to extremes to avoid whatever it is that they fear, even though they realize that these feelings are excessive or unreasonable. The most common phobias involve animals, particularly dogs, snakes, insects, and mice; the sight of blood; closed spaces (claustrophobia); heights (acrophobia); air travel and being in open or public places or situations from which one perceives it would be difficult or embarrassing to escape (agoraphobia).

Although various medications have been tried, none is effective by itself in relieving phobias. The best approach is behavioral therapy, which consists of gradual, systematic exposure to the feared object (a process called systematic desensitization). Numerous studies have proved that exposure—especially in vivo exposure, in which individuals are exposed to the actual source of their fear rather than simply imagining it—is highly effective. Medical hypnosis—the use of induction of an altered state of consciousness—also can help.

Panic Attacks and Panic Disorder

Individuals who have had panic attacks describe them as the most frightening experiences of their lives. Without reason or warning, their hearts race wildly. They may become light-headed or dizzy. Because they can't catch their breath, they may start breathing rapidly and hyperventilate. Parts of their bodies, such as their fingers or toes, may tingle or feel numb. Worst of all is the terrible sense that something horrible is about to happen: that they will die, lose their minds, or have a heart attack.

 Individuals of different ethnic and racial backgrounds may experience panic symptoms differently. In one cross-cultural study of undergraduates, Asians tended to report symptoms such as dizziness, unsteadiness, choking, and feeling terrified more frequently than did Caucasians. African Americans reported feeling less nervous than Caucasians. However, panic symptoms were equally severe across all racial and ethnic groups.[24]

Most attacks reach peak intensity within ten minutes. Afterward, individuals live in dread of another one. In the course of a lifetime, your risk of having a single panic attack is 7 percent.

Panic disorder develops when attacks recur or apprehension about them becomes so intense that individuals cannot function normally. Full-blown panic disorder occurs in about 2 percent of all adults in the course of a lifetime and usually develops before age 30. Women are more than twice as likely as men to experience panic attacks, although no one knows why. Parents, siblings, and children of individuals with panic disorders also are more likely to develop them than are others.

The two primary treatments for panic disorder are (1) cognitive-behavioral therapy (CBT), which teaches specific strategies for coping with symptoms like rapid breathing, and (2) medication. Treatment helps as many as 90 percent of those with panic disorder either improve significantly or recover completely, usually within six to eight weeks. Individuals with a greater internal locus of control (discussed in Chapter 1) may respond better to CBT.

Generalized Anxiety Disorder

About 10 million adults in the United States suffer from a generalized anxiety disorder (GAD), excessive or unrealistic apprehension that causes physical symptoms and lasts for six months or longer. It usually starts when people are in their twenties. Unlike fear, which helps us recognize and avoid real danger, GAD is an irrational or unwarranted response to harmless objects or situations of exaggerated danger. The most common symptoms are faster heart rate, sweating, increased blood pressure, muscle aches, intestinal pains, irritability, sleep problems, and difficulty concentrating.

Worry is a normal part of daily life, but individuals with generalized anxiety disorder worry constantly about everything that might go wrong.

generalized anxiety disorder (GAD) An anxiety disorder characterized as chronic distress.

obsessive-compulsive disorder (OCD) An anxiety disorder characterized by obsessions and/or compulsions that impair one's ability to function and form relationships.

panic disorder An anxiety disorder in which the apprehension or experience of recurring panic attacks is so intense that normal functioning is impaired.

Chronically anxious individuals worry—not just some of the time, and not just about the stresses and strains of ordinary life—but constantly, about almost everything: their health, families, finances, marriages, potential dangers. Treatment for GAD may consist of a combination of psychotherapy, behavioral therapy, and antianxiety drugs.

Obsessive-Compulsive Disorder

As many as 1 in 40 Americans has a type of anxiety called obsessive-compulsive disorder (OCD). Some of these individuals suffer only from an obsession, a recurring idea, thought, or image that they realize, at least initially, is senseless. The most common obsessions are repetitive thoughts of violence (for example, killing a child), contamination (becoming infected by shaking hands), and doubt (wondering whether one has performed some act, such as having hurt someone in a traffic accident).

Most people with OCD also suffer from a *compulsion*, a repetitive behavior performed according to certain rules or in a stereotyped fashion. The most common compulsions involve handwashing, cleaning, hoarding useless items, counting, or checking (for example, making sure dozens of times that a door is locked).

Individuals with OCD realize that their thoughts or behaviors are bizarre, but they cannot resist or control them. Eventually, the obsessions or compulsions consume a great deal of time and significantly interfere with normal routines, job functioning, or usual social activities or relationships with others. A young woman who must follow a very rigid dressing routine may always be late for class, for example; a student who must count each letter of the alphabet as he types may not be able to complete a term paper.

Treatment may consist of cognitive therapy to correct irrational assumptions, behavioral techniques such as progressively limiting the amount of time someone obsessed with cleanliness can spend washing and scrubbing, and medication. Using neuroimaging techniques, researchers have found significant changes in activity in certain regions of the brain after four weeks of daily therapy in patients with obsessive-compulsive disorder.

Attention Disorders

Attention-deficit/hyperactivity disorder (ADHD) is the most common mental disorder in childhood. About one in ten school-age children suffer from ADHD and show marked differences in their brain chemistry.[25] Contrary to previous beliefs, most children do not outgrow it. For as many as two-thirds of youngsters, ADHD persists into adolescence and young adulthood. About 4 percent of college students have ADHD and another 11 percent have ADHD symptoms.[26]

 ADHD looks and feels different in adults. Hyperactivity is more subtle, an internal fidgety feeling rather than a physical restlessness. As youngsters with ADHD mature, academic difficulties become much more of a problem. Students with ADHD may find it hard to concentrate, read, make decisions, complete complex projects, and meet deadlines. The academic performance and standardized test scores of college students with ADHD are significantly lower than those of their peers.

Relationships with peers also can become more challenging. Young people with ADHD may become frustrated easily, have a short fuse, and erupt into angry outbursts. Some become more argumentative, negative, and defiant than most other teens. Sleep problems, including sleeping much more or less than normal, are common. The likelihood of developing other emotional problems, including depression and anxiety disorders, is higher. As many as 20 percent of those diagnosed with depression, anxiety, or substance abuse also have ADHD.

The risk of substance use disorders for individuals with ADHD is twice that of the general population. According to several reports, between 15 and 25 percent of adults with substance use disorders have ADHD. In addition, individuals with ADHD start smoking at a younger age and have higher rates of smoking and drinking. (The use of stimulant medication to treat ADHD does not increase the risk of substance abuse.)

attention-deficit/ hyperactivity disorder (ADHD) A spectrum of difficulties in controlling motion and sustaining attention, including hyperactivity, impulsivity, and distractibility.

The medications used for this disorder include stimulants (such as Ritalin), which improve behavior and cognition for about 70 percent of adolescents. Extended-release preparations (including a skin patch) are longer acting, so individuals do not have to take these medications as often as in the past. As discussed in Chapter 12, misuse of prescription stimulants by students without ADHD is a growing problem on college campuses.

 According to recent research, college students who have not been diagnosed with ADHD but use prescription stimulants may be self-medicating themselves for attention problems. In one survey, 10 percent of those who had never been diagnosed with ADHD had high levels of ADHD symptoms. However, it's not clear whether they suffer from true ADHD or are using medication to deal with short-term academic challenges. The dangers of doing so include drug abuse and addiction (discussed in Chapter 12).[27]

Although many students take stimulants to improve performance, they generally get poorer grades, perhaps because they fall behind and then take stimulants in order to cram and catch up.

An alternative nonstimulant treatment is Strattera (atomoxetine), which treats ADHD and coexisting problems such as depression and anxiety. Its effects are more gradual, and it does not seem to have any known potential for abuse. Adverse effects include drowsiness, loss of appetite, nausea, vomiting, and headaches. Its long-term effects are not known. A promising new approach is transcendental meditation (TM), which may calm anxiety and improve ability to concentrate.[28]

 In the ACHA survey, 5 percent of students reported that ADHD had affected their academic performance.[29] Undergraduates with ADHD are at higher risk of becoming smokers, abusing alcohol and drugs, and having automobile accidents. The normal challenges of college—navigating the complexities of scheduling, planning courses, and honing study skills—may be especially daunting.

Psychological therapies have not been studied extensively in adolescents and young adults with ADHD. However, if you have ADHD, check with your student health or counseling center to see if any special services are available.

Many students with ADHD benefit from strategies such as sitting in the front row to avoid distraction, recording lectures if they have difficulty listening and taking notes at the same time, being allowed extended time for tests, and taking oral rather than written exams.[30] Some students have tried to feign ADHD to qualify for such special treatment or to obtain prescriptions for stimulants. However, a thorough examination by an experienced therapist can usually determine whether a student actually suffers from ADHD.[31]

Autism and Autism Spectrum Disorders

Autism, a complex neurodevelopmental disability that causes social and communication impairments, is a "spectrum" disorder that includes several disorders with similar features. These problems affect all racial, ethnic, and socioeconomic groups but are four times more likely to occur in boys than girls.

The CDC estimates that between about 1 in 80 and 1 in 240, with an average of 1 in 110, children in the United States have an autism spectrum disorder. Autism rates have risen steadily in recent decades, but the reasons why are not clear. There is no scientific evidence that any part of a vaccine or combination of vaccines causes autism, nor is there proof that any material used to produce the vaccine, such as thimerosal, a mercury-containing preservative, plays a role in causing autism. Although past studies linked vaccines to autism, further investigations have refuted these findings.[32]

Symptoms, which include repetitive patterns of thoughts and behavior and inability to communicate verbally, usually start before age three and can create delays or problems in many different skills that develop from infancy to adulthood. The earlier that interventions begin, the more effective they have proved to be.[33]

Individuals with **Asperger syndrome**, the mildest of the autism spectrum disorders, have autism-like problems in social interaction and communication but normal to above-average intelligence. However, they usually are very rigid and literal and may have trouble understanding nonverbal communications, such as body language. One of their most distinctive symptoms is having such an obsessive interest in a single object or topic that they ignore other objects, topics, or thoughts.

Treatments for managing autism spectrum disorders include behavioral therapy to reinforce wanted behaviors and reduce unwanted behaviors; speech–language therapy to improve ability to communicate and interact with others; physical therapy to build motor control and improve posture and balance; and school-based educational programs. There are no medications specifically for the treatment of autism, but various medicines can help manage associated symptoms.

Schizophrenia

Schizophrenia, one of the most debilitating mental disorders, profoundly impairs an individual's sense of reality. As the National Institute of Mental Health (NIMH) puts it, schizophrenia, which is characterized by abnormalities in brain structure and chemistry, destroys "the inner unity of the mind" and weakens "the will and drive that constitute our essential character." It affects every aspect of psychological functioning, including the ways in which people think, feel, view themselves, and relate to others.

The symptoms of schizophrenia include:

- **Hallucinations.**
- **Delusions.**
- **Inability to think** in a logical manner.
- **Talking** in rambling or incoherent ways.
- **Making odd or purposeless movements** or not moving at all.
- **Repeating others' words** or mimicking their gestures.
- **Showing few, if any, feelings;** responding with inappropriate emotions.

- **Lacking will or motivation** to complete a task or accomplish something.
- **Functioning at a much lower level** than in the past at work, in interpersonal relations, or in taking care of themselves.

Schizophrenia is one of the leading causes of disability among young adults. The mean age for schizophrenia to develop is 21.4 years for men and 26.8 years for women. Although symptoms do not occur until then, they are almost certainly the result of a failure in brain development that occurs very early in life. The underlying defect is probably present before birth. The risk increases along with the age of a father at the birth of his first child.[34] Schizophrenia has a strong genetic basis and is not the result of upbringing, social conditions, or traumatic experiences.

For the vast majority of individuals with schizophrenia, antipsychotic drugs are the foundation of treatment. Newer agents are more effective in making most people with schizophrenia feel more comfortable and in control of themselves, helping organize chaotic thinking, and reducing or eliminating delusions or hallucinations, allowing fuller participation in normal activities.

Suicide

Suicide is not in itself a psychiatric disorder, but it is often the tragic consequence of emotional and psychological problems. Every year 30,000 Americans—among them many young people who seem to have "everything to live for"—commit suicide, and an estimated 811,000 attempt to take their own lives. There may be 4.5 million suicide "survivors" in the United States.

 The suicide rate for African American and Caucasian men peaks between ages 20 and 40. It rises again after age 65 among white men and after age 75 among blacks. In general, whites are at highest risk for suicide, followed by American Indians, African Americans, Hispanic Americans, and Asian Americans. Internationally, suicide rates are highest in Germany, Scandinavia, Eastern Europe, and Japan; average in the United States, Canada, and Great Britain; and low in Italy, Spain, and Ireland.

Asperger syndrome is a high-functioning form of autism characterized by difficulty interacting socially, repetitive behaviors, clumsiness, and delays in motor development.

schizophrenia A general term for a group of mental disorders with characteristic psychotic symptoms, such as delusions, hallucinations, and disordered thought patterns during the active phase of the illness, and a duration of at least six months.

At all ages, men *commit* suicide three to four times more frequently than women, but women attempt suicide much more often than men (Table 3.1). Elderly men are ten times more likely to take their own lives than elderly women. (See Chapter 20 for more on depression and suicide in older men and women.)

Suicide in the Young

Suicide rates among youths between ages 10 and 19 in the United States have risen after a decade-long decline. In a national survey, an estimated 15 percent of high school students seriously considered suicide, and 7 percent attempted suicide at least once. Girls and black and Hispanic students were most likely to attempt suicide. Up to 50 percent of adolescents who attempt suicide try again to take their own lives. An estimated 11 percent of those who attempt suicide eventually die by suicide.

The controversy about the use of antidepressants in children and teens may play a role in the spike in youth suicide. Although several re-analyses and reviews have confirmed that these medications can themselves increase the likelihood of suicide in individuals younger than age 20, this risk is small. In many cases, the benefits may well outweigh the risk, but there is a need for careful monitoring for warning signs of suicide whenever a child or teen begins antidepressant therapy.

 Native American communities have especially high rates of suicide among both young men and women. Young African American men, historically at low suicide risk, are narrowing the gap with their white peers, while suicide by Hispanic young men has declined. The lowest rates are for Asian Pacific males and African American females.

Firearms and suffocation (mainly by hanging) are the most common methods of suicide among young people. In recent years, deaths with firearms have decreased, in part because of laws restricting access to guns by youngsters.

Researchers also have identified factors that protect young people from suicide. Number one for both boys and girls was feeling connected to their parents and family. For girls, emotional well-being was also protective; grade-point average was an additional protective factor for boys.

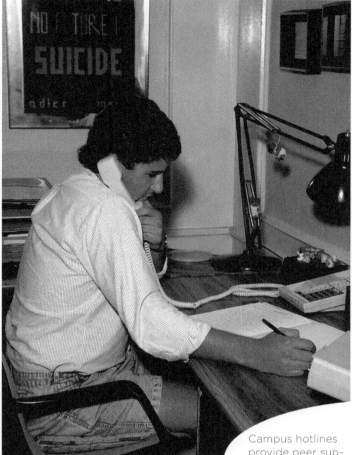

© Mary Kate Denny/PhotoEdit

Campus hotlines provide peer support to students who may be feeling overwhelmed but don't know where to turn for help.

Table 3.1 **Suicide Risk**

	Who Attempts Suicide?	**Who Commits Suicide?**
Sex	Female	Male
Age	Under 35	Under 20 or over 60
Means	Less deadly, such as a wrist slashing	More deadly, such as a gun
Circumstances	High chance of rescue	Low chance of rescue

From HALES, *An Invitation to Health*, 15E. © 2013 Cengage Learning.

Suicide on Campus

More than 1,100 college students take their own lives every year; 1.5 percent attempt to do so. In a recent survey, 12 percent of students reported suicidal thoughts; 25 percent of these had more than one episode.[35] The rates of self-harm without intent to die are even higher.[36]

The reasons that students consider or attempt suicide vary, but the most significant is untreated depression. Two-thirds of individuals who kill themselves experienced depressive symptoms at the time of their deaths. However, rates of suicide attempts and completions are consistently lower than among college-age peers who are not in college.

Suicide rarely stems from a single cause. Researchers have identified several common ones for college students, including the following:

- Depression or depressive symptoms.
- Family history of mental illness.
- Personality traits, such as hopelessness, helplessness, impulsivity, and aggression.
- Alcohol use and binge drinking. Among college students, binge drinkers are significantly more likely to contemplate suicide, to have attempted suicide in the past, and to believe they would make a future suicide attempt than non-binge drinkers.
- Ineffective problem solving and coping skills.
- Recent sexual or physical victimization; being in an emotionally or physically abusive relationship;
- Family problems.
- Exposure to trauma or stress.
- Feelings of loneliness or social isolation.
- Harassment because of sexual orientation.

 The stress of acculturation (the psychosocial adjustments that occur when an ethnic minority interacts with the ethnic majority, discussed in Chapter 4) may also play a role. Blacks who take their own lives tend to be younger, less likely to have been depressed, and less likely to have financial problems, chronic illness, or substance abuse problems. While alcohol and cocaine play a role in more than 40 percent of suicides by European American youths, they are involved in less than 18 percent of suicides of African Americans.

Although many schools offer counseling and crisis services, students often don't know where to turn when they feel hopeless or are thinking about suicide. In a study of undergraduates, as suicidal thoughts increased, students' help-seeking decreased. Negative feelings or stigma, both about themselves and about getting mental health care, contributed to the inability or unwillingness to reach out for professional help.[37]

Factors That Lead to Suicide

Researchers have looked for explanations for suicide by studying everything from phases of the moon to seasons (suicides peak in the spring and early summer) to birth order in the family. They have found no conclusive answers. However, the most important risk factors for suicide appear to be impulsivity, high levels of arousal and aggression, and past suicidal behavior.[38] (See Table 3.2 on page 78.)

Mental Disorders More than 95 percent of those who commit suicide have a mental disorder. Two in particular—depression and alcoholism—account for two-thirds of all suicides. Suicide also is a risk for those with other disorders, including schizophrenia, posttraumatic stress disorder, personality disorders, and untreated depression. The lifetime suicide rate for people with major depression is 15 percent.

Substance Abuse Many of those who commit suicide drink beforehand, and their use of alcohol may lower their inhibitions. Since alcohol itself is a depressant, it can intensify the despondency suicidal individuals are already feeling. Alcoholics who attempt suicide often have other risk factors, including major depression, poor social support, serious medical illness, and unemployment. Drugs of abuse also can alter thinking and lower inhibitions against suicide.

Hopelessness The sense of utter hopelessness and helplessness may be the most common contributing factor in suicide. When hope dies, individuals view every experience in negative terms and come to expect the worst possible outcomes for their problems. Given this way of thinking, suicide often seems a reasonable response to a life seen as not worth living. Optimism, on the other hand, correlates with fewer thoughts of suicide by college students.

Combat Stress According to a congressional report, veterans who have been exposed to the violence and trauma of combat or deployment in a war zone may account for as many as 20 percent of suicides. Conditions that may increase a veteran's risk of suicide include depression, PTSD, traumatic brain injury, and lack of social support.[39] In response to this, the Veterans Administration has set up a Suicide Prevention Hotline number: 1-800-274-TALK.

Family History One of every four people who attempt suicide has a family member who also tried to commit suicide. While a family history of suicide is not in itself considered a predictor of suicide, two mental disorders that can lead to suicide—depression and bipolar disorder (manic depression)—do run in families.

Physical Illness People who commit suicide are likely to be ill or to believe that they are. About 5 percent actually have a serious physical disorder, such as AIDS or cancer. While suicide may seem to be a decision rationally arrived at in persons with serious or fatal illness, this may not be the case. Depression, not uncommon in such instances, can warp judgment. When the depression is treated, the person may no longer have suicidal intentions.

Brain Chemistry Investigators have found abnormalities in the brain chemistry of individuals who complete suicide, especially low levels of a metabolite of the neurotransmitter serotonin. There are indications that individuals with a deficiency in this substance may have as much as a ten times greater risk of committing suicide than those with higher levels.

Access to Guns For individuals already facing a combination of predisposing factors, access to a means of committing suicide, particularly to guns, can add to the risk. Unlike other methods of suicide, guns almost always work. Suicide rates among children, women, and men of all ages are higher in states where more households have guns. Although only 5 percent of suicide attempts involve firearms, more than 90 percent of these attempts are fatal. States with stricter gun-control laws have much lower rates of suicide than states with more lenient laws.

Your Strategies for Prevention

Steps to Prevent Suicide

If you worry that someone you know may be contemplating suicide, express your concern. Here are some specific guidelines:

- **Ask concerned questions.** Listen attentively. Show that you take the person's feelings seriously and truly care.
- **Don't offer trite reassurances.** Don't list reasons to go on living, try to analyze the person's motives, or try to shock or challenge him or her.
- **Suggest solutions or alternatives to problems.** Make plans. Encourage positive action, such as getting away for a while to gain a better perspective on a problem.
- **Don't be afraid to ask whether your friend has considered suicide.** The opportunity to talk about thoughts of suicide may be an enormous relief and—contrary to a long-standing myth—will not fix the idea of suicide more firmly in a person's mind.
- **Don't think that people who talk about killing themselves never carry out their threat.** Most individuals who commit suicide give definite indications of their intent to die.
- **Watch out for behavioral clues.** If your friend begins to behave unpredictably or suddenly emerges from a severe depression into a calm, settled state of mind, these could signal increased danger of suicide. Don't leave your friend alone. Call a suicide hotline, or get in touch with a mental health professional.

If you are thinking about suicide ...

- **Talk to a mental health professional.** If you have a therapist, call immediately. If not, call a suicide hotline.
- **Find someone you can trust and talk honestly about what you're feeling.** If you suffer from depression or another mental disorder, educate trusted friends or relatives about your condition so they are prepared if called upon to help.
- **Write down your more uplifting thoughts.** Even if you are despondent, you can help yourself by taking the time to retrieve some more positive thoughts or memories. A simple record of your hopes for the future and the people you value in your life can remind you of why your own life is worth continuing.
- **Avoid drugs and alcohol.** Most suicides are the results of sudden, uncontrolled impulses, and drugs and alcohol can make it harder to resist these destructive urges.
- **Go to the hospital.** Hospitalization can sometimes be the best way to protect your health and safety.

Table 3.2 **Risk Factors for Suicide**

Biopsychosocial Risk Factors

- Mental disorders, particularly depressive disorders, schizophrenia, and anxiety disorders
- Alcohol and other substance use disorders
- Hopelessness
- Impulsive and/or aggressive tendencies
- History of trauma or abuse
- Some major physical illness
- Previous suicide attempt
- Family history of suicide

Environmental Risk Factors

- Job or financial loss
- Relational or social loss
- Easy access to lethal means
- Local clusters of suicide that have a contagious influence

Sociocultural Risk Factors

- Lack of social support and sense of isolation
- Stigma associated with help-seeking behavior
- Barriers to accessing health care, especially mental health and substance abuse treatment
- Certain cultural and religious beliefs (for instance, the belief that suicide is a noble resolution of a personal dilemma)
- Exposure to suicide, including through the media, and the influence of others who have died by suicide

SOURCE: NATIONAL STRATEGY FOR SUICIDE PREVENTION: GOALS AND OBJECTIVES FOR ACTION, 2001 U.S. DEPARTMENT OF HEALTH AND HUMAN SERVICES

Other Factors Individuals who kill themselves have often gone through more major life crises—job changes, births, financial reversals, divorce, retirement—in the previous six months, compared with others. Long-standing, intense conflict with family members or other important people may add to the danger. In some cases, suicide may be an act of revenge that offers the person a sense of control—however temporary or illusory. For example, some may feel that, by rejecting life, they are rejecting a partner or parent who abandoned or betrayed them.

Overcoming Problems of the Mind

About 80 percent of those with mental disorders eventually seek treatment, but many suffer for years, even decades. As discussed earlier in this chapter, college students are especially likely to delay getting help for a psychological problem.

The median delay for all disorders is nearly ten years. Those with social phobia and separation anxiety disorders may not get help for more than 20 years. The earlier in life that a disorder begins, the longer that individuals tend to delay treatment.

Without treatment, mental disorders take a toll on every aspect of life, including academics, relationships, careers, and risk-taking. Symptoms or episodes of a disorder typically become more frequent or severe. Individuals with one mental disorder are at high risk of having a second one (this is called comorbidity).

Getting Help for a Psychological Problem

Sometimes we all need outside help from a trained, licensed professional to work through personal problems. Here is what you need to know if you are experiencing psychological difficulties.

Consider therapy if you

- Feel an overwhelming and prolonged sense of helplessness and sadness, which does not lift despite your efforts and help from family and friends.
- Find it difficult to carry out everyday activities such as homework, and your academic performance is suffering.
- Worry excessively, expect the worst, or are constantly on edge.
- Are finding it hard to resist or are engaging in behaviors that are harmful to you or others, such as drinking too much alcohol, abusing drugs, or becoming aggressive or violent.
- Have persistent thoughts or fantasies of harming yourself or others.

Most people who have at least several sessions of psychotherapy are far better off than individuals with emotional difficulties who do not get treatment. According to the American Psychological Association, 50 percent of patients noticeably improve after eight sessions, while 75 percent of individuals in therapy improved by the end of six months.

Where to Turn for Help

As a student, your best contact for identifying local services may be your health education instructor or department. The health instructors can tell you about general and mental health counseling available on campus, school-based support groups, community-based programs, and special emergency services. On campus, you can also turn to the student health services or the office of the dean of student services or student affairs. (See "Help Yourself" in *Labs for IPC*.)

Within the community, you may be able to get help through the city or county health department and neighborhood health centers. Local hospitals often have special clinics and services; and there are usually local branches of national service organizations, such as United Way or Alcoholics Anonymous, other 12-step programs, and various support groups. You can call the psychiatric or psychological association in your city or state for the names of licensed professionals. (Check the telephone directory for listings.) Your primary physician may also be able to help.

Search the Internet for special programs, found either by the nature of the service, by the name of the neighborhood or city, or by the name of the sponsoring group. In addition to suicide-prevention programs, look for crisis intervention, violence prevention, and child-abuse prevention programs; drug-treatment information; shelters for battered women; senior citizen centers; and self-help and counseling services. Many services have special hotlines for coping with emergencies. Others provide information as well as counseling over the phone.

Types of Therapists   Only professionally trained individuals who have met state licensing requirements are certified as psychiatrists, psychologists, or social workers. Before selecting any of these mental health professionals, be sure to check the person's background and credentials.

Psychiatrists are licensed medical doctors (M.D.) who complete medical school; a year-long internship; and a three-year residency that provides training in various forms of psychotherapy, psychopharmacology, and both outpatient and inpatient treatment of

David Buffington/Digital Vision/Getty Images

Therapists may have degrees in psychology, psychiatry, social work, or nursing, but all must have supervised clinical training and meet state licensing requirements.

mental disorders. They can prescribe medications and make medical decisions. *Board-certified* psychiatrists have passed oral and written examinations following completion of residency training.

Psychologists complete a graduate program (including clinical training and internships) in human psychology but do not study medicine and cannot prescribe medication. They must be licensed in most states in order to practice independently.

Certified social workers or **licensed clinical social workers (LCSWs)** usually complete a two-year graduate program and have specialized training in helping people with mental problems in addition to conventional social work.

Psychiatric nurses have nursing degrees and have passed a state examination. They usually have special training and experience in mental health care, although no specialty licensing or certification is required.

Marriage and family therapists, licensed in some but not all states, usually have a graduate degree, often in psychology, and at least two years of supervised clinical training in dealing with relationship problems.

psychiatrist Licensed medical doctor with additional training in psychotherapy, psychopharmacology, and treatment of mental disorders.

psychologist Mental health care professional who has completed doctoral or graduate program in psychology and is trained in psychotherapeutic techniques, but who is not medically trained and does not prescribe medications.

certified social worker or licensed clinical social worker (LCSW) A person who has completed a two-year graduate program in counseling people with mental problems.

psychiatric nurse A nurse with special training and experience in mental health care.

marriage and family therapist A psychiatrist, psychologist, or social worker who specializes in marriage and family counseling.

Other therapists include pastoral counselors, members of the clergy who offer psychological counseling; hypnotherapists, who use hypnosis for problems such as smoking and obesity; stress-management counselors, who teach relaxation methods; and alcohol and drug counselors, who help individuals with substance abuse problems. Anyone can use these terms to describe themselves professionally, and there are no licensing requirements.

Choosing a Therapist Ask your physician or another health professional. Call your local or state psychological association. Consult your university or college department of psychology or health center. Contact your area community mental health center. Inquire at your church or synagogue.

- A good rapport with your psychotherapist is critical. Choose someone with whom you feel comfortable and at ease.

- Ask the following questions:

  - Are you licensed?

  - How long have you been practicing?

  - I have been feeling (anxious, tense, depressed, etc.), and I'm having problems (with school, relationships, eating, sleeping, etc.). What experience do you have helping people with these types of problems?

  - What are your areas of expertise— phobias? ADHD? depression?

  - What kinds of treatments do you use? Have they proved effective for dealing with my kind of problem or issue?

  - What are your fees? (Fees are usually based on a 45-minute to 50-minute session.) Do you have a sliding-scale fee policy?

  - How much therapy would you recommend?

  - What types of insurance do you accept?

As you begin therapy, establish clear goals with your therapist. Some goals require more time to reach than others. You and your therapist should decide at what point you might expect to begin to see progress.

As they begin therapy, some people may have difficulty discussing painful and troubling experiences. Feelings of relief or hope are positive signs indicating that you are starting to explore your thoughts and behaviors.

psychotherapy Treatment designed to produce a response by psychological rather than physical means, such as suggestion, persuasion, reassurance, and support.

psychodynamic Interpreting behaviors in terms of early experiences and unconscious influences.

Types of Therapy

The term **psychotherapy** refers to any type of counseling based on the exchange of words in the context of the unique relationship that develops between a mental health professional and a person seeking help. The process of talking and listening can lead to new insight, relief from distressing psychological symptoms, changes in unhealthy or maladaptive behaviors, and more effective ways of dealing with the world. "Spirituality oriented" psychotherapy pays particular attention to the roles that religion and spiritual and religious beliefs play in an individual's psychological life.40

Landmark research has shown that psychotherapy does not just benefit the mind but actually changes the brain. In studies comparing psychotherapy and psychiatric medications as treatments for depression, both proved about equally effective. But a particular group of patients—those who had lost a parent at an early age or had experienced childhood trauma, including physical or sexual abuse—gained greater benefits with talk therapy.

The most common goal of psychotherapy is to improve quality of life. Most mental health professionals today are trained in a variety of psychotherapeutic techniques and tailor their approach to the problem, personality, and needs of each person seeking their help. Because skilled therapists may combine different techniques in the course of therapy, the lines between the various approaches often blur.

Brief or short-term psychotherapy typically focuses on a central theme, problem, or topic and may continue for several weeks to several months. The individuals most likely to benefit are those who are interested in solving immediate problems rather than changing their characters, who can think in psychological terms, and who are motivated to change.

Psychodynamic Psychotherapy For the most part, today's mental health professionals base their assessment of individuals on a **psychodynamic** understanding that takes into account the role of early experiences and unconscious influences in *actively* shaping behavior. (This is the *dynamic* in psychodynamic.) Psychodynamic treatments work toward the goal of providing greater insight into problems and bringing about behavioral change. Therapy may be brief, consisting of 12 to 25 sessions, or may continue for several years.

Cognitive-BehavioralTherapy(CBT)

Cognitive-behavioral therapy (CBT) focuses on inappropriate or inaccurate thoughts or beliefs to help individuals break out of a distorted way of thinking. The techniques of **cognitive therapy** include identification of an individual's beliefs and attitudes, recognition of negative thought patterns, and education in alternative ways of thinking. Individuals with major depression or anxiety disorders are most likely to benefit, usually in 15 to 25 sessions. However, many of the positive messages used in cognitive therapy can help anyone improve a bad mood or negative outlook.

Behavioral therapy strives to substitute healthier ways of behaving for maladaptive patterns used in the past. Its premise is that distressing psychological symptoms, like all behaviors, are learned responses that can be modified or unlearned. Some therapists believe that changing behavior also changes how people think and feel. As they put it, "Change the behavior, and the feelings will follow." Behavioral therapies work best for disorders characterized by specific, abnormal patterns of acting—such as alcohol and drug abuse, anxiety disorders, and phobias—and for individuals who want to change bad habits.

Interpersonal Therapy (IPT)

Interpersonal therapy (IPT), originally developed for research into the treatment of major depression, focuses on relationships in order to help individuals deal with unrecognized feelings and needs and improve their communication skills. IPT does not deal with the psychological origins of symptoms but rather concentrates on current problems of getting along with others. The supportive, empathic relationship that is developed with the therapist, who takes an even more active role than in psychodynamic psychotherapy, is the most crucial component of this therapy. The emphasis is on the here and now and on interpersonal—rather than intrapsychic—issues. Individuals with major depression, chronic difficulties developing relationships, and chronic mild depression are most likely to benefit. IPT usually consists of 12 to 16 sessions.

Other Treatment Options

Psychiatric Drugs Medications that alter brain chemistry and relieve psychiatric symptoms have brought great hope and help to millions of people. Thanks to the recent development of a new generation of more precise and effective **psychiatric drugs**, success rates for treating many common and disabling disorders—depression, panic disorder, schizophrenia, and others—have soared. Often used in conjunction with psychotherapy, sometimes used as the primary treatment, these medications have revolutionized mental health care.

At some point in their lives, about half of all Americans will take a psychiatric drug. The reason may be depression, anxiety, a sleep difficulty, an eating disorder, alcohol or drug dependence, impaired memory, or another disorder that disrupts the intricate chemistry of the brain.

Psychiatric drugs are now among the most widely prescribed drugs in the United States. Serotonin-boosting medications (SSRIs) have become the drugs of choice in treating depression. They also are effective in treating obsessive-compulsive disorder, panic disorder, social phobia, posttraumatic stress disorder, premenstrual dysphoric disorder, and generalized anxiety disorder. In patients who don't respond, psychiatrists may add another drug to boost the efficacy of the treatment.

 According to various studies, 5 to 7 percent of college students take antidepressant medications. Direct-to-consumer advertisements for antidepressant drugs can influence students' perceptions of what is wrong with them. In one study, college women were more likely to rate themselves as having mild-to-moderate depression as a result of reading pharmaceutical company information for popular antidepressants.

Alternative Mind-Mood Products People with serious mental illnesses, including depression and bipolar disorder, often use at least one alternative health-care practice, such as yoga or meditation. In a recent survey of women with depression, about half (54 percent) reported trying herbs, vitamins, and manual therapies such as massage and acupressure. Some "natural" products, such as herbs and enzymes, claim to have

cognitive therapy A technique used to identify an individual's beliefs and attitudes, recognize negative thought patterns, and educate in alternative ways of thinking.

behavioral therapy A technique that emphasizes application of the principles of learning to substitute desirable responses and behavior patterns for undesirable ones.

interpersonal therapy (IPT) A technique used to develop communication skills and relationships.

psychiatric drugs Medications that regulate a person's mental, emotional, and physical functions to facilitate normal functioning.

Your Strategies for Prevention

Before Taking a Psychiatric Drug

Before taking any psychoactive drug (one that affects the brain), talk to a qualified health professional. Here are some points to raise:

- **What can this medication do for me?** What specific symptoms will it relieve? Are there other possible benefits?

- **When will I notice a difference?** How long does it take for the medicine to have an effect?

- **Are there any risks?** What about side effects? Do I have to take it before or after eating? Will it affect my ability to study, work, drive, or operate machinery?

- **Is there a risk of suicide or increased aggression?** What should I do if I start thinking about taking my own life or of harming others?

psychological effects. However, they have not undergone rigorous scientific testing.

St. John's wort has been used to treat anxiety and depression in Europe for many years. Data from clinical studies in the United States do not support the efficacy of St. John's wort for moderate to severe depression. In ten carefully controlled studies, the herb did not prove more effective than a placebo. However, more than two dozen studies have found that St. John's wort was similar in efficacy to standard antidepressants. Side effects include dizziness, abdominal pain and bloating, constipation, nausea, fatigue, and dry mouth. St. John's wort should not be taken in combination with other prescription antidepressants. St. John's wort can lower the efficacy of oral contraceptives and increase the risk of an unwanted pregnancy.

Build Your Future

Taking Care of Your Mental Health

Like physical health, psychological well-being is not a fixed state of being, but a process. The way you live every day affects how you feel about yourself and your world. Here are some basic guidelines that you can rely on to make the most of the process of living. Check those that you commit to making part of your mental and psychological self-care:

_____ **Accept yourself.** As a human being, you are, by definition, imperfect. Come to terms with the fact that you are a worthwhile person despite your mistakes.

_____ **Respect yourself.** Recognize your abilities and talents. Acknowledge your competence and achievements, and take pride in them.

_____ **Trust yourself.** Learn to listen to the voice within you, and let your intuition be your guide.

_____ **Love yourself.** Be happy to spend time by yourself. Learn to appreciate your own company and to be glad you're you.

_____ **Stretch yourself.** Be willing to change and grow, to try something new and dare to be vulnerable.

_____ **Look at challenges as opportunities for personal growth.** "Every problem brings the possibility of a widening of consciousness," psychologist Carl Jung once noted. Put his words to the test.

_____ **When your internal critic**—the negative inner voice we all have—starts putting you down, force yourself to think of a situation that you handled well.

_____ **Set a limit on self-pity.** Tell yourself, "I'm going to feel sorry for myself this morning, but this afternoon, I've got to get on with my life."

_____ **Think of not only where but also who you want to be a decade from now.** The goals you set, the decisions you make, the values you adopt now will determine how you feel about yourself and your life in the future.

Recognizing Depression

Depression comes in different forms, just like other illnesses such as heart disease. Not everyone with a depressive disorder experiences every symptom. The number and severity of symptoms may vary among individuals and also over time.

Read through the following list, and check all the descriptions that apply.

- ☐ I am often restless and irritable.
- ☐ I am having irregular sleep patterns—either too much or not enough.
- ☐ I don't enjoy hobbies, my friends, family, or leisure activities any more.
- ☐ I am having trouble managing my diabetes, hypertension, or other chronic illness.
- ☐ I have nagging aches and pains that do not get better no matter what I do.
- ☐ Specifically, I often experience:
  - ☐ Digestive problems
  - ☐ Headache or backache
  - ☐ Vague aches and pains like joint or muscle pains
  - ☐ Chest pains
  - ☐ Dizziness
- ☐ I have trouble concentrating or making simple decisions.
- ☐ Others have commented on my mood or attitude lately.
- ☐ My weight has changed a considerable amount.

- ☐ I have had several of the symptoms I checked above for more than two weeks.
- ☐ I feel that my functioning in my everyday life (work, family, friends) is suffering because of these problems.
- ☐ I have a family history of depression.
- ☐ I have thought about suicide.*

Checking several items on this list does not mean that you have a depressive disorder because many conditions can cause similar symptoms. However, you should take this list with you to discuss with your health-care provider or mental health therapist. Even though it can be difficult to talk about certain things, your health-care provider is knowledgeable, trained, and committed to helping you.

If you can't think of what to say, try these conversation starters:

"I just don't feel like myself lately."

"My friend (parent, roommate, spouse) thinks I might be depressed."

"I haven't been sleeping well lately."

"Everything seems harder than before."

"Nothing's fun anymore."

If you are diagnosed with depression, remember that it is a common and highly treatable illness with medical causes. Your habits or personality did not cause your depression, and you do not have to face it alone.

*University of Michigan Depression Center, 800-475-MICH, www.med.umich .edu/depression

Making Change Happen

Your Psychological Self-Care Pyramid

Your physical well-being and psychological health are so intimately related that to a significant degree they are expressions of each other. Yes, grave diseases can occur despite a healthy mental outlook, and physically healthy people can experience psychological difficulties. But overwhelming evidence demonstrates that physical health affects mood and thoughts, and mood and thoughts affect physical health.

"Your Psychological Self-Care Pyramid" from *Labs for IPC* deals with optimizing your psychological health to benefit body, mind, and spirit. It will teach you how to infuse your life with mentally rewarding and stimulating activities that not only provide balance, prevent the blahs, and add zest but also, if continued, form a lifelong foundation for optimal mental health. Here's a preview.

Get Real

In this stage you rate yourself from 0 to 10, with 0 being the low end and 10 the high end, on the degree to which you now include or exhibit in your weekly life the 13 elements of Your Psychological Self-Care Pyramid shown in *Labs for IPC*. Here are three examples:

- **Self-knowledge and self-control.** ____
  You make your inner world of feelings and thoughts and your relationship to the outer world a source of ongoing contemplation. You seek self-understanding and systematically develop your ability to consider and weigh actions before taking them.

- **Community.** ____
  You have a circle of trusted friends and participate in a larger social milieu. You look out for and assist the interests of the community as a whole, not merely those of your circle of immediate friends.

- **Generosity.** ____
  You are giving of your time and your self both toward others and toward yourself. You give materially when this is advisable but more than that when asked you give that which is most precious—that is, who you are.

You will then examine your self-ratings. Are some unacceptably lower than you would like them to be? Completing this lab will address this concern for the short run and, if you continue the activities, for the future.

Get Ready

In this stage you examine your schedule and create pockets of time for the activities that serve as building blocks of Your Psychological Self-Care Pyramid and for journaling about your experiences doing so.

Get Going

In this stage you begin the exercises related to each of the areas you want to bolster by engaging in related activities for at least five minutes four times per week. *Immediately after* completing the exercise or at some other point the *same* day, you will make an entry of at least five lines in your *IPC Journal* and reflect on your experiences . . .

Lock It In

Just as you can use the USDA Food Pyramid to guide your eating choices every day, pay attention to Your Psychological Self-Care Pyramid. Here is one of the steps that can ensure that you are providing adequate daily nourishment for your mind and spirit.

- **Rate yourself.** Every four weeks rate yourself between 0 and 10, with 0 being the low end and 10 the high end, on each element of Your Psychological Self-Care Pyramid. Record your scores.

Atonement and wisdom

Generosity; forgiveness; gratitude

Goals; self-knowledge and self-control; self-expression and achievement; community

Attention; order; physical activity; rest and relaxation; happiness, joy, and laughter

Making This Chapter Work for You

Review Questions

1. Depression
   a. is not likely to occur in young adults.
   b. is twice as common in men as women.
   c. has the same symptoms in men and women.
   d. is more likely to occur again in those who suffer a first episode.

2. Which statement about depression treatment is true?
   a. Psychotherapy and drug therapy are effective in treating depression, but only about 50 percent of people seek treatment.
   b. Antidepressants help about 90 percent of individuals feel better within four weeks.
   c. Jogging has only a small benefit for most depressed individuals.
   d. With the right therapy, depression will not reoccur.

3. Neurons
   a. transmit information within the brain and throughout the body by means of electrical impulses and chemical messengers.
   b. are specialized support cells that travel through the spinal cord, carrying signals related to movement.
   c. are protein molecules designed to bind with neurotransmitters.
   d. cross a synapse before reuptake.

4. Students with attention-deficit/hyperactivity disorder
   a. perform as well on standardized tests as students without ADHD.
   b. have an increased risk of substance use disorders.
   c. have a decreased risk of developing depression or anxiety disorders.
   d. constitute 10 percent of the student population.

5. Some characteristic symptoms of major depression are
   a. difficulty concentrating, lack of energy, and eating more than usual.
   b. exaggerated sense of euphoria and energy.
   c. palpitations, sweating, numbness, and tingling sensations.
   d. talking in rambling ways, inability to think in a logical manner, and delusions.

6. Which of the following statements is true?
   a. Individuals with phobias are most likely to benefit from psychiatric medications.
   b. Antidepressant medications now require a warning label about the increased risk of suicidal thoughts.
   c. Only children have attention disorders.
   d. Interpersonal therapy focuses on the role of early experiences and unconscious influences in shaping patterns of behavior, such as repeated failed relationships.

7. Which of the following statements about anxiety disorders is true?
   a. Anxiety disorders are the least prevalent type of mental illness.
   b. An individual suffering from a panic attack may mistake her symptoms for a heart attack.
   c. The primary symptom of obsessive-compulsive disorder is irrational, intense, and persistent fear of a specific object or situation.
   d. Generalized anxiety disorders respond to systematic desensitization behavior therapy.

8. A mental disorder can be described as
   a. a condition associated with migraine headaches and narcolepsy.
   b. a condition that is usually caused by severe trauma to the brain.
   c. a behavioral or psychological disorder that impairs an individual's ability to conduct one or more important activities of daily life.
   d. a psychological disorder that is easily controlled with medication and a change in diet.

9. A person may be at higher risk of committing suicide if
   a. he is taking blood pressure medication.
   b. he lives in a rural environment and is married.
   c. he has been diagnosed with hyperactivity disorder.
   d. he has lost his job because of alcoholism.

10. Which of these therapies focuses on recognizing negative thought patterns and changing those patterns?
    a. psychodynamic psychotherapy
    b. behavioral activation
    c. interpersonal therapy
    d. cognitive therapy

Critical Thinking

1. Jake, who took antidepressants to recover from depression in high school, began feeling the same troubling symptoms. A physician at the student health center prescribed the same medication that had helped him in the past, but this time Jake noticed the warning about an increased risk of suicide. He has had thoughts of killing himself, and he worries whether or not to start the medication. When he did some online research, he learned that the risk of suicide is greater if depression is untreated than it is with medication. How would you counsel Jake? How would you weigh the risks and benefits of taking an antidepressant? Do you know someone who might benefit from taking antidepressants but is afraid to take them because of the possible risk of suicide? What might you say to this person based on what you have read in this chapter?

2. Research has indicated that many homeless men and women are in need of outpatient psychiatric care, often because they suffer from chronic mental illnesses or alcoholism. Yet government funding for the mentally ill is inadequate, and homelessness itself can make it difficult, if not impossible, for people to gain access to the care they need. How do you feel when you pass homeless individuals who seem disoriented or out of touch with reality? Who should take responsibility for their welfare? Should they be forced to undergo treatment at psychiatric institutions?

SOURCE: From HALES, *An Invitation to Health*, 15E. © 2013 Cengage Learning.

REVIEW QUESTIONS

Chapter 3: Caring For Your Mind

MULTIPLE CHOICE

1 **Neuropsychiatry is the scientific field that studies**

A. the brain and the body
B. the brain and the mind
C. the brain and the spirit
D. the brain and the psyche

2 The basic working units of the brain are called

A. glia
B. nuclei
C. axon terminals
D. neurons

3 **In the brain, if there is a malfunction in the release of a neurotransmitter, in its reuptake or elimination, it is likely that the individual will suffer**

A. abnormal thinking or feeling behaviors
B. from major bipolar disorders
C. neuron loss and brain atrophy
D. dysfunction of the heart rate and breathing

4 **The brains of teens rely more on the**

A. brainstem
B. frontal cortex
C. cerebrum
D. amygdala

5 **Women have higher rates of all the following *except***

A. alcohol and substance abuse
B. migraines
C. anxiety disorders
D. Alzheimer's disease

6 Among the strongest factors that put college students at risk for mental problems is

A. sexual-identity crisis
B. stress
C. homesickness
D. romantic breakup

7 One of the main contributors to depression among college students is

A. stress

B. substance abuse

C. lack of sleep

D. all of the choices

8 Which condition is characterized by experiencing feelings of great energy and euphoria alternated with feelings of depression and despair?

A. major depression

B. panic attacks

C. bipolar disorder

D. acrophobia

9 An irrational, intense, and persistent fear of certain objects is known as

A. a panic attack

B. a phobia

C. anxiety

D. an obsession

10 Which psychotherapy technique utilizes the patient's earliest experience and unconscious influences?

A. cognitive-behavioral therapy

B. interpersonal therapy

C. behavioral therapy

D. psychodynamic therapy

DISCUSSION QUESTIONS

1. Discuss at least five characteristics of a mentally healthy individual.

- _____
- _____
- _____
- _____
- _____
- _____
- _____
- _____

2. Describe at least five factors that could predict the possibility that a person would commit suicide.

- _____
- _____
- _____
- _____
- _____
- _____
- _____
- _____
- _____

3. Describe at least five symptoms that could predict the possibility of a person having schizophrenia.

_____

_____

_____

_____

_____

_____

QUESTIONS FOR WRITING AND DISCUSSION

1. What do you think college campus health services could do to reduce the effects of stress for students? Outline your plan using information from your own experience as well as from this chapter.

2. Do you know someone with one of these mental health issues addressed in this chapter? If so, outline the symptoms and suggest a treatment plan using information in this chapter to formulate your response.

3. Choose one of the mental health issues in the chapter and conduct further research using a variety of sources. Present your research to your class or write a report.

READING FOR
MAIN IDEAS

THEME *Communication and Conflict Across Cultures*

UNIT
2

Index Stock Imagery/Photolibrary/Getty Images

Understanding
EXPLICIT MAIN IDEAS

🟦 Why Do You Need to Know This?

Did you know that you have already begun to develop the skill of finding explicit main ideas in previous chapters? Now that you have learned about patterns in writing, you are ready to zero in on the author's most important point. Recognizing main ideas is a complex skill that develops with practice. If you have to make one statement about a reading, the main idea statement would be the one to make. In any given reading, in all disciplines, a successful college student must answer this question: What is the author's most important point about the topic?

When you communicate with other people, have you ever been surprised that they do not see things as you do? Being aware of someone's main idea in a conversation is the foundation for good

IN THIS CHAPTER YOU WILL LEARN

- To identify the author's purpose in a reading
- To understand and locate an author's explicit main idea
- To understand graphics: identifying the main idea in visuals aids

A READING STUDY STRATEGY

- Summarizing to express the author's main idea and major details

VOCABULARY STRATEGIES

- Identifying common root words
- Increasing your discipline-specific vocabulary: social sciences

> " **A WORLD COMMUNITY CAN EXIST ONLY WITH WORLD COMMUNICATION, WHICH MEANS SOMETHING MORE THAN EXTENSIVE SHORT-WAVE FACILITIES SCATTERED ABOUT THE GLOBE. IT MEANS COMMON UNDERSTANDING, A COMMON TRADITION, COMMON IDEAS, AND COMMON IDEALS.** "
>
> ROBERT M. HUTCHINS American University President (1899–1977)

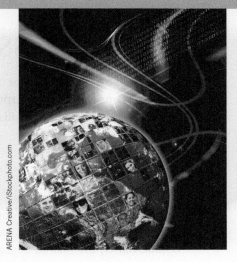

ARENA Creative/iStockphoto.com

communication as a student, employee, friend, or acquaintance.

In Chapter 3, you will turn your attention away from your own brain and how it works and consider how other people think and react when communicating with each other. Others may think differently from you for a variety of reasons. To be an educated and informed global citizen, it is necessary to know something about other people and places. Even if you have not traveled far from home, learning about how other people think impacts how you view the world. With the knowledge that people do think differently because of cultural or even gender influences, how can you use this information to become a better student, a better employee, and a better citizen?

✓ CHECK YOUR PRIOR KNOWLEDGE

Jot down some ideas about communication challenges between genders and different cultures. Do not edit your list—just brainstorm!

_____

_____

_____

_____

_____

_____

_____

_____

_____

_____

_____

_____

_____

❖ PRE-ASSESSMENT

Read the passage and then answer the questions that follow. Don't worry if you do not know what all the terms mean. The purpose of this Pre-Assessment is to find out how much you already know about the reading skills and strategies introduced in this chapter.

The Differences Between Boys and Girls . . . at the Office
by Marjory Weinstein

1   It turns out your problems communicating with those of the opposite gender don't end at the kitchen table or on that bad blind date. It happens in the office, too, and all the time. Connie Glaser, the Atlanta-based speaker and author of the upcoming *Gender Talk Works (If You Do It Right): 7 Steps for Cracking the Gender Code at Work,* says corporate miscommunications between the sexes may abound but there's hope.

2   Since discussion about gender differences is rife with controversy, a better way to look at it, Glaser says, is through the lens of culture. Each gender is a culture unto itself, one that comes with certain norms and standards that can be misunderstood by those of the opposite sex.

3   To that effect, Glaser cites what happened when a mass e-mail led to a mass settlement for Chevron about a decade ago. The story concerns a mass e-mail proclaiming "25 Reasons Beer Is Better Than Women." The e-mail wasn't so funny to four female employees who filed a suit that cost Chevron $2.5 million, Glaser says, but "in the male culture, this was just off-handed humor, and whoever initiated it probably didn't see anything offensive about it."

4   The differences in how men and women sometimes interpret humor can even affect how each chooses to exert power at work. While a man might casually chide a fellow co-worker at the coffee machine about something he said at a meeting, a woman, Glaser says, generally wouldn't think of doing that. "In the female culture, the relationship, the connectedness, the rapport is ultimately the most important thing," she explains. "That's what really gives women their base of power and influence. In the male culture, the sense of hierarchy and status is much more important, so you see that kind of joking around to establish a kind of status among themselves. With females, you don't see that—you see an effort to flatten [the hierarchy] out."

5   Communication is the source of many gender-related workplace differences. According to Glaser, a group of women may be more likely to change the topic of conversation to include a male co-worker who has just joined them as a way of making sure he feels included. Women often will hold back in meetings as well, for fear of interrupting.

6   To ensure men and women under your corporate roof understand where one another is coming from, Glaser suggests organizing a program where gender issues can be discussed.

7   "You need to have the gender talk," she says. "You need to put these issues on the table in an upbeat and constructive kind of way to minimize that kind of conflict and misunderstanding or worse."

SOURCE: Weinstein, Marjery, "The differences between boys and girls . . . at the office," *Training*, Vol. 43, Issue 11, Nov. 2006. Reprinted with permission of Training Magazine.

COMPREHENSION CHECK

Circle the best answer to the following questions.

Reading Comprehension

1 What is the topic of this reading?

A. Gender and communication in the workplace

B. Men, women, and communication

C. Women and gender issues

D. Business, women, and communication

2 What is the overall pattern of organization of this reading?

A. Definition and example

B. Comparison and contrast

C. Simple listing

D. Classification

3 In the following sentence, what is the relationship between ideas?

Each gender is a culture unto itself, one that comes with certain norms and standards that can be misunderstood by those of the opposite sex.

A. Comparison and contrast

B. Cause and effect

C. Simple listing

D. Definition

4 In the following sentence, what is the relationship between ideas?

While a man might casually chide a fellow co-worker at the coffee machine about something he said at a meeting, a woman, Glaser says, generally wouldn't think of doing that.

A. Cause and effect

B. Comparison and contrast

C. Simple listing

D. Definition

5 What is the author's main point in this reading?

A. Gender differences have many causes.

B. Communication problems can be avoided if men listen.

C. Communication is a problem for men and women.

D. Corporate miscommunications between the sexes may abound but there's hope.

(Continued)

6 Looking at your answer to question 5, in which paragraph is the same point made by the author in one sentence?

A. Paragraph 1
B. Paragraph 3
C. Paragraph 4
D. It is not in any paragraph.

7 What is the directly stated main idea in paragraph 4?

A. The differences in how men and women sometimes interpret humor can even affect how each chooses to exert power at work.
B. While a man might casually chide a fellow co-worker at the coffee machine about something he said at a meeting, a woman, Glaser says, generally wouldn't think of doing that.
C. "In the female culture, the relationship, the connectedness, the rapport is ultimately the most important thing," she explains.
D. "With females, you don't see that—you see an effort to flatten [the hierarchy] out."

8 What is the directly stated main idea in paragraph 5?

A. Communication is the source of many gender-related workplace differences.
B. According to Glaser, a group of women may be more likely to change the topic of conversation to include a male co-worker who has just joined them as a way of making sure he feels included.
C. A combination of A and B.
D. Women often will hold back in meetings as well, for fear of interrupting.

Vocabulary Comprehension

9 In the following sentence, what is the meaning of the underlined word?

"In the male culture, the sense of hierarchy and status is much more important, so you see that kind of joking around to establish a kind of status among themselves."

A. Culture
B. Embarrassment
C. Rank
D. Bossiness

10 In the word *gender* (as in the sentence below), what does the root word *gen* mean?

It turns out your problems communicating with those of the opposite gender don't end at the kitchen table or on that bad blind date.

A. Death
B. Life
C. Brain-related
D. Kind

AUTHOR'S PURPOSE

In this chapter and the next, you will develop skills to zero in on the author's most important point about a passage. What you have learned so far will aid you in determining the most important point in a reading. First, however, you need to consider why an author has written a passage to begin with. This is called **author's purpose.** The purpose an author has for writing is very important to consider in order to help you determine the main idea.

When an author writes, he or she has a purpose in mind. By thinking about *why* an author has written something, you can understand the basic motivation behind the task of writing to begin with. This motivation and how the author arranges his or her ideas, the pattern of organization, are key steps to getting to the heart of the reading: the most important point. There are four main purposes an author may have in writing (Table 3.1):

FIGURE 3.1 Purpose for Writing. An Author Has a Main Purpose for Writing, but Sometimes Purposes May Intertwine.

- To inform

- To instruct

- To persuade

- To entertain

Of course, all authors try to be informative and entertaining to some extent. For our purposes, however, there is a distinct difference between these four reasons for writing. These different reasons for writing can often be recognized by the use of specific language that reveals the author's purpose. Sometimes an author can have more than one purpose. For example, an author can aim to inform *and* persuade. However, as in patterns of organization, one purpose is predominant, and this purpose is reflected in the author's most important point.

To Inform

deadlyphoto.com/Alamy

An author may write to inform or explain. In other words, an author wants to present information in an objective manner without imposing his or her opinion on the reader. The author provides information only and does not want to convince the reader of any point of view. The sole purpose of the writing is to convey information in an unbiased, open-minded manner. If an author wants to inform, his or her purpose is objective with no agenda or point of view to put forward that would persuade the reader. The author presents just the facts and does not provide any sort of personal opinion about the facts; the author does not take any sides.

Newspaper stories or articles are examples of writing where an author's purpose is to inform. Remember how you used journalists' prompts to develop questions from topics or headings when you read? These same prompts are used to write news stories. The story will contain information about who, what, where, when, why, or how. Nowhere in news articles does the author say what he or she thinks or what you, the reader, should think. You are left to form your own conclusion based on the provided information. The author may quote someone else's opinion but will not state his or her own.

Similarly, the purpose of most authors of textbooks is to inform. The author of an introductory biology textbook, for example, does not tell you what to think about DNA synthesis; he or she just gives you the facts—his or her purpose is purely to inform. The author of the textbook chapter on mental stress in the Unit 1 Textbook Application presents information in order to inform.

To Instruct

A second purpose an author may have for writing is to instruct the reader about how to do something or how something works. Instructional writing usually follows a sequence or process order. Like informative writing, the author does not provide an opinion about the process or set of instructions. Instead, he or she presents the information in a factual, step-by-step manner and with a neutral tone or attitude.

Instructional writing can be found in many different types of reading. Office systems texts or other technical classes may have instructional writing. The writing will tell you how to do something or how something works. How to assemble something is a classic example of an instructional purpose.

To Persuade

Sometimes an author wants to persuade the reader to adopt a position on an issue. The author wants to convince the reader about something. Even if the author's argument is one with which you agree, if that author tries to get the reader to choose a side—usually the author's side—then his or her main purpose is to persuade. In persuasive writing, an author uses biased words, also called **loaded** or **slanted language,** that reveal the author's position on an issue. Not only does an author use words that sometimes indicate the bias or one-sidedness of a position on an issue, but he or she also may use words or phrases such as *should, ought to,* or *must.* Words like these always reveal a persuasive purpose, as the author is putting forward an opinion. The author's intent, then, is to change the reader's mind. (Be careful, though, that provocative words like *should* or *ought to* are in the author's voice, and do not express the opinion of someone about whom the author is writing.)

Just as a news story is a good example of informative writing, a newspaper editorial is a good illustration of a persuasive piece of writing. Editorials, usually in the middle of the first section of the newspaper, contain essays that express the opinions of the writers about some topic currently in the news. The authors of these essays take a stand on the issue and try to persuade the reader to agree with and accept their point of view; their purpose is to convince the reader to agree with them.

In college, you are likely to read persuasive pieces in classes where a central focus is on issues open to debate, such as those offered in disciplines like sociology, history, psychology, and the sciences. Persuasive pieces in textbooks tend to be an added feature of a chapter rather than the main content of the chapter. You will likely read many persuasive essays in your English classes, though some of these pieces will also have the purpose to inform.

To Entertain

Usually in academic writing, an author's primary purpose will be to inform, instruct, or persuade. Magazines, novels, and stories that are read for recreation usually have the purpose of entertaining a reader. In addition to providing entertainment, these types of readings may also inform, instruct, or persuade. The point of a story or poem can be informative or persuasive as well as entertaining. However, originally the definition of *entertain* meant to engage a reader—to grab the reader's attention. So, if you are interested in a topic about which you are reading, you are entertained. For the purposes of academic reading, however, to inform, to instruct, and to persuade are the primary purposes used.

TABLE 3.1 Author's Purpose

AUTHOR'S PURPOSE	TYPICAL READING MATERIAL	VOCABULARY
To Inform	Textbooks Newspapers Nonfiction books	Straightforward language
To Instruct	Manuals, diagrams "How-to" passages Steps in a process Instructions for assembly or task How something works	Detailed language explaining a process or how to do or assemble something *First, second, next, finally,* or numbers
To Persuade	Persuasive essays Editorials Written debates	*Ought to, should, must* Words that express emotion or point of view, such as adjectives like *terrible, wonderful, suspicious,* etc.
To Entertain	Literature Poetry Fiction Magazines	Symbolism, figurative language, description, humor

Cultura Creative/Alamy

On Your Own DETERMINING AN AUTHOR'S PURPOSE

For these short passages, identify the author's primary purpose and write *I* to inform, *IN* to instruct, *P* to persuade, or *E* to entertain next to the passage. The first two are sample items that have been completed for you, followed by an explanation of the answer.

__P__   To eradicate sex-selective abortion, <u>we must convince</u> the world that destroying female fetuses is <u>horribly wrong</u>. <u>We need</u> something akin to the abolitionist movement: a moral campaign waged globally, with victories declared one conscience at a time.
—"Should Sex-Selective Abortions Be Outlawed" by Nicholas Eberstadt, *CQ Global Researcher*, May 23, 2008.

The author of this passage takes a position that sex-selective abortion is wrong and must be stopped. Notice the wording (*we must convince, horribly wrong, we need*) that shows persuasive intent underlined above.

__I__   Most people know that humor or sarcasm can easily fall flat when expressed via e-mail, yet psychologists find that most people are still confident that they will be understood. Psychologist Justin Kruger calls this "everyday egocentrism"—the natural tendency we all have to see things from our own perspective. "Because we know we're trying to be sarcastic or funny, we egocentrically assume our audience will, as well," he says. "It's a hurdle that we can't completely overcome, even when we are trying to put ourselves in someone else's shoes," he says.
—"The Ego in Cyberspace," by Marina Krakovsky, *Psychology Today Magazine*, May/Jun 2005.
Last Reviewed 5 Sep 2007 (http://www.psychologytoday.com).

The author does not take a position on the issue here. Rather, she reports what psychologists have discovered. Just because she quotes what a psychologist says, the author herself is reporting the comments to inform the reader—notice the straightforward language.

___ 1.   In a study of adults, Kruger, a professor at the University of Illinois at Urbana-Champaign, found a simple way to make sure written words hit their mark. His team asked senders to read their sarcastic or serious e-mails aloud just before sending them. One group had to read the statements in a tone inconsistent with the intended meaning (reading a sarcastic statement in a serious tone or vice versa). "By forcing participants to get beyond their own subjective interpretation of the e-mail message, overconfidence disappeared," Kruger says.
—"The Ego in Cyberspace," by Marina Krakovsky, *Psychology Today Magazine*, May/Jun 2005.
Last Reviewed 5 Sep 2007 (http://www.psychologytoday.com).

___ 2.   If someone goes to every class and reads every chapter in the book and does everything the teacher asks of him and more, then he should be getting an A like his effort deserves. If a student's maximum effort can only be average in a teacher's mind, then something is wrong.
—"Student Expectations Seen as Causing Grade Disputes," by Max Roosevelt,
The New York Times, February 17, 2009 (http://www.nytimes.com).

___ 3.   Wash hands the right way—for 20 seconds with soap and running water.

Washing your hands the right way can stop the spread of illness-causing bacteria. Here's how to do it.

- Wet your hands with warm or cold running water and apply soap.
- Rub your hands together to make a lather and scrub them well. Be sure to scrub the backs of your hands, between your fingers, and under your nails. Bacteria can hide out here too!
- Continue rubbing hands for at least 20 seconds. Need a timer? Hum "Happy Birthday" from beginning to end twice.
- Rinse your hands well under running water.
- Dry your hands using a clean towel or air dry.

—FoodSafety.gov (http://www.foodsafety.gov/keep/basics/clean/index.html).

___ 4.   Medical technology today allows parents to test early in pregnancy for fetal abnormalities, hereditary illnesses, and even the sex of the fetus, raising horrifying questions about eugenics and population control. In some countries, a growing number of women apparently are terminating pregnancies when they learn the fetus is female. The resulting sex imbalance in countries like China and India is not only disturbing but also leads to further injustices, such as the abduction of girls for forced marriages.

—"Should Sex-Selective Abortions Be Outlawed" by Nicholas Eberstadt,
CQ Global Researcher, May 23, 2008.

___ 5.   Every year, after the lottery, Mr. Summers began talking again about a new box, but every year the subject was allowed to fade off without anything's being done. The black box grew shabbier each year: by now it was no longer completely black but splintered badly along one side to show the original wood color, and in some places faded or stained.

— "The Lottery" by Shirley Jackson, Original Publication: *The New Yorker*, Vol. XXIV, No. 18, June 26,
1948, pgs. 25–28. Farrar, Straus and Giroux, LLC

___ 6.   Most parents who give their children exotic names are striving for individuality. There are certain advantages to being the only Shalice Jadzia Washington in the school, or on the payroll. Unusual names also don't hold a lot of predispositions that common names do. Danelle Duran named her son Ukiah in part because it was the only name everyone could agree to; no one associated the name with jocks, hicks or nerds, she said.

—From ADLER/PROCTOR, *Looking Out, Looking In*, 13E. © 2011 Cengage Learning.

___ 7.   Unique names can have serious consequences, however. They are harder to pronounce, which can be frustrating, especially for younger children and for teachers coping with a new class at the beginning of the school year. On a more serious note, studies have shown that people tend to negatively judge people with unusual names solely on the basis of the name.

—From ADLER/PROCTOR, *Looking Out, Looking In*, 13E. © 2011 Cengage Learning.

(Continued)

___ 8.   A recent study by researchers at the University of California, Irvine, found that a third of students surveyed said that they expected B's just for attending lectures, and 40 percent said they deserved a B for completing the required reading.

—"Student Expectations Seen as Causing Grade Disputes," by Max Roosevelt, *The New York Times*, February 17, 2009 (http://www.nytimes.com).

___ 9.   "Navigation to nowhere" perfectly sums up the experience of many parents I have interviewed about their attempts to secure mental health services for their children. As a country, it's really in our interest to provide them with a compass.

—"Children in the Mental Health Void," by Judith Warner, *The New York Times*, February 19, 2009 (http://www.nytimes.com).

___ 10. **Develop a Family Disaster Plan**

Families can cope with disaster by preparing in advance and working together as a team. Create a family disaster plan including a communication plan, disaster supplies kit, and an evacuation plan. Knowing what to do is your best protection *and* your responsibility.

- Find out what could happen to you
- Make a disaster plan
- Complete the checklist
- Practice your plan

—Centers for Disease Control (CDC) (http://emergency.cdc.gov/preparedness/plan/).

MAIN IDEA

The **main idea** is the single-most important point the author makes about the topic. This point reflects the pattern of organization of the passage, the author's purpose for writing, and is general enough that all the supporting points function to back it up.

Everything you read has a point. The most important point the author makes about the subject or topic in a reading passage, or even a paragraph, is called the main idea. There are different words for *main idea,* depending on what type of main idea is at issue. A main idea of an essay or long passage is called the **thesis.** A thesis can be explicit or directly stated in a sentence, or it can be implied (or suggested). The main idea of a paragraph, if explicit (directly stated in one sentence), is called the **topic sentence.** A topic sentence is a sentence that states the author's most important point about the **topic.** The important point to keep in mind is that the main idea is *the* important point, regardless of how long a passage or section is.

Purpose Is Linked to Main Idea

An author has a topic about which he or she is writing. In addition, an author always has a purpose for writing about the topic. The author wants to inform, instruct, persuade, or entertain the reader with regard to the topic. Based on this purpose, the author chooses words or a writing style to express his or her intent. Furthermore, to communicate with the reader, the author arranges the information, or supporting details, in a deliberate pattern of organization. All these intentions are intertwined in

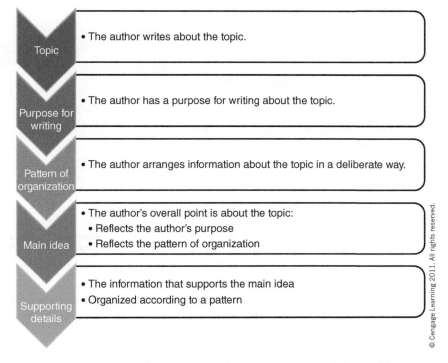

FIGURE 3.2 The Relationships Among Topic, Purpose, Pattern, Point, and Support

the mind of the author and between the ideas in the reading (see Figure 3.2). First and foremost, the author wants to communicate the most important point about the reading to the reader. This most important point, or main idea, is about the topic, in accord with the purpose for writing and reflective of the pattern of organization.

If an author's purpose is to instruct, for example, the topic of the reading will be how to understand or do something. The pattern of organization will likely be sequence or process order since how to do something involves steps and procedures. The main idea will be a general statement about the topic, such as, "Follow these three steps to communicate productively with coworkers." The supporting details will be the steps to follow in order to have productive communication with coworkers.

If the author's purpose is to inform or to persuade, the topic of the reading may be anything. The pattern of organization will take one of the forms you learned in Chapter 2. The main idea will reflect the author's stance: either presenting information or presenting a point of view about the topic. The supporting details will follow the pattern of organization that best conveys the author's purpose in writing.

The Difference Between Topic and Main Idea

The topic of a reading passage is the subject of the passage. Topic can be determined by answering this question: Who or what is the passage about? It is important to remember that the topic is always expressed as a word or phrase.

The main idea, on the other hand, is the author's most important point about the topic. The main idea can be determined by answering this question: What is the author's most important point about the topic? It is important to remember that the main idea is always expressed as a sentence.

Put a check mark beside each of the following statements that could be a main idea statement:

___1 . How to prepare for an exam

___2 . Exam preparation follows several general steps.

___3 . These are important steps.

___4 . To prepare for an exam involves important steps, such as taking good notes and using spaced practice to learn.

___5 . How do you prepare for an exam?

You learned in Unit 1 that both topic and patterns of organization can apply to different lengths of text. The same applies to main idea (Figure 3.3). There is a main idea of a whole reading. A main idea can also be found in a subsection of a reading and a paragraph. Unlike a topic, however, a main idea is always expressed as a sentence; main idea is a sentence about the topic. Table 3.2 summarizes key terms for a main idea and their definitions.

Applications of patterns of organization and topic

FIGURE 3.3 Patterns and Topic Apply to All Parts of a Reading

TABLE 3.2 Key Terms for Main Idea

TERM	DEFINITION
Main idea	The most important point
Topic sentence	The most important point of a paragraph *when directly stated*
Thesis	The most important point of an essay or longer reading
Explicit (directly stated) main idea	The most important point expressed in one sentence in the reading

Finding the Main Idea

Determining the main idea involves thinking through information the author provides. The first step is to determine the topic: About whom or what is the passage written? Next, consider why the author wrote the passage: What is the author's purpose for writing? Then, consider how the author arranges information about the topic and in accord with his or her purpose: What is the pattern of organization? Then, ask: What is the author's most important point about the topic? This is the main idea.

Once you have determined the main idea, you can ask yourself several questions to verify your answer. Follow the checklist in the Quick Tips box to catch any errors. The main idea sentence must make complete sense by itself and contain the topic; after all, the main idea is the author's most important point about the topic. In addition, the main idea must be general enough to cover all the supporting details, as these details function to support the main idea. Also, keep in mind that the main idea reflects both the pattern of organization and the author's purpose for writing.

QUICK TIPS STEPS TO FINDING THE MAIN IDEA

1. What is the topic?

2. What is the author's purpose?

3. What is the pattern of organization?

4. What is the author's most important point about the topic?

5. The answer to question 4 is the main idea.

6. Find that same answer to question 4 in a sentence in the reading. This is the explicit main idea.

To make sure you have understood the main idea, ask yourself the following questions.

☑ Is your main idea a complete sentence (not a phrase)?

☑ Does your main idea sentence contain the topic?

☑ Does your main idea sentence make sense by itself? (Would someone who hadn't read the passage understand the main point without major clarification?)

☑ Does your main idea sentence reflect the author's structure? (If it is cause and effect, does the sentence show a cause and effect relationship between ideas?)

☑ Does your sentence reflect the author's purpose? (If the author's purpose is informative, your sentence should not include words like *should, must, ought to*, as they indicate an opinion or intent to persuade.)

☑ Do the major supporting points provided back up or support the more general sentence you say is the main point?

Where Are Explicit Main Ideas Located?

An author always has a point to communicate to you, the reader. The author's most important point can apply to a whole reading, a subsection of a reading, or a paragraph within a reading.

EXPLICIT MAIN IDEA IN A WHOLE READING: THE THESIS

The main idea for a whole reading, usually called a *thesis,* can be located anywhere in the passage. Most often, the main idea appears in the introduction. The second-most likely place for an explicit main idea is in the conclusion. However, the main idea can also be in the middle of the reading. While this may seem overwhelming, remember to follow the steps for determining the main idea, and the process will be easier for you.

Remember from Chapter 1 that previewing is an essential reading strategy to get an overview of the structure of a reading. The reason that previewing involves reading the entire introductory paragraph as well as the entire concluding paragraph is because the author's most important point, or main idea, of the reading is most likely to be in one of these two spots.

EXPLICIT MAIN IDEA IN A SUBSECTION OF A READING

If the reading has a subsection indicated by a heading, this subsection can also have an overall main idea. Think of a subsection in a reading as a complete, shorter reading within a longer reading. The same process is followed to determine the main idea of a subsection as with a longer reading (or within a paragraph, for that matter). Look at a subheading, for example, in a textbook and consider what the author's most important point is about that subsection. Sometimes authors will state a main idea of a subsection in a sentence of one paragraph and provide other paragraphs to clarify the idea. (See "Patterns That Explain" in Chapter 2.)

EXPLICIT MAIN IDEA IN A PARAGRAPH: THE TOPIC SENTENCE

An explicit main idea in a paragraph is called a *topic sentence*. A topic sentence is a sentence stating the most important point about the topic. As with a main idea, or thesis, in a whole reading, most often a topic sentence is the first or last sentence in a paragraph. Sometimes, however, the topic sentence can be in the middle of a paragraph (see Table 3.3).

Look for transition words that indicate a supporting detail to narrow your scope. If there is a transition, or signal word or phrase, such as *in addition, furthermore,* or *second,* this point would be a supporting point rather than a main point. Look for the sentence that is the general point under which these examples might fall.

Remember that the main idea sentence (topic sentence) is never a question. However, the topic sentence is often the answer to a question posed at the beginning of a paragraph. The topic sentence always contains the topic and the point made about the topic in a paragraph. In addition, the main idea reflects the author's purpose and the organizational pattern of the paragraph. Keep in mind that even if you see more than one pattern of organization or mixed patterns, or a transition word or phrase that indicates a certain pattern of organization, the pattern reflected in the topic sentence is the most important pattern because this is the main point of the paragraph—this is the overall point about the topic.

In some cases, clues or signal words can point you to the main idea. These words are the clue to finding the main idea. They are often referred to as *summative words* because they summarize the author's most important point about the passage. Summative words are usually indicating a main idea at the end of the paragraph, but not always.

Summative Words: Words and Phrases Indicating a Main Idea Sentence

- The point is
- Clearly
- To sum up
- The key is . . .
- In conclusion

- What this means is . . .
- In reality
- Obviously
- In short

- In summary
- It is clear that . . .
- The fact is
- Overall

TABLE 3.3 Where Are Topic Sentences Located?

Finding the main idea in a paragraph is a very important skill because a topic sentence is the main point of a paragraph—and a main point in a paragraph becomes a major supporting detail of a whole article.

At the beginning	MAIN IDEA Details	<u>Most people know that humor or sarcasm can easily fall flat when expressed via e-mail, yet psychologists find that most people are still confident that they will be understood.</u> Psychologist Justin Kruger calls this "everyday egocentrism"—the natural tendency we all have to see things from our own perspective. "Because we know we're trying to be sarcastic or funny, we egocentrically assume our audience will, as well," he says. It's a hurdle that we can't completely overcome, even when we are trying to put ourselves in someone else's shoes, he says. — Marina Krakovsky, "The Ego in Cyberspace"
In the middle	Details MAIN IDEA Details	"Birds of a feather flock together." "Familiarity breeds contempt." "Opposites attract." Are these statements true? <u>Actually, the folklore about friendship is, at best, a mixture of fact and fiction.</u> As you might expect, we look for friends and lovers who will be kind and understanding and who appear to have attractive personalities. — From COON, *Introduction to Psychology*, 12E. © 2010 Cengage Learning.
At the end	Details MAIN IDEA	Once initial contact has been made, it's time to get to know each other. This is done mainly through the process of self-disclosure, as you begin to share private thoughts and feelings and reveal yourself to others. To get acquainted, you must be willing to talk about more than just the weather, sports, or nuclear physics. In general, as friends talk, they gradually deepen the level of liking, trust, and self-disclosure. We more often reveal ourselves to persons we like than to those we find unattractive. Disclosure also requires a degree of trust. Many people play it safe, or "close to the vest," with people they do not know well. <u>Indeed, self-disclosure is governed by unspoken rules about what's acceptable.</u> — From COON, *Introduction to Psychology*, 12E. © 2010 Cengage Learning.

On Your Own DETERMINING TOPIC SENTENCES WITHIN PARAGRAPHS

For each of the paragraphs in this reading, determine the topic and the pattern of organization. Circle transitions if these clues are in the paragraph. Then, underline the topic sentence and compare your answers with a partner.

(Continued)

1.   "Mark is a nervous guy." "Karen is short-tempered." "You can always count on Wes." Statements that contain or imply the word *is* lead to the mistaken assumption that people are consistent and unchanging—an incorrect belief known as static evaluation. Instead of labeling Mark as permanently and totally nervous, it would be more accurate to outline the particular situations in which he behaves nervously. The same goes for Karen, Wes, and the rest of us: We are more changeable than the way static, everyday language describes us.

—From ADLER/PROCTOR, *Looking Out, Looking In*, 13E. © 2011 Cengage Learning.

Topic: _____

Pattern of organization: _____

2.   First, for a prospective job an interview on campus may be the first step. Next, this initial interview is followed by an interview at the company's headquarters. This interview could last anywhere from a few hours to an entire day. Interviews involve meeting with a number of people: hiring managers, the prospective immediate supervisor, and potential colleagues and associates. All will provide their impressions of your qualifications and "fit" within the company. Third, follow-up interviews may take place after you make the initial cut. Then, job offers usually come by phone, or in person at the follow-up interview. Getting a job that you want often involves having a series of face-to-face interviews.

Topic: _____

Pattern of organization: _____

3.   "The squeaky wheel gets the grease." This is one of my favorite American aphorisms. We don't always like it, but we recognize the common-sense truth in it—that the person who speaks up, or even complains, can get what he or she wants. On the other hand, one of my favorite Chinese aphorisms is, "The bird that flies first gets the bullet." If you speak first and "stick your neck out," you may pay the price. Better to stay quiet and see where the group is going. Another favorite is the Japanese saying, "The nail that stands up gets pounded down." If you draw too much attention to yourself, you will be brought down into line with the others. In each country where they originate, these sayings represent knowledge that everyone knows to be true—maybe not in every situation, but often enough to have found expression in a common saying.

—"Developing Cross-Cultural Awareness and Understanding," by Theresa Kneebone, *Independent School*, Vol. 67, Issue 1, Fall 2007, pp. 80–91 (http://www.nais.org).

Topic: _____

Pattern of organization: _____

4.   However, as Voltaire said, "Common sense is not so common." Many of the guidance systems we rely on don't set a true course when we find ourselves in a different context. This can be true for students attending a new school or for someone living with a new roommate or for those of us who move to a new region or country. In new surroundings, the "common understanding" that has guided us for so long may no longer apply. Consider that, for international students at North American independent schools, all of the above may be true. International students find themselves not only dealing with the

"normal" challenges of childhood/young adulthood and of entering a new school, but also of navigating the additional challenges of coming from a cultural background that is different from those of their fellow students—and speaking a different language.

—"Developing Cross-Cultural Awareness and Understanding," by Theresa Kneebone,
Independent School, Vol. 67, Issue 1, Fall 2007, pp. 80–91 (http://www.nais.org).

Topic: _____

Pattern of organization: _____

5.   A person's behavior and attitudes are formed by more than his or her cultural background. They are formed by personality, family background, education, and experience. For example, if, on average, Chinese students have a greater comfort with silence than U.S. students, does that mean all Chinese students will be quiet? Or, as I have sometimes been asked by teachers, "I have had a lot of shy kids in my classes; why would you think this student is quiet because she's Chinese? Why should I assume she's different than the other quiet kids in my class?" My answer is this: I don't know if she's quiet because of her cultural background and the respect for silence in China, or if it is because she's 14 years old, or if it is because she doesn't know the topic that is being discussed. But without understanding the whole context of her experience and background, we may be missing an important part of the picture. Increasing our cross-cultural awareness can give us additional tools to support not only our international students, but students of every background.

—"Developing Cross-Cultural Awareness and Understanding," by Theresa Kneebone,
Independent School, Vol. 67, Issue 1, Fall 2007, pp. 80–91 (http://www.nais.org).

Topic: _____

Pattern of organization: _____

6.   Many international students, especially those from Asian countries, come from school systems that emphasize mastery of knowledge. There is often the rote memorization of facts and information that come from texts and teachers. The written language itself is learned through hours of practice and memorization. A Chinese or Japanese character written out of the exact stroke order is incorrect. Rigorous national examinations and competition for entry into top national schools have created the need to master the exact skill and knowledge tested for in the exam system.

—"Developing Cross-Cultural Awareness and Understanding," by Theresa Kneebone,
Independent School, Vol. 67, Issue 1, Fall 2007, pp. 80–91 (http://www.nais.org).

Topic: _____

Pattern of organization: _____

7.   This difference in assumptions about what constitutes a "good teacher" or "good student" can lead to confusion and misunderstanding among teachers and students from different backgrounds. Teachers in the U.S. may say to international students, "If you don't understand, ask." The responsibility is now upon the students to seek the teacher's help. But years of acculturation are not overcome that easily, so the teacher is sometimes left wondering why some students didn't speak up when asked directly about a

(Continued)

problem. The students may expect that the teacher will tell them specifically what they need to know or that the teacher will understand the subtext of their indirect answer. The students may be uncomfortable being put on the spot in a way that reveals their ignorance and, therefore, causes a loss of face for themselves and for their teacher.

—"Developing Cross-Cultural Awareness and Understanding," by Theresa Kneebone,
Independent School, Vol. 67, Issue 1, Fall 2007, pp. 80–91 (http://www.nais.org).

Topic: _____

Pattern of organization: _____

8.   International students have also expressed distress about going from strong students in their home environments to struggling to express themselves in a second language and new culture. Even if they feel comfortable with the vocabulary, they don't always catch cultural references or non-verbal cues (eye contact, personal body space) and have found it difficult to understand and to make themselves understood. This doesn't happen all the time, but, when it does, it can lead to feelings of frustration and isolation.

—"Developing Cross-Cultural Awareness and Understanding," by Theresa Kneebone,
Independent School, Vol. 67, Issue 1, Fall 2007, pp. 80–91 (http://www.nais.org).

Topic: _____

Pattern of organization: _____

9.   When at a job interview, remember first of all to be nice to everyone you meet at your prospective job site, since you never know who will report to the committee or hiring manager. Second, be sure to research the company that you want to join. It is painfully obvious to hiring professionals if an interviewee does not know anything about the company. If you don't know anything about the company, just how interested do you appear? Also, ask questions and present yourself in a professional, energetic manner that will show your prospective employer your level of professionalism, interest, and preparation. Most importantly, anticipate interview questions and prepare for them! There are many reference books and online sources that will help you understand the general questions that are a part of most interviews; prepare your answers in advance, so you can talk fluently and convincingly to make a good impression. Clearly, there are many important factors to succeeding in a job interview—remember that practice is your most important ally.

Topic: _____

Pattern of organization: _____

10.   **Emotive language** seems to describe something but actually announces the speaker's attitude toward it. If you approve of a friend's roundabout approach to a difficult subject, you might call her "tactful"; if you don't approve of it, you might accuse her of "beating around the bush." Whether the approach is good or bad is more a matter of opinion than of fact, although this difference is obscured by emotive language.

—From ADLER/PROCTOR, *Looking Out, Looking In*, 13E. © 2011 Cengage Learning.

Topic: _____

Pattern of organization: _____

Thinking It Through FINDING THE MAIN IDEA OF A WHOLE READING

Here you will apply the steps of finding the main idea of a whole article—the thesis—as well as finding the main idea of each paragraph. Begin by previewing the article to figure out the topic, the pattern of organization, the author's purpose, and the author's main idea. Jot down your responses or discuss your ideas with a partner. Then look at the explanation following the reading.

1. **What is the topic of the article?** _____

2. **What is the pattern of organization suggested by the topic?** _____

3. **What is the author's purpose?** _____

4. **What is the author's main idea about the topic (in your own words)?** _____

5. **Underline the thesis of the article—the sentence that has the same ideas as you wrote in question 4.**

After you've previewed the article to answer these questions, read the article completely to check your answers. Make adjustments to your answers if your reading has revealed something new. Next, find the topic sentence in paragraphs 2 through 5 and list the major supporting details of each of these paragraphs in the margin. Finally, check your answers at the end of this section.

His *Brain*, Her *Brain*
by Nancy Shute

1   Anyone who's heard a group of men discuss the virtues of high-end stereo equipment will have little trouble believing that men's and women's brains work differently. That's also no surprise to scientists, who have spent the past two decades trying to figure out which aspects of cognition and behavior are determined by nature and which by nurture. The verdict: Female and male brains differ in both structure and function, and many of those variations start in the womb. It's no longer: "Is there a difference?" It's: "What do these differences mean?"

2   Male and female brains differ in how they're built, with some parts larger in men, others larger in women. The variation is most striking in overall size. Women's brains are about 10 percent smaller than men's, a fact that in centuries past provided ammunition for the argument that women were by nature mentally deficient. Yet, despite this difference, women do just as well as men on intelligence tests. Researchers at the University of California–Irvine say they have figured out one possible explanation: In January, they reported that men have more gray matter in the brain, and women have more white matter. Gray matter forms the brain's information-processing centers, and white matter serves as wiring to connect the processing centers. "Female brains might be more efficient," says Richard Haier, the psychologist who led the study. Women also tend to use their frontal lobes for intellectual performance, while the gray matter used by men is distributed throughout the

(Continued)

brain. That has implications for treating diseases like stroke and Alzheimer's, Haier says; treatments could be targeted to protect or restore those critical regions.

3   DIVERGENCE. When it comes to putting brains to work, women and men have their own areas of expertise. Men do better than women at spatial tasks such as thinking about rotating or manipulating an object. They're also better at navigating along a route and at high-end mathematical reasoning; men have scored more perfect 800 scores on the math portion of the SAT than women have every year since 1964. Women excel at tests that measure word recall and at other tests of verbal memory. They're also better at remembering landmarks and where objects are located. It used to be thought that these differences in cognitive skills didn't emerge until puberty, but researchers have found the same differences in very young children.

4   The big question, of course, is whether the differences in his and her brains cause the variation in cognitive skills or whether society pushes women toward verbal, people-oriented tasks, and men toward quantitative fields like engineering. Few women in science have forgotten the infamous Teen Talk Barbie of 1992, which chirped, "Math is hard!" And although the number of women in the sciences has increased steadily over the past 30 years—women now compose the majority in medical schools and graduate programs in biology—they are still underrepresented in math, engineering, and physics.

5   In 1980, psychologists Julian Stanley and Camilla Benbow ignited a firestorm when they proposed that gifted boys did better at math than gifted girls because of a "math gene." The nature vs. nurture debate continues 25 years later, but it is becoming more pragmatic as researchers use MRIs and other brain-imaging tools that show differences in male and female brains even when performance is identical. "In the early 80s, we were worried that sex differences in the brain would be used against us as women," says Jill Becker, a psychologist at the University of Michigan. "We're all more comfortable with diversity these days, and we've come to accept that there are many different ways of solving a problem. No two brains are the same."

SOURCE: *"His Brain, Her Brain."* By Shute, Nancy, *U.S. News & World Report*, 00415537, 3/7/2005, Vol. 138, Issue 8. Reprinted by permission of U.S. News & World Report.

Check Your Answers

1. **What is the topic of the article?** *Men, women, and brains*

2. **What is the pattern of organization suggested by the topic?** *Comparison and contrast*

3. **What is the author's purpose?** *To inform*

4. **What is the author's main idea about the topic (in your own words)?** *Male and female brains are different physically and as evidenced by how we behave.*

5. **Underline the thesis of the article—the sentence that has the same ideas as you wrote in question 4.** *The thesis is in the first paragraph: The verdict: Female and male*

brains differ in both structure and function, and many of those variations start in the womb.

Main Ideas and Supporting Details by Paragraph

PARAGRAPH 1

Thesis: *The verdict: Female and male brains differ in both structure and function, and many of those variations start in the womb.*

PARAGRAPH 2

Topic Sentence: *Male and female brains differ in how they're built, with some parts larger in men, others larger in women.*

Supporting Details

1. *Size*
   a. *Women's brains are 10 percent smaller.*
   b. *Women do as well as men on IQ tests.*
2. *Men have more gray matter—the brain's information-processing centers—and women have more white matter, connecting the processing centers.*
3. *Women's brains might be more efficient.*
   a. *Women use their frontal lobes.*
   b. *Men use matter distributed throughout the brain.*
4. *This knowledge impacts treating diseases of the brain.*

PARAGRAPH 3

Topic Sentence: *When it comes to putting brains to work, women and men have their own areas of expertise.*

Supporting Details

1. *Men are better at spatial tasks, navigating, and high-end math.*
2. *Women are better at words, verbal memory, and remembering landmarks and objects.*

PARAGRAPH 4

Topic sentence: *The big question, of course, is whether the differences in his and her brains cause the variation in cognitive skills or whether society pushes women toward verbal, people-oriented tasks, and men toward quantitative fields like engineering.*

Supporting Detail

The number of women in science has increased in the last 30 years, but is not equal to the number of men in math, engineering, and physics.

(Continued)

PARAGRAPH 5

Topic Sentence: *The nature vs. nurture debate continues 25 years later, but it is becoming more pragmatic as researchers use MRIs and other brain-imaging tools that show differences in male and female brains even when performance is identical.*

Supporting Details

1. *In the past, people were concerned that sex differences in the brain would result in discrimination.*

2. *Today, there's more tolerance of differences.*

On Your Own FINDING THE MAIN IDEA

This is a reading about global business customs and etiquette. Answer the six questions that follow after previewing the reading. Then read the passage and answer the questions in the margins. You will apply the steps to finding the main idea or thesis of the whole article and also find the main idea of each paragraph or subsection.

1. What is the topic of the whole article? _____

2. What is the overall pattern of organization? _____
_____

3. What is the author's purpose (to inform us or to persuade us)? _____

4. How many major subsections are there in this article? _____
_____

5. What is the author's main idea about the topic (in your own words)? _____
_____
_____

Global Business Customs and Etiquette
by Lillian Chaney and Jeanette Martin

1　　The number of Americans who work for foreign employers and the number of foreign companies who have built plants in the United States is increasing. Due to the global business boom and increasing international travel, it is more and more important to learn about the customs of people of other cultures. Building global business relationships depends on your ability to learn cultural similarities and differences in greeting behavior, introductions, and business card exchange. Successful intercultural encounters also depend on knowledge of gift-giving customs so that we do not unintentionally offend people in other cultures. Professionals whose responsibilities include international travel or assisting others with travel arrangements will benefit from knowledge of global business customs and etiquette.

Greetings and Introductions

What is the topic of paragraph 2?

What is the pattern of organization in paragraph 2?

Underline the topic sentence in paragraph 2.

2   Customary greetings vary from culture to culture and are important for building relationships in all cultures. The informality of American greetings is not shared by many cultures. While Americans often say "Hi!" to complete strangers, in most countries of the world saying "Hi" to strangers is uncommon. Additionally, people of the United States are sometimes perceived as insincere in their ritualistic greeting of "Hello, how are you?" in some Latin American countries because it does not indicate a sincere inquiry about the state of the other person's health. In general, when greeting someone for the first time, it is better to use peoples' titles with their last name rather than using their first name, a common practice in the United States. An appropriate greeting to use would be "Hello, I'm pleased to meet you, Mr. Oguzhan" when greeting people.

What is the main idea of paragraph 3?

3   Introductions are part of making a positive initial impression when interacting with others in business and social settings. One difference between cultures is the use of titles when making introductions.

What is the topic of paragraph 4?

What is the pattern of organization in paragraph 4?

Underline the topic sentence in paragraph 4.

4   Remember that titles are important in most of the world. In the U.S., there is sometimes a prevailing view that a relaxed standard on the use of titles leads to a more relaxed interaction among people. In most other cultures, however, the use of titles helps to formalize relationships and establish a comfort of a different sort.

What is the topic of paragraph 5?

5   In many European countries like Germany and Italy, titles are used with a person's last name when

(Continued)

What is the pattern of organization in paragraph 5?

Write the main idea of paragraph 5 in your own words.

What is the topic of paragraph 6?

What is the pattern of organization in paragraph 6?

Underline the topic sentence in paragraph 6.

introducing people to show respect. Similarly, in the African countries of Nigeria and Kenya, titles are used with last names until a relationship has been established and you are asked to address them by their first name. Since surnames are reversed in such Asian countries as China and Japan, address "Sung Lo Chang" as "Mr. Sung." In Latin American countries people add their mother's maiden name to their surname, so you would address Teresa Gomez Sanchez as Señorita Gomez. In Iraq and India, titles such as *Professor* are used with the last name as part of introductions.

6   Introductions are accompanied by a handshake, an embrace, kiss, or bow, depending on the culture. The handshake usually accompanies a verbal greeting in many parts of the world including Nigeria, Kenya, Saudi Arabia, Egypt, and Finland. The duration and vigorousness of the handshake can be different. The U.S. handshake is moderately firm compared to the light, quick grasp of the French; the soft or gentle grasp of the British; and the firm grasp of the Germans. Although embracing and kissing when being introduced are inappropriate in business situations in the United States, it is common in many South American and Middle Eastern countries as well as in some African countries and parts of Europe. Middle Eastern men will shake hands and kiss on both cheeks as they embrace. Russians are famous for their bear hug often followed by a strong handshake between male friends. People of Latin America, the Mediterranean, and parts of Africa embrace, often accompanied with a slap on the back. In Japan and China, the bow, rather than the handshake, is customary. The handshake, though, is often combined with a bow during international business encounters so that each *culture* shows the proper respect. In India, the traditional greeting is the Namaste, which one says while pressing palms together with fingers up and hands placed below the chin. A slight bow accompanies this gesture when greeting supervisors or others to whom you wish to show respect.

Business Cards

7   In the United States, businesspeople exchange business cards only if there is a reason to do so. Card exchange is an expected part of business introductions, though, in most countries of the world. Since the business card plays such an important role in relationship building, it is wise to have cards for every country you plan to visit printed in the local language on the back of your cards. Although it is permissible in the United States to glance at a business card and place it in a pocket, this practice is not universally accepted around the world. In countries like Japan, for example, the examination of the business card is done with great deliberation. The Japanese will examine the card carefully for clues to hierarchy within the firm and will make a comment about your position with the company or ask a question about some other information on the card before putting it away. In addition, it is customary to use both hands when presenting your card in Japan or South Korea and to position the card so that the other person can read it. In the Middle East, Southeast Asia, and African cultures (except Israel), use only your right hand to present and accept business cards as the left hand is reserved for taking care of bodily functions. Because of the negative associations with certain colors in many countries, use white paper with black ink for your business cards. Since rank, title and profession are important in other cultures, be sure to include your position, title, degrees, all phone numbers (with international codes) and e-mail address on your business cards.

What is the topic of paragraph 7?

What is the pattern of organization in paragraph 7?

Underline the topic sentence in paragraph 7.

Gift-Giving Customs

8   Since gift giving is an integral part of building global relationships, it is important to understand the subtleties of the gift-giving art. Consider the appropriateness or inappropriateness of certain gifts and cultural gift-giving guidelines.

9   Appropriate business gifts for U.S. persons to give when visiting abroad include flowers, chocolates, or something that is unique to the United States such as

What is the main idea of paragraph 8?

Underline the main idea of this subsection in paragraph 8.

(Continued)

What is the topic of paragraph 9?

What is the pattern of organization in paragraph 9?

Write the main idea of paragraph 9 in your own words.

Native American art or jewelry, DVDs of U.S. movies, U.S.-made sports equipment, or California wines. However, avoid giving California wines to the French, as fine wines are that country's specialty. In addition, avoid gifts of liquor or wine in all Islamic cultures as alcohol is forbidden by their religion. Other gifts to avoid include a knife or handkerchief in South American countries. The knife would be interpreted as wanting to end a relationship, and a handkerchief is associated with tears. Gifts to avoid in India are those made of cowhide, because the cow is sacred. Be aware of superstitions and taboos related to gifts. For example, when giving a gift in China or Saudi Arabia, avoid anything with an eagle on it as the eagle in these countries signifies bad luck. Also, avoid giving a clock in China as the clock is considered a symbol of bad luck. (In Korea, though, the clock is a symbol of good luck.) Further, be aware of the significance of numbers in gift giving: Three is a lucky number in Thailand, eight and nine are considered lucky in Hong Kong, but four is the most negative number in China, so do not give four of anything.

What is the topic of paragraph 10?

What is the pattern of organization in paragraph 10?

Underline the topic sentence in paragraph 10.

10   While flowers make appropriate gifts in most cultures, learning cultural taboos related to color and variety is important. Red roses, for example, are associated with romance in the United States as well as in some other cultures and are inappropriate for business gifts. In China white is the color of mourning, and gladioli are often used in funeral sprays; thus, a gift of white gladioli is inappropriate in that country. In most European counties, carnations are used in cemeteries only and make inappropriate gifts. Another flower variety associated with funerals in Belgium, Japan, and Italy is the chrysanthemum, which makes it an inappropriate business gift in those countries. A flower shop in the country you are visiting is probably the best source of information concerning local customs about giving flowers as gifts.

What is the topic of paragraph 11?

What is the pattern of organization in paragraph 11?

Underline the topic sentence in paragraph 11.

11   Knowing proper guidelines for gift giving is important. In the United States business gifts are most often limited to about $25 and are opened in front

of the giver. The verbal expression of thanks is followed by a note of appreciation. Gifts are also opened in the presence of the giver in Belgium and in Brazil. In the Arabian countries, presenting the gift in the presence of other people is important so it will not be viewed as a bribe. In Taiwan, Hong Kong, and Korea, on the other hand, gifts are not opened in the presence of the giver. In addition, you should accept the gift with both hands in these countries. Another important point to remember is that in some Asian countries a gift is declined out of politeness at least once before they accept the gift; you are expected to do likewise. A special caution to those visiting Islamic countries: Exercise restraint in expressing admiration for their personal possessions as they will feel obligated to give them to you.

12   Following the preceding suggestions related to global business customs and etiquette will increase your chances of success in intercultural encounters.

Can you find a sentence in paragraph 1 that states this same point made in paragraph 12? Why do you think the author states the same point at the beginning and at the end?

SOURCE: Repubished with permission of OfficePro, from "Global Business Customs And Etiquette," by Chaney, Lillian H., Martin, Jeanette S., *OfficePro*, 66(4), May 2006; permission conveyed through Copyright Clearence Center, Inc.

UNDERSTANDING GRAPHICS

FINDING THE MAIN IDEA IN VISUAL AIDS

To find the main idea in a graphic, consider the same steps you would when reading text. To read for the main idea in graphics:

1. Determine the topic.
2. Determine the pattern of organization.
3. Determine the most important point.

Now, consider the answers to those questions for Figure 3.4. This pie chart shows the distribution of the world's population by continent—this is the topic. The pattern of organization is comparison and contrast because the pie chart compares the population ratios around the world. When you examine the pie chart closely, what do you see as the main idea? Which piece of the pie chart is the largest? The main idea is that the majority of the world's population is in Asia.

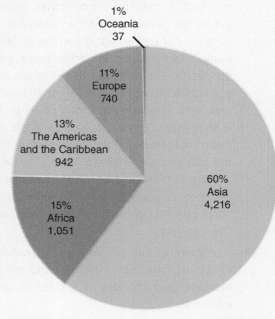

Based on statistics from www.nationsonline.org/oneworld/world_population.htm

FIGURE 3.4 Distribution of Global Population by Continent (in Millions), 2011

CONTINENT	NUMBER OF PEOPLE (IN MILLIONS)
Asia	4,216
Africa	1,051
The Americas and the Caribbean	942
Europe	740
Oceania	37

SUMMARIZING TO EXPRESS MAIN IDEA AND SUPPORTING DETAILS

There are three main ways to represent an author's ideas in paragraph form. You learned in Chapter 2 about paraphrasing. A paraphrase is the same length as the original and functions to clarify the whole passage by representing the author's ideas in your own words. **Paraphrasing** involves rewording the main idea as well as both major and minor supporting details.

Another type of summary strategy is the abstract. An **abstract** is a highly condensed summary of a long reading that highlights only the major points in an otherwise detailed passage. Abstracts are usually written as a summary of a research study. An example of an abstract is in Chapter 2: "Gender Differences Among Adolescents with Gambling-Related Problems" on page 97. This abstract was from a long paper on the subject and summarized the main points so a reader will know the fundamental findings of the research before reading the study.

The third method of restating an author's ideas is **summarizing.** This involves putting an author's main idea and major supporting details in your own words. A summary, like a paraphrase, represents an author's ideas in your own words. Unlike a paraphrase, a summary consists of only the author's most important point and major supporting points. All minor details, such as lists and examples, are left out of a summary. Be careful not to add information to the summary that the author has not stated. If you must take direct wording from a passage an author has written, be very sure to use quotation marks to announce that these are the author's words and not your words.

Summarizing is an excellent method for learning information because, as you know from Chapter 1, to learn new information, you need to process it in an organized format, so your brain can retrieve it more effectively. Summarizing allows you to do this because you have to put an author's main idea and major supporting details into your own words and use the same pattern of organization the author uses. Also, because you have to be clear on the main idea and major supporting points, summarizing allows you to determine if you *truly* understand what you have read. You cannot summarize without good comprehension. If you cannot summarize, recheck your notes and reread the passage, concentrating again on what's important. Creating a paraphrase of a reading can help you summarize: If you can rewrite a passage, you will be more certain that you understand it. Then, focus on just the major points and try your summary again.

A summary is written in paragraph format. A good rule is to make your summary about one-fourth as long as the original reading. However, the length of any summary depends on the number of details in the original reading. If the original reading is dense with information, your summary will be longer than a quarter of the original piece. If the original reading contains a lot of minor supporting details, your summary may be quite short.

QUICK TIPS SUMMARY ESSENTIALS

 A summary is a shortened passage, written in paragraph form, that condenses the major points of a reading.

A summary includes transitions, or signal words, to show the relationship between ideas.

A summary of a reading must make sense on its own.

A summary must reflect the structure the author intended in the original passage as well as the author's purpose for writing.

A summary does not contain minor details.

Main idea + major supporting details in paragraph form = summary.

How to Write a Summary

To write a summary, you need to apply everything you have learned so far about approaching a reading. In addition, you will need to use your skills of determining the main idea of a passage, as this is the foundation of a summary. Furthermore, you have to separate major details from minor details.

1. Find the topic of the reading.
2. Determine the author's purpose.
3. Determine the pattern of organization.
4. Determine the main idea.
5. Identify the major supporting details.
6. Paraphrase 4 and 5 into your own words, paying attention to the pattern of organization.

Thinking It Through SUMMARIZING A READING

Summary writing sounds complicated, but it is not as difficult as it first appears. You will see all the steps of summary writing modeled here, and then you will write a summary of the main points of the article "His Brain, Her Brain," by Nancy Shute from page 195. You have already determined the thesis as well as the main ideas and major supporting points in the reading. Now all you need to do is arrange these points into paragraph form. Because the original article is about a page in length, you will aim for about half a page in length for the summary. A summary begins with the main idea of the entire reading and then moves into the major supporting points. You do not want to be repetitive or add unnecessary details and lists. As you can see, finding the main ideas of paragraphs is an excellent tool in writing a summary because a topic sentence is the main point of a paragraph—*and a main point in a paragraph becomes a major supporting detail of a whole article.*

Remember, in a summary, you aim to paraphrase ideas. So paraphrase the main idea sentences rather than copying a topic sentence. Go back to the article on page 195 where you have underlined the main points and listed the major details of each paragraph. Then write down just the major ideas.

Title and author:_____

THE MAIN IDEAS AS EXPRESSED BY THE AUTHOR	YOUR PARAPHRASED MAIN IDEAS AND MAJOR SUPPORTING DETAILS
Thesis:	
Topic sentence of paragraph 2:	Your paraphrase of the main idea: The supporting details of paragraph 2:
Topic sentence of paragraph 3:	Your paraphrase of the main idea: The supporting details of paragraph 3:
Topic sentence of paragraph 4:	Your paraphrase of the main idea: The supporting details of paragraph 4:
Topic sentence of paragraph 5:	Your paraphrase of the main idea: The supporting details of paragraph 5:

(Continued)

Compare your answers with those that follow.

Title and author: <u>"His Brain, Her Brain," by Nancy Shute</u>

THE MAIN IDEAS AS EXPRESSED BY THE AUTHOR	YOUR PARAPHRASED MAIN IDEAS AND MAJOR SUPPORTING DETAILS
Thesis: The verdict: Female and male brains differ in both structure and function, and many of those variations start in the womb.	*Male and female brains are different physically, and differences are evident from how we behave.*

Topic sentence of paragraph 2: Male and female brains differ in how they're built, with some parts larger in men, others larger in women.	*Male and female brains differ in structure and size.*
	
	1. Size
	  a. Women's brains are 10 percent smaller.
	  b. Women do as well on IQ tests.
	
	2. Men have more gray matter—the brain's information-processing centers—and women have more white matter, connecting the processing centers.
	
	3. Women's brains might be more efficient.
	  a. Women use their frontal lobes.
	  b. Men use matter distributed throughout the brain.
	
	4. This knowledge impacts treating diseases of the brain.

Topic sentence of paragraph 3: When it comes to putting brains to work, women and men have their own areas of expertise.	*Because of their brain differences, men and women are good at different things.*
	
	1. Men are better at
	  ■ *spatial tasks*
	  ■ *navigating*
	  ■ *high-end math*
	
	2. Women are better at
	  ■ *words and verbal memory*
	  ■ *remembering landmarks and objects*

THE MAIN IDEAS AS EXPRESSED BY THE AUTHOR	YOUR PARAPHRASED MAIN IDEAS AND MAJOR SUPPORTING DETAILS
Topic sentence of paragraph 4: The big question, of course, is whether the differences in his and her brains cause the variation in cognitive skills or whether society pushes women toward verbal, people-oriented tasks, and men toward quantitative fields like engineering.	*The question is whether differences in the brain cause differences in ability between men and women or whether it is environment or nurture that explains these differences.* 1. *The number of women in science has increased in last 30 years but is still not equal to the number of men in math, engineering, and physics.*
Topic sentence of paragraph 5: The nature vs. nurture debate continues 25 years later, but it is becoming more pragmatic as researchers use MRIs and other brain-imaging tools that show differences in male and female brains even when performance is identical.	*Today, while the nature-versus-nurture debate continues, technology that allows imaging of the brain can confirm gender brain differences, even when the performance is the same.* 1. *In the past, people were concerned that sex differences in the brain would result in discrimination.* 2. *Today, there's more tolerance of differences.*

Put these ideas into paragraph form to create your summary. Be sure to use appropriate transition words to show the connections between the ideas.

_____

_____

_____

_____

_____

_____

_____

_____

_____

_____

_____

_____

(Continued)

Compare your summary with that written by a partner or others in your small group. Do you all have the main points in your summaries? Whose summary seems most precise and clear? Why? Now compare your summary to this example of a summary. Remember, summaries can be worded differently, but they must all contain the main idea and the major supporting details.

In "His Brain, Her Brain," Nancy Shute discusses the differences between male and female brains. Male and female brains are different physically, and these differences are evident from how we behave. <u>First</u>, male and female brains differ in structure and size. Women's brains are 10 percent smaller than men's, but men and women do equally well on IQ tests. <u>Whereas</u> men have more gray matter (which is in the brain's information-processing centers), women have more white matter, connecting the processing centers of the brain. <u>In addition</u>, women's brains might be more efficient <u>because</u> they use their frontal lobes more, <u>whereas</u> men use matter distributed throughout the brain. This information impacts the treatment of diseases of the brain. <u>Second, because</u> of their brain differences, men and women are good at different things. <u>While</u> men generally are better at spatial tasks like navigating and high-end math, women are better at using words and verbal memory, and at remembering landmarks and objects. <u>Third</u>, the question arises about whether differences in the brain cause differences in ability between men and women or whether it is environment that explains these differences. <u>Although</u> the number of women in science has increased in the last 30 years, their numbers still do not equal those of men in the fields of math, engineering, and physics. <u>Last</u>, today, while the nature-versus-nurture debate continues, technology that allows imaging of the brain can confirm gender brain differences, even when the performance is the same. <u>Whereas</u> in the past people were concerned that sex differences in the brain would result in discrimination, today there's more tolerance of differences.

Note the underlined transition words that help create flow in the preceding summary.

On Your Own SUMMARIZING A READING

Return to the On Your Own, "Finding the Main Idea," on page 198. Using the main ideas you found for each paragraph, combine these to write a summary of the whole reading. Remember, the main ideas of the body paragraphs become supporting details of a whole reading! Keep in mind that there are 12 paragraphs, with an introductory and concluding paragraph. Also, there are three subsections, so you will want to aim for three paragraphs in your summary. First cite the title of the reading and the authors' names. Then state the thesis of the reading. Next, organize the supporting details (the main ideas of each of the body paragraphs) into a paragraph for each subsection. Remember to use transition words to connect your ideas.

_____
_____
_____
_____
_____
_____
_____
_____
_____
_____
_____
_____
_____
_____
_____
_____
_____
_____
_____
_____
_____

VOCABULARY STRATEGY

RECOGNIZING ROOT WORDS

In Chapter 2, you learned to focus on prefixes and suffixes in a word, just as you learned to look at supporting details in a reading. Here, you will look at the main part of a word, its root, just like you have been examining the main idea of a reading. Many languages have contributed to English and continue to expand and enhance our language. The most common languages that form the basis of English are Latin and ancient Greek, as well as words that come from older versions of the English and French languages. Many of the words we use today originate from these sources.

Root words are the primary units in words. *Primary* refers to the part of a word that cannot be reduced to a smaller unit. Consider the word *prescription*. This word can be divided into three parts.

pre	+	**script**	+	**ion**
prefix	+	root word	+	suffix
before	+	to write	+	means the word is a noun

So, if directly translated, *prescription* means something that was written before. Consider that doctors write prescriptions to make a patient better. A prescription is written before a person regains his or her health.

In some cases, root words can function as prefixes, or at the beginning rather than the end of the word. The word *autobiographical* is a word that contains two roots. In this case, *auto* functions as a prefix.

auto	+	**bio**	+	**graphic**	+	**al**
prefix	+	root word	+	root word	+	suffix
self	+	life	+	to write	+	indicates an adjective

A direct "translation" of *autobiographical* is "self, life, and writing." Autobiographical writing is writing about one's own life. Notice how a root word is not on its own but rather is accompanied by prefixes and suffixes. You will need to use your knowledge of both prefixes and suffixes when identifying root words.

Table 3.4 shows some common root words found in academic reading. In every chapter, you have a list of the common word parts used in a variety of disciplines, so you may see some of these root words appear in other chapters. Be alert to these roots and open to noticing and learning others as they come up in your reading. Once you begin to look for them, you will realize how common they are.

TABLE 3.4 Common Root Words

ROOT WORD	MEANING	EXAMPLE	PREFIX AND/OR SUFFIX
anthrop	man/human	Anthropology—the study of humans *Anthropology is the academic study of humans and culture.*	ology = study of
astro	star	Astronaut—one who travels space *Astronauts are specifically trained to cope with the rigors of space travel.*	naut = sailor (as in nautical = water)
bio	life	Biology—the study of life *Biology is the science of life.*	ology = study of
demos	people	Democracy—government run by the people *To live in a democracy provides freedoms and options not found in political systems of dictatorship.*	cracy = govern, rule
derma	skin	Epidermis—outer layer of skin *A dermatologist is a medical specialist in the study of the epidermis.*	epi = over, on

ROOT WORD	MEANING	EXAMPLE	PREFIX AND/OR SUFFIX
gamy	spouse	Monogamy—one spouse *Monogamy is the only acceptable legal union in the United States; not so in other countries.*	mono = one
gen	race, kind, grow	To generate—to grow *Studies have suggested that antidepressant medication prompts neurons to generate new connections, which takes time.*	erate = verb form
hydro	water	Hydrate—to fill with water *To hydrate before long-distance running is as important as it is to all endurance sports.*	ate = verb form
hypno	sleep	Hypnotism—the act of putting to sleep/trance *The warmth and gentle hum in the classroom were hypnotic.*	ism = noun ending ic = adjective ending
man(u) script	hand write	Manuscript—written by hand *The manuscript was irreplaceable because no copies had been generated.*	
pod/ped	foot *ped* also means "child"	Pedal—operated by foot; pediatrics—study of child medicine *The pediatric nurse was an expert in dealing with the traumatized child.*	al = adjective ending iatrics = from the Greek *iatros*, meaning "healer" or "physician" ic = adjective ending
psycho	mind	Psychology—the study of the mind *To understand the criminal mind it is necessary to contemplate the psychology of the antisocial act.*	ology = study of
pop	people	Populace—a group of people *The populace was excited to welcome the dignitaries to the capital city.*	ace = noun ending
script	write	Prescription—to write before (pre) *The experts prescribed alternatives to our existing reliance on fossil fuels.*	pre = before ion = noun ending ed = verb ending
spec	look	Spectator—someone who looks *The spectator watched the game with great interest.*	or = noun ending

(Continued)

ROOT WORD	MEANING	EXAMPLE	PREFIX AND/OR SUFFIX
terra	earth	Extraterrestrial—from outside the earth *The terraforming of Mars by making it livable to external life conjures images of extraterrestrial civilizations seen in bad science-fiction movies.*	extra = beyond ial = adjective ending ing = verb ending
thermo meter	heat measure	Thermometer—measure of heat *The thermometer indicates that the outside temperature is hovering above freezing.*	
ver	truth	Verify—to determine truth *To verify your risk in assuming a loan of some proportion, banks check three credit-reporting agencies.*	ify = verb ending
zoo	animal	Zoology—the study of animals *The late Steve Irwin, known as the "Crocodile Hunter," made the study of zoology fascinating and accessible to countless people.*	ology = the study of
FAMILY RELATIONSHIPS			
mater/matri	mother	Maternal—motherly *Her maternal instincts compelled her to become a teacher.*	al = adjective
pater/patri	father	Paternity test—test of fatherhood *Before accepting responsibility for child support payments, the millionaire insisted on taking a paternity test to assure the child's parentage.*	ity = noun ending
frater/fratri	brother	Fraternity—brotherhood club *Fraternity hazing, of long concern, is being banned on an increasing number of college campuses.*	ity = noun ending
soror	sister	Sorority—sisterhood club *Sororities have become increasingly popular, although they are not as numerous as fraternities on college campuses.*	ity = noun ending

On Your Own RECOGNIZING ROOT WORDS

Choose 10 of the root words listed in Table 3.4. Without using the dictionary, write down at least one word that you know containing this root. Next to the word, write a definition using the meaning listed in the chart. Then, write your word in a sentence, providing context clues that clearly reveal the word's meaning. Share your sentences with a partner or in class discussion.

Original Word from Chart	Your New Word	Your Definition
1.		
2.		
3.		
4.		
5.		
6.		
7.		
8.		
9.		
10.		

INCREASE YOUR DISCIPLINE-SPECIFIC VOCABULARY

SOCIAL SCIENCES: ANTHROPOLOGY AND GENDER STUDIES

The social sciences, like any other discipline, have specific terminology that students need to learn to be conversant in these disciplines. Familiarizing yourself with these common word parts will help prepare you for terms you are certain to encounter again and again in your college-level reading (see Table 3.5).

TABLE 3.5 Vocabulary Associated with Social Science, Anthropology, and Gender Studies

WORD PARTS	MEANING	VOCABULARY
anthrop	man/human	anthropology, misanthrope, anthropoid, philanthropist, anthropomorphic
cide	to kill	genocide, suicide, homicide
cracy, crat	to rule/govern	democracy, autocracy, democrat, bureaucracy, bureaucrat
dem	people	demographic, democracy, endemic, epidemic, democrat
gamy	spouse	monogamy, bigamy, polygamy
gen	birth, race, kind, grow	engender, generate, generation, gene, genius, hydrogen, generous, gentleman, genocide
gyn	woman/female	gynecology, misogyny, polygyny
mit, mis, miss	to send	emissary, intermittent, missive, omit, premise, remission, transmit, commit, promise, submit, missionary
poly	many	polygyny, polyandry, polygamy, polymorphous
pop	people	populate, populace, popular

Key Terms—Social Science, Anthropology, and Gender Studies

- **Kinship:** family relationship or ancestry.

- **Ethnocentrism:** the belief that one's own culture is superior to another's culture.

- **Cultural Relativism:** the objective mindset of not judging another culture based on beliefs and/or customs.

- **Division of Labor:** the subsistence roles in any given culture based on gender.

- **Feminism:** the political movement geared to define, establish, or defend political, economic or social roles of women.

- **Chauvinism:** an attitude of superiority towards the opposite sex (usually attributed to males)

- **Gender:** the social differences, acculturation, and division of labor between males and females.

- **Sex:** the biological differences between males and females.

- **Acculturation:** the process by which one culture absorbs and adopts cultural traits from another culture.

- **Affirmative action:** policies designed to correct past prejudice, discrimination or unfairness in employment, opportunity, housing, education, and other societal institutions.

APPLICATIONS

APPLICATION ①

This is a passage about online dating in the United States and abroad excerpted from *Choices in Relationships: An Introduction to Marriage and the Family* by David Knox and Caroline Schacht. Preview the passage and answer the following questions.

1. What is the topic of the article? _____

2. What is the pattern of organization suggested by the topic? _____
   _____

3. What is the author's purpose? _____

4. What is the author's main idea about the topic (in your own words)? _____
   _____

5. Underline the thesis of the passage—the sentence that has the same ideas as you wrote in question 4.

The Internet—Meeting Online and After
by David Knox and Caroline Schacht

Topic of paragraph 1:

Underline the main idea of paragraph 1.
What does the prefix *de-* mean in *decreasing*? What does the suffix *-ing* indicate?

What does the prefix *com-* mean in *compatibility*? What does the suffix *-y* indicate?

Topic of paragraph 2:

Underline the main idea of paragraph 2.

1   Although some individuals feel "We could never let any-one know we met over the Internet," such stigmatization is **decreasing**. Almost three-fourths (74%) of single Americans have used the Internet to find a romantic partner, and 15% report that they know someone who met their spouse or significant other online. Over 16 million U.S. adults report that they have been online looking for a partner. Three to six percent of marriages or long-term relationships began online. eHarmony founder, Dr. Neil Clark Warren, has advertised that their broad-based **compatibility** system, in which they claim to match highly compatible singles, will possibly reduce the divorce rate in the United States by 1%. There is no evidence to support this claim. But one thing is certain, internet dating in all its configurations and with all its pros and cons is becoming increasingly popular.

2   Persons who are busy, don't have time for traditional dating, or who are shy may also be attracted to finding a partner online. Online meetings will continue to increase as people delay getting married and move beyond contexts

where hundreds or thousands of potential partners are available (the undergraduate coed classroom filled with same-age potential mates is rarely equaled in the workplace after college). The profiles that individuals construct or provide for others are an example of impression **management**—presenting an image that is perceived to be what the target audience wants. In this regard, men tend to emphasize their status characteristics (for example, income, education, career), whereas women tend to emphasize their youth, trim body, and beauty.

What does the root man *mean in* management?

3   It takes time and effort to meet someone at a coffee shop for an hour, only to discover that the person has habits (for example, does or does not smoke) or values (too religious or too agnostic) that would eliminate them as a potential partner. One can spend a short period of time and literally scan hundreds of potential partners without leaving the house. For noncollege people who are busy in their job or career, the Internet offers the chance to meet someone outside their immediate social circle. "There are only six guys in my office," noted one Internet user. "Four are married and the other two are alcoholics. I don't go to church and don't like bars so the Internet has become my guy store." An example is a woman who devoted a month to doing nothing but finding a mate on the Internet. She sifted through hundreds of guys, ended up seeing 8 of them, settled on two of them and ended up marrying one of them. She said of the experience, "I was exhausted. But I found my man." A primary attraction of meeting someone online is its efficiency.

Topic of paragraph 3:

Underline the main idea of paragraph 3.

4   Another advantage of looking for a partner online is that it removes emotion/chemistry/first meeting magic from the mating equation so that individuals can focus on finding someone with common interests, background, values, and goals. In real life, you can "fall in love at first sight" and have zero in common. Right Mate at Heartchoice.com not only provides a way to meet others but a free "Right Mate Checkup" to evaluate similarities with a potential partner. Some websites exist to target specific interests such as black singles (BlackPlanet.com), Jewish singles (Jdate.com), and gay people (Gay.com). In one study on online dating, women received an average of fifty-five replies compared to men who reported receiving thirty-nine replies. Younger women (average age of 35), attractive women, and those who wrote longer profiles were more successful in **generating** replies.

Topic of paragraph 4:

Underline the main idea of paragraph 4.

What does the root gen *mean in* generating?

(Continued)

Internet Use: The Downside

Topic of paragraph 5:

Underline the main idea of paragraph 5.
What does the prefix *mis-* mean in *misrepresentation*?

5   Lying occurs in Internet dating (as it does in non-Internet dating). Hall et al. identified seven categories of **misrepresentation** used by 5,020 individuals who posted profiles in search of an Internet date. These included personal assets ("I own a house at the beach"), relationship goals ("I want to get married'), personal interests ("I love to exercise"), personal attributes ("I am religious"), past relationships ("I have only been married once"), weight, and age. Men were most likely to misrepresent personal assets, relationship goals, personal interests, and personal attributes, whereas women were more likely to misrepresent weight. Heino et al. interviewed 34 online dating users and found that there is the assumption of exaggeration and a compensation for such exaggeration. The female respondents noted that men exaggerate how tall they are, so the women downplay their height. If a man said he was 5'11" the woman would assume he was 5'9".

Topic of paragraph 6:

Underline the main idea of paragraph 6.

6   Toma and Hancock examined the role of an online daters' physical attractiveness in the probability that they would be deceptive in their profile self-presentation. Sixty-nine online daters had their photograph taken in the lab. Independent judges rated the online daters' physical attractiveness. Results showed that the lower the online daters' attractiveness, the more likely they were to enhance their profile photographs and lie about their physical descriptors (height, weight, age).

Topic of paragraph 7:

Underline the main idea of paragraph 7.
What does the root *ver* mean in the word *veracity*?

7   Some online daters lack **veracity** and lie about being single. "Saleh" was married yet maintained fifty simultaneous online relationships with other women. He allegedly wrote intoxicating love letters, many of which were cut and paste jobs, to various women. He made marriage proposals to several and some bought wedding gowns in anticipation of the wedding. Although Saleh is an "Internet guy," it is important to keep in mind that people not on the Internet may also be very deceptive and cunning. To suggest that the Internet is the only place where deceivers lurk is to turn a blind eye to those people met through traditional channels.

Topic of paragraph 8:

Underline the main idea of paragraph 8.

8   A theme of the website WildXAngel.com is that it is important to be cautious of meeting someone online. The website features horror stories of some people who met online. Although the Internet is a good place to meet new people, it also allows someone you rejected or an old lover to monitor your online behavior. Most sites note when you have been online last, so if you reject someone online by saying, "I'm really not ready for a relationship," that

same person can log on and see that you are still looking. Some individuals become obsessed with a person they meet online and turn into a cyberstalker when rejected. Some people use the Internet to try on new identities. For example a person who feels he or she is attracted to same sex individuals may present a gay identity online. Clearly, caution is required when surfing online social sites.

9   There are other disadvantages to online meeting. These include the potential to fall in love too quickly as a result of intense mutual disclosure; not being able to assess "chemistry" or to observe nonverbal cues and gestures or how a person interacts with your friends or family; and the tendency to move too quickly (from e-mail to phone to meeting to first date) to **matrimony**, without spending much time to get to know each other.

Topic of paragraph 9:

Underline the main idea of paragraph 9.
What does the root word *matri* mean in *matrimony*?
What is the connection between the root word and the meaning of the word today?

10   Another disadvantage of using the Internet to find a partner is that having an unlimited number of options sometimes results in not looking carefully at the options one has. Wu and Chiou studied undergraduates looking for romantic partners on the Internet who had 30, 60, and 90 people to review and found that the more options the person had, the less time the undergraduate spent carefully considering each profile. The researchers concluded that it was better to examine a small number of potential online partners carefully than to be distracted by a large pool of applicants, which does not permit the time for close scrutiny.

Topic of paragraph 10:

Underline the main idea of paragraph 10.

11   McGinty noted the importance of not giving out home or business phone numbers or addresses, always meeting the person in one's own town with a friend, and not posting photos that are "too revealing," as these can be copied and posted elsewhere. Safety is important when using Internet dating sites. It is recommended to take it slow—after connecting in an email through the dating site, move to instant messages, phone calls, texting, **Skyping**, then meet in a public place with friends near. She recommends being open and honest: "Let them know who you are and who you are looking for," she suggests.

Topic of paragraph 11:

Underline the main idea of paragraph 11.

What part of speech does the suffix *-ing* indicate in *Skyping*?

12   The Internet may also be used to find out information about a partner. Argali.com can be used to find out where the Internet mystery person lives, Zabasearch.com for how long the person has lived there, and Zoominfo.com for where the person works. The person's birth date can be found at Birthdatabase.com. Women might want to see if any red flags have been posted on the Internet at Dontdatehimgirl.com.

Topic of paragraph 12:

Underline the main idea of paragraph 12.

(Continued)

Topic of paragraph 13:

Underline the main idea of
paragraph 13.

What does the root word *spec*
mean in *spectacular*?

Topic of paragraph 14:

Underline the main idea of
paragraph 14.
What does the root word *nov*
mean in *innovation*?

Topic of paragraph 15:

Underline the main idea of
paragraph 15.

What does the root word *pop*
mean in *populace*?

13   For individuals who learn about each other online, what is it like to finally meet? Baker is clear: "If they have presented themselves accurately and honestly online, they encounter few or minor surprises at the first meeting offline or later on in further encounters." About 7% end up marrying someone they met online. As you can see, meeting online can be a successful, and sometimes **spectacular**, experience.

Speed-Dating

14   Dating **innovations** that involve the concept of speed include the eight-minute date. The website http://www.8minutedating.com identifies these "Eight-Minute Dating Events" throughout the country, where a person has eight one-on-one dates at a bar that last eight minutes each. If both parties are interested in seeing each other again, the organizer provides contact information so that the individuals can set up another date. Speed-dating is time-effective because it allows daters to meet face-to-face without burning up a whole evening. Adams et al. interviewed participants who had experienced speed-dating to assess how they conceptualized the event. They found that women were more likely to view speed-dating as an investment of time and energy to find someone (58% versus 25%), whereas men were more likely to see the event as one of exploration (75% versus 17%). Wilson et al. collected data on nineteen young men who had three-minute social exchanges with nineteen young women and found that those partners who wanted to see each other again had more in common than those who did not want to see each other again.

High End Matchmaking

15   Wealthy busy clients looking for marriage partners pay Selective Search (www.selectivesearch.com) $20,000 to find them a mate. The Chicago based service personally interviews the client and then searchers the data base (for men there are 140,000 women in the database) for a partner. The women selected may also be personally interviewed again to ensure a match. Barbie Adler is the CEO of Selective Search and notes that 1,221 marriages and 417 babies have occurred to date. Almost ninety percent (88%) of clients meet their eventual spouse within the first nine months. In short, high end matchmaking may not be for the general **populace** but can work well.

International Dating

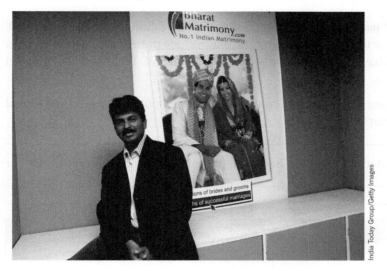

International dating sites are popular outside of the United States, too. Murugavel Jankiraman, CEO of the successful Bharat Matrimony, (Bharatmatrimony.com), poses in Chennai, Tamil Nadu, India in front of a wedding photograph of a couple who met using his Web site.

16   Go to Google.com and type in "international brides," and you will see an array of sites dedicated to finding foreign women for Americans. Dating sites are flourishing outside U.S. **territory**. Not listed is Ivan Thompson, who specializes in finding Mexican women for his American clients. As documented in the movie *Cupid Cowboy*, Ivan takes males (one at a time) to Mexico (Torreón is his favorite place). For $3,000, Ivan places an ad in a local newspaper for a young (age 20 to 35), trim (less than 130 pounds), single woman "interested in meeting an American male for romance and eventual marriage" and waits in a hotel for the phone to ring. They then meet and interview "candidates" in the hotel lobby. Ivan says his work is done when his client finds a woman he likes.

SOURCE: From KNOX/SCHACHT, *Choices in Relationships: An Introduction to Marriage and the Family*, 11E. © 2013 Cengage Learning.

Topic of paragraph 16:

Underline the main idea of paragraph 16.
What does the root word *terr* mean in *territory*?

(Continued)

COMPREHENSION CHECK

1. On a separate sheet of paper, write a summary of the article following the steps outlined. Remember to paraphrase the authors' wording and only include the major supporting points. Each paragraph should have a main point; there are 16 paragraphs, so your summary should be about a page in length.

2. Do you think that dating Web sites will continue to grow in popularity in international markets? Why or why not? _____

_____

3. What are the pros to Internet dating? What are the cons? Use this chart to organize your thoughts. _____

_____

PROS	CONS

4. In your opinion, do the pros outweigh the cons in Internet dating? _____

_____

5. What are the qualities that make American dating Web sites successful?

_____

_____

_____

_____

_____

_____

_____

_____

_____

_____

READING GRAPHICS

Consider Table 3.6 shown here.

TABLE 3.6 Internet Users and Population Statistics for Asia

ASIA REGION	POPULATION (2011 EST.)	POP. % WORLD	INTERNET USERS, LATEST DATA	PENETRATION (% POPULATION)	USERS % WORLD	FACEBOOK DEC. 31, 2011
Asia Only	3,879,740,877	56.0 %	**932,393,209**	24.0 %	44.2 %	183,963,780
Rest of World	3,050,314,277	44.0 %	**1,178,372,601**	38.6 %	55.8 %	615,128,380
WORLD TOTAL	6,930,055,154	100.0 %	**2,110,765,810**	30.5 %	100.0 %	799,092,160

SOURCE: http://www.internetworldstats.com/stats3.htm Copyright © 2012, Miniwatts Marketing Group. All rights reserved.

1. What is the topic of this table? _____
   _____

2. What is the pattern of organization of Table 3.6? _____
   _____

3. What is the main idea of Table 3.6? _____
   _____
   _____

4. Based on information in this reading as well as information you gain from this chart, what do you predict will be the trends in international social networking? _____
   _____

(Continued)

DEVELOPING YOUR COLLEGE-LEVEL VOCABULARY

Here are some prefixes, suffixes, and root words you encountered in this reading. Complete the chart, using the word part to create a new word. Then, use your new word in a sentence, clearly showing its meaning with context clues. The first one is completed as an example.

WORD PART	WORD	MEANING	NEW WORD	SENTENCE
de	decreasing	away from	decipher	To decipher what's true and what's false in an online profile is often difficult.
1. man	management			
2. gen	generating			
3. -mis	misrepresentation			
4. ver	veracity			
5. matri	matrimony			
6. -ing	Skyping			
7. spec	spectacular			
8. nov	innovation			
9. pop	populace			
10. terra	territory			

THEMATIC CONNECTIONS

1. If you were a CEO of a matchmaking company, which countries would you target for business and why? In which countries would you not invest? Why not?

2. In this chapter, you have learned about gender communication as well as cross-cultural communication. How might you design a dating site for an international audience taking into account both cultural and gender differences? Choose a country to target, and discuss some ideas for tailoring your dating site to that specific audience.

3. If you were going to design a social networking or dating site for an American audience, how would you market your site to both male and female consumers?

4. Do you know anyone who has experience with online dating? Outline his or her experience and explain why online dating did or did not work.

APPLICATION ②

Communications Textbook

This is an excerpt from a communications college textbook, *Looking Out, Looking In* by Ronald B. Adler and Russell F. Proctor II. Preview the reading and consider the topic, the pattern of organization, the authors' purpose, and the authors' main idea. Write down your responses or discuss your ideas with a partner.

1. Overall topic: _____

2. Overall pattern of organization:_____

3. Author's purpose: _____

4. Overall main idea (thesis): _____
   _____
   _____

Next, find the important characteristics of each paragraph as you work through the margin questions. Last, discuss the Comprehension Check and/or write a summary of the whole passage as assigned.

Culture, Gender, and Identity
by Ronald B. Adler and Russell F. Proctor II

1   We have already seen how experiences in the family, especially during childhood, shape our sense of who we are. Along with the messages we receive at home, many other forces shape our identity, and thus our communication, including age, physical ability/disability, sexual orientation, and socioeconomic status. Along with these forces, culture and **gender** are powerful forces in shaping how we view ourselves and others and how we communicate. We will examine each of these forces now.

What does the root word *gen* mean in the word *gender*?

Culture

2   Although we seldom recognize the fact, our sense of self is shaped, often in subtle ways, by the culture in which we have been reared. Most Western cultures are highly individualistic, whereas other traditional cultures—most Asian ones, for example—are much more collective. When asked to identify themselves, individualistic people in the United States, Canada, Australia, and Europe would probably respond by giving their first name, **surname**, street, town, and country. Many Asians do it the other way around. If you ask Hindus for

Underline the main idea of paragraph 2.

What is a synonym for the word *surname*?

(Continued)

their identity, they will give you their caste and village as well as their name. The Sanskrit formula for identifying one's self begins with lineage and goes on to state family, house, and ends with one's personal name. When members of different cultures were asked to create an "I am" list, those from collectivist cultures make far more group references than those from individualistic cultures.

Underline the main idea of paragraph 3.

3   These conventions for naming aren't just cultural curiosities: They reflect a very different way of viewing one's self and of what kinds of relationships are important. In collective cultures, a person gains identity by belonging to a group. This means that the perceived degree of **interdependence** among members of the society and its **subgroups** is high. Feelings of pride and self-worth are likely to be shaped not only by what the individual does but also by behavior of other members of the community. This linkage to others explains the traditional Asian denial of self-importance—a strong contrast to the self-promotion that is common in individualistic Western cultures. In Chinese written language, for example, the pronoun *I* looks very similar to the word for selfish. [Table 3.7 summarizes some differences between individualistic cultures and more collective ones.]

What do the prefixes *inter-* and *sub-* mean in *interdependence* and *subgroups*?

4   This sort of cultural difference isn't just a matter of interest to **anthropologists.** It shows up in the level of comfort or anxiety that people feel when communicating. In collective societies, there is a higher degree of communication apprehension. For example, as a group, residents of China, South Korea, and Japan exhibit a significantly higher degree of anxiety about speaking out than do members of individualistic cultures, such as the United States and Australia. It's important to realize that different levels of communication apprehension don't mean that shyness is a "problem" in some cultures. In fact, just the opposite is true: In these societies **reticence** is valued. To avoid being a standout, it's logical to feel nervous when you make yourself appear different by calling attention to yourself. A self-concept that includes "assertive" might make a Westerner feel proud, but in much of Asia it would more likely be cause for shame. As you can see, cultural difference is apparent in the comfort level people feel when interacting with others.

What does the root *anthro* mean in *anthropologists*?

Underline the main idea of paragraph 4.

Using context clues, what does the word *reticence* mean?

What type of context clue did you use?

5   The difference between individualism and collectivism shows up in everyday interaction. Communication researcher Stella Ting-Toomey has developed a theory that explains cultural differences in important norms, such as honesty and directness. She suggests that in individualistic Western cultures where there is a strong "I" orientation, the norm of speaking directly is honored, whereas in collectivistic cultures, where the main desire is to build connections between the self and others, indirect approaches that maintain harmony are considered more desirable. "I gotta be me" could be the motto of a Westerner, but "If I hurt you, I hurt myself" is closer to the Asian way of thinking.

Underline the main idea of paragraph 5.

6   You don't need to travel overseas to appreciate the influence of culture on the self. Within societies, **co-cultural** identity plays an important role in how we see ourselves and others. For example, ethnicity can have a powerful effect on how people think of themselves and how they communicate. There's no surprise here: If society keeps reminding you that your ethnicity is important, then you begin to think of yourself in those terms. If you are part of the dominant majority, you probably aren't as conscious of your ethnicity. Nonetheless, it plays an important part in your self-concept. Being part of the majority increases the chances that you have a sense of belonging to the society in which you live and of entitlement to being treated fairly. Members of less privileged ethnic groups often don't have these feelings.

What does the word co-cultural mean?

Underline the main idea of paragraph 6.

Sex and Gender

7   One way to appreciate the tremendous importance of gender on your sense of self is to imagine how your identity would be different if you had been born as a member of the opposite sex. Would you express your emotions in the same way? Deal with conflict? Relate to friends and strangers? The answer is almost certainly a resounding "no." Clearly, one's identity and sense of self is powerfully affected by gender.

Underline the main idea of paragraph 7.

8   From the earliest months of life, being male or female shapes the way others communicate with us, and thus how they shape our sense of self. Think about the first questions most people ask when a child is born. One of them is almost always "Is it a boy or a girl?" After most people know what the baby "is," they often behave accordingly. They use different pronouns

Underline the main idea of paragraph 8.

(Continued)

and often choose gender-related nicknames. With boys, comments often focus on size, strength, and activity; comments about girls more often address beauty, sweetness, and facial responsiveness. It's not surprising that these messages shape a child's sense of identity and how he or she will communicate. The **implicit** message is that some ways of behaving are masculine and others feminine. Little girls, for example, are more likely to be reinforced for acting "sweet" than are little boys. The same principle operates in adulthood: A man who stands up for his beliefs might get approval for being "tough" or "persistent," whereas a woman who behaves in the same way could be described by critics as a "nag" or "bitch." It's not hard to see how the gender roles and labels like these can have a profound effect on how men and women view themselves and on how they communicate.

What is a synonym for the word implicit*?*

9   Self-esteem is also influenced by gender. In a society that values competitiveness more in men than in women, it isn't surprising that the self-esteem of adolescent young men is closely related to having abilities that are superior in some way to those of their peers, whereas teenage women's self-worth is tied more closely to the success of their social relationships and verbal skills. Research also suggests that young women struggle more with self-esteem issues than do young men. For example, the self-esteem of about two-thirds of the males in one study (ages 14 to 23) increased. The same study revealed that about 57 percent of females in the same age group grew to feel *less* good about themselves.

Underline the main idea of paragraph 9.

10   Don't resign yourself to being a prisoner of expectations about your gender. Research demonstrates that our sense of self is shaped strongly by the people with whom we interact and by the contexts in which we communicate. For example, a **nonaggressive** young man who might feel **unwelcome** and **inept** in a macho environment might gain new self-esteem by finding others who appreciate his style of communicating. A woman whose self-esteem is stifled by the limited expectations of bosses and coworkers can look for more hospitable places to work. Children usually can't choose the reference groups that shape their identities, but adults can.

Underline the main idea of paragraph 10.

What do the prefixes non-*in* nonaggressive, un- *in* unwelcome, *and* in- *in* inept *mean?*

SOURCE: From ADLER/PROCTOR, *Looking Out, Looking In*, 13E.
© 2011 Cengage Learning.

COMPREHENSION CHECK

1 Fill in this chart with details that differentiate collective cultures from individualistic cultures.

CRITERIA	COLLECTIVE CULTURES	INDIVIDUALISTIC CULTURES
Self-identity		
Communication style		
Everyday interaction		
Communication apprehension		

2 Reread paragraph 6 and relate the ideas made here to American society. How might this theory apply to the following groups:

a. European Americans
b. Haitian Americans
c. Native Americans

d. African Americans
e. Mexican Americans
f. Korean Americans

_____

_____

_____

_____

3 In a paragraph, summarize how <u>culture</u> plays a role in the development of personal identity. _____

_____

_____

_____

_____

_____

4 In a paragraph, summarize how <u>gender</u> plays a role in the development of personal identity. _____

_____

_____

_____

_____

(Continued)

5   Consider the information in Table 3.7. Do you agree with the in-group and out-group perceptions? Add another example of a cultural difference in nonverbal communication.

TABLE 3.7 Cultural Differences in Nonverbal Communication Can Lead to Misunderstandings

Behaviors that have one meaning for members of the same culture or co-culture can be interpreted differently by members of other groups.

BEHAVIOR	PROBABLE IN-GROUP PERCEPTION	POSSIBLE OUT-GROUP PERCEPTION
Avoidance of direct eye contact (Latino/a)	Used to communicate attentiveness or respect	A sign of inattentiveness; direct eye contact is preferred.
Aggressively challenging a point with which one disagrees (African American)	Acceptable means of dialogue; not regarded as verbal abuse or a precursor to violence	Arguments are viewed as inappropriate and a sign of potential imminent violence.
Use of finger gestures to beckon others (Asian)	Appropriate if used by adults for children, but highly offensive if directed at adults	Appropriate gesture to use with both children and adults
Silence (Native American)	Sign of respect, thoughtfulness, and/or uncertainty/ambiguity	Interpreted as boredom, disagreement, or refusal to participate
Touch (Latino/a)	Normal and appropriate for interpersonal interactions	Deemed appropriate for some intimate or friendly interactions; otherwise perceived as a violation of personal space
Public display of intense emotions (African American)	Accepted and valued as measure of expressiveness; appropriate in most settings	Violates expectations for self-controlled public behaviors; inappropriate in most public settings
Touching or holding hands of same-sex friends (Asian)	Acceptable in behavior that signifies closeness in platonic relationships	Perceived as inappropriate, especially for male friends
Your Example:		

READING GRAPHICS

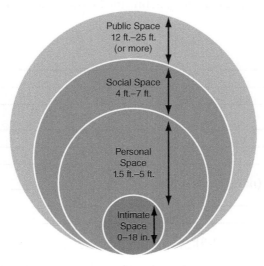

FIGURE 3.5 Proxemics: Interpersonal Distances.

Based on Edward T. Hall's concept of proxemics in The Hidden Dimension. Hall coined the term proxemics in 1963 to denote the different kinds of distance that occur between people. These distances vary between cultures.

1. What is the topic of Figure 3.5? _____

2. What is the pattern of organization of this figure? _____

3. What is the main idea of Figure 3.5? _____
_____

4. These proxemics relate to American culture. Draw a diagram for interpersonal space for any culture, based on information in this reading, Table 3.7, Cultural Differences in Nonverbal Communication Can Lead to Misunderstandings, or your own experiences.

(Continued)

DEVELOPING YOUR COLLEGE-LEVEL VOCABULARY

In your own words and based on the reading, define the following key terms from context clues.

1. Culture (paragraph 1): _____
   _____
   _____

2. Identity (paragraph 1): _____
   _____
   _____

3. Individualistic cultures (paragraphs 2, 3): _____
   _____
   _____

4. Collective cultures (paragraphs 2, 3): _____
   _____
   _____

5. Anthropologist (paragraph 4): _____
   _____
   _____

6. Communication apprehension (paragraph 4): _____
   _____
   _____

7. Co-culture (paragraph 6): _____
   _____
   _____

8. Gender (paragraph 7): _____
   _____
   _____

9. Sex (paragraph 7): _____
   _____
   _____

OUR MULTICULTURAL LANGUAGE

Although the term *multicultural* has only recently come into popular usage, our society and our language have always been multicultural (Carnes, 1994). Do you know the cultural origins of the following everyday words?

1.	brocade	3.	cotton	5.	khaki	7.	skunk	9.	noodle
2.	chocolate	4.	klutz	6.	silk	8.	gingham	10.	Zombie

Source: From WOOD, *Interpersonal Communication*, 7E. © 2013 Cengage Learning.

THEMATIC CONNECTIONS

1. Think of a time where there was a cultural difference between you and someone else. What was the situation? What was the misunderstanding? Why did the misunderstanding occur?

2. Imagine you are the CEO of an international business. Choose the geographical arena that you serve, and outline an action plan for relating to your new employees based on a cultural worldview.

3. Reread the article about "Global Business Customs and Etiquette" on page 198. Discuss a culture mentioned in this reading and outline the "worldview" of that group, based on information you have read about in Application 2.

4. Think of your upbringing. Do you feel that your identity is strongly affected by your gender?

5. Talk to a relative, friend, or coworker from a different generation than yours (a generation is roughly defined as a 25-year span). In your estimation, has the role of gender changed in its power to dictate behavior and shape self-image? Is there less power to gender roles now than in previous generations in the United States?

6. In paragraph 10, the author mentions a "macho environment." Is this environment lessening in recent years? Should we seek to lessen it?

7. Do different co-cultures in the United States emphasize masculinity differently? Choose an American subculture, and outline expected behaviors for males and females.

8. In which American subculture are the differences between the sexes in terms of social roles most pronounced? In which subculture are the differences between the sexes in terms of social roles least pronounced? Support your perspective using specific examples.

9. Think about cultural holidays or religious holidays in which you participate: St. Patrick's Day, Cinco de Mayo, Kwanza, Purim, Ramadan, and others. How do you relate your participation in these festivities to your personal identity?

Answers to Our Multicultural Language: 1, Spanish; 2, Nahuatl (Native American); 3, Arabic; 4, Yiddish; 5, Hindi; 6, Greek; 7, Algonquin (Native American); 8, Malay; 9, German; 10, Bantu (Congolese).

WRAPPING IT UP

In the following study outline, fill in the definitions and a brief explanation of the key terms in the "Your Notes" column. Use the strategy of spaced practice to review these key terms on a regular basis. Use this study guide to review this chapter's key topics.

KEY TERM OR CONCEPT	YOUR NOTES
Author's purpose	
To inform	
To instruct	
To persuade	
To entertain	
Main idea	
Topic sentence	
Thesis	
Summary	
Root word	

GROUP ACTIVITY: CULTURAL ANTHROPOLOGIST PROJECT

Cultural anthropologists study different cultures throughout the world. One of the important aspects of being a cultural anthropologist is to try to see other cultures objectively and not impose ethnocentric judgments and cultural norms onto others.

Use a search engine to find additional information about another culture on the Internet. Present your findings to the class for group discussion. Topics might include the following:

- Intercultural business
- Intercultural dating
- Norms and behaviors in other cultures that differ from yours

- Gender issues in communication
- Communication issues in relationships
- Subcultures in the United States

REFLECTIVE JOURNAL QUESTIONS

1. In your other classes, how can finding the main idea in readings help you to prepare for class discussions and tests? How will you employ this strategy in your college reading?

2. Choose a passage of about a page in length from a text you are reading for another class. Summarize this passage using the skills you have learned.

THEMATIC CONNECTIONS

Respond to one of the following questions. Prepare notes for class discussion or write a response to submit to your instructor.

1. What do you believe is the most significant reason for gender miscommunication? What do you think can be done to lessen the "war between the sexes"?

2. Several readings in this chapter concern differences between cultures and how those differences impact communication. Based on these readings, choose three strategies you think would be effective in increasing understanding within and among subcultures in our country.

3. What are the qualities needed for an individual to overcome communication problems with other cultures, in business or dating, for example? Choose three qualities (behaviors, techniques, or attitudes) that characterize successful intercultural communication. Support your answer with specific examples.

ADDITIONAL SKILL AND STRATEGY PRACTICE

Finding Directly Stated Main Ideas

Using all you have learned about finding main ideas in this chapter, underline the topic sentence in the following paragraphs.

1. Persons like Eduardo have an **ambivalent attachment style**, marked by mixed emotions about relationships. Conflicting feelings of affection, anger, emotional turmoil, physical attraction, and doubt leave them in an unsettled, ambivalent state. Often, ambivalent persons regard themselves as misunderstood and unappreciated. They tend to see their friends and lovers as unreliable and unable or unwilling to commit themselves to lasting relationships. Ambivalent persons worry that their romantic partners don't really love them or may leave them. Although they want to be extremely close to their partners, they are also preoccupied with doubts about the partner's dependability and trustworthiness.

   —From COON, *Introduction to Psychology*, 12E. © 2010 Cengage Learning.

2. Similarity refers to how alike you are to another person in background, age, interests, attitudes, beliefs, and so forth. In everything from casual acquaintance to marriage, similar people are attracted to each other. And why not? It's reinforcing to see our beliefs and attitudes shared by others. It shows we are "right" and reveals that they are clever people as well!

   —From COON, *Introduction to Psychology*, 12E. © 2010 Cengage Learning.

3. Inflammatory speech by young people is nothing new, and neither is adults' desire to suppress it. In 1908, the Wisconsin Supreme Court ruled that school officials could suspend two students who ridiculed their teachers in a poem in a local newspaper. Seven years later, a California appellate court said a student could be suspended for criticizing school officials in an assembly.

   —"Cyberbullying" by litteri, T.J., *CQ Researcher*, 18, 385–408, May 2, 2008 (Retrieved from http://library.

   cqpress.com).

4. *So similarity also influences mate selection?* Yes, in choosing a mate we tend to marry someone who is like us in almost every way, a pattern called homogamy (huh-MOG-ah-me). Studies show that married couples are highly similar in age, education, ethnicity, and religion. To a lesser degree, they are also similar in attitudes and opinions, mental abilities, status, height, weight, and eye color. In case you're wondering, homogamy also applies to unmarried couples who are living together Homogamy is probably a good thing. The risk of divorce is highest among couples with sizable differences in age and education.

   —From COON, *Introduction to Psychology*, 12E. © 2010 Cengage Learning.

5. OK, so he (or she) is someone you are familiar with, appears to share a lot in common with you, and is hot to boot. What else do you need to know before taking it to the next level? Well, it would be nice to know if he or she is also the least bit interested in you. In fact, reciprocity, which occurs when people respond to each other in similar ways, may be the most important factor influencing the development of friendships. Most people find it easier to reciprocate to someone else's overtures than to be the initiator. That way, at least the embarrassment of an outright rejection can be avoided.

   —From COON, *Introduction to Psychology*, 12E. © 2010 Cengage Learning.

6. Self-disclosure involves an exchange of personal information, but other exchanges also occur. In fact, many relationships can be understood as an ongoing series of social exchanges (transfers of attention, information, affection, favors, and the like between two people). In many social

exchanges, people try to maximize their rewards while minimizing their "costs." When a friendship or love relationship ceases to be attractive, people often say, "I'm not getting anything out of it anymore." Actually, they probably are, but their costs—in terms of effort, irritation, or lowered self-esteem— have exceeded their rewards.

—From COON, *Introduction to Psychology*, 12E. © 2010 Cengage Learning.

7.   Charlene's **avoidant attachment style** reflects a fear of intimacy and a tendency to resist commitment to others. Avoidant persons tend to pull back when things don't go well in a relationship. The avoidant person is suspicious, aloof, and skeptical about love. She or he tends to see others as either unreliable or overly eager to commit to a relationship. As a result, avoidant persons find it hard to completely trust and depend on others. Avoidant persons get nervous when anyone gets too close emotionally. Basically, they avoid intimacy.

—From COON, *Introduction to Psychology*, 12E. © 2010 Cengage Learning.

8.   *How could emotional attachments early in life affect adult relationships?* It appears that we use early attachment experiences to build mental models about affectionate relationships. Later, we use these models as a sort of blueprint for forming, maintaining, and breaking bonds of love and affection. Thus, the quality of childhood bonds to parents or other caregivers may hold a key to understanding how we approach romantic relationships. Maybe it's no accident that persons who are romantically available are often described as "unattached."

—From COON, *Introduction to Psychology*, 12E. © 2010 Cengage Learning.

9.   Aggression is expressed in many forms. One pervasive form is **bullying**, any behavior that deliberately and repeatedly exposes a person to negative experiences. Bullies tend to deal with everyday situations by resorting to aggression. Bullying can be *verbal* (name-calling, insults, teasing) or *physical* (hitting, pushing, confining), and it can also be *direct* ("in your face") or *indirect* (intentional exclusion, spreading rumors). Whereas male bullies are more likely to engage in direct aggression, female bullies tend to specialize in indirect aggression. Bullying is a worldwide phenomenon. It first appears in early childhood, continues throughout adolescence into adulthood and the workplace, and can even be found online, in the form of *cyberbullying*.

—From COON, *Introduction to Psychology*, 12E. © 2010 Cengage Learning.

10.   Is it any wonder that people who were the victims of violence during childhood are likely to become violent themselves? Social learning theorists predict that people growing up in nonaggressive cultures will themselves be nonaggressive. Those raised in a culture with aggressive models and heroes will learn aggressive responses. Considered in such terms, it is no wonder that America has become one of the most violent of all countries. A violent crime occurred every 23 seconds in the United States during 2008. Approximately 38 percent of U.S. households own at least one firearm. Nationally, 70 percent agree that when a boy is growing up, it is "very important" for him to have a few fistfights. Children and adults are treated to an almost nonstop parade of aggressive models, in the media as well as in actual behavior. We are, without a doubt, an aggressive culture.

—From COON, *Introduction to Psychology*, 12E. © 2010 Cengage Learning.

POST-ASSESSMENT   PSYCHOLOGY MAGAZINE

Preview the following article and then read it all the way through. Then go to the end of the article and answer the questions. This assessment will help you determine your strengths and weaknesses in understanding, learning, and applying the skills and strategies discussed in this chapter.

The Pitfalls of E-mail
by Marina Krakovsky

1   We assume that the opportunity to edit our written words means we put our best foot forward, but a recent study suggests that communicating via e-mail alone can doom a relationship.

2   [1]Janice Nadler, a social psychologist and Northwestern University law professor, paired Northwestern law students with those from Duke University and asked each pair to agree on the purchase of a car. [2]Researchers instructed each team to bargain entirely through e-mail, but half the subjects were secretly told to precede the negotiation with a brief getting-to-know-you chat on the phone. [3]The results were dramatic: Negotiators who first chatted by phone were more than four times likelier to reach an agreement than those who used only e-mail. [4]In the study, which will appear in the *Harvard Negotiation Law Review*, subjects who never spoke were not only more likely to hit an impasse but they often felt resentful and angry about the negotiation.

3   [1]While all sorts of online exchanges can be misunderstood, social scientists say that face-less strangers are especially likely to run into problems. [2]"Through that initial phone call, people become real," says Susan Barnes, a professor of communication at Rochester Institute of Technology in New York. [3]Simply foregoing common pleasantries can make a message come across as rude—especially if communicators don't know each other. [4]A rushed e-mail may give the impression that the exchange is unimportant. [5]And, because first impressions set the tone for subsequent interaction, Barnes says, the exchange can quickly go downhill.

4   [1]Nadler says the missing element in electronic communication is rapport, that in-sync state that's easier to establish in person or by phone. [2]Facial expressions, gestures, tone of voice—all these social cues are missing in e-mail (and smiley-face "emoticons" can do only so much to replace them). [3]But because messages travel almost instantly, people act as if they're in a face-to-face conversation, says David Falcone, a psychology professor at La Salle University in Philadelphia. [4]Because of this illusion of proximity, we're duped into thinking we can communicate about touchy subjects, such as disagreements or criticisms, and that the tone of our writing will be perceived correctly.

5   [1]Furthermore, says Nadler, just because we can send a message anytime doesn't mean someone is there to receive it. [2]Yet people often fear a delayed reply is a potential blow-off.

6   [1]And when we feel slighted, we are more apt to throw a fit via e-mail than we would by phone. [2]"The anonymity of e-mail leads to rudeness," says Barnes, adding we may not feel accountable, especially if we've never actually spoken to the other person. [3]Even if we mean well, the lack of second-by-second feedback, by which we constantly adjust our words in conversation, can cause us to go on blithely composing messages that will rub the recipient the wrong way. [4]John Suler, a psychologist at New Jersey's Rider University who specializes in cyberspace behavior, believes that talking first on the phone might set expectations at an appropriate level—an effect that then carries over into the e-mail relationship.

7   [1]The less we know someone, the more likely we are to engage in what therapists call transference, the tendency to project our desires or fears onto another person. [2]Without social cues, says Falcone, these tendencies can run wild, causing us to interpret messages in ways that are "overly self-affirming and, potentially, extremely inaccurate." [3]Suler adds that in the negotiation study, the initial phone call may have served as a "transference antidote," making the partners more real to each other.

COMPREHENSION CHECK

Circle the best answer to the following questions.

Reading Comprehension

1   **What is the topic of this reading?**

   A. E-mail

   B. E-mail, relationships, and communication

   C. E-mails and relationships

   D. Relationships and cyberspace

2   **What is the overall pattern of organization?**

   A. Comparison and contrast

   B. Sequence or process order

   C. Cause and effect

   D. Definition and example

3   **What is the author's purpose in writing this article?**

   A. To inform

   B. To persuade

   C. To entertain

   D. To persuade and inform

(Continued)

4 **Which sentence expresses the thesis of the article?**

   A. We assume that the opportunity to edit our written words means we put our best foot forward, but a recent study suggests that communicating via e-mail alone can doom a relationship.

   B. Negotiators who first chatted by phone were more than four times likelier to reach an agreement than those who used only e-mail.

   C. And when we feel slighted, we are more apt to throw a fit via e-mail than we would by phone.

   D. The less we know someone, the more likely we are to engage in what therapists call transference, the tendency to project our desires or fears onto another person.

5 **What is the topic sentence of paragraph 3?**

   A. Sentence 1
   B. Sentence 2
   C. Sentence 3
   D. Sentence 4

6 **What is the topic sentence of paragraph 4?**

   A. Sentence 1
   B. Sentence 2
   C. Sentence 3
   D. Sentence 4

7 **What is the topic sentence of paragraph 6?**

   A. Sentence 1
   B. Sentence 2
   C. Sentence 3
   D. The main idea is implied.

8 **What is the topic sentence of paragraph 7?**

   A. Sentence 1
   B. Sentence 2
   C. Sentence 3
   D. The main idea is implied.

Vocabulary Comprehension

9 **What does the word *psychologist* mean, based on the root word?**

Janice Nadler, a social <u>psychologist</u> and Northwestern University law professor, paired Northwestern law students with those from Duke University and asked each pair to agree on the purchase of a car.

A. One who studies communication
B. One who studies the mind
C. The study of society
D. One who communicates

10 **What is the meaning of the underlined word in the following sentence from paragraph 7?**

The less we know someone, the more likely we are to engage in what therapists call <u>transference</u>, the tendency to project our desires or fears onto another person.

A. The measure of how much we know another person.
B. Making another person fearful in light of our desires.
C. Feeling afraid of another person's empowerment through therapy.
D. Projecting our own fears onto another person.

4

Understanding
IMPLIED MAIN IDEAS

✳ Why Do You Need to Know This?

What do you do when an author suggests a main idea, but you cannot find it explicitly stated in one sentence in the reading? In this chapter, you will strengthen your skills by making inferences to understand an author's implied main idea. Finding implied main ideas is often perceived to be difficult and, initially, it is. However, you will learn that implied main ideas are not that difficult to find. The key is to always consider *in your head* what the point is in any reading based on topic and structure. If you approach any reading this way, confirming if the point is explicit or implied is not so hard; you have already inferred the main point. Furthermore, you draw conclusions and make inferences about situations and people's behaviors

IN THIS CHAPTER, YOU WILL LEARN

- To make reasonable inferences and draw logical conclusions
- To locate and understand an author's implied main idea
- To understand graphics: identifying implied main ideas in visual aids and cartoons

A READING STUDY STRATEGY

- Identifying common poetic and literary devices to unlock the meaning of stories and poems

VOCABULARY STRATEGIES

- Identifying and describing subtleties in figurative language
- Increasing your discipline-specific vocabulary: literature

Robert Churchill/iStockphoto.com

" **THE NOSE OF A MOB IS ITS IMAGINATION. BY THIS, AT ANY TIME, IT CAN BE QUIETLY LED.** "
EDGAR ALLAN POE American poet, critic, and short-story writer (1809–1845)

all the time outside of reading. For example, you may look at facial expressions and body language to make an inference about how someone is feeling. In doing this, you have formulated an implied main idea about that person's emotions. In any given reading, a successful college student must answer this question, when reading: What is the author's most important point about the topic?

In this chapter, you will read about how people think and behave in groups as a result of peer pressure or conformity. Sometimes people have psychological reactions that you do not expect. Sometimes the consequences are both surprising and destructive. If you witnessed a crime, you would go for help . . . wouldn't you? If you were the victim of a crime, you would be safer with a lot of other people around, wouldn't you?

✔ **CHECK YOUR PRIOR KNOWLEDGE**

Jot down some ideas about how people behave in groups. Do not edit your list—just brainstorm!

_____

_____

_____

_____

_____

_____

_____

_____

_____

_____

_____

_____

_____

❧ PRE-ASSESSMENT   ONLINE ACADEMIC SUMMARY

Read the passage and then answer the questions that follow. Don't worry if you do not know what all the terms mean. The purpose of this Pre-Assessment is to find out how much you already know about the reading skills and strategies introduced in this chapter.

Milgram's Experiment on Obedience to Authority
by Gregorio Billikopf Encina

1   Why is it so many people obey when they feel **coerced**? Social psychologist Stanley Milgram researched the effect of authority on obedience. He concluded people obey either out of fear or out of a desire to appear cooperative—even when acting against their own better judgment and desires. Milgram's classic yet controversial experiment illustrates people's reluctance to confront those who abuse power.

2   Milgram recruited subjects for his experiments from various walks in life. Respondents were told the experiment would study the effects of punishment on learning ability. They were offered a token cash award for participating. Although respondents thought they had an equal chance of playing the role of a student or of a teacher, the process was rigged so all respondents ended up playing the teacher. The learner was an actor working as a cohort of the experimenter.

3   "Teachers" were asked to administer increasingly severe electric shocks to the "learner" when questions were answered incorrectly. In reality, the only electric shocks delivered in the experiment were single 45-volt shock samples given to each teacher. This was done to give teachers a feeling for the jolts they thought they would be discharging.

4   Shock levels were labeled from 15 to 450 volts. Besides the numerical scale, verbal anchors added to the frightful appearance of the instrument. Beginning from the lower end, jolt levels were labeled: "slight shock," "moderate shock," "strong shock," "very strong shock," "intense shock," and "extreme intensity shock." The next two anchors were "Danger: Severe Shock," and, past that, a simple but ghastly "XXX."

5   In response to the supposed jolts, the "learner" (actor) would begin to grunt at 75 volts; complain at 120 volts; ask to be released at 150 volts; plead with increasing vigor, next; and let out agonized screams at 285 volts. Eventually, in desperation, the learner was to yell loudly and complain of heart pain.

6   At some point the actor would refuse to answer any more questions. Finally, at 330 volts the actor would be totally silent—that is, if any of the teacher participants got so far without rebelling first.

7   Teachers were instructed to treat silence as an incorrect answer and apply the next shock level to the student.

8   If at any point the innocent teacher hesitated to inflict the shocks, the experimenter would pressure him to proceed. Such demands would take the form of increasingly severe statements, such as "The experiment *requires* that you continue."

9   What do you think was the average voltage given by teachers before they refused to administer further shocks? What percentage of teachers, if any, do you think went up to the maximum voltage of 450?

10   *Results from the experiment.* Some teachers refused to continue with the shocks early on, despite urging from the experimenter. This is the type of response Milgram expected as the norm. But Milgram was shocked to find those who questioned authority were in the minority. Sixty-five percent (65%) of the teachers were willing to progress to the maximum voltage level.

11   Participants demonstrated a range of negative emotions about continuing. Some pleaded with the learner, asking the actor to answer questions carefully. Others started to laugh nervously and act strangely in diverse ways. Some subjects appeared cold, hopeless, somber, or arrogant. Some thought they had killed the learner. Nevertheless, participants continued to obey, discharging the full shock to learners. One man who wanted to abandon the experiment was told the experiment must continue. Instead of challenging the decision of the experimenter, he proceeded, repeating to himself, "It's got to go on, it's got to go on."

12   Milgram's experiment included a number of variations. In one, the learner was not only visible but teachers were asked to force the learner's hand to the shock plate so they could deliver the punishment. Less obedience was extracted from subjects in this case. In another variation, teachers were instructed to apply whatever voltage they desired to incorrect answers. Teachers averaged 83 volts, and only 2.5 percent of participants used the full 450 volts available. This shows most participants were good, average people, not evil individuals. They obeyed only under coercion.

13   In general, more submission was elicited from "teachers" when (1) the authority figure was in close proximity; (2) teachers felt they could pass on responsibility to others; and (3) experiments took place under the auspices of a respected organization.

14   Participants were debriefed after the experiment and showed much relief at finding they had not harmed the student. One cried from emotion when he saw the student alive, and explained that he thought he had killed him. But what was different about those who obeyed and those who rebelled? Milgram divided participants into three categories:

15   *Obeyed but justified themselves.* Some obedient participants gave up responsibility for their actions, blaming the experimenter. If anything had happened to the learner, they reasoned, it would have been the experimenter's fault. Others had transferred the blame to the learner: "He was so stupid and stubborn he deserved to be shocked."

16   *Obeyed but blamed themselves.* Others felt badly about what they had done and were quite harsh on themselves. Members of this group would, perhaps, be more likely to challenge authority if confronted with a similar situation in the future.

17   *Rebelled.* Finally, rebellious subjects questioned the authority of the experimenter and argued there was a greater <u>ethical imperative</u> calling for the protection of the learner over the needs of the experimenter. Some of these individuals felt they were accountable to a higher authority.

(Continued)

18   Why were those who challenged authority in the minority? So entrenched is obedience it may void personal codes of conduct.

COMPREHENSION CHECK

Circle the best answer to the following questions.

Reading Comprehension

1 **What is the author's purpose in writing?**

A. To persuade

B. To inform

C. To instruct

D. To entertain

2 **In this reading, the supporting information to back up the author's claim is organized according to which pattern?**

A. Comparison and contrast

B. Definition and example

C. Sequence or process order

D. Simple listing

3 **What is the topic of this reading?**

A. Obedience to authority

B. People and cruelty

C. Humans and experiments for research

D. Humans and learning

4 **What is the thesis of the whole reading or most important point about the topic?**

A. Humans are unlikely to bow to social conformity.

B. Humans learn from their environment and this learning overcomes conformity.

C. Stanley Milgram researched obedience to authority and concluded people obey either out of fear or out of a desire to appear cooperative—even when acting against their own better judgment and desires.

D. Human culture is corrupt and evil is innate.

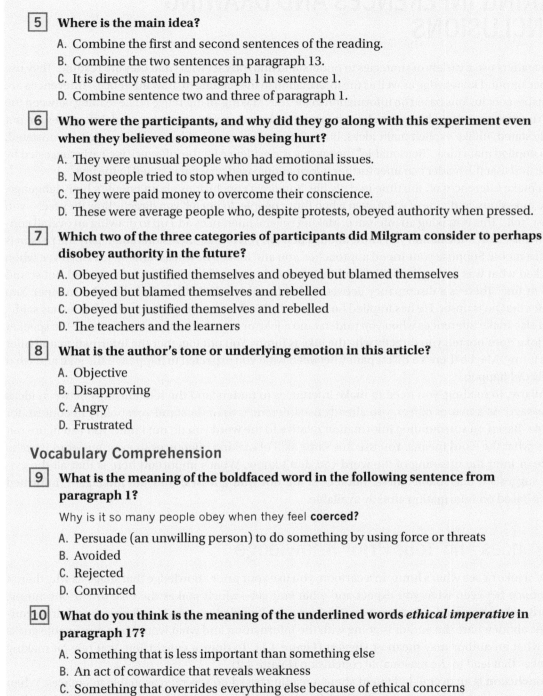

5 **Where is the main idea?**

A. Combine the first and second sentences of the reading.

B. Combine the two sentences in paragraph 13.

C. It is directly stated in paragraph 1 in sentence 1.

D. Combine sentence two and three of paragraph 1.

6 **Who were the participants, and why did they go along with this experiment even when they believed someone was being hurt?**

A. They were unusual people who had emotional issues.

B. Most people tried to stop when urged to continue.

C. They were paid money to overcome their conscience.

D. These were average people who, despite protests, obeyed authority when pressed.

7 **Which two of the three categories of participants did Milgram consider to perhaps disobey authority in the future?**

A. Obeyed but justified themselves and obeyed but blamed themselves

B. Obeyed but blamed themselves and rebelled

C. Obeyed but justified themselves and rebelled

D. The teachers and the learners

8 **What is the author's tone or underlying emotion in this article?**

A. Objective

B. Disapproving

C. Angry

D. Frustrated

Vocabulary Comprehension

9 **What is the meaning of the boldfaced word in the following sentence from paragraph 1?**

Why is it so many people obey when they feel **coerced**?

A. Persuade (an unwilling person) to do something by using force or threats

B. Avoided

C. Rejected

D. Convinced

10 **What do you think is the meaning of the underlined words *ethical imperative* in paragraph 17?**

A. Something that is less important than something else

B. An act of cowardice that reveals weakness

C. Something that overrides everything else because of ethical concerns

D. Something that is tempting and encourages rebellion

MAKING INFERENCES AND DRAWING CONCLUSIONS

Active readers use a variety of strategies to understand and interact with what they are reading. They use their background knowledge as well as the information in the reading to draw inferences. **Inferences** are reasonable conclusions based on information in the text. Making an inference is like reading between the lines: You make a reasonable guess about information based on what you have read. Inferences are not directly stated, unlike explicit main ideas, but inferences are *reasonable* conclusions that are unstated, like an implied main idea. "Reasonable" means that the evidence for the inference is clearly suggested by the text and that the reader can infer further information based on what is stated in the text.

You make inferences all the time in daily life. You draw conclusions about people's body language, facial expressions, and tone of voice even when those people do not tell you directly how they feel—you can just "tell." This is making an inference. Making several inferences add up to drawing an overall conclusion. Based on information you know about a person, you draw conclusions about *why* the person is in such a mood. Suppose your friend approached you and looked downcast and upset. However, when you asked what was wrong, he said, "Nothing, everything's fine," but his tone of voice did not sound happy or fine. There is a discrepancy between what he said and what you feel about his manner. You can infer that he is upset. He has implied he is upset by his downcast mood, despite what he has said.

You also make inferences when you understand a joke or see what's funny in a cartoon. The speaker of the joke does not tell you directly why the joke is funny. You put together the information and infer what's funny. Maybe there's a discrepancy between what you expected to happen in the joke and what actually did happen.

Similarly, in reading, you need to make inferences to understand the relationships between ideas in a passage. As a matter of fact, you already use inferences to understand vocabulary in context, for example. Based on surrounding information relative to the word you do not know, you can figure out or infer what the word means. You use this same skill of making inferences to examine word parts to deduce or infer the meaning of the word you don't know. What's important here is that all the evidence suggests a reasonable guess. Inferences are not wild guesses; they are intelligent, informed guesses based on information already available.

Inferences and Your Prior Knowledge

To "get" a joke or see what's funny in a cartoon, you use your prior knowledge that suggests why there's a difference between what you expect and what you get—which makes the joke or cartoon funny. Similarly, when you read a passage, you use your prior knowledge to make inferences and draw conclusions about where the author is going with the information and what would be a reasonable guess about what an author may mean or suggest (Figure 4.1). To draw a conclusion, you rely on making inferences that lead to the reasonable conclusion (Figure 4.2).

A **conclusion** is an overall judgment about a reading based on several reasonable inferences. When you determine an overall implied main idea of a whole reading, you are drawing a conclusion based on both stated and unstated main ideas in each of the reading's body paragraphs. You know from Chapter 3 that the main ideas of body paragraphs in a reading become the major supporting details for the whole

Inference

FIGURE 4.1 Inferring with Background Knowledge

Conclusion

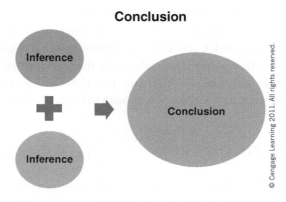

FIGURE 4.2 Inferences Lead to Conclusions

reading. When you consider a series of main ideas in the body paragraphs of a longer passage, you can infer or deduce what the author's overall point may be. In doing this, you have inferred the **implied main idea** of a reading. This is called an *implied* main idea because the author strongly implies or suggests the overall point. The overall point is not a wild guess, but a guess predicated on a series of pieces of information: the topic, how it is organized, the author's purpose, and the major supporting details.

Making inferences and drawing conclusions in reading are common. Here are a few ways readers make inferences:

- Using context clues
- Using word structure clues (structural analysis)
- Predicting what will happen next in a reading
- Predicting how the information in a reading will be structured
- Determining implied main ideas
- Determining the mood or tone of a reading from the author's choice of word
- Understanding how a character feels
- Understanding events in a reading and why they happened
- Comprehending the author's side on an issue
- Relating to a reading by using background knowledge

QUICK TIPS
STEPS TO MAKING INFERENCES AND DRAWING CONCLUSIONS

1. Consider what each sentence says about the topic.

2. Ask yourself this question: What is a reasonable conclusion to make about this passage based on the information provided in the text?

Most of the time, an author intends to make a deliberate impression and intends for the reader to draw certain inferences and conclusions. Sometimes, however, readers draw conclusions that the author did not intend. As a reader, you must be careful to draw reasonable conclusions based on reasonable inferences. In other words, the evidence in the text must provide the support for your conclusion. You cannot make a reasonable inference based on background knowledge or guessing alone—you must be able to support your conclusion with evidence from the reading.

Thinking It Through   MAKING REASONABLE INFERENCES AND DRAWING LOGICAL CONCLUSIONS

Here is a passage from a historical overview of the Salem witch trials. You can read the entire article in Application 1 at the end of this chapter.

> The Salem witch trials occurred in colonial Massachusetts between 1692 and 1693. More than 200 people were accused of practicing witchcraft—the Devil's magic—and 20 were executed. Eventually, the colony admitted the trials were a mistake and compensated the families of those convicted. Since then, the story of the trials has become synonymous with paranoia and injustice, and it continues to beguile the popular imagination more than 300 years later.

SOURCE: "A Brief History of the Salem Witch Trials" by Jess Blumberg. Copyright 2012 Smithsonian Institution. Reprinted with permission from Smithsonian Enterprises. All rights reserved. Reproduction in any medium is strictly prohibited without permission from Smithsonian Institution. Such permission may be requested from Smithsonian Enterprises.

Put a check mark next to the inferences that are reasonable, based on the text.

___ 1. The Salem witch trials lasted for a short period of time.

___ 2. Most people who were accused were not convicted of witchcraft.

___ 3. Practicing the "Devil's magic" was a crime punishable by death.

___ 4. The people who engaged in these accusations eventually realized that there were other explanations for the bizarre behavior thought to be caused by the devil.

___ 5. Families probably received money as compensation for those executed for witchcraft years later.

___ 6. The families of those compensated were happy about the compensation.

___ 7. There were crimes more severe than practicing witchcraft, crimes that ensured a more brutal penalty.

If you put a check mark beside the first five of these statements, you are correct. The first five statements are reasonable inferences based on the text. Here is why:

1. The Salem witch trials occurred only during the years of 1692 and 1693—a relatively short period of time.

2. If only 20 people were executed while 200 were accused of witchcraft, 1 in 10 being convicted indicates that most people were not convicted of the crime of which they were accused.

3. Because those convicted of witchcraft during this period were executed, it is reasonable to assume that practicing the "Devil's magic" was a crime punishable by death.

4. Because the passage states that "Eventually, the colony admitted the trials were a mistake," it is reasonable to assume that some other rational explanation was thought to have accounted for these accusations as being other than possession by the devil.

5. Compensation usually refers to money, though this is not directly stated.

Statements 6 and 7 are not reasonable inferences.

6. This is unreasonable as it would be unlikely that the families would feel okay about losing a loved one to such a punishment.

7. This is an unreasonable inference because there is no punishment that would be more severe than execution.

Now, which of the following statements would be a reasonable conclusion based on the paragraph? Put a check mark next to the reasonable conclusions.

___ 1. The Salem witch trials were a short but frenzied period of mass hysteria and paranoia.

___ 2. The devil probably left the Salem area, accounting for the short period of time in which the witch trials took place.

___ 3. People need to learn about the Salem witch trials to be aware of how the powers of paranoia and mass hysteria can result in terrible injustice.

___ 4. Only a small number of those who were accused were actually convicted of practicing witchcraft because the people of Salem were fair and just.

___ 5. While we may not believe we could act in such an unjust way, history tells us that we can and do; the Salem witch trials are but one example of the power of the group.

Because reasonable conclusions are based on what is suggested or explicitly stated in the text, some of the statements are not reasonable. Consider these explanations.

(Continued)

1. This is a reasonable conclusion because the trial only lasted a year (based on an inference explained above). However, the number of people accused and the number of people convicted strongly suggests that the people of Salem were hysterical and panic-stricken, resulting in the trials.

2. Personal beliefs aside, based on the evidence provided in the text, there is no suggestion of this being a reasonable conclusion to draw. In contrast, there are several statements that suggest the people of Salem were at fault, rather than the devil himself:
   a. Eventually, the colony admitted the trials were a mistake and compensated the families of those convicted.
   b. Story of the trials has become synonymous with paranoia and injustice.
   c. It continues to beguile the popular imagination more than 300 years later.

3. This is a reasonable conclusion to draw because the Salem witch trials are a classic case of what group behavior can lead to when people are scared. This conclusion is strongly suggested by the last two sentences in the passage, as well as the number of people accused and the number executed in just one year's time.

4. This is not an accurate conclusion. According to the passage, while the people of Salem eventually realized that the witch trials were unjust, the enormous number of people accused (200) and the number of people convicted (20) suggests that the people of Salem were neither fair nor just.

5. This is a reasonable conclusion to draw. Again, the last two sentences state that the trials are known for the degree of paranoia and injustice. While we may not execute people for being witches these days, the historical event suggests that human nature may play a part in what happened then, and we need to learn from these events so they are not repeated in a different form.

On Your Own MAKING REASONABLE INFERENCES AND DRAWING LOGICAL CONCLUSIONS

Next are two paragraphs from the same reading about the Salem witch trials. With a partner, write three reasonable inferences based on this passage. In addition, write two reasonable conclusions you can draw based on inferences you can make based on the passage. Be prepared to defend your answers, citing evidence from the paragraphs. Discuss your answers in a small group or in class discussion.

1   In 1689, English rulers William and Mary started a war with France in the American colonies. Known as King William's War to colonists, it ravaged regions of upstate New York, Nova Scotia, and Quebec, sending refugees into the county of Essex and, specifically, Salem Village in the Massachusetts Bay Colony. (Salem Village is present-day Danvers, Massachusetts; colonial Salem Town became what's now Salem.)

2   The displaced people created a strain on Salem's resources. This aggravated the existing rivalry between families with ties to the wealth of the port of Salem and those who still depended on agriculture. Controversy also brewed over Reverend Samuel Parris, who became Salem Village's first ordained minister in 1689, and was disliked because of his rigid ways and greedy nature. The Puritan villagers believed all the quarreling was the work of the devil.

Inference 1: _____

_____

Inference 2: _____

_____

Inference 3: _____

_____

Conclusion 1: _____

_____

_____

_____

Conclusion 2: _____

_____

_____

_____

IMPLIED MAIN IDEA

Now that you have some practice making reasonable inferences and drawing logical conclusions, determining implied main ideas will be clearer. An **implied main idea** is a formulated main idea statement, created by the reader when an author does not directly state his or her main point in one sentence within a reading. To determine an implied main idea *is to draw a logical conclusion.* To find implied main ideas, a reader needs to use all the skills outlined in the previous chapters: identifying topic, recognizing patterns of organization, knowing an author's purpose and seeing the relationships between ideas, recognizing supporting points, and using steps to figure out the author's most important point about the topic. Implied main ideas can be made with one of three methods:

1. Topic + existing sentence = implied main idea

2. Sentence + sentence = implied main idea

3. General statement based on supporting details = implied main idea

Method 1: Topic + Existing Sentence = Implied Main Idea

There may be a sentence in the passage that contains the author's most important point about the topic but refers to the topic itself by a pronoun (*he, she, it, they, this,* etc.). To express a complete thought, the reader needs to add the topic to the sentence that contains the point (Figure 4.3).

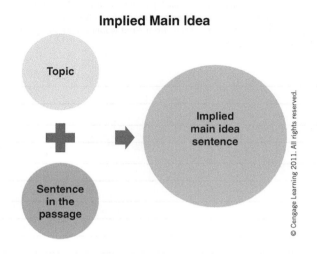

FIGURE 4.3 Method 1 for Finding Implied Main Idea

We seldom know the real reasons for others' actions. That is why we tend to infer causes from *circumstances.* However, in doing so, we often make mistakes. The most common error is to attribute the actions of others to internal causes. This mistake is called the **fundamental attribution error.** We tend to think the actions of others have internal causes even if they are actually caused by external forces or circumstances. One amusing example of this error is the tendency of people to attribute the actions of actors in television programs to the personality of the actor rather than the obvious external cause (that they are playing a character).

—From COON, *Introduction to Psychology,* 12E. © 2010 Cengage Learning.

In this passage, the topic is the fundamental attribution error. The fourth sentence defines this psychological phenomenon. The definition of the fundamental attribution error is "to attribute the actions of others to internal causes."

Notice, however, the sentence that follows the definition: "This mistake is called the **fundamental attribution error.**" So, the definition of the fundamental attribution error *precedes* the boldfaced term. To accurately and completely state the main idea of this paragraph, the topic, fundamental attribution error, is inserted in the definition sentence to completely state the author's most important point in this paragraph. To correctly state the main idea, then, you insert the topic into the existing sentence because topic is *always* included in the main idea.

The fundamental attribution error is to attribute the actions of others to internal causes.

Method 2: Sentence + Sentence = Implied Main Idea

The second type of implied main idea exists when the author's most important point is divided into two sentences (Figure 4.4). These sentences must be combined to state the main idea accurately in a single sentence.

Sentence + Sentence

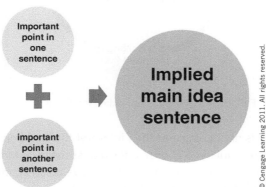

FIGURE 4.4 Method 2 for Finding Implied Main Idea

In social situations, people look to others in the crowd to determine whether or not to intervene in an emergency. Diffusion of responsibility occurs when they determine others will take action, so the individual does nothing. "Someone else must have called the police, so I don't need to do anything," the onlooker reasons to himself. As a result, if everyone assumes this, the police never do get called.

Here, the topic is diffusion of responsibility. The point is that, when in a crowd, people assume others have taken action and so do nothing. This thought is expressed by the first and second sentences. Combine the two sentences to state the main idea:

Diffusion of responsibility occurs in social situations when people look to others in the crowd to determine whether or not to intervene in an emergency, assume others have taken action, and so do nothing.

Method 3: General Statement Based on Supporting Details = Implied Main Idea

The third type of implied main idea occurs when the author presents a series of supporting details only (Figure 4.5). The reader can fairly easily understand what the overall point is but has nothing stated in the passage to work with as in methods 1 and 2 above.

Supporting Details

FIGURE 4.5 Method 3 for Finding Implied Main Idea

Notice something is happening and then interpret the situation as an emergency. Assume personal responsibility to choose a form of assistance. Most importantly, implement assistance. Do not assume that others have taken action to intervene in the emergency as they may be a part of the Bystander Effect.

Here, the topic is the Bystander Effect and steps to take to overcome it. The author's point is that *certain steps can be taken to overcome the Bystander Effect.* No sentence in the paragraph mentions this idea. Instead, the writer presents a sequence of things to do to counteract the assumption that others are reacting. The main idea is inferred from the details:

There are steps that can be taken to overcome the Bystander Effect.

or

The Bystander Effect can be overcome by becoming aware of these steps.

Here is another example of using method 3 to create an implied main idea statement.

One way to avoid the Bystander Effect is to be aware of the phenomenon. Another safeguard is to be aware of what is going on around you when an emergency occurs. Be aware of what other people are doing and how they are reacting. Furthermore, make sure that help has been summoned, even if you are the one to call for assistance. Last, spread the word about this phenomenon, so others may react effectively in emergency situations as well.

In this example, the author has provided four suggestions for avoiding the Bystander Effect:

1. Be aware of the phenomenon.
2. Be aware of what is going on around you when an emergency occurs.

3. Make sure that help has been summoned.

4. Spread the word about this phenomenon.

What is a general statement about the topic "avoiding the Bystander Effect" that would be general enough to cover the four supporting points? Write your idea here.

_____

_____

Here is one way of stating the main idea:

> In order to avoid the Bystander Effect, follow these suggestions.

Another way of stating the implied main idea is this:

> There are four pieces of information to be aware of to help avoid the Bystander Effect.

Each person will have a different sentence for expressing the main idea based on supporting details. The point is that each of these sentences will convey the same overall idea, even if they are not worded in exactly the same way.

Steps to Finding the Implied Main Idea

The steps for figuring out an implied main idea are very similar to those for finding an explicitly stated main idea, with one additional step.

1. What is the topic?

2. What is the author's purpose?

3. What is the overall structure or pattern of organization?

4. What is the author's most important point about the topic?

5. Write your own statement of main idea when the author does not do so directly.

In Chapter 3, you went back to the reading and found a sentence that stated what you had answered for question 4. In the case of an implied main idea, of course, the sentence that states the main point cannot be found. You will need to use your skills of paraphrasing to come up with a statement that encapsulates the author's most important point, so you need to write your own statement of the main idea.

Finding implied main ideas is not really harder than finding directly stated main ideas. When you go back and look for your idea of the point of the passage, you see that the author does not state that idea in just one sentence; instead, the author presents all the information you need to understand the point of the passage—and you need to write the main idea yourself.

QUICK TIPS WRITING IMPLIED MAIN IDEA STATEMENTS

When you write your own implied main idea statements, follow these guidelines.

 Method 1: Add the topic to a sentence in the passage that comes close to stating the point you have constructed in your mind.

 Method 2: Combine two sentences to create your statement of the main point.

 Method 3: Check to see if the reading is a series of supporting points that all logically fall under the general statement you have constructed as the main idea, taking into account that all major supporting points are equal in importance.

Keep in mind the following:

 Notice if any passage is a list of something and has a general, overriding point that can be summed up in a general statement.

☑ Turn the topic into a question; then answer the question. There you have the main idea!

☑ Think in terms of summative words or phrases and imagine explaining the point of a passage to a peer. Start your thinking with "The point is . . ." or "In conclusion, . . .," or "To sum up, . . ."

☑ In contrast patterns, half of the point is often mentioned in one sentence, and the other half in a second sentence. When you see a contrast pattern, consider the possibility of using method 2.

 When in doubt, try beginning your implied main idea statement with "There are . . . ." This way, you will know you are creating a sentence, not a phrase.

On Your Own FINDING IMPLIED MAIN IDEAS IN PARAGRAPHS

Determine the topic, pattern of organization, and implied main idea of each of the following paragraphs. Make sure to note the major supporting details that back up the main point. Be alert for transitions that indicate a major supporting point and clarify the pattern of organization used in the paragraph. Identify which of the three methods you used to formulate the implied main idea sentence.

- Method 1: topic + existing sentence
- Method 2: sentence + sentence
- Method 3: general statement based on supporting details

Discuss your answers with a partner or in class discussion.

1.   Like all acts of terrorism, the 2001 attacks on the World Trade Center and the Pentagon were examples of human behavior at its worst. But like all tragedies, they drew responses that provide inspiring examples of human behavior at its best. Michael Benfante and John Cerqueira were working in the World Trade Center when one of the hijacked planes struck their building. They headed for a stairwell, but they didn't just save themselves. Although it slowed their own escape, they chose to carry Tina Hansen, a wheelchair-bound co-worker, down sixty-eight flights of stairs to safety. David Theall was in his Pentagon office when another hijacked plane hit the building not far from his desk. He could have escaped the rubble immediately, but he first located a dazed officemate and led him, along with seven other coworkers, to an exit. And no one will ever forget the heroism of the hundreds of New York City firefighters, police officers, and emergency workers who risked their lives, and lost their lives, while trying to save others. Acts of selflessness and sacrifice were common that day and in the days and weeks and months that followed. Police officers, medical personnel, search-and-rescue specialists, and just ordinary people came to New York from all over the United States to help clear wreckage, look for survivors, and recover bodies. Donations of more than $1 billion poured in to the Red Cross and other charitable organizations to help victims; one celebrity telethon raised $150 million in two hours. There was also a dramatic increase in many other forms of prosocial behavior, including volunteering to work for all kinds of charities.

—From BERNSTEIN/PENNER/CLARKE-STEWART/ROY, *Psychology*, 7E. © 2006 Cengage Learning.

Topic: _____

Pattern of organization: _____

Main idea: _____

_____

Method for implied main idea: _____

2.   The presence of others also has a strong influence on the tendency to help. Somewhat surprisingly, though, their presence actually tends to inhibit helping behavior. One of the most highly publicized examples of this phenomenon was the Kitty Genovese incident, which occurred on a New York City street in 1964. During a thirty-minute struggle, a man stabbed Genovese repeatedly, but none of the dozens of neighbors who witnessed the attack intervened or even called the police until it was too late to save her life. A similar case occurred in November 2000, in London, when a ten-year-old boy who had been stabbed by members of a street gang lay ignored by passersby as he bled to death. After each case, journalists and social commentators expressed dismay about the apathy and callousness that seems to exist among people who live in big cities. But psychologists believe that something about the situation surrounding such events deters people from helping.

—From BERNSTEIN/PENNER/CLARKE-STEWART/ROY, *Psychology*, 7E. © 2006 Cengage Learning.

(Continued)

Topic: _____

Pattern of organization: _____

Main idea: _____

_____

Method for implied main idea: _____

3.   Some states have adopted laws with broadened scopes. Arkansas, for example, last year added cyberbullying to its anti-bullying policies and included provisions for schools to act against some off-campus activities. The measure applies to actions originating on or off school grounds "if the electronic act is directed specifically at students or school personnel and is maliciously intended for the purpose of disrupting school, and has a high likelihood of succeeding in that purpose."

—"Cyberbullying" by litteri, T.J., *CQ Researcher*, 18, 385–408, May 2, 2008
(Retrieved from http://library.cqpress.com).

Topic: _____

Pattern of organization: _____

Main idea: _____

_____

Method for implied main idea: _____

4.   Terrorism on the Internet extends far beyond Web sites directly operated or controlled by terrorist organizations. Their supporters and sympathizers are increasingly taking advantage of all the tools available on the Web. "The proliferation of blogs has been exponential," says Sulastri Bte Osman, an analyst with the Civil and Internal Conflict Programme at Nanyang Technological University in Singapore. Just two years ago, Osman could find no extremist blogs in the two predominant languages of Indonesia and Malaysia; today she is monitoring 150.

—B. Mantel, "Terrorism and the Internet, *CQ Global Researcher* 3, November 1, 2009, pp. 285–310.
(Retrieved from http://library.cqpress.com/globalresearcher/).

Topic: _____

Pattern of organization: _____

Main idea: _____

_____

Method for implied main idea: _____

5.   Cyberbullying isn't just a problem among adolescents. Adults engage in it, too. From online vigilantism and angry blogs to e-stalking and anonymous ranting on newspaper Web sites, grownups can be as abusive as the meanest schoolhouse tyrant.

—"Cyberbullying" by litteri, T.J., *CQ Researcher*, 18, 385–408, May 2, 2008
(Retrieved from http://library.cqpress.com).

Topic: _____

Pattern of organization: _____

Main idea: _____

_____

Method for implied main idea: _____

6.   Following the trials and executions, many involved, like Judge Samuel Sewall, publicly confessed error and guilt. On January 14, 1697, the General Court ordered a day of fasting and soul-searching for the tragedy of Salem. In 1702, the court declared the trials unlawful. And in 1711, the colony passed a bill restoring the rights and good names of those accused and granted £600 restitution to their heirs. However, it was not until 1957—more than 250 years later—that Massachusetts formally apologized for the events of 1692.

Topic: _____

Pattern of organization: _____

Main idea: _____

_____

Method for implied main idea: _____

7.   In August 1992, to mark the 300th anniversary of the trials, Nobel Laureate Elie Wiesel dedicated the Witch Trials Memorial in Salem. Also in Salem, the Peabody Essex Museum houses the original court documents, and the town's most-visited attraction, the Salem Witch Museum, attests to the public's enthrallment with the 1692 hysteria.

Topic: _____

Pattern of organization: _____

Main idea: _____

_____

Method for implied main idea: _____

8.   When teams are unable to effectively work together, moaning, complaining, and blaming others is one hallmark. In addition, dysfunctional teams engage in reluctance to make decisions and, instead, defer to the team captain for advice and direction. Furthermore, struggling teams practice avoidant behavior and tend not to stretch players' individual abilities that would otherwise occur through teamwork and camaraderie. If players are not communicating well, they tend to avoid one another. This makes developing individual abilities that help the team unlikely. Last, not being

(Continued)

up-front and honest dismantles any team spirit formerly present. As you can see, there are many characteristics of this type of conflict.

Topic: _____

Pattern of organization: _____

Main idea: _____

_____

Method for implied main idea: _____

9.   High team effectiveness results when team members seek new approaches to situations and engage in honest evaluation. Furthermore, good teamwork involves approaching new situations with accountability and responsibility not only towards individual performance, but that of the team as a whole. Another characteristic of the effective team is that a unified group will lead to synergy and understanding since everyone seeks challenge and knows how to work together to surmount difficulties.

Topic: _____

Pattern of organization: _____

Main idea: _____

_____

Method for implied main idea: _____

10.   Many people are unsure of themselves in a group situation. They may look to the group leader for direction or for guidance. Sometimes, people unsure of a group and the appropriate behavior follow the example of the group. However, this can be disastrous if the phenomenon of the Bystander Effect is in place.

Topic: _____

Pattern of organization: _____

Main idea: _____

_____

Method for implied main idea: _____

Thinking It Through FINDING THE IMPLIED MAIN IDEA OF A LONGER READING

This is a passage from a psychology text called *Introduction to Psychology: Gateways to Mind and Behavior with Concept Maps and Reviews,* 13th edition, about conformity and how people react to the pressure of groups. Respond to these questions, and then compare your responses to those following the reading.

1. Preview the article, noting the italicized question prompts. How many major sections are in this reading?

_____

2. What is the topic of the reading? _____

3. What is the author's purpose? _____

As you read the article, find the topic, pattern of organization, and the main idea of each paragraph. If the paragraph's main idea is explicit, underline it and write "explicit" in the space for "Method." If the paragraph's main idea is implied, identify which of the three methods you used to create it:

■ Method 1: topic + existing sentence

■ Method 2: sentence + sentence

■ Method 3: general statement based on supporting details

Also determine the main idea of each subsection and then the thesis of the article.

The Asch Experiment

How strong are group pressures for conformity?

Topic: _____

Pattern: _____

Main idea: _____

_____

Method: _____

1   One of the first experiments on conformity was staged by a famous researcher. His name was Solomon Asch (1907–1996). To fully appreciate it, imagine yourself as a subject. Assume that you are seated at a table with six other students. Your task is actually quite simple: You are shown three lines on a card and you must select the line that matches a "standard" line.

(a)
Standard Line

(1)   (2)   (3)
Comparison Lines

From COON, Introduction to Psychology: Gateways to Mind and Behavior with Concept Maps and Reviews, 13E. © 2013 Cengage Learning.

FIGURE 4.6 Stimuli Used in Solomon Asch's Conformity Experiments

(Continued)

Topic: _____
Pattern: _____
Main idea: _____
_____
Method: _____

2   As the testing begins, each person announces an answer for the first card. When your turn comes, you agree with the others. "This isn't hard at all," you say to yourself. For several more trials, your answers agree with those of the group. Then comes a shock: All six people announce that line 1 matches the standard, and you were about to say line 2 matches. Suddenly, you feel alone and upset. You nervously look at the lines again. The room falls silent. Everyone seems to be staring at you. The experimenter awaits your answer. Do you yield to the group?

Topic: _____
Pattern: _____
Main idea: _____
_____
Method: _____

3   In this study, the other "students" were all actors who gave the wrong answer on about a third of the trials to create group pressure. Real students conformed to the group on about one third of the critical trials. Of those tested, 75 percent yielded at least once. People who were tested alone erred in less than 1 percent of their judgments. Clearly, those who yielded to group pressures were denying what their eyes told them.

Are some people more susceptible to group pressures than others?

Topic: _____
Pattern: _____
Main idea: _____
_____
Method: _____

4   People with high needs for structure or certainty are more likely to conform. So are people who are anxious, low in self-confidence or concerned with the approval of others. People who live in cultures that emphasize group cooperation (such as many Asian cultures) are also more likely to conform.

Topic: _____
Pattern: _____
Main idea: _____
_____
Method: _____

5   In addition to personal characteristics, certain situations tend to encourage conformity—sometimes with disastrous results. "Groupthink" offers a prime example.

SOURCE: From COON, *Introduction to Psychology: Gateways to Mind and Behavior with Concept Maps and Reviews*, 13E. © 2013 Cengage Learning.

1. What is the main idea of the first section (paragraphs 1 through 3)?_____
_____

2. What is the main idea of the second subsection (paragraphs 4 and 5)? _____
_____

Check Your Answers

1. **How many major sections are in this reading?** *There are two major subsections of the reading, indicated by the two italicized question prompts:*

   ■ *How strong are group pressures for conformity?*

   ■ *Are some people more susceptible to group pressures than others?*

2. **What is the topic of the passage?** *Conformity and the Asch experiment*

3. **What is the author's purpose?** *The author is informing us about conformity and the results of the experiment.*

PARAGRAPH 1

The topic is experiments about conformity conducted by Solomon Asch. The pattern is example/illustration or clarification. The author begins to describe an experiment conducted by Solomon Asch, who is renowned for his seminal studies on conformity. The first two sentences in paragraph 1 need to be combined to express the most important point. Here is the main idea statement, using method 2:

> One of the first experiments on conformity was staged by a famous researcher named Solomon Asch.

PARAGRAPH 2

This passage is Asch's experiment on conformity and pressure to yield to the group. The pattern is sequence. You will have to use method 3 to construct the main idea because each sentence in this paragraph provides a detail about the sequence of the conformity experiment.

> Solomon Asch's experiment on conformity tested the reaction of subjects to yield to group pressure.

PARAGRAPH 3

In paragraph 3, the topic is the conformity study and yielding to group pressure. This is an effect paragraph, outlining the findings of Asch's conformity study. The author's point is that subjects in the study went against their awareness of the correct answer and were swayed by group pressure to answer incorrectly a large percentage of the time. The last sentence begins with the word "clearly," which you know often indicates the author's summative main idea statement. However, what is missing from the concluding sentence? While this sentence summarizes the point or outcome of the experiment, it does not include all of the topic. So we need to add the complete topic to the last sentence, using method 1:

> Clearly, those who yielded to group pressures *in Asch's study on conformity* were denying what their eyes told them.

(Continued)

Can you answer the question posed before paragraph 1: ***How strong are group pressures for conformity?***

Revisiting the main ideas of each of the three paragraphs following this question, can you come up with one sentence in answer? You need to mention Solomon Asch's study on conformity, yielding to group pressure, and the results of group pressure being that subjects eschewed, or ignored, what their eyes saw and went along with the group.

> *In Solomon Asch's study on conformity, group pressure is powerful since subjects ignored what they saw to conform to the group.*

PARAGRAPH 4

The topic is characteristics of people likely to conform. The author lists these characteristics: people with high needs for structure or certainty, who are anxious, low in self-confidence or concerned with the approval of others, and those who live in cultures that emphasize group cooperation. Using method 3, you can create a general statement to express the main idea or you could string together the three characteristics.

> There are several characteristics that increase the likelihood of conformity.

or

> People who are most likely to conform are those who have a high need for structure or certainty, who are anxious or lack self-confidence and need approval, or those who live in cultures that value group cooperation.

PARAGRAPH 5

The topic is other factors that influence conformity. This paragraph functions to add another characteristic and clarifies or adds to the previous paragraph—the pattern of organization is example/illustration or clarification. The main idea is explicit in the first sentence.

Can you answer the question posed before paragraph 4: ***Are some people more susceptible to group pressures than others?***

Revisiting the main ideas of each of the two paragraphs following this question, can you come up with one sentence in answer? You need to mention that certain personality characteristics influence conformity and that certain situations increase conformity. You can either make a general statement using method 3 or string together the key characteristics and the situational influence using method 3:

> Certain personality characteristics as well as situational factors influence conformity.

or

> People who are characterized by a high need for structure or certainty, who are anxious or lack self-confidence and need approval, or who live in cultures that value group cooperation as well as situational factors influence conformity.

THE THESIS

Keeping in mind all the main ideas you found for each of the paragraphs and for the answers to the italicized questions in the reading, now consider the thesis of the whole reading. Because the article has subheadings, each subsection has equal importance to the whole. The first section poses the question "How strong are group pressures for conformity?"; the second subsection poses the question "Are some people more susceptible to group pressures than others?" Look at the main ideas of each subsection again:

- In Solomon Asch's study on conformity, group pressure is powerful since subjects ignored what they saw to conform to the group.
- Certain personality characteristics as well as situational factors influence conformity.

With these statements in mind, answer the following questions:

1. What is the author's overall main idea about the topic?

2. Can you find a sentence in the reading that echoes what you wrote (explicit thesis)? If not, is there a sentence that almost states the most important point but may need the topic inserted into this existing sentence (method 1)? If not, can you find two sentences to combine to express the main idea that you paraphrased (method 2)? If not, you have written a general statement that sums up the overall point of the reading (method 3).

    The overall main idea, then, is as follows:

> In Solomon Asch's study, group pressure is powerful since subjects ignored what they saw to conform to the group, heightened by certain personality characteristics as well as situational factors that influence conformity.

When passages contain implied main ideas, each reader will state the point in a slightly different way with slightly different sentences. But, in essence, the points are all saying the same thing. Notice how an implied thesis statement is like writing a summary in one sentence!

FINDING THE IMPLIED MAIN IDEA
On Your Own OF A WHOLE READING

With a partner or small group, determine the main idea of each subsection in the following passage about social influence and power from the psychology textbook: *Introduction to Psychology: Gateways to Mind and Behavior with Concept Maps and Reviews,* 13th edition. Then, determine the main idea of the entire passage. In this passage, the author raises two questions. You know that the main idea is never in question form; the main idea is the answer to the questions posed about the topic.

Respond to the questions that follow. After doing so, read the passage and find the topic, pattern of organization, and the implied main idea of each paragraph. If the paragraph's main idea is explicit, underline it and write "explicit" in the space for "Method." If the paragraph's main idea is implied, identify which of the three methods you used to create it:

- Method 1: topic + existing sentence
- Method 2: sentence + sentence
- Method 3: general statement based on supporting details

1. Preview the article, noting subheadings. How many major sections are in this reading?

_____

2. What is the topic of the reading? _____

3. What is the author's purpose? _____

Topic: _____
Pattern: _____
Main idea: _____
_____
_____
_____
Method: _____

Social Influence—Follow the Leader

What Is Social Influence?

1   No topic lies nearer the heart of social psychology than social influence. This is changes in behavior induced by the actions of others. When people interact, they almost always affect one another's behavior. For example, in a classic sidewalk experiment, various numbers of people stood on a busy New York City street. On cue, they all looked at a sixth floor window across the street. A camera recorded how many passersby also stopped to stare. The larger the influencing group, the more people were swayed to join in staring at the window.

Are There Different Kinds of Social Influence?

Topic: _____
Pattern: _____

2   The gentlest form of social influence is *mere presence* (changing behavior just because other

people are nearby). We *conform* when we spontaneously change our behavior to bring it into agreement with others. Compliance is a more directed form of social influence. We *comply* when we change our behavior in response to another person who has little or no social power, or authority. Obedience is an even stronger form of social influence. We *obey* when we change our behavior in direct response to the demands of an authority. The strongest form of social influence is *coercion,* or changing behavior because you are forced to.

Social Power

3   The people we encounter on any given day vary in their power to influence us. Here's something to think about: Strength is a quality possessed by individuals; power is always social—it arises when people come together and disappears when they disperse. In trying to understand the ways in which people are able to influence one another, it is helpful to distinguish among five types of **social power.** It refers to the capacity to control, alter, or influence the behavior of another person:

- **Reward power**—This lies in the ability to reward a person for complying with desired behavior. Teachers try to exert reward power over students with grades. Employers command reward power by their control of wages and bonuses.

- **Coercive power**—This is based on an ability to punish a person for failure to comply. Coercive power is the basis for most laws, in that fines or imprisonment are used to control behavior.

- **Legitimate power** is accepting a person as an agent of an established social order. For example, elected leaders and supervisors have legitimate power. So does a teacher in the classroom. Outside the classroom that power would have to come from another source.

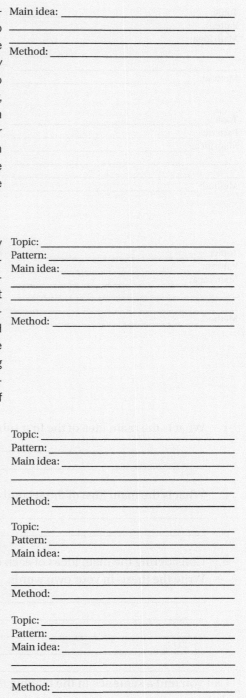

Main idea: _____
_____
_____
Method: _____

Topic: _____
Pattern: _____
Main idea: _____
_____
_____
Method: _____

Topic: _____
Pattern: _____
Main idea: _____
_____
_____
Method: _____

Topic: _____
Pattern: _____
Main idea: _____
_____
_____
Method: _____

Topic: _____
Pattern: _____
Main idea: _____
_____
_____
Method: _____

(Continued)

Topic: _____
Pattern: _____
Main idea: _____
_____
_____
Method: _____

Topic: _____
Pattern: _____
Main idea: _____
_____
_____
Method: _____

Topic: _____
Pattern: _____
Main idea: _____
_____
_____
Method: _____

- **Referent power**—This type of power is based on respect for or identification with a person or a group. The person "refers to" the source of referent power for direction. Referent power is responsible for much of the conformity we see in groups.

- **Expert power** is based on recognition that another person has knowledge necessary for achieving a goal. We allow teachers, lawyers, and other experts to guide behavior because of their ability to produce desired results. Physicians, psychologists, programmers, and plumbers have expert power.

4   A person who has power in one situation may have very little in another. In those situations in which a person has power, she or he is described by a specific term. He or she is described as an authority. Regardless of whether the people around you are authorities, friends, or strangers, their mere presence is likely to influence your behavior.

SOURCE: From COON, Introduction to Psychology: Gateways to Mind and Behavior with Concept Maps and Reviews, 13E. © 2013 Cengage Learning.

1. What is the main idea of the first subsection?
_____
_____

2. What is the main idea of the second subsection?
_____
_____

3. Considering the main ideas of each of the subsections, what is the thesis of this reading? Write the thesis in your own words. _____
_____
_____
_____
_____

Can you find a sentence in the reading that echoes what you wrote (explicit thesis)? If not, is there a sentence that almost states the most important point but may need the topic inserted into this existing sentence (method 1)? If not, can you find two sentences to combine to express the main idea that you paraphrased (method 2)? If not, you have written a general statement that sums up the overall point of the reading (method 3).

On Your Own

MORE PRACTICE WITH FINDING IMPLIED MAIN IDEAS OF A WHOLE READING

Becoming good at formulating the implied main idea of a passage becomes easier with practice. With a partner or as your instructor assigns, read the following excerpt from *The Tipping Point* by Malcolm Gladwell. Malcolm Gladwell is the author of four *New York Times* best-selling nonfiction books: *Blink, The Tipping Point, Outliers,* and *What the Dog Saw.* This excerpt concerns the dark side of human nature where people behave in ways that betray both their upbringing and personality. When put in specific situations that overwhelm what we would normally be like, are we all capable of uncharacteristic behavior? In the passage, Bernie Goetz is referenced in paragraph 2. Bernie Goetz became a household name in 1984 for taking the law into his own hand and shooting three young men who tried to mug him on a New York subway train.

Find the implied main idea for each of the following paragraphs. Use method 3, constructing a general statement about the most important point. Just because the paragraphs are long does not mean that they are difficult to work with. Just remember to take it step by step: consider the topic, determine the pattern, and then figure out the main point using your own words.

From *The Tipping Point*
by Malcolm Gladwell

1   In the early 1970's, a group of social scientists at Stanford University, led by Philip Zimbardo, decided to create a mock prison in the basement of the university's psychology building. They took a thirty-five-foot section of corridor and created a cell block with a prefabricated wall. Three small, six- by nine-foot cells were created from laboratory rooms and given steel-barred, black-painted doors. A closet was turned into a solitary confinement cell. The group then advertised in the local papers for volunteers, men who would agree to participate in the experiment. Seventy-five people applied, and from those Zimbardo and his colleagues picked the 21 who appeared the most normal and healthy on psychological tests. Half of the group were chosen, at random, to be guards, and were given uniforms and dark glasses and told that their responsibility was to keep order in the prison. The other half was told that they were to be prisoners. Zimbardo got the Palo Alto Police Department to "arrest" the prisoners in their homes, cuff them, bring them to the station house, charge them with fictitious crime, fingerprint them, then blindfold them and bring them to the prison in the Psychology Department basement. Then they were stripped and given a prison uniform to wear, with a number on the front and back that was to serve as their only means of identification for the duration of their incarceration.

Implied Main Idea: _____

_____

_____

(Continued)

2   The purpose of the experiment was to try to find out why prisons are such nasty places. Was it because prisons are full of nasty people, or was it because prisons are such nasty environments that they make people nasty? In the answer to that question is obviously the answer to the question posed by Bernie Goetz and the subway cleanup, which is how much influence does immediate environment have on the way people behave? What Zimbardo found out shocked him. The guards, some of whom had previously identified themselves as pacifists, fell quickly into the role of hard-bitten disciplinarians. The first night they woke up the prisoners at two in the morning and made them do pushups, line up against the wall, and perform other arbitrary tasks. On the morning of the second day, the prisoners rebelled. They ripped off their numbers and barricaded themselves in their cells. The guards responded by stripping them, spraying them with fire extinguishers, and throwing the leader of the rebellion into solitary confinement. "There were times when we were pretty abusive, getting right in their faces and yelling at them," one guard remembers. "It was part of the whole atmosphere of terror." As the experiment progressed, the guards got systematically crueler and more sadistic. "What we were unprepared for was the intensity of the change and the speed at which it happened," Zimbardo says. The guards were making the prisoners say to one another they loved each other, and making them march down the hallway, in handcuffs, with paper bags over their heads. "It was completely the opposite from the way I conduct myself now," another guard remembers. "I think I was positively creative in terms of my mental cruelty." After 36 hours, one prisoner began to get hysterical, and had to be released. Four more then had to be released because of "extreme emotional depression, crying, rage, and acute anxiety." Zimbardo had originally intended to have the experiment run for two weeks. He called it off after six days. "I realize now," one prisoner said after the experiment was over, "that no matter how together I thought I was inside my head, my prisoner behavior was often less under my control than I realized." Another said: "I began to feel that I was losing my identity, that the person I call _ _ _, the person who volunteered to get me into this prison (because it was a prison to me, it still is a prison to me, I don't regard it as an experiment or a simulation . . .) was distant from me, was remote, until finally I wasn't that person. I was 416. I was really my number and 416 was really going to have to decide what to do."

Implied Main Idea: _____

_____

_____

3   Zimbardo's conclusion was that there are specific situations so powerful that they can overwhelm our inherent predispositions. The key word here is situation. Zimbardo isn't talking about environment, about the major external influences on all of our lives. He's not denying that how our parents raise us affects what we are, or that the kind of schools we went to, the friends we have, or the neighborhoods we live in affect our behavior. All of these things are undoubtedly important. Nor is he denying that our genes play a role in determining who we are. Most psychologists believe that nature—genetics—accounts for about half of the reason why we tend to act the way we do. His point is simply that

there are certain times and places and conditions when much of that can be swept away, that there are instances where you can take normal people from good schools and happy families and good neighborhoods and powerfully affect their behavior merely by changing the immediate details of their situation.

Implied Main Idea: _____

_____

_____

Find the main idea of the whole reading passage. Consider the main ideas of each of the paragraphs and then state one overall point that sums up the paragraphs.

Implied Thesis: _____

_____

_____

_____

_____

UNDERSTANDING GRAPHICS

FINDING IMPLIED MAIN IDEAS IN VISUAL AIDS AND CARTOONS

By considering the title, identifying the topic, identifying the organizational pattern, and looking at the relationship between ideas, a reader can infer the overall point made in any graphic. In Figure 4.7, "The Bystander Effect," the point is partially stated at the top of the chart: "Fewer people help if others seem available." Using method l, add the topic to this existing information:

> The greater the number of people who witness an emergency event, the fewer the number of people who will be likely to help as a result of the Bystander Effect.

Or

> The Bystander Effect is a social phenomenon whereby the greater the number of people who witness an emergency event, the less likely any of those people will be to help.

FIGURE 4.7 The Bystander Effect

Understanding the main idea of cartoons usually requires figuring out what the implied main idea is. Of course, you need to have some prior knowledge in order to get the joke and the joke is often the main idea. To get the joke, you make an inference. Remember, an inference is a reasonable guess based on information provided together with your own prior knowledge. Consider this cartoon.

What is the topic? The topic is apathy, or not taking action. The superhero, "Whatever Man," takes no action even though the frantic citizen is urgently alerting him to a robot trying to destroy the city. The joke is that the superhero is lounging on a park bench, rather than trying to help solve the problem, which is the opposite of a superhero's role. The implied main idea is that by doing nothing, Whatever Man contributes to, rather than solves, the problem; traditionally, superheroes right the world's wrongs, whereas this superhero is apathetic in the face of imminent destruction.

"Hey, I'm Whatever Man. I possess vast powers of indifference."

◆ VOCABULARY STRATEGY

UNDERSTANDING FIGURATIVE LANGUAGE

When an author has an implied main idea, he or she does not directly state the point of the passage in one sentence within the reading. Similarly, when an author uses figurative language, the reader needs to make an inference to figure out the main idea. It is important to understand how figurative language is used in readings. **Figurative language** functions to provide a vivid mental image in the mind of the reader. It is not meant to be interpreted literally and involves using a comparison between two things, different enough that when compared, the suggested similarities are interesting or thought-provoking. In using this language, authors *show* rather than *tell* how they feel or how a character feels.

Literal language does not use literary devices; it is language that is very straightforward and clear, or the dictionary definition. Figurative language, on the other hand, involves mental images or literary devices to make a point. Figurative language uses words and meanings that are different from literal meanings to make a point. Figurative language is the opposite of literal language.

Literature is a specific type of writing that relies heavily on word choice as well as the use of figurative language. Figurative language also reveals the **tone** or **mood** of the reading or situation, which is the underlying emotion, similar to an implied main idea. Writers in other disciplines sometimes use figurative language when they want to explain or draw attention to a particular point in a memorable or more effective way. Here are the most common types of figurative language.

- **Metaphor** is a form of figurative language that compares two objects or ideas in order to emphasize a particular quality they have in common despite their essential differences.

  > That man is a tiger when it comes to business.

  In this example, the man is compared to a tiger. In Western culture, a tiger symbolizes power and aggression. So, in this metaphor, the man is being described as aggressive, powerful, and in charge. Here is another example of a straight metaphor.

  > Mother was my rock when I went through the crisis.

  This statement compares the mother to a rock. A rock is solid and unmoving and secure. Mother provided support, something that is solid and secure, during a crisis.

- Like a metaphor, a **simile** compares two dissimilar entities. However, unlike a metaphor, a simile uses the words *like, as,* or *than* to express the point of similarity in the two things compared. Consider these two examples, similar to the earlier examples of metaphor. Note the use of *like, as,* and *than.*

  > She was as aggressive as a tiger when it came to business.
  > Mother was like the Rock of Gibraltar when I went through the crisis.
  > She was more aggressive than a tiger, and those in business learned to fear her.

Whether an author uses metaphor or simile depends on her or his desired effect, which might be very subtle. Both are indirect comparisons between two seemingly unlike things; both function to create a strong mental image in the mind of the reader. The only difference between the two is that the use of certain words (*like, as, than*) signals a simile, while a metaphor is expressed as a direct equivalency—one thing is the same as another.

■ **Personification** gives living characteristics to inanimate objects. Consider this example:

> The chair flew across the room when he slammed into it.

Here, an inanimate object—a chair—is given characteristics held only by certain living creatures—birds. In this sentence, the writer creates for the reader a vivid mental image about *how* the chair moved. It moved as if it were flying, which implies speed and perhaps even grace. Take a look at this example of personification.

> As I stood on the bridge, I watched the river dancing beneath my feet.

In this sentence, the river is given a characteristic held only by living creatures—the ability to dance. Rhythmic, patterned movement is implied through the use of personification in this example.

■ **Hyperbole** is exaggeration for literary effect. Consider these two examples of hyperbole:

> I was so famished I could eat the food of a dozen lumberjacks.
> She waited an eternity for him to return from the outing.

Most readers would not believe that any one individual could eat as much food as 12 presumably large, strong men. The exaggeration functions to show how hungry the person was. Similarly, in the second example, the hyperbole functions to emphasize the length of the wait.

On Your Own RECOGNIZING FIGURATIVE LANGUAGE

With a partner or in a small group, identify figurative language in the following passages. Look for metaphors, similes, personification, and hyperbole. In some passages, there may be examples of more than one type of figurative language. Paraphrase what you think the author's "message" is in the passage. Afterward, discuss your answers with a partner or in class discussion.

1. A word is not a crystal, transparent and unchanged; it is the skin of a living thought, and may vary greatly in color and content according to the circumstances and the time in which it is used.

—Oliver Wendell Holmes, opinion, *Towne v. Eisner*, January 7, 1918

Figurative language: _____

_____

Message: _____

_____

2.   Melting pot Harlem—Harlem of honey and chocolate and caramel and rum and vin-
      egar and lemon and lime and gall . . . where the subway from the Bronx keeps right on
      downtown.

                                        —Langston Hughes, *Freedomways,* Summer, 1963

Figurative language: _____

_____

Message: _____

_____

3.   I would rather be ashes than dust! I would rather that my spark burn out in a brilliant
      blaze than it be stifled by dry-rot. I would rather be a superb meteor, every atom of me
      in magnificent glow, than a sleepy and permanent planet.

                                                        —Jack London, 1916

Figurative language: _____

_____

Message: _____

_____

4.   The mind I love must have wild places, a tangled orchard where dark damsons drop
      in the heavy grass, an overgrown little wood, the chance of a snake or two, a pool that
      nobody's fathomed the depth of, and paths threaded with flowers planted by the mind.

                                                    —Katherine Mansfield

Figurative language: _____

_____

Message: _____

_____

5.   He looked like the love thoughts of women. He could be a bee to a blossom—a pear
      tree blossom in the spring. He seemed to be crushing scent out of the world with his
      footsteps. Crushing aromatic herbs with every step he took. Spices hung about him. He
      was a glance from God.

                            —Zora Neale Hurston, *Their Eyes Were Watching God*

Figurative language: _____

_____

Message: _____

_____

(Continued)

6.   A tearing wind last night. A flurry of red clouds, hard, a watercolour mass of purple and black, soft as a water ice, then hard slices of intense green stone, blue stone and a ripple of crimson light.

—Virginia Woolf, in her diary, August 17, 1938

Figurative language: _____

_____

Message: _____

_____

7.   To be, or not to be, that is the question:
Whether 'tis nobler in the mind to suffer
The slings and arrows of outrageous fortune,
Or to take arms against a sea of troubles
And by opposing end them.

—William Shakespeare, *Hamlet*

Figurative language: _____

_____

Message: _____

_____

8.   Life's but a walking shadow, a poor player
That struts and frets his hour upon the stage,
And then is heard no more. It is a tale
Told by an idiot, full of sound and fury,
Signifying nothing.

—William Shakespeare, *Macbeth*

Figurative language: _____

_____

Message: _____

_____

⭐ READING STUDY STRATEGY

READING AND UNDERSTANDING LITERATURE

Some readings that are instructive, informative, persuasive, or entertaining do not have explicit main ideas. Likewise, in literary readings, the author does have a point for the reader to consider, but the point is not directly stated. As such, the point or message of a story, poem, play, novel, or literary passage is unstated or implied.

Furthermore, like an implied main idea, in a story or poem, an author's work may have several points that are supported by the information in the reading. These points, or statements of or about the theme, are reasonable if the rest of the passage supports them.

The main idea of a literary piece is referred to as its **theme.** The theme of a piece of literature is somewhat similar to the main idea of a piece of nonfiction writing: it answers the questions: What is the author's most important point? What message is he or she communicating?

The theme of a piece of literature—a novel, a poem, a play, or other imaginative work—is rarely stated explicitly. In your college literature classes, you will often need to figure out an author's most important point, or theme, and because that theme will most likely only be implied, you will need to make inferences and draw reasonable conclusions. These reasonable conclusions need to be based on evidence contained in the reading. Determining the theme of a literary selection and determining implied main ideas in a reading from another academic discipline require the same skill of inference.

QUICK TIPS   STEPS TO FINDING THE MAIN IDEA OF A LITERARY SELECTION

To figure out the main idea, or theme, of a literary work, consider these steps:

1. Determine the message, moral, abstract principle, or statement about life that the author is communicating. This is the theme, or implied main idea, of the reading.

2. Write your perception of the author's theme in statement format.

3. Determine whether your theme statement makes sense in and of itself.

4. Reread the selection several times to determine whether the information in the literary work functions to support your theme statement.

Questions to Consider When Reading Literature

There are several questions to consider when reading literature for your college classes. The term *literature* refers to short stories, novels, plays, descriptive passages, or poetry. Keeping these questions in mind will help you comprehend literary selections more fully.

- **What does the title reveal about the literary work?** The author chose the title for a specific reason. It can help you understand the theme of the work—the message the author is communicating.

- **Who are the characters?** Understanding who plays a part in a short story, novel, narrative poem, or dramatic work may help in clarifying the course of events or the author's point in writing the piece.

- **What is the setting?** Generally speaking, the setting of a short story, novel, narrative poem, or play refers to the time and place in which the events recounted occur. Setting is important not only to the plot of a piece of literature, but also to its mood or tone. For example, if a passage were set in a prison environment, the mood of the piece might be one of confinement and lost hope, or perhaps of violence, hatred, and resentment. Setting, then, can be more than mere physical location and placement in time.

- **What is the point of view?** The author tells the story from a particular point of view. Consider the following possibilities:

  - Is the story told from a first-person perspective ("I")?
  - Is the story told from a second-person perspective ("you")?
  - Is the story told from a third-person perspective ("he," "she," "it," or "they")?

  If the story is told from a third-person point of view, is the narrator reporting events as if watching a video of the action, or is the narrator reporting events and can also tell us what the characters are thinking? An "omniscient" narrator is one who knows all (*omni* means all; *scient* means knowing).

- **What is the author or narrator's attitude (tone) toward the subject?** A writer's choice of words and his or her choice of sentence structure, or style, allow you to also make an inference, or educated guess, as to the author's relationship to the written piece. **Tone** is the author's attitude toward his or her subject as revealed by his or her choice of words and writing style. An author might be critical, objective, angry, sad, excited, or disapproving, for example.

  The **mood** or underlying emotion of a story, play, or poem is also communicated by the author's choice of words and writing style, and is linked with tone. Whereas tone suggests the author's attitude toward the subject matter, usually in informative and persuasive text, mood suggests the underlying emotion of a poem, story, or literary piece. The author's tone is important in creating mood in a work of literature.

- **What is the main conflict? Conflict** is the tension that is created by or between two opposing forces. A literary selection may feature one or more types of conflict. In the first type, human versus human, the protagonist (central character or hero) is in opposition to an antagonist who is another character in the piece. In a second type of conflict, human versus an external force or entity, the protagonist is pitted against something external to himself or herself, such as the environment or a social tradition. A third type of conflict, human versus self, is internal to the protagonist. He or she may struggle with his or her conscience, thoughts, impulses, or desires.

- **What is the plot, or sequence of events?** You also want to be able to paraphrase what happens in the literary piece. The **plot** is the series of actions and events that make up a story—how the action develops over time.

- **What is the high point?** Central to understanding what happens in a piece of literature is identifying the high point of the action, known as the **climax.** At this point, the action reaches its most exciting and suspenseful point, after which the resolution, or ending, takes place.

- **What is the resolution?** (How does it end)? Do the characters reconcile their differences? Or does the resolution leave the reader wondering what might happen next? The ending of a piece of literature is important in determining the author's message; how the piece ends is deliberate, informing the reader of the author's purpose and the author's message.

- **What figurative language, poetic devices, or symbols has the author used?** Literature often uses figurative language (discussed earlier) and imagery—words and phrases that appeal to the reader's senses and that conjure up images and associations in his or her mind. Similarly, authors often create **symbols,** which are events, objects, or even characters that represent something beyond their immediate or apparent purpose. For example, the American flag is an object associated with the United States—a piece of fabric with an interesting pattern that is hoisted on a pole and saluted or sung about at sporting events. But the American flag is also a symbol of freedom, justice, liberty, and all the abstract ideals for which the country stands.

  In addition, authors may use other poetic devices to achieve a certain effect related to rhyme or meter. A **poetic device** is a technique that provides a special effect. Rhyme and meter have to do with the sound of words in a literary piece. **Assonance** is the repetition of vowel sounds for effect, or vowel rhyme.

  > The f<u>a</u>t c<u>a</u>t s<u>a</u>t on the r<u>a</u>t.
  > The gr<u>ie</u>ving w<u>ea</u>ver wh<u>ee</u>led his wares in the wilderness.

  Notice that the second example has a repetition of vowel sounds—the long /*e*/ sound in *grieve* and *weave*. However, that example also has a repetition of the sound associated with the letter *w (/wuh/)*. This is known as alliteration.

  Alliteration is the repetition of initial consonant sounds.

  > The <u>sl</u>ithering <u>sn</u>eaky <u>sn</u>ake <u>sn</u>uck through the <u>sl</u>imy <u>s</u>ewer.
  > The <u>ch</u>uckling <u>ch</u>erub <u>ch</u>ortled with <u>Ch</u>arles.

  The poetic technique of assonance is often used in combination with alliteration.

- **What is the author's message, or moral, that is being communicated?** Based on your answers to all these questions when reading to understand literature, you need to determine what the author's theme or message is.

QUICK TIPS QUESTIONS TO CONSIDER WHEN READING LITERATURE

1. What does the title reveal?

2. Who are the characters?

3. What is the setting?

4. What is the point of view?

5. What is the author's attitude (tone) toward the subject?

6. What is the main conflict?

7. What is the plot, or sequence of events?

8. What is the climax or high point of the action?

9. What is the resolution?

10. What figurative language, poetic devices, or symbols has the author used?

11. What is the message or moral that the author is communicating?

Thinking It Through ANALYZING A POEM

Here is a poem by Gwendolyn Brooks about a woman who went against the crowd and made her own choices. For some background information about Brooks, her life, her literary contributions, and her place in American literary history, see the practice exercise in Chapter 6 on page 446.

Sadie and Maud
by Gwendolyn Brooks

Maud went to college.
Sadie stayed home.
Sadie scraped life
With a fine-toothed comb.

5   She didn't leave a tangle in
Her comb found every strand.
Sadie was one of the livingest chicks
In all the land.
Sadie bore two babies

10   Under her maiden name.
Maud and Ma and Papa
Nearly died of shame.
When Sadie said her last so-long
Her girls struck out from home.

15   (Sadie left as heritage
Her fine-toothed comb.)
Maud, who went to college,
Is a thin brown mouse.
She is living all alone

20   In this old house.
_____

SOURCE: "Sadie and Maud" by Gwendolyn Brooks. Reprinted by consent of Brooks Permissions.

1. **What does the title reveal?** *The title reveals that the poem concerns two females, Sadie and Maud.*

2. **Who are the characters?** *The characters are Sadie and Maud, who are sisters. We can assume Sadie and Maud are sisters from lines 11 and 12.*

3. **What is the setting?** *There is no specific location where the story the poem tells takes place; rather, the poet gives a kind of review of the two sisters' lives. However, we can infer the approximate time the action takes place because Ma and Pa "nearly died of shame" (line 8) when Sadie bore a child outside of marriage. The events in the poem take place during a time when choices outside of culturally accepted norms (such as having children out of wedlock) are a source of shame. The poet grew up in the 1940s and 1950s, when women had to choose between having a domestic life and having a career.*

4. **What is the point of view?** *The poem has a third-person narrator.*

5. **What is the author's attitude toward the subject (tone)?** *The poet seems sympathetic toward Sadie. The image of Sadie's "combing" life (getting down to life's roots—its basics) is a positive one; also, the made-up adjective "livingest" (line 7) suggests unbridled enthusiasm and vibrancy. In contrast, the poet seems disapproving of Maud, as the speaker describes her as a "thin, brown mouse" (line 18), living in isolation, perhaps deprived of the support human relationships provide. Brooks presents two contrasting lifestyles in this poem. From her word choice, however, we can infer with whom her sympathy lies. This, in turn, helps us infer the message of the poem.*

6. **What is the main conflict?** *The conflict in the poem is between Sadie and her family's opinion about her choices. The conflict can be categorized as human versus external force or entity, in this case, Sadie's environment—the family and the society to which she belongs. There is also a conflict between Sadie and Maud, as Maud joins the parents in condemning Sadie for her lifestyle.*

(Continued)

7. **What is the plot, or sequence of events, in the story the poem relates?** *The two sisters live very different lives: Maud is described as a "thin brown mouse" (line 18) and Sadie is described as "one of the livingest chicks/In all the land" (lines 7–8). We can assume Sadie took risks in her life and Maud did not. We also know that "Sadie bore two babies/Under her maiden name" (lines 9–10) and that she passed on her lifestyle to her own two children because she "left as heritage/Her fine-toothed comb" (lines 15–16). Maud, who has chosen a higher road than her sister, outlives Sadie, but winds up alone in an old house.*

8. **What is the climax (or high point of the action) in the literary work?** *The first two stanzas of the poem lead up to the climax. The climax of the poem occurs when Sadie passes on her "fine-toothed comb" to her daughters, implying that Sadie dies relatively young. From that point, the reader learns that Maud lived a submissive and colorless life, educated but alone.*

9. **What is the resolution of the literary work?** *Sadie seems to have lived a wild life without regard for the opinions of others. Maud did everything she was supposed to do, but is alone. This ending leaves the reader thinking about which sister lived the fullest life.*

10. **What figurative language, poetic devices, or symbols has the poet used?** *The poet repeats the symbol of the "fine-toothed comb." This symbol suggests a comparison between Sadie's outlook on life and a fine-toothed comb, which implies having as many experiences as possible and not missing any opportunities. Sadie did not miss anything that life had to offer, including bringing new life into the world, and passed on her willingness to embrace life fully to her daughters. In contrast, the speaker in the poem tells us little about Maud other than to describe her at the end of the poem as a "thin brown mouse" (line 18), a metaphor that suggests that Maud was timid and meek, lived a lonely and unfulfilling life, and conformed to the expectations of others. This view is supported by the fact that Maud lives alone "in this old house" (line 20), devoid of any fresh experiences and without human contact. In addition, because the poem uses rhyming words like "home" and "comb," "strand" and "land," "name" and "shame," and "mouse" and "house" at the end of each stanza, the poet used the technique of assonance, where vowel sounds are repeated.*

11. **What is the author's message or moral that is being communicated?** *Because Maud is left with little at the end of the poem, the poet seems to be suggesting that living life to the fullest without worrying about others' opinions is worthwhile. This theme statement could also be worded in the following ways:*
    - Do what you feel is best in life and do not worry about the opinions of others.
    - Life is to be lived to the fullest.
    - Have the courage to make your own choices.
    - Different choices make different people happy.

On Your Own ANALYZING A POEM

Here's another poem by Gwendolyn Brooks about more choices in life. Using the questioning technique you learned from the Quick Tips on page 284, analyze this poem and determine the theme and the statement that can be made about the theme.

We Real Cool
The Pool Players Seven at the Golden Shovel
by Gwendolyn Brooks

    We real cool. We
    Left school. We

    Lurk late. We
    Strike straight. We

5   Sing sin. We
    Thin gin. We

    Jazz June. We
    Die soon.

SOURCE: Gwendolyn Brooks, "We real cool." From *The Bean Eaters* by Gwendolyn Brooks. Reprinted by consent of Brooks Permissions.

1. What does the title reveal? _____
_____
_____
_____

2. Who are the characters? _____
_____
_____
_____

3. What is the setting? _____
_____
_____
_____

4. What is the point of view? _____

5. What is the author's attitude toward the subject (tone)? _____
_____
_____
_____

(Continued)

6. What is the main conflict? _____
_____
_____
_____

7. What is the plot, or sequence of events? _____
_____
_____
_____

8. What is the climax (or high point) of action? _____
_____
_____
_____

9. What is the resolution? _____
_____
_____
_____

10. What figurative language, poetic devices, or symbols has the author used? _____
_____
_____

11. What is the author's message or moral that is being communicated? _____
_____
_____
_____

12. In this poem, does the poet approve of the boys' choices? Support your answer with specific references to the poem. _____
_____
_____
_____

INCREASE YOUR DISCIPLINE-SPECIFIC VOCABULARY

LITERATURE

Literature can be a part of college study as well as a part of daily life. Like other disciplines, literature has specific key terms—particular vocabulary—that are used to discuss the literary work. You have learned many key concepts for reading literature in this chapter. Here is a list of word parts that relate to reading literature along with more key terms for understanding literature.

TABLE 4.1 Vocabulary Associated with Literature

WORD PART	MEANING	VOCABULARY
chron	time	anachronism, chronic, chronological, synchronize
cur	to run	cursive, discourse, concourse, concur, concurrent, curriculum, precursor, currency, occurrence
log	speech, word	analogy, dialogue, monologue, prologue, epilogue, apology, eulogy
loqu, loc	to speak	soliloquy, colloquial, eloquent, loquacious, ventriloquist
phon	sound	phonetics, phonics, symphony, megaphone, microphone, telephone
sed, sid, sess	to sit	assess, insidious, obsession, preside, president, sedentary, sedative, session, subside, reside, residue
syn, sym, syl	together, with	symbol, syndrome, synopsis, syntax, synthesis, symmetry, synonym, photosynthesis
ten, tain, tin	to hold	abstain, contents, detain, pertain, sustain, tenacious, tenure, contain, tenet
tort	to twist	contort, distort, retort, torment, torture, torch, tortoise
vert, vers	to turn	verse, adversary, aversion, controversy, divert, introvert, perverse, anniversary, reverse, subversive, diverse, universe

(Continued)

Key Terms—Literature

- **Analogy:** this is a general term for a comparison created between two things.

- **Genre:** refers to a type or category of writing, such as drama, poetry, essay, or story and novel.

- **Antagonist:** this is the character or force that is in conflict with the hero or heroine.

- **Protagonist:** the protagonist is the main character in a piece of literature.

- **Foreshadowing:** the literary technique of suggesting a future plot or character development in order to build dramatic tension.

- **Motif:** an element that recurs in a literary work or a series of works.

- **Pathos:** a sense of pity or sympathy for a character, scene, or situation in a literary work.

- **Dramatic Irony:** a term in a literary work for the actions or thoughts of characters that have a different meaning to the audience than for the characters themselves.

- **Soliloquy:** a dramatic device where a character talks out loud to reveal his or her thoughts to the audience.

- **Tragedy:** a dramatic term to characterize a plot where the ending is tragic or unhappy for the main character.

APPLICATIONS

APPLICATION ①

This reading about the Salem witch trials in the late 1600s in Massachusetts is taken from *Smithsonian* magazine. Answer the questions about the overall reading; then read through the passage, making notations in the margin as you uncover important information. Afterward, answer the questions following the reading.

1. What is the topic of the reading? _____

2. What is the pattern of organization? _____

3. What is the author's purpose? _____

4. What is the main idea of the reading in your own words? _____

_____

_____

_____

A Brief History of the Salem Witch Trials
One town's strange journey from paranoia to pardon
by Jess Blumberg

1   The Salem witch trials occurred in colonial Massachusetts between 1692 and 1693. More than 200 people were accused of practicing witchcraft—the Devil's magic—and 20 were executed. Eventually, the colony admitted the trials were a mistake and <u>compensated</u> the families of those convicted. Since then, the story of the trials has become <u>synonymous</u> with paranoia and injustice, and it continues to <u>beguile</u> the popular imagination more than 300 years later.

Paragraph 1: What is the main idea?

What method did you use?

The Granger Collection

(Continued)

What is the main idea of
this subsection?

Paragraph 2: What is the main
idea?

What method did you use?

Paragraph 3: What is the main
idea?

What method did you use?

Paragraph 4: What is the
main idea?

What method did you use?

Paragraph 5: What is the
main idea?

What method did you use?

What is the main idea of
this subsection?

Paragraph 6: What is the main
idea?

Salem Struggling

2   Several centuries ago, many practicing Christians, and those of other religions, had a strong belief that the Devil could give certain people known as witches the power to harm others in return for their loyalty. A "witchcraft craze" <u>rippled</u> through Europe from the 1300s to the end of the 1600s. Hundreds of thousands of supposed witches—mostly women—were executed.

3   In 1689, English rulers William and Mary started a war with France in the American colonies. Known as King William's War to colonists, it <u>ravaged</u> regions of upstate New York, Nova Scotia and Quebec, sending refugees into the county of Essex and, specifically, Salem Village in the Massachusetts Bay Colony. (Salem Village is present-day Danvers, Massachusetts; colonial Salem Town became what's now Salem.)

4   The displaced people created a strain on Salem's resources. This aggravated the existing rivalry between families with ties to the wealth of the port of Salem and those who still depended on agriculture. Controversy also brewed over Reverend Samuel Parris, who became Salem Village's first ordained minister in 1689, and was disliked because of his <u>rigid</u> ways and greedy nature. The Puritan villagers believed all the quarreling was the work of the Devil.

5   In January of 1692, Reverend Parris' daughter Elizabeth, age 9, and niece Abigail Williams, age 11, started having <u>"fits."</u> They screamed, threw things, uttered peculiar sounds, and contorted themselves into strange positions, and a local doctor blamed the supernatural. Another girl, Ann Putnam, age 11, experienced similar episodes. On February 29, under pressure from magistrates Jonathan Corwin and John Hathorne, the girls blamed three women for afflicting them: Tituba, the Parrises' Caribbean slave; Sarah Good, a homeless beggar; and Sarah Osborne, an elderly, impoverished woman.

Witch Hunt

6   All three women were brought before the local magistrates and interrogated for several days, starting on March 1, 1692. Osborne claimed innocence, as did Good. But Tituba confessed, "The Devil came to me and bid me serve him." She described elaborate images of black dogs, red cats, yellow birds, and a "black man" who wanted her to sign his book. She admitted that she signed the book and said there were several other

witches looking to destroy the Puritans. All three women were put in jail.

7 <u>With the seed of paranoia planted</u>, a stream of accusations followed for the next few months. Charges against Martha Corey, a loyal member of the Church in Salem Village, greatly concerned the community; if she could be a witch, then anyone could. Magistrates even questioned Sarah Good's 4-year-old daughter, Dorothy, and her timid answers were construed as a confession. The questioning got more serious in April when Deputy Governor Thomas Danforth and his assistants attended the hearings. Dozens of people from Salem and other Massachusetts villages were brought in for questioning.

8 On May 27, 1692, Governor William Phipps ordered the establishment of a Special Court of Oyer (to hear) and Terminer (to decide) for Suffolk, Essex, and Middlesex counties. The first case brought to the special court was Bridget Bishop, an older woman known for her gossipy habits and promiscuity. When asked if she committed witchcraft, Bishop responded, "<u>I am as innocent as the child unborn</u>." The defense must not have been convincing, because she was found guilty and, on June 10, became the first person hanged on what was later called Gallows Hill.

9 Five days later, respected minister Cotton Mather wrote a letter imploring the court not to allow <u>spectral</u> evidence—testimony about dreams and visions. The court largely ignored this request and five people were sentenced and hanged in July, five more in August, and eight in September. On October 3, following in his son's footsteps, Increase Mather, then president of Harvard, denounced the use of spectral evidence: "It were better that ten suspected witches should escape than one innocent person be condemned."

10 Governor Phipps, in response to Mather's plea and his own wife being questioned for witchcraft, prohibited further arrests, released many accused witches, and dissolved the Court of Oyer and Terminer on October 29. Phipps replaced it with a Superior Court of Judicature, which <u>disallowed</u> spectral evidence and only condemned 3 out of 56 defendants. Phipps eventually pardoned all who were in prison on witchcraft charges by May 1693. But the damage had been done: 19 were hanged on Gallows Hill, a 71-year-old man was pressed to death with heavy stones, several people died in jail, and

What method did you use?

Paragraph 7: What is the main idea?

What method did you use?

Paragraph 8: What is the main idea?

What method did you use?

Paragraph 9: What is the main idea?

What method did you use?

Paragraph 10: What is the main idea?

What method did you use?

(Continued)

nearly 200 people, overall, had been accused of practicing "the Devil's magic."

Restoring Good Names

What is the main idea of this subsection?

11   Following the trials and executions, many involved, like judge Samuel Sewall, publicly confessed error and guilt. On January 14, 1697, the General Court ordered a day of fasting and soul-searching for the tragedy of Salem. In 1702, the court declared the trials unlawful. And in 1711, the colony passed a bill restoring the rights and good names of those accused and granted £600 <u>restitution</u> to their heirs. However, it was not until 1957—more than 250 years later—that Massachusetts formally apologized for the events of 1692.

Paragraph 11: What is the main idea?

12   In the 20th century, artists and scientists alike continued to be fascinated by the Salem witch trials. Playwright Arthur Miller resurrected the tale with his 1953 play *The Crucible*, using the trials as an allegory for the McCarthyism paranoia in the 1950s. Additionally, numerous hypotheses have been devised to explain the strange behavior that occurred in Salem in 1692. One of the most concrete studies, published in *Science* in 1976 by psychologist Linnda Caporael, blamed the abnormal habits of the accused on the fungus ergot, which can be found in rye, wheat, and other cereal grasses. Toxicologists say that eating ergot-contaminated foods can lead to muscle spasms, vomiting, delusions, and hallucinations. Also, the fungus thrives in warm and damp climates—not too unlike the swampy meadows in Salem Village, where rye was the staple grain during the spring and summer months.

What method did you use?

Paragraph 12: What is the main idea?

What method did you use?

Paragraph 13: What is the main idea?

13   In August 1992, to mark the 300th anniversary of the trials, Nobel Laureate Elie Wiesel dedicated the Witch Trials Memorial in Salem. Also in Salem, the Peabody Essex Museum houses the original court documents, and the town's most-visited attraction, the Salem Witch Museum, attests to the public's <u>enthrallment</u> with the 1692 hysteria.

What method did you use?

COMPREHENSION CHECK

Answer the following questions, using your skills of inference and drawing conclusions. Remember: Inferences and conclusions must be based on information provided in the passage, as well as your own knowledge. Be prepared to defend your answer by referring to information in the reading.

1 What was the historical reason that the Salem witch trials began? _____
_____
_____
_____
_____

2 Why did the people of Salem react as they did? _____
_____
_____
_____
_____

3 Why did the trials last for only a short period of time? _____
_____
_____
_____
_____

4 What do you think accounted for the "publicly confessed error and guilt" (paragraph 11)
on the parts of the judges and others involved?

_____
_____
_____
_____
_____

5 What might account for people's continued fascination with the Salem witch trials?

_____
_____
_____
_____

6 Explain the 1976 study that suggested that ingestion of ergot might account for the
abnormal behavior. _____
_____
_____
_____
_____
_____

(Continued)

READING GRAPHICS

1. What is the implied main idea of this
   cartoon? _____
   _____
   _____
   _____
   _____

2. How does this cartoon relate to the reading?
   _____
   _____
   _____
   _____
   _____

"Hey, we're sheep. *Everything* seems like a good idea."

Leo Cullum/New Yorker Cartoon/Cartoonbank.com

DEVELOPING YOUR COLLEGE-LEVEL VOCABULARY

Answer the following questions about language in the reading.

Paragraph 1

1. What does the word *compensated* mean in context? _____

2. What does the word *synonymous* mean in context? _____

3. What does the word *beguile* mean in context? _____

Paragraph 2

4. What is a synonym for the word *rippled*? _____

Paragraph 3

5. What is implied by the word *ravaged*? _____

Paragraph 4

6. What is a synonym for *rigid* in this context? _____

Paragraph 5

7. What is implied by the word *fits*? _____

Paragraph 7

8. What is meant by the metaphor "With the seed of paranoia planted ..."? _____
   _____

9. What two things are being compared? _____
_____

Paragraph 8

10. What is meant by the expression "I am as innocent as the child unborn"? _____
_____

Paragraph 9

11. What does the adjective *spectral* mean in context? _____

Paragraph 10

12. What is the meaning of the prefix *dis-* in *disallow*? _____

Paragraph 11

13. What does the word *restitution* mean in context? _____

Paragraph 12

14. Explain the "allegory" in the following quote: "Playwright Arthur Miller resurrected the tale with his 1953 play *The Crucible,* using the trials as an allegory for the McCarthyism paranoia in the 1950s." _____
_____

Paragraph 13

15. What does the word *enthrallment* mean in context? _____

THEMATIC CONNECTIONS

1. What other historical events might compare with the Salem witch trials? Was the human motivation the same or similar for the other historical event(s) as they were in the Salem witch trials?

2. Can you relate on some level to either the persecutors or the persecuted in the Salem witch trials? Write about or discuss an event in your life that affected you and compelled you to contemplate the darker side of human nature.

3. Have humans evolved since the times of the Salem witch trials? Are we more humane and understanding now? Explain your answer using real-world examples where possible.

APPLICATION ②

This Application features a famous short story published around the time of World War II. It concerns appearances and reality, people's inhumanity to each other, and a variety of other themes. Read the story, practicing the skills you learned in this chapter related to understanding literature. After reading, respond to the questions following the story.

The Lottery
by Shirley Jackson

1   The morning of June 27th was clear and sunny, with the fresh warmth of a full-summer day; the flowers were blossoming profusely and the grass was richly green. The people of the village began to gather in the square, between the post office and the bank, around ten o'clock; in some towns there were so many people that the lottery took two days and had to be started on June 26th, but in this village, where there were only about three hundred people, the whole lottery took less than two hours, so it could begin at ten o'clock in the morning and still be through in time to allow the villagers to get home for noon dinner.

   The children assembled first, of course. School was recently over for the summer, and the feeling of liberty sat uneasily on most of them; they tended to gather together quietly for a while before they broke into boisterous play, and their talk was still of the classroom and the teacher, of books and reprimands. Bobby Martin had already stuffed his pockets full of stones, and the other boys soon followed his example, selecting the smoothest and roundest stones; Bobby and Harry Jones and Dickie Delacroix—the villagers pronounced this name "Dellacroy"—eventually made a great pile of stones in one corner of the square and guarded it against the raids of the other boys. The girls stood aside, talking among themselves, looking over their shoulders at the boys and the very small children rolled in the dust or clung to the hands of their older brothers or sisters.

   Soon the men began to gather, surveying their own children, speaking of planting and rain, tractors and taxes. They stood together, away from the pile of stones in the corner, and their jokes were quiet and they smiled rather than laughed. The women, wearing faded house dresses and sweaters, came shortly after their menfolk. They greeted one another and exchanged bits of gossip as they went to join their husbands. Soon the women, standing by their husbands, began to call to their children, and the children came reluctantly, having to be called four or five times. Bobby Martin ducked under his mother's grasping hand and ran, laughing, back to the pile of stones. His father spoke up sharply, and Bobby came quickly and took his place between his father and his oldest brother.

   The lottery was conducted—as were the square dances, the teen club, the Halloween program—by Mr. Summers, who had time and energy to devote to civic activities. He was a round-faced, jovial man and he ran the coal business, and people were sorry for him, because he had no children and his wife was a scold. When he arrived in the square, carrying the black wooden box, there was a murmur of conversation among the villagers, and he waved and called, "Little late today, folks." The postmaster, Mr. Graves, followed him, carrying a three-legged stool, and the stool was put in the center of the square and Mr. Summers set the black box down on it. The villagers kept their distance, leaving a space between themselves and the stool, and when Mr. Summers said, "Some of you fellows want to give me a hand?" there was a hesitation before two men, Mr. Martin and his oldest son, Baxter, came forward to hold the box steady on the stool while Mr. Summers stirred up the papers inside it.

5   The original paraphernalia for the lottery had been lost long ago, and the black box now resting on the stool had been put into use even before Old Man Warner, the oldest man in town, was born. Mr. Summers spoke frequently to the villagers about making a new box, but no one liked to upset even as much tradition as was represented by the black box. There was a story that the present box had been made with some pieces of the box that had preceded it, the one that had been constructed when the first people settled down to make a village here. Every year, after the lottery, Mr. Summers began talking again about a new box, but every year the subject was allowed to fade off without anything's being done. The black box grew shabbier each year: by now it was no longer completely black but splintered badly along one side to show the original wood color, and in some places faded or stained.

Mr. Martin and his oldest son, Baxter, held the black box securely on the stool until Mr. Summers had stirred the papers thoroughly with his hand. Because so much of the ritual had been forgotten or discarded, Mr. Summers had been successful in having slips of paper substituted for the chips of wood that had been used for generations. Chips of wood, Mr. Summers had argued, had been all very well when the village was tiny, but now that the population was more than three hundred and likely to keep on growing, it was necessary to use something that would fit more easily into the black box. The night before the lottery, Mr. Summers and Mr. Graves made up the slips of paper and put them in the box, and it was then taken to the safe of Mr. Summers' coal company and locked up until Mr. Summers was ready to take it to the square next morning. The rest of the year, the box was put way, sometimes one place, sometimes another; it had spent one year in Mr. Graves's barn and another year underfoot in the post office, and sometimes it was set on a shelf in the Martin grocery and left there.

There was a great deal of fussing to be done before Mr. Summers declared the lottery open. There were the lists to make up—of heads of families, heads of households in each family, members of each household in each family. There was the proper swearing-in of Mr. Summers by the postmaster, as the official of the lottery; at one time, some people remembered, there had been a recital of some sort, performed by the official of the lottery, a perfunctory, tuneless chant that had been rattled off duly each year; some people believed that the official of the lottery used to stand just so when he said or sang it, others believed that he was supposed to walk among the people, but years and years ago this part of the ritual

(Continued)

had been allowed to lapse. There had been, also, a ritual salute, which the official of the lottery had had to use in addressing each person who came up to draw from the box, but this also had changed with time, until now it was felt necessary only for the official to speak to each person approaching. Mr. Summers was very good at all this; in his clean white shirt and blue jeans, with one hand resting carelessly on the black box, he seemed very proper and important as he talked interminably to Mr. Graves and the Martins.

Just as Mr. Summers finally left off talking and turned to the assembled villagers, Mrs. Hutchinson came hurriedly along the path to the square, her sweater thrown over her shoulders, and slid into place in the back of the crowd. "Clean forgot what day it was," she said to Mrs. Delacroix, who stood next to her, and they both laughed softly. "Thought my old man was out back stacking wood," Mrs. Hutchinson went on, "and then I looked out the window and the kids was gone, and then I remembered it was the twenty-seventh and came a-running." She dried her hands on her apron, and Mrs. Delacroix said, "You're in time, though. They're still talking away up there."

Mrs. Hutchinson craned her neck to see through the crowd and found her husband and children standing near the front. She tapped Mrs. Delacroix on the arm as a farewell and began to make her way through the crowd. The people separated good-humoredly to let her through: two or three people said, in voices just loud enough to be heard across the crowd, "Here comes your, Missus, Hutchinson," and "Bill, she made it after all." Mrs. Hutchinson reached her husband, and Mr. Summers, who had been waiting, said cheerfully, "Thought we were going to have to get on without you, Tessie." Mrs. Hutchinson said, Grinning, "Wouldn't have me leave m'dishes in the sink, now, would you, Joe?," and soft laughter ran through the crowd as the people stirred back into position after Mrs. Hutchinson's arrival.

10   "Well, now," Mr. Summers said soberly, "guess we better get started, get this over with, so's we can go back to work. Anybody ain't here?"

"Dunbar," several people said. "Dunbar. Dunbar."

Mr. Summers consulted his list. "Clyde Dunbar," he said. "That's right. He's broke his leg, hasn't he? Who's drawing for him?"

"Me. I guess," a woman said, and Mr. Summers turned to look at her. "Wife draws for her husband," Mr. Summers said. "Don't you have a grown boy to do it for you, Janey?" Although Mr. Summers and everyone else in the village knew the answer perfectly well, it was the business of the official of the lottery to ask such questions formally. Mr. Summers waited with an expression of polite interest while Mrs. Dunbar answered.

"Horace's not but sixteen yet," Mrs. Dunbar said regretfully. "Guess I gotta fill in for the old man this year."

15   "Right," Mr. Summers said. He made a note on the list he was holding. Then he asked, "Watson boy drawing this year?"

A tall boy in the crowd raised his hand. "Here," he said. "I'm drawing for my mother and me." He blinked his eyes nervously and ducked his head as several voices in the crowd said things like "Good fellow, Jack," and "Glad to see your mother's got a man to do it."

"Well," Mr. Summers said, "guess that's everyone. Old Man Warner make it?"

"Here," a voice said, and Mr. Summers nodded.

A sudden hush fell on the crowd as Mr. Summers cleared his throat and looked at the list. "All ready?" he called. "Now, I'll read the names—heads of families first—and the men come up and take a paper out of the box. Keep the paper folded in your hand without looking at it until everyone has had a turn. Everything clear?"

20   The people had done it so many times that they only half listened to the directions: most of them were quiet, wetting their lips, not looking around. Then Mr. Summers raised one hand high and said, "Adams." A man disengaged himself from the crowd and came forward. "Hi, Steve," Mr. Summers said, and Mr. Adams said, "Hi, Joe." They grinned at one another humorlessly and nervously. Then Mr. Adams reached into the black box and took out a folded paper. He held it firmly by one corner as he turned and went hastily back to his place in the crowd, where he stood a little apart from his family, not looking down at his hand.

"Allen," Mr. Summers said. "Anderson . . . Bentham."

"Seems like there's no time at all between lotteries anymore," Mrs. Delacroix said to Mrs. Graves in the back row.

"Seems like we got through with the last one only last week."

"Time sure goes fast," Mrs. Graves said.

25   "Clark . . . Delacroix."

"There goes my old man," Mrs. Delacroix said. She held her breath while her husband went forward.

"Dunbar," Mr. Summers said, and Mrs. Dunbar went steadily to the box while one of the women said. "Go on, Janey," and another said, "There she goes."

"We're next," Mrs. Graves said. She watched while Mr. Graves came around from the side of the box, greeted Mr. Summers gravely, and selected a slip of paper from the box. By now, all through the crowd there were men holding the small folded papers in their large hands, turning them over and over nervously. Mrs. Dunbar and her two sons stood together, Mrs. Dunbar holding the slip of paper.

"Harburt . . . Hutchinson."

30   "Get up there, Bill," Mrs. Hutchinson said, and the people near her laughed.

"Jones."

"They do say," Mr. Adams said to Old Man Warner, who stood next to him, "that over in the north village they're talking of giving up the lottery."

Old Man Warner snorted. "Pack of crazy fools," he said. "Listening to the young folks, nothing's good enough for them. Next thing you know, they'll be wanting to go back to living in caves, nobody work anymore, live that way for a while. Used to be a saying about 'Lottery in June, corn be heavy soon.' First thing you know, we'd all be eating stewed chickweed and acorns. There's always been a lottery," he added petulantly. "Bad enough to see young Joe Summers up there joking with everybody."

"Some places have already quit lotteries," Mrs. Adams said.

(Continued)

35   "Nothing but trouble in that," Old Man Warner said stoutly. "Pack of young fools."

"Martin." And Bobby Martin watched his father go forward. "Overdyke . . . Percy."

"I wish they'd hurry," Mrs. Dunbar said to her older son. "I wish they'd hurry."

"They're almost through," her son said.

"You get ready to run tell Dad," Mrs. Dunbar said.

40   Mr. Summers called his own name and then stepped forward precisely and selected a slip from the box. Then he called, "Warner."

"Seventy-seventh year I been in the lottery," Old Man Warner said as he went through the crowd. "Seventy-seventh time."

"Watson." The tall boy came awkwardly through the crowd. Someone said, "Don't be nervous, Jack," and Mr. Summers said, "Take your time, son."

"Zanini."

After that, there was a long pause, a breathless pause, until Mr. Summers, holding his slip of paper in the air, said, "All right, fellows." For a minute, no one moved, and then all the slips of paper were opened. Suddenly, all the women began to speak at once, saying, "Who is it?," "Who's got it?," "Is it the Dunbars?," "Is it the Watsons?" Then the voices began to say, "It's Hutchinson. It's Bill." "Bill Hutchinson's got it."

45   "Go tell your father," Mrs. Dunbar said to her older son.

People began to look around to see the Hutchinsons. Bill Hutchinson was standing quiet, staring down at the paper in his hand. Suddenly, Tessie Hutchinson shouted to Mr. Summers. "You didn't give him time enough to take any paper he wanted. I saw you. It wasn't fair!"

"Be a good sport, Tessie," Mrs. Delacroix called, and Mrs. Graves said, "All of us took the same chance."

"Shut up, Tessie," Bill Hutchinson said.

"Well, everyone," Mr. Summers said, "that was done pretty fast, and now we've got to be hurrying a little more to get done in time." He consulted his next list. "Bill," he said, "you draw for the Hutchinson family. You got any other households in the Hutchinsons?"

50   "There's Don and Eva," Mrs. Hutchinson yelled. "Make them take their chance!"

"Daughters draw with their husbands' families, Tessie," Mr. Summers said gently. "You know that as well as anyone else."

"It wasn't fair," Tessie said.

"I guess not, Joe," Bill Hutchinson said regretfully. "My daughter draws with her husband's family; that's only fair. And I've got no other family except the kids."

"Then, as far as drawing for families is concerned, it's you," Mr. Summers said in explanation, "and as far as drawing for households is concerned, that's you, too. Right?"

55   "Right," Bill Hutchinson said.

"How many kids, Bill?" Mr. Summers asked formally.

"Three," Bill Hutchinson said.

"There's Bill, Jr., and Nancy, and little Dave. And Tessie and me."

"All right, then," Mr. Summers said. "Harry, you got their tickets back?"

60   Mr. Graves nodded and held up the slips of paper. "Put them in the box, then," Mr. Summers directed. "Take Bill's and put it in."

"I think we ought to start over," Mrs. Hutchinson said, as quietly as she could. "I tell you it wasn't fair. You didn't give him time enough to choose. Everybody saw that."

Mr. Graves had selected the five slips and put them in the box, and he dropped all the papers but those onto the ground, where the breeze caught them and lifted them off.

"Listen, everybody," Mrs. Hutchinson was saying to the people around her.

"Ready, Bill?" Mr. Summers asked, and Bill Hutchinson, with one quick glance around at his wife and children, nodded.

65   "Remember," Mr. Summers said, "take the slips and keep them folded until each person has taken one. Harry, you help little Dave." Mr. Graves took the hand of the little boy, who came willingly with him up to the box. "Take a paper out of the box, Davy," Mr. Summers said. Davy put his hand into the box and laughed. "Take just one paper," Mr. Summers said. "Harry, you hold it for him." Mr. Graves took the child's hand and removed the folded paper from the tight fist and held it while little Dave stood next to him and looked up at him wonderingly.

"Nancy next," Mr. Summers said. Nancy was twelve, and her school friends breathed heavily as she went forward switching her skirt, and took a slip daintily from the box. "Bill, Jr.," Mr. Summers said, and Billy, his face red and his feet overlarge, nearly knocked the box over as he got a paper out. "Tessie," Mr. Summers said. She hesitated for a minute, looking around defiantly, and then set her lips and went up to the box. She snatched a paper out and held it behind her.

"Bill," Mr. Summers said, and Bill Hutchinson reached into the box and felt around, bringing his hand out at last with the slip of paper in it.

The crowd was quiet. A girl whispered, "I hope it's not Nancy," and the sound of the whisper reached the edges of the crowd.

"It's not the way it used to be," Old Man Warner said clearly. "People ain't the way they used to be."

70   "All right," Mr. Summers said. "Open the papers. Harry, you open little Dave's."

Mr. Graves opened the slip of paper and there was a general sigh through the crowd as he held it up and everyone could see that it was blank. Nancy and Bill Jr. opened theirs at the same time, and both beamed and laughed, turning around to the crowd and holding their slips of paper above their heads.

"Tessie," Mr. Summers said. There was a pause, and then Mr. Summers looked at Bill Hutchinson, and Bill unfolded his paper and showed it. It was blank.

"It's Tessie," Mr. Summers said, and his voice was hushed. "Show us her paper, Bill."

Bill Hutchinson went over to his wife and forced the slip of paper out of her hand. It had a black spot on it, the black spot Mr. Summers had made the night before with the heavy pencil in the coal company office. Bill Hutchinson held it up, and there was a stir in the crowd.

75   "All right, folks," Mr. Summers said. "Let's finish quickly."

(Continued)

Although the villagers had forgotten the ritual and lost the original black box, they still remembered to use stones. The pile of stones the boys had made earlier was ready; there were stones on the ground with the blowing scraps of paper that had come out of the box. Mrs. Delacroix selected a stone so large she had to pick it up with both hands and turned to Mrs. Dunbar. "Come on," she said. "Hurry up."

Mrs. Dunbar had small stones in both hands, and she said, gasping for breath, "I can't run at all. You'll have to go ahead and I'll catch up with you."

The children had stones already. And someone gave little Davy Hutchinson a few pebbles.

Tessie Hutchinson was in the center of a cleared space by now, and she held her hands out desperately as the villagers moved in on her. "It isn't fair," she said. A stone hit her on the side of the head. Old Man Warner was saying, "Come on, come on, everyone." Steve Adams was in the front of the crowd of villagers, with Mrs. Graves beside him.

80   "It isn't fair, it isn't right," Mrs. Hutchinson screamed, and then they were upon her.

SOURCE: "The Lottery" from *The Lottery* by Shirley Jackson. Copyright © 1948, 1949 by Shirley Jackson. Copyright renewed 1976, 1977 by Laurence Hyman, Barry Hyman, Mrs. Sarah Webster and Mrs. Joanne Schnurer. Reprinted by permission of Farrar, Straus and Giroux, LLC and Penguin Books Ltd.

COMPREHENSION CHECK

Answer the following questions. Discuss your answers with a partner or in class discussion.

1 What does the title reveal about the story?_____
_____
_____

2 Who are the characters in the story?_____
_____
_____

3 Where does the story take place (setting)? _____
_____
_____
_____

4 What is the point of view?_____
_____
_____

5 What is the author's attitude (tone) toward the subject?_____
_____
_____

6 What is the main conflict in the story?_____

_____

7 What is the plot, or sequence of events, in the story?_____

_____

_____

_____

_____

_____

_____

_____

8 What is the climax (or high point) of the action in the story?_____

_____

_____

9 What is the resolution of the story?_____

_____

10 Were you surprised by the ending? If not, at what point in the story did you guess the ending? _____

11 A scapegoat is a person or group made to bear the blame for others or to suffer in their place. Who do you think is the scapegoat in this story? _____

12 Why does the town go through the ritual of the lottery every year? _____

_____

13 What is the significance of the lighthearted exchange once Tessie arrives in paragraphs 8 and 9? _____

_____

14 What is the significance of the character of Old Man Warner? _____

_____

15 What message, or moral, is Jackson communicating?_____

_____

_____

_____

_____

_____

READING GRAPHICS

Mike Baldwin/www.CartoonStock.com

1. What is the implied main idea of this cartoon? _____
   _____
   _____

2. How does the implied main idea of this cartoon relate to the story? _____
   _____
   _____

DEVELOPING YOUR COLLEGE-LEVEL VOCABULARY

1. In paragraph 9, what type of figurative language is used in this quote from the story?
   "… soft laughter ran through the crowd as the people stirred back into position after
   Mrs. Hutchinson's arrival." _____

2. What two things are being compared? _____
   _____

3. What other figurative language, poetic devices, or symbols has the author used? _____
   _____
   _____
   _____
   _____
   _____

THEMATIC CONNECTIONS

1. This story was published in 1948. Do you think Shirley Jackson was making a comment on events that took place around this time? If so, what events do you think she was commenting on?

2. Do you think the story is only about the time period following World War II, or is the author making a larger statement about human nature? If so, what statement is she making?

3. What other events in human history can be compared to the lottery?

4. What might be a connection between Jackson's message in the story and the study conducted by Milgram on obedience to authority from the Pre-Assessment in this chapter?

5. How would you explain the behavior of the characters in "The Lottery"? Is it comparable to the behavior of the people of Salem during the times of the witch trials or to the participants in Milgram's study?

6. Can you relate any event or experience in your life to this short story? Was there a time when you or someone you know engaged in group behavior either as a victim or a perpetrator? What have you learned from that experience?

7. Is this short story realistic? How is it or how is it not realistic as a commentary on group behavior?

8. Would "The Lottery" be as relevant today as it was post–World War II when it was first published?

WRAPPING IT UP

In the following study outline, fill in the definitions and a brief explanation of the key terms in the "Your Notes" column. Use the strategy of spaced practice review these key terms on a regular basis. Use this study guide to review this chapter's key topics.

KEY TERM OR CONCEPT	YOUR NOTES
Inference	
Conclusion	
Implied main idea	
Method 1 for implied main idea	
Method 2 for implied main idea	
Method 3 for implied main idea	
Figurative languag	
Metaphor	
Simile	
Personification	
Hyperbole	
Theme	
Characters	
Setting	
Point of view	
Tone	
Mood	
Conflict	
Plot	

KEY TERM OR CONCEPT	YOUR NOTES
Climax	
Resolution	
Symbol	
Assonance	
Alliteration	

GROUP ACTIVITY: GROUP BEHAVIOR

Use a search engine to find information about the Bystander Effect, group behavior, or another topic introduced in this chapter on the Internet. Present your findings to the class for group discussion.

Alternatively, find a poem online, in a book, or in a magazine. Analyze your poem, following the criteria outlined in the study strategy for understanding literature. Find several examples of figurative language in the poem and interpret their meaning.

REFLECTIVE JOURNAL QUESTIONS

1. Analyze a piece of fiction or a movie using the criteria for reading literature outlined in this chapter.
2. A significant amount of college reading involves understanding implied main ideas. Choose a reading assigned for another class and find the implied main idea. What are the inferences you made as a reader that allowed you to draw the conclusion you did about the main idea?

THEMATIC CONNECTIONS

Respond to one of the following questions. Prepare notes for class discussion or write a response to submit to your instructor.

1. What do you believe is the most significant reason that people choose to behave in ways they know are wrong? Provide three examples of errors in judgment that you have made in your own life, and describe how you would make different choices now.
2. Several readings in this chapter concern group behavior. Based on these readings, explain three strategies you think would be effective in educating people about group behavior. Use specific examples of how such education might change your community.
3. What are the qualities needed for an individual to overcome being prone to group pressure? Choose three qualities (behaviors, techniques, or attitudes) that characterize a person who has risen above this influence. Support your answer with specific examples.

ADDITIONAL SKILL AND STRATEGY PRACTICE

Implied Main Idea

Determine the implied main idea of each of the following paragraphs. Identify which of the three methods you used to create the implied main idea:

- Method 1: topic + existing sentence

- Method 2: sentence + sentence

- Method 3: general statement based on supporting details

1.   Take a moment to make a list of your closest friends. What do they have in common (other than the joy of knowing you)? It is likely that their ages are similar to yours and you are of the same sex and ethnicity. There will be exceptions, of course. But similarity on these three dimensions is the general rule for friendships.

—From COON, Introduction to Psychology, 12E. © 2010 Cengage Learning.

---

2.   Cyberterrorism is generaly defined as highly damaging computer attacks by private individuals designed to generate terror and fear to achieve political or social goals. Thus, criminal hacking—no matter how damaging—conducted to extort money or for bragging rights is not considered cyberterrorism. (Criminal hacking is common. A year ago, for instance, criminals stole personal credit-card information from the computers of RBS WorldPay and then used the data to steal $9 million from 130 ATMs in 49 cities around the world.) Likewise, the relatively minor denial-of-service attacks and Web defacements typically conducted by hackers aligned with terrorist groups also is not considered cyberterrorism.

—B. Mantel, "Terrorism and the Internet, CQ Global Researcher 3, November 1, 2009, pp. 285–310.
(Retrieved from http://library.cqpress.com/globalresearcher/).

---

3.   Moderate self-disclosure leads to increased reciprocity (a return in kind). In contrast, overdisclosure exceeds what is appropriate for a relationship or social situation, giving rise to suspicion and reducing attraction. For example, imagine standing in line at a store and having the stranger in front of you say, "Lately I've been thinking about how I really feel about myself. I think I'm pretty well adjusted, but I occasionally have some questions about my sexual adequacy."

—From COON, Introduction to Psychology, 12E. © 2010 Cengage Learning.

---

4.   A decade ago, terrorist organizations operated or controlled only about a dozen Web sites. Today there are more than 7,000. Terrorist groups use the Internet for many activities, ranging from raising funds to explaining how to build a suicide bomb. They find the Internet appealing

for the same reasons everyone else does: It's cheap, easily accessible, unregulated and reaches a potentially enormous audience. As terrorist content spreads to chat rooms, blogs, user groups, social networking sites and virtual worlds, many experts, politicians and law enforcement officials are debating how government and industry should respond. Some want Internet companies to stop terrorists from using the Web, while others say that is not the role of Internet service providers. As governments enact laws based on the belief that the Internet plays a significant role in promoting terrorism, critics say the new measures often overstep free-speech and privacy rights.

—B. Mantel, "Terrorism and the Internet, *CQ Global Researcher* 3, November 1, 2009, pp. 285–310.
(Retrieved from http://library.cqpress.com/globalresearcher/).

5.   When self-disclosure proceeds at a moderate pace, it builds trust, intimacy, reciprocity, and positive feelings. When it is too rapid or inappropriate, we are likely to "back off" and wonder about the person's motives. It's interesting to note that on the Internet (and especially on social networking websites like Facebook) people often feel freer to express their true feelings, which can lead to genuine, face-to-face friendships. However, it can also lead to some very dramatic overdisclosure.

—From COON, *Introduction to Psychology*, 12E. © 2010 Cengage Learning.

6.   The U.S. Department of State has begun its own modest online effort. In November 2006 it created a Digital Outreach Team with two Arabic-speaking employees. The team now has 10 members who actively engage in conversations on Arabic-, Persian- and Urdu-language Internet sites, including blogs, news sites and discussion forums. Team members identify themselves as State Department employees, but instead of posting dry, policy pronouncements they create "engaging, informal personas for [their] online discussions." The team's mission is "to explain U.S. foreign policy and to counter misinformation," according to the State Department.

—B. Mantel, "Terrorism and the Internet, *CQ Global Researcher* 3, November 1, 2009, pp. 285–310.
(Retrieved from http://library.cqpress.com/globalresearcher/).

7.   In North American culture, most male friendships are *activity based.* That is, men tend to do things together—a pattern that provides companionship without closeness. The friendships of women are more often based on *shared feelings and confidences.* If two female friends spent an afternoon together and did not reveal problems, private thoughts, and feelings to one another, they would assume that something was wrong. For women, friendship is a matter of talking about shared concerns and intimate matters.

—From COON, *Introduction to Psychology*, 12E. © 2010 Cengage Learning.

(Continued)

8.   In the end, individual governments' direct role in providing an online alternative narrative to terrorist ideology may, out of necessity, be quite small because of the credibility issue, say analysts. Instead, they say, governments could fund Internet literacy programs that discuss hate propaganda, adjust school curriculums to include greater discussion of Islam and the West and encourage moderate Muslim voices to take to the Web. Cilluffo, of the Homeland Security Policy Institute, said the United Nations could lead the way, sponsoring a network of Web sites, publications and television programming.

—B. Mantel, "Terrorism and the Internet, *CQ Global Researcher* 3, November 1, 2009, pp. 285–310.
(Retrieved from http://library.cqpress.com/globalresearcher/).

_____

_____

9.   According to social exchange theory, we unconsciously weigh social rewards and costs. For a relationship to last, it must be *profitable* (its rewards must exceed its costs) for both parties. For instance, Troy and Helen have been dating for 2 years. Although they still have fun at times, they also frequently argue and bicker. If the friction in their relationship gets much stronger, it will exceed the rewards of staying together. When that happens, they will probably split up.

—From COON, *Introduction to Psychology*, 12E. © 2010 Cengage Learning.

_____

_____

10.   In Maryland, lawmakers approved a bill in April that requires public schools to develop a policy barring cyberbullying and other kinds of intimidation. The bill says that even if the bullying occurs off school grounds, administrators can report it if it "substantially disrupts the orderly operation of a school."

—"Cyberbullying" by litteri, T.J., *CQ Researcher*, 18, 385-408, May 2, 2008
(Retrieved from http://library.cqpress.com).

_____

_____

POST-ASSESSMENT

Preview the following article and then read it all the way through. Then go to the end of the article and answer the questions. This assessment will help you determine your strengths and weaknesses in understanding, learning, and applying the skills and strategies discussed in this chapter.

Study: Office Bullies Create Workplace "War Zone"
by Jeanna Bryner

1   The office might be far from the playground, but it's not off limits to bullies. From a screaming boss to snubbing colleagues, bullies can create a "war zone" in the workplace.

2   In a recent study, bullied employees likened their experiences to a battle, water torture, a nightmare, or a noxious substance. Understanding the seriousness of workplace bullying and what it feels like to get bullied could help managers put the brakes on the behavior, shown to afflict 25 to 30 percent of employees sometime during their careers.

3   "Many Americans are familiar with sexual and racial harassment, but not generalized workplace bullying," said study team member Sarah Tracy of Arizona State University. Bullying can lead to higher company costs including increased employee illness, use of sick days, and medical costs, ultimately affecting productivity, she added.

4   Workplace bullying can include "screaming, cursing, spreading vicious rumors, destroying the target's property or work product, excessive criticism, and sometimes hitting, slapping, and shoving." Subtle behaviors, such as silent treatment, disregard of requests, and exclusion from meetings, count as bullying.

Bully Icons

5   The scientists interviewed 17 women and 10 men ranging from 26 to 72 years old, who had experienced bullying. Often, people have trouble putting into words their emotions surrounding bully behavior. So the researchers analyzed the metaphors found throughout the participants' descriptions of bullying.

6   More than any other metaphor, participants characterized bullying as a contest or battle, with a female religious educator saying, "I have been maimed . . . I've been character assassinated." Others expressed feeling "beaten, abused, ripped, broken, scared, and eviscerated," the researchers stated in the upcoming issue of the journal *Management Communication Quarterly.*

7   The bullies were described as two-faced actors, narcissistic dictators and devils, leading workers to feel like vulnerable children, slaves, and prisoners in these situations. As one employee explained, "I feel like I have 'kick me' tattooed on my forehead."

(Continued)

Bully-Proof Office

8   How can you take the bite out of a bully-fied office? "An important first step of changing workplace bullying is helping people to understand that it's more than just kid stuff," Tracy told *LiveScience*.

9   Early intervention can nip bullying in the bud before it escalates into an established pattern, one resulting in high company costs. The problem is that most bully victims keep their mouths shut, whispering their horrid experiences to close friends rather than higher-ups. The use of metaphors, the researchers suggested, is more subtle and more likely to seep into conversations both public and private.

10   The scientists will continue examining the prevalence and impact of workplace bullying. In another research project, which will be published in an upcoming issue of the *Journal of Management Studies*, they found that out of more than 400 U.S. workers surveyed, 25 percent were bullied at work.

SOURCE: "Study: Office Bullies Create Workplace 'Warzone'," by Jeanna Bryner from *LiveScience*, Oct 31. 2006. Reprinted by permission.

COMPREHENSION CHECK

Circle the best answer to the following questions.

Reading Comprehension

1   **What is the implied meaning of the following sentence?**

In a recent study, bullied employees likened their experiences to a battle, water torture, a nightmare, or a noxious substance.

A. To go to work was a very unpleasant experience.
B. Employees need to go along with what others in the group do.
C. Employees should do what they think is best, regardless of others' actions.
D. Bullies should go along with the group unless they know better.

2   **What is the pattern of organization in this reading?**

A. Comparison and contrast
B. Definition and example
C. Sequence or process order
D. Cause and effect

3   **Which of the following would make a reasonable alternative title for this reading?**

A. To Hell and Back: My Day at the Office
B. Bullying Is Cruel
C. Bullies Should Be Punished
D. Monkey See, Monkey Do

4 **What is the most important point about the topic?**

A. In a recent study, bullied employees likened their experiences to a battle, water torture, a nightmare, or a noxious substance.

B. Many Americans are familiar with sexual and racial harassment, but not generalized workplace bullying.

C. Understanding the seriousness of workplace bullying and what it feels like to get bullied could help managers put the brakes on the behavior.

D. From a screaming boss to snubbing colleagues, bullies can create a "war zone" in the workplace.

5 **Where is the main idea?**

A. Combine the first and second sentences of paragraph 8.

B. Combine the two sentences in paragraph 10.

C. It is directly stated in paragraph 1.

D. Combine the two sentences in paragraph 2.

6 **It is stated, "Often, people have trouble putting into words their emotions surrounding bully behavior. So the researchers analyzed the metaphors found throughout the participants' descriptions of bullying." Why?**

A. Metaphors reveal the bullying episodes.

B. Metaphors create a mental image that clearly reflects the emotions of the victims.

C. The participants in the study could not use literal language.

D. The degree of bullying was insufficient for the participants to use figurative language.

7 **What is the implied main idea of paragraph 9?**

A. Early intervention can nip bullying in the bud before it escalates into an established pattern, but the problem is that most bully victims keep their mouths shut.

B. The use of metaphors prevents the employees from speaking up about the bullying.

C. To see the bullying behavior clearly, employees should use metaphors.

D. Early intervention is blocked by all the metaphors.

8 **What method of determining the implied main idea did you use to figure out the main idea of paragraph 9?**

A. Method 1

B. Method 2

C. Method 3

D. The main idea is directly stated.

(Continued)

Vocabulary Comprehension

9 **What is the author's tone in this reading?**

A. Sad

B. Angry

C. Lighthearted

D. Amused

10 **What is the meaning of the simile in the following sentence from paragraph 7?**

As one employee explained, "I feel like I have 'kick me' tattooed on my forehead."

A. The employee wanted to kick the bully.

B. The employee was tired of all the bullying.

C. The employee wanted to complain to the boss about mistreatment.

D. The employee felt like he was a target for excessive bullying.

READING FOR
MAIN IDEAS

THEME *Communication and Conflict Across Cultures*

TEXTBOOK APPLICATION

Chapter 27: The Limits of Liberalism: The 1970s from *HIST* by Kevin M. Schultz

This history textbook chapter concerns the political and social landscape in the United States in the 1970s. This chapter tackles such topics as Richard Nixon's presidency and his policies in the United States and abroad, the Watergate scandal, the economic conditions of the 1970s, and how later presidents Ford and Carter approached the problems. The chapter also considers political activism as an evolution of 1960s activism along with the rise of the "New Right." You will not learn only about American history reading this chapter, but also about international and domestic politics, conflict, social movements, and economics and business.

You now have a foundation in applying reading strategies and assessing text structure and supporting points from your study of Chapters 1 and 2. In addition, you have a strong understanding of both explicit and implied main ideas as well as fundamental strategies for understanding vocabulary. Now you have to continue to gain practice in transferring these skills to real college textbook chapters. This may seem a difficult task, but you have enough preparation now to practice here and succeed. The trick is to look at the sections in the text logically and to use what you have learned.

Apply what you have learned about prereading strategies, structure, relationships between ideas, and finding main ideas—both explicit and implied. In addition, apply your knowledge of vocabulary strategies and reading graphics.

There are five major learning objectives in this chapter. The predominant patterns of organization, as is typical in history, are cause and effect and sequence. Can you predict the pattern of organization of each section from its heading?

1. Survey the chapter.

2. Take each section one at a time, turning the headings into questions. The outline on the next page is a list of headings from this chapter. The first three headings are turned into question format as a model. Complete the rest of the outline.

3. Read each section first, looking for the answers to the questions.

4. As you read, jot down major points that answer the question posed by your guide question.

5. Circle any vocabulary that is unfamiliar and use context clues or word structure clues to help you make a guess as to the word's meaning. In addition, be alert to any figurative language.

A. PRESIDENT NIXON

1. Nixon's Foreign Policy
   a. Ping-Pong Diplomacy
   b. SALT and the Cold War
   c. Latin America and Africa
2. Nixon the Accidental Liberal
   a. Increasing the Size of Government

B. WATERGATE

C. THE TROUBLED ECONOMY AND POLITICS ADRIFT

1. Economic Woes
   a. Oil Embargo
   b. The Decline of Cities
2. President Ford
   a. Domestic Policy
   b. Foreign Policy
3. President Carter
   a. The Election of 1976
   b. Domestic Policy
   c. Foreign Policy

D. THE RISE OF IDENTITY POLITICS

1. Identifying with a Group
   a. African American Activism
   b. Affirmative Action
   c. The Chicano Movement
   d. Red Power
2. The Women's Movement
   a. ERA and Equal Rights
   b. *Roe v. Wade*
   c. Social and Economic Participation
   d. The Sexual Revolution
3. The Gay Liberation Movement
4. High Tide of Environmentalism
5. Popular Culture

E. THE RISE OF THE NEW RIGHT

1. Economic and Political Conservatism
2. The Religious Right
   a. "Family Values"

F. AND IN THE END

Who was President Nixon?

What was Nixon's foreign policy?

What was ping-pong diplomacy?

INCREASE YOUR DISCIPLINE-SPECIFIC VOCABULARY

HISTORY

Key Terms

The terms listed are used on the page indicated. Define each of these terms.

KEY TERM	DEFINITION
Strategic Arms Limitation Talks (SALT), p. 323	
Détente, p. 323	
Stagflation, p. 325	
Watergate, p. 324	
Oil embargo, p. 325	
Three Mile Island, p. 327	
Camp David Accords, p. 327	
Affirmative Action, p. 329	
Equal Rights Amendment (ERA), p. 330	
Roe v. Wade, p. 330	
Stonewall Inn, p. 331	
Moral Majority, p. 333	

After you read and take notes, answer the mutiple-choice questions about this chapter on page 334. Your notes should be a helpful guide to answering these questions. Following the quiz, your instructor will help you assess the strengths and weaknesses in your understanding of this textbook chapter.

The Limits *of* Liberalism: *The* 1970s

Learning Outcomes

After reading this chapter, you should be able to do the following:

LO **1** Evaluate Richard Nixon as president, focusing on his policies in the United States and abroad.

LO **2** Describe the events of Watergate and its ramifications for the country.

LO **3** Describe the economic conditions of the 1970s, including stagflation and the end of the post–World War II economic boom, and describe how Presidents Ford and Carter attempted to confront the problem.

LO **4** Describe the perpetuation of 1960s-style activism and how it transformed into a politics of identity in the 1970s.

LO **5** Evaluate the reaction to the 1960s social movements and describe the rise of the New Right.

> **66** *Without a magnetic social vision to unify the populace, the 1970s came to be characterized as a time of turning inward.* **99**

The social activism of the late 1960s continued into the 1970s, but during the 1970s that activism ran into roadblocks. A variety of minority movements seemed poised to fracture any national unity that had been created in the struggle for African American civil rights, and the postwar economic boom came to a startling end in 1973, raising poverty and unemployment as contentious and serious issues. American politicians learned the limits of politics' ability to create change, and they simultaneously learned that they could not publicly discuss these limits and expect to be reelected.

What do you think?

Americans' inability to buy gas whenever they wanted to was the first sign that the country's position as most powerful nation in the world was faltering.

Strongly Disagree						Strongly Agree
1	2	3	4	5	6	7

This awareness of limits had many sources. The war in Vietnam ended in 1975, but only after it had increased friction and schisms between Americans and diminished American expectations of imperial power. In addition, the countless fabrications that Johnson and Nixon had fed the public about the progress of the war made many Americans suspicious of their country's leaders. Meanwhile, the civil rights movement had succeeded in winning political rights for African Americans, but it then faced social and economic limits that tested the reality of America's commitment to racial equality. And a series of new social movements—by women, Chicanos, American Indians, and others—that followed in the wake of the civil rights movement seemed to cast African Americans as just another minority group vying for institutional recognition. Interest in other causes, such as environmentalism, exploded during the 1970s as well. All this turmoil and diverse social action provoked a backlash from voters, who, by 1980, were willing to overlook one Republican president's shady dealings in order to elect another conservative to the nation's highest office. Many Americans had tired of calls for social justice, and this sheer exhaustion led many to turn inward, contributing to what one writer called the "me generation."

At the same time, while the economy had remained healthy during the 1960s, it soured badly during the 1970s, officially ending the long post–World War II boom. The economic decline lasted the entire decade, casting a pall over the other events of the era. While the causes of the downturn are complex, a significant part was played by the demise of American manufacturing. Companies moved out of the Northeast and Midwest, heading to the South or the West in order to find better weather, cheaper labor, and fewer unions. This demographic and economic shift created "the Sunbelt," a region stretching from Florida to California. As more companies moved to the Sunbelt, American politics and culture took on the traditionally southern cast of anti-elitism and antigovernment individualism. "Get government off our backs" became a staple slogan of the late 1970s—one that epitomized a tax revolt that opened the door for a rightward shift in American politics that Americans still live with today.

LO¹ President Nixon

Richard Nixon, who had made his political name as a rabid anticommunist during the McCarthy years, who had served dutifully as Eisenhower's vice president throughout most of the 1950s, and who had nearly beaten Kennedy in the presidential race of 1960, finally won the office he so ardently sought in 1968. Some historians cite that year as the beginning of "the seventies."

As president, Nixon capitalized on divisions within the Democratic Party over the Vietnam War to beat the Democratic nominee, Hubert Humphrey. This son of a California grocer is considered one of our most complex presidents, reviled by liberals but not necessarily beloved by conservatives either. He was brilliant but unprincipled. Nixon responded to problems with a creativity and drive that stemmed not from concern for social justice, but from a persistent fear of how history would judge him. He was driven by a long-smoldering resentment against what he saw as "the Eastern Establishment," which he defined as the bankers, politicians, and businessmen who had controlled American social, cultural, and political life for years. More than anything else,

Nixon hated the Democratic establishment, which he thought was perpetually out to get him. His mistrust and suspicion would score him significant political gains in matters of foreign policy and the environment. But it would also lead to his historic downfall.

Nixon's Foreign Policy

Nixon's greatest triumphs as president were in foreign policy. As explained in the last chapter, his Vietnamization plan simultaneously pulled American troops out of Vietnam and increased the American military presence in other nations of Southeast Asia. Nevertheless, by 1972, Vietnamization was in fact removing American troops from the country. The last of them left Vietnam in 1973. Most Americans were relieved to be removed from a situation that was perceived as a stalemated "quagmire," where American soldiers were dying while fighting a war that could not be won.

Ping-Pong Diplomacy

As Vietnam simmered down as a national issue, Nixon saw that relations between China and the Soviet Union were beginning to break down. The two communist superpowers were still at odds, and, attempting to push the two further apart, Nixon began talks with China. His first step was to accept an invitation to send the American table tennis team to compete in a friendly international event in China. This gave his foreign policy toward China its name: Ping-Pong Diplomacy. The players were the first Americans invited into China since its

>> In efforts to redirect the Cold War, Nixon became the first president to visit China, meeting with Mao Zedong and Zhou Enlai in 1972. With regard to Chinese-Soviet relations, Nixon confided to Zhou that if Moscow marched either east or west, he was ready to "turn like a cobra on the Russians."

© AFP/Getty Images

founding as a communist country in 1949. In 1972, Nixon himself went to China, and the two nations increased trade and cultural exchanges. They also agreed that the Soviet Union should not be allowed to expand farther into Asia.

SALT and the Cold War

Increasingly worried about the cost of the arms race, Nixon also made overtures to the Soviet Union. Just months after going to China, Nixon went to Moscow to meet with Soviet premier Leonid Brezhnev. In this meeting he agreed to sell excess American wheat to the Soviets. The fact that their country needed wheat was an early sign that Soviet-style communism was not performing well economically, even though the Soviets attempted to hide this fact. Under the auspices of the Strategic Arms Limitation Talks (SALT), the two leaders also agreed to freeze the number of long-range missile launchers and build certain new missiles only after they had destroyed the same number of older missiles. This did not signify an end to the Cold War, but it did demonstrate that the nations' leaders were beginning to recognize the problems inherent in an unchecked arms race.

Thus, within four years, Nixon, perceived as a hard-nosed anticommunist Republican, had removed the American presence in Vietnam, ceding it to communists, and made overtures to both China and the Soviet Union. This softened approach toward America's supposed enemies was executed largely by Nixon's assistant for national security affairs and, later, his secretary of state, Henry Kissinger. These more relaxed relations are labeled détente (a French term meaning "a relaxing" or "an easing").

Latin America and Africa

As the Cold War cooled with China and the Soviet Union, it heated up in Latin America and Africa. Each time a nation in one of these regions elected a leftist—potentially communist—regime, the United States actively supported coups and the installation of new governments that would support U.S. interests. These new right-wing regimes routinely punished political opponents. For instance, the United States supported the ousting of Chile's Salvador Allende in 1973, opting instead to provide assistance to the authoritarian regime of General Augusto Pinochet. In Africa, the United States tolerated the racist regime of South Africa and sided with anticommunists in the Angolan civil war. But, taking a lesson from Vietnam, Nixon was leery of using American troops in these situations.

Nixon the Accidental Liberal

While Nixon's foreign policies often represented significant breakthroughs, his domestic policies were even more transformative, although not always in the way Nixon's supporters had hoped. Upon entering office, Nixon claimed to be a typical small-government Republican. In reality, Nixon's relentless preoccupation with and fear of being defeated for reelection led him to advocate many goals of the left and of the Democratic Party. Cagily, however, while Nixon sought to increase budgets for liberal causes, he made these increases contingent upon greater local control. This put Democrats in a tough political position, because they could not reject funds for causes they had long advocated, but they could not control how those funds were spent locally. In this way, Nixon became an advocate of many liberal causes, but he did so while weakening the supposed Eastern Establishment he despised.

Increasing the Size of Government

For instance, Nixon signed into law the National Environmental Policy Act (1970), which established the Environmental Protection Agency (EPA). He endorsed the Occupational Safety and Health Administration (OSHA), which sought to make workplaces safer. He doubled the budgets of the National Endowment for the Humanities (NEH) and the National Endowment for the Arts (NEA). Nixon also became the first president to embrace affirmative action, as discussed later in the chapter.

But each of these progressive developments came at a cost to the liberals who had long advocated them. For instance, Nixon's increases to the National Endowment for the Humanities were earmarked for popular artists in Middle America or for local museums, instead of the large museums in New York and Boston, which championed abstract art that was appreciated mostly by the well educated and affluent. Politically, Democrats could not reject his proposal to increase funding for the arts. It was a stroke of political genius: Nixon got credit for being a proponent of the arts, at the same time draining support from his nemesis, the eastern liberal elite.

Strategic Arms Limitation Talks (SALT) Sessions held between President Nixon and Soviet premier Leonid Brezhnev, in which the two leaders agreed to freeze the number of long-range missile launchers and build certain new missiles only after they had destroyed the same number of older missiles

détente French term meaning "a relaxing" or "an easing"; refers to more relaxed relations with America's supposed enemies, China and the Soviet Union

LO² Watergate

Before Nixon could do more, he became mired in scandal. During his successful reelection bid in 1972, five men were arrested breaking into the Democratic National Committee offices at the Watergate Hotel in Washington, D.C. One of the burglars worked directly for Nixon's Committee to Re-Elect the President (CREEP), a fact that did not impede Nixon's landslide victory in the election. But print journalists, spurred by the investigative reporting of the Washington Post's Bob Woodward and Carl Bernstein, continued to follow the story and discovered that orders for the break-in had been issued from high up in the Nixon White House. The Senate convened hearings, which were televised nationally.

> **❝I have never been a quitter. To leave office before my term is completed is abhorrent to every instinct in my body. But as President, I must put the interest of America first.❞**
>
> —*Richard M. Nixon, resignation speech 1974*

While the testimony never revealed whether or not Nixon had ordered the break-in, what did emerge were Nixon's suspicious nature and illegal spying on Americans. Watergate became an investigation about much more than a simple break-in. The Senate learned that the president had taped nearly every conversation that had happened in the White House. When the Senate demanded to see the tapes, Nixon fired the special prosecutor leading the Senate's investigation, prompting a series of sympathy resignations within his own administration.

As the scandal mushroomed, Nixon's vice president, Spiro Agnew, admitted to tax evasion and bribery. He resigned and was replaced by Gerald Ford. The credibility of the entire administration was under attack. Americans watched the scandal with alarm. It seemed to confirm many people's beliefs that American leaders were untrustworthy. After the Supreme Court ordered Nixon to turn over the White House tapes, it was evident that he was going to be impeached. Nixon instead chose to resign from office, which he did after a speech to the nation on August 9, 1974. His new vice president, Gerald Ford, became president. To understand the reasons why Watergate was so pivotal to the 1970s political culture, see "The reasons why . . ." box on the facing page.

AP Photo

>> **President Nixon resigning, August 9, 1974. A scandal surrounding a break-in of the Democratic party headquarters in the Watergate Hotel during the 1972 presidential election led to numerous revelations of presidential abuse. Before Nixon was indicted, he resigned, and was pardoned by President Gerald Ford a month later.**

LO³ The Troubled Economy and Politics Adrift

The backdrop for all this commotion was an economic recession that officially ended the great post–World War II economic boom. The two presidents that succeeded Nixon, Gerald Ford and Jimmy Carter, had little success in solving this problem.

Economic Woes

In the late 1960s, Vietnam, the Great Society, and the costs of the arms race had diverted a lot of money from federal coffers, and Johnson had refused to raise taxes to pay for these expensive ventures.

{ *The reasons why . . .* }

There were at least four reasons why the Watergate scandal was so pivotal in American life:

The death of political idealism. The disclosures of Watergate put the nail in the coffin of the political idealism of the early 1960s. During that earlier period, social movements like the civil rights movement turned to the federal government and the American system of law to advocate change. After the decade of lies about the Vietnam War, the Watergate scandal validated many Americans' darkest suspicions that a politician's first priority was not to serve the public, but simply to get reelected.

Americans turn inward. These suspicions led many Americans to turn away from politics, often choosing to search for answers to large social problems through the individual groups that gave them their identity. This, in turn, helped lead to the rise of identity politics, an effort to create social change not through politics but instead by changing American culture and society. America's politics seemed corrupt.

The irony. One major irony of the Watergate scandal was that it served Republican ends. Since at least the New Deal, Republicans had been advocating a smaller role for government. The disaffection toward politics inspired by Nixon, a Republican, was a long-term boon to the Republican Party. After Watergate, many people began to see government as part of the problem rather than part of the solution, and thus they too began advocating for smaller government.

New political scrutiny. Meanwhile, before Watergate, presidents were usually given a wide berth by the media and forgiven their personal flaws, which frequently went unreported. After Watergate, every dimension of a politician's life was deemed newsworthy. President Ford, who became president after Nixon resigned, was a talented athlete and former college football star at the University of Michigan, but he was widely portrayed as a goof and a bumbling klutz. Where there once had been deference and respect, now there was cynicism and ire.

Furthermore, by the early 1970s, America's industrial sector was weakening due to the rise of foreign competition and decreasing demand for American goods. The economy was cooling after its long period of post–World War II growth. With the United States borrowing tremendous amounts of money, the value of the dollar decreased, meaning that it took more dollars to pay for the same goods. This condition is called inflation. Nixon did not really know what to do to control the problem. First, he made it more difficult to borrow money, which, he hoped, would lower the amount of investments and keep dollars spare. However, all this did was constrict the economy, leading to an economic recession.

In 1971, facing reelection, Nixon initiated the first-ever peacetime wage and price freeze. He also accepted large federal deficits. These initiatives reversed the economy long enough for him to win reelection in 1972, but his economic plan was erratic and short term, confidence remained low, and the American industrial sector was beginning to decline in the face of cheaper prices on imported foreign goods.

Oil Embargo

The whole problem was compounded after the Yom Kippur War of 1973, which provoked the oil-rich nations of the Middle East to punish the United States for supporting Israel, a nation with friendly ties to the United States since its founding, in 1948. Oil prices quadrupled. Gas became hard to find, and long lines of drivers were seen waiting at filling stations. Other sources of energy were not immediately available. Beyond the daily frustrations of expensive gas at the pump, the oil embargo raised the cost of making goods and moving them from one place to another. Prices of all consumer goods went up. Thus, the American economy entered a complicated cycle in which prices kept going up (inflation) but the economy began losing jobs (or stagnating). Economists called this unique condition **stagflation**.

Stagflation is notoriously difficult to fight, because most of the tools the government has to control the economy—such as regulating the interest it charges banks to borrow money from the Federal Reserve banks—are primarily designed to either slow growth and end inflation, or increase growth and boost inflation. Tools to lower inflation while growing the economy do not exist. The economy would continue to perform badly throughout the 1970s, bringing to an abrupt halt the consistent economic growth the country had enjoyed since 1946.

stagflation
Economic cycle in which prices keep going up (inflation) while the economy is losing jobs (or stagnating)

The Decline of Cities

Another force compounded these economic pressures. Since the Second World War, Americans had been leaving cities at alarming rates, heading to the suburbs, where good schools, bigger homes, and larger spaces beckoned. Stagflation slowed the American economy down, especially the manufacturing sector that was overwhelmingly based in large northeastern and midwestern cities like Chicago and Philadelphia. As these sectors declined in productivity, many Americans lost their jobs and left the industrial cities of the North in search of work in the South or Southwest. As businesses left, the tax base left with them, making the 1970s the roughest time in the history of most American cities. During the 1970s, more than 1 million residents left New York City; it took the city nearly two decades to make up that population loss.

President Ford

After Watergate and the Vietnam War had discredited the role that government might play in solving deep social problems, the two presidents who followed Nixon appeared to be rudderless and without confidence that the American people would listen to, much less enact, their attempts to solve the country's problems. For his part, President Ford was the first president never subjected to a national election. A good-natured, well-liked man who self-effacingly admitted that he was "a Ford, not a Lincoln," Gerald Ford weathered the wrath of the American public in the aftermath of Watergate. And one of his first acts as president did not generate widespread goodwill: Ford offered Nixon a full presidential pardon. This action ended the possibility of criminal proceedings and, perhaps, of finding out whether or not Nixon had ordered the Watergate break-in. But the pardon did allow the nation to move beyond political scandal in order to focus on the dire problems of the economy and the Cold War. Unfortunately, Ford was unable to take complete control of either.

Domestic Policy

Ford's chief domestic problem was stagflation, but, like Nixon, Ford had little luck tackling it. At first, he encouraged Americans to save rather than spend their money. Then he offered a large tax cut. Neither measure worked to improve the sagging economy. With little national support, Ford regularly vetoed congressional bills, only to have his vetoes overridden.

Foreign Policy

Ford had better luck overseas. He laid the basis of another arms agreement with the Soviets, which was finalized as SALT II a few years later, under President Carter. Ford's secretary of state Henry Kissinger negotiated between Israel and Egypt, leading to a short-term break in hostilities in the Middle East.

President Carter

In 1976, Ford stood little chance of reelection. Affable and open as he was, even within his party he faced a strong challenge from California's former governor, Ronald Reagan, a symbol of the new Sunbelt conservatism that would dominate the 1980s and 1990s.

The Election of 1976

The Democrats, for their part, took a chance and won. They nominated a little-known, one-term Georgia governor named Jimmy Carter. Carter struck a note with the electorate because he appeared to be honest, was a "born again" Christian, was progressive on issues of poverty and treatment of minorities, and was a southerner capable of talking to the demographically growing southern half of the nation (Map 27.1). Carter won the election, in which he competed against the ghost of Nixon as much as against Ford.

Domestic Policy

Domestically, Carter faced the same economic conditions that Nixon and Ford had: stagflation. Carter could not manage it either, and when he proposed to increase government spending to create jobs (à la the New Deal), inflation skyrocketed. He then made the ultimate political blunder when he asked the nation to sacrifice on behalf of the "common purpose" and offered a list of small and specific proposals as to how that might be done. These modest proposals did not capture the public's imagination, and his political inexperience in Washington, D.C., contributed to his making several gaffes, which repeatedly made him look weak and ineffectual.

Carter was further burdened by the nationwide energy crisis, which had surged after the Yom Kippur War of 1973 and had not subsided since. By 1977, elementary and high schools were forced to close because there was not enough energy to heat them. Carter's ambitious plan to remedy the crisis combined higher taxes and a vigorous search for alternative fuels. This plan was met with general disapproval by Congress and did not pass. Making matters worse, the meltdown of a nuclear reactor at **Three Mile Island**, Pennsylvania, in 1979 discredited nuclear power, a potentially viable alternative to oil. With an economy this troubled, Carter could not advocate any of the plans he had for expanding American social justice.

Three Mile Island
Nuclear reactor in Pennsylvania that suffered a meltdown in 1979

Camp David Accords
1978 peace agreement between Israel and Egypt, brokered by President Carter

Foreign Policy

Carter made more progress abroad. His longest-lasting achievement in foreign policy was in establishing human rights as an element of American policy. Doing so energized him to (1) call for the end of apartheid in South Africa, (2) give up control of the Panama Canal, and (3) cite human rights considerations as a factor in the granting of American aid. In the Middle East, Carter oversaw a peace agreement between Israel and Egypt, called the **Camp David Accord**, in late 1978. But this accomplishment was overshadowed just six months later when Islamic militants took fifty-two hostages from the American Embassy in Tehran, the capital of Iran. The militants were part of a coup in which fundamentalist Islamists seized power from the American-supported dictatorship, in place since 1953. The terrorists held the American hostages for more than a year. Each day that went by, Carter seemed more and more unable to handle the problem. But the inability to bring together the nation was not Carter's doing alone.

LO⁴ The Rise of Identity Politics

One historian has described the social movements of the 1960s as a "coming together" of sorts, when large gestures—the civil rights movement, the War on Poverty—were intended to create a more unified and inclusive nation. The 1970s, however, served as a spin cycle, scattering the social energy of the sixties in a thousand different directions. Without a magnetic social vision to unify the populace, the 1970s came to be characterized as a time of turning inward or, to use a term from the era, a celebration of the culture of narcissism. People's interest in pet causes flourished, as did a variety of new faiths, most of which prioritized personal renewal or an individual relationship with God.

© Dirck Halstead/Time Life Pictures/Getty Images

>> President Jimmy Carter, wearing the kind of sweater he urged all Americans to wear, in order to reduce their consumption of energy.

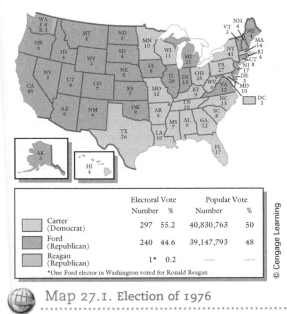

	Electoral Vote		Popular Vote	
	Number	%	Number	%
Carter (Democrat)	297	55.2	40,830,763	50
Ford (Republican)	240	44.6	39,147,793	48
Reagan (Republican)	1*	0.2	----	----

*One Ford elector in Washington voted for Ronald Reagan

© Cengage Learning

Map 27.1. Election of 1976

Many of these themes were manifested in the southern tilt of American culture that began in the 1970s, and many of these melded seamlessly into the political New Right, which prioritized, above all, individual rights.

Identifying with a Group

One of the most contentious and transformative sociopolitical events of the decade was the codification of identity politics. In other words, there was a resurgence of people's practicing politics and voting based on their identification with a particular group, rather than with the entire nation as a whole. Identity politics had been made acceptable by Catholics and Jews in the postwar era and had been made both politically potent and divisive by African Americans, Mexican Americans, Native Americans, and others following the civil rights movement, especially in the militancy that emerged in the late 1960s.

African American Activism

America's black population was the first to embrace this brand of politics, which intended to change the culture as well as public policy. Despite the federal laws passed in the 1960s, racism against America's black people persisted. For the most part, racism was no longer legally codified or socially acceptable at the broad institutional level, but it remained entrenched in the personal-level institutions of society and culture. Thus, many African American activists broadened their focus from just politics to politics and culture, hoping to change the way Americans thought about their nation. Cultural acceptance was different from political acceptance. Political acceptance concerned the enforcement of color-blind laws, while social acceptance depended on an awareness of differences and a conscious decision to ignore them.

In response to this heightened awareness, "Black is beautiful" became a widespread call in the black community. Africa became a destination for many Americans seeking to understand their cultural past, a sentiment epitomized in and popularized by Alex Haley's 1976 bestseller, Roots. Attending historically black colleges acquired cultural cachet. Black Studies writers and professors established this field as an accepted academic discipline within America's colleges. The cultural politics of the Black Freedom Movement surpassed attempts to create protective legal structures to ensure equal access.

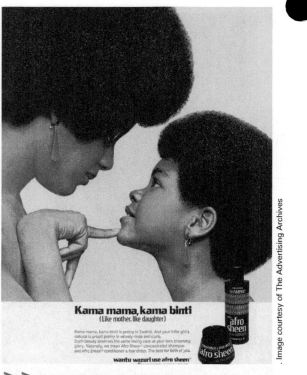

Image courtesy of The Advertising Archives

Kama mama, kama binti
(Like mother, like daughter)

>> In the 1970s, products like Afro-Sheen built their ad campaigns on heightened awareness and acceptance of African roots among black people.

Social and economic acceptance required different methods.

Affirmative Action

Amid this transition toward greater interest in changing American culture, federal and state governments attempted to rectify the continuing effects of racism. Because many white Americans were afraid of dropping property values if their neighborhoods became racially integrated, and because of deeply entrenched fears of interracial mingling, schools generally remained segregated. To remedy this persistent problem, cities such as Boston and Los Angeles began busing students from one school district to another in order to desegregate schools. This action provoked much ire from parents, black and white, who had their children bused far from home. Riots erupted in Boston, and the level of suspicion increased between the groups on either side of the color line

Meanwhile, the federal government developed programs of **affirmative** action, in which employers were supposed to ensure that a certain percentage of employees were minorities, or that a certain percentage of government contracts were given to minority-owned businesses. In another example of Nixon's ruthless politics, affirmative action's federal origins can be traced to his proclaimed free-market administration. He did this to cause political rifts between white and black laborers, which would, and did, break up a Democratic political coalition that was first formed by President Roosevelt in the 1930s.

Affirmative action also became policy in many of the nation's universities. In 1978, the Supreme Court upheld the legality of some elements of affirmative action, but disallowed the use of exact quotas, in a case that emerged when a white student claimed he was denied entrance to medical school because of the color of his skin. The case, *Regents of the University of California v. Bakke*, not only codified affirmative action in American education but also dramatically displayed the overwhelming backlash against affirmative action brought forward by many white Americans. Some members of this furious group were the children of turn-of-the-century immigrants who, ignoring the centuries of racism and favoritism inherent in America's institutions, claimed to have never wronged America's racial minority groups during the time of slavery and conquest. They claimed that they were not responsible for paying the debt for America's offenses during the precolonial and colonial eras.

The Chicano Movement

After the variety of successes won by labor leaders César Chávez and Dolores Huerta in the late 1960s, in 1970 a more radical aspect of the Chicano movement emerged and was embodied by the organization La Raza. This term literally means "the Race," although colloquially it is synonymous with "the People." *La Raza* explicitly focused on electing Mexican American politicians to office in the West and Southwest. Demonstrating their frustration with the persistent racism that they had confronted throughout their history, members of *La Raza* rejected the name "Mexican American" in favor of the more particular "Chicano," a term derived from barrio slang.

Red Power

Heartened by African American and Chicano efforts toward social, cultural, and economic equality, many American Indians sought political redress as well. Many Indians lived at the poverty level, and most Indian reservations had no industry of any kind. The crushing poverty inspired protests. Holding several sit-ins of their own, in 1969 a group of activists

affirmative action
Program meant to ensure that a certain percentage of a company's employees are minorities or that a certain percentage of government contracts are given to minority-owned businesses

© Bettmann/CORBIS

>> In 1969, a group of activists called "Indians of All Tribes" occupied Alcatraz Island, demanding the land be returned to the tribes that had once occupied it.

Roe v. Wade
Supreme Court decision of 1973 that struck down laws in forty-six states that limited a woman's access to a safe, legal abortion

called "Indians of All Tribes" occupied Alcatraz Island in San Francisco Bay. Demanding the land be returned to the tribes that had once occupied it, they intended to make an Indian cultural center out of the former prison.

The protest recalled the pan-Indian resistance of the early 1800s, although in 1970s language. Indeed, the activists boldly declared "Red Power!" echoing Stokely Carmichael's Black Power campaign of the late 1960s. In 1968, a group of Native Americans coordinated the American Indian Movement and began a series of audacious political protests, including occupying the federal Bureau of Indian Affairs building, Mount Rushmore, and Wounded Knee, South Dakota. The protests provoked headlines and benefited several moderate groups helping to craft laws in Washington, D.C. They wrote a dozen new laws and steered more than $100 million to educational and health programs on Indian reservations. Furthermore, the number of Americans who identified as Indians more than doubled between 1970 and 1990.

The Women's Movement

The politics of identity moved beyond racial groups too. Throughout the 1970s, American women continued to press for increased political and economic rights.

ERA and Equal Rights

Throughout the 1970s, women fought against sexual harassment in the workplace and for greater awareness of women's health issues. They also secured congressional approval of the Equal Rights Amendment to the U.S. Constitution, which would have made it illegal to discriminate based on sex. Furthermore, in 1972, Congress passed Title IX of the Higher Education Act, which obligated universities to spend the same amount of money on women's athletics that they spent on men's athletics.

Roe v. Wade

The most controversial milestone of the women's movement was a landmark legal case. In 1973, the Supreme Court handed down a decision in **Roe v. Wade** that struck down laws in forty-six states that limited a woman's access to a safe, legal abortion. The decision, which referenced a woman's right to privacy, extending that right to her reproductive

system, stunned the opposition, who generally felt abortion was morally equivalent to murder. The debate about abortion has increased the polarization between the left and the right ever since.

Social and Economic Participation

In a change perhaps more profound than the debates about laws that delineated women's place in American society, in the 1970s women began to play a more active role in the economy and in forming the parameters of American social life. Like other minority groups, they fomented a social movement that existed outside of normal politics. For instance, consistently struggling against a "glass ceiling" that limited their ability to rise beyond a certain corporate level, in the 1970s women fought for and sometimes won the right to earn pay equal to that of men. Some companies opened day-care centers and job-training programs specifically for working mothers. Beyond economics, the 1970s saw a rise in the use of gender-neutral terms (for instance, using the terms *firefighter* and *flight attendant* in place of *fireman* and *stewardess*).

© Image courtesy of The Advertising Archives

>> The image of the ideal man transitioned from the masculine if inarticulate swashbuckler of the 1940s to the man who was more "in touch with his feelings."

The Sexual Revolution

Some women also embraced their own sexuality in what was called the sexual revolution. There was a new cultural atmosphere in which women more openly discussed their sexual needs and desires, while sometimes flouting conventional arrangements, such as maintaining a single partner in a traditionally identifiable relationship. Divorce became more common. Breaking such long-standing taboos began a fundamental transformation in American gender relations. The image of the ideal man transitioned from the masculine if inarticulate swashbuckler of the 1940s to the man who was more "in touch with his feelings." Women forthrightly demanded equality in their private as well as their public lives, although in the 1970s, women were not always in agreement as to what exactly that meant.

The Gay Liberation Movement

Also in the 1970s, gay men and lesbians began to demand equality as people living outside what had been perceived as the heterosexual norm. As barriers against racial and religious minorities collapsed, as women advocated and sometimes won equality, gay men and women still faced considerable legal discrimination. For example, consensual sex between two people of the same sex was illegal in nearly every state. In 1969, a police raid on the bar at the **Stonewall Inn** in New York City sparked the gay liberation movement. Gay men fought back against the police raid, proclaiming "Gay Power." The riot propelled many gay men and lesbians into politics and political activism, advocating for legal equality such as marriage rights. In 1977, Harvey Milk, on

>> In 1977, Harvey Milk became the first openly gay politician elected to public office in the United States. His sign, "I'm from Woodmere, NY," suggests that anyone from anywhere can be gay, challenging the notion that only freaks from radical locales are homosexuals.

© Terry Schmitt/San Francisco Chronicle/Corbis

being elected to the Board of Supervisors in San Francisco, became the first openly gay person to win a major political campaign. He was assassinated shortly thereafter and is an iconic martyr of the gay rights movement, which continues today.

> **Stonewall Inn**
> Site in New York City of the riots that ignited the Gay Liberation Movement in the late 1960s and 1970s; at the time of the riots, all fifty states had antisodomy laws, and police busts of gay bars were routine

High Tide of Environmentalism

Demanding respect for the environment was another facet of 1970s social activism. Launched in 1962 by Rachel Carson's book *Silent Spring*, the environmental movement grew through the 1960s. In 1970, the United States celebrated the first "Earth Day," which stimulated greater awareness of humans' treatment of the land, sea, and air. Vital to 1970s environmentalism was advocacy of preserving unspoiled lands and promoting ecologically sound practices in industry, manufacturing, and automobile use.

Beyond creating valuable awareness, the political record of the environmental movement is mixed. Environmentalists cheered when Richard Nixon established the Environmental Protection Agency in 1970 and when Congress passed eighteen environmental laws throughout the decade. They rued the construction of the Trans-Alaska Pipeline in 1973, however. Other defeats loomed as well. Most damning was the sense that, in an era when Americans were searching for belonging, the cause of environmentalism asserted a species-wide identity, something too diffuse and broad to command much allegiance.

Popular Culture

American popular culture also reflected the broader, inward-focused trend of the 1970s, often in increasingly flashy ways that demonstrated a more complicated morality, where one might feel like cheering for the traditional bad guy. The music of the 1960s icons Sly and the Family Stone, for example, transitioned from celebrating American unity and possibility in the 1960s to being more introspective and aware of the limits of broad social change in the 1970s. In one poignant instance, Sly changed the lyrics of one of his most popular 1960s songs from "Thank You (Falettinme Be Mice Elf Agin)" to, in 1971, "Thank You for Talkin' to Me Africa." In addition to demonstrating the decline of hope for broad social change, the changed lyrics also capture the rise of identity politics, with Sly looking for his roots in Africa rather than the United States.

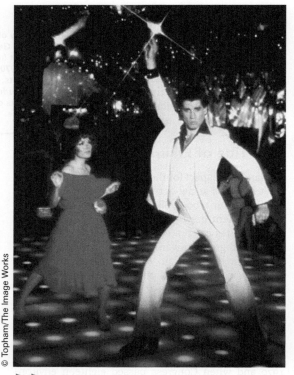

© Topham/The Image Works

>> John Travolta in *Saturday Night Fever* (1979) does most of his dancing by himself.

In the later 1970s, disco music throbbed in America's cities, articulating an individual desire to dance on one's own and pursue individual rather than societal goals. The 1979 film *Saturday Night Fever* enshrined disco music as a typical "seventies" cultural form, but the film also displayed as its depressing backdrop the decline and plight of American cities of the Northeast. In other landmark films of the era, such as *The Godfather, The Godfather, Part II,* and *Bonnie and Clyde, viewers* feel compelled to root for the success and freedom of violent criminals who defy traditional American morals. Thus the moral complexity of the period, with its dramatically changing social and economic background, inspired many vibrant contributions to the popular culture that also reflected the era's malaise.

LO⁵ The Rise of the New Right

All these calls for change led to a combative conservative reaction. This movement, collectively dubbed the "New Right" by the press, scrubbed all

potential intellectual elitism from conservatism, an elitism symbolized by William F. Buckley's National Review magazine, founded in the 1950s. Instead, through a variety of grassroots movements, social conservatives opposed abortion and what they saw as the moral decline of society, while economic conservatives urged tax cuts to limit the size and reach of government. Both types of conservatives continued to urge an aggressive stance against the Soviet Union. Both also strove to diminish government intervention in people's lives. The expansion of the federal state during the 1960s and what conservatives saw as the loosening of laws regarding morality spurred this new coalition, which would continue to grow for the remainder of the century.

Economic and Political Conservatism

A key dimension of 1970s conservatism arose in opposition to what were viewed as excessive tax policies in an era of inflation. If government was deemed corrupt, went the refrain, why should a significant percentage of our income go to taxes? This sentiment was most evident in California, where skyrocketing house prices meant dramatic increases in property taxes. When homeowners could not pay these higher property taxes, they revolted and passed Proposition 13, which limited all further increases on property taxes to 2 percent a year. Within months, nearly three-quarters of other states passed similar laws.

The Republican Party capitalized on this populist anger, positioning itself as the antigovernment party. The state of California had a large economic surplus, so the decline in property taxes there did not limit services. In many other places, however, states could not afford to pay for public schools, road maintenance, or effective fire and police departments. In a familiar theme of the 1970s and 1980s, Americans would have to turn inward—to their communities—to solve these institutional problems. Those cities and towns that could afford a good level of local control thrived; those that could not faced dire straits.

The Religious Right

Some of the shock troops of the New Right were evangelical Christians, a growing force in the 1970s. These Protestant evangelicals poured their efforts into three things: (1) forming an intense personal relationship with Jesus; (2) gathering converts, usually former mainline or liberal Protestants; and (3) advancing a political agenda that stressed traditional "family values" that countered the women's rights movement and the gay liberation movement. This new crop of evangelicals especially targeted feminism and was visibly enraged by the Supreme Court's Roe v. Wade decision, which has since served as a rallying cry for the entrance of the fundamentalist movement into American politics.

Institutionally, conservative Christians led by Rev. Jerry Falwell founded the **Moral Majority** political lobbying group in 1979, which, alongside tax-revolting economic conservatives, formed the other arm of the Republican party and helped elect Ronald Reagan to the presidency in 1980. Culturally, evangelicals became increasingly visible in popular music and fiction. Diminished were the paramount religious divisions between mainline Protestants, Catholics, and Jews, which had defined American religious life in the 1950s; surging were new divisions between conservatives and liberals of all faiths, but especially Protestants. Not only did the appearance of a more public aspect of faith reflect the "southernization" of American culture, but it also demonstrated the inward turn that took place in the 1970s, as religion became a realm of division and exclusion rather than one of inclusion and community building.

"Family Values"

Predictably, the women's movement served as a touchstone for strong opposition. While many women sought to take advantage of the new opportunities open to them, a substantial percentage wanted to preserve the traditional roles of American womanhood. If securing the right to low-wage work was what the women's movement was about, some of these women thought the cost of equality too high. Others cited biblical passages about a woman's obligation to submit to her husband. Still others saw the women's movement and the sexual revolution as putting traditional families in jeopardy, by encouraging women to focus on themselves rather than their children. Phyllis Schlafly, a conservative activist, headed up the opposition. She founded STOP-ERA, claiming that the women in NOW were using politics to remedy their personal problems. She also asserted that the women in the women's

movement were all lesbians, a mischaracterization intended to capitalize on America's homophobia. But Schlafly's tactics were effective. When Schlafly began STOP-ERA in 1972, thirty of the necessary thirty-eight states had approved the amendment. After she began her organization, the amendment languished, finally expiring without passage in 1982.

> **Moral Majority**
> Conservative political organizations begun by Rev. Jerry Falwell in 1979 and consisting of evangelical Christians who overwhelmingly supported the Republican Party

And in the end . . .

At the end of the 1970s, the dominant news story was the Iranian hostage crisis that emerged during the final year of Carter's presidency. The crisis would help propel into office a president who projected a more positive image of the United States and who promised to return America to a perceived greatness of old. But rather than serving as a definitive transition, the election of Ronald Reagan solidified the changes that had taken place during the 1970s.

Reagan emblematized the return to political conservatism that had gathered strength in the 1970s, and he projected the Sunbelt image of a tough leader, unwilling to grant any ground to anti-establishment forces. He also saw government as more of a problem than a solution to many of society's problems, and favored low taxes. Reagan also paid homage (if usually only that) to minorities whose concerns had come to the forefront of 1970s identity politics. For instance, he appointed Sandra Day O'Connor as the first female associate justice to the U.S. Supreme Court. Many Americans were delighted to leave the 1970s behind, but the decade's legacy influenced developments for the remainder of the twentieth century.

What else was happening . . .	
1970	The Beatles split up.
1971	London Bridge is purchased by an American and shipped to Lake Havasu City, Arizona, to be displayed as a tourist attraction.
1974	Art Fry invents Post-it- Notes by using a colleague's "failed" adhesive while working at 3M.
1975	*Popular Electronics* announces Altair, the first "personal computer."

SOURCE: From SCHULTZ, *HIST* (with History CourseMate with eBook Printed Access Card), 2E. © 2012 Cengage Learning.

REVIEW QUESTIONS

MULTIPLE-CHOICE QUESTIONS

1 **The activism of the 1960s ran into roadblocks in the 1970s, which included all of the following, EXCEPT**

A. the economic boom of the 1960s had turned into a recession.
B. ethnic groups seemed poised to fracture any national unity the struggle for black civil rights had initially created.
C. American politics had reached its limits.
D. a conservative movement began to push back against the demands of women and minorities.
E. the civil rights activists had already achieved all their goals.

2 **When the last American troops came home from Vietnam in 1973,**

A. most Americans were relieved to be removed from what seemed like a quagmire.
B. protests over the Vietnamization of the conflict grew.
C. pro-war Americans protested at the airport.
D. South Vietnam was a stable and defensible nation.
E. most Americans considered the war "won."

3 **Nixon's goal in improving relations with China was to**

A. try to take the Soviet Union's place as China's closest ally.
B. have a chance to visit China during his administration.
C. drive a further wedge between China and the Soviet Union.
D. be able to invite the Chinese table tennis team to the United States.
E. try to convince the Chinese to trade with the United States and help cut trade protections between the two countries.

4 **Americans reeled from an embargo on oil deliveries to the United States from the oil-producing countries in the Middle East because those countries**

A. resented the help America had given Israel during the 1967 and 1973 wars.
B. wanted to convince the United States to stay out of Middle Eastern affairs.
C. they believed the United States had pushed Israel to begin the 1973 war.
D. they wanted to see Americans begging for help.
E. they resented the friendly relationship between Israeli prime minister Golda Meir and the American press.

5 **Stagflation is an economic crisis that combines**

A. low prices and economic growth.
B. steady prices and decreasing output.

C. runaway high prices and declining jobs.

D. unemployment with a contraction in the money supply.

E. a contraction in the labor market combined with excessive regulation.

6 **The Watergate scandal began with a break-in at the**

A. *Washington Post.*

B. Democratic National Committee headquarters.

C. National Endowment for the Arts headquarters.

D. Republican National Headquarters.

E. *National Review.*

7 **The action(s) that Gerald Ford took that probably had the people of America too angry to elect him president was/were**

A. his pardon of Richard Nixon.

B. his decision to attempt to try Nixon.

C. his fumbling speeches that made him a laughingstock across America.

D. his pardon of Spiro Agnew.

E. his direct meeting with Ho Chi Minh.

8 **Which of the following did *not* happen during Carter's presidency?**

A. Some public schools had to close because there was not enough energy to heat them.

B. There was a meltdown of a nuclear reactor at Three Mile Island in Pennsylvania, raising profound concerns about the safety of nuclear energy.

C. His administration was finally able to get stagflation under control.

D. Carter signed the SALT II agreement with the Soviet Union, although it fell apart years later.

E. He achieved his goal of establishing human rights as an element of American policy.

9 **The most controversial issue to arise in regard to the desegregation attempts by the federal government was**

A. busing children to achieve integrated schools.

B. interracial marriage.

C. desegregating elementary schools.

D. desegregating high schools.

E. interracial sports in public schools.

10 **Conservatives in the 1970s**

A. obediently toed the Republican party line.

B. shared a centuries-old, monolithic understanding of the meaning of conservatism.

C. were the most cohesive political group America had ever seen.

D. tended to focus on a particular aspect of society.

E. found an especially effective liberal opponent in the columnist and author, William F. Buckley.

Discussion Questions

1. How did America's involvement with Israel lead to the oil embargo of 1973? What were the results of the embargo in the United States?

_____
_____
_____

2. What were Nixon's reasons for visiting China in 1972? Was he successful? Explain.

_____
_____
_____

3. Gerald Ford (Republican) and Jimmy Carter (Democrat) both failed to win their bids for reelection. Apart from the differences between these two presidents, what shared circumstances may have jeopardized their chances at a second term?

_____
_____
_____

4. How did the evangelical movement, the growing fundamentalist aspect of religion, and the case of *Roe v. Wade* change the American cultural landscape?

_____
_____
_____

5. What was Secretary of State Henry Kissinger's role in the achievement of détente during Nixon's presidency?

_____
_____
_____

6. How would one account for the liberal policies of Republican president Richard Nixon?

_____
_____
_____

SOURCE: From SCHULTZ, HIST (with History CourseMate with eBook Printed Access Card), 2E. © 2012 Cengage Learning.

READING FOR
STUDY

THEME *Education and Responsibility*

UNIT

3

Dan Tero/iStockphoto.com

5

Understanding
TEXT MARKING AND ANNOTATION

✻ Why Do You Need to Know This?

Now that you have developed reading skills to identify patterns, to see the relationships between ideas, and to determine main ideas, if you were asked *how* to read and learn a passage for school, would you still say "just read it"? Chapters 5 and 6 explore reading for study. Many students are unaware that there is an effective method of reading for college success. This requires that you apply active reading and study strategies *while* reading. These strategies involve varying your reading rate to suit the assignment, identifying and

IN THIS CHAPTER, YOU WILL LEARN

- To vary your reading rate
- To monitor and overcome comprehension problems
- To use text marking and annotation strategies
- To understand graphics: reading complex tables

READING STUDY STRATEGIES

- Reading rate
- Comprehension monitoring

VOCABULARY STRATEGIES

- Improving your college-level vocabulary by using the dictionary
- Increasing your discipline-specific vocabulary: business and economics

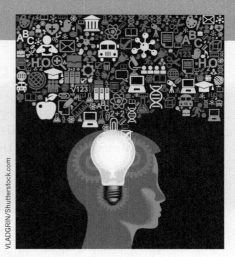

VLADGRIN/Shutterstock.com

"EDUCATION IS NOT RECEIVED. IT IS ACHIEVED."

ANONYMOUS

overcoming comprehension problems, and using text marking to comprehend and learn. In fact, you have already started using these strategies in previous chapters in the Applications.

This chapter's theme concerns education and motivation—not just within yourself, but from a global perspective. Being aware of how our education system succeeds as well as how it can be improved is useful as you engage in the education process. Where does the United States succeed? Where does it fall short? What are the challenges for those in our educational system? How do these challenges affect you?

✓ **CHECK YOUR PRIOR KNOWLEDGE**

Jot down some facts you know about the challenges within the U.S. educational system and how to be successful in school. Do not edit your list—just brainstorm!

_____

_____

_____

_____

_____

_____

_____

_____

_____

_____

_____

_____

_____

_____

_____

_____

❖ PRE-ASSESSMENT

EDUCATION MAGAZINE

Read the passage, marking the key points and then answer the questions that follow. Don't worry if you do not know what all the terms mean. The purpose of this Pre-Assessment is to find out how much you already know about the reading skills and strategies introduced in this chapter.

Losing Global Ground
by Lynn Olson

1   For decades, a highly qualified workforce has helped fuel economic prosperity in the United States. But now other countries are catching up with and even surpassing America's performance.

2   On a variety of measures, "the U.S. has been joined by a number of other countries," says Alan P. Wagner, a professor of educational administration at the State University of New York at Albany, "and particularly in the younger age groups, there is evidence of higher levels of performance elsewhere."

3   For example:

- Although the <u>achievement gap</u> opens before children even reach school, U.S. support for early-childhood education lags well behind that of other developed nations.
- While U.S. children in elementary school perform relatively well on international tests of achievement, particularly in reading, American 15-year-olds perform in the middle of the pack on tests of science and mathematics, with one-quarter performing at the lowest achievement levels.
- At a time when a high school diploma is typically the minimum requirement for a decent job, the United States has slipped to 11th among 30 Organization for Economic Cooperation and Development countries in the proportion of 25- to 34-year-olds with that <u>credential</u>.
- Long a leader in higher education, the United States has dropped to seventh in the proportion of 25- to 34-year-olds with a college degree.

4   "These results cannot simply be tied to money," says Barbara Ischinger, who heads the education directorate for the OECD. "Only Luxembourg, Switzerland, and Norway spend more per student in the primary through secondary grades than the United States does," according to OECD data.

5   The United States, however, devotes only half of its expenditures to teacher compensation, a share that is below those of all but five OECD countries.

6   Perhaps most troubling, America's older adults, ages 35 to 64, have higher rates of college completion than its younger generation—a trend opposite the direction in other industrialized nations.

7   "Are we going to react in a way that's too little, too late?" asks Thomas J. Tierney, the president of the Bridgespan Group, a nonprofit management-consulting organization based in Boston. "I think the choice is ours."

SOURCE: Lynn Olson, "Losing Global Ground," Reprinted with permission from Education Week, Vol. 26, No. 17, January 4, 2007.

COMPREHENSION CHECK

Circle the best answer to the following questions.

Reading Comprehension

1 **What is the main idea of this article?**

A. The United States should spend more on education of youth to raise math scores.

B. The United States spends too much on educating its youth, despite poor math scores.

C. The United States ranks in the lowest six countries on math scores despite being one of the highest-ranking countries for education spending.

D. There is no correlation (statistical relationship) between spending on education and test scores.

2 **According to this article, at what point do U.S. children begin to lose ground in education as compared with children in other countries?**

A. U.S. children fall behind at the age of 15, when the math tests are tabulated.

B. U.S. children are at a disadvantage before school even begins.

C. As compared with other countries, U.S. children lag behind from middle school and upward.

D. U.S. children begin strongly in academics and then fall sharply during high school.

3 **To what does the author attribute the loss of a strong foothold in high international ranking for U.S. children at the beginning of their schooling?**

A. Reading scores are low for U.S. elementary children as compared with others internationally of the same age.

B. U.S. early childhood education is comparatively underfunded as compared with other countries.

C. Science and mathematics are not sufficiently emphasized in U.S. high schools.

D. The United States spends too much on education; the problem stems from another source.

(Continued)

4 **You can infer from the passage that**

A. U.S. graduation rates from high school as measured by those holding the degree by the ages of 25–34 used to be among the highest among nations participating in this assessment.

B. U.S. high school graduation rates are on the rise as a result of the economic necessity for Americans to have this minimum requirement to get jobs.

C. In several other countries, attaining a high school diploma does not necessarily lead to good employment.

D. In the United States, high school graduation does not necessarily lead to good employment.

5 **To what does the study attribute the decline in U.S. educational achievement?**

A. The United States is not spending enough money on education.

B. Only half of the money used for education pays teachers.

C. U.S. students are less motivated than students in other countries.

D. In the United States, an education is not required to earn a decent living.

6 **To the author, the most troubling implication of the decline in higher education among U.S. students is that**

A. other countries are surpassing the United States.

B. the majority of other countries fall below the United States in higher education.

C. U.S. higher education rates are increasing, albeit at a slow pace.

D. older Americans have a higher rate of college education as compared with the young, implying that the United States is in a decline.

7 **Go back and look at the text marking you completed—the important points in the article. Based on your text marking, which is the best representation of the major points of this article?**

A. **Main Idea:** The United States is losing ground on international education surveys and needs to determine why.

   A. The United States was once "highly qualified."

   B. Other countries are surpassing us educationally.

   C. Results/problems (effects) of the survey

      1. U.S. early childhood achievement is lower

      2. U.S. elementary test results are okay, but science and math achievement scores for 15-year-olds are very low compared with other countries.

      3. The United States slipped to 11th out of 30 in adults with high school diplomas—a minimal requirement to get a decent job.

      4. U.S. adults have higher rates of college completion compared with U.S. youth—the opposite of which is true in other countries.

   D. Causes of problem/solution

While the United States spends at the top range on education, only half goes to promoting good teachers. This is not the case in other countries.

B. **Main Idea:** The United States needs to spend more money on education because we're losing ground in competence internationally.
   A. The United States was once "highly qualified."
   B. Other countries are surpassing us educationally.
   C. Comparisons and contrasts in the survey
      1. The United States scores higher than five other countries.
      2. The United States scores lower than 23 other countries.
      3. U.S. early childhood achievement is lower.
      4. U.S. 15-year-old math scores are lower.
      5. U.S. elementary school reading test scores are higher.
      6. The United States has slipped in comparison to other countries in high school graduation rates.
      7. Older adults in the United States are more likely to have completed college than younger adults.

Vocabulary Comprehension

8 **What does the term *achievement gap* mean in this context?**

  A. An observable educational disparity between two groups
  B. An observable economic divide between two cultures
  C. An implied cultural gap
  D. An implied generation gap

9 **What does the root word *cred* mean in the word *credential* in paragraph 3?**

  A. credit
  B. to believe
  C. to know
  D. to lack

READING STUDY STRATEGIES

MONITORING YOUR READING

College reading is far more difficult than reading in high school. Because college reading is intensive and complex, it is important to develop the reading tools you will need to increase your chances of success. One of these tools is to consciously vary your reading rate according to the complexity of your college-level reading as well as your purpose for reading. In addition, a successful college student is aware of the degree of his or her understanding. Not only is she aware of the level of her understanding while reading complex college assignments, but the successful student also draws on an arsenal of strategies to fix comprehension problems.

READING RATE

To navigate these complex waters, you must vary your **reading rate,** or the rate or speed at which you read, depending on several factors related to the reading passage you are tackling. The most important factors that affect reading rate are

- your purpose for reading (Table 5.1);
- your prior knowledge related to the topic;
- the level of comprehension the reading passage requires.

For example, reading a complex text for school requires that you slow down your reading pace to absorb the complex ideas. Reading a text for school if you have a lot of prior knowledge about the subject may mean that you can read faster and still absorb the new information. Reading a novel or magazine for fun means you can read relatively quickly, as you do not necessarily have to "learn" the information.

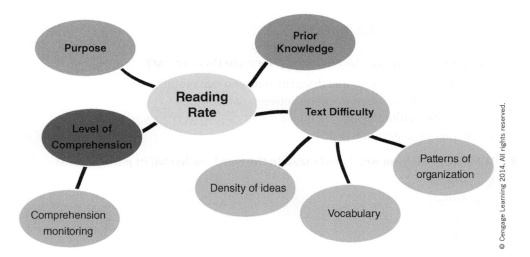

Several factors influence your comprehension, or understanding, of what you read.

- Your purpose for reading
- The amount and detail expected of your prior knowledge (what you already know about the topic)
- The amount of comprehension monitoring, or being aware of what you're thinking and understanding (or not understanding) while reading
- The difficulty of the subject matter (material) in a text
    - The intricacy and density of ideas, or the large amount of what is important to learn within a passage
    - The level of complex vocabulary in a text
    - The complexity, or sheer number and overlap, of patterns of organization

QUICK TIPS CALCULATING READING RATE

To calculate how many words per minute you read, follow this procedure:

- Divide the total words read by the time it took you to read them. (For example, 1140 ÷ 10 minutes = 114 words per minute.)

Calculate the number of words in a reading by using this formula.

1. Count the number of words in three different, full lines in the text.

    Line 1: _____ words

    Line 2: _____ words

    Line 3: _____ words

2. Add the total number of words in the three sample sentences: _____ words.

3. Divide by 3: _____ words on average in each sentence.

4. Now, count the number of lines on a page: _____ lines.

5. Calculate the average number of words on a page.

    _____ (average number of words in a line) × _____ (average number of lines per page) × average number of words per page

6. Multiply the average number of words per page by how many pages are in your reading:

    _____ (average number of words per page) × _____ (number of pages in the reading) × number of words in the reading

7. Read the passage.

8. Time how many minutes and seconds it took to read: _____ minutes _____ seconds

9. To find your reading rate, divide the number of words you read by the number of minutes it took you to read the passage:

$$\frac{\text{Number of words read}}{\text{Number of minutes it took to read}} = \text{Reading rate}$$

TABLE 5.1 Average Reading Rates Depending on Your Purpose

Memorization	Fewer than 100 wpm	Intensive college study
Learning	100–200 wpm	College reading to take notes
Comprehension	200–400 wpm	College reading to understand information (not necessarily be able to recall all or most of it)
Skimming	400–700 wpm	To preview or survey a reading

COMPREHENSION MONITORING

To be active in reading, it is most important to use the appropriate strategies to fix the problem. You have to know what to do about not understanding what you are reading to begin to grasp the ideas.

First, do not expect to read everything in college at the same speed. Information that you are familiar with, find interesting, or that is clearly written and explained is easier to read. Read at a pace that allows you to concentrate and move along quickly to complete the assignment. If the topic of a reading is something about which you have little or no prior knowledge, slow down your reading pace and allow yourself to struggle with the material until you grasp the major points and see the relationships between ideas. Be aware of whether you are concentrating sufficiently and understanding what you are reading. You will have to work harder with unfamiliar subjects.

Second, expect to use prereading, during reading, and postreading strategies when reading to learn information. In previous chapters, you focused on reading strategies: prereading strategies like surveying and previewing in Chapter 1, paraphrasing information in Chapter 2, summarizing in Chapter 3, and reading literature in Chapter 4. In this chapter, you will learn what to do *during* reading to ensure you are an active reader. In Chapter 6, you will learn how to study *after* reading.

Before
- Generate background knowledge
- Set purpose for reading
- Preview

During
- Answer questions to guide reading
- Mark text
- Annotate/take notes

After
- Rewrite notes to solidify ideas and learn
- Use spaced practice to absorb ideas fully
- Predict test questions and practice answering them

Third, have a repertoire of strategies to use when you do not understand the information. As you know from Chapter 1, being aware of what you are thinking about during thinking is called **metacognition.** If you are aware of reading comprehension problems and you use strategies to deal with those problems, you are being metacognitively aware. This is vital to success in college reading. Table 5.2 outlines some tips to fix common comprehension problems.

TABLE 5.2 Tips to Fix Common Comprehension Problems

YOUR PROBLEM	THE CAUSE	WHAT TO DO TO FIX IT
I am not understanding the reading.	Difficult content	1. Slow down. 2. Turn headings into questions to focus your reading. 3. Use text aids, such as chapter outlines and summaries, to provide an overview. 4. Write down specific questions to ask in class. 5. Ask a study partner to clarify. 6. Read a simplified text on the topic first.
It seems that everything is important.	Idea density	1. If you are reading science or technical material, everything, or much of it, may be important! 2. Outline or map the material after marking the text to separate main ideas from supporting ones. 3. Be clear on the pattern of organization to guide your understanding of what is important. 4. Look at the big picture. Instead of deciding that everything in a paragraph is important, consider the main ideas of a subsection of the reading. 5. Focus on key terms. 6. Focus on how the key terms relate to structure or organization (i.e., if the pattern is cause and effect, focus only on those two elements in the text).
There are so many vocabulary words and terms I don't know.	Vocabulary level	1. Look for text clues to unlock the meaning of unfamiliar words from context. 2. Focus on word parts to determine basic meaning and part of speech. 3. Use a dictionary, but pay attention to refocusing concentration repeatedly. 4. Keep reading and see if you get the "gist." 5. Use the text aids, such as glossary, index, sidebars, and summaries to see if you can find an overview for terminology.

(Continued)

TABLE 5.2 Tips to Fix Common Comprehension Problems *(Continued)*

YOUR PROBLEM	THE CAUSE	WHAT TO DO TO FIX IT
I don't know how to organize my notes or what to mark in the text.	Patterns of organization	1. Turn the topic or subheading into a question: The answer to the question is the main idea. 2. Recall that structure is revealed in the answer to the question or main idea. 3. Focus on the relationships between ideas that reflect the organization of the subsection. 4. Use only the information in your notes that reflects the main pattern of organization. 5. Draw the information in a web or chart to clarify the relationship between ideas.
I have no idea what the text is discussing.	Prior knowledge	1. Read chapter summaries and outlines. 2. Read information on the same topic from an "easier" source so you have some background. 3. Read or skim previous chapters to understand context. 4. Ask your instructor for an overview of content. 5. Keep reading to see if your questions are clarified later in the text. 6. Ask a study partner to explain the information or visit your college's support services.
I can't concentrate on reading and "drift off."	Comprehension monitoring	1. Preview to get an overview. 2. Focus your mind by text marking and other active reading strategies. 3. Ask questions and focus by finding the answers in the text. 4. Write notes or annotate as you read to force focus. 5. Read engaging text about the topic to generate interest. 6. Review your study environment, goals, time management, and other controllable study strategies to make sure you are setting yourself up for success.

MARKING AND ANNOTATING TEXT

Text marking, often referred to simply as **underlining,** is a term used to express a reader's interaction with written information as a part of an effective comprehension strategy. **Annotating** a text refers to transcribing the text marking into notes in the margin (or on a separate piece of paper). Marking the text is the process of sorting important from unimportant information in a reading. And in the sorting, you are learning the information and preparing it for storage in your long-term memory. Part of the learning process when you read material is to interact with the text by marking it and annotating it. While it may be a cumbersome method to begin with, marking your textbook and written notes provides the backbone of good study skills. It is essential to learning the material. It is the hallmark of active reading to organize information to help your brain process it. Marking the text and making annotations is the first step in organizing information for study and learning.

To be able to mark text and annotate it effectively, you must have a solid grounding in several comprehension skills. You must be about to

- recognize the pattern of organization of a text;
- see the relationships between ideas in a passage;
- pinpoint the main idea and major supporting points that support the most important point.

And these are all skills you learned in Chapters 1 through 4, so you already have a strong foundation to be successful at marking. Efficient and effective text marking will follow naturally after practice.

QUICK TIPS   THE SOUL METHOD OF TEXT MARKING AND ANNOTATING

The more you mark text and create annotations, the more information you will learn and retain. SOUL is an acronym (the first letter of each word is combined to form an easy-to-remember word) to help you remember the key points in text marking. SOUL stands for

Select. Make sure you are selective about choosing the key points.

Organize. Make sure you organize the key points based on the author's structure.

Understand. Make sure you understand what you're writing by paraphrasing the author's language.

Learn. Use your study notes to prepare for tests and learn the information.

Why Use Text Marking and Annotation?

Using a pen to mark text forces the reader to pay attention to the reading. It is not possible to underline points or mark the text in any way without thinking about what you are doing. Therefore, this method almost guarantees concentration on the subject. Losing one's concentration is a big problem when studying and with school work in general. If your mind wanders, it may be a while before you catch yourself. Even then, it may be a challenge to get yourself back on track. Text marking promotes active learning, making the most of the time you spend on your work.

Text marking is an effective strategy because you learn to selectively identify the most important information in the reading. Because marking the text is a selective strategy (you choose only certain things to mark with your pen), you are doing the groundwork for note taking. If you learn to use effective text-marking strategies, the follow-up strategies of annotating and then rewriting those annotations by summarizing, outlining, and mapping, as well as creating study guides, will be made much easier. You will learn more about summarizing, outlining and mapping as well as creating study guides in Chapter 6.

How to Mark a Text

In the first half of this textbook, you learned to locate and understand important information. In doing that, you underlined main ideas and identified supporting points. Now you will develop those skills by learning a system for marking text. Initially, you must preview and then read the entire reading (including subsections). After completing all of the steps for determining the most important information, as described in Chapters 1–4, go back and mark the text for main ideas and supporting details. Once your skill at doing this improves, you will be able to mark the text *as you read it the first time.*

There are endless text-marking methods and techniques available. But remember: You are identifying important information—not learning a whole new language. The bottom line is that you need to find out what works for you. As your ability improves, you will develop your own methods to improve on the simple method outlined in this chapter. Remember, in its pure form, text marking identifies major ideas—nothing more, nothing less.

Follow these steps to mark a text:

1. Preview the reading.

2. Read the paragraph or passage in its entirety.

3. Determine the author's purpose.

4. Determine the topic of the reading.

5. Determine the pattern of organization.

6. Determine the main idea.

7. Go back and mark the text.

8. After you mark the text, annotate (make notes, paraphrasing the topic, main idea and major and minor details) in the margins or on a separate piece of paper.

When you mark text, use a pen or pencil; a highlighter can make it difficult to see the relationship between ideas because everything (main ideas and details) is in the same color. Even if you use a different color for the main idea and supporting details, the act of interrupting your flow of concentration can disrupt your comprehension of the reading. Remember how limited your working memory capacity is and how quickly information can be bumped from this area. By trying this method of just using a pen or pencil, your concentration will not be disturbed.

Annotating a Text

After you mark a text, you can **annotate** it—that is, write notes, paraphrasing the topic, the main idea, and major and minor details in the margin or on a separate sheet of paper, based on your marking of the text.

As you get better at annotating, a variety of symbols and abbreviations can expand or add to your marking and annotating strategy. For example, if a passage is unclear, put a question mark (?) in the margin. If there is an interesting or surprising fact in a reading, put an exclamation mark (!) in the margin to draw your attention. If you come across an important definition, highlight this with "def" in the margin. You will develop other techniques as you need them.

QUICK TIPS SUGGESTED TECHNIQUES FOR MARKING A TEXT

☑ Circle concepts or key terms. A concept is an idea or, simply, the topic of the passage.

☑ Underline main ideas only. Underlining is a way of marking the text to determine main ideas and supporting details. You shouldn't underline anything but the main idea itself, however, because this would be confusing.

☑ Enumerate (1, 2, 3 or A, B, C) major supporting details in the margin (or, if there's space, above the supporting detail).

☑ Use lowercase alphabetical notations for minor supporting details (a, b, c) (or numbers, if you use uppercase alphabetical notations for major details).

After you have marked the text, you can **annotate** it—that is, write notes, paraphrasing the topic, the main idea, and major and minor supporting details in the margin or on a separate sheet of paper, based on your marking of the text.

Thinking It Through MARKING TEXT IN A PARAGRAPH

You will now see text marking in action in this paragraph from a sociology textbook. What you have learned so far in previous chapters will guide you. Try answering the questions that follow before you read the explanations.

1. **What is the author's purpose?** _____

2. **What is the topic?** _____

3. **What is the pattern of organization?** _____

4. **What is the main idea?** _____

5. **What are the major and minor supporting details?** _____

(Continued)

1   To sociologists, the most common educational institution, the school, is a specialized structure with a special function: preparing children for active participation in adult activities. In simpler societies, however, education of the young is everybody's task in the village or settlement. Children learn through direct demonstration around the hearth or in pastures or fields. For example, among the Maasai, boys learn to hunt from their uncles and fathers; girls learn their roles by helping their mothers perform their tasks. However, in urban industrial societies with a great deal of division of labor and highly developed social institutions, schools of all kinds, including universities, have become highly specialized institutions designed to teach young people the skills and values the society wishes to foster. The typical school has a clearly defined authority system and set of rules. In fact, sociologists often cite schools as examples of bureaucratic organizations.

—From KORNBLUM, *Sociology in a Changing World*, 9E. © 2012 Cengage Learning.

1. **What is the author's purpose?** *The author's purpose is to inform.*

2. **What is the topic?** *Education in industrialized and nonindustrialized societies*

3. **What is the pattern of organization?** *Comparison and contrast*

4. **What is the main idea?** *Here, the main idea is a combination of sentences 1 and 2 (you know that comparison and contrast patterns often involve method 2 of determining an implied main idea from Chapter 4). Main Idea: School in industrial societies is a specialized structure with a special function, but in simpler societies, education of the young is everybody's task in the village or settlement.*

5. **What are the major and minor supporting details?** *Look at the outline of the major details. This outline follows the text markings. These are the annotations you would create based on the text marking:*

   1. *In simpler societies (nonindustrial) children learn through direct demonstration around the hearth or in pastures or fields.*
      a. *Among the Maasai, boys learn to hunt from their uncles and fathers.*
      b. *Girls learn their roles by helping their mothers perform their tasks.*

   2. *In industrial societies, schools are highly specialized institutions designed to teach young people the skills and values the society wishes to foster.*
      a. *The typical school has a clearly defined authority system and set of rules.*
      b. *Sociologists often cite schools as examples of bureaucratic organizations.*

With a clear understanding of the relationship between ideas in the paragraph, you can mark the text. Notice that the text markings are transcribed in the margins. These notes are called *annotations.*

To sociologists, the most common educational institution, the (school) is a specialized structure with a special function: preparing children for active participation in adult activities. In (simpler societies) however, education of the young is everybody's task in the village or settlement. ¹Children learn through direct demonstration around the hearth or in pastures or fields. For example, among the Maasai, ᵃboys learn to hunt from their uncles and fathers; ᵇgirls learn their roles by helping their mothers perform their tasks. ²However, in urban (industrial societies) with a great deal of division of labor and highly developed social institutions, schools of all kinds, including universities, have become highly specialized institutions designed to teach young people the skills and values the society wishes to foster. ᵃThe typical school has a clearly defined authority system and set of rules. ᵇIn fact, sociologists often cite schools as examples of bureaucratic organizations.

Main Idea: *School in industrial societies is a specialized structure with a special function, but in simpler societies, education of the young is everybody's task in the village or settlement.*

1. Nonindustrial children learn through direct demonstration

   a. Maasai boys learn to hunt from uncles and fathers

   b. Girls learn roles by helping mothers

2. Industrial societies have highly specialized schools to teach skills and values

   a. Clearly defined authority system and rules

   b. Bureaucratic organizations

So, text marking and annotating are putting into practice a system for interacting with what you read using all your reading comprehensions skills.

On Your Own MARKING TEXT IN PARAGRAPHS

Read the following paragraphs from a sociology textbook and answer the questions that follow each passage. Then, mark the text following the model in "Thinking It Through: Marking Text in a Paragraph". After marking the text, fill out the outline template, transcribing your text markings into the outline format.

(Continued)

Passage 1

Main Idea:

Supporting Detail 1:

Supporting Detail 2:

From this functionalist perspective, another primary function of schools is to help assimilate the children of immigrants into U.S. society. Through language instruction and socialization of students into "the American way of life," schools have been active agents in the assimilation of waves of immigrants over the past 150 years of U.S. history. But debates over bilingual education and interpretations of American history (for example, the treatment of Native Americans by the U.S. government) in school curricula are indications that the assimilation function is also subject to controversy.

—From KORNBLUM, *Sociology in a Changing World*, 9E. © 2012
Cengage Learning.

1. What is the author's purpose? _____

2. What is the topic? _____

3. What is the pattern of organization? _____

4. Underline the main idea.

Passage 2

Main Idea:

Supporting Detail 1:

Supporting Detail 2:

Supporting Detail 3:

Supporting Detail 4:

Sociologists summarize the explicit, or manifest, functions of education in the United States and most other highly developed nations as follows:

- Formal education transmits the culture of a society to new generations.

- It prepares future generations for appropriate occupational and citizenship roles.

- Educational institutions continually evaluate and select competent individuals.

- Education transmits the requisite social skills for functioning in society.

—From KORNBLUM, *Sociology in a Changing World*, 9E.
© 2012 Cengage Learning.

1. What is the author's purpose? _____

2. What is the topic? _____

3. What is the pattern of organization? _____

4. Underline the main idea.

Passage 3

In addition to these manifest functions, however, there are many latent functions that are implicit in the way we actually go about organizing the education of our children. A latent function of schools is to help reproduce the existing class structure of societies, for example. Parents with knowledge and sufficient wealth can send their children to better public schools by moving to suburban communities that pay teachers more and recruit more highly qualified teachers than are available in central cities, where there are higher concentrations of students from poor backgrounds with less preparation for school. A latent function of institutions of higher education is to bring young men and women from similar class and cultural backgrounds together in an informal "marriage market." Of course, there are many exceptions to these latent functions; people from different class backgrounds may find each other in college, for example, but the basic trends remain in effect, often despite educators' efforts to foster greater equality of access and educational outcomes.

Main Idea:

Supporting Detail 1:

Minor detail:

Minor detail:

Supporting Detail 2:

Supporting Detail 3:

Minor detail:

Minor detail:

—From KORNBLUM, *Sociology in a Changing World*, 9E. © 2012 Cengage Learning.

1. What is the author's purpose? _____

2. What is the topic? _____

3. What is the pattern of organization? _____

4. Underline the main idea.

Thinking It Through MARKING AND ANNOTATING A LONGER TEXT

Marking a longer text requires the same thought process for marking individual paragraphs. The only difference when interacting with a longer text is that you need to consider what the purpose, topic, pattern, and point are for the entire passage as well as for individual paragraphs. With a longer passage, the main idea of the body paragraphs becomes supporting details for the longer passage.

Here is a newspaper article on a subject many of us can relate to: math anxiety. Preview the reading and then read through the article, identifying the pattern of organization, main idea, and the supporting points in each paragraph. Then go back and selectively mark the text. Afterward, transcribe the key points into the margin.

Before you begin, answer the following questions.

1. **What is the topic of this article?**_____

2. **How is the article structured?**_____

3. **Why did the author write the article?**_____

4. **What is the thesis (the most important point) of the article?**_____

Math Anxiety Saps Working Memory Needed to Do Math
by Julie Steenhuysen

1   Worrying about how you'll perform on a math test may actually contribute to a lower test score, U.S. researchers said.

2   Math anxiety—feelings of dread and fear and avoiding math—can sap the brain's limited amount of working capacity, a resource needed to compute difficult math problems, said Mark Ashcroft, a psychologist at the University of Nevada Las Vegas who studies the problem.

3   "It turns out that math anxiety occupies a person's working memory," said Ashcroft, who spoke on a panel at the annual meeting of the American Association for the Advancement of Science in San Francisco.

4   Ashcroft said while easy math tasks such as addition require only a small fraction of a person's working memory, harder computations require much more.

5   Worrying about math takes up a large chunk of a person's working memory stores as well, spelling disaster for the anxious student who is taking a high-stakes test.

6   Stress about how one does on tests like college entrance exams can make even good math students choke. "All of a sudden they start looking for the short cuts," said University of Chicago researcher Sian Beilock.

7   Although test preparation classes can help students overcome this anxiety, they are limited to students whose families can afford them.

8   Ultimately, she said, "It may not be wise to rely completely on scores to predict who will succeed." While the causes of math anxiety are unknown, Ashcroft said people who manage to overcome math anxiety have completely normal math proficiency.

Now compare your text marking and your annotations with those shown here. Remember, marking and annotations will be different among individuals. Notice how the SOUL method of marginal note taking works in this example. The notes and text markings are *selective*: Only important information has been chosen. The notes are organized to reflect how the author has arranged the information. The understanding of the material is apparent because the notes are written in a paraphrased format; they are rewritten using similar, but not identical, wording. And the notes are now clear so the information can be learned. The very act of writing the notes after marking the text is a step in learning the information.

Math Anxiety Saps Working Memory Needed to Do Math
by Julie Steenhuysen

Topic: Math anxiety

Author's Purpose: To inform

Thesis: Worrying about how you'll perform on a math test may actually contribute to a lower test score.

1   Worrying about how you'll perform on a math test may actually contribute to a lower test score, U.S. researchers said.

2   Math anxiety—feelings of dread and fear and avoiding math—can sap the brain's limited amount of working capacity, a resource needed to compute difficult math problems, said Mark Ashcroft, a psychologist at the University of Nevada Las Vegas who studies the problem.

1. Math anxiety is feelings of dread and fear and avoiding math.

3   "It turns out that math anxiety occupies a person's working memory," said Ashcroft, who spoke on a panel at the annual meeting of the American Association for the Advancement of Science in San Francisco.

2. Math anxiety occupies working memory.

4   Ashcroft said while easy math tasks such as addition require only a small fraction of a person's working memory, harder computations require much more.

3. Easy math occupies a small amount of working memory, but hard math occupies much more working memory.

(Continued)

4. Worrying takes up additional working memory.	5 (Worrying about math) takes up a large chunk of a person's working memory stores as well, spelling disaster for the anxious student who is taking a high-stakes test.
5. Stress can affect even good students.	6 (Stress about) how one does on (tests) like college entrance exams can make even good math students choke. "All of a sudden they start looking for the short cuts," said University of Chicago researcher Sian Beilock.
6. Test preparation classes can help but cost money.	7 Although (test preparation) classes can help students overcome this anxiety, they are limited to students whose families can afford them.
7. People who overcome math anxiety are unharmed in their math performance.	8 Ultimately, she said, "It may not be wise to rely completely on scores to predict who will succeed." While the causes of math anxiety are unknown, Ashcroft said people who manage to (overcome math anxiety) have completely normal math proficiency.

On Your Own MARKING AND ANNOTATING A LONGER TEXT

Here is an excerpt from a college text, *Psychology*, that contrasts the different learning outcomes and learning methods in the United States and some Asian cultures, specifically Taiwan and Japan. Textbook material can be more complex and information-dense than other reading material, but the process of text marking will be the same. Use the SOUL method when you mark this reading; the difference is not in what you do, but how much you mark in the text.

1. **Read the textbook excerpt, then go back and selectively mark the text.**

2. **Transcribe the key points into the margin, using the SOUL method.**

3. **Compare your notes with those of a classmate or a small group of peers.**

Before you begin, as always, answer the following questions:

■ What is the topic of this article? _____

■ How is the article structured? _____

■ What is the author's purpose? _____

Using Research on Learning
to Help People Learn

1   Teaching and training—explicit efforts to assist learners in mastering a specific skill or body of material —are major aspects of socialization in virtually every culture. So the study of how people learn has important implications for improved teaching our schools and for helping people develop skills ranging from typing to tennis.

Classrooms Across Cultures

2   Many people are concerned that schools in the United States are not doing a very good job. The average performance of U.S. students on tests of reading, math, and other basic academic skills has tended to fall short of that of youngsters in other countries, especially some Asian countries. In one comparison study, Harold Stevenson (1992) followed a sample of pupils in Taiwan, Japan, and the United States from first grade, in 1980, to eleventh grade, in 1991. In first grade, the Asian students scored no higher than their U.S. peers on tests of mathematical aptitude and skills, nor did they enjoy math more. However, by fifth grade the U.S. students had fallen far behind. Corresponding differences were seen in reading skills.

3   Some possible causes of these differences were found in the classroom itself. In a typical U.S. classroom session, teachers talked to students as a group. The students then worked at their desks independently. Reinforcement or other feedback about performance on their work was usually delayed until the next day or, often, not provided at all. In contrast, the typical Japanese classroom placed greater emphasis on cooperative work among students. Teachers provided more immediate feed-back on a one-to-one basis. And there was an emphasis on creating teams of students with varying abilities, an arrangement in which faster learners help teach slower ones.

(Continued)

However, before concluding that the differences in performance are the result of social factors alone, we must consider another important distinction: The Japanese children practiced more. They spent more days in school during the year and on average spent more hours doing homework.

4   Although the significance of these cultural differences in learning and teaching is not yet clear, the educational community in the United States is paying attention to them. Psychologists and educators are also considering how other principles of learning can be applied to improve education. Anecdotal and experimental evidence suggests that some of the most successful educational techniques are those that apply basic principles of operant conditioning, offering frequent testing, positive reinforcement for correct performance, and immediate corrective feedback following mistakes. Research in cognitive psychology also suggests that students are more likely to retain what they learn if they engage in numerous study sessions rather than in a single "cramming" session on the night before a quiz or exam. To encourage this more beneficial "distributed practice" pattern, researchers say, teachers should give enough exams and quizzes (some unannounced, perhaps) that students will be reading and studying more or less continuously. And because learning is aided by repeated opportunities to use new information, these exams and quizzes should cover material from throughout the term, not just from recent classes. Such recommendations are not necessarily popular with students, but there is good evidence that they promote long-term retention of course material.

—From BERNSTEIN/PENNER/CLARKE-STEWART/ ROY, Psychology, 7E. © 2006 Cengage Learning.

UNDERSTANDING GRAPHICS

READING COMPLEX TABLES

Reading complex tables requires some careful investigation to determine the key points. With complex tables, you will benefit from marking the information in the table in order to pinpoint the most important information, just as you do in written text. First, read for main ideas by determining the topic, pattern of organization, and most important point. In the case of a complex table, such as Table 5.3, you have to look more closely at the information to get the most important points. You will add three more steps to draw your conclusion:

- Determine the meaning of each of the columns in the table.
- Determine what each of the columns tells you as a whole about the topic.
- Make a reasonable inference.

These steps are applied to Table 5.3 (on the following page) here.

1. **Determine the topic.** *The actual and projected numbers for enrollment in all degree-granting postsecondary institutions, by race/ethnicity: fall 1993 through fall 2018, in the thousands.*

2. **Determine the pattern of organization.** *Comparison and contrast and sequence.*

3. **Determine the most important point.** *All degree-granting postsecondary institutions are expected to increase in enrollment in all racial/ethnic groups.*

4. **Determine the overall point of each of the columns.**
   a. *The first column concerns the years of enrollment—the actual statistics span 1993–2007; the estimated (projected) enrollment rates per year from 2008 to 2018.*
   b. *The second column shows total enrollment rates and projected trends.*
   c. *The third column shows White enrollment rates.*
   d. *The fourth column shows African American enrollment rates.*
   e. *The fifth column shows Hispanic graduation rates.*
   f. *The sixth column indicates Asian/Pacific Islander enrollment rates.*
   g. *The seventh column shows American Indian/Alaskan native enrollment rates.*

5. **Determine the overall point of each of the columns as they relate to the whole.** *These figures show that all racial and ethnic enrollment rates are expected to increase between 2008 and 2018, and they have continued to rise between 1993 and 2007. While their enrollment numbers are not as large as those of other groups, Asian/Pacific Islanders and American Indian/Alaskan native students have the highest rate of expected enrollment growth between 2007 and 2018. White and Hispanic student enrollment rates are expected to increase at a rate of approximately 2 million students.*

6. **What is a reasonable inference about future trends?** *This information indicates that the enrollment rates of students are likely to continue to rise in the coming years.*

(Continued)

TABLE 5.3 Actual and Projected Numbers for Enrollment in All Degree-Granting Postsecondary Institutions, by Race/Ethnicity: Fall 1993 through Fall 2018

YEAR	TOTAL	RACE/ETHNICITY				
		WHITE	BLACK	HISPANIC	ASIAN/PACIFIC ISLANDER	AMERICAN INDIAN/ ALASKANATIVE
ACTUAL						
1993	14,305	10,600	1,413	989	724	122
1994	14,279	10,427	1,449	1,046	774	127
1995	14,262	10,311	1,474	1,094	797	131
1996	14,368	10,264	1,506	1,166	828	138
1997	14,502	10,266	1,551	1,218	859	142
1998	14,507	10,179	1,583	1,257	900	144
1999	14,791	10,282	1,643	1,319	913	145
2000	15,312	10,462	1,730	1,462	978	151
2001	15,928	10,775	1,850	1,561	1,019	158
2002	16,612	11,140	1,979	1,662	1,074	166
2003	16,911	11,281	2,068	1,716	1,076	173
2004	17,272	11,423	2,165	1,810	1,109	176
2005	17,487	11,495	2,215	1,882	1,134	176
2006	17,759	11,572	2,280	1,964	1,165	181
2007	18,248	11,756	2,383	2,076	1,218	190
PROJECTED						
2008	18,699	11,981	2,462	2,170	1,255	192
2009	19,037	12,196	2,482	2,219	1,266	216
2010	19,126	12,182	2,507	2,259	1,292	220
2011	19,286	12,182	2,561	2,324	1,324	223
2012	19,462	12,177	2,627	2,398	1,358	227
2013	19,710	12,210	2,708	2,484	1,397	230
2014	19,928	12,226	2,778	2,568	1,434	234
2015	20,097	12,212	2,838	2,646	1,469	238
2016	20,254	12,194	2,895	2,720	1,502	242
2017	20,446	12,211	2,951	2,794	1,536	246
2018	20,620	12,228	2,995	2,863	1,568	251

SOURCES: U.S. Department of Education, National Center for Education Statistics, Integrated Post Secondary Data System, "Fall Enrollment Survey" (IPEDS-EF:93–99), and Spring 2001 through Spring 2008; and Enrollment in Degree-Granting Institutions by Race/Ethnicity Model, 1980–2007. (This table was prepared January 2009.) http://nces.ed.gov/programs/projections/projections2018/tables/table_22.asp?referrer=list.

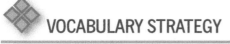

VOCABULARY STRATEGY

IMPROVING YOUR COLLEGE-LEVEL VOCABULARY

In college texts, you will encounter many words you do not know. One strategy for understanding these key terms is to use the key terms features in your textbook. Another strategy you can use is to practice and apply the vocabulary strategies of using context clues, recognizing words parts, and understanding figurative language. However, sometimes you need to be active in expanding your vocabulary by using a dictionary and learning more complex words through study.

Using a Dictionary

Every college student needs to own a good college dictionary. Using this resource is vital to building your college vocabulary. Online dictionaries are convenient and easy to access; however, if you don't know how to spell the word in question, it is difficult to use an online resource. A book, however, provides the assurance that if you come close to spelling the word correctly, you can often find it.

A dictionary will help you understand different ways a particular word can be used in different contexts. And, a dictionary identifies what part of speech a word is—noun, pronoun, verb, article, adjective, adverb, conjunction, interjection. A dictionary can provide information about the origin of a word—whether it is derived from Latin, Greek, old English, French, or another language. As valuable a reference tool as a dictionary is, it is a last resort for learning the meaning of an unfamiliar word because of the disruption the "looking-it-up" process causes to your comprehension and working memory. Better strategies for learning the meaning of new words are using context clues and structural analysis—examination of word parts. The dictionary is a first resort, however, for spelling help (besides a spell-check program) and learning the part of speech or origin of a word.

Guide words at the top of each page in the dictionary indicate which alphabetical words listings are on that page. For example, if a guide word on the top left of the page is *independence* and the guide word on the top right of the page is *individual,* and the word you wanted to find was *indignant,* you are on the right page! *Indignant* would fall between *independence* and *individual.* Most dictionaries list entries in boldface print. Following the word is its phonetic pronunciation and its part of speech. After this is the definition of the word and an example of how the word is used. Many dictionaries include the word's origin and how the parts of the word originally came to be. Abbreviations for the word origins can usually be found at the beginning of a dictionary (*L, OFr, Gr, OE* stands for Latin, Old French, Greek, Old English, respectively). Last, additional forms of the word are provided as well as synonyms.

in•dig•nant [in-**dig**-n*uh* nt]—***adjective*** Feeling or showing anger because of something unjust, filled with indignation. *He was indignant when insulted unjustly.*

Origin: 1590. From L-the Latin *indignus, indignare,* to be displeased, unworthy
Related forms: in.dig.nant.ly, adverb
Synonyms: enraged, furious, livid, angry, resentful, mad

(●) DENOTES SYLLABLE BREAKS

PRONUNCIATION

PART OF SPEECH

Bi●as [bahy-uhs]n. 1. A diagonally
line usually across fabric. 2. Taking a side
on an issue or an inclination to adopt a
point of view.-v. -ased or -assed, -as'ing
or as'sing. To be biased; prejudice. [Ofr.
Middle French biais, oblique.]

ALTERNATE FORMS
OF WORD

ETYMOLOGY (word's history)

Recognizing Common College Vocabulary

Here is a list of the top 100 vocabulary words according to JustColleges.com. While there is no doubt vocabulary is acquired through encountering words you do not know within passages you are reading, some of you may desire to begin to expand your vocabulary by learning the top 100 words found across the disciplines. Use your knowledge of word parts to make educated guesses as to the meanings of the following words, or look them up in a dictionary. You might consider setting a goal of learning five new words from this list per week. In any case, learning any of these words cannot hurt.

SAT—THE TOP 100 VOCABULARY WORDS

Extensive reading is the best way to develop your command of tough vocabulary. But cramming Shakespeare and Milton before the test is not very practical. So, we've done a little investigating and have compiled the top 100 vocabulary words of all time. Use this list to strengthen your vocabulary and prepare for the test day challenge.

1. **abbreviate:** (v) to shorten, abridge
2. **abstinence:** (n) the act of refraining from pleasurable activity, e.g., eating or drinking
3. **adulation:** (n) high praise
4. **adversity:** (n) misfortune, an unfavorable turn of events
5. **aesthetic:** (adj) pertaining to beauty or the arts
6. **amicable:** (adj) friendly, agreeable
7. **anachronistic:** (adj) out-of-date, not attributed to the correct historical period
8. **anecdote:** (n) short, usually funny account of an event
9. **anonymous:** (adj) nameless, without a disclosed identity
10. **antagonist:** (n) foe, opponent, adversary
11. **arid:** (adj) extremely dry or deathly boring

12. **assiduous:** (adj) persistent, hard-working

13. **asylum:** (n) sanctuary, shelter, place of refuge

14. **benevolent:** (adj) friendly and helpful

15. **camaraderie:** (n) trust, sociability amongst friends

16. **censure:** (v) to criticize harshly

17. **circuitous:** (adj) indirect, taking the longest route

18. **clairvoyant:** (adj) exceptionally insightful, able to foresee the future

19. **collaborate:** (v) to cooperate, work together

20. **compassion:** (n) sympathy, helpfulness, or mercy

21. **compromise:** (v) to settle a dispute by terms agreeable to both sides

22. **condescending:** (adj) possessing an attitude of superiority, patronizing

23. **conditional:** (adj) depending on a condition, e.g., in a contract

24. **conformist:** (n) person who complies with accepted rules and customs

25. **congregation:** (n) a crowd of people, an assembly

26. **convergence:** (n) the state of separate elements joining or coming together

27. **deleterious:** (adj) harmful, destructive, detrimental

28. **demagogue:** (n) leader, rabble-rouser, usually appealing to emotion or prejudice

29. **digression:** (n) the act of turning aside, straying from the main point, esp. in a speech or argument

30. **diligent:** (adj) careful and hard-working

31. **discredit:** (v) to harm the reputation of, dishonor or disgrace

32. **disdain:** (v) to regard with scorn or contempt

33. **divergent:** (adj) separating, moving in different directions from a particular point

34. **empathy:** (n) identification with the feelings of others

35. **emulate:** (v) to imitate, follow an example

36. **enervating:** (adj) weakening, tiring

37. **enhance:** (v) to improve, bring to a greater level of intensity

38. **ephemeral:** (adj) momentary, transient, fleeting

39. **evanescent:** (adj) quickly fading, short-lived, esp. an image

40. **exasperation:** (n) irritation, frustration

41. **exemplary:** (adj) outstanding, an example to others

42. **extenuating:** (adj) excusing, lessening the seriousness of guilt or crime, e.g., of mitigating factors

43. **florid:** (adj) red-colored, flushed; gaudy, ornate

44. **fortuitous:** (adj) happening by luck, fortunate

(Continued)

45. **frugal:** (adj) thrifty, cheap
46. **hackneyed:** (adj) clichéd, worn out by overuse
47. **haughty:** (adj) arrogant and condescending
48. **hedonist:** (n) person who pursues pleasure as a goal
49. **hypothesis:** (n) assumption, theory requiring proof
50. **impetuous:** (adj) rash, impulsive, acting without thinking
51. **impute:** (v) to attribute an action to a particular person or group
52. **incompatible:** (adj) opposed in nature, not able to live or work together
53. **inconsequential:** (adj) unimportant, trivial
54. **inevitable:** (adj) certain, unavoidable
55. **integrity:** (n) decency, honesty, wholeness
56. **intrepid:** (adj) fearless, adventurous
57. **intuitive:** (adj) instinctive, untaught
58. **jubilation:** (n) joy, celebration, exultation
59. **lobbyist:** (n) person who seeks to influence political events
60. **longevity:** (n) long life
61. **mundane:** (adj) ordinary, commonplace
62. **nonchalant:** (adj) calm, casual, seeming unexcited
63. **novice:** (n) apprentice, beginner
64. **opulent:** (adj) wealthy
65. **orator:** (n) lecturer, speaker
66. **ostentatious:** (adj) showy, displaying wealth
67. **parched:** (adj) dried up, shriveled
68. **perfidious:** (adj) faithless, disloyal, untrustworthy
69. **precocious:** (adj) unusually advanced or talented at an early age
70. **pretentious:** (adj) pretending to be important, intelligent, or cultured
71. **procrastinate:** (v) to unnecessarily delay, postpone, put off
72. **prosaic:** (adj) relating to prose; dull, commonplace
73. **prosperity:** (n) wealth or success
74. **provocative:** (adj) tending to provoke a response, e.g., anger or disagreement
75. **prudent:** (adj) careful, cautious
76. **querulous:** (adj) complaining, irritable
77. **rancorous:** (adj) bitter, hateful
78. **reclusive:** (adj) preferring to live in isolation

79. **reconciliation:** (n) the act of agreement after a quarrel, the resolution of a dispute

80. **renovation:** (n) repair, making something new again

81. **resilient:** (adj) quick to recover, bounce back

82. **restrained:** (adj) controlled, repressed, restricted

83. **reverence:** (n) worship, profound respect

84. **sagacity:** (n) wisdom

85. **scrutinize:** (v) to observe carefully

86. **spontaneity:** (n) impulsive action, unplanned events

87. **spurious:** (adj) lacking authenticity, false

88. **submissive:** (adj) tending to meekness, to submit to the will of others

89. **substantiate:** (v) to verify, confirm, provide supporting evidence

90. **subtle:** (adj) hard to detect or describe; perceptive

91. **superficial:** (adj) shallow, lacking in depth

92. **superfluous:** (adj) extra, more than enough, redundant

93. **suppress:** (v) to end an activity, e.g., to prevent the dissemination of information

94. **surreptitious:** (adj) secret, stealthy

95. **tactful:** (adj) considerate, skillful in acting to avoid offense to others

96. **tenacious:** (adj) determined, keeping a firm grip on

97. **transient:** (adj) temporary, short-lived, fleeting

98. **venerable:** (adj) respected because of age

99. **vindicate:** (v) to clear from blame or suspicion

100. **wary:** (adj) careful, cautious

SOURCE: "Top 100 vocabulary words for the SAT" (http://www.justcolleges.com). Used with permission.

USING THE DICTIONARY WITH THE TOP
On Your Own 100 VOCABULARY WORDS

Choose five words from the Top 100 Vocabulary Words list. Look these words up in the dictionary and provide the following information for each.

- Word
- Pronunciation
- Part of speech
- Etymology (word origin)
- Related forms
- Synonyms

INCREASE YOUR DISCIPLINE-SPECIFIC VOCABULARY

BUSINESS AND ECONOMICS

As you know, every discipline has specific vocabulary. Business and financial disciplines draw heavily on Greek and Latin roots. Familiarize yourself with these word parts and common core vocabulary to gain an advantage in college reading (Table 5.4).

TABLE 5.4 Vocabulary Associated with Business and Economics

WORD PARTS	MEANING	VOCABULARY
auto	self	**autocratic, autonomy, automatic, automated, automobile, autopsy**
bene	well, good	**benefit, benefactor, benevolent, beneficial, benign, benediction**
capit	head	**capital, capitalism, capital punishment, capitulate**
con, com, col,	together, with	**conflict, conform, conscientious, consult, contingent, continuous, conversation, conviction, commiserate, concur, condone, consensus, collaborate,**
cor corpus	body	**correlate corporation, corporate, incorporate, corporal punishment, corpse**
cred	to believe	**credit, incredible, credentials, discredit**
equ	equal	**equate, equivalent, equitable, inadequate, equilibrium, equity**
manu	hand	**manuscript, manual, manage, manager, manufacture,**
post	after	**posterity, posterior, postdate, postscript, preposterous, postpone**
pre, ante	before	**precedent, precise, precocious, prejudice, prescribe, anteroom, antecedent, antique**

Key Terms—Business and Economics

- **Capital:** all human, equipment and skills used to produce goods and services.
- **Collateral:** any money or goods acceptable to a lender to guarantee repayment of a loan.
- **Consumer:** the public who purchases goods or services.
- **Entrepreneur:** a person who assumes, manages and organizes a risk in an enterprise or business.
- **Federal Reserve:** the central governmental monetary body.
- **Gross domestic product (GDP):** the final monetary value of goods and services produced in a fiscal (financial) year.
- **Inflation:** an increase in overall price of goods and services.
- **Profit:** the difference between money made from and expended to produce goods or services.
- **Revenue:** money produced by a body from producing goods and services.
- **Tariff:** a tax imposed on the importing of goods.

APPLICATIONS

APPLICATION ①

This reading is an article from the magazine *U.S. News & World Report* on college graduation challenges in the United States. Read the article after you preview it. Then, using the techniques you have learned in this chapter, mark the text and annotate in the margins. Use the SOUL method to mark the text and take notes. In addition, circle any words that are unfamiliar to you and use vocabulary strategies or a dictionary to find their meaning.

Once you have completed your text marking and annotation, compare your text and notes in small groups or with a partner. Remember: The notes should contain roughly the same information, but because you are paraphrasing the ideas, the wording may be a bit different.

Get In, Show Up, Drop Out
by Alex Kingsbury

1   For years, universities have known that one freshman does not a graduate make. Yet the focus of policymakers and teachers throughout the education pipeline has been to get students accepted to college. An admirable goal, experts say, but one that may be fruitless, even detrimental, unless students finish with a degree.

2   The numbers are stark. Only 63 percent of all students entering four-year colleges have their degrees within six years, according to government statistics. Rates for black and Hispanic students are less than 50 percent, and the gap between minority and white students is growing. It is these disturbing trends that have prompted William Bowen, president of the Andrew W. Mellon Foundation and one of the nation's foremost education researchers, to announce a major research initiative into *the* subject last week in a speech to the Goldman Sachs Foundation. "We need to understand with greater precision what happens to these students along the way in their academic careers that makes them drop out," says Bowen, whose previous studies on affirmative action, collegiate athletics, and socioeconomic diversity in admissions have been influential in higher education.

Behind South Korea

3   Motivating the project, which will most likely focus on 20 large public universities, are several worrying—and not unrelated— trends: the growing inequities of higher education, especially between students from different racial and socioeconomic backgrounds, and the lagging competitiveness of the nation. In 2003, just 39 percent of American adults ages 25 to 34 had a degree, compared with 53 percent in Canada, 52 percent in Japan, and 47 percent in South Korea. Couple that with the fact that 100 new universities will break ground in China in the next decade, and the need for action is clear, Bowen says.

4   The ramifications for students who fail to obtain a degree are serious. College graduates earn far more than non-graduates over their lifetimes. And students who attend college, incur debt, and fail to emerge with a degree can be worse off than when they applied in the first place.

5   While family income, financial aid, and the education level of one's parents have been contributing factors, the underlying causes—and possible solutions—are far from evident. Most frustrating, researchers say, is the lack of usable data on who actually drops out of college and why. "Colleges have long felt that they are not responsible for tracking completion rates and dealing with the issue," says Yolanda Kodrzycki, an economist with the Federal Reserve Bank of Boston, who has studied regional variations in minority completion rates. But the answers won't be readily apparent. Researchers typically must track students over six years to get good data.

SOURCE: Alex Kingsbury, "Get in, show up, drop out." *U.S. News & World Report* 139.20 (Nov 28, 2005): p39. Reprinted by permission of U.S. News & World Report.

(Continued)

TABLE 5.5 Actual and Alternative Projected Numbers for Enrollment in Public 4-Year Degree-Granting Postsecondary Institutions, by Sex and Attendance Status: Fall 1992 through Fall 2017 [in Thousands]

YEAR	TOTAL	MEN		WOMEN	
		FULL-TIME	PART-TIME	FULL-TIME	PART-TIME
Actual					
1992	5,900	2,005	760	2,090	1,045
1993	5,852	1,989	750	2,085	1,027
1994	5,825	1,966	738	2,100	1,022
1995	5,815	1,951	720	2,134	1,009
1996	5,806	1,943	703	2,163	997
1997	5,835	1,951	687	2,214	984
1998	5,892	1,959	685	2,260	988
1999	5,970	1,984	686	2,309	991
2000	6,055	2,009	683	2,363	1,001
2001	6,236	2,082	687	2,450	1,017
2002	6,482	2,167	706	2,557	1,052
2003	6,649	2,225	713	2,639	1,072
2004	6,737	2,260	717	2,684	1,076
2005	6,838	2,295	724	2,726	1,091
2006	6,955	2,339	740	2,765	1,111
Middle alternative projections					
2007	6,981	2,376	738	2,768	1,098
2008	7,092	2,417	746	2,819	1,110
2009	7,204	2,455	753	2,872	1,125
2010	7,290	2,488	761	2,906	1,134
2011	7,379	2,518	773	2,942	1,146
2012	7,473	2,544	786	2,983	1,159
2013	7,575	2,567	802	3,033	1,174

| YEAR | TOTAL | MEN | | WOMEN | |
		FULL-TIME	PART-TIME	FULL-TIME	PART-TIME
2014	7,666	2,583	816	3,079	1,188
2015	7,738	2,592	828	3,118	1,201
2016	7,806	2,601	839	3,153	1,213
2017	7,874	2,614	850	3,184	1,226

SOURCE: U.S. Department of Education, National Center for Education Statistics, Integrated Postsecondary Education Data System, "Fall Enrollment Survey" (IPEDS-EF:92–99), and Spring 2002 through Spring 2007; and Enrollment in Degree-Granting Institutions Model, 1980–2006. (This table was prepared November 2007.)

NOTE: Detail may not sum to totals because of rounding. Some data have been revised from previously published figures. Data for 1999 were imputed using alternative procedures.

COMPREHENSION CHECK

1. Why do you think only 63 percent of students entering four-year colleges have their degrees within six years?

2. Why do you think the graduation rates for African American and Hispanic students are less than 50 percent? What can be done to close the achievement gap between white and minority students?

3. The rates of graduation in several other countries were cited in this reading. Compare these graduation rates to those of the United States. What do you think accounts for this disparity or difference?

4. Several Asian countries have high university graduation rates. What is the likely trend in these countries in coming years? What impact might this trend have on the United States?

5. Does the author offer any explanation for U.S. drop-out rates? Does he offer any solution? How do you explain the educational attainment in the United States and what solution would you offer to reverse these trends?

READING GRAPHICS

Table 5.5 examines the enrollment figures and projected trends for four-year universities by gender and part- or full-time status. Despite what you read in Application 1 regarding graduation rates in four-year colleges, enrollment numbers continue to climb! Examine Table 5.5, marking the information that is important.

1. Determine the topic. _____

2. Determine the pattern of organization. _____

(Continued)

3. Determine the most important point._____
_____

4. Write down the most important point of each of the columns represented in Table 5.5, using this table.

YEAR	TOTAL	MEN FULL-TIME	MEN PART-TIME	WOMEN FULL-TIME	WOMEN PART-TIME

5. Determine what the meaning of each of the columns tells you as a whole about the topic.
_____

6. Make a reasonable inference about future trends as noted in the table.
_____
_____
_____
_____
_____
_____

7. Unlike this table, the reading does not discuss sex in light of dropout and graduation rates. Do you think sex or gender is involved in rates of graduation and rates of dropping out in

college? _____
_____
_____
_____
_____

DEVELOPING YOUR COLLEGE-LEVEL VOCABULARY

Here are some words that you will most likely encounter in your college reading from the Application reading. For each set of words, write one sentence using sufficient context clues to make clear each word's meaning.

1. Paragraph 1: *pipeline, fruitless, detrimental*

_____
_____
_____
_____

2. Paragraph 2: *initiative, precision, affirmative, socioeconomic*

_____
_____
_____
_____

3. Paragraph 3: *inequities, lagging*

_____
_____
_____
_____

4. Paragraph 4: *ramifications, incur*

_____
_____
_____
_____

5. Paragraph 5: *variations, readily*

_____
_____
_____
_____

(Continued)

THEMATIC CONNECTIONS

1. Relate the information in this reading to the Pre-Assessment in this chapter. Do the authors hold the same point of view about U.S. education? Explain your answer.

2. Do you know people who have enrolled in and then dropped out of college during their freshman year? Explain why you believe they dropped out.

3. What do you think it takes to stay enrolled in college and graduate?

4. Why do you think so many students dropped out during their freshman year?

APPLICATION ②

Here is a psychology textbook passage that concerns the topic of motivation for achievement. Apply the skills you have developed in this chapter to this textbook passage.

1. Mark the text in its entirety, or mark a subsection of the text as assigned by your instructor.

2. Create notes in the margins.

Development of Achievement Motivation
by Douglas A. Bernstein, Louis A. Penner, Alison Clarke-Stewart, and Edward J. Roy

1   Achievement motivation tends to be learned in early childhood, especially from parents. For example, in one study young boys were given a difficult task at which they were sure to fail. Fathers whose sons scored low on achievement motivation tests often became annoyed as they watched their boys. They discouraged them from continuing, interfered, and even completed the task themselves. A different pattern of behavior appeared among parents of children who scored high on tests of achievement motivation. Those parents tended to encourage the child during difficult tasks, especially new ones; give praise and other rewards for successes; encourage the child to find ways to succeed rather than merely complaining about failure; and prompt the child to go on to the next, more difficult challenges. Other research with adults shows that even the slightest cues that bring a parent to mind can boost people's efforts to achieve a goal.

2   More general cultural influences also affect the development of achievement motivation. For example, subtle messages about a culture's view of how achievement occurs often appear in the books children read and the stories they hear. Does the story's main character work hard and overcome obstacles, thus creating expectations of a payoff for persistence? Is the character a

(Continued)

loafer who wins the lottery, suggesting that rewards come randomly, regardless of effort? If the main character succeeds, is it the result of personal initiative, as is typical of stories in individualist cultures? Or is success based on ties to a cooperative and supportive group, as is typical of stories in collectivist cultures? These themes appear to act as blueprints for reaching culturally approved goals. It should not be surprising, then, that ideas about how people achieve differ from culture to culture. In one study, for example, individuals from a Saudi Arabia and from the United States were asked to comment on short stories describing people who succeeded at various tasks. Saudis tended to see the people in the stories as having succeeded because of the help they got from others, whereas Americans tended to attribute success to the personal traits of each story's main character. Achievement motivation is also influenced by how much a particular culture values achievement. For example, the motivation to excel is likely to be especially strong in cultures in which demanding standards lead students to fear rejection if they fail to attain high grades.

3   It is possible to increase achievement motivation among people whose cultural training did not foster it in childhood. In one study, high school and college students with low achievement motivation were helped to develop fantasies about their own success. They imagined setting goals that were difficult, but not impossible. Then they imagined themselves concentrating on breaking a complex problem into small, manageable steps. They fantasized about working hard, failing but not being discouraged, continuing to work, and finally feeling elated at success. Afterward, the students' grades and academic success improved, suggesting an increase in their achievement motivation. In short, achievement motivation is strongly influenced by social and cultural learning experiences, as well as by the beliefs about oneself that these experiences help to create. People who come to believe in their ability to achieve are more likely to do so than those who expect to fail.

SOURCE: From BERNSTEIN/PENNER/CLARKE-STEWART/ROY, Psychology, 7E. © 2006 Cengage Learning.

COMPREHENSION CHECK

[1] To what extent do you think effort equates with success? Are there situations where effort does not equate with success?

[2] Many Americans grow up with the mindset that they can do *anything* as long as they put their mind to it. Do you believe this is true? Provide several specific, supporting examples to prove your point of view.

[3] The reading discusses child-rearing techniques that produce children with a likelihood for success. Outline the ideal parental environment and its effect on a receptive child.

[4] Explain how or if it is possible to increase achievement motivation among people whose cultural training did not foster it in childhood.

READING GRAPHICS

"Maybe they didn't try hard enough."

Al Ross/The New Yorker/www.CartoonBank.com

1. How does this cartoon function to clarify the main point of the passage for readers? _____
_____
_____

2. What does this cartoon suggest about the American view of motivation and achievement? _____
_____
_____

3. Do you think achievement is all about effort or is that not enough? _____
_____
_____

(Continued)

DEVELOPING YOUR COLLEGE-LEVEL VOCABULARY

Define the following key terms or phrases from the reading. No specific definitions are provided. Write your own definition based on information provided in the reading. Compare your definitions with a partner, in a small group, or in class discussion.

1. Paragraph 1: *achievement motivation:* _____
   _____

2. Paragraph 2: *cultural influences:* _____
   _____

3. Paragraph 3: *cultural training:* _____
   _____

THEMATIC CONNECTIONS

1. This reading discusses achievement motivation in different cultures. Discuss the cross-cultural differences between any culture discussed in this passage and that of the United States.

2. Do you think that American "achievement motivation" is still as strong as it used to be, or is the motivation waning? Support your answer with examples.

3. This reading discusses how mindset can influence achievement motivation. Describe how you were raised and its effect on your motivation to be successful.

WRAPPING IT UP

In the following study outline, fill in the definitions and a brief explanation of the key terms in the "Your Notes" column. Use the strategy of spaced practice to review these key terms on a regular basis. Use this study guide to review this chapter's key topics.

KEY TERM OR CONCEPT	YOUR NOTES
Reading rate	
Comprehension monitoring	
Text marking	
Underlining	
Annotating	
SOUL method of note taking	

GROUP ACTIVITY: COLLEGE ADMISSIONS

In groups of three or four (or as your instructor assigns), arrive at a consensus of opinion in the following role-play scenario involving the issue of what it takes to be successful in college.

As a team, you and your group are the admissions committee for your small college. There is a limit to how many applicants you can accept per year because funding is low. All students are required to "give back" to the college through some sort of service work.

Consider the following applicants to your college. Only three can be admitted for this upcoming semester. Who will get in? Be prepared to discuss your group's reasons and justify your choices. What do your groups' choices reveal about what you consider important for college success?

Maria
- College degree from Mexico
- Wants to come to the United States to learn the language
- Qualifies for a scholarship
- Majored in biology
- Intends to stay for two years only

Fred
- High school athlete
- Earns average grades
- Works hard for grades
- Limits outside employment to concentrate on sports

Ty
- Tested very high on college aptitude test
- Was in a "gifted" program until halfway through junior high school
- Earned poor but passing high school grades
- Reports he didn't study
- Has high school discipline record
- Wants to major in music

Keisha
- Works 40 hours per week as nurse's aide
- Earned average ACT/SAT scores
- Earned high school grade point average of 2.0
- Wants to go into nursing
- Works very hard at school-related tasks
- Is active in high school extracurricular clubs

Ashley
- Is single parent of two small children
- Has been out of school for 6 years
- Left high school in grade 11
- Received a GED (General Education Diploma) after the birth of first child
- Earned grade point average of 3.0 before dropping out
- Earned average ACT/SAT scores
- Wants to get certification in early childhood education

Louisa
- Age 58
- Wants to earn a degree in business
- Wants to open her own restaurant
- Has never attended college
- Works as a waitress full-time
- Has grown children but often must care for grandson

Randolph	▪ Earned a high school equivalency diploma (GED) at age 24 while incarcerated for breaking and entering
	▪ Has long history of petty crime; attributes this to growing up in a dysfunctional home
	▪ Is described as an "excellent, motivated student" by his instructor in the prison program
	▪ Has decided to go to college to better himself and make a good life for his young son
	▪ Wants to major in computer technology*

*Activity adapted from "Who Stays? A Values-Clarification Exercise," by Dave Ellis, from *Becoming a Master Student*.

REFLECTIVE JOURNAL QUESTIONS

1. What is the main reason you are in college? How do you intend to "beat the odds" by being one who graduates? What is your goal if not to graduate with a certificate, a 2-year, or a 4-year degree?

2. What do you find difficult about marking a text? Do you think text marking is important even if instructors provide handouts or PowerPoint slides? Why or why not?

3. Mark a textbook assignment for another class. How has this activity helped you understand or learn the material more effectively than if you had just read the assignment?

THEMATIC CONNECTIONS

Respond to one of the following questions. Prepare notes for class discussion, or write a response to submit to your instructor.

1. What do you believe is the most significant problem in education today? What do you think we need to do to address this problem? Support your answer with specific examples.

2. Recall your own experience and that of your peers in high school. Do you think you were adequately prepared for the demands of college? Give three specific examples to support your claim.

3. What are the qualities needed to succeed in college? Choose three qualities (behaviors or attitudes) that characterize a successful college student. Support your answer with specific examples.

4. Many of the graphics you have reviewed in this chapter suggest increasing postsecondary educational enrollment, but evidence suggests that actual graduation rates are declining in the United States. Explain the possible connection between increased enrollment but high dropout rates.

ADDITIONAL SKILL AND STRATEGY PRACTICE

A. Text Marking

Follow these steps you learned in this chapter for marking the following passage from a sociology textbook.

STEPS FOR MARKING A TEXT

1. Preview the reading.
2. Read the passage in its entirety.
3. Determine the author's purpose. _____
4. Determine the topic of the reading. _____
5. Determine the pattern of organization. _____
6. Underline the thesis of the whole passage and main idea of each paragraph.
7. Go back and mark the text.
8. After you mark the text, annotate (make notes, paraphrasing the topic, main idea and major and minor details) in the margins or on a separate piece of paper.

Who Goes to School?
William Kornblum

1   The idea that all children should be educated is a product of the American and French Revolutions of the late eighteenth century. In the European monarchies, the suggestion that the children of peasants and workers should be educated would have been considered laughable. In those societies, children went to work with adults at an early age, and adolescence was not recognized as a distinct stage of development. Formal schooling, which was generally reserved for the children of the elite, typically lasted three or four years, after which the young person entered a profession.

2   Even after the creation of republics in France and the United States and the beginning of a movement for universal education, the development of a comprehensive system of schools took many generations. In the early history of the United States, the children of slaves, Native Americans, the poor, and many immigrant groups, as well as almost all female children, were excluded from educational institutions. The norm of segregated education for racial minorities persisted into the twentieth century and was not overturned until 1954, in the Supreme Court's famous ruling in *Brown v. Board of Education of Topeka*. Even after that decision, it took years of civil rights activism to ensure that African Americans could attend public schools with whites. Thus, although the idea of universal education in a democracy arose early, it took many generations of conflict and struggle to transform it into a strong social norm.

3   The idea of mass education based on the model created in the United States and other Western nations has spread throughout the world. Mass education differs from elite education, which is designed to prepare a small number of privileged individuals (generally sons of upper-class families) to run the institutions of society (for example, the military, the clergy, the law). Mass education focuses instead on the socialization of all young people for membership in the society. It is seen as a way for young people to become citizens of a modern nation-state. Mass education establishes an increasingly standardized curriculum and tries to link mastery of that curriculum with personal and national development.

—From KORNBLUM, *Sociology in a Changing World*, 9E. © 2012 Cengage Learning.

✤ POST-ASSESSMENT   EDUCATION MAGAZINE

Preview the following article and then read it all the way through, marking the text. Then go to the end of the article and answer the questions. This assessment will help you determine your strengths and weaknesses in understanding, learning, and applying the skills and strategies discussed in this chapter.

Linking Learning to Earning
by Lynn Olson

1   Educating young people to high levels is a <u>moral imperative</u>, but statistics suggest it's also an economic one—for individuals and for society.

2   A college graduate in the United States earns, on average, $23,441 more per year than a high school graduate, and $31,595 more than a high school dropout.

3   College graduates also are more likely than high school graduates to have full-time, year-round employment, and are about 20 percent more likely to be fully employed as those without a high school diploma.

4   Those statistics don't even reflect the cost burdens to states in the form of public assistance, publicly financed health insurance, and increased incarceration rates for those who drop out of high school.

5   A recent study by the Federal Reserve Bank of Cleveland found that one of the biggest factors explaining differences in income across states is the educational attainment of their citizens [Figure 5.1].

6   Yet, with few exceptions, publicly supported education systems are not well aligned with workforce and economic-development systems at any level of government, according to a report from the New York City-based Workforce Strategy Center. And none of those systems is adequately responsive to the labor market, the center found.

7   A 2006 survey of 431 human-resources officials for the Conference Board, a business-research group based in New York, found that about seven in ten employers <u>deemed</u> the professionalism and work ethic of high school graduates deficient, as well as their critical-thinking and problem-solving skills. Eight in ten found the written communications of recent graduates <u>wanting</u>.

8   Moreover, 28 percent of those surveyed projected that, over the next five years, their companies would reduce the hiring of new entrants with only a high school diploma.

9   "Greater communication and collaboration between the business sector and educators is critical to ensure that young people are prepared to enter the workplace of the 21st century," says Richard E. Cavanagh, the president and chief executive officer of the Conference Board. "Less-than-intense preparation in critical skills can lead to unsuccessful futures for America's youth, as well as a less competitive U.S. workforce."

10   Twenty-one states have defined workforce readiness, according to the policy survey of 50 states and the District of Columbia for *Quality Counts 2007*. Thirty-five states give students the option of earning a standard high school diploma with a concentration or specialization in a career-technical field.

11   Inadequate workforce readiness has implications far beyond states' own borders. "The fact is that a school in Ohio is not competing against a school in Michigan," says James E. Whaley, the president of the Iselin, N.J.-based Siemens Foundation. "It's competing against a school in Shanghai. Companies are looking for the best talent all over the world, and if they find it, they're going to move there."

SOURCE: Linking Learning to Earning, By Lynn Olson, in Education Week at Edweek.org, Published: January 4, 2007, Vol. 26, Issue 17, Pages 66–68, http://www.edweek.org/ew/articles/2007/01/04/17work-force.h26.html.

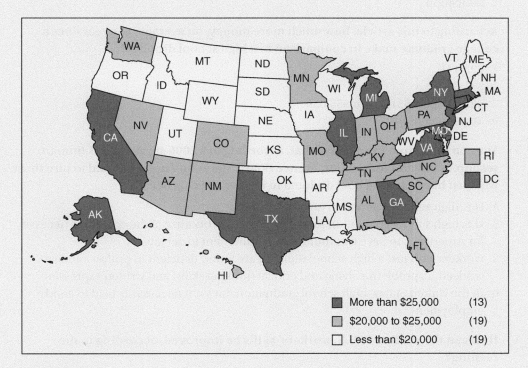

FIGURE 5.1

The College Advantage

Across the nation, adults with bachelor's degrees earn substantially more than those with only a high school diploma. But that earnings advantage varies by state, according to 2005 data from the U.S. Census Bureau. SOURCE: As originally published in Education Week, January 4, 2007. Reprinted with permission from Editorial Projects in Education.

(Continued)

COMPREHENSION CHECK

Circle the best answer to the following questions.

Reading Comprehension

1 **What is the main idea of the article?**

A. Educating our youth is not only morally correct but a distinct economic advantage for society.

B. If you want to make more money, move to the coastal states.

C. Education and income do not seem to be statistically related.

D. Most people would rather have a higher income than a higher amount of education.

2 **According to this article, how much more money, on average, per year does a college graduate make in comparison to a high school dropout?**

A. $23,441

B. $31,595

C. $23,441 plus $31,595 or $55,036

D. 20 percent more

3 **You can infer from the passage that, according to a 2006 survey of 431 human resources officials for the Conference Board, fewer businesses intend to hire those who just have a high school diploma in the next 5 years because**

A. U.S. high school graduation rates are falling.

B. U.S. high school graduation rates are on the rise because of the economic necessity for Americans to have this minimum requirement to get jobs.

C. workers with just a high school diploma are found deficient in professionalism, work ethic, problem-solving and critical thinking skills, and written expression.

D. in the United States, high school graduation does not necessarily lead to good employment.

4 **How can the decline in U.S. workers' skills be improved, according to the reading?**

A. The government needs to provide money for everyone to attend college.

B. We need to teach technical skills for workplace readiness in high school.

C. We need to make the educational competencies for jobs lower in the United States.

D. We need to make the educational competencies for jobs higher in the United States.

5 To the author, the most troubling implication of this decline in skills among U.S. workers is that

A. other countries are surpassing us in skill and U.S. jobs will be outsourced.
B. the majority of other countries fall below us in skills.
C. our skill rates are increasing, albeit at a slow pace.
D. there is competition between the states for wages.

6 In Figure 5.1, "The College Advantage," what is the most important point?

A. New Mexico ranks below other states in income.
B. Coastal states pay more than landlocked states.
C. Vermont is the highest-ranking state for income.
D. While college graduates make more money than high school graduates, the amount varies widely from state to state.

7 In Figure 5.1, "The College Advantage," you can infer that

A. the United States needs to spend more on education.
B. college educations are more common in Georgia and Texas than in Utah and Idaho.
C. the variation in earnings nationally with a college diploma suggest that in states where graduates earn the most, college educations are more in demand, less common or the population is higher, yielding more jobs for graduates.
D. the United States needs to equalize jobs between different educational levels.

8 Go back and look at what you marked as the important points in the article. Then, based on your text marking, which is the best representation of major points of this article?

A. **Main Idea:** College graduates earn more than high school graduates.
   A. College graduate versus high school graduate
      1. Earns $23,442 more
      2. More likely to have full-time employment
   B. College graduate versus high school dropout
      1. Earns $31,595 more
      2. 20 percent more likely to be employed
      3. Education
   C. Workforce issues and educational system
      1. Not working together
      2. Greater preparation of workplace skills needed
      3. 21 states identified workplace readiness skills
      4. 35 states have workplace skills in high school programs
   D. Study: Employers perception of high school graduates
      1. Not professional
      2. Poor work ethic

(Continued)

   3. Lack critical thinking/problem-solving skills
   4. Poor writing
   5. 28 percent said their companies would decrease hiring over 5 years
   E. Outcome: To make more money, Americans should get more education.
B. **Main Idea:** As the job market becomes global, there is an economic need to attain higher education not only for the individual, but also for society.
   A. College graduate versus high school graduate
      1. Earns $23,442 more
      2. More likely to have full-time employment
   B. College graduate versus high school dropout
      1. Earns $31,595 more
      2. 20 percent more likely to be employed
   C. Dropouts cause strain on the state
      1. Public assistance
      2. Publicly financed health insurance
      3. Increased incarceration rate
   D. State income differential based on educational level attained
   E. Workforce issues and educational system
      1. Not working together
      2. Greater preparation of workplace skills needed
      3. 21 states identified workplace readiness skills
      4. 35 states have workplace skills in high school programs
   F. Study: Employers perception of high school graduates
      1. Not professional
      2. Poor work ethic
      3. Lack critical thinking/problem-solving skills
      4. Poor writing
      5. 28 percent said their companies would decrease hiring over 5 years
   G. Outcome: If situation does not improve, American jobs will be outsourced to better skilled workers in other countries.

Vocabulary Comprehension

9 **In the first sentence, the author uses the term *moral imperative*. What does she mean?**

   A. An economic motivation
   B. A motive based on immoral behavior
   C. A principle that urges one to take action
   D. A global issue

10 In paragraph 7, the author uses the words *deemed* and *wanting*. What do these words mean in context?

A. Attributed, lacking

B. Confused, needing

C. Suggested, desiring

D. Implied, inferring

6

Understanding
TEXT NOTE TAKING

Why Do You Need to Know This?

How important is taking good notes in college?

**IN THIS CHAPTER,
YOU WILL LEARN**

- Comprehension strategies for different college subjects
- Note-taking strategies for college reading
  - □ Outlining
  - □ Mapping
  - □ Charts
  - □ Double-column notes
- To understand graphics: reading and understanding maps

READING STUDY STRATEGIES

- College reading in the disciplines
- Using textbook features

VOCABULARY STRATEGIES

- Learning college vocabulary
- Focusing on key terms
- Increasing your discipline-specific vocabulary: science and mathematics

Good notes are the foundation of good study skills. Furthermore, effective note taking is the culmination of all you have learned so far. In Chapter 5, you learned about active reading strategies for marking the text. In this chapter, you will expand on your strategies by incorporating note taking from readings to learn. Readings in each college discipline tend to reflect particular patterns of organization. A smart note taker pays attention to this organization to create effective notes, marking key points and representing the author's structure. Repetition is the hallmark of studying—that is how the brain learns information. Learning information *is* repetition—repeating

> "THE SALVATION OF MANKIND LIES ONLY IN MAKING EVERYTHING THE CONCERN OF ALL."
>
> ALEXANDER SOLZHENITSYN, Russian novelist (1918–2008)

information until you can seamlessly retrieve it from your long-term memory. Because your brain requires organized information to learn, once you learn and incorporate solid note-taking methods into your study strategies, you will find immediate improvement in the speed and accuracy of your learning for college classes.

In Chapter 5, you read about the system of education from a domestic and global perspective and how this system affects you. Chapter 6 is about social responsibility. This chapter raises some serious concerns about our world and what each of us can do to improve it. What about others in our community? How do our actions and decisions affect others in our global community? How do our actions and decisions affect our own success?

CHECK YOUR PRIOR KNOWLEDGE

Jot down what you think about our responsibility to each other, our society, and our world. Do not edit your list—just brainstorm!

_____
_____
_____
_____
_____
_____
_____
_____
_____
_____
_____
_____
_____

PRE-ASSESSMENT   MANAGEMENT TEXTBOOK

Read the passage and then answer the questions that follow. Don't worry if you do not know what all the terms mean. The purpose of this Pre-Assessment is to find out how much you already know about the reading skills and strategies introduced in this chapter.

Arguments for and against Social Responsibility
by Ricky W. Griffin

1   On the surface, there seems to be little disagreement about the need for organizations to be socially responsible. In truth, though, those who oppose broad interpretations of social responsibility use several convincing arguments. Some of the more salient arguments on both sides of this contemporary debate are summarized in Figure 6.1 and further explained in the following sections.

Arguments for Social Responsibility

2   People who argue in favor of social responsibility claim that, because organizations create many of the problems that need to be addressed, such as air and water pollution and resource depletion, they should play a major role in solving them. They also argue that, because <u>corporations</u> are legally defined entities with most of the same privileges as private citizens, businesses should not try to avoid their obligations as citizens. Advocates of social responsibility point out that, whereas governmental organizations have stretched their budgets to the limit, many large businesses often have surplus revenues that could be used to help solve social problems. For example, IBM routinely donates surplus computers to schools, and many restaurants give leftover food to homeless shelters.

FIGURE 6.1 Arguments for and against Social Responsibility

3   While many people want everyone to see social responsibility as a desirable aim, there are in fact several strong arguments that can be used both for and against social responsibility. Hence, organizations and their managers should carefully assess their own values, beliefs, and priorities when deciding which stance and approach to take regarding social responsibility.

4   Although each of the arguments just summarized is a distinct justification for socially responsible behaviors on the part of organizations, another more general reason for social responsibility is profit itself. For example, organizations that make clear and visible contributions to society can achieve an enhanced reputation and garner greater market share for their products. Although claims of socially responsible activities can haunt a company if they are exaggerated or untrue, they can also work to the benefit of both the organization and society if the advertised benefits are true and accurate.

Arguments against Social Responsibility

5   Some people, however, including the famous economist Milton Friedman, argue that widening the interpretation of social responsibility will undermine the U.S. economy by detracting from the basic mission of business: to earn profits for owners. For example, money that Chevron or General Electric contributes to social causes or charities is money that could otherwise be distributed to owners as a dividend. A few years ago, shareholders of Ben & Jerry's Homemade Holdings expressed outrage when the firm refused to accept a lucrative exporting deal to Japan simply because the Japanese distributor did not have a strong social agenda.

6   Another objection to deepening the social responsibility of businesses points out that corporations already wield enormous power and that their activity in social programs gives them even more power. Still another argument against social responsibility focuses on the potential for conflicts of interest. Suppose, for example, that one manager is in charge of deciding which local social program or charity will receive a large grant from her business. The local civic opera company (a not-for-profit organization that relies on contributions for its existence) might offer her front-row tickets for the upcoming season in exchange for her support. If opera is her favorite form of music, she might be tempted to direct the money toward the local company, when it might actually be needed more in other areas.

7   Finally, critics argue that organizations lack the expertise to understand how to assess and make decisions about worthy social programs. How can a company truly know, they ask, which cause or program is most deserving of its support or how money might best be spent? For most of the money to support breeding programs in zoos and to help educate people about the tiger. But conservationists criticize the firm and its activities, arguing that the money might be better spent instead on eliminating poaching, the illegal trade of tiger fur, and the destruction of the tiger's natural habitat.

SOURCE: From GRIFFIN, *Management*, 8E. © 2005 Cengage Learning.

(Continued)

COMPREHENSION CHECK

Circle the best answer to the following questions.

Reading Comprehension

1 **What is the main point of this reading?**

A. The arguments against businesses adopting a socially responsible agenda are convincing.

B. The arguments for a business adopting a socially responsible agenda are convincing.

C. Most businesses agree that social responsibility is important; however, there are convincing arguments in opposition to social responsibility as directives for businesses.

D. Both perspectives for and against social responsibility are reasonable to and agreed upon by the business community.

2 **Which of the following is *not* one of the major arguments in favor of social responsibility?**

A. Businesses create the problems and should help solve them.

B. Businesses have the resources to solve the problems.

C. Corporations are comprised of citizens, after all.

D. There is a potential for conflicts of interest.

3 **Which of the following is *not* one of the major arguments against social responsibility?**

A. The purpose of U.S. business is to make profits.

B. It is the job of the government and general population to solve problems.

C. If a business were to be involved in social programs, it would have too much power.

D. There is a potential for conflict of interest.

4 **The pattern of organization in this reading is predominantly**

A. problem/solution.

B. cause and effect.

C. comparison and contrast.

D. sequence or process order.

5 **According to the passage, Ben & Jerry's Homemade Holdings (an ice cream company) refused to export to Japan because the distributor in Japan did not have a "strong social agenda." According to the reading, what were the results of this decision?**

A. The company was praised by the public.

B. The shareholders were furious because they lost money.

C. Sales declined.

D. The Japanese distributors retaliated, or exacted revenge.

6 **The example of ExxonMobil contributing money to promote education about tigers, an endangered species, was met with criticism from whom?**

A. Those who oppose social responsibility in business

B. The shareholders in ExxonMobil

C. Conservationists who probably support social responsibility but who took issue with how the money was spent

D. The management of ExxonMobil itself

7 **If you were studying for a test on this material, which is the best outline of this passage, considering the pattern of organization?**

A.

  I. Arguments for social responsibility

   A. Businesses need to solve the problems they create.

   B. Corporations are citizens.

   C. Businesses have money.

   D. Businesses have an obligation to help government and citizens.

  II. Arguments against social responsibility

   A. Profits are the main focus.

   B. Too much power results from involvement.

   C. Conflicts of interest might arise.

   D. Management might lack expertise in choosing worthy programs to which to contribute.

B.

  I. Causes of business problems with social responsibility

   A. If the purpose of businesses is to create profit, then they need to at least solve the problems they create.

   B. If involvement in social programs gives too much power, then they need to understand that, first and foremost, businesses are citizens.

   C. If there are conflicts of interest, then they need to use financial resources to solve the problems.

   D. If businesses lack expertise in choosing worthy programs to become involved with, they need to partner with government and the general population.

(Continued)

8 If you were studying for a test on this material, which is the best visual representation of notes on this passage, considering the pattern of organization?

A.

ARGUMENTS FOR SOCIAL RESPONSIBILITY	ARGUMENTS AGAINST SOCIAL RESPONSIBILITY
• Businesses need to solve the problems they create.	• Profits are the main focus of a business.
• Corporations are citizens.	• Too much power results from involvement.
• Businesses have money.	• Conflicts of interest might arise.
• Businesses have an obligation to help government and citizens.	• Management might lack expertise in selecting worthy programs.

B.

Arguments for social responsibility
- Businesses need to solve the problems they create.
- Corporations are citizens.
- Businesses have money.
- Businesses have an obligation to help government and citizens.

Arguments against social responsibility
- Profits are the main focus.
- Too much power results from involvement.
- Conflicts of interest might arise.
- Management might lack expertise in selecting worthy programs.

C.

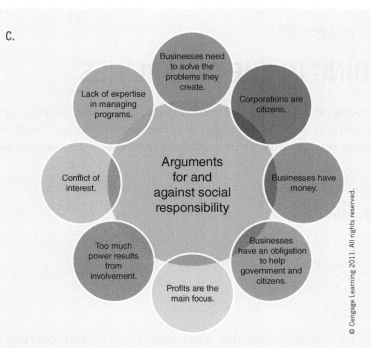

D. Both a and b

Vocabulary Comprehension

9 **In the following sentence from paragraph 1, what does the word *salient* mean?**

Some of the more <u>salient</u> arguments on both sides of this contemporary debate are summarized in Figure 6.1 and further explained in the following sections.

A. Disturbing
B. Historic
C. Confusing
D. Prominent

10 **What does the root word *corp* mean in the word *corporation* in paragraph 2?**

A. Business
B. Stratification
C. Body
D. Like or kind

⭐ READING STUDY STRATEGIES

COLLEGE READING IN THE DISCIPLINES

Not only are tests and note taking more involved and demanding in college, but the reading tasks are harder and more time consuming as well. The demands of college reading far exceed those of high school. The demands of college reading are greater because of the increased awareness needed to understand the following:

- Difficult subject matter in texts in general

- Complexity and density of material

- Vocabulary level

- Complex patterns of organization

- Need for prior (background) knowledge

- Comprehension monitoring

Being aware of your purpose for reading, monitoring your comprehension, and observing an organized study methodology is integral to success. Active reading techniques, such as marking and annotating the text, are vital to a successful study strategy for college students. To create good study notes to learn college material, it is helpful to learn what is expected of you in different college disciplines. The Increase Your Discipline-Specific Vocabulary features in each chapter help to expose you to typical word parts of vocabulary across the college curricula. Table 6.1 shows an overview of the typical demands, by content area, of college-level coursework—the majority of which is reading based!

TABLE 6.1 Varying Your Reading Strategies: The Challenges of College Reading

SUBJECT AREA	READING AND STUDY STRATEGIES	OBJECTIVES/ASSIGNMENTS/TESTS
HUMANITIES Art Literature Music Philosophy Cultural History	• Determine author's (or philosopher's, or artist's) point of view. • Draw logical inferences and conclusions. • Identify objectives for reading and assignments.	• Analyze, evaluate, or interpret information. • Synthesize with other work. • Write, read, and participate in discussions.

SUBJECT AREA	READING AND STUDY STRATEGIES	OBJECTIVES/ASSIGNMENTS/TESTS
	• Keep track of personal reactions in your notes. • Relate the current work to other works.	
SOCIAL SCIENCES Psychology Sociology Anthropology History Government Some medical fields (see also Natural Sciences)	• Learn facts and definitions. • Recognize common patterns (compare/contrast, cause/effect, sequence, definition, etc.). • Compare and contrast theories. • Build new information on concepts already learned. • Distinguish fact from opinion.	• Generate complex answers and questions. • Compare/contrast, analyze, synthesize, and evaluate material.
MATHEMATICS Information Systems Technical fields (see also Sciences)	• Know terms and symbols. • Translate math language into common language. • Identify and compare/contrast new problems. • Look for patterns: classification, process or sequence order, problem/solution.	• Solve problems (application). • Identify strategies for problem solving (comprehension). • Evaluate effectiveness of problem-solving strategies (evaluation). • Compare problem types (analysis, synthesis).
NATURAL SCIENCES Biology Astronomy Physical Science Physics Chemistry Some medical fields (see also Social Sciences) Technical fields (see also Mathematics)	• Look for common patterns (sequence or process order/classification/description/cause and effect). • Define terms. • Check comprehension by providing examples or compare and contrast concepts and processes. • Study from sample problems.	• Focus on problem solving and definitions. • Solve problems, classify information, and apply theory to individual case studies. • Compare types of problems: synthesis, analysis. • Describe processes: comprehension.

(Continued)

SUBJECT AREA	READING AND STUDY STRATEGIES	OBJECTIVES/ASSIGNMENTS/TESTS
BUSINESS AND MANAGEMENT	• Learn facts and definitions. • Recognize common patterns (comparison and contrast, cause and effect, sequence or process order, definition, etc.). • Compare and contrast theories. • Build new information on concepts already learned. • Distinguish fact from opinion. • Understand theory as it applies to real-life situations.	• Generate complex answers and questions. • Compare/contrast, analyze, synthesize, and evaluate material. • Solve problems (application). • Identify strategies for problem solving (comprehension). • Evaluate effectiveness of problem-solving strategies (evaluation). • Compare problem types (analysis, synthesis).

Many students are surprised at the differences between high school and college work and testing. Instead of memorizing facts and reading a few pages of a textbook each week for each class, you are faced with vast amounts of reading each week for every class. Some estimates suggest that high school reading equals about 10 pages of text per week for each class. Often, teachers in high school expect students to learn the material from class lectures and discussions and do not require study and learning from textbook reading as well.

In college, a student can expect to be assigned a chapter of dense, complex material per class each week. Instructors expect a student to learn the information presented in class lectures and discussion *as well as* additional information presented in the textbook, whether or not it is even discussed in class. This is why it is important to read and take notes from your textbook. Reading, marking the text, and taking notes for study equates to interacting with the material three times. Remember that repetition is the hallmark of learning, so following this process will help you learn the information you need to learn and thereby be successful in your classes.

USING TEXTBOOK FEATURES

While college reading can be a challenge, you can use features in a typical textbook chapter and textbook as a whole to guide your learning and increase your comprehension. Using textbook features to your advantage is one characteristic of a successful student. Furthermore, a successful student uses the features available in his or her textbooks as a basis for text note taking. When you use these features to understand the author's train of thought, you unearth a useful framework that you can use to decipher and write down the author's most important points.

A textbook feature is any feature of a textbook provided to aid the student in learning material presented. There are many types of textbook features, and most textbooks have several in common. Most, however, do not have all of these features. Some features you can expect to encounter within a chapter follow.

1. **Chapter introductions** introduce the information in the chapter, usually with a real-life application. These introductions function to prime the brain for accepting the new information by outlining important information for the student.

2. **Chapter outline, objectives, or goals** are usually presented as an outline of key subjects or topics to be discussed in the chapter. Try the technique of turning these objectives into questions to pinpoint key information in the chapter for study.

3. **Key terms and their definitions in the text margins** (or otherwise emphasized) are very useful for students as these definitions and explanations are often exactly the ones that need to be learned for classes.

4. **Boxes and charts** often summarize information in a chapter or prompt you to reflect on the chapter contents and should be examined closely. Like key terms in the margin, these boxes emphasize the key information of the chapter and sum up important concepts.

5. **Graphic aids or visuals** represent important information related to the content of the chapter.

6. **Featured readings or applications** are passages inserted into a textbook chapter that apply the ideas of the chapter to a case study, a real-life scenario, or another discipline. This feature usually applies to content area texts like psychology or biology texts rather than skills texts, like reading and English texts. These features allow you to apply what you've learned to actual situations, enhancing your ability to apply and analyze the chapter information.

7. **Chapter summaries** usually appear at the end of the chapters and present a condensed version of key information. This feature usually applies to content area texts like psychology or biology texts rather than skills texts, like reading and English texts. These are very important because, as you know, summaries are the main ideas and major supporting details in a reading. Most often, the chapter summaries will answer the questions that can be posed by turning the chapter outline, objectives, or goals into questions.

8. **Study questions, review exercises, and other learning devices** are found at the end of the chapter. These devices allow students to test whether or not they really know the information and to make predictions about test questions. They also provide a structured review in preparation for a test or activity related to the chapter.

In addition to the features found within a chapter, textbooks have other learning tools that apply to all chapters within the book.

1. The **table of contents,** at the front of the textbook, allows you to find the location and sequence of both topics and readings in the text.

2. A **glossary,** at the back of the textbook, provides the definitions of all the key concepts and vocabulary outlined in all the chapters. This is like a dictionary just for that textbook.

3. The **index,** at the back of the textbook, allows you to look up a specific concept or topic and find on which pages this concept was discussed. This is very useful in answering think-and-search-type questions (see Chapter 8 "Question-Answer Relationships") or reading to better understand a concept.

4. An **appendix (or appendices)** varies from book to book and includes other relevant information that expands on the information discussed in the textbook.

On Your Own FINDING TEXTBOOK FEATURES

Look at this chapter as well as the Textbook Applications to determine if these chapters contain these features. Put a check mark in the box that indicates the chapter contains the feature in the left-hand column.

FEATURE	MINDSCAPES	TEXTBOOK APPLICATION 1: CARING FOR YOUR MIND	TEXTBOOK APPLICATION 2: THE LIMITS OF LIBERALISM: THE 1970S	TEXTBOOK APPLICATION 3: EQUITY AND EDUCATIONAL PRACTICE	TEXTBOOK APPLICATION 4: LAW AND MEDICINE
Chapter introduction					
Chapter outline, objectives, or goals					
Key terms (in the margins, in a list or otherwise emphasized)					
Boxes and charts					
Graphic aids or visuals					
Featured readings or applications					

Chapter summaries					
Study questions, review exercises, and other learning aids					

Flip through *Mindscapes* or another textbook and put a check mark in the appropriate box if the text contains the features in the left-hand column.

	MINDSCAPES	TEXTBOOK 1	TEXTBOOK 2
Table of contents			
Glossary			
Index			
Appendix (appendices)			

TAKING NOTES

In addition to using textbook features to your advantage, a successful college student knows effective methods to take notes both in class and from the assigned reading. To be a successful college student, you must be able to translate your skills in identifying key points into taking good notes and proving your knowledge on tests. Taking good notes during class is one of the best ways to ensure study success. Successful students not only take notes during a class but also rewrite these notes after class and take additional notes from class readings that may or may not be discussed by the instructor. It is well worth your while to take these kinds of notes and even rewrite them because you know that repetition is learning. Because you learn by repeating the processing of information, writing information in the form of notes is study time very well spent.

Double-Column Notes

Despite the attraction of using spiral-bound notebooks for note taking, using loose-leaf paper is better because it allows you to insert hand-outs from class or your notes from the readings after or with the notes from your class lectures. So before your classes begin, stock up on loose-leaf paper!

To take double-column notes, divide your paper into two columns, using a ruler to mark off one-third (1/3) of the page from the left margin. Ignore the red line about one inch from the left of the page (see Figure 6.2).

Now, you have two columns. The column on the left is narrower than the column on the right. The left-hand column should remain blank during active note taking. Later, after you have recorded your notes, go back and write the topic (perhaps in question form) in this left-hand column.

The right-hand column is for your notes. Write on one side of the page only, so you have room to write additional information on the reverse of the page if necessary. This method is effective because it allows you to test yourself. Once you have written the topics in question form in the left-hand column, you can cover up the right-hand column of notes with a spare sheet of paper and test your memory and understanding of the information. Then you can uncover your notes and verify your answers.

In Figure 6.3, the marginal notations on the left side of the page can be turned into these questions.

- What is the legislative branch?
- What is the executive branch?
- What is the judicial branch?

COURSE	DATE
Key column:	Notes column:
Write key terms here	Write full notes here
1/3 of page	2/3 of page

FIGURE 6.2 Setting Up a Page for Double-Column Notes

POLY SCI 102	9-15-2010
Legislative	Makes laws
	Congress
	Senate
	House of Rep
Executive	Enforces law
	President
	Vice President
	Cabinet
Judicial	Interprets laws
	Supreme Court
	Circuit Court
	District Court

FIGURE 6.3 Double-Column Notes on the Branches of Government

Cornell Notes

Cornell notes are similar to basic double-column notes except you create a section at the bottom of the page where you write a summary of the information on the page (see Figure 6.4). As you know, a summary is a consolidation of the main idea and major supporting points. Look at the example in Figure 6.5.

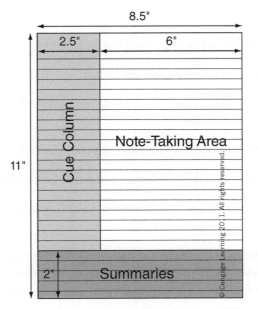

FIGURE 6.4 Setting Up a Page for Cornell Notes

Psychology 101	11-7-2012
What is Community Psychology?	Community psychology—A movement to minimize or prevent psychological disorders through
	1. changes in social systems
How are changes made?	2. and through community mental health programs
	Community mental health movement:
What is the Community Mental Health Movement?	1. arose during 1960s to make treatment available within communities
	2. antipsychotic drugs became available
	3. deinstitutionalization process led to community health need
	a. psychosocial rehabilitation for mentally ill in halfway houses
	b. community services do not seek to cure but aid in coping

Community psychology is a movement to minimize or prevent psychological disorders
through changes in social systems and through community mental health programs.
This movement arose during 1960s to make treatment available within communities.
As antipsychotic drugs became available, the deinstitutionalization process led to
community health needs, such as psychosocial rehabilitation for the mentally ill in halfway
houses. These community services do not seek to cure but aid in coping.

FIGURE 6.5 Double-Column Notes for Psychology

QUICK TIPS TAKING GOOD NOTES IN COLLEGE CLASSES

☑ Listen actively and with concentration during lectures.

☑ Focus on the key points outlined in the lecture.

☑ Look for the structure of the lecture by noticing how the lecturer formulates the "title" of the information presented.

☑ Write down only main ideas and major supporting details.

☑ Write down information that the lecturer or writer emphasizes or repeats.

☑ Write down brief examples or page references in case you need to refresh your memory later.

☑ Practice formulating your own shorthand versions of common words. Example: Write the first several letters of a common word, then abbreviate the ending that shows the part of speech: *attent'n* (attention), *eval'n* (evaluation), *speak'g* (speaking), *effect'v* (effective). You can develop your own methods of shorthand or learn some abbreviations from a good source.

☑ Write in phrases rather than sentences.

☑ Skip several lines after each topic so you can plug in more information later.

☑ Write topic-based questions in the left-hand margin, and rewrite, highlight, or clarify your notes as soon as possible after taking them to consolidate the information on the page and in your memory.

NOTE TAKING FROM READING

Follow these four steps to learn information in preparation for study:

1. Read the passage, using all the techniques and strategies you have learned so far.

2. Go back and mark the text.

3. Write notes in the margin or on a separate piece of paper based on your marking of the text.

4. Rewrite your marginal notations and organize them further to make study notes.

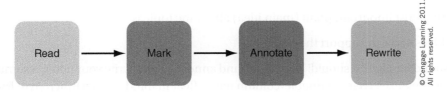

Effective learning involves a four-step process for note-taking.

You know that studying is repetition to enable you to accurately and effectively retrieve new information from your long term memory. Good note taking is an essential part of this learning process.

You have developed skills in marking and annotating your college texts. Given your awareness of the challenges of college-level reading, the next step is to transcribe, or rewrite, your text marking and annotations into a study format. Remember: The very act of this transcription *is* studying because the more information is repeated, the more you will retain it—and the more accurate will be your retrieval of the information when the time comes to repeat it on a test. In transcribing your notes, you are rehearsing the information, which means encoding the material, storing it in your long-term memory, and then retrieving it. It is this repetitive process that yields higher recall the more it is practiced.

After underlining and annotating, transcribe your main ideas and major and minor details into one of the following formats. All of these formats help you to understand and remember the main ideas and supporting details. You learned and practiced summarizing in Chapter 3, so you understand what to include in a good summary. Unlike summaries, these other formats do not need to be written in full sentences, nor do transition words need to be used. Like summaries, these methods involve recognizing main ideas and major supporting details. However, depending on your note-taking assignment, these methods may also include minor supporting details. Note-taking formats include:

- Outlines

- Maps

- Charts

- Double-column notes

- Summaries

There are many note-taking systems; the most popular and, in many experts' views, the most effective type of note taking is double-column note taking. Double-column notes are not just for taking notes in class; they are also good for taking notes from reading. This method is particularly effective because it provides a study method within the structure of the notes.

To take good notes from a reading, regardless of the exact form, you need to have all your powers of thinking as well as all your reading strategies on target. Good notes depend on structure, or patterns of organization, topic, main ideas and seeing the relationships between those ideas—in short, everything you have learned in this book so far. Good notes reflect the bones, or skeleton, of the reading or lecture. To take good notes, identify:

1. Who or what the subject or topic is

2. How the author or the speaker is structuring the information—the pattern of organization

3. What the most important point (main idea) about the topic is

4. What ideas serve to support the main idea

Does this sound familiar? It should! Then, mark and annotate. Last, write your notes: a summary, an outline, graphic organizer, chart, or double-column notes. Bear in mind the SOUL acronym from Chapter 5 as you consider this next step of creating notes: Be selective, organize, understand, and learn.

QUICK TIPS USING THE SOUL METHOD FOR TAKING NOTES

 The more effort you put into transcribing your notes into one of these formats (summary, outline, graphic organizer, chart, or double-column notes), the more information you will learn and retain.

 Read actively, using strategies such as turning subheadings into questions, looking for the answers, and underlining, when taking notes from a reading.

Make sure you are SELECTIVE about choosing the key points.

> ☑ Make sure you ORGANIZE the key points based on the author's structure.
>
> ☑ Make sure you UNDERSTAND what you are writing (paraphrase the author's language).
>
> ☑ Use your study notes to prepare for tests and LEARN the information.

Outlines

Outlines are useful as a means of organizing information and showing the relationship between ideas. Outlines can also help you in your writing to present material in a logical format and to define the relationship between major and minor supporting details. The most common type of outline is the **alphanumeric outline** (*alpha* = alphabet; *numeric* = numbers). The alphanumeric outline uses both letters of the alphabet (uppercase and lowercase) and numbers (Arabic and Roman numerals).

- Roman numerals (I, II, III, IV, V, VI, etc.)
  - ☐ Capitalized letters (A, B, C, etc.)
    - Arabic numerals (1, 2, 3, etc.)
      - ☐ Lowercase letters (a, b, c, d, etc.)

The basic premise is that the more general a point, the closer it falls to the left of the outline. Similarly, the more detailed or minor a point, the more indented it is toward the right of the page. This structure demonstrates the relationship between topics, main ideas, and major as well as minor details.

I. Topic 1
  A. Main idea 1
    1. Major supporting detail
    2. Major supporting detail
      a. Minor detail
      b. Minor detail
  B. Main idea 2
    1. Major supporting detail
      a. Minor detail
      b. Minor detail
II. Topic 2
  A. Main idea 3
    1. Major supporting detail
    2. Major supporting detail

To determine how much information to include in an outline (or any other note-taking method), you need first to be aware of the purpose of the assignment. If the test will cover information from a whole chapter of a college text, do you need to learn main ideas as well as major supporting details? If the test will cover information from a subsection of text or an article, do you need to learn minor details as well as the main ideas and major details?

Thinking It Through CREATING AN OUTLINE

Here is a passage with details about the topic of the economic hardships of families. Notice how the text is marked to indicate the main idea (underlined), the major details (numbers), and minor details (letters in lowercase). To illustrate the relationship between ideas in an outline, sentences are placed in the appropriate location in the outline. In reality, you would paraphrase the ideas in the original before inserting these ideas into your outline. Here, to show how each sentence can be inserted into an outline format, showing the relationship between ideas, this outline is not paraphrased.

Basic Needs Budgets show that it takes an income of about 1.5 to 3.5 times the official poverty level ($22,050 a year for a family of four), depending on locality, to cover the cost of a family's minimum day-to-day needs. The largest expenses are typically ᵃchild care and ᵇhousing. ᶜHealth care and ᵈtransportation can cost nearly as much—and in some cases more. ¹While the struggle to make ends meet is particularly difficult for single parents, paying the bills is a tough challenge for two-parent families as well. ²The cost of living varies dramatically both within and across states. To make ends meet in the large, ᵃhigh-cost cities of Chicago, New York, and San Francisco, for example, a two-parent family with two children (one preschool-aged and one school-aged) needs an income of $52,000 to $67,000 a year. Some ᵇsmaller cities, such as Burlington, VT, cost just as much. ᶜThat means two full-time workers earning at least $13 an hour each.

SOURCE: Adapted from "Budgeting for Basic Needs: A Struggle for Working Families," by Kinsey Alden Dinan, March 2009, National Center for Children in Poverty.

Topic: *Basic Needs Budgets*

Main Idea: *Basic Needs Budgets show that it takes an income of about 1.5 to 3.5 times the official poverty level ($22,050 a year for a family of four), depending on locality, to cover the cost of a family's minimum day-to-day needs.*

Supporting Detail 1: *Large expenses for family whether single parent or two-parent*

    Minor detail: *child care*

    Minor detail: *housing*

    Minor detail: *health care*

    Minor detail: *transportation*

Supporting Detail 2: *Cost of living expenses vary within and across states*

    Minor detail: *High-cost cities of Chicago, New York, and San Francisco, a two-parent family with two children) needs an income of $52,000 to $67,000 a year.*

    Minor detail: *Smaller cities, such as Burlington, VT, cost just as much.*

    Minor detail: *That means two full-time workers need to earn at least $13 an hour each.*

On Your Own CREATING AN OUTLINE

Create an outline of the following paragraph. First, mark the text. Next, fill in the outline template with the appropriate information from the paragraph.

After the cost of child care, housing is generally families' next largest expense, with rent and utilities comprising about 20 percent of a family's total basic budget. Food and transportation are significant costs too, rivaling the cost of housing in some places. Transportation costs can be especially burdensome in rural areas where parents often have to drive long distances to reach their jobs. In some of the highest cost cities, on the other hand, public transportation makes commuting much more affordable.

SOURCE: Adapted from "Budgeting for Basic Needs: A Struggle for Working Families," by Kinsey Alden Dinan, March 2009, National Center for Children in Poverty.

Topic: _____

Main Idea: _____

_____

   Supporting Detail 1:_____

_____

   Supporting Detail 2: _____

_____

      Minor detail: _____

_____

      Minor detail: _____

_____

Graphic Organizers: Webs, Clusters, Maps

The purpose of this type of note taking is the same as that of an outline: to show the relationships between ideas. As you can see from the header, there are many types of graphic organizers. What you call a graphic organizer depends on the subject in which it is used. For example, in English or writing classes, the term *cluster diagram* is commonly used as a prewriting technique. Like an outline, each of these methods of organizing ideas relies on depicting the relationships between ideas in a reading passage, so the important point to remember here is that the structure of your graphic reflects the pattern of organization. Graphic organizers come in a variety of formats to suit the structural pattern of the text from which you are note taking (Figure 6.6). First, decide on the pattern of organization; then determine which type of visual would best suit the structure of the information. Notice how each of these visuals suggests a pattern of organization.

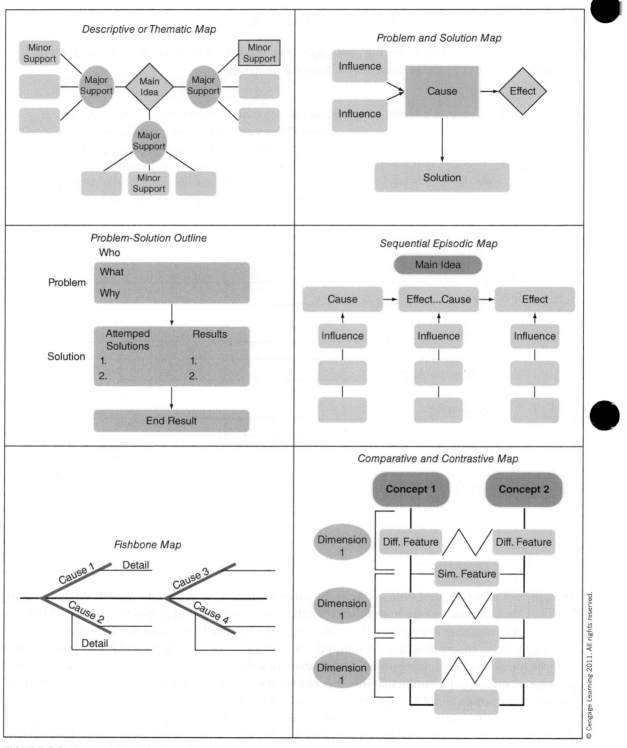

FIGURE 6.6 Types of Graphic Organizers

Charts and Tables

Charts and tables are useful to represent text that has a two-part structure, like comparison or contrast, cause and effect, or problem and solution patterns. Charts also work well for a sequential pattern because they usually are arranged in columns and rows that allow the reader to see the similarities or differences side-by-side, or the causes that lead to the effects, or problems that lead to solutions, or steps in a process. However, charts can be made for other patterns of organization, too. Here is an example of a simple chart that can be effective for study. Notice how the major details would be written in the appropriate box—causes, immediate effects, or long-term effects.

ECONOMIC CAUSES AND EFFECTS OF WORLD WAR II—BRITAIN AND GERMANY		
CAUSES OF WW II	IMMEDIATE EFFECTS	LONG-TERM EFFECTS
Britain		
Germany		

Double-Column Notes

Double-column notes are an excellent note-taking method for reading as well as for taking class notes. You use the same format for note taking from readings as that for lecture or class note taking (see page 406). Additionally, you can use the left-hand margin to write the topic related to the information; or, as you would while previewing or text marking and annotating, you can write a question in the left-hand margin that can be used as a memory prompt to help in studying.

QUICK TIPS NOTE-TAKING METHODS

✓ Present your material in a logical form.

✓ Show the relationships between ideas in writing.

✓ Follow the organization of the writing.

✓ Reflect main ideas, supporting details, and pattern of organization.

Thinking It Through TAKING NOTES FROM A READING

First mark the text, then annotate in the margins. Next, compare your text marking and annotations with the four methods of representing information: outline, chart, double-column notes, and graphic organizer. What you have written in the margin should be the same information as in all of the note-taking methods because marking and annotating text pulls the same information as any of the types of note taking. Remember: All note-taking formats represent main ideas and major details.

Community Psychology: From Treatment to Prevention
by Douglas A. Bernstein, Louis A. Penner,
Alison Clarke-Stewart, and Edward J. Roy

1   It has long been argued that even if psychologists knew exactly how to treat every psychological problem, there would never be enough mental health professionals to help everyone who needs them. This view fostered the rise of **community psychology,** a movement that aims both to treat troubled people in their home communities and to promote social and environmental changes that can minimize or prevent psychological disorders.

Community psychology:
A movement to minimize or prevent psychological disorders through changes in social systems and through community mental health programs.

2   One aspect of community psychology, the community mental health movement, arose during the 1960s as an attempt to make treatment available to people in their own communities. As antipsychotic drugs became available, and as concern grew that patients were not improving—and might be getting worse—after years of confinement in mental hospitals, thousands of these patients were released. The plan was that they would receive drugs and other mental health services in newly funded community mental health centers. This deinstitutionalization process did spare patients the boredom and isolation of the hospital environment, but the mental health services available in the community never matched the need for them. Some former hospital patients and many people whose disorders might once have sent them to mental hospitals are now living in halfway houses and other community-based facilities where they receive psychosocial rehabilitation. These community support services are not designed to "cure" them but to help them cope with their problems and develop the social and occupational skills necessary for semi-independent living. All too many others with severe psychological disorders are to be found enduring the dangers

of homelessness on city streets or of confinement in jails and prisons.

3   Community psychology also attempts to prevent psychological disorders by addressing unemployment, poverty, overcrowded substandard housing, and other stressful social problems that may underlie some disorders. Less ambitious, but perhaps even more significant, are efforts to detect psychological problems in their earliest stages and keep them from becoming worse as well as to minimize the long-term effects of psychological disorders and prevent their recurrence. Examples include prevention of depression and suicide programs, including Project Head Start, that help preschoolers whose backgrounds hurt their chances of doing well in school and put them at risk for delinquency; identification of children who are at risk for disorder or delinquency because of aggressiveness, parental divorce, or being rejected or victimized at school; interventions to head off anxiety disorders or schizophrenia in children and adults; and programs designed to prevent drug abuse and promote health consciousness in ethnic minority communities.

SOURCE: From BERNSTEIN/PENNER/CLARKE-STEWART/ROY, *Psychology*, 7E. © 2006 Cengage Learning.

1. **Outline Example.** In this outline, the main points of the reading are listed from general to specific. Roman numeral topics are followed by alphabetized main points. Enumerated major supporting points are indented as well as alphabetized minor details to show the relationships between ideas as they become more and more specific.

    I. Community Psychology
        A. Movement that aims to treat troubled people in their home communities
        B. Also aims to promote social and environmental changes that can minimize or prevent psychological disorders
    II. Community Mental Health Movement
        A. Arose during 1960s to make treatment available within communities
        B. Antipsychotic drugs became available
        C. Deinstitutionalization process led to community health need
            1. Psychosocial rehabilitation for mentally ill in halfway houses
            2. Community services do not seek to cure but aid in coping
    III. Community psychology attempts to prevent psychological disorders through changes in social and environmental influence
        A. Employment
        B. Poverty
        C. Overcrowded housing
        D. Other stressful social problems   *(Continued)*

    E. Detection of psychological problems in early stages

    F. Minimize long-term effects of mental illness and prevent recurrence

        1. Prevention of depression and suicide

        2. Programs—Project Head Start (at-risk children)

        3. Identify children at risk for disorder or delinquency

            a. Aggressiveness

            b. Divorce

            c. Rejected or victimized at school

            d. Interventions to stop anxiety disorders or schizophrenia from progressing

            e. Programs to prevent drug abuse and promote health consciousness in ethnic and minority communities

2. **Graphic Organizer (Web, Cluster, Map) Example.** In this example, the overall definition is put at the top of the web. Branching off the definition are the two parts of the discussion: the history of community mental health and the social/environmental changes the community psychology movement hopes to promote.

3. **Chart Example.** In this example, the definition and goal of the community mental health movement are put at the top of the chart. Below these headings are sections about the history of the movement and the action plan to realize the goal of the movement.

Definition	Goals
Community psychology is a movement to minimize or prevent psychological disorders through changes in social systems and through community mental health programs.	A. Promotion of social and environmental changes to minimize/prevent psychological disorders B. Treatment for troubled people in their home communities

Background	Action Plan to Promote Change

Community mental health movement:
A. Arose during 1960s to make treatment available within communities
B. Antipsychotic drugs became available
C. Deinstitutionalization process led to community health need
   1. Psychosocial rehabilitation for mentally ill in halfway houses
   2. Community services do not seek to cure but aid in coping
	A. Employment
	B. Poverty
	C. Overcrowded housing
	D. Other stressful social problems
	E. Detection of psychological problems in early stages
	F. Minimize long-term effects of mental illness and prevent recurrence
	   1. Prevention of depression and suicide
	   2. Programs—Project Head Start (for at-risk children)
	   3. Identify children at risk for disorder or delinquency
	      a. Aggressiveness
	      b. Divorce
	      c. Rejected or victimized at school
	      d. Interventions to stop anxiety disorders or schizophrenia from progressing
	      e. Programs to prevent drug abuse and promote health consciousness in ethnic and minority communities

4. **Double-Column Notes Example.** In this example, the key points of the reading are preceded by question prompts to aid in studying and learning the new information.

What is community psychology?	**community psychology:** A community-based movement to minimize or prevent psychological disorders
How are changes made?	Through changes in social systems and through community mental health programs

(Continued)

What is the Community Mental Health Movement? *How do community mental health programs promote social and environmental changes to help people?*	Community Mental Health Movement: • Arose during 1960s to make treatment available within communities • Antipsychotic drugs became available • Deinstitutionalization process led to community health need • Psychosocial rehabilitation for mentally ill in halfway houses • Community services do not seek to cure but aid in coping • Employment • Poverty • Overcrowded housing • Detection of psychological problems in early stages • Minimize long-term effects of mental illness and prevent recurrence

In what ways are long-term effects of mental health issues addressed?	• Prevention of depression and suicide
	• Programs—Project Head Start (at-risk children)
	• Identify children at risk for disorder or delinquency
	  • Aggressiveness
	  • Divorce
	  • Rejected or victimized at school
	  • Interventions to stop anxiety disorders or schizophrenia from progressing
	  • Programs to prevent drug abuse and promote health consciousness in ethnic and minority communities

On Your Own TAKING NOTES FROM A READING

Here is an article about the psychological effects of a natural disaster—a hurricane. The article comes from the American Psychological Association and discusses how to cope with trauma. Mark the text and annotate in the margins. Then, choose one (or all) of the methods of representing text in a note-taking system and complete your notes based on your text marking and annotating. Afterward, compare your work with that of a classmate to strengthen your skills.

Managing Traumatic Stress: After the Hurricanes

1   The effects of the recent hurricanes will be long-lasting and the resulting trauma can reverberate even with those not directly affected by the disaster.

2   It is common for people who have experienced traumatic situations to have very strong emotional reactions. Understanding normal responses to these abnormal events can aid you in coping effectively with your feelings, thoughts, and behaviors, and help you along the path to recovery.

How Should I Help Myself and My Family?

3   Many people already possess the skills of resilience and will bounce back on their own, given time. There also are a number of steps you can take to help restore emotional well-being and a sense of control following a natural disaster, including the following:

• Give yourself time to heal. Anticipate that this will be a difficult time in your life. Allow yourself to mourn the losses you have experienced. Try to be patient with changes in your emotional state.

• Ask for support from people who care about you and who will listen and empathize with your situation. But keep in mind that your typical support system may be weakened if those who are close to you also have experienced or witnessed the trauma.

(Continued)

- Communicate your experience in whatever ways feel comfortable to you, such as by talking with family or close friends, or keeping a diary.

- Find out about local support groups that often are available, such as for those who have suffered from natural disasters. These can be especially helpful for people with limited personal support systems.

- Try to find groups led by appropriately trained and experienced professionals such as psychologists. Group discussion can help people realize that other individuals in the same circumstances often have similar reactions and emotions.

- Try to find groups led by appropriately trained and experienced professionals such as psychologists. Group discussion can help people realize that other individuals in the same circumstances often have similar reactions and emotions.

- Engage in healthy behaviors to enhance your ability to cope with excessive stress. Eat well-balanced meals and get plenty of rest. If you experience ongoing difficulties with sleep, you may be able to find some relief through relaxation techniques. Avoid alcohol and drugs.

- Establish or reestablish routines such as eating meals at regular times and following an exercise program. This can be especially important when the normal routines of daily life are disrupted. Even if you are in a shelter and unable to return home, establish routines that can bring comfort. Take some time off from the demands of daily life by pursuing hobbies or other enjoyable activities.

- Help those you can. Helping others, even during your own time of distress, can give you a sense of control and can make you feel better about yourself.

- Avoid major life decisions such as switching careers or jobs if possible because these activities tend to be highly stressful.

When Should I Seek Professional Help?

4   Many people are able to cope effectively with the emotional and physical demands brought about by a natural disaster by using their own support systems. It is not unusual, however, to find that serious problems persist and continue to interfere with daily living. For example, some may feel overwhelming nervousness or lingering sadness that adversely affects job performance and interpersonal relationships.

5   Individuals with prolonged reactions that disrupt their daily functioning should consult with a trained and experienced mental health professional. Psychologists and other appropriate mental health providers help educate people about common responses to extreme stress. These professionals work with individuals affected by trauma to help them find constructive ways of dealing with the emotional impact.

6   With children, continual and aggressive emotional outbursts, serious problems at school, preoccupation with the traumatic event, continued and extreme withdrawal, and other signs of intense anxiety or emotional difficulties all point to the need for professional assistance. A qualified mental health professional such as a psychologist can help such children and their parents understand and deal with thoughts, feelings and behaviors that result from trauma.

UNDERSTANDING GRAPHICS

READING AND UNDERSTANDING MAPS

Just as authors are deliberate in choosing how to convey their intended meaning and purpose by using a certain pattern of organization and illustrating their main idea with effective supporting points, they are also deliberate in choosing the type of graphic that conveys their point most effectively. One format that is commonly used in college textbooks is maps. Maps can show a variety of relationships between ideas and can effectively show the reader locations and geographical trends. What is the overall point and what are the reasonable conclusions of Figure 6.7, based on the critical thinking questions provided?

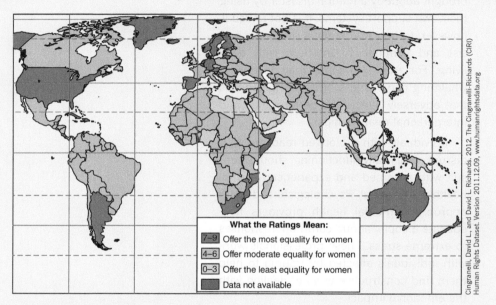

Cingranelli, David L. and David L. Richards. 2012. The Cingranelli-Richards (CIRI) Human Rights Dataset. Version 2011.12.09. www.humanrightsdata.org

What the Ratings Mean:

7–9 Offer the most equality for women
4–6 Offer moderate equality for women
0–3 Offer the least equality for women
     Data not available

FIGURE 6.7 Status of Women's Rights Around the Globe

1. **What is the topic of the map?** *the status of women's rights around the globe*

2. **Which countries offer the most support for women?** *Countries that are progressive in women's rights are purple: United States, Argentina, Australia, New Zealand, South Africa, Liberia, Costa Rica, Greenland, Iceland, Spain, Finland, Scandinavia (Norway, Sweden, Denmark).*

3. **Which countries offer the least support for women?** *Countries that are the least progressive in women's rights are green: Nigeria, Zambia, Libya, Egypt, Saudi Arabia, Iran, Turkey, and a few Southeast Asian countries.*

4. **Where is the United States in relation to neighboring countries with regard women's rights?** *The United States has a high rating of equality compared to Mexico and Canada.*

5. **What might account for the difference in rates of equality across the globe?** *Possible answers are the economy, religion, political affiliations, laws, or culture.*

VOCABULARY STRATEGY

STUDYING VOCABULARY

The demands of college reading require comprehension of the material, above all. However, memorization does play a role in solidifying concepts for study. There are several strategies for learning the key terms or definitions that are frequently found in textbook passages. To be a successful student, you need to review these key terms as part of your spaced practice study strategy.

The best way to increase your vocabulary is to read a lot. Circle or write down new words that you encounter in both your academic and leisure reading. Look up these words in the dictionary later. Use the new words you encounter as frequently as you can in your speaking and writing to absorb them into your daily vocabulary. Previous vocabulary strategy sections in this text discussed unlocking the meaning of new words by using context clues and word parts (prefixes, roots, and suffixes). The dictionary is another outstanding tool. Every college student should purchase a good dictionary and use it with regularity. However, using a dictionary disrupts your concentration when you are trying to focus on and read text for college classes as you learned in Chapter 5. Also, dictionaries, unless specialized to a certain field, can fall short when you are trying to learn key terms in a specific discipline. For example, if you look up "Bystander Effect" in a typical college dictionary, you will not find it listed. If you do a search on the Internet for this term, you will find it has a specific meaning in sociology as well as a specific meaning in biological science. It is essential that the meanings of key terms be learned as they relate to what you are studying.

Textbook Glossaries

To ensure that you understand a key term or definition, make use of textbook's glossary. As you learned earlier in the chapter, textbooks have many learning aids, from chapter outlines at the front of each chapter, to chapter summaries and comprehension questions at the end of each chapter. These text aids are there to be used; when employed as intended, they will increase your comprehension of the material. One often overlooked and underused text aid in your college books is the glossary. A *glossary* is a list of all key terms and important concepts in the textbook. Glossary terms are often put in boldface in the margins of the chapters. These terms are given such special attention because they are important! If you use your textbook's glossary, you will be certain to have the correct definition for the term within that specific subject.

Learning Key Terms

Just like any learning, vocabulary and key terms must be reviewed repeatedly to be processed into your long-term memory. The Wrapping It Up exercise at the end of each of the chapters in this textbook provides one simple way to learn key terms. It is best to set aside a specific period of time each day to study vocabulary and key terms for each of your courses. Set a goal for how many words you would like to learn each study period. Fifteen minutes is a good amount of time each day for vocabulary review. Study vocabulary key terms in clusters. At the end of a few days, spend the 15 minutes going over the entire list of new words or key terms.

In order for you to review them effectively, you must keep the list of words you have targeted to learn in one place. You cannot be flipping through your notes to find highlighted or circled words. At first, you may feel that writing out all the key terms and definitions is time consuming. However, writing out all the key terms and definitions is *not* a waste of time because the act of writing these notes *is* learning; repetition by writing is an active form of learning.

METHOD 1: DEDICATED NOTEBOOK FOR VOCABULARY

One way to list and learn vocabulary is to use a notebook specifically for this purpose. Use a smaller notebook, so you can carry it with you to review whenever you have even a small chunk of time.

Much as you do when you set up double-column notes, draw a line one-third of the way from the left-hand side of the page. In this column, write the vocabulary word or key term. Write the definition of the word or explanation of the concept or key term on the right-hand side of the page. Cover the right-hand side to test yourself on your recall of the word or term's meaning.

METHOD 2: VOCABULARY CARDS

Index cards or flash cards are an effective tool to use for learning new general vocabulary as well as key terms. Because they are portable and can be secured with a rubber band, index cards can be carried with you for a quick review between classes, on public transportation, during breaks at work, and even when standing in line at the store! Keep your cards arranged in alphabetical order so a term or word can be found easily. You should be systematic about reviewing each word in the deck at least every couple of weeks, and more frequently as the test nears. Once a test has passed, keep your cards for review for the cumulative (final) exam. It is a morale booster to keep your vocabulary cards so you can admire the growing pile as you proceed from semester to semester. Remember, too, that college classes are cumulative in terms of content and skill development, so the key terms you learn for biology as a first-year student you will be expected to know for subsequent classes.

On one side of the index card (the blank side), write the key term or word. On the reverse (lined) side, write the definition of the key term with an example. If the targeted item is a single word, write its definition on the lined side along with a sentence using the word that provides enough context to clearly point to the word's meaning. Some students also find that simple drawings or diagrams are helpful in solidifying definitions as they learn. Test yourself by trying to repeat the definition; then look at the reverse of the card to verify your answer. See Figure 6.8 for an example.

Definition   **Crisis**

An event or series of events that represents a critical threat to the health, safety, security, or well-being of a community or other large group of people, usually over a wide area. Armed conflicts, epidemics, famine, natural disasters, environmental emergencies, and other major harmful events may involve or lead to a humanitarian crisis.

FRONT OF INDEX CARD	BACK OF INDEX CARD
Crisis	• Critical threat to (a) health, (b) safety, (c) security of large group • armed conflicts, epidemics, famine, natural disasters, environmental emergencies • 'humanitarian' crisis

FIGURE 6.8 Vocabulary Card Example

Index cards come in several colors. Try choosing a specific color for each subject you are learning and alternate these decks for study. For example, white index cards can be for biology, pink for psychology, green for history, and so on.

On Your Own CREATING VOCABULARY CARDS

Complete vocabulary concept cards for each of the terms and their definitions below.

1. Hazard: Any phenomenon that has the potential to cause disruption or damage to people and their environment.

FRONT OF INDEX CARD	BACK OF INDEX CARD

(Continued)

2. Vulnerability: (1) The conditions determined by physical, social, economic, and environmental factors or processes that increase the susceptibility of a community to the impact of hazards. (2) The degree to which a population or an individual is unable to anticipate, cope with, resist, and recover from the impact of a disaster.

FRONT OF INDEX CARD	BACK OF INDEX CARD

INCREASE YOUR DISCIPLINE-SPECIFIC VOCABULARY

SCIENCE AND MATHEMATICS

The sciences and mathematics disciplines have complex vocabulary. Learning these key terms and affixes will help you to understand scientific readings. Once you familiarize yourself with these affixes and fundamental terminology, navigating complex readings will be easier.

TABLE 6.1 Vocabulary Associated with Science and Mathematics

WORD PART	MEANING	VOCABULARY
ambi, amb, amphi	around, about, both	ambidextrous, ambiguity, ambivalent, amphibian, ambitious, amphitheater, amble, ambient, ambulance
aqua, hydro, hydra, hydr	water	aquarium, aquatic, aquamarine, aquiline, Hydrate, hydrant, hydraulics, hydrophobia, hydroponic, dehydrate
astro, aster	star	astronomy, astrology, astronaut, astronomical, asterisk, asteroid
bio	life	biology, biography, autobiography, biopsy
cosmo, cosm	universe, order	cosmos, cosmology, microcosm, macrocosm, cosmopolitan, cosmonaut
geo, ge, terra, ter	earth, ground	geography, geology, territory, extra-terrestrial, terracotta, terrarium, terrain
grav	heavy	gravity, gravitate, grave, aggravate
luc, lum, lus, lun	light, moon	luminous, illuminate, luster, translucent, lucid, elucidate, lunatic, lunacy, lunar
meter	measure	thermometer, barometer, speedometer, metric, symmetrical, trigonometry, kilometer, metronome, perimeter, parameter, diameter, odometer, geometry
thermo	heat	thermometer, thermal, thermostat, geothermal, hypothermia, thermos

(Continued)

Key Terms—Science and Mathematics

- **Average:** the sum of the addends.

- **Mean:** the sum of the addends divided by the number of addends.

- **Median:** the middle number that separates the data into equal parts.

- **Mode:** the number of greatest frequency in a set of numbers.

- **Mutation:** the genetic change of an organism resulting in an offspring that is different from the parents.

- **Genes:** elements in chromosomes that contain hereditary information.

- **Chromosome:** thread-like material that contains genetic information—each cell in the human body is comprised of 46 chromosomes.

- **Element:** a fundamental substance that cannot be separated into another substance—there are more than one hundred elements.

- **Atom:** the smallest unit of an element that still contains the properties of that element.

- **Magma:** molten or liquefied rock.

APPLICATIONS

APPLICATION (1)

This application is a report on a study concerning the lowering teen birth rate in the United States. Such a reduction in teenagers becoming parents has broad implications for our society in terms of social responsibility and health care, not to mention education and mental health.

Apply active reading strategies as you review the article. Then complete the chart following the reading to practice your note-taking skills.

Report: Teen Birth Rate Hits Record Low
by Jennifer Kerr

1   Fewer high school students are having sex these days, and more are using condoms. The teen birth rate has hit a record low.

2   More young people are finishing high school, too, and more little kids are being read to, according to the latest government snapshot on the well-being of the nation's children. It's good news on a number of key wellness indicators, experts said of the report being released Friday.

3   "The implications for the population are quite positive in terms of their health and their well-being," said Edward Sondik, director of the National Center for Health Statistics. "The lower figure on teens having sex means the risk of sexually transmitted diseases is lower."

4   In 2005, 47 percent of high school students—6.7 million—reported having had sexual intercourse, down from 54 percent in 1991. The rate of those who reported having had sex has remained the same since 2003.

5   Of those who had sex during a three-month period in 2005, 63 percent—about 9 million—used condoms. That's up from 46 percent in 1991.

6   The teen birth rate, the report said, was 21 per 1,000 young women ages 15 to 17 in 2005—an all-time low. It was down from 39 births per 1,000 teens in 1991.

7   "This is very good news," said Sondik. "Young teen mothers and their babies are at a greater risk of both immediate and long-term difficulties."

8   The birth rate in the 15 to 19 age group was 40 per 1,000 in 2005, also down sharply from the previous decade.

9   Education campaigns that started years ago are having a significant effect, said James Wagoner, president of Advocates for Youth, a Washington-based nonprofit group that focuses on prevention of teen pregnancy and sexually transmitted diseases.

10   "I think the HIV/AIDS epidemic and the efforts in the 80s and 90s had a lot to do with that," Wagoner said of the improved numbers on teen sex, condoms, and adolescent births.

11   "We need to encourage young teens to delay sexual initiation and we need to make sure they get all the information they need about condoms and birth control," he said.

(Continued)

12   The report was compiled from statistics and studies at 22 federal agencies, and covered 38 key indicators, including <u>infant mortality</u>, academic achievement rates, and the number of children living in poverty.

13   Other highlights:

- The percentage of children covered by health insurance decreased slightly. In 2005, 89 percent of children had health insurance coverage at some point during the year, down from 90 percent the previous year.
- The percentage of <u>low birthweight</u> infants (born weighing less than 5 pounds, 8 ounces) increased. It was 8.2 percent in 2005, up from 8.1 percent in 2004.
- More youngsters are getting reading time. Sixty percent of children ages 3 to 5 (and not in kindergarten) were read to daily by a family member in 2005, up from 53 percent in 1993.
- The percentage of children who had at least one parent working year round and full-time increased to 78.3 percent in 2005, up from 77.6 percent the previous year.
- More young people are completing high school. In 2005, 88 percent of young adults had finished high school—up from 84 percent in 1980.

SOURCE: Jennifer Kerr, "Report: Teen birth record hits new low," Associated Press, 2007. Reprinted by permission of The Associated Press.

COMPREHENSION CHECK

1   Summarize the key points in the preceding reading passage in the chart that follows. Draw from your text marking to represent the major points.

ISSUE	PAST	2005	IMPLICATIONS
Teen sexual activity			
Condom use			
Teen birth rate			
Children's health coverage			

ISSUE	PAST	2005	IMPLICATIONS
Low birth weight			
Preschool literacy			
Working parents			
High school completion			
Overall trends			

(Continued)

READING GRAPHICS

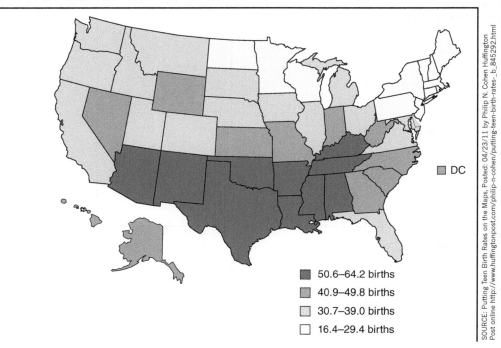

SOURCE: Putting Teen Birth Rates on the Maps, Posted: 04/23/11 by Philip N. Cohen Huffington
Post online http://www.huffingtonpost.com/philip-n-cohen/putting-teen-birth-rates-_b_845292.html

☐ DC

■ 50.6–64.2 births
■ 40.9–49.8 births
☐ 30.7–39.0 births
☐ 16.4–29.4 births

FIGURE 6.9 Teen birth rates across the U.S. Teen birth rates are the number of births per 1,000 women ages 15 to 19

1. Based on information in Figure 6.9, in which region of the United States are the most births for teenage mothers? _____

2. In which region of the United States are the least births for teenage mothers? _____
   _____

3. What do you think may account for the disparity between the regions and their birth rates in questions 1 and 2? _____
   _____

4. Locate your state on Figure 6.9 and determine the teenage birth rate. How does your state relate to the rest of the country? _____
   _____

5. Given the teen birth rate numbers in the reading, where do you suppose most births to teenage mothers took place? _____
   _____

6. This reading looks at teen birth rates nationally. Which region on the map of the United States do you suppose has the greatest decline in teenage birth rates? Which U.S. region do

you suppose has experienced little change? Justify your assumptions. _____

_____

_____

DEVELOPING YOUR COLLEGE-LEVEL VOCABULARY

Define the following key terms from the reading.

1. In paragraph 2, what does *indicators* mean? _____

_____

2. What does *implications* mean in paragraph 3? What other word has the same root?_____

_____

3. What does the term *teen birth rate* mean in paragraph 6? _____

_____

4. What does the term *infant mortality* mean in paragraph 12? _____

_____

5. What does the term *low birthweight* mean in paragraph 13? _____

_____

THEMATIC CONNECTIONS

Here is current information from the Center for Disease Control (CDC), a governmental agency dedicated to health, that recently released statistics showing that the teenage birth rate continues to decline. Look at the information and answer the questions that follow.

DATA FROM THE NATALITY DATA FILE, NATIONAL VITAL STATISTICS SYSTEM
• The teenage birth rate declined 8 percent in the United States from 2007 through 2009, reaching a historic low at 39.1 births per 1,000 teens aged 15–19 years.
• Rates fell significantly for teenagers in all age groups and for all racial and ethnic groups.
• Teenage birth rates for each age group and for nearly all race and Hispanic origin groups in 2009 were at the lowest levels ever reported in the United States.
• Birth rates for teens aged 15–17 dropped in 31 states from 2007 through 2009; rates for older teenagers aged 18–19 declined significantly in 45 states during this period.

SOURCE: NCHS Data Brief, Number 58, February 2011, U.S. Teenage Birth Rate Resumes Decline, http://www.cdc.gov/nchs/data/databriefs/db58.htm

1. Given the information, what is the trend for teenage birth rates in the United States overall?

2. The reading states that teen birth rates for teens 15–17 in 2005 were 21 births per 1,000; the new statistics cite that between 2007 and 2009, the birthrate for teens reached "a historic low" at 39.1 births per 1,00 for teens 15–19. How do you reconcile these numbers?

3. In your experience, has the teenage pregnancy rate increased in your community? Why do you think it has risen or lowered?

APPLICATION ②

This reading concerns the global issue of population explosion. Use active reading strategies to review the information in the passage. Answer the questions following the reading.

World Population Hits 7 Billion
by Haya El Nasser, *USA Today*

1   You are one of 7 billion people on Earth.

2   This historic milestone is rekindling age-old debates over birth control, protecting natural resources and reducing consumption. It also has many wondering whether the Earth can support so many people.

3   About half were added just in the past 40 years, and 3 billion more are expected by 2100.

4   Global population has swelled in record time since 1987, when it hit 5 billion.

5   "Currently, world population is growing at the most rapid pace in history," says Carl Haub, a demographer at the Population Reference Bureau. "In 1900, we were at 1.6 billion. In 99 years, we flipped the numbers to 6.1 billion."

6   The world is adding more people in less time but the annual growth rate is slowing down—from 2.1% in the late 1960s to 1.2% today—reflecting lower birth rates.

7   "In 1999, when we passed the 6 billion mark, the world economy was in hyperdrive," says Robert Lang, urban sociologist at the University of Nevada–Las Vegas. "Now we pass the 7 billion mark in a recession and there's much pessimism."

8   Recessions and depressions tend to slow population growth, especially in developed nations. Currently, growth is highest in poorest countries where health care advances are keeping people alive longer while birth rates are still relatively high.

9   The result is a yawning age gap. The share of the population 65 and older is at 21% in Germany and 23% in Japan. In countries such as Gambia and Senegal, only 2% are in that age group.

10   Many of the programs to reduce population growth have been successful, Haub says.

11   "I can only imagine what population size would have been today if that had not happened," he says.

12   However many more people are added in the next century, more will live in cities. Even in developing nations, a growing share of the population lives in urbanized areas, a shift that is leading to denser living and putting more pressure to reduce energy use and build new infrastructure.

13   "Seven billion people are 7 billion good reasons for sustainable infrastructure development," says Daryl Dulaney, president and CEO of Siemens Industry, a leading supplier of transportation and building technology.

14   Only 28.8% of the world's population lived in urban areas in 1950. Today, just over 50% do, and the United Nations projects that almost 69% will by 2050, when the population is expected to reach 9.3 billion. The number of people who live in cities by then will almost equal today's world population.

15   That's why Siemens created the Infrastructure and Cities Sector this month.

16   "From a city's perspective, what this is doing is putting additional pressure to be competitive in the world," says Dulaney, who heads Siemens' new division in the USA. "Global companies can go anywhere. If America is going to compete to attract businesses ... the way they compete is with infrastructure, a good quality of life."

17   Cities in developing nations have an edge of sorts because they're building from scratch and can apply the latest green technologies. In developed nations such as the USA, the challenge is to retrofit old buildings, power grids and roads.

18   Many are doing it. Siemens installed 40,000 new lights in Houston's traffic signal system, cutting energy use and saving $1.4 million a year, Dulaney says. Dallas is getting a smart grid that will integrate water, electrical and other services.

19   "With 19th-century technology, the planet could not have handled 2 billion people," Lang says. "It would have consumed every stick of wood, which was a principal source of fuel."

(Continued)

20 Groups such as the Population Institute, an organization that advocates family planning around the world, are calling for more international support to reduce births.

21 "People in the developing world are on the front line of climate change and food insecurity," says Robert Walker, executive vice president. "Of all the very significant challenges that we face in the world today, many of those issues appear to be almost insurmountable challenges. Population growth is not."

COMPREHENSION CHECK

1. Select the major points in the passage by marking the text. In the margin of the reading, create an outline or on a separate piece of paper, create double-column notes as you would use to study the key points.

READING GRAPHICS

This application discusses the increasing pressure for protecting natural resources and reducing consumption. Figure 6.10 shows the global CO_2 (carbon dioxide) emissions.

1. In the green bar graph in the bottom right of the map, what might the CM (as in 1CM, 3CM, and so on) mean?_____

2. Why do the gray-colored countries produce the most CO_2?

3. What countries are expected to rise in their temperature by 5 to 10 centimeters by the end of the twenty-first century? _____
_____
_____

4. What is the relationship between regions that will experience a rise in temperature and those countries that are the regions of widespread poverty? _____
_____
_____

5. Which continents contribute the most CO_2 emissions? _____
_____
_____

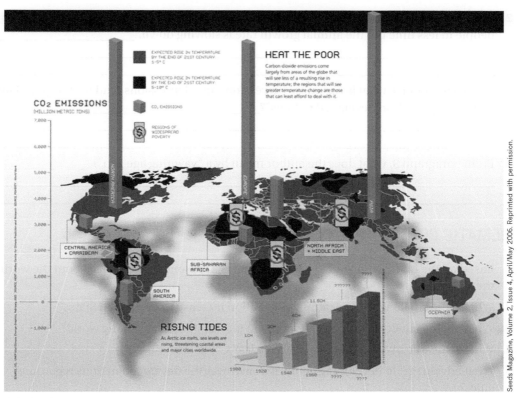

FIGURE 6.10 CO$_2$ Emissions

Seeds Magazine, Volume 2, Issue 4, April/May 2006. Reprinted with permission.

6. What is the relationship between the information in this map and the information in the reading? _____
_____
_____
_____
_____
_____

DEVELOPING YOUR COLLEGE-LEVEL VOCABULARY

Interpret the following key phrases or passages from the reading.

1. What does the following quote mean from paragraph 5, "Currently, world population is growing at the most rapid pace in history." _____
_____
_____

(Continued)

2. What does the following statement mean from paragraph 6: "The world is adding more people in less time but the annual growth rate is slowing down."_____

_____

_____

3. From paragraph 8, what is meant by "Recessions and depressions tend to slow population growth, especially in developed nations"?_____

_____

_____

4. From paragraph 9, what does the author mean by a "yawning age gap"? _____

_____

_____

THEMATIC CONNECTIONS

1. Based on the information in the passage, what is a reasonable inference about the world in the year 2100?
2. What is the challenge for sustaining population increase in the United States?
3. What are the challenges of rapid population growth in the developing world?
4. What is the role of the city in coming decades?
5. What advantage do developing countries have over the developed nations regarding cities?

WRAPPING IT UP

In the following study outline, fill in the definitions and a brief explanation of the key terms in the "Your Notes" column. Alternatively, create vocabulary cards to learn these key terms. Use the strategy of spaced practice to review these key terms on a regular basis. Use this study guide to review this chapter's key topics.

KEY TERM OR CONCEPT	YOUR NOTES
Double-column notes	
Cornell notes	
Outline	
Graphic organizers	
Glossary	
Key terms	

GROUP ACTIVITY: RESEARCHING A SOCIAL ISSUE

This assignment requires you to conduct some research on your own. Choose a topic within the broad theme of social responsibility. Your instructor may have you present your research findings in class as a part of a discussion forum on issues of concern in the world today—and our responsibility as global citizens to be aware of and address them.

Steps For Conducting Research

1. Find an article of two to three pages in length on a topic of your choice concerning an aspect of social responsibility or issue of concern in our culture or for the world. You do not have to agree with the author of the article.

2. If the reading you've found is longer than two to three pages, choose subsections that comprise the required length.

3. Print out the article to attach to the back of the form you will submit.

4. The following Research Reading Assignment directions can be copied on your own paper—each section is worth points.

5. Indicate your bibiographic information described in the Research Reading Assignment. If you choose a website, include the author, periodical, date, and URL or Internet website address.

6. The vocabulary section requires you choose five words central to understanding your topic. For example, if you are researching global warming, you may choose a key term such as *greenhouse effect*. Indicate the part of speech of the word or key term; use a dictionary if necessary. Then use the word or key term in an original sentence, providing context clues that demonstrate your understanding of the word's meaning. If the sentence does not contain context clues, you will not receive full points.

7. Construct an outline, map, chart, or double-column notes of the author's point of view, or thesis and major arguments. Do *not* include your opinion.

8. In the last section, present your opinion, based on the author's major points. This section should be well organized and several paragraphs long to receive full points.

    Here are the major sections of your report.

Research Reading Assignment

Bibliographic Information (2 points). Website, author, date, publication, pages.
Vocabulary (5 points). Choose five challenging words central to your article or topic. For each word, provide the meaning and part of speech and use the word in an original sentence.

WORD	PART OF SPEECH	MEANING	SENTENCE
1.			
2.			
3.			
4.			
5.			

Note Taking (10 points). Compose an outline, map, double-column notes, or a chart of major points in a clear, well-organized format. (Notes must not include your ideas—only those of the reading passage.)

Critique (8 points). Write several paragraphs reacting to the article you read. Take issue with or express support for particular supporting arguments made by the author. It is also appropriate to relate the information in your article to class or to your life experiences.

REFLECTIVE JOURNAL QUESTIONS

1. What do you think is the most valuable benefit of note taking? What is the most frustrating aspect of note taking? What techniques have you already been using and which ones will you start to use now that you've learned about them?

2. Take notes on both a reading assignment and a class lecture about the same topic in another class. How are these two sets of notes alike? How are they different?

THEMATIC CONNECTIONS

Respond to one of the following questions. Prepare notes for class discussion or create a polished essay of several paragraphs to support your thesis. Type your essay, and be sure to proofread it before you submit it to your instructor.

1. In your opinion, what is the most significant social problem in our country today? What are some ways to address this issue of social concern?

2. Recalling your own experience and that of your associates, what are young people or older people most concerned about with regard to the state of our country or world? What issues are young people most apathetic about and why?

3. What are the qualities needed in an individual who works to change injustice? Choose three qualities (behaviors or attitudes) that characterize a successful leader, whether in civil rights, environmental issues, or any other social concern. Support your answer with specific examples.

ADDITIONAL SKILL AND STRATEGY PRACTICE

A. Using Graphic Organizers to Take Notes

This passage concerning literature in the contemporary age comes from a chapter in a humanities textbook, *The Humanities in the Western Tradition*. This section of the chapter outlines the contributions of major African American women writers and their efforts to unveil social injustice through their work. Read the passage and then complete the graphic organizer that follows.

Racial Injustice
by Marvin Perry, J. Wayne Baker, and Pamela Pfeiffer Hollinger

1   The closing decades of the twentieth century were marked by the unprecedented achievement of African American women writers who overcame racial discrimination to become award-winning poets, novelists, screenplay writers, and governmental emissaries. Through their works, they not only brought attention to the plight of African Americans, but they also created a new awareness of the important role that African American culture plays in American life.

2   Gwendolyn Brooks (1917–2000), whose work spans five decades, was the first African American writer to win a Pulitzer Prize (1950) and to be appointed to the American Academy of Arts and Letters (1976). She won her Pulitzer for her collection of poems, *Annie Allie* (1949), but between it and her last two volumes of poetry, she proved to be less a literary integrationist and more of a "black" author, who poetically demanded an inquiry into the denial of citizens' rights for ordinary African Americans. In all her works, Brooks explores African American culture and the impact of

racial identity on a black person's thought and behavior. For example, in her novel, *Maud Martha* (1953), Brooks deals with the racial prejudice that Maud experiences, from both within and without the black community, and how she comes to view herself as less appealing than other girls because her skin is darker. In her collection of poems, *The Bean Eaters* (1960), Brooks offers insights into the attitudes of elderly African Americans who, although poverty-stricken, are content with their lives, and in *We Real Cool* (1966), her stream of consciousness poems, she reveals the inner thoughts of impoverished, inner-city blacks who have become hooligans. In all, Brooks wrote twenty-one volumes of poetry, and in 1994 she was awarded the National Endowment for the Humanities *Jefferson Lectureship*—the highest humanities award granted by the federal government.

3　　The autobiographical works of the African American poet, novelist, actress, and screenplay writer Maya Angelou (1928–) are concerned with issues pertaining to racial, sexual, and economic oppression. In *I Know Why the Caged Bird Sings* (1970), the first of her autobiographical volumes (which was nominated for the National Book Award), she recounts her childhood through her teenage years, including her early years with her grandmother in rural Arkansas and living in St. Louis with her mother, where her mother's boyfriend, Mr. Freeman, raped her at age eight. As a consequence, Angelou became mute—except with her older brother, Bailey, who had given her the nickname Maya (short for "my sister"), because he could not pronounce her given name of Marguerite. Angelou relates how she refused to testify in court that he had previously molested her, prior to the rape, thus compounding the guilt and shame that she already felt. Because justice was not done in the courts, Mr. Freeman was subsequently a victim of a vigilante murder. In the eight years after the rape, Angelou tells us she became a savvy, street-smart teenager, and following her move to San Francisco to study dance, she challenged wartime racist hiring policies by becoming a streetcar conductor at age fifteen. A year later for eight months, she hid her unwanted pregnancy from her family so that she could graduate from high school. During the 1960s, Angelou was the Northern Coordinator for Dr. Martin Luther King's Southern Christian Leadership Conference. Later, she held appointments under U.S. Presidents Gerald Ford and Jimmy Carter and was invited to read her poem, "On the Pulse of the Morning," for President Bill Clinton's inauguration in 1993. Her screenplay, *Georgia, Georgia,* was the first original screenplay by an African American woman to be made into a motion picture; her collection of poems, *Just Give Me a Cool Drink of Water 'Fore I Die,* was nominated for the Pulitzer Prize; and she penned and produced a television miniseries entitled *Three Way Choice.* The latest volume of her autobiography, *A Song Flung Up to Heaven,* was published in 2002.

—From PERRY, The Humanities in the Western Tradition, 1E. © 2003 Cengage Learning.

1. Based on the information provided in this reading, determine the key points about the careers and accomplishments of Gwendolyn Brooks and Maya Anjelou. Write down your key points in the graphic organizer below.

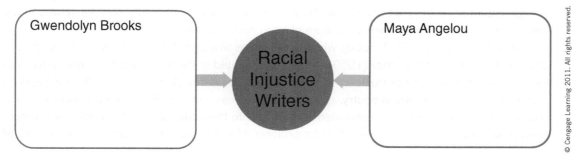

✤ POST-ASSESSMENT

PHYSICAL SCIENCE TEXTBOOK

Preview the following article and then read it all the way through. Then go to the end of the article and answer the questions. This assessment will help you determine your strengths and weaknesses in understanding, learning, and applying the skills and strategies discussed in this chapter.

Future Use of Natural Resources
by Stanley Chernicoff, Haydn A. Fox, and Lawrence H. Tanner

1   The United States has about 50 billion barrels of known oil reserves recoverable by current methods and may have an additional, as-yet-undiscovered, 35 billion barrels. The world's oil reserves total approximately 700 billion barrels. At the current worldwide petroleum use rate of nearly 21 billion barrels per year, these reserves will last only 35 years or so. Although shortages and price increases may eventually reduce the rate of oil consumption, somewhat extending the life of current supplies, ways must be found to extend the finite crude oil supply or to develop alternative energy sources before the reserves run out during the twenty-first century.

2   Large new petroleum finds are unlikely; virtually all potential oil-producing rock formations have already been explored. One way to maximize our oil reserves, however, is to extract as much as possible from known reservoir rocks.

3   Currently economical methods of oil extraction remove only 20 percent to 30 percent of the oil within the rocks. As oil shortages increase, it may become more economical to use already-available enhanced recovery methods that can reclaim as much as 50 percent of the oil. Extraction of more than that percentage is virtually impossible, because the oil tends to adhere tightly to the rock particles.

4   Other technological initiatives seek alternatives to petroleum for transportation energy. These options include the liquification and gasification of coal as fuel, and the development of practical electric automobiles, solar-powered buses, and trains propelled by powerful electromagnets.

5   The supply of mineral resources remains adequate, although some are located in remote places. Valuable deposits of important metals and nonmetals are still being discovered. Indeed, major ore bodies have recently been unearthed in Chile, Australia, and Siberia. Extensive outcrops rich in zinc, lead, copper, nickel, cobalt, and uranium have also been found in Antarctica, along with a 120-kilometer (70-mile) long, 100-meter (300-feet)-thick deposit of iron, which is large enough to meet the world's iron demand for 200 years.

6   Soon we may be able to mine the vast mineral deposits on the sea floor, which in some places is covered by billions of nodules of manganese oxide, some approaching the size of bowling balls. These nodules, which contain lesser amounts of iron, nickel, copper, zinc, and cobalt, accumulate where deep-sea sedimentation occurs slowly enough to allow them to grow without being buried. Collectively, they may represent the Earth's largest mineral deposit.

(Continued)

7   Most mineral resources can be recycled. Steel from "tin" cans, automobiles, and old bridges, mercury from discarded thermometers, copper from electrical wire, and platinum from the catalytic converters of abandoned automobiles can all be reclaimed for reuse. Recycling offers several benefits: It reduces the volume of waste requiring disposal, causes less land area to be disturbed by new mining operations, and minimizes the energy needed to mine and refine new ores. Scrap aluminum recycling, for example, uses only one-twentieth the energy needed to mine and process an equivalent amount of new aluminum from bauxite.

8   Everything we have, or can make, comes from the Earth. Now that you understand the processes that built, moved, and shaped the continents and ocean floors, and the vast amount of time over which the Earth and its resources developed, you can appreciate why we must act wisely in managing the materials that make our modern lives possible. If we fail in this task, most assuredly, little will remain for future generations. Industry, local governments, and the world community of nations must cooperate to ensure that the search for, development of, and use of the planet's resources do not squander those precious resources or irreversibly damage our shared environment. With the knowledge you have acquired from your <u>geology</u> training, you are now prepared to contribute to the ongoing debate about the need to balance resource development and environmental protection. By all means, use your training and make yourself be heard.

SOURCE: From CHERNICOFF, *Earth*, 1E. © 2002 Cengage Learning.

COMPREHENSION CHECK

Circle the best answer to the following questions.

Reading Comprehension

1 **What is the main point of this passage?**

A. While mineral supplies are adequate, methods to find or to replace crude oil supplies must be found because we're running out.

B. When crude oil supplies are depleted, we will use our abundant mineral supplies.

C. Both mineral and crude oil supplies can be regenerated.

D. The ocean is, as yet, an unexploited source of mineral supplies.

2 **Which of the following is *not* one of the possible alternatives for crude oil?**

A. Liquification and gasification of coal as fuel

B. Minerals

C. Development of electric automobiles

D. Solar-powered buses

3 **Which of the following is *not* one of the major reasons for the petroleum crisis?**

A. All potential oil-producing rock formations have been explored.

B. The petroleum use worldwide is almost 21 billion barrels per year.

C. The world's oil reserves are about 700 billion barrels.

D. As-yet-undiscovered oil reserves are pending.

4 **How much oil is left?**

A. There is enough to last a century.
B. There is enough to last a couple of decades.
C. There is enough to last 35 years.
D. There is enough to last 50 years.

5 **The pattern of organization in this passage is predominantly**

A. problem/solution.
B. definition.
C. comparison and contrast.
D. sequence or process order.

6 **According to the text, what is the significance of the nodules of manganese oxide?**

A. These nodules on the ocean floor may be the world's largest mineral deposit.
B. Because most minerals can be recycled, efforts to exploit the ocean are not underway.
C. While mineral resources are adequate, scientists hope to conserve land mining and turn to ocean mining.
D. Geologists hope to uncover crude oil where the manganese oxide is found.

7 **According to the passage, because oil shortages are increasing, scientists may need to extract more oil from rocks. You can infer that this means**

A. reclaiming 50 percent of the oil through enhanced recovery methods is a technology we do not yet have.
B. extraction of 50 percent is impossible because oil adheres to rock particles.
C. currently, economical methods remove only 20 to 30 percent, which is the best we can do.
D. more money will be needed to employ the technology we already have to maximize oil output from rocks.

8 **If you were studying for a test over this information, which is the best chart of this passage, considering the pattern of organization?**

A.

PROBLEMS WITH OIL	PROBLEMS WITH MINERAL RESOURCES
1. The United States has 50 billion barrels.	1. The supply is adequate, although most reserves are in remote places.
2. Potential reserves = 35 billion barrels.	2. The world's iron reserves = 200 years' worth.
3. The world's reserves = 700 billion barrels.	
4. Twenty-one billion barrels of petroleum are used per year.	
5. The world's reserves will last 35 years.	

(Continued)

SOLUTIONS TO OIL SHORTAGE	SOLUTIONS USING MINERAL RESOURCES
1. Maximize reserves with enhanced recovery method. 2. Seek alternatives for transportation energy.	1. Mine ore deposits in Chile, Australia, and Siberia. 2. Mine deposits in Antarctica. 3. Mine deposits on sea floor. 4. Continue recycling.

B.

EFFECT OF OIL SHORTAGE	EFFECT OF MINERAL SHORTAGE
1. The United States has 50 billion barrels. 2. Potential reserves = 35 billion barrels. 3. The world's reserves = 700 billion barrels. 4. Twenty-one billion barrels of petroleum are used per year. 5. The world's reserves will last 35 years.	1. The supply is adequate, although most reserves are in remote places. 2. The world's iron reserves = 200 years' worth.

Vocabulary Comprehension

9 **What does the root word *solar* mean as used in paragraph 4?**

A. The sun
B. The earth
C. The sky
D. Water

10 **What does the root word *geo* mean in the word *geology* in paragraph 8?**

A. The sun
B. The Earth
C. The sky
D. Water

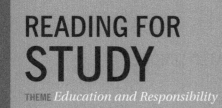
TEXTBOOK APPLICATION

Chapter 4: Equity and Education Practice from *Diverse Histories, Diverse Perspectives* by Grace Huerta

This textbook chapter from *Educational Foundations* concerns the concepts of equal opportunity and its relationship to schooling in the United States. The interrelationships among poverty, segregated communities, and segregated schools are explored as well as how the social issue of poverty affects schooling and educational outcomes.

Your instructor may assign a subsection of this chapter for you to complete with a small group. Alternatively, your instructor may require you to complete activities independently during or outside of class.

Apply what you have learned about text marking and note taking for study from this unit. In addition, use the strategies you have learned for mastering new vocabulary and decoding graphic material in texts. Then, build a detailed outline, graphic organizer, chart, or double-column notes. Remember to apply the SOUL system as you pull out key points: Be *selective* about what you include, *organize* the information in an appropriate format for the pattern of organization, make sure you *understand* what you write by paraphrasing the key information, and then use your notes to *learn* the new information. In addition, create vocabulary cards to learn key terms, making sure to look up the unfamiliar words to arrive at an accurate definition given the context.

There are seven major subsections in this chapter. Survey the chapter, paying special attention to the headings of the sections. Then, depending on the assignment, preview a subsection of the chapter. In this chapter, the predominant patterns of organization will be cause and effect and definition and example. As part of your survey of the text chapter, review the discussion questions and summary at the end of the chapter. Then read and mark the text. Next, complete the following note-taking exercise(s) as your instructor assigns.

As your instructor assigns, identify the following in each subsection.

WHAT IS EQUAL OPPORTUNITY?

1. Define the term *equal opportunity*.

2. List the points mentioned in this section that dispute the notion of "equal opportunity."

POVERTY, SEGREGATED COMMUNITIES, AND SEGREGATED SCHOOLS

1. Poverty and Minority Students

   - Outline of the effects of poverty as they relate to schooling.

2. Poverty in Inner Cities

   - List the challenges faced by inner cities.

3. Regional Diversity in Public Schools

   - Based on the information in Tables 4.2 and 4.3 and the text, create a chart comparing and contrasting the racial composition of U.S. public schools by region and the racial composition of extreme-poverty schools by region.

4. Low-Income Status and Free Lunch

   - Create a web of the major information in this subsection.

SOCIAL AND EDUCATIONAL OUTCOMES OF DESEGREGATION

   - Complete double-column notes of the key information in this section.

INTERSECTIONS BETWEEN EDUCATIONAL PRACTICE AND SOCIOECONOMIC STATUS

1. Ability Grouping and Tracking of Students

   - Construct an outline or chart of the causes and effects of ability grouping and tracking.

2. Advantages of Students with a High Socioeconomic Background

   - List the advantages in outline or chart format. Alternatively, create a web of this information.

3. Dropout Rates and Their Relationship to Poverty, Segregation, and Race.

   - Use a note-taking method, identifying the *causes* of poverty, segregation, and race as they relate to the *effects* of higher dropout rates.

   - List the major points in the feature "From Preservice to Practice."

THE NO CHILD LEFT BEHIND ACT AND EDUCATION EQUITY

   - Construct a chart that compares and contrasts the goals of the No Child Left Behind Act with the reality of its implementation in schools.

IMPLICATIONS FOR EDUCATORS

Choose one of these subsections and use a suitable note-taking method to represent key points.

1. Making Decisions About Employment

2. Dealing with Classroom Size

3. Effects of Ability Grouping and Tracking

4. Bring Communities Together

ENGAGING FAMILY AND COMMUNITY

Choose one of these subsections and use a suitable note-taking method to represent key points.

1. Funds of Knowledge

2. Using Funds of Knowledge in the Classroom

INCREASE YOUR DISCIPLINE-SPECIFIC VOCABULARY

EDUCATION AND SOCIAL SCIENCE

The terms listed are used on the page indicated. Define each of these terms. Definitions are on the pages indicated.

Key Terms

Create vocabulary concept cards or use a similar study method to learn the definitions of the following key terms.

1. Equal opportunity, p. 454

2. Meritocracy, p. 455

3. Poverty threshold, p. 455

4. Free or reduced-price lunch, p. 458

5. Ability grouping, p. 460

6. Tracking, p. 460

7. Teacher expectations, p. 461

8. Self-fulfilling prophecy, p. 461

9. Funds of knowledge, p. 466

After preparing your notes on this chapter, you should be able to respond to the discussion questions and multiple-choice questions following the reading to assess your learning.

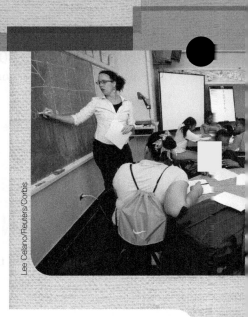
4

Equity and Educational Practice

Lee Celano/Reuters/Corbis

FIRST PERSON

Minority Communities "Don't Care About Kids" and Other Myths

Looking back on my own elementary educational experiences, my first memories are of Santa Barbara Avenue Elementary School and Transfiguration Catholic School in South Central Los Angeles, where I attended from kindergarten to grade 6. The playgrounds of this public school and this private school were unused sections of parking lots and concrete courtyards. My teachers were mostly white and very strict. Our classes focused on such skills as reading, writing, and mathematics and, in the case of my Catholic school, catechism. Textbooks never went home because there weren't enough, or they simply did not travel well with their frayed spines. Once we were at school, our teachers demanded that we stay quiet, listen, and read. When we weren't reading, we were told to write. Spankings happened.

These inner-city public and private schools did not have a music program or wonderful play gyms or green fields to enjoy at recess. We had tetherball poles and one chain-link backstop. Hopscotch and four-square lines were painted on gravel. At both schools, the auditorium served as lunchroom, library, nurse's office, and assembly hall.

The majority of the local community consisted of the urban, working poor. Our neighbors were African American and Latina/o families and kids. The neighborhood was neat, but the old rental houses and bungalows were accented with black security doors and windows. Everyone always seemed to be going to work or returning from work in run-down cars.

After school, we kids were expected to go home and finish our chores. I was lucky. My mom was there when I arrived, while my dad worked at the market, stacking produce. By the time I was in the fourth grade, my mom made sure we completed our homework first, chores second. My chores were to vacuum, help with the laundry, take out the trash, pick up dog poop, ride my bike to the market for groceries, or deliver cash payments to the gas and electric companies.

CHAPTER OBJECTIVES

- Readers will analyze the concept of equal opportunity and its relationship to schooling in the United States.

- Readers will consider the interrelationship among poverty, segregated communities, and segregated schools.

- Readers will understand how poverty affects public schools in regions across the United States.

- Readers will analyze the educational outcomes and graduation rates of students from low socioeconomic backgrounds and communities.

- By exploring a sociocultural approach to understanding family social networks and knowledge construction, readers will explore the funds-of-knowledge approach to parent outreach and curriculum development.

452

My parents did not have credit cards or a checking account because of their distrust of banks (both had experienced the Great Depression). Everything was paid for in cash—and sometimes in pennies. My best toy, my bike, was cheap, but the lock was expensive. Kids' bikes, including mine, were always getting stolen in the neighborhood. Nevertheless, we all had bikes to help out with jobs and errands (my mom did not drive, and my dad was often at work).

We had no parks or community center in our local neighborhood. We did have a free clinic, where I remember sitting for hours in the waiting room with my mom and brothers when we needed immunizations. A USC Mobile Dentist also came to our neighborhood once or twice a year. We would line up for hours to let the dental students have a crack at our mouths.

For fun, we played in the streets or in our neighbor's little backyard. The game of choice, our only choice, was kickball. There were no organized leagues of any sort, for boys or girls. We girls often had to fight for a chance to play kickball with the boys. When they wouldn't let us play, we'd find a yard with a garage to bounce a handball against, or we simply went home—to read.

Come nightfall, we stayed inside. We knew there were robberies because we'd hear our parents talking about them. Occasionally, we would see men hanging out in the alley behind our garage, drinking "tall boys" of Colt 45. Our parents instructed us to not talk to them, although they didn't explain why.

In the evenings, we did not attend social or community activities, scouts, or boys' or girls' clubs because there were none. Instead, we watched black-and-white TV shows such as *Father Knows Best* and *The Flintstones* or listened to the radio as the Dodgers played baseball. Once in a while, my mother watched a telenovela. We listened to Dad's jazz, Mom's Latin music, or my brothers' Smokey Robinson and the Doors albums. Mostly, I read books checked out from our small school library, sometimes the same ones over and over again. Or I would read the newspapers my dad brought home from work.

Some evenings were punctuated by the sounds of police helicopters and ambulances and what I thought were firecrackers, although one of my brothers would later correct me: "No, that's a gun shot." I heard them while reading my Scholastic paperback books.

But by the next morning, we were back on the streets, zooming off to school on our bikes. Our community embraced us during the day; at night, we respected the darkness. But I was not afraid, nor was I taught to be afraid, of our community.

As I reflect on growing up among our African American and Latina/o neighbors and classmates, I recall what we shared as a community. We did not have much, but everyone worked hard to have what we needed—rent money, food, clothing, and (most important) love and unity. I don't remember ever being on welfare or using food stamps.

In retrospect, I learned much from inner-city life. I learned responsibility. Among minority neighbors interconnected in a struggle, I observed people with a work ethic, people who were creative in making ends meet. Our community was proud and resilient. In fact, I did not know that people thought less of us until we left South Central L.A. and got a taste of "upward" mobility in a suburb just a few miles away.

Even though I spent my early years living in a ghetto or barrio or whatever label I would soon become familiar with, my South Central Los Angeles community gave me what it could give. Without romanticizing the struggles of living in a segregated place where there was some violence and many school resources were lacking, I would simply say that South Central L.A. life gave me a sense of community.

But today, given our increasingly competitive and technological society, is a sense of community enough? In this chapter, I explore the outcomes of poverty and segregation that communities and schools experience when cohesiveness simply cannot overcome the effects of long-term inequities. What are the ramifications of maintaining a segregated educational system that continues to sort and stratify the working poor from those who have access to a variety of educational and employment opportunities?

What Is Equal Opportunity?

What does the term **equal opportunity** mean exactly? In essence, it refers to the idea that all the people in a society have the chance to pursue any occupation or economic status they choose. This does not ensure that everyone who graduates from high school will make a million dollars as a company's chief executive officer. But it does mean that we all have an equal chance to pursue goals related to educational objectives and to compete for economic rewards—whatever our race, class, sex, language, and physical ability.

People often use the metaphor of "participating on a level playing field" when they discuss equal opportunity. To ensure that a level playing field is provided to all "players," we must extend the metaphor further. How do coaches and teachers determine which players and students step onto the field or into a college preparatory classroom? What prior training experiences do the participants bring to the field or classroom? Players and students with more refined skills are likely to have had extra training opportunities, equipment, and resources with which to prepare and practice. Other players and students who are just as potentially talented will not have had any prior training and therefore may not have developed the skills needed to play on the field or take college preparatory classes.

Who selects the coaches and teachers to make such judgments about players and students and determines what criteria or standards will be applied? What kind of training did the coaches and teachers receive, and what measures do they use to identify select players and students to advance onto the "field"? What resources were available to assist them in their own preparation?

In other words, although we may believe that the "playing field is level" and that all participants can compete, there will be players and students who are not equally prepared to compete. Inequality comes into play when families and communities do not have the economic status needed to access equal educational opportunities both in and outside of school settings. These players and students languish on the sidelines with limited access to training and sanctioned learning experiences, because they did not have the resources to hone their skills and thus fall further and further behind.

Factors that dramatically impede access to a level playing field include stereotypes about economic status and racial bias. Such assumptions suggest that certain groups have less motivation and intellectual capacity and thus are themselves solely responsible for their lack of educational achievement and economic resources. Often individuals are blamed or celebrated for their life's successes and failures, regardless of the quality of educational experiences they accessed. This notion of **meritocracy**—success based solely on one's own ability or on another metaphor, "pulling oneself up by the bootstraps"—ignores the fact that some schools are better funded, hire better-qualified teachers, secure more resources, and employ better leaders than other schools do.

What, then, is the responsibility of an education system that is charged with equally preparing students to pursue the educational paths and employment of their choice? Do schools actively pursue equal opportunities for their students, or do they simply reproduce the economic class distinctions evident in society today?

PAUSE & REFLECT

Americans often maintain that success is based exclusively on an individual's own merits. Do you agree or disagree with this position? How do a community and its institutions affect and contribute to the success of individuals in a society?

Poverty, Segregated Communities, and Segregated Schools

To live in poverty means different things to different people. The U.S. government has identified a poverty threshold, or baseline, that is the lowest annual income a family needs to meet its most basic needs. According to a 2002 U.S. Bureau of the Census report, the 2001 **poverty threshold** for a family of four was $18,267. The report adds that compared to other developed countries, the United States has the highest child poverty rates, with estimates ranging from 17 to 22 percent.

Poverty and Minority Students

Poverty is more evident among U.S. minority students (see Table 4.1) and among families with a single mother as head of the household than it is among white students. African American students living in households headed by women increased from 38 percent to 54 percent from 1973 to 1994. During the same period, among Latinos, the percentage of single mothers who headed households nearly doubled from 20 percent to 39 percent (Hauser, Simmons, & Pager, 2004).

Equally important is the economic segregation of communities, which affects the extent to which school systems can provide equal educational opportunities, particularly for black and Latina/o students

TABLE 4.1 Percent Poor in Schools Attended by K–12 Students, by Race and Year

| | Percent Poor* | | | | |
	Whites	**Blacks**	**Latinos**	**Asians**	**Native Americans**
1996-1997	19	43	46	29	31
1998-1999	20	39	44	26	35
2000-2001	19	45	44	26	31
2002-2003	23	49	48	27	39

*These numbers include both students eligible for and students receiving free and reduced price lunch.

Source: NCES Common Care of Data.

whose schools reflect that segregation. Public school populations are now 41 percent minority students, and most of these minority students attend schools in which they are the *majority*. Because of high poverty levels, limited employment, inaccessible housing, as well as homelessness, the poor are excluded from living in middle-class communities and attending school with middle-class students. As a result, many poor, minority children live and attend schools isolated from middle-class, Euro-American communities (Orfield & Lee, 2005). Conversely, many whites have little, if any experience living in diverse, less affluent communities.

Poverty in Inner Cities

This is not to say that predominantly African American or Latina/o communities are inferior and maintain inferior schools. Nor are all-white communities and schools superior. After all, school segregation by race is only one form of separatism. Economic class, as well as locale, segregates schools. However, since the 1970s and "white flight" (the shift of white families out of metropolitan centers and into suburbs), large populations of African American and Latina/o students remain in central cities.

These communities face a number of overwhelming challenges that are not easily overcome, such as dilapidated housing, inadequate social services and health care, and job shortages (Karnasiewicz, 2005; Rothstein, 2004). In addition to poverty, inner-city students must confront poor health care and nutrition, crime and gang violence, and defeatist beliefs that can demoralize anyone caught in the cycle of poverty. Low-income white families must also send their children to schools severely damaged by economically segregated communities, thus debunking the myth that segregation is only a racial issue.

Regional Diversity in Public Schools

Shifts in immigration have transformed U.S. schools beyond almost anyone's expectations. Since the 1970s, African American student populations have grown slowly, while Latina/o and Asian populations have increased rapidly, with Euro-American enrollments, in proportion to the total, having declined. As illustrated in Table 4.2, enrollment statistics for the 2002–2003 school year show the diverse nature of U.S. public schools; Latinos are the largest minority group at 18 percent, and African Americans follow at 17 percent. These two groups now represent one-third of the total public school population.

The country's the two most populous regions, the West and the South, teach a combined 54 percent of the nation's public school students. Thirty percent of African American and Latina/o students live in the western and southern states. Also, Asian/Pacific Islanders now outnumber African American students in the West. In the Northeast, African American students represent 16 percent of the student population, although growth in the Latina/o student population, at 13 percent, continued to increase in 2002–2003.

In the West, South, and Northeast, public school students are more likely to attend culturally diverse, biracial schools than are students in midwestern states, where Euro-American, white students represent 70 percent of the public school population (Orfield & Lee, 2005). Given these ongoing trends, with concentrations of Latinos in the West and of African Americans in the South (and with Latina/o populations increasing in such states as Georgia and North Carolina), what remains constant is the need to provide equitable education and resources to our increasingly diverse, yet economically segregated, communities nationwide.

As noted in Table 4.3, African American and Latina/o students make up 80 percent of the student population in schools that serve neighborhoods where

TABLE 4.2 Racial Composition of U.S. Public Schools by Region, 2002–2003

Region	Total Enrollment	White	Black	Latina/o	Asian	Native American
West	11,086,700	48	7	35	8	2
Border	3,518,342	70	21	4	2	3
Midwest	9,850,818	75	15	7	3	1
South	13,880,097	51	27	19	2	0
Northeast	8,296,140	66	16	13	5	0
Alaska	134,364	59	5	4	6	26
Hawaii	183,829	20	2	5	72	1
Bureau of Indian Affairs	46,126	0	0	0	0	100
U.S. total	46,996,416	59	17	18	4	1

Note: Definition of the regions: **South:** Alabama, Arkansas, Florida, Georgia, Louisiana, Mississippi, North Carolina, South Carolina, Tennessee, Texas, and Virginia; **Border:** Delaware, Kentucky, Maryland, Missouri, Oklahoma, and West Virginia; **Northeast:** Connecticut, Maine, Massachusetts, New Hampshire, New Jersey, New York, Pennsylvania, Rhode Island, and Vermont; **Midwest:** Illinois, Indiana, Iowa, Kansas, Michigan, Minnesota, Nebraska, North Dakota, Ohio, South Dakota, and Wisconsin; **West:** Arizona, California, Colorado, Montana, Nevada, New Mexico, Oregon, Utah, Washington, and Wyoming. Note: Hawaii and Alaska, which have very distinctive populations are treated separately and the District of Columbia is treated as a city rather than a state.

Sources: NCES Common Core of Data (2002–2003); Orfield & Lee (2005).

TABLE 4.3 Racial Composition of Extreme-Poverty Schools by Region, 2002–2003 (percentage of students in schools with 90 to 100 percent poor students)

Region	White	Black	Latina/o	Asian	Native American	Total
West	7	9	76	6	2	100
Border	66	27	5	1	2.2	100
Midwest	13	54	30	2	2	100
South	7	62	31	1	0.2	100
Northeast	9	55	34	2	0.3	100
Racial composition of extreme-poverty schools	16	39	41	2	1	100

Note: Definition of the regions: **South:** Alabama, Arkansas, Florida, Georgia, Louisiana, Mississippi, North Carolina, South Carolina, Tennessee, Texas, and Virginia; **Border:** Delaware, Kentucky, Maryland, Missouri, Oklahoma, and West Virginia; **Northeast:** Connecticut, Maine, Massachusetts, New Hampshire, New Jersey, New York, Pennsylvania, Rhode Island, and Vermont; **Midwest:** Illinois, Indiana, Iowa, Kansas, Michigan, Minnesota, Nebraska, North Dakota, Ohio, South Dakota, and Wisconsin; **West:** Arizona, California, Colorado, Montana, Nevada, New Mexico, Oregon, Utah, Washington, and Wyoming. *Note:* Hawaii and Alaska, which have very distinctive populations, are treated separately, and the District of Columbia is treated as a city rather than as a state.

Sources: NCES Common Core of Data (2002–2003); Orfield & Lee (2005).

extreme poverty exists; 90 to 100 percent of the students in such schools were identified as poor in 2002–2003 (NCES, 2003). In the Midwest, Northeast, and South, African Americans represent 50 to over 60 percent of the students who attend the public schools affected by poverty. As for the West, Latina/o students account for 76 percent of the student population who attend extreme-poverty schools. This information helps explain why issues arising from poverty are often associated with minority populations as they experience numerous economic challenges related to the regions where they live and the schools they attend.

Bob Daemmrich/Alamy

Low-Income Status and Free Lunch

Middle-school students enjoy a quick lunch before their next class.

Across the nation, another measure of a family's low-income status is the percentage of students eligible for **free or reduced-price lunch** at school. In 2003, 40 percent of U.S. fourth graders were eligible for the program, including 70 percent of African American students, 71 percent of Latina/o students, and 23 percent of white students (NCES, 2003).

From PRESERVICE to PRACTICE

Where Should I Teach?

As soon as senior Devin McNabb finished his student teaching assignment and physical education degree, he was thrilled to be graduating from college. "Sure, college was fun, but I'm ready to get a job. I need to make some money. Plus, I want to be a football coach," he told his fellow classmates. But his friends also wanted to know where Devin would apply for a job.

"Well, I want to go back to Shoshoni, Wyoming, where I grew up. It's a small, rural town, but it's in the country, not far from national parks. There are a few schools there, a few businesses, and not much else. But most of my family still lives there," Devin explained.

Devin later found out that it would be tough to get a job back in his hometown. He wanted to coach football. In fact, his old high school coach was still there, and it did not look like he was planning to retire soon. To make matters worse, Devin found out from his uncle, who worked at the local school district, that there were no secondary physical education jobs openings for the fall semester. His uncle added, "You could move back anyway and substitute teach and do some ranch-hand work until something opens up in the school district."

Devin was devastated. No way did he want to substitute teach. He had his heart set on moving back to the country and coaching. He grew weary of listening to his education professors spewing data about poor, inner-city schools with large minority populations. There were no minority students at his high school. There were only a handful of English language learners where he student taught. Devin felt uncomfortable with the idea of working in a big city with people he knew very little about, except from TV and a multicultural education class he had taken in college.

Devin's college would soon be offering a job fair for teachers. There would be representatives from a number of school districts across the nation. His friend Lindsay asked if he would like to attend the job fair with her. She was eager to meet district representatives from Las Vegas. She explained to Devin, "I got on the Internet and looked up school districts in Las Vegas. Did you know that some districts offer beginning teachers close to $40,000 in salary?"

"That beats the beginning salary back home by at least $10,000," Devin admitted, but he still had his heart set on Wyoming. Lindsay argued, "But the needs are in the big cities. The students need us there."

Questions for Reflection
1. What do you think Devin should do?
2. Given the diverse opportunities and challenges associated with the teaching profession, what factors should new teachers consider as they apply for their first teaching positions?

In essence, as the proportion of minority students (African Americans and La-tinos) increases, so does the proportion of students eligible for free or reduced-price school lunch. According to a 2003 survey by the National Center for Educa-tional Statistics, 47 percent of African American and 51 percent of Latina/o students attended high-poverty schools, with more than 75 percent of the students eligible for the lunch program. By contrast, only 5 percent of Euro-American stu-dents attended high-poverty schools.

School location also is a factor when identifying student poverty rates. In 2003, minority fourth graders were more likely than Euro-American fourth graders to be eligible for free or reduced-price lunch in schools located in urban, rural, and inner-city (or center-city) areas. Within these school settings, the NCES study also found that minority students were more likely than Euro-American students to be enrolled in high-poverty schools with large concentra-tions of other African American and Latina/o students. For example, 61 percent of African American and 64 percent of Latina/o students attended the highest-poverty urban schools, compared to 12 percent of Euro-American students. At the same time, 38 percent of African American and 39 percent of Latina/o fourth graders attended schools in which 90 percent of the students were members of minority groups (NCES, 2003).

Social and Educational Outcomes of Desegregation

The desegregation of the public schools during the 1960s was driven by law to enable minority students, particularly African American and Latina/o students, to attend middle-class schools with access to better resources, improved program-ming, and highly qualified teachers. Students were bused from their community schools in high-poverty areas in hopes that they would have equal educational opportunities to compete with their white peers.

Over time, research concerning desegregated schools has established that social and educational outcomes have been positive. Findings show that with increased ethnic and racial exposure, the cycle of lifelong segregation in communities and schools can be interrupted, if not broken. Such exposure empowers students' social, as well as cognitive, development as they become more familiar and comfortable living and working with diverse groups, and especially as they challenge the perpetuation of racism within insulated communities and schools (Orfield & Lee, 2005; Kurlaender & Yun, 2001; Wells & Crain, 1994).

Research highlighting the benefits of desegregated schools can also be found in the context of higher education, as illustrated in the study of affirmative action. For example, in *Grutter v. Bollinger*, 539 U.S. 306 (2003), the U.S. Supreme Court ruled in support of affirmative action, and the majority opinion expressed the conviction that all students benefit from the knowledge gained from cross-cultural interactions. According to expert testimony and reports presented in the trial, this evidence established that a diverse student population advances learning and helps prepare all students to take part in a diverse society and workforce (Chang, Witt, Jones, & Hakuta, 2003).

A 2004 review of the desegregation research by Willis Hawley of the University of Maryland (in Orfield & Lee, 2005, p. 42) also reported the following:

- African American and Hispanic students learn somewhat more in schools that are majority white than in schools that are predominantly nonwhite. This ap-pears to be particularly the case for higher-ability African American students.

- The earlier students experience desegregated learning environments, the greater the positive impact on their achievement.
- The integration of schools that remain majority white appears to have no negative effect on white students. However, white students in predominantly nonwhite schools may achieve at lower levels than students from similar socioeconomic backgrounds who attend majority white schools.

What this and other research reveals is that given the economic inequities that affect communities and their schools, segregation will only continue to exacerbate the discrepancies between the educational access, opportunities, and the economic outcomes of students living in poverty and those of students who are middle-class.

PAUSE & REFLECT

In what way has desegregation helped close the achievement gap between minority and mainstream students? Given your own educational experiences, do you believe that desegregated schools can help improve cross-cultural relationships? How so?

Intersections Between Educational Practice and Socioeconomic Status

Ironically, some educational policies, practices, and programs that are useful and effective for teachers and for students preparing to go to college may simultaneously limit access to equal educational opportunities for disadvantaged students. For example, ability grouping, ineffective counseling, unwarranted teacher expectations, and tracking can have a negative effect on some students' academic achievement and on their graduation and college attendance rates. A continuing challenge for schools is to resolve this dilemma, which, like widely divergent funding for school expenditures in different communities, is an outgrowth of differences in socioeconomic status.

Ability Grouping and Tracking of Students

The term **ability grouping** refers to the practice of sorting elementary or secondary students on the basis of their skills into specific groups within a class. **Tracking** is the sorting of secondary students into specific academic curricula, such as vocational, college preparatory, and general education programs. Students are identified and assessed for such placements via standardized tests and teachers' informal assessments, such as ongoing observations and skill demonstrations.

Research shows that as early as the 1920s, there is a correlation or relationship between family income and the levels, or tracks, into which students are grouped in school (Oakes, 1985). In other words, students placed in high-ability groups or in a college preparatory track often have families with high incomes. Students whose families have low incomes are generally tracked in vocational or general education courses of study or in low-ability groups. Children are readily aware that their families' economic status may differ from that of their peers. Being from a different ethnic group, not having the best clothing or the "hottest" technology, or living in a section of the community that others try to avoid can all serve as identifiers of a student's economic status.

Ability grouping and tracking can have a profound effect on student self-perceptions, **teacher expectations**, and instructional design. That is, if poor students are identified as low achievers, teacher expectations regarding their performance may be lower than what they might expect from the other student populations they serve. Given these perceived deficits, how teachers design and deliver instruction to students from low socioeconomic backgrounds can affect students' academic performance and, ultimately, their life outcomes. For example, instruction may be limited to remedial work and rote learning. This kind of instruction often does not meet the goal of equal educational access and equal opportunity to achieve in school.

Placement in low-achieving groups or tracks leaves students vulnerable to the teacher perception that it is the students' *behaviors* that impede their learning, rather than the institutional and educational programming, teacher quality, and resources available to them in the school system. By contrast, college-bound students with high socioeconomic status are expected to excel in well-funded, computer-loaded schools with highly qualified teachers. Those with behavior problems are perceived as merely bored or perhaps even gifted.

Compounding this, students can be poorly counseled, on the basis of their sociocultural, economic status, into educational programs that limit equal educational opportunities and access to the curriculum. English-language learners are often tracked into ESL *and* remedial content-area classes because of their emergent English skills. However, they may possess literacy skills in their native language or in other content areas such as math and science that do not require remediation. In addition, counselors may assume that children from wealthy families should be counseled into a college-track program, whereas children from poor families must pursue vocational education programs.

Student responses to ability grouping and tracking may be life-altering. Consigned to a lower economic and educational standing than that of their peers, these students may fall victim to a **self-fulfilling prophecy;** that is, their teachers' low expectations for their educational success may convince them that they will never do well in school—and so they don't. Teachers may even subscribe to these beliefs, coming to assume that all students living in poverty have little or no interest in learning, have poor skills, and will ultimately fail in school. The curriculum and instruction that such teachers provide may reflect their low expectations. They may not advocate for these students, design rigorous and challenging lessons, or provide high-quality feedback, thus contributing to the students' sense that school is irrelevant to their lives.

Advantages of Students with a High Socioeconomic Background

Charter schools, magnet programs, and voucher-funded private schools provide additional outlets for students from high socioeconomic backgrounds to access specialized college preparatory programs. Wealthier families can help support their college-bound learners through summer school programs and workshops, tutoring, advance placement courses offered at local colleges, and college entrance exam preparation courses. Wealthier families can also purchase computers and other technologies that provide tremendous opportunities for students to develop skills critical to college and career advancement.

Economic status and educational opportunity are intertwined variables that have important ramifications for the maintenance of educational equity. Though well intended, such practices as ability grouping, tracking, and unenlightened counseling have served only to pigeonhole students and, along with unwarranted low expectations communicated by teachers, have predetermined the futures of many students before they even entered high school.

Dropout Rates and Their Relationship to Poverty, Segregation, and Race

Research continues to establish the interrelationships among academic outcomes, poverty, segregation, and race. Graduation rates differ among minority groups. In 2001, slightly over 50 percent of African American, Latina/o, and Native American students graduated from high school, and Asian students had the higher graduation rate at 77 percent. Euro-American students followed at 75 percent (Orfield et al., 2004).

Schools with high rates of poverty (as determined by the proportion of students receiving free and reduced-price lunches) generally have high minority student populations. And urban or central school districts with "minority majority" populations, limited economic resources, and large numbers of unqualified teachers often have the highest dropout rates. Urban high schools with high rates of poverty and large numbers of students who do not graduate have been described as "dropout factories" (Balfanz & Legters, 2004).

Despite the attention given to test-driven initiatives such as the No Child Left Behind Act, high dropout rates continue to plague both the poor and minority groups. This has tremendous ramifications for our society's future workforce and for its technological, global economy. And more important, we cannot begin to measure the trauma the dropout phenomenon inflicts on the lives of individual students and their families.

In the United States, there are 24 central or urban school districts whose responsibility is to teach more than 4.5 million students in predominantly (50 to 90 percent) minority schools (Balfanz & Legters, 2004). Many of these districts include high-poverty schools. For example, in such western cities as Dallas, El Paso, and Santa Ana, 100 percent of Latina/o students attend schools whose student population is a "minority majority." In 15 other school districts, 90 percent of Latina/o students go to schools where over 50 percent of their classmates are members of minority groups (NCES, 2003).

Within these large central and urban districts are segregated communities where more than three-quarters of minority students are enrolled in the public schools. Add to this the effects of poverty and inadequate school resources, and it comes as no surprise that schools in these districts have some of the highest dropout rates. These cities include Chicago, Los Angeles, and New York City.

In comparison, high graduation rates tend to be found in predominantly Euro-American, white suburban school districts with low rates of reduced-price or free-lunch participation. These large suburban school districts include Baltimore County (Maryland), Ft. Bend (outside Houston, Texas), and Jordan (outside Salt Lake City, Utah). It is rare for large numbers of white students to attend predominantly minority schools, although there are a handful of exceptions, such as Dekalb County, Georgia; Long Beach, California; Northside, Texas; and Prince George's County, Maryland (NCES, 2003).

Conversely, minority students are concentrated in urban, central schools, segregated from middle- or upper-income white peers who attend suburban schools. Such communities generally have ample educational resources and can attract qualified teachers who foster a school climate that stresses academic achievement and college preparation.

From PRESERVICE to PRACTICE

Empowerment of a Dropout

Marilee Coles just completed her first year as a second-grade teacher. She and her husband Mark, also a teacher, were excited about having their first summer off. With their savings, they looked forward to turning their unfinished basement into a family room for their two small children before the next winter. Their funds for the project, however, were limited. They worried that they could not afford the bid a professional construction company submitted. With a growing family and a pressing need for more space in their two-bedroom bungalow, Marilee wondered how they could ever afford to get the job done before the next snow fell.

When Marilee mentioned her concerns to a friend at church, her friend Denise recommended that Marilee and her husband hire a young man by the name of Cesar to complete the job. But Cesar worked with a licensed contractor and could not tackle Marilee's basement until after the company's larger jobs were completed. This meant that he worked during the late afternoons and early evenings.

Cesar and his boss offered Marilee and Mark a bid that was within their budget. A contract was signed, and the work began. Cesar redesigned the basement framing, began measuring and cutting the drywall, and constructed the new walls and door frames. Marilee soon learned that Cesar was quick and accurate with his measurements and vision for design. He could multitask, and he made framing suggestions that offered the best use of space for the kids' play area and a small study. Cesar worked "clean" and efficient, never left a mess, and always explained and met the day's goals.

Marilee and Mark soon became friends with Cesar. They learned he was 19 years old and a high school dropout. They were shocked to learn this, because he was such a creative and fast thinker and was a true craftsman. They asked Cesar, "Why did you quit school?" He replied, "I was in the lower-track classes it seems like all of my life. All I remember about high school was doing worksheets and answering problems in my textbooks—and dressing and undressing for gym. We never had computers or small classes. A lot of my classes were taught by substitutes. Nobody talked to me about college. After a while, I just stopped caring about school. My folks didn't go to college either, so they were happy that I became a construction apprentice. That way, I could help them with the rent and my little brother's medical bills. What can I say? High school offered nothing to me, and I guess I had nothing to offer high school."

Marilee and Mark decided to investigate construction management classes offered at a local vocational school. And they wondered about the GED. They planned to talk with Cesar again and learn more about his aspirations. Maybe his company would help support further education for someone who was clearly one of their best employees.

Questions for Reflection

1. Why do you think Cesar lost interest in high school?
2. What stereotypes about dropouts does his experience challenge?
3. What kinds of interventions do you think teachers could utilize to better engage students like Cesar so that they wouldn't drop out?

The No Child Left Behind Act and Educational Equity

Even though it appears that the No Child Left Behind (NCLB) Act initiative seeks to improve low-achieving schools, it does not address the larger challenges facing segregated, poverty-strained communities and schools. The No Child Left Behind Act represents the current trend in the accountability movement (Orstein & Levine, 2006). Such schools are vulnerable to not meeting "adequate yearly progress" test standards and will be identified as failing. The NCLB law requires often segregated, poor, urban school districts to make greater annual progress than affluent suburban schools. Schools that do not make adequate progress must report this to the communities and face, after much scrutiny, the possible closure of the school.

In addition, although securing "highly qualified" teachers is another goal of this law, research reveals that most teachers who work in segregated, poor schools do not intend to remain in the districts for their entire careers. Consequently, NCLB may have a negative impact on the retention of teachers in districts that experience high teacher turnover (Rothstein, 2004). Federal, state, and local leaders need to explore together how best to assist segregated, low-income schools in ways that support equal opportunity and positive educational outcomes, such as examining school funding, program design, and instructional practices.

Implications for Educators

With the link firmly established between low-income communities and low-quality schools that affect the education and long-term income of students, what can educators do to break the cycle of "social reproduction"? Let's examine factors that teachers should consider when making decisions about employment, school programming and practices relevant to equal opportunity, community development, and academic achievement for all learners.

Making Decisions About Employment

New teachers who research the areas where they believe they want to work are the most likely to remain committed to serving diverse communities if they decide to do so. They come prepared to seek ways to pursue academic excellence despite the obstacles of poverty and segregation (Kozol, 2005). Although such urban school districts as Los Angeles and New York City may offer relatively high salaries and incentives for new educators, without the awareness and commitment to the school and community that educational equity requires, your job effectiveness, satisfaction, and even attendance may fall short.

Dealing with Classroom Size

Class size remains an issue that has a major influence on the quality of instruction that a teacher provides. With large classes come less individual and small-group instruction, fewer opportunities to provide feedback to students, limited access to instructional materials and technology, and the need to devote much more time to instructional planning, professional development, and interaction with families. Class size is an important negotiating point for teachers and the unions that represent them.

New teachers are often invited by their administrators to admit additional students to their classrooms. Although accepting more students into a class may seem like an appropriate response, educators must reflect on the ramifications. With larger classes, are instructors able to ensure that all students will receive an equitable and effective educational experience, an experience that will not require the teacher to compromise on expectations, instructional design, and student feedback? No beginning teacher wants to challenge an administrator who seeks to balance the needs of the campuswide community, but new educators can collaborate with administrators, department chairs, and colleagues to keep class sizes from limiting the quality of education they deliver.

Strategies such as designing team-teaching programs, sharing jobs, employing paraprofessionals, and using university clinical teachers and mentoring programs can help minimize the problems associated with a high student-to-teacher ratio. After-school and summer tutoring programs (such as Upward Bound) and early intervention programs (such as Head Start) can offer educational support for students attending overcrowded, low-achieving schools.

Effects of Ability Grouping and Tracking

Instructional practices such as ability grouping and tracking often do not promote educational equity, as we noted earlier. In 1992, the NEA adopted a resolution that denounced the practice of tracking not simply because it groups students according to ability but also because it segregates students along the lines of race, class, and sex. Research shows that tracking and ability grouping have not improved the academic achievement of students with either advanced or low skills (Oakes, 1985).

Not all educators support the elimination of tracking and ability grouping. Supporters of programs for the gifted and talented argue that ability grouping makes it easier for teachers to design instruction for students who can progress quickly. Other proponents of grouping contend that because students possess different levels of academic potential and skills, instruction should be tailored to those different levels of skills and abilities. However, although educational researchers and teachers agree that students have different abilities and needs, the long-term effects of tracking and ability grouping tend to further entrench low teacher expectations and to distance many students from a rigorous, academic curriculum.

Students soon recognize when their school programs are not serving them equitably. They realize when the programs they are enrolled in are not preparing them for college or equipping them for careers of their choice. Thus, it comes as no surprise that students who are continually assigned to low-level classes develop feelings of resentment about schooling and express their defiance in unproductive ways. Or they simply stop attending school.

Bring Communities Together

It becomes imperative, then, that new teachers, who are often "saddled" with teaching low-level classes or groups, begin a dialogue with administrators, chairs, colleagues, and families about how all students can have access to the core curriculum as much as possible. Asking questions about what content objectives and teaching strategies can be used in the classroom can help better shape instructional practice. Asking the students themselves what content areas are relevant to their interests can also help teachers make the "instructional turns" needed to reexamine content integration and methods.

Working more closely with counselors, curriculum specialists, and administrators can help you begin the dialogue about closing the gaps between communities, educational opportunities, and access to resources. By exploring how school programs are delivered and to whom, educators can design policies that ensure that students will have access to a broad range of curriculum choices that introduce them to more learning and life opportunities. Even though confronting the systemic challenges inflicted by a legacy of poverty and segregation is primarily the responsibility of our political leadership, this does not absolve educators, as advocates for their students, from pursuing equal opportunity in the local community and in the classroom. Questioning longstanding practices that research shows perpetuate segregation and class stratification is one way to begin that advocacy.

PAUSE & REFLECT

What forms of tracking have you observed in the public schools? How is tracking useful for students and for classroom teachers? On the other hand, how does tracking promote unequal access to the curriculum and limit students' college and career opportunities?

How can teachers begin to work in a community that is segregated? Why is there a continual disconnect between educators and the families and students they serve? For that matter, why are new teachers resistant to teaching in communities that have the most needs?

One faulty assumption that troubles some educators is the idea that low-income students and their families have no intellectual interests or skills. These educators believe that low-income, minority students bring little or no knowledge to the classroom, at least not the kinds of knowledge sanctioned by the schools. This emphasis on deficits offers justification for educators to lower their expectations for students, while maintaining an uninformed and inaccurate view of low-income minority families and their children. Indeed, given these assumptions, who *would* want to teach in these communities?

Funds of Knowledge

One way to confront these damaging stereotypes is to develop an understanding of communities and families. To begin, educators can adopt an instructional philosophy that is focused on family knowledge as well as classroom knowledge. This student-centered approach can help educators understand the histories of families, which include culture, social networks, language, religion, labor, skills, and other interests and concerns.

By developing their knowledge about families, educators can arrive at a better understanding of what skills students bring to the classroom. These skills, also known as **funds of knowledge,** consist of those historically acquired and accumulated practices (skills and strategies) that are critical to a household's operation and happiness (Moll & González, 2004). Funds of knowledge can be appreciated by

Secondary students using their funds of knowledge by helping a teacher repair her car in the faculty parking lot.

visiting the homes of students, interviewing family members, engaging with community members, and participating in community activities. It is critical for educators working in a segregated community to enter that community. Limiting interactions to those that take place in a classroom cannot help educators and the community to strategize how to interrupt poverty and segregation.

Ethnographic research shows us that funds of knowledge are abundant and diverse among low-income communities and families. For example, families often create social networks with other families, and as they develop social relationships, they exchange resources (Moll et al., 1992). A key characteristic of these exchanges is *reciprocity*. Vélez-Ibáñez (1988) explains that reciprocity represents an "attempt to establish a social relationship on an enduring basis. Whether symmetrical or asymmetrical, the exchange expresses and symbolizes human social interdependence" (p. 142). Each reciprocal exchange among a community of families and friends can reveal specific knowledge and skills in many arenas, including music, art, dance, language translation, culinary practices, fashion design, building renovation, automobile repair, agricultural practices, and business and finance.

Using Funds of Knowledge in the Classroom

According to Tenery (2005), several kinds of funds of knowledge lend themselves to instructional practice:

- *The strategizing household.* To maintain their own economic security, families may pool resources, divide household chores, and trade and exchange goods and services. Students therefore have responsibilities and have expectations placed on them by the community, which can also be mirrored in school leadership settings, such as in student government or classroom situations.

From PRESERVICE to PRACTICE

Excerpts from Martha Tenery's Home Visit: La Visita

As I got out of my Honda Accord holding a manila folder, I wanted nothing more than to be inconspicuous. Instead, I stuck out like a sore thumb: a tall, blonde-haired, blue-eyed Anglo teacher in the middle of a Mexican barrio. With permission from the school district, I had arranged an interview with the parents of one of my students.

I left school alone at 3:30 p.m., armed with an address and a map of the neighborhood for my first home visit. I had never before ventured outside the school into this neighborhood, and I was nervous. Making matters worse, I could not find my student's street and trailer, as spaces were out of numerical order. I stopped and asked, unsure which language to use in addressing community members. As I finally approached the address, a middle-aged Mexican woman in a sleeveless cotton dress pulled back a blue homemade curtain and looked out her window. Two children, my student and a younger child, took turns peeking out.

I wondered what the family would think of me and if they would be suspicious of my motives. I worried that I was imposing on their family time and wondered what to say. This meeting was simply about getting to know them better. I planned to follow up with more interviews later.

By the time I reached the house, the door was already swinging open, and the mother smiled as she invited me in. I introduced myself and consciously allowed the parents to start the conversation. Our talk flowed naturally and centered on background information, medical problems, salaries, and their personal lives. I was impressed with how openly and warmly they received me. Two men were seated in the living room, and they stood to greet me and shake my hand. We exchanged introductions, and I explained that I hoped to be a better teacher from what I learned from them.

María's father, after introducing himself, began telling me about a palace his brother had built in Cholula, just eight blocks from their house. He told María to find the *Selecciones (Reader's Digest)* magazine that featured her uncle. María went to the chest of drawers and rummaged through papers, notebooks, books from Mexico, a *Lengua Española* book, an English workbook, and all kinds of worksheets before coming across the magazine her father had requested. The feature in *Selecciones* told of a palace with fifteen rooms and several staircases built over a period of six years by a man of striking resemblance to María's father. Our conversation evolved into a discussion of other areas of interest in Puebla, tourist sites in Mexico, import and property taxes, and a description of his job. He purchases televisions, radios, stereos, appliances, and clothes—either on sale or used—in Tucson and sells them in Mexico. Consequently, he travels frequently between Mexico and Tucson [to maintain their lives together].

Questions for Reflection

1. In your preservice experiences, have you met with families of students? In what ways can you relate to Martha's experience?
2. Martha and Maria's father talk a lot about his life but don't talk about Maria as a student. Why is it important for Martha, as a teacher, to understand Maria's home life and family history?

- *Domains of knowledge.* Low-income households often confront unstable work situations due to layoffs and unemployment. As a result, families must strategize within a community to find work or exchange labor for goods and services. Families' specific domains of knowledge, such as construction and home repair, can be developed into hands-on instructional lessons that incorporate mathematics and science.

- *Interactional patterns.* Large families, combined households, and temporary guests can result in adults cohabitating in a single residence to meet rental or mortgage expenses. Because families rely on social networks to adapt to such challenges as unemployment and child care, maintaining positive social relations is an important part of daily life. Thus, youth engage in cross-generational relationships with parents and relatives, while assisting with such household responsibilities as cooking, cleaning, child care, yard work, home repairs, and animal care. These skills can be used in instructional designs that emphasize cooperative learning, group projects and presentations, hands-on activities, and the development of leadership and peer mentoring skills informed by interactional patterns taking place at home.

- *Cultural practices.* Within the intimacy of family households, cultural traditions are evident in such forms as language, literacy practices (reading, writing, and media use), as well as cultural and religious customs. These practices affirm families' cultural identity and solidarity. Family traditions such as coming-of-age celebrations (quinceañeras) and family visits (visitas de respeto) offer a feeling of unity, tradition, and cultural maintenance (Tenery, 2005). Preserving native language, religion, and traditions helps families retain a connection to their homelands and to relatives who still reside there. Instructional strategies that integrate or introduce histories, language, and culturally relevant content to students can help engage them in learning that is pertinent to their knowledge base.

Teacher educators often highlight the importance of parent outreach and collaboration. Teachers have opportunities to work positively within communities because of their teacher preparation, knowledge, and ability to interact closely and consistently with students and their families. University researchers and community activists do not always have such long-term access.

Therefore, teachers must use these opportunities to collaborate within segregated communities by conducting home visits to explore families' funds of knowledge. As trust develops, teachers can plan instruction based on strengths found in the homes to better meet the needs of students and community.

Classroom instruction that is designed in ways that are relevant to the students' domains of knowledge, cultural practices, and interactional patterns is significant to the lives of students and can also be integrated within a school's core curriculum. By implementing a funds-of-knowledge approach to family outreach, teachers can become better informed about the many aspects of student and family life. For example, a student may be a caregiver, translator, dancer, and DJ. A parent may be a wife, mother, aunt, seamstress, Catholic, and household bookkeeper. Home and school interviews and observations can empower teachers to dispel previously held assumptions about low-income, segregated communities. By identifying students' funds of knowledge, educators can confront stereotypes regarding race, culture, and poverty within their own curriculum.

SUMMARY

This chapter discusses the challenges associated with providing equal educational opportunities for all learners. Although the ideal of equal opportunity is for all people to be able to pursue the education, occupation, or economic status that they choose, factors such as racism, poverty, and segregation have interfered with the realization of such goals. The interconnectedness of racism, poverty, and segregation also affect the educational access of minority students, many of whom live in low-income communities and attend school there. With severely limited educational resources, these schools struggle to deliver a college preparatory curriculum within programs that tend to track, or group, many students in low-level or vocational courses of study. Staffed by teachers who hold low expectations for stu-

dents, these segregated schools do not offer them the benefits of programming and interactions that middle-class students experience in desegregated schools.

Strategies that new educators can consider when seeking employment in low-income, segregated school settings include researching and posing questions to administrators, department chairs, and colleagues about program design, class size, and resource access. Team teaching, job sharing, mentoring, and tutoring can help provide better instruction to students with the greatest needs. Interacting within the community using a funds-of-knowledge approach to family outreach can also help establish rapport with students, as well as inform teachers how to design instruction that capitalizes on student knowledge and affirms cultural practices.

DISCUSSION QUESTIONS

1. How has the United States responded to the need to provide equal educational opportunities to segregated communities? How do the educational experiences in low-income segregated communities differ from those available in more affluent, mainstream communities?

2. In what ways does poverty affect a community of learners? How does the No Child Left Behind Act support students' access to an equitable education? How does it constrain that access?

3. Compare and contrast regional differences in the percentage of minority students enrollment and in socioeconomic status. How do these differences affect diverse students' access to educational resources and master teachers?

4. How do educational practices such as tracking promote or detract from students' equal educational access to the curriculum and to career opportunities?

5. What are funds of knowledge? Describe an example of such "funds" that you have become aware of as a consequence of your own experiences in the community where you live. How can a funds-of-knowledge approach to parent and student outreach and curriculum development help close the achievement gap between minority and mainstream students?

ACTIVITIES

1. Read and explore the work on tracking done by Jeannie Oakes, a professor at the University of California at Los Angeles. Create a poster board that highlights her key findings and suggestions about multitracking and year-round schooling.

2. Interview two or three public school teachers. Describe their experiences with tracking. How do they differentiate the curriculum to ensure that all students have access to it? What do they see as the strengths and weaknesses of tracking?

3. Research and identify the most recent graduation rates of three states across the country. Consult the National Center for Educational Statistics website at http://nces.ed.gov. Compare and contrast your findings. Describe some of the factors that contribute to these differences.

4. With permission from a school principal and family members, conduct a funds-of-knowledge home visit with a student's family. Generate an interview and a two- or three-page report based on your findings.

REVIEW QUESTIONS

Multiple Choice Questions

1 _____ refers to the idea that anyone in a group has the chance to pursue the lifestyle, status, or occupation they choose.

A. Meritocracy
B. Liberty
C. Equal opportunity
D. Empowerment

2 About what percentage of public school students today are from a racial minority?

A. 20 percent
B. 30 percent
C. 40 percent
D. 50 percent

3 Regarding patterns of student populations in public schools since the 1970s, which one of the following statements is TRUE?

A. African American and Euro-American populations have grown slowly.
B. Latino and Asian populations have grown slowly.
C. Euro-American populations have grown slowly.
D. Latino and Asian populations have increased rapidly.

4 Regarding regional diversity in public schools, which of the following statements is FALSE?

A. The two most populous regions, the West and the South, teach a combined 54 percent of the nation's public school students.
B. Asians outnumber African American students in the West.
C. Alaska is the region with the highest enrollment of Native Americans.
D. Schools in the Northeast are the least likely to be culturally diverse or biracial.

5 Among schools where a very high proportion of the students live in poverty, about what percentage of the student population is either Latino or African American?

A. 50
B. 65
C. 75
D. 80

6 Other factors being equal, which of the following children is LEAST likely to be receiving a free or reduced-cost lunch at school?

A. Adrianna, who attends a suburban public school
B. Bobby, who attends an inner-city public school
C. Carlos, who attends a rural public school
D. Darlene, who attends a central-city school

7 During which decade did the most intensive effort to desegregate public schools occur?

A. 1950s
B. 1960s
C. 1970s
D. 1980s

8 The secondary students in Monroe County School District are sorted into specific academic curricula called "vocational," "general education," and "college prep." Which educational practice is the Monroe County District using?

A. Ability grouping
B. Mainstreaming
C. Scaffolding
D. Tracking

9 Regarding the No Child Left Behind initiative and educational equity, which of the following statements is FALSE?

A. Research shows that many teachers working in segregated, poverty-strained schools do not intend to remain in these districts for their long-term careers.
B. The NCLB should have a positive impact on the retention of teachers in districts that experience high teacher turnover.
C. Compared to those schools with more resources, segregated, poverty-strained schools are more at risk of failing to meet standards for adequate yearly progress.
D. The NCLB law often requires segregated, poor, urban school districts to make greater annual progress than affluent suburban schools.

10 Regarding ethnographic research on funds of knowledge among low-income communities and families, which of the following statements is FALSE?

A. Funds of knowledge among these groups are abundant and diverse.
B. Families often create social networks with other families that involve the exchange of resources.
C. A key characteristic of familial exchanges is reciprocity.
D. Familial exchanges are mostly symmetrical, rather than asymmetrical.

READING
CRITICALLY

THEME *Crime, Medicine, and Ethics*

UNIT
4

Purestock/Alamy

Understanding
ARGUMENTS

✳ Why Do You Need to Know This?

IN THIS CHAPTER, YOU WILL LEARN

- About reading controversial text
- To differentiate between prescriptive and descriptive writing
- To map arguments
- To distinguish between fact and opinion statements
- To determine the main types of support for arguments: facts, reasons, examples, testimony, and counterargument
- To understand graphics: distinguish fact from opinion in visual material

READING STUDY STRATEGIES

- Techniques for reading essays, newspaper articles, editorials, research studies, and online sources

VOCABULARY STRATEGIES

- Understanding and identifying connotation and denotation
- Recognizing loaded language
- Increasing your discipline-specific vocabulary: criminal justice and law

How does a good reader approach different types of reading?

Reading textbooks or any material for which the author's purpose is to inform requires the comprehension skills you have acquired so far. But what about readings in which authors take a position on an issue and then proceed to defend that position? Understanding arguments heightens your skills of critical reading and thinking: analysis, synthesis, and evaluation. Learning how to "map" an argument helps you lay out the structure of a persuasive reading, react to the supporting arguments, and hone or refine your own points of view.

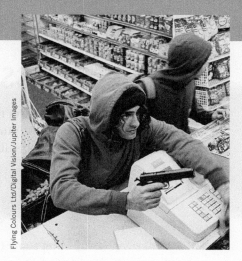

"INJUSTICE ANYWHERE IS A THREAT TO JUSTICE EVERYWHERE."

MARTIN LUTHER KING, JR. (1929–1968) U.S. civil rights leader and Nobel Prize Winner

What it means to be an "informed citizen" has many interpretations. The informed citizen searches for information, digests it, and actively participates in the community. One of the foundations of a civilized society is a fair and equitable justice system. Your education as an informed citizen will help you assess the pros and cons of the U.S. justice system. While this system is not perfect, there is at least some concern and support for its continual improvement. As DNA testing moves to the forefront of forensic evidence in legal trials, we learn more about culpability in crime. Is everyone in our prisons guilty of the crimes for which they are convicted? To what degree are those convicted falsely accused? What accounts for the phenomenon whereby an individual confesses to a crime he or she did not commit?

CHECK YOUR PRIOR KNOWLEDGE

Jot down some facts you know about our system of crime and punishment. Do not edit your list—just brainstorm!

_____

_____

_____

_____

_____

_____

_____

_____

_____

_____

_____

_____

_____

_____

✤ PRE-ASSESSMENT

ONLINE SCIENCE MAGAZINE

Read the passage and then answer the questions that follow. Don't worry if you do not know what all the terms mean yet. The purpose of this Pre-Assessment is to find out how much you already know about the reading skills and strategies introduced in this chapter.

Innocent Suspects Confess Under Pressure
by the LiveScience Staff

1   A new study finds that some people under <u>interrogation</u> will confess to crimes they did not commit, either to end the questioning or because they become convinced they did it.

2   An unrelated study last year found it is fairly easy to create false memories in people in a lab setting.

3   Lack of sleep and isolation contribute to false confessions, the scientists say in the new study, announced today. A suspect's mental status and lack of education play roles.

4   Police are often not qualified to judge truth versus deception, the researchers argue. In the latest issue of the journal *Psychological Science in the Public Interest,* the scientists call for videotaping of confessions so they can be properly analyzed by experts.

5   "Modern police interrogations involve the use of high-impact social influence tech-niques [and] sometimes people under the influence of certain techniques can be induced to confess to crimes they did not commit," write Saul Kassin of Williams College and Gisli Gudjonsson of King's College, University of London.

6   A University of Michigan study last year reached the same conclusion in analyzing 328 cases since 1989 in which DNA-exonerated [*sic*] defendants were convicted of rape, murder, and other serious crimes.

SOURCE: "Innocent Suspects Confess Under Pressure," by LiveScience Staff, July 26, 2005, © TechMediaNetwork 2012. All Rights Reserved. Reprinted by permission.

COMPREHENSION CHECK

Circle the best answer to the following questions.

Reading Comprehension

1   **What is the main idea of this passage?**
   A. The University of Michigan study reached the same conclusions as this study.
   B. Scientists have called for the videotaping of confessions as a result of this study.
   C. A new study finds some people under interrogation will confess to crimes they did not commit, either to end the questioning or because they become convinced they did it.
   D. A suspect's mental status and lack of education play a role in false confessions.

2 **Why have scientists called for videotaping of confessions so these confessions can be properly analyzed by experts?**

A. Police are not qualified to provide expert opinions on truth telling or deception of those interviewed.
B. Further studies need be conducted on this subject.
C. Scientists want to find out why people confess to crimes they have not committed.
D. A second study needs to be undertaken to double-check the results of the first study.

3 **What is a reasonable inference you can draw about the following sentence from paragraph 3?**

Lack of sleep and isolation contribute to false confessions, the scientists say in the new study, announced today.

A. Police exhaust suspects to make them confess.
B. Confessions obtained under compromising conditions are not accurate.
C. Suspects are tired of having to confess.
D. Confessions are not reliable.

4 **What type of support is used in the sentence in question 3?**

A. Facts
B. Reasons
C. Testimony
D. Examples

5 **Is this statement from paragraph 4 fact or opinion?**

Police are often not qualified to judge truth versus deception, the researchers argue.

A. Fact
B. Opinion
C. Both fact and opinion
D. Neither fact nor opinion

6 **Is this statement from paragraph 5 fact or opinion?**

Modern police interrogations involve the use of high-impact social influence techniques [and] sometimes people under the influence of certain techniques can be induced to confess to crimes they did not commit.

A. Fact
B. Opinion
C. Both fact and opinion
D. Neither fact nor opinion

(Continued)

7 What is the *main* type of support used in the statement in question 6?

A. Facts

B. Reasons

C. Testimony

D. Examples

8 This is a summary of a real research study. Original research studies include several sections: an abstract of the study, an introduction, a description of the study's participants and the method used to gather data, a presentation of the results of the study, and a discussion of those results and their implications for the discipline. What parts of the original study are probably used in this article?

A. Subjects and method

B. Hypothesis and results

C. The abstract and hypothesis

D. Discussion and abstract

Vocabulary Comprehension

9 What does the word *interrogation* mean in paragraph 1?

A. Interruption

B. Threat

C. Condemnation

D. Questioning

10 What is the connotation of the word *interrogation* as in question 9?

A. A session of questions that a person questioned considers secret or personal

B. A session of questions where answers are viewed as doubtful

C. A joke or jest

D. A session of questions that is lighthearted

 READING STUDY STRATEGIES

HOW TO READ A VARIETY OF SOURCES

A successful college reader adjusts his or her approach depending on the type of reading that is assigned. You are now familiar with the kinds of textbooks that make up the majority of assigned reading for college-level courses. You also have developed skills to enhance your understanding of literature. Reading essays, newspaper articles and editorials, and research studies from professional journals require specific reading strategies. Understanding and applying these strategies will help you understand the key points of each of these types of reading.

How to Read an Essay

Reading an essay is like reading a textbook in that the reader must determine the topic, main idea, structure, and relationships between ideas. In an essay, the main idea is called a **thesis.** Every detail in the essay functions to support the thesis. As you know, not every paragraph of an essay has an important point. Some paragraphs function to clarify or expand upon a point made in an earlier paragraph (see the discussion of clarification pattern of organization in Chapter 2). In an essay, an author's purpose may be to inform, to instruct, to persuade, or even to entertain.

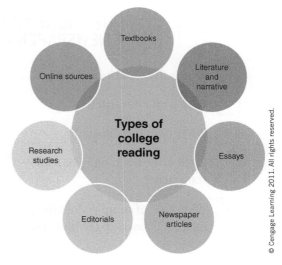

QUICK TIPS QUESTIONS TO ASK WHEN READING AN ESSAY

☑ Why is the topic important?

☑ Who wrote the essay?

☑ Where was it published?

☑ What is the author's thesis?

☑ What is the author's purpose: to inform, instruct, persuade, or entertain?

☑ What type of support does the author include to back up the thesis?

☑ How does the information in the essay affect your understanding of other information about the topic?

☑ Could the essay be biased as a result of who the writer is or where the essay was published?

How to Read a Newspaper Article

Newspaper articles provide excellent examples of highlighting the most important point. A newspaper article contains a **lead statement** that summarizes the most important points of the article in the first line. Journalists are taught to put the lead at the beginning of an article, so a reader immediately gets the key point at the very beginning of the story. The main idea, then, is explicitly stated in the opening of the article. The rest of the article functions to provide supporting details and explanation.

What are the lead statements in the online newspaper articles in this chapter's Pre- and Post-Assessments? Application 2 also is a newspaper article. Can you locate the lead statement in that reading?

QUICK TIPS QUESTIONS TO ASK WHEN READING A NEWSPAPER ARTICLE

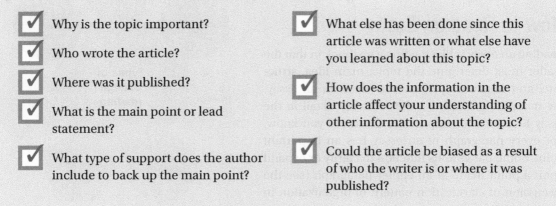

- ☑ Why is the topic important?
- ☑ Who wrote the article?
- ☑ Where was it published?
- ☑ What is the main point or lead statement?
- ☑ What type of support does the author include to back up the main point?

- ☑ What else has been done since this article was written or what else have you learned about this topic?
- ☑ How does the information in the article affect your understanding of other information about the topic?
- ☑ Could the article be biased as a result of who the writer is or where it was published?

How to Read a Newspaper Editorial

An **editorial** is a commentary on an issue, usually placed in the op-ed section of a newspaper. In the op-ed (opinion-editorial) section, editors and commentators provide opinion articles expressing their points of view on the current topics reported by the press. Editorials attempt to persuade readers to accept a particular point of view. In contrast, news stories function to inform and present the information objectively, or without apparent bias. Because the intent of an editorial is to persuade, the author takes a side on a controversial issue. A **controversial issue** is one for which there are at least two primary points of view, or sides, a person can hold. Like reading essays, reading editorials requires you to find the thesis (if it is directly stated) and the supporting details, or supporting arguments, that support the thesis.

QUICK TIPS QUESTIONS TO ASK WHEN READING AN EDITORIAL

- ☑ Why is the topic important?
- ☑ Who wrote the editorial?
- ☑ Where was it published?
- ☑ What is the author's point of view?
- ☑ What type of support does the author include to back up his or her point of view?

- ☑ How does the information in the editorial affect your understanding of other information about the topic?
- ☑ Could the editorial be biased as a result of who the writer is or where the editorial was published?

How to Read a Research Study

In college coursework, especially in the social and natural sciences, information is presented to the reader as a research study. For the general public, the results of a study often are condensed and abbreviated, as in the Pre- and Post-Assessments in this chapter. The authors of these articles, from online magazines such as *Live Science* and other sources, report the main points of a study. These sources present material in a journalistic fashion and, therefore, do not bury the lead statement. Also, these summarized newspaper studies have an informative rather than persuasive purpose. To excel in college reading, it is necessary to know and understand the structure of research studies and how to find the details that support the key point.

Research studies follow a similar approach insofar as they usually begin with an **abstract** that is a summary of key findings. This general overview is followed by more detailed information in the method and results sections. The discussion section at the end of a study discusses the implications—what the results imply, or suggested outcomes of the research. In other words, the author draws conclusions for the reader based on the evidence presented from the research.

THE STRUCTURE OF A RESEARCH STUDY

Research studies for both the natural sciences and the social sciences have the same structure.

- The **abstract** is a summary of the key points of the study. The abstract contains the **hypothesis,** or the expected findings the researchers anticipated or predictions tested in the study, as well as their purpose for conducting the study.

- The **introduction** provides background knowledge for the reader and explains the motivation of the researcher or research team in conducting the study. This section also contains both a review of the results of previous research studies about the topic as well as the hypothesis (prediction to be tested).

- The **method** section outlines, in sequence, the steps of the process used in conducting the study; it also discusses the participants (subjects) who were involved in the study and how the data were gathered.

- The **results** section describes in detail what the researcher(s) found. It often presents data in statistical format and may feature charts, tables, or other graphics.

- The **discussion** section interprets the statistical information in the results section and discusses the findings of the study based on the hypothesis, previous research related to the topic, and implications and suggestions for further research to be conducted.

- The **references** section, which concludes the research article, lists the sources used actively in the study. Some research articles also include a bibliography (list of materials available in print, online, or in other media formats) of background readings related to the topic.

HOW TO APPROACH RESEARCH STUDY READING

1. Read the abstract to get an overview of the study. This allows you to preview the study.

2. Read the introduction to clarify the subject of the study. Focus on the last paragraph or so, where the hypothesis is usually discussed.

3. Read the discussion section to gain understanding of how the research concluded and the overall findings of the study.

4. Go back and read the methods section. This information is very detailed and contains all the steps in the research process.

5. Read the results for major findings. Unless you are proficient in statistics, this section is very dense; read for an overall grasp of the outcomes rather than for mathematical details, unless you are reading the study for a class that requires detailed knowledge of the results.

6. Carefully reread the discussion to solidify the information and implications (what the findings suggest) of the study.

7. If your purpose for reading the study is more specific, go back and read the entire document again. Take notes.

QUICK TIPS
QUESTIONS TO ASK WHEN READING A RESEARCH STUDY

- ☑ Why is the study important?
- ☑ Who wrote the study?
- ☑ Where was it published?
- ☑ What is the hypothesis?
- ☑ Are the methods appropriate to the research?
- ☑ How does the information in the study affect your understanding of other information about the topic?

- ☑ Are the results significant?
- ☑ What are the implications of the study? (See the discussion section.)
- ☑ What else has been done since this study was conducted or what else have you learned about this topic?
- ☑ Could the data be biased as a result of the methods used, who the researchers are, or where the study was published?

How to Read Online Sources

Reading research suggests that reading online sources is different from reading print materials. Unlike reading print sources, reading online is "nonlinear." When you read a book or an article in print, you follow a reading sequence—beginning at the start of the text and progressing through the text systematically. However, when you read information online, you frequently jump around from source to source using hyperlinks that direct you to a different Web page. To read effectively online you need to be able to

- Use background knowledge to focus on the task (see Chapter 1).

- Locate information.

- Pose appropriate questions (see Chapter 1).

- Differentiate between fact and opinion (see Chapter 7).

- Think critically—analyze, synthesize and evaluate online material. (For more on critical thinking, see Chapter 8).

- Be familiar with changing technology and have some proficiency in navigating the Web.

Reading online and sifting between good and poor material requires some thought; not all online sources are created equal for academic reference. There is a difference between reading a blog on a certain topic and reading research conducted by an authority. How can you tell if an online source is reliable or not?

USING APPROPRIATE ONLINE SOURCES IN RESEARCH

To be an effective learner, you need to differentiate between academic and credible sources and those that express and opinion and are not necessarily factual or verifiable content. Just as you would assess the credibility of an author of a print source, you should also assess the credibility of an online source. These two considerations are important because they influence your judgment about whether the argument is a good source to cite for college research. If the author has authority by virtue of his or her background, experience, or expertise, then this authority lends some weight to the author's point of view and supporting arguments. If the author does not have the background, experience, or expertise to pass judgment on the issue, then this weakens the author's argument.

Here are the different types of sites you will find on the Internet:

- **.com sites:** These are commercial sites that may or may not provide reliable information.

- **.gov sites:** These are government Web sites that can be relied on to provide factual or reliable information.

- **.org sites:** These are sites originally intended for non-profit organizations. While these sites may provide reliable information, the information may be biased, as in a political Web site.

- **.net sites:** These sites were originally created for organizations involved in network technologies, such as an Internet service provider. Now, however, .net can include general-purpose domain sites. Verify the source.

- **.edu sites:** These sites are intended for educational institutions. These sites are of academic origin, but they may be biased.

However, just because you find a site that may look credible and reliable, you will need to critically evaluate the content of the site to make sure.

QUICK TIPS   FIVE STEPS TO EVALUATING AN ONLINE SOURCE FOR QUALITY

- **Type of site:** Check the type of site—is it a .com site, a .edu site, a .net site, or a .gov site? Is the publishing source reliable or not?

- **Author's credibility:** Check the author—is the author a credible voice?—is he or she an expert in the field or an authority whom you can believe? Is the author biased? Is there a biographical note about the author to help you make this judgment?

- **References:** Does the piece cite credible references? Credible sources cite reliable references.

- **Content:** Is the content reliable? Is the content accurate? Can the information be verified or proven?

- **Currency:** Is the information current? Can you find date references to verify the currency and accuracy of the information?

READING CONTROVERSIAL TEXT

In the first six chapters of *Mindscapes,* you learned new strategies to read and determine what is important to learn in college-level texts across the disciplines. In this chapter and in Chapter 8, you will learn techniques to delve even further into a reading in order to make judgments about it rather than simply understand it. In order to do this, you must use everything you have learned so far in this textbook. To read critically, you learned to employ the following steps.

1. Determine the topic.

2. Determine the pattern of organization.

3. Determine the author's most important point, or thesis.

4. Determine the supporting points that back up the core idea.

Now you will apply this method to controversial text—text in which a point of view about an issue is presented.

Prescriptive Versus Descriptive Writing

If the author's purpose is to persuade the reader to accept a particular position about an issue or to move the reader to a particular action, then that author gives the reader a *prescription,* so to speak. The author *prescribes* a stance, perspective, or course of action. This type of writing is called **prescriptive**—just as a doctor writes a prescription to make you better, so a writer outlines a *prescription* that, in her or his opinion, will address an issue in such a way as to make it better. You can recognize prescriptive writing from the use of phrases such as *we should, we ought to, we need to,* and so on. These are phrases that indicate a value judgment or opinion about an issue. Prescriptive writing is persuasive writing.

In contrast, if an author presents information about an issue without taking a particular side—presents just the facts and no personal opinion about the facts—he or she is *not* trying to convince or persuade. **Descriptive** or informative writing is used in a newspaper article or research study. The author writes to describe a situation or to inform the reader about something. There is no prescription for addressing the issue or proposal made for a course of action. The author may report on research that may lead to a point of view, but the author of the article writes objectively—without bias—and lets the results of the study speak for themselves. Discussion or interpretation sections of a research study, however, do present opinion, specifically that of the researcher or research team. Descriptive writing is informative writing.

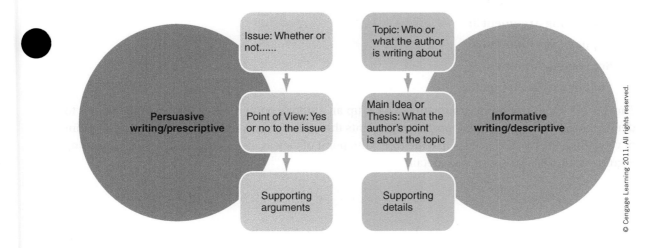

Some of the terms and concepts discussed thus far in this book are referred to differently in prescriptive writing. For example, the topic is called the **issue.** Similarly, the thesis or main idea is referred to as the **author's point of view.** Supporting details are called **supporting arguments** or **premises.**

An issue (or topic) is the subject of the debate. It is useful to use the phrase *whether or not . . .* when formulating the issue of a reading, so that the thesis, or author's point of view, is easier to identify. For example, if the issue at hand is whether or not gun control laws should be strengthened, an author's point of view is either (1) yes, gun control laws should be strengthened, or (2) no, gun control laws should not be strengthened. It is worth your time to carefully consider the issue in an argument to determine both the author's point of view and the support he or she presents for that point of view.

Mapping Arguments

To be a critical reader and thinker and to take your understanding of a reading to the next level, you need to develop skills to read and understand arguments. In an argument, the author's paramount purpose is always to persuade. The author's secondary purpose may be to inform, instruct, or entertain; his or her primary purpose, however, is to convince you to agree with his or her thesis or point of view. In arguments, the point of view has to do with the side the author takes on the issue, or what the topic of the argument is. The author then defends his or her point of view with supporting arguments.

To outline or represent the key point in an argument, follow this template.

Mapping Arguments

1. **Issue:** Whether or not . . . [summarize the topic of the argument]

2. **Author's Point of View:** the author's conclusion(s) about the issue

   Supporting Argument 1:

   Supporting Argument 2:

   Supporting Argument 3:

   Supporting Argument 4:

   Supporting Argument 5:

   Supporting Argument 6:

There may or may not be six arguments to back up an author's point of view; it is up to the reader to determine how many major supporting arguments the author makes to substantiate his or her point of view. Remember: The issue is like the topic; the point of view is like the main idea; the supporting arguments are like the supporting details.

Thinking It Through MAPPING AN ARGUMENT

The Innocence Project, started by lawyer Barry Scheck, uses law students to research criminal cases for death row convicts. The research uses DNA testing, previously unavailable when these inmates were convicted of their crimes, to exonerate, or to find those convicts not guilty, *after* conviction. The passage has been translated into an argument mapping format. Notice how clearly the major points and author's point of view or conclusion about the issue are represented in this method of note taking.

The Causes of Wrongful Conviction
by the Staff of the Innocence Project

1   As the pace of DNA exonerations has grown across the country in recent years, wrongful convictions have revealed disturbing fissures and trends in our criminal justice system. Together, these cases show us how the criminal justice system is broken—and how urgently it needs to be fixed.

2   We should learn from the system's failures. In each case where DNA has proven innocence beyond doubt, an overlapping array of causes has emerged—from mistakes to misconduct to factors of race and class.

Countless Cases

3   Those exonerated by DNA testing aren't the only people who have been wrongfully convicted in recent decades. For every case that involves DNA, there are thousands that do not.

4   Only a fraction of criminal cases involve biological evidence that can be subjected to DNA testing, and even when such evidence exists, it is often lost or destroyed after a conviction. Since they don't have access to a definitive test like DNA, many wrongfully convicted people have a slim chance of ever proving their innocence.

Common Causes

5   Here you will find further information about seven of the most common causes of wrongful convictions:

- Eyewitness Misidentification
- Unvalidated or Improper Forensic Science
- False Confessions/Admissions
- Government Misconduct
- Informants or Snitches
- Bad Lawyering

6   These factors are not the only causes of wrongful conviction. Each case is unique and many include a combination of the above issues. Review our case profiles to learn how the common causes of wrongful convictions have affected real cases and how these injustices could have been prevented.

7   To stop these wrongful convictions from continuing, we must fix the criminal justice system. The Innocence Commission is a reform that can help identify and address the fundamental flaws in the criminal justice system that lead to wrongful convictions.

SOURCE: http://www.innocenceproject.org/understand/

Example of Mapping Arguments
1. **Issue: Whether or not . . .** *we need to fix our justice system*
2. **Author's Point of View (conclusion about the issue):** *Our justice system needs to be fixed.* (first and last paragraph)

(Continued)

Supporting Argument 1: *We should learn from the system's failures.*

Supporting Argument 2: *Those exonerated by DNA testing aren't the only people who have been wrongfully convicted in recent decades.*

Supporting Argument 3: *Only a fraction of criminal cases involve biological evidence that can be subjected to DNA testing, and even when such evidence exists, it is often lost or destroyed after a conviction.*

Supporting Argument 4: *There are many other causes of wrongful convictions.*

All of these arguments directly support the conclusion (thesis) that the justice system needs to be reformed. All of these arguments rely on fact as a basis of support.

On Your Own MAPPING AN ARGUMENT

With a partner or individually as your instructor assigns, mark the text of the following passage from the Innocence Project Web site. Read to find and mark the author's point of view and the major arguments that support that point of view. Then use the mapping arguments template to outline the major arguments in support of the point of view.

Government Misconduct
by the Staff of the Innocence Project

1   Some wrongful convictions are caused by honest mistakes. But in far too many cases, the very people who are responsible for ensuring truth and justice—law enforcement officials and prosecutors—lose sight of these obligations and instead focus solely on securing convictions.

2   The cases of wrongful convictions uncovered by DNA testing are filled with evidence of negligence, fraud or misconduct by prosecutors or police departments.

3   While many law enforcement officers and prosecutors are honest and trustworthy, criminal justice is a human endeavor and the possibility for negligence, misconduct and corruption exists. Even if one officer of every thousand is dishonest, wrongful convictions will continue to occur.

4   DNA exonerations have exposed official misconduct at every level and stage of a criminal investigation.

5   Common forms of misconduct by law enforcement officials include:

- Employing suggestion when conducting identification procedures
- Coercing false confessions

- Lying or intentionally misleading jurors about their observations
- Failing to turn over exculpatory evidence to prosecutors
- Providing incentives to secure unreliable evidence from informants

6   Common forms of misconduct by prosecutors include:

- Withholding exculpatory evidence from defense
- Deliberately mishandling, mistreating or destroying evidence
- Allowing witnesses they know or should know are not truthful to testify
- Pressuring defense witnesses not to testify
- Relying on fraudulent forensic experts
- Making misleading arguments that overstate the probative value of testimony

Necessary Oversight

7   We need to find solutions to fix these problems. One way to put checks on the enormous power of prosecutors and law enforcement officials would be to establish **criminal justice reform commissions.**

SOURCE: http://www.innocenceproject.org/understand/Government-Misconduct.php

1. **Issue:** _____

_____

2. **Author's Point of View (conclusion about the issue):** _____

_____

   Supporting Argument 1: _____

_____

_____

   Supporting Argument 2: _____

_____

_____

   Supporting Argument 3: _____

_____

_____

   Supporting Argument 4: _____

_____

_____

If you determined that the major arguments in this passage support the point of view that governmental misconduct in criminal prosecutions need reform, you are correct.

Fact and Opinion

Determining the issue, point of view, and supporting arguments is the first step to understanding persuasive writing. But to be a critical reader, you also need to recognize different types of supporting arguments and begin to evaluate their strengths and weaknesses. You need to consider the effectiveness of an author's argument by understanding the difference between fact and opinion.

On one level, fact versus opinion is an easy concept to grasp. After all, a **fact** is something that can be proven; an **opinion** is one person's belief, or something that cannot be proven. The truth is that statistics, or factual results in the form of numbers, so often used to back up an argument and support an author's perspective, can be used in a variety of ways and in a variety of forums, depending on how they are interpreted. For our purpose, facts are straightforward, provable, and documented pieces of information—facts exist, are known to exist, or can be verified, or proven, to exist. Statistics are facts; how they are interpreted is often a matter of opinion, as they are often used to convince a reader of a point of view.

Opinions, on the other hand, are someone's *interpretation* of facts. Opinion statements cannot be verified or proven. You may well agree with someone's opinion; you may even see the opinion as obvious and true. But an opinion *can* be debated. In other words, someone can argue the opposite point of view, or counterargue, and still, in his or her opinion, be "right."

Opinions involve a value judgment, and they are often signaled by words or phrases such as *in my opinion, the truth is, I think, we should, we must,* or *we ought to.* All of these phrases indicate an opinion, regardless of how convincing that opinion is. Furthermore, anything that has not yet happened must be opinion because it cannot be verified, even if it seems very likely. Thus, projections about population growth in the year 2050 are opinions, even if they are based on reasonable deductions and are mathematically probable. "Probable" is not fact, but opinion.

QUICK TIPS DIFFERENCES BETWEEN FACTS AND OPINIONS

Facts	Opinions
☑ Can be proven or verified	☑ Are someone's interpretation of facts
☑ May be statistics, but their *interpretation* is opinion	☑ Involve a value judgment
	☑ Are signaled by words and phrases like *the truth is, I think, we ought to, we should,* etc.

On Your Own RECOGNIZING FACT AND OPINION

Put an *F* next to the statements that are facts. Put an *O* next to the statements that are opinions. Put an *F/O* next to statements that contain both fact and opinion. The first three are done for you as examples.

_F_ 1. Snitches contribute to wrongful convictions in 15 percent of cases.

_O_ 2. Forensic scientists and prosecutors presented fraudulent, exaggerated, or otherwise tainted evidence to the judge or jury, which led to the wrongful conviction.

_F/O_ 3. . . . more innocent people gain their freedom through postconviction testing. They are not proof, however, that our system is righting itself.

_____ 4. The average sentence served by DNA exonerees has been 12 years.

_____ 5. The common themes that run through these cases cannot be ignored and continue to plague our criminal justice system.

_____ 6. Exonerations have been won in 31 states and Washington, D.C.

_____ 7. These stories are becoming more familiar as more innocent people gain their freedom through postconviction testing.

_____ 8. False confessions are another leading cause of wrongful convictions. Twenty-five percent of cases involve a false confession or incriminating statement made by the defendant.

_____ 9. Whenever snitch testimony is used, the Innocence Project recommends that the judge instruct the jury that most snitch testimony is unreliable, as it may be offered in return for deals, special treatment, or the dropping of charges.

_____ 10. Prosecutors should also reveal any incentive the snitch might receive, and all communication between prosecutors and snitches should be recorded.

UNDERSTANDING GRAPHICS

DISTINGUISHING FACT FROM OPINION IN VISUALS

When reading graphics, it is also important to determine what is fact and what is opinion. Any projection of a future trend is, of course, opinion, as it has not yet happened. However, a projection might be a *reasonable inference,* or an educated guess, based on facts that can be verified. To obtain future projection numbers, researchers use statistics to determine what is *likely* to happen (opinion) based on what has *already* happened (fact). To determine facts versus opinions in graphics, follow these steps.

1. Determine the topic, structure, and most important point of the visual.

2. Determine which part of the information is verifiable, or fact, and which part of the information is a projection, or a reasonable inference (therefore an opinion), based on already verified factual information.

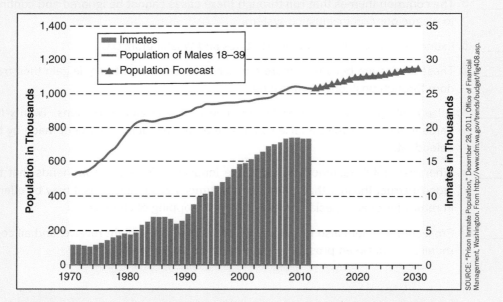

FIGURE 7.1 Prison Inmate Population Compared to Age 18 to 39 Male Population

- From 1970 through 1988, the prison inmate population closely tracked the population group most susceptible to incarceration—males age 18–39.
- The Sentencing Reform Act stabilized and lowered the prison caseload in the mid- to late 1980s, while new policies, including an emphasis on drug crimes beginning in the late 1980s had a dramatic impact on the size of the prison population.
- 2007—Offender Reentry Initiative is implemented and expected to reduce future inmate caseloads through education, work force skills, and treatment programs.

—Office of Financial Management, http://www.ofm.wa.gov/trends/budget/fig408.asp

● Look at Figure 7.1 tracing males in the population between the ages of 18 and 39 in the United States from 1970 to 2010, and the projected population up until 2030. Consider how this general population relates to the inmate population from 1970 to 2010. Keep in mind these facts related to Figure 7.1: two federal influential initiatives are cited following the graphic: The Sentencing Reform Act promoted consistency in federal sentencing and abolished federal parole, and the Offender Reentry Initiative provided multifaceted support for adults and juvenile offenders reentering society.

To determine fact versus opinion in graphics, follow these steps to answer the questions.

1.   **What is the topic, structure, and most important point of the visual?**
     This is the prison inmate population from 1970 to 2010 as well as males aged 18–39 between the same years and projected through 2030. The pattern is compare and contrast as well as sequence. The most important point is that from 1970 through 1988, the prison inmate population mirrors the vulnerable population of males 18–39. After this point, the prison population rose disproportionately when compared with the population of males in the United States. According to the bulleted information, incarceration rates rose due to new laws.

2.   **Which part of the information is verifiable, or fact, and which part of the information is a projection or a reasonable inference (therefore an opinion), based on already verified factual information?**
     Up until 2010, the information in the graphic is factual; from 2010 to 2030, the information is opinion.

3.   **What can you infer regarding the future relationship between the young male population and that of the prison population, based on the bulleted information provided with the graphic?**
     It is reasonable to conclude that the prison population will decrease in relation to the rise of the population in this age group. According to the bulleted information, the Offender Reentry Initiative is likely to reduce the inmate population as alternatives to incarceration are implemented as well as improved rehabilitation methods.

Types of Support for Arguments

Recognizing a fact and an opinion as well as a mixed statement that contains both fact and opinion is the first step in evaluating an argument. However, understanding different ways that an author presents both facts and opinions to support his or her point of view will help you become a more informed critical reader. You know that an author can use facts to support his or her point of view, which is his or her opinion. An author will also use other types of support to lend credence or believability to his or her argument. When an author backs up the main idea (i.e., his or her point of view), one of these five types of support can be used.

1. **Facts.** As you learned, facts are supporting points that can be verified, or proved. Make sure the facts that are used to reinforce the point are directly related to the point. Statistics are a type of supporting fact. While these numbers or results could be verified (i.e., they can be traced to a study or report), do not always assume statistics prove the main idea without question. For example, statistics used out of their original context can be misleading. Often there are statistics from another source that could be used for equally verifiable counterargument! Furthermore, the *interpretation* of statistics blurs the line between fact and fiction or opinion. For example, consider the research study in Application 1 on page 513. Notice how the results and discussion sections are combined. While the results are fact insofar as the analysis is based on statistics, what these results mean (the discussion) is open to interpretation! Similarly, while textbooks appear to contain factual, objective information, be aware that the author may be biased if all opposing points of view on the subject are not mentioned.

2. **Reasons.** Authors also use *reasons* to support their point of view. Reasons are opinions based on facts. Reasons are logical arguments, although they are not usually verifiable (provable). In other words, a counterargument could use equally valid reasons to support the opposing point of view.

3. **Examples.** *Examples* are supporting points that illustrate or clarify the author's point of view. These may be logical and reasonable, but cannot be verified like facts or statistics. Examples often support reasons. Examples are usually found in a series of specific statements or descriptions that support an overall point.

4. **Testimony.** This type of support is used when an author cites an expert witness or someone seen to be an authoritative source to comment on, and back up, the overall point. Testimony can also be a quote from someone involved in an issue. Testimony may be based on facts to some extent, but it is *someone's opinion based on facts*. Testimony can also derive from eyewitness accounts that are not always accurate. While eyewitness testimony can carry substantial weight, particularly if the testimony was reported to an official source, this does not mean that the report is accurate or indisputable. The eyewitness could have misconstrued the event or misrepresented the information. An example of testimony is testimony in court, in which a person testifies by answering the questions of a prosecutor or defense attorney, or an expert witness passes judgment relevant to the trial proceedings.

5. **Counterarguments.** A writer can use counterargument (as do lawyers in court) to first outline what the opposing side argues and *then prove the opposing side wrong or point out errors in reasoning.* This is a very effective method of debate because it undercuts the arguments of the opposing side. To counterargue, an author can use facts, reasons, examples, or testimony.

In the following example, note how the author first reports a misconception on the side of those who are in favor of the death penalty, then goes on to argue why those in favor of the death penalty are wrong. Also note that the author is arguing *against* the death penalty, but saying what those *in favor of* the death penalty say and arguing that they are wrong.

> Those who argue for the death penalty cite that it costs tax payers less to execute an inmate than to incarcerate the inmate for life. Frankly, this argument is, at best, misguided and, at worst, wrong since it costs far more to finance the legal appeals process for a prisoner on death row whose life ends in execution than it does to finance a life sentence.

This example is one of fact and opinion.

> **Opinion:** This argument is, at best, misguided and, at worst, wrong . . .

> **Fact:** It costs far more to finance the legal appeals process for a prisoner on death row whose life ends in execution than it does to finance a life sentence.

However, the author does not provide specifics to support her saying that it costs more for taxpayers to support someone on death row than to keep that prisoner incarcerated for life. The author could provide some substantial or specific facts to support the claim that life-in-prison sentences cost taxpayers less money by citing documented costs of housing a prisoner for life in prison compared with the total cost of housing a prisoner, funding the legal appeals process, and, ultimately, executing the prisoner. As a critical reader, you do not want to accept what an author writes at face value. Chapter 8 will give you the tools to evaluate an argument effectively. However, Table 7.1 lists some initial questions you can ask yourself regarding an author's point of view and supporting arguments to begin to delve beneath the surface of what is said and formulate your own opinion about an argument.

TABLE 7.1 Identifying the Type of Support for a Point of View

FACT	OPINION		FACT OR OPINION	
FACTS	REASONS	EXAMPLES	TESTIMONY	COUNTERARGUMENT
• Numbers • Statistics • Verifiable events	• Informed opinion • Logical arguments • Reasoned conclusions	• Lists in support • Names • Dates • Events • Specific cases	• Expert witnesses • Expert opinion	• Laying out the other side's points and finding fault with them
IS THE SUPPORT EFFECTIVE? ASK THESE QUESTIONS				
Are the facts verifiable? Are the statistics interpreted and, therefore, part opinion?	Are the arguments logical? Are the conclusions reasonable?	Are the lists or other examples directly relevant to the point being proven?	Are the experts qualified to pass judgment?	Are the opponents' points clearly and convincingly disproven?

Thinking It Through   IDENTIFYING FACT, OPINION, AND SUPPORT FOR POINT OF VIEW

Here is an excerpt from an article about an inmate who was exonerated (later found to be not guilty) well into his prison sentence. Notice the commentary that indicates whether a particular sentence or phrase is fact or opinion; also, note the types of support the author uses for his arguments.

Wrongly Convicted
by Terry Golway

1   Scott Fappiano spent more than 20 years in prison in New York. He was convicted of a brutal crime in 1985—the rape of a woman married to a police officer in Brooklyn.

Fact: can be verified

2   His trial was not exactly open and shut. Although the victim identified Fappiano as her attacker by looking at photographs, he was, in fact, about five inches shorter than the man she had described, and he had shorter hair. Extensive blood tests failed to establish any connection between Fappiano and the crime. Nevertheless, in 1985 he was convicted of the crime and sentenced to 50 years.

Opinion

Counterargument—citing the "other side's" perspective and then undercutting the argument

Fact—but this information is support for the opinion that the trial was not "exactly open and shut." Therefore, the support is examples.

3   He is free today because a group called The Innocence Project took up his case, demanded DNA testing, and proved what Fappiano had said all along: He was innocent. The State of New York, which had custody of him for nearly half of his 44 years on earth, released him earlier this year.

Fact that he is free and that he was backed by the Innocence Project and had DNA testing done; opinion that it is *because* of the Innocence Project that he is free. The author uses reasons to support his claim that the Innocence Project directly freed the inmate.

4   What do you say when you have spent more than 20 years in prison for a crime you didn't commit? Scott Fappiano simply said he was glad his ordeal was over and that the injustice had come to an end. His 69-year-old mother said she felt that her son had been kidnapped, but finally had returned.

While he may well feel this way, this is his opinion; the type of support for his claim that he is glad to be free is reasons.

That the mother said this may be a fact, but her feelings are an opinion; it is the mother's testimony or direct speech that she feels her son was "kidnapped."

5   In a sense, he was kidnapped—an innocent person taken away against his will by an
imperfect justice system, imperfect because
it is administered by flawed human beings
who probably get it right most of the time
but clearly not all of the time.

Opinion—the author uses reasons to support his claim that the justice system was imperfect.

6   Scott Fappiano received a long sentence
for a crime he did not commit. How many
prisoners in the United States today have
received a far worse sentence—death—for
crimes they did not commit? At a time when
Americans have embraced the death penalty with unseemly enthusiasm, this question
ought to haunt prosecutors, judges, and juries.

Fact that he received a long sentence.

Opinion—notice the phrase "ought to," which implies a value judgment; the support for the claim is a reason why society should rethink the death penalty.

SOURCE: "Wrongly Convicted," by Terry Golway of The Innocence Project. From *America*, 195. 15 (Nov 13, 2006): 8. Reprinted by permission of the author.

You can see from the example that finding facts and opinions can sometimes be straightfor-ward; sometimes, it is complicated to separate what is a logical reason from a fact, since some statements can blur that line.

On Your Own IDENTIFYING FACT, OPINION, AND SUPPORT FOR POINT OF VIEW

Consider the rest of the "Wrongly Convicted" passage here. In the margins, note whether each passage is a fact or opinion. Highlight facts and underline opinions. Also, identify the type of support used in each section of the reading. The first two paragraphs have been completed as examples.

	FACT OR OPINION?	TYPE OF SUPPORT?
1 Death penalty advocates argue that the system has built-in checks and procedures that nearly elim-inate the chance that an innocent person could be convicted of a capital crime and sentenced to death. But is that really the case?	Opinion	Testimony

(Continued)

	FACT OR OPINION?	TYPE OF SUPPORT?
2 In 1991 a man named Jeffrey Mark Deskovic was convicted of raping and murdering a young woman in Peekskill, N.Y. New York did not have a death penalty statute at the time <u>because two successive New York governors, Hugh Carey and Mario Cuomo, vetoed death-penalty legislation annually. Had they not done so, Jeffrey Mark Deskovic surely would have received a death sentence.</u>	Fact Fact/Opinion Opinion	Fact. Paragraph 2 is a counterargument to the statement in paragraph 1. Reason
3 But he did not commit that crime. He maintained his innocence for years and asked the local prosecutor, Jeanine Pirro, to examine DNA evidence that he believed would prove his case. The prosecutor's office declined to do so. But earlier this year, the Innocence Project took up Deskovic's case, a new prosecutor looked at the DNA evidence, and Deskovic was cleared of the crime after spending 15 years in prison.		
4 Without the support of the Innocence Project, Deskovic, Fappiano, and other wrongly convicted people in New York and elsewhere might still be in prison. The staff and lawyers of this not-for-profit legal clinic deserve the gratitude of all who pray for justice, for the clinic's mission is nothing less than the overturning of injustice. In the last year alone, the Innocence Project has helped free five prisoners wrongly convicted of murder in New York.		
5 The Innocence Project relies on DNA evidence to return the unjustly convicted to freedom. Since 1989, nearly 200 people have been released, because of DNA evidence, from prison for crimes they did not commit. The Innocence Project is pushing for the routine collection of genetic material from convicted felons. That seemingly sensible proposition, however, has drawn some opposition from civil libertarians, who fear the growth of government-maintained DNA databases.		

	FACT OR OPINION?	TYPE OF SUPPORT?
6 With two million people serving time in American prisons, the Innocence Project's mission could hardly be more urgent. How many of those two million have been wrongly convicted? The number certainly is small, but the presence of even one innocent person in prison mocks the very notion of justice. Once imprisoned, as Deskovic discovered, inmates and their continued pleas of innocence generally go unheard. Judges, prosecutors, and the public at large generally do not regard convicted felons as sympathetic or credible figures.		
7 All of this, of course, takes on even greater import when the death penalty becomes part of the equation. We know, thanks to the Innocence Project, that people have been wrongly convicted of crimes. Shouldn't that give death penalty supporters pause? Do they believe that the system is flawless, or do they believe that the occasional innocent executed in the name of justice is the tragic price we must pay for law and order?		
8 After Deskovic was released earlier this year, Barry Scheck, a lawyer who has been one of the driving forces behind the Innocence Project, directed his remarks to death penalty supporters. "This is the fifth man to be exonerated in a murder case in New York State in the past 10 months," he noted. "And for all those who are thinking that it might be a good idea to reinstate capital punishment in this state, please, please, please look at the evidence in front of you."		
9 The evidence in front of New Yorkers—in front of all of us—was a live human being wrongly sent to prison for murder he didn't commit. He lost 15 years of his life thanks to a miscarriage of justice.		
10 But at least he did not lose his life. Do we really wish to take that risk?		

SOURCE: Wrongly Convicted By Terry Golway of The Innocence Project. From *America*, 195. 15 (Nov 13, 2006): 8. Reprinted by permission of the author.

Thinking It Through　**MAPPING AN ARGUMENT AND RECOGNIZING SUPPORT**

After you have applied your skills of marking the text and annotating in the margins, consider the types of support the author uses for each argument he makes to back up his point of view. In this activity and the next, you will read two articles featuring opposing positions about harsh penalties for juvenile offenders. Should we allow life without parole for serious juvenile offenses, or should we take the position that juveniles deserve a second chance to show they can be rehabilitated?

Read the author's summary of the issue in the abstract preceding the argument against implementing life without parole (LWOP) for juvenile offenders. Think about what you already know about this issue, and then read the article and write the answers to the questions in the margin. Consider these questions as you read: What is the author's point of view? What are the key arguments the author uses to support his point of view? What types of support are used to back up each key argument? Are these supports fact or opinion? Afterward, read the explanation following the reading.

The types of support and whether the arguments are fact or opinion are indicated in the margin. The mapping of the argument follows the passage.

LWOP for Juveniles Is Morally Wrong
Should Juveniles Be Given Life Without Parole?
By John Coleman

1　　The 1990s produced a rush of legislation to curb perceived crime, with lawmakers and politicians becoming tougher on crime to benefit their political agendas. States passed laws allowing juveniles to be tried as adults as well as habitual offender laws, allowing juveniles who repeatedly committed crimes to be given a sentence of life without parole (LWOP). The sentence is being tested before the Supreme Court. Those arguing against LWOP cite that giving a juvenile a life sentence with no chance of parole is cruel and unusual punishment, according to the Constitution. Juveniles are not as mentally capable as adults and are more likely to act on impulse and fall prey to peer pressure, which is why they should be treated differently than adults.

2　　Currently, 109 prisoners in the United States are serving life-sentences without parole for non-homicide offenses, committed as juveniles; 77 of them are in Florida.　　　　　Fact

Many States Are Not Using This Sentence

3   A number of states (Texas, Colorado) have, legisla-
tively, recently rescinded life-sentence without parole
for juveniles, even in cases which involved homicide
or felony murder charges. In these two states, however, there are provisions for life sentence for juveniles
which only allow a possible parole after 40 years in
prison. A bill proposing a similar outlawing of life-
sentence without parole for juveniles is now pending before the California Assembly. California has
239 prisoners who were sentenced to life-sentences
without parole as juveniles. Nationally the number runs
to 1,755.

Fact

Fact

Fact

4   Every state permits life sentences for juveniles.
Forty-five states allow life-sentences without parole
for juveniles. In some cases of felony-murder, passive accomplices (e.g., "look-outs" in armed robberies) who had no idea a homicide was going to occur
and did not directly wield any weapon have received
life-sentences without parole.

Fact

5   Every other country has banned life-sentence
without parole for juveniles.

Fact

Juveniles Can Be Rehabilitated

6   Juveniles have not developed in the same way
as adults. They are more given to impulsivity, reck-
lessness and are more susceptible to peer pressure.
They are inherently less responsible—which does not
mean entirely un-responsible! Neuroscientists have
shown that brain regions and systems responsible
for foresight, self-regulation, risk assessment, responsiveness to social influences continue to mature until
early adulthood.

Opinion—reasons

Fact

7   Minors need to be considered differently than
adults in sentencing due to differences in brain
development, emotional maturity and their greater
capacity for rehabilitation. As Alison Parker, Deputy Director of the U.S. Program at Human Rights
Watch has put it: "Children are different than adults.

Opinion—reasons

(Continued)

They need to be punished for serious crimes but the punishment they receive needs to acknowledge their capacity for rehabilitation and life without parole does not do that."

Opinion—testimony

SOURCE: Adapted from: John Coleman, "Life Without Parole For Juveniles: Morally Wrong," America Magazine, April 13, 2010. Reproduced by permission of America Press. For subscription information, visit www.americamagazine.org.

Example of Mapping Arguments

1. **Issue: Whether or not** . . . *juveniles should be given life without parole.*

2. **Author's Point of View (conclusion about the issue):** *Life without parole for juveniles is morally wrong* (stated in the title and last paragraph)

   > **Supporting Argument 1:** *Many states have rescinded (repealed) LWOP for juveniles.*

   > **Supporting Argument 2:** *Forty-five states allow life-sentences without parole for juveniles. In some cases of felony-murder, passive accomplices (e.g., "look-outs" in armed robberies) who had no idea a homicide was going to occur and did not directly wield any weapon have received life-sentences without parole.*

   > **Supporting Argument 3:** *Every other country has banned life-sentence without parole for juveniles.*

   > **Supporting Argument 4:** *Juveniles' brain development is not mature, according to neuroscientists.*

   > **Supporting Argument 5:** *Minors need to be considered differently than adults in sentencing due to differences in brain development, emotional maturity, and their greater capacity for rehabilitation.*

All of these arguments directly support the conclusion (thesis) that life without parole is morally wrong for juvenile offenders. Arguments 1 through 4 rely on fact as a basis of support. Argument 5 uses reasons and testimony for the point of view.

Notice how each of the supporting arguments functions to support the point of view directly. You should be able to say, "Therefore, life without parole for juveniles is morally wrong" after each argument is expressed. Double-check the arguments above. Does each argument logically lead to the conclusion?

MAPPING AN ARGUMENT
On Your Own **AND RECOGNIZING SUPPORT**

As you read, note whether the arguments are fact or opinion. After reading, identify the major arguments and determine the type of support used for each by completing the chart that follows the reading. Follow these steps to guide your reading and mapping of the argument.

1. **What is the issue?**

2. **What is the author's point of view about the issue?**

3. **What are the key arguments the author uses to support his point of view?**

4. **Given the key arguments in support of the author's point of view, what type of support is used to back up each argument? Is each type of support fact or opinion?**

Harsh Punishment Is the Best Way to Prevent Juvenile Crime
by Kenneth W. Sukhia

1   Despite recent positive trends, our nation continues to record one of the highest violent crime rates in the world. Since 1960, the population of the United States has increased some 43%, yet the number of violent crimes has increased over 500%. While violent crime is a rarity in some countries, in America someone falls prey to a crime of violence every 17 seconds and one of us is murdered every 25 minutes.

2   No small contributor to this epidemic has been the astounding increase in juvenile crime. . . .

Swift and Certain Punishment

3   As discussed by [researcher] Eugene Methvin in the Summer of 1997 issue of *Policy Review*, studies at the University of Southern California and by criminologist Marvin Wolfgang in Philadelphia revealed that swift and certain punishment for convicted felons in the early stages of their criminal activity is a most effective means of suppressing crime.

4   In his *Policy Review* article, Methvin cited numerous studies confirming that society's failure to take punitive action in dealing with first-time youthful offenders is a primary factor contributing to the development of habitual criminals. As Mr. Methvin noted, "a troublesome youngster typically has ten or 12 contacts with the criminal-justice system and many more undiscovered offenses before he ever receives any formal 'adjudication,' or finding of guilt, from a judge. He quickly concludes that he will never face any serious consequences for his delinquency."

(Continued)

Recommendations for Improving the Situation

1. Long Term.

5   Given the disparity between the number of violent crimes committed by juveniles and the number of facilities available to detain them over the last decade . . . , juvenile offenders have been taught to believe through repeated brushes with the system that unless they commit murder, they stand little or no chance of being incarcerated for their crimes.

6   The long-term solution to the problem of juvenile crime clearly falls largely outside the law enforcement system. It requires strengthening of the basic institutions of family, schools, religious organizations and community groups which are responsible for instilling values and helping to raise law-abiding citizens. From a law enforcement perspective, however, there can be no meaningful deterrent to ongoing juvenile crime as long as juvenile offenders believe they will never be subjected to meaningful punishment for their crimes.

2. Build More Youth Detention Facilities.

7   Accordingly, we must commit to the building of a sufficient number of youth detention facilities to provide an adequate deterrent to those who would commit crime.

3. To Protect the Innocent, Violent Juvenile Offenders Must Be Punished and Removed from Society.

8   We must insure that violent and hardened juvenile offenders, who are responsible for a large share of the violent crime increase in Florida and our nation, are removed from society and punished. Increasingly, these violent criminals are being transferred to the adult system which seems incapable of imposing adequate punishment, and which fails to incarcerate 85 percent of the juveniles certified for adult treatment. . . .

9   A weak and indulgent response to juvenile crime serves an injustice to both the society which suffers from the effects of such crime and to the juvenile offender who is encouraged through repeated conduct which goes unpunished to escalate his criminal activity. To fail to act responsibly to address this crucial problem is to disserve both the law-abiding public and our state's youthful offenders.

SOURCE: Adapted from "TESTIMONY OF KENNETH W. SUKHIA BEFORE THE SUBCOMMITTEE ON CRIME OF THE UNITED STATES HOUSE JUDICIARY COMMITTEE," http://judiciary.house.gov/legacy/106-325.htm.

1. **Issue: Whether or not . . .** _____

2. **Author's Point of View (conclusion about the issue):** _____
_____

Now map the argument using the following chart.

SUPPORTING ARGUMENT	TYPE OF SUPPORT	FACT OR OPINION
1.		
2.		
3.		
4.		
5.		
6.		

Which of the two points of view about whether or not juveniles deserve harsh punishments do you believe provides the best support and the most convincing argument?

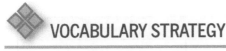

VOCABULARY STRATEGY

RECOGNIZING BIAS AND TONE: DENOTATION, CONNOTATION, AND LOADED LANGUAGE

A critical reader pays attention to the language an author uses to influence the emotions of a reader and that is, therefore, "high-inference" language. To draw these inferences as a critical reader, you need to understand the difference between denotative and connotative language. In addition, you need to understand how an author's use of language reveals his or her bias and tone.

Connotation and Denotation

The **connotative** meaning of words refers to the varied emotions, or references, a word may conjure in the mind of the reader. The connotation of a word has to do with the associations that are created in the mind of the reader. Many connotations of language can be attributed to culture or the learned associations passed on within a group of people from generation to generation.

The **denotative** meaning of a word is the straightforward, dictionary definition of that word. The denotative value of a word does not have anything "read" into it. Literal language and the denotative meanings of words are the same thing.

Consider the following example.

> The word *moon* on a denotative level means "a natural satellite revolving around a planetary body."

This is a dictionary definition of the word *moon*: the information is scientific, objective, detached. However, on a connotative level, the word *moon* may imply or symbolize several different meanings: Notice the symbolism in the photo of the tarot card on the following page. In this example, associations that are typically made with the word *moon* are communicated: These are the connotative "meanings" or values of the word. Read the following examples that further illustrate the connotative implications of the word *moon*.

- The word *moon* derives from the Greek word *luna.* We know this when we stop and think because the adjective for *moon* is *lunar.* From the same root comes the English word *lunatic,* an adjective, and the word *lunacy,* a noun—both indicating insanity.

- When you consider the moon, especially a full moon, as it often appears in popular culture, such as in films, it can symbolize romance, the unknown, or the unapproachable. Sometimes the word *moon* even connotes horrific happenings: Consider the image of a wolf howling at the moon and the derivation of werewolves, as in the tarot card.

- Because almost all gods of the moon are female in traditional cultures, (and therefore appropriately termed *goddesses*), the moon sometimes can symbolize the feminine. It is often connected with the fertility cycle and the female menstrual cycle, which parallel the cycle of the moon, intuition, and the subconscious.

Clearly, we can see that the denotative and connotative meanings of the word *moon* are very different.

Some words have positive connotations; some words have negative connotations. Some words have neutral connotations. The emotional load of a word has to do with personal bias as well as cultural bias. Most people who share a cultural tradition have learned the connotations of certain words. For example, consider these words:

- communism

- democracy

- God

While the words themselves have neutral denotations, what you associate with the word may be either positive or negative, depending on your background and culture. For the majority of U.S. citizens, the first word would have negative connotations (because most of them have been taught that communism is "bad"), and the two following words would have positive connotations.

Some words have connotations that may be positive or negative, depending on a person's point of view and life experience. For example, what kinds of connotations do *dentist, welfare,* and *money* carry for you?

Bias and Tone

In controversial writing—writing in which an author has a point of view about an issue—**bias,** or the side the author takes on an issue, is directly related to the **tone,** or underlying attitude, he or she has about his or her subject (see Chapter 4's Vocabulary Strategy). Bias and tone, then, are directly related. If an author has a distinct point of view about an issue, then he or she has an attitude or underlying opinion about that issue. In persuasive or prescriptive writing, an author's primary purpose is to get the reader to agree with his or her point of view. In neutral or objective writing, the author conveys facts with little or no underlying attitude.

The author has two elements at his or her disposal to persuade the reader to accept his or her point of view about an issue: the choice of words and the style of writing.

In a persuasive piece of writing, an author's choice of words, or diction, is extremely important. After all, the author has only words to convince the reader! Because the author only has words and a style in which those words are arranged, he or she will be very deliberate in selecting particular vocabulary to covey his or her message. Most authors are acutely aware of the connotations of the words and phrases they choose.

Loaded Language

Heavily biased words and phrases are referred to as **loaded language,** or words and phrases that an author chooses to convey a point of view and that reveal bias. A word or phrase is considered loaded if it suggests strong connotations—whether negative or positive—beyond its strict dictionary, or denotative, definition (see Table 7.2). A reader who is not aware of loaded language can misconstrue the author's point. Persuasive writing is manipulative, which is not always a negative. After all, it is the author's job to persuade. He or she will use whatever means are available to do so.

Loaded language reveals a great deal about an author's attitude or tone. You can tell whether an author is angry, sad, frustrated, excited, arrogant, disturbed by, or disgusted with a subject from her or his diction—her or his choice of words. Also, you can make an inference about the author's political position or social position, level of education, worldview, and so on from the sort of language that she or he uses. Furthermore, the author's choice of words and style of writing may reveal the nature of the audience for whom her or his writing is intended.

TABLE 7.2 Looking at Language Critically

CONNOTATION	DENOTATION	LOADED LANGUAGE	TONE	BIAS
The suggested implications of a word or phrase, either positive or negative, based on cultural conditioning or individual experience	The dictionary or literal interpretation of a word without symbolic or emotional load	A word or phrase carries connotation—either positive or negative associations—beyond its strict denotative meaning	The author's underlying attitude or emotion toward the subject as revealed by words or writing style	The author's side on an issue as revealed by choice of words and tone

Consider this extract from a reading presented earlier in this chapter. Determine the author's underlying attitude, or tone, as well as which words in particular have connotations that reveal his feelings about the issue, or loaded language:

> At a time when Americans have embraced the death penalty with unseemly enthusiasm, this question ought to haunt prosecutors, judges, and juries.

Here, the author is certainly not objective. He is clearly opposed to the death penalty. His tone is one of horror regarding the errors made in death penalty cases. How do we know this? Consider the phrases "this question ought to haunt prosecutors" and "unseemly enthusiasm." *Haunt* is an interesting word to choose—it implies that some grave injustice has been done and that those in error shall not rest and will be tormented by their unjust deeds. *Haunt* is a heavily loaded word that tells us that the author is opposed to the death penalty. Similarly, *unseemly* means "not decent or proper." Here, the writer clearly is critical of those Americans who support the death penalty, isn't he? Again, the author chose to use words that convey disgust and horror at the justice system and toward Americans who support the death penalty. His tone is one of anger and outrage as well as horror and shock.

Consider the following examples. What do the circled loaded words or phrases imply about the author's attitude toward the subject?

> What do you say when you have spent more than 20 years in prison for a crime you didn't commit? Scott Fappiano simply said he was glad his ordeal was over and that the injustice had come to an end. His 69-year-old mother said she felt that her son had been kidnapped, but finally had returned.

What is the author's tone? The tone evident in this passage is one of anger. In this case, the state is regarded as a criminal.

> The staff and lawyers of this not-for-profit legal clinic deserve the gratitude of all who pray for justice, for the clinic's mission is nothing less than the overturning of injustice.

What is the author's tone? The tone in this passage is one of thankfulness and gratitude toward those who serve justice over injustice.

> Soon afterward, Texas exonerated Ernest Willis from his arson/murder death sentence when prosecutors agreed with the same expert and science offered in Willingham's case. Nothing could be done for Willingham—likely an innocent man—because the state had already killed him.

What is the author's tone? The tone in this passage is one of anger: The state is guilty of murder.

On Your Own RECOGNIZING LOADED LANGUAGE

Independently or with a partner, consider the following passages. What is the author's tone in each? What loaded language reveals that tone? Underline loaded words or phrases that suggest tone. Write the tone suggested by the words in the space provided. Be prepared to discuss your ideas with the class.

1. How many of those two million have been wrongly convicted? The number certainly is small, but the presence of even one innocent person in prison mocks the very notion of justice.

    Tone: _____

2. All of this, of course, takes on even greater import when the death penalty becomes part of the equation. We know, thanks to the Innocence Project, that people have been wrongly convicted of crimes. Shouldn't that give death penalty supporters pause? Do they believe

    (Continued)

that the system is flawless, or do they believe that the occasional innocent executed in the name of justice is the tragic price we must pay for law and order?

Tone: _____

3.   And for all those who are thinking that it might be a good idea to reinstate capital punishment in this state, please, please, please look at the evidence in front of you.

Tone: _____

4.   The evidence in front of New Yorkers—in front of all of us—was a live human being wrongly sent to prison for murder he didn't commit. He lost 15 years of his life thanks to a miscarriage of justice.

Tone: _____

5.   Forensic scientists and prosecutors presented fraudulent, exaggerated, or otherwise tainted evidence to the judge or jury, which led to the wrongful conviction.

Tone: _____

INCREASE YOUR DISCIPLINE-SPECIFIC VOCABULARY

CRIMINAL JUSTICE AND LAW

Legal language is the foundation of criminal justice and law coursework and readings, of course. However, legal language is also embedded in our everyday language: on the news, in politics and government, in the newspaper and other media, as well as in daily conversation. While you may not have a background in Latin and ancient Greek, some familiarity with these word parts derived from these languages will inform your understanding of legal terminology you may encounter.

TABLE 7.3 Vocabulary Associated with Criminal Justice and Law

WORD PARTS	MEANING	VOCABULARY
cede, ceed	go, give away	antecedent, exceed, precede, precedent, recede, succeed
circum	around	circumstance, circuit, circumnavigate, circumspect, circumference
graph, gram	to write	graphic, demographic, stenographer, telegraph, autograph, biography, monograph
jud, judi, judic	law, judge	judge, judiciary, judgment, adjudicate, judicious, prejudice
leg	law	legal, legality, legislate, legislature, legalize, illegal
mort	death	mortal, moratorium, immortal, mortification, mortuary, mortician, postmortem
pend, pen	to hang	suspended, pendant, pending, pendulum, impending, interdependent
sub	under	subpoena, subject, subjugate, submerge, subsist, subterfuge, subversive
super	above, over	supreme court, soprano, superimpose, supersonic, superstition, superior, supervise
ver	truth	verify, verdict, veracity, very, veritable

(Continued)

Key Terms—Criminal Justice and Law

- *Acquittal:* the court ruling that a defendant is not guilty

- *Adjudicate:* to settle a case or make a decision via a court of law

- *Culpability:* guilt, blame, fault

- *Felony:* a serious crime punishable by death or prison sentence

- *Litigation:* a legal process in a court of law

- *Misdemeanor:* a crime of less seriousness than a felony but more serious than a violation

Latin Legal Terms

- *Bona fide:* in good faith

- *Habeas corpus:* a legal order to produce before the court to determine if the defendant needs to be held in custody

- *Mens rea:* guilty mind—the accused had the intention to commit the crime.

- *Pro bono:* for the public good. This term is used when a lawyer represents a client free of charge.

APPLICATIONS

APPLICATION (1)

Academic Research Study

Here is a research study on the subject of false confessions. References to the work of this author, Saul Kassin, are in the readings for the Pre-Assessment in this chapter. Follow the process for reading research studies shown here. Then answer the questions that follow the study.

1. Read the abstract to get an overview of the study. Reading the abstract is like previewing the study.

2. Read the introduction to clarify the subject of the study. Focus on the last paragraph, where the hypothesis is usually discussed.

3. Read the discussion section to understand the research conclusions and the overall findings of the study.

4. Go back and read the methods section. This information is very detailed and contains all the steps in the research process.

5. Read the results section for major findings. Unless you are proficient in statistics, this section is very dense, so read it for an overall grasp of the outcomes rather than for mathematical details, unless you are reading the study for a class that requires detailed knowledge of the results.

6. Carefully reread the discussion section to solidify your understanding of the information as well as the implications of the study.

7. If your purpose for reading the study is more detailed, go back and read through the study again. Take notes.

The Social Psychology of False Confessions: Compliance, Internalization, and Confabulation
by Saul M. Kassin and Katherine L. Kiechel

1   *An experiment demonstrated that false incriminating evidence can lead people to accept guilt for a crime they did not commit. Subjects in a fast- or slow-paced reaction time task were accused of damaging a computer by pressing the wrong key. All were truly innocent and initially denied the charge. A confederate then said she saw the subject hit the key or did not see the subject hit the key. Compared with subjects in the slow-pace/no-witness group, those in the fast-pace/witness group were more likely to sign a confession, internalize guilt for the event, and confabulate details in memory consistent with that belief. Both legal and conceptual implications are discussed.*

(Continued)

2   In criminal law, confession evidence is a potent weapon for the prosecution and a recurring source of controversy. Whether a suspect's self-incriminating statement was voluntary or coerced and whether a suspect was of sound mind are just two of the issues that trial judges and juries consider on a routine basis. To guard citizens against violations of due process and to minimize the risk that the innocent would confess to crimes they did not commit, the courts have erected guidelines for the admissibility of confession evidence. Although there is no simple litmus test, confessions are typically excluded from trial if elicited by physical violence, a threat of harm or punishment, or a promise of immunity or leniency, or without the suspect being notified of his or her Miranda rights.

3   To understand the psychology of criminal confessions, three questions need to be addressed: First, how do police interrogators elicit self-incriminating statements (i.e., what means of social influence do they use)? Second, what effects do these methods have (i.e., do innocent suspects ever confess to crimes they did not commit)? Third, when a coerced confession is retracted and later presented at trial, do juries sufficiently discount the evidence in accordance with the law? General reviews of relevant case law and research are available elsewhere (Gudjonsson, 1992; Wrightsman & Kassin, 1993). The present research addresses the first two questions.

4   Informed by developments in case law, the police use various methods of interrogation, including the presentation of false evidence (e.g., fake polygraph, fingerprints, or other forensic test results; staged eyewitness identifications), appeals to God and religion, feigned friendship, and the use of prison informants. A number of manuals are available to advise detectives on how to extract confessions from reluctant crime suspects (Aubry & Caputo, 1965; O'Hara & O'Hara, 1981). The most popular manual is Inbau, Reid, and Buckley's (1986) *Criminal Interrogation and Confessions,* originally published in 1962, and now in its third edition.

5   After advising interrogators to set aside a bare, soundproof room absent of social support and distraction, Inbau et al. (1986) describe in detail a nine-step procedure consisting of various specific ploys. In general, two types of approaches can be distinguished. One is *minimization,* a technique in which the detective lulls the suspect into a false sense of security by providing face-saving excuses, citing mitigating circumstances, blaming the victim, and underplaying the charges. The second approach is one of *maximization,* in which the interrogator uses scare tactics by exaggerating or falsifying the characterization of evidence, the seriousness of the offense, and the magnitude of the charges. In a recent study (Kassin & McNall, 1991), subjects read interrogation transcripts in which these ploys were used and estimated the severity of the sentence likely to be received. The results indicated that minimization communicated an implicit offer of leniency, comparable to that estimated in an explicit-promise condition, whereas maximization implied a threat of harsh punishment, comparable to that found in an explicit-threat condition. Yet although American courts routinely exclude confessions elicited by explicit threats and promises, they admit those produced by contingencies that are pragmatically implied.

6   Although police often use coercive methods of interrogation, research suggests that juries are prone to convict defendants who confess in these situations. In the case of *Arizona* v. *Fulminante* (1991), the U.S. Supreme Court ruled that under certain conditions, an improperly admitted coerced confession may be considered upon appeal to have been nonprejudicial, or "harmless error." Yet mock-jury research shows that people find it hard to believe that anyone would confess to a crime that he or she did not commit (Kassin & Wrightsman, 1980, 1981; Sukel & Kassin, 1994). Still, it happens. One cannot estimate the prevalence of the problem, which has never been systematically examined, but there are numerous documented instances on record (Bedau & Radelet, 1987; Borchard, 1932; Rattner, 1988). Indeed, one can distinguish three types of false confession (Kassin & Wrightsman, 1985): *voluntary* (in which a subject confesses in the absence of external pressure), *coerced-compliant* (in which a suspect confesses only to escape an aversive interrogation, secure a promised benefit, or avoid a threatened harm), and *coerced-internalized* (in which a suspect actually comes to believe that he or she is guilty of the crime).

7   This last type of false confession seems most unlikely, but a number of recent cases have come to light in which the police had seized a suspect who was vulnerable (by virtue of his or her youth, intelligence, personality, stress, or mental state) and used false evidence to convince the beleaguered suspect that he or she was guilty. In one case that received a great deal of attention, for example, Paul Ingram was charged with rape and a host of satanic cult crimes that included the slaughter of newborn babies. During 6 months of interrogation, he was hypnotized, exposed to graphic crime details, informed by a police psychologist that sex offenders often repress their offenses, and urged by the minister of his church to confess. Eventually, Ingram "recalled" crime scenes to specification, pleaded guilty, and was sentenced to prison. There was no physical evidence of these crimes, however, and an expert who reviewed the case for the state concluded that Ingram had been brainwashed. To demonstrate, this expert accused Ingram of a bogus crime and found that although he initially denied the charge, he later confessed and embellished the story (Ofshe, 1992: Wright, 1994).

8   Other similar cases have been reported (e.g., Pratkanis & Aronson, 1991), but, to date, there is no empirical proof of this phenomenon. Memory researchers have found that misleading postevent information can alter actual or reported memories of observed events (Loftus, Donders, Hoffman, & Schooler, 1989; Loftus, Miller, & Burns, 1978; McCloskey & Zaragoza, 1985)—an effect that is particularly potent in young children (Ceci & Bruck, 1993; Ceci, Ross, & Toglia, 1987) and adults under hypnosis (Dinges et al., 1992; Dywan & Bowers, 1983; Sheehan, Statham, & Jamieson, 1991). Indeed, recent studies suggest it is even possible to implant false recollections of traumas supposedly buried in the unconscious (Loftus, 1993). As related to confessions, the question is, can memory of one's own actions similarly be altered? Can people be induced to accept guilt for crimes they did not commit? Is it, contrary to popular belief, possible?

9   Because of obvious ethical constraints, this important issue has not been addressed previously. This article thus reports on a new laboratory paradigm used to test the

(Continued)

following specific hypothesis: The presentation of false evidence can lead individuals who are vulnerable (i.e., in heightened state of uncertainty) to confess to an act they did not commit and, more important, to internalize the confession and perhaps confabulate details in memory consistent with that new belief.

Method

10   Participating for extra credit in what was supposed to be reaction time experiment, 79 undergraduates (40 male, 39 female) were randomly assigned to one of four groups produced by a 2 (high vs. low vulnerability) x 2 (presence vs. absence of a false incriminating witness) factorial design.

11   Two subjects per session (actually, 1 subject and a female confederate) engaged in a reaction time task on an IBM PS2/Model 50 computer. To bolster the credibility of the experimental cover story, they were asked fill out a brief questionnaire concerning their typing experience and ability, spatial awareness, and speed of flexes. The subject and confederate were then taken another room, seated across a table from the experimenter, and instructed on the task. The confederate was read aloud a list of letters, and the subject was to type these letters on the keyboard. After 3 minutes, the subject and confederate were to reverse roles. Before the session began, subjects were instructed on proper use of the computer and were specifically warned not to press the "ALT" key positioned near the space bar because doing so would cause the program to crash and data to be lost. After 60 seconds, the computer supposedly ceased to function, and a highly distressed experimenter accused the subject of having pressed the forbidden key. All subjects initially denied the charge, at which point the experimenter tinkered with the keyboard, confirmed that data had been lost, and asked, "Did you hit the ALT key?"

12   Two forensically relevant factors were independently varied. First, we manipulated subjects' level of *vulnerability* (i.e., their subjective certainty concerning their own innocence) by varying the pace of the task. Using a mechanical metronome, the confederate read either at a slow and relaxed pace of 43 letters per minute or at a frenzied pace of 67 letters per minute (these settings were established through pretesting). Two-way analyses of variance revealed significant main effects on the number of letters typed correctly (*Ms* = 33.01 and 61.12, respectively; [$1l$, 71] = 278.93, $p < .001$) and the number of typing errors made (*Ms* = 1.12 and 10.90, respectively; $F[1, 71] = 38.81$, $p < .001$), thus confirming the effectiveness of this manipulation.

13   Second, we varied the use of *false incriminating evidence,* a common interrogation technique. After the subject initially denied the charge, the experimenter turned to the confederate and asked, "Did you see anything?" In the false-witness condition, the confederate "admitted" that she had seen the subject hit the ALT key that terminated the program. In the no-witness condition, the same confederate said she had not seen what happened.

14   As dependent measures, three forms of social influence were assessed: compliance, internalization, and confabulation. To elicit *compliance,* the experimenter handwrote a standardized confession ("I hit the ALT key and caused the program to crash. Data were lost.")

and asked the subject to sign it, the consequence of which would be a phone call from the principal investigator. If the subject refused, the request was repeated a second time.

15   To assess *internalization,* we unobtrusively recorded the way subjects privately described what happened soon afterward. As the experimenter and subject left the laboratory, they were met in the reception area by a waiting subject (actually, a second confederate who was blind to the subject's condition and previous behavior) who had overheard the commotion. The experimenter explained that the session would have to be rescheduled, and then left the room to retrieve his appointment calendar. At that point, the second confederate turned privately to the subject and asked, "What happened?" The subject's reply was recorded verbatim and later coded for whether or not he or she had unambiguously internalized guilt for what happened (e.g., "I hit the wrong button and ruined the program"; "I hit a button I wasn't supposed to."). A conservative criterion was employed. Any reply that was prefaced by "he said" or "I may have" or "I think" was not taken as evidence of internalization. Two raters who were blind to the subject's condition independently coded these responses, and their agreement rate was 96 percent.

16   Finally, after the sessions seemed to be over, the experimenter reappeared, brought the subjects back into the lab, reread the list of letters they had typed, and asked if they could reconstruct how or when they hit the ALT key. This procedure was designed to probe for evidence of *confabulation,* to determine whether subjects would "recall" specific details to fit the allegation (e.g., "Yes, here, I hit it with the side of my hand right after you called out the A."). The interrater agreement rate on the coding of these data was 100 percent.

17   At the end of each session, subjects were fully and carefully debriefed about the study—its purpose, the hypothesis, and the reason for the use of deception by the experimenter and first confederate. Most subjects reacted with a combination of relief (that they had not ruined the experiment), amazement (that their perceptions of their own behavior had been so completely manipulated), and a sense of satisfaction (at having played a meaningful role in an important study). Subjects were also asked not to discuss the experience with other students until all the data were collected. Four subjects reported during debriefing that they were suspicious of the experimental manipulation. Their data were excluded from all analyses.

Results and Discussion

18   Overall, 69 percent of the 75 subjects signed the confession, 28 percent exhibited internalization, and 9 percent confabulated details to support their false beliefs. More important, between-group comparisons provided strong support for the main hypothesis. As seen in Table 7.4, subjects in the slow-pace/no-witness control group were the least likely to exhibit an effect, whereas those in the fast-pace/witness group were the most likely to exhibit the effect on the measures of compliance ($x^2[3] = 23.84$, $p < .001$), internalization ($I[3] = 37.61$, $p < .001$), and confabulation ($x^2[3] = 18.0$, $p < .005$).

19   Specifically, although 34.78 percent of the subjects in the slow-pace/no-witness group signed the confession, indicating compliance, not a single subject in this group exhibited internalization or confabulation. In contrast, the two in dependent variables had a powerful combined effect.

(Continued)

TABLE 7.4 Percentage of Subjects in Each Cell Who Exhibited the Three Forms of Influence

FORM OF INFLUENCE	NO WITNESS		WITNESS	
	SLOW PACE	FAST PACE	SLOW PACE	FAST PACE
Compliance	35[a]	65[b]	89[bc]	100[c]
Internalization	0[a]	12[ab]	44[bc]	65[c]
Confabulation	0[a]	0[a]	6[a]	35[b]

NOTE: Percentages not sharing a common subscript differ at p < .05 via chi-square test of significance.

SOURCE: From Saul M. Kassin and Katherine L. Kiechel, "The Social Psychology of False Confessions: Compliance, Internalizations, and Confabulation" *Psychological Science*, 7(3), pp 125–128, copyright © 1996 by Sage. Reprinted by permission of SAGE Publications.

20   Out of 17 subjects in the fast-pace/witness cell, 100 percent signed a confession, 65 percent came to believe they were guilty (in reality, they were not), and 35 percent confabulated details to support their false belief (via chi-square tests, the differences in these rates between the slow-pace/no-witness control group and fast-pace/witness group were significant at ps < .001, .001, and .005, respectively).

21   Additional pair-wise comparisons revealed that the presence of a witness alone was sufficient to significantly increase the rates of compliant and internalized confessions, even in the slow-pace condition ($x^2[1]$ = *12.18, p* < .005, and $x^2[1]$ = 16.39, *p* < .001). There were no sex differences on any s (i.e., male and female subjects exhibited comparable confession rates overall, and were similarly influenced by the independent variables).

22   The present study provides strong initial support for the provocative notion that the presentation of false incriminating evidence—an interrogation ploy that is common among the police and sanctioned by many courts—can induce people to internalize blame for outcomes they did not produce. These results provide an initial basis for challenging the evidentiary validity of confessions produced by this technique. These findings also demonstrate, possibly for the first time, that memory can be altered not only for observed events and remote past experiences, but also for one's own recent actions.

23   An obvious and important empirical question remains concerning the external validity of the present results: To what extent do they generalize to the interrogation behavior of actual crime suspects? For ethical reasons, we developed a laboratory paradigm in which subjects were accused merely of an unconscious act of negligence, not of an act involving

explicit criminal intent (e.g., stealing equipment from the lab or cheating on an important test). In this paradigm, there was only a minor consequence for liability. At this point, it is unclear whether people could similarly be induced to internalize false guilt for acts of omission (i.e., neglecting to do something they were told to do) or for acts that emanate from conscious intent.

24   It is important, however, not to overstate this limitation. The fact that our procedure focused on an act of negligence and low consequence may well explain why the compliance rate was high, with roughly two-thirds of all subjects agreeing to sign a confession statement. Effects of this sort on overt judgments and behavior have been observed in studies of conformity to group norms, compliance with direct requests, and obedience to the commands of authority. But the more important and startling result—that many subjects privately internalized guilt for an outcome they did not produce, and that some even constructed memories to fit that false belief—is not seriously compromised by the laboratory paradigm that was used. Conceptually, these findings extend known effects of misinformation on memory for observed events (Loftus et al., 1978; McCloskey & Zaragoza, 1985) and for traumas assumed to be buried in the unconscious (Loftus, 1993). Indeed, our effects were exhibited by college students who are intelligent (drawn from a population in which the mean score on the Scholastic Aptitude Test is over 1300), self-assured, and under minimal stress compared with crime suspects held in custody, often in isolation.

25   At this point, additional research is needed to examine other common interrogation techniques (e.g., minimization), individual differences in suspect vulnerability (e.g., manifest anxiety, need for approval, hypnotic susceptibility), and other risk factors for false confessions (e.g., blood alcohol level, sleep deprivation). In light of recent judicial acceptance of a broad range of self-incriminatory statements, increasing use of videotaped confessions at the trial level (Geller, 1993), and the U.S. Supreme Court's ruling that an improperly admitted coerced confession may qualify as a mere "harmless error" (Arizona v. Fulminante, 1991), further research is also needed to assess the lay jury's reaction to this type of evidence when presented in court.

References

Arizona v. Fulminante, 59 U.S.L.W. 4235 (1991).

Aubry, A., & Caputo, R. (1965). Criminal interrogation. Springfield, IL: Charles C. Thomas.

Bedau, H., & Radelet, M. (1987). Miscarriages of justice in potentially capital cases. Stanford Law Review, 40, 21–179.

Borchard, E. M. (1932). Convicting the innocent: Errors of criminal justice. New Haven, CT: Yale University Press.

Ceci, S. I., & Bruck, M. (1993). Suggestibility of the child witness: A historical review and synthesis. Psychological Bulletin, 113, 403–439.

Ceci, S. I., Ross, D. F., & Toglia, M. P. (1987). Suggestibility of children's memory: Psycholegal implications. Journal of Experimental Psychology: General, 116, 38–49, 203.

Dinges, D. F., Whitehouse, W. G., Orne, E. C., Powell, I. W., Orne, M. T., & Erdelyi, M. H. (1992). Evaluating hypnotic memory enhancement (hypernesia and reminiscence) using multitrial forced recall. Journal of Experimental Psychology: Learning, Memory, and Cognition, 18, 1139–1147.

Dywan, J., & Bowers, K. (1983). The use of hypnosis to enhance recall. Science, 222, 184–185.

(Continued)

Geller, W. A. (1993). *Videotaping interrogations and confessions* (National Institute of Justice: Research in Brief). Washington, DC: U.S. Department of Justice.

Gudjonsson, G. (1992). *The psychology of interrogations, confessions, and testimony.* London: Wiley.

Inbau, F. E., Reid, J. E., & Buckley, J. P. (1986). *Criminal interrogation and confessions* (3rd ed.). Baltimore, MD: Williams & Wilkins.

Kassin, S. M., & McNall, K. (1991). Police interrogations and confessions: Communicating promises and threats by pragmatic implication. *Law and Human Behavior, 15,* 233–251.

Kassin, S. M., & Wrightsman, L. S. (1980). Prior confessions and mock juror verdicts. *Journal of Applied Social Psychology, 10,* 133–146.

Kassin, S. M., & Wrightsman, L. S. (1981). Coerced confessions, judicial instruction, and mock juror verdicts. *Journal of Applied Social Psychology, 11,* 489–506.

Kassin, S. M., & Wrightsman, L. S. (1985). Confession evidence. In S. M. Kassin & L. S. Wrightsman (Eds.), *The psychology of evidence and trial procedure* (pp. 67–94). Beverly Hills, CA: Sage.

Loftus, E. F. (1993). The reality of repressed memories. *American Psychologist, 48,* 518–537.

Loftus, E. F., Donders, K., Hoffman, H. G., & Schooler, J. W. (1989). Creating new memories that are quickly accessed and confidently held. *Memory and Cognition, 17,* 607–616.

Loftus, E. F., Miller, D. G., & Burns, H. I. (1978). Semantic integration of verbal information into visual memory. *Journal of Experimental Psychology: Human Learning and Memory, 4,* 19–31.

McCloskey, M., & Zaragoza, M. (1985). Misleading postevent information and memory for events: Arguments and evidence against memory impairment hypotheses. *Journal of Experimental Psychology, 114,* 3–18.

Ofshe, R. (1992). Inadvertent hypnosis during interrogation: False confession due to dissociative state; misidentified multiple personality and the satanic cult hypothesis. *International Journal of Clinical and Experimental Hypnosis, 40,* 125–156.

O'Hara, C. E., & O'Hara, G. L. (1981). *Fundamentals of criminal investigation.* Springfield, IL: Charles C. Thomas.

Pratkanis, A., & Aronson, E. (1991). *Age of propaganda: The everyday use and abuse of persuasion.* New York: W. H. Freeman.

Rattner, A. (1988). Convicted but innocent: Wrongful conviction and the criminal justice system. *Law and Human Behavior, 12,* 283–293.

Sheehan, P. W., Statham, D., & Jamieson, G. A. (1991). Pseudomemory effects and their relationship to level of susceptibility to hypnosis and state instruction. *Journal of Personality and Social Psychology, 60,* 130–137.

Sukel, H. L., & Kassin, S. M. (1994, March). *Coerced confessions and the jury: An experimental test of the "harmless error" rule.* Paper presented at the biennial meeting of the American Psychology Law Society, Santa Fe, NM.

Wright, L. (1994). *Remembering Satan.* New York: Alfred A. Knopf.

Wrightsman, L. S., & Kassin, S. M. (1993). *Confessions in the courtroom.* Newbury Park, CA: Sage.

COMPREHENSION CHECK

1 What is the topic of the research study? _____

_____

_____

INTRODUCTION

2 Why have courts established guidelines for confessions? _____

_____

_____

_____

3　What are the three criteria for exclusion of confessions from trial? _____
_____
_____
_____

4　What three questions need to be addressed in order to understand the psychology of
confessions? _____
_____
_____
_____

5　This study focuses on which two of these three questions? _____
_____

6　List some commonly used police methods for eliciting confessions from suspects.
_____
_____

7　What are the two main approaches commonly used to elicit confessions in police
interrogations? _____
_____
_____
_____

8　Despite the fact that police use coercive methods to elicit confessions (what does
coercive mean?), do juries tend to convict on these confessions? Explain your answer.
_____
_____
_____
_____
_____

9　What are the three types of false confessions? _____
_____
_____
_____
_____

10　Coerced-internalized confessions are the most extreme. Does evidence support that
such confessions are rare? Explain your answer._____
_____

(Continued)

_____
_____
_____

11 What is the hypothesis of this study? _____
_____
_____
_____
_____

METHOD

12 How do the researchers "test" compliance, internalization, and confabulation?
_____
_____
_____
_____
_____
_____
_____
_____
_____
_____
_____

13 Who were the subjects of this study? _____
_____

14 What were the main steps of the research study? _____
_____
_____
_____
_____
_____
_____
_____

_____

_____

_____

15 How did the researchers mimic police procedures for securing a confession?_____

_____

_____

_____

_____

_____

_____

RESULTS AND DISCUSSION

16 What provokes people to assume (internalize) blame for crimes they did not commit? _____

_____

_____

_____

17 How does the study suggest one's own memory can be "altered"? _____

_____

_____

_____

18 What major question does the study raise in terms of predicting false confessions for an actual crime?_____

_____

_____

19 How do the researchers account for subjects having such a high rate of compliance?

_____

_____

_____

20 What further research is necessary? _____

_____

_____

(Continued)

READING GRAPHICS

Consider Figure 7.2 and answer the questions that follow.

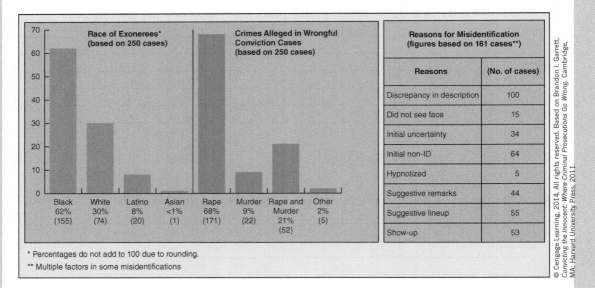

* Percentages do not add to 100 due to rounding.

** Multiple factors in some misidentifications

FIGURE 7.2 Testing the Reliability of Eyewitnesses

Race of Exonerees

1. What is the topic, structure, and most important point of this part of the figure? _____
_____
_____

2. Is the information fact or opinion? _____
_____

Crimes Alleged in Wrongful Conviction Cases

3. What is the topic, structure, and most important point of this part of the figure? _____
_____
_____

4. Is the information fact or opinion? _____
_____

Reasons for Misidentification

5. What is the topic, structure, and most important point of this part of the figure? _____
_____
_____

6. Is the information fact or opinion? _____
   _____

7. How does Figure 7.2 relate to the research study? _____
   _____
   _____
   _____
   _____
   _____

DEVELOPING YOUR COLLEGE-LEVEL VOCABULARY

1. What is *compliance*? _____
   _____

2. What is *internalization*? _____
   _____

3. What is *confabulation?* _____
   _____

4. What is the authors tone in this study? _____

5. Based on the language used in this study, is the author biased? _____
   _____

THEMATIC CONNECTIONS

1. How does the information in the study affect your understanding of other information about the topic?

2. Could the data be biased as a result of the methods used, who the researchers are, or where the study was published? Justify your answers using specific examples.

3. How do the findings in this study affect your understanding of the phenomenon of false confessions?

4. Do you think you would be susceptible to giving a false confession under duress? Explain why or why not.

5. What kind of support is used in this study?

APPLICATION ②

This reading is a newspaper story about a theory that links crime rates to exposure to lead during childhood. While the reporting of the story is factual and objective and the purpose is to inform, Rick Nevin's theory is one that is provocative and controversial: Nevin contends that lead exposure is linked with U.S. crime rates.

According to the FDA, lead was banned in house paint in 1978 and from gasoline by 1995. In addition, food canners stopped using lead solder in 1991. However, lead paint is still prevalent in old homes across the United States. Because lead affects the functioning of neurotransmitters in the brain, lead exposure can result in a host of medical and cognitive problems, from memory impairment and hyperactivity to impaired cognitive development resulting in lowered IQ, compounded by an array of other physical and neurological problems.

Following the reading, map the support for the theory as presented in this article. Note the lead statement, or the story writer's statement of main idea.

Theory Links Lead Exposure, Crime
by Shankar Vedantam

1   Rudy Giuliani never misses an opportunity to remind people about his track record in fighting crime as mayor of New York City from 1994 to 2001.

2   "I began with the city that was the crime capital of America," Giuliani, now a candidate for president, recently told Fox's Chris Wallace. "When I left, it was the safest large city in America. I reduced homicides by 67 percent. I reduced overall crime by 57 percent."

3   "Although crime did fall dramatically in New York during Giuliani's tenure, a broad range of scientific research has emerged in recent years to show that the mayor deserves only a fraction of the credit that he claims. The most compelling information has come from an economist in Fairfax who has argued in a series of little-noticed papers that the "New York miracle" was caused by local and federal efforts decades earlier to reduce lead poisoning.

4   The theory offered by the economist, Rick Nevin, is that lead poisoning accounts for much of the variation in violent crime in the United States. It offers a unifying new neurochemical theory for fluctuations in the crime rate, and it is based on studies linking children's exposure to lead with violent behavior later in their lives.

Findings Hold Across Countries

5   What makes Nevin's work persuasive is that he has shown an identical, decades-long association between lead poisoning and crime rates in nine countries.

6   "It is stunning how strong the association is," Nevin said in an interview. "Sixty-five to ninety percent or more of the substantial variation in violent crime in all these countries was explained by lead."

7   Through much of the 20th century, lead in U.S. paint and gasoline fumes poisoned toddlers as they put contaminated hands in their mouths. The consequences on crime, Nevin found, occurred when poisoning victims became adolescents. Nevin does not say that lead is the only factor behind crime, but he says it is the biggest factor.

8   Giuliani's presidential campaign declined to address Nevin's contention that the mayor merely was at the right place at the right time. But William Bratton, who served as Giuliani's police commissioner and who initiated many of the policing techniques credited with reducing the crime rate, dismissed Nevin's theory as absurd. Bratton and Giuliani instituted harsh measures against quality-of-life offenses, based on the "broken windows" theory of addressing minor offenses to head off more serious crimes.

9   Many other theories have emerged to try to explain the crime decline. In the 2005 book *Freakonomics*, Steven D. Levitt and Stephen J. Dubner said the legalization of abortion in 1973 had eliminated "unwanted babies" who would have become violent criminals. Other experts credited lengthy prison terms for violent offenders, or demographic changes, socioeconomic factors, and the fall of drug epidemics. New theories have emerged as crime rates have inched up in recent years.

Crime Tied to Lead Levels in Gas?

10   Most of the theories have been long on intuition and short on evidence. Nevin says his data not only explain the decline in crime in the 1990s, but the rise in crime in the 1980s and other fluctuations going back a century. His data from multiple countries, which have different abortion rates, police strategies, demographics, and economic conditions, indicate that lead is the only explanation that can account for international trends.

11   Because the countries phased out lead at different points, they provide a rigorous test: In each instance, the violent crime rate tracks lead poisoning levels two decades earlier.

12   "It is startling how much mileage has been given to the theory that abortion in the early 1970s was responsible for the decline in crime" in the 1990s, Nevin said. "But they legalized abortion in Britain, and the violent crime in Britain soared in the 1990s. The difference is our gasoline lead levels peaked in the early '70s and started falling in the late '70s, and fell very sharply through the early 1980s and was virtually eliminated by 1986 or '87.

13   "In Britain and most of Europe, they did not have meaningful constraints [on leaded gasoline] until the mid-1980s and even early 1990s," he said. "This is the reason you are seeing the crime rate soar in Mexico and Latin America, but [it] has fallen in the United States."

14   Lead levels plummeted in New York in the early 1970s, driven by federal policies to eliminate lead from gasoline and local policies to reduce lead emissions from municipal incinerators. Between 1970 and 1974, the number of New York children heavily poisoned by lead fell by more than 80 percent, according to data from the New York City Department of Health.

Steep Drop in Crime During '90s

15   Lead levels in New York have continued to fall. One analysis in the late 1990s found that children in New York had lower lead exposure than children in many other big U.S. cities,

(Continued)

possibly because of a 1960 policy to replace old windows. That policy, meant to reduce deaths from falls, had an unforeseen benefit—old windows are a source of lead poisoning, said Dave Jacobs of the National Center for Healthy Housing, an advocacy group that is publicizing Nevin's work. Nevin's research was not funded by the group.

16   The later drop in violent crime was dramatic. In 1990, 31 New Yorkers out of every 100,000 were murdered. In 2004, the rate was 7 per 100,000—lower than in most big cities. The lead theory also may explain why crime fell broadly across the United States in the 1990s, not just in New York.

17   The centerpiece of Nevin's research is an analysis of crime rates and lead poisoning levels across a century. The United States has had two spikes of lead poisoning: one at the turn of the 20th century, linked to lead in household paint, and one after World War II, when the use of leaded gasoline increased sharply. Both times, the violent crime rate went up and down in concert, with the violent crime peaks coming two decades after the lead poisoning peaks.

Metal Linked to Aggression

18   Other evidence has accumulated in recent years that lead is a neurotoxin that causes impulsivity and aggression, but these studies have also drawn little attention. In 2001, sociologist Paul B. Stretesky and criminologist Michael Lynch showed that U.S. counties with high lead levels had four times the murder rate of counties with low lead levels, after controlling for multiple environmental and socioeconomic factors.

19   In 2002, Herbert Needleman, a psychiatrist at the University of Pittsburgh, compared lead levels of 194 adolescents arrested in Pittsburgh with lead levels of 146 high school adolescents: The arrested youths had lead levels that were four times higher.

20   "Impulsivity means you ignore the consequences of what you do," said Needleman, one of the country's foremost experts on lead poisoning, explaining why Nevin's theory is plausible. Lead decreases the ability to tell yourself, "If I do this, I will go to jail."

21   Nevin's work has been published mainly in the peer-reviewed journal *Environmental Research*. Within the field of neurotoxicology, Nevin's findings are unsurprising, said Ellen Silbergeld, professor of environmental health sciences at Johns Hopkins University and the editor of *Environmental Research*.

22   "There is a strong literature on lead and sociopathic behavior among adolescents and young adults with a previous history of lead exposure," she said.

What Explains Current Crime Trends?

23   Two new studies by criminologists Richard Rosenfeld and Steven F. Messner have looked at Giuliani's policing policies. They found that the mayor's zero-tolerance approach to crime was responsible for 10 percent, maybe 20 percent, at most, of the decline in violent crime in New York City.

24   Nevin acknowledges that crime rates are rising in some parts of the United States after years of decline, but he points out that crime is falling in other places and is still low overall by historical measures. Also, the biggest reductions in lead poisoning took place by the

mid-1980s, which may explain why reductions in crime might have tapered off by 2005. Lastly, he argues that older, recidivist offenders—who were exposed to lead as toddlers three or four decades ago—are increasingly accounting for much of the violent crime.

25   Nevin's finding may even account for phenomena he did not set out to address. His theory addresses why rates of violent crime among black adolescents from inner-city neighborhoods have declined faster than the overall crime rate—lead amelioration programs had the biggest impact on the urban poor. Children in inner-city neighborhoods were the ones most likely to be poisoned by lead, because they were more likely to live in substandard housing that had lead paint and because public housing projects were often situated near highways.

26   Chicago's Robert Taylor Homes, for example, were built over the Dan Ryan Expressway, with 150,000 cars going by each day. Eighteen years after the project opened in 1962, one study found that its residents were 22 times more likely to be murderers than people living elsewhere in Chicago.

27   Nevin's finding implies a double tragedy for America's inner cities: Thousands of children in these neighborhoods were poisoned by lead in the first three quarters of the last century. Large numbers of them then became the targets, in the last quarter, of Giuliani-style law enforcement policies.

COMPREHENSION CHECK

Map the major points supporting the Rick Nevin's theory that lead exposure increases crime.

Issue: Whether or not . . ._____

_____

Rick Nevin's point of view (conclusion about the issue): _____

_____

   Supporting Argument 1: _____

   _____
   _____
   _____
   _____
   _____
   _____

   Supporting Argument 2: _____

   _____
   _____

(Continued)

_____

_____

Supporting Argument 3: _____

_____

_____

_____

_____

_____

Supporting Argument 4: _____

_____

_____

_____

_____

Supporting Argument 5: _____

_____

_____

_____

_____

_____

Supporting Argument 6: _____

_____

_____

_____

Supporting Argument 7: _____

_____

_____

_____

_____

_____

Supporting Argument 8: _____

_____

_____

_____

_____

_____

Supporting Argument 9: _____

_____

_____

_____

_____

Supporting Argument 10: _____

_____

_____

_____

_____

Supporting Argument 11: _____

_____

_____

_____

_____

_____

READING GRAPHICS

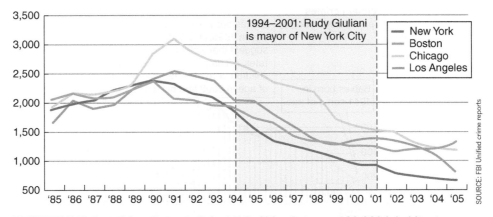

FIGURE 7.3 Violent Crime Rates In Select U.S. Cities Rate per 100,000 inhabitants

NOTE: The New York crime figure for 2001 does not include the 2,823 homicides reported as a result of the events of September 11, 2001

(Continued)

1. Determine the topic, structure, and most important point of Figure 7.3.

_____

_____

_____

_____

_____

In 1994, economist Rick Nevin began probing the link between lead and crime, comparing lead levels in both paint and gasoline with violent-crime rates. What he found was starting: As lead levels rose and fell, so did crime—but with a 23-year lag as children exposed to lead as babies came of age.

Gasoline lead
(in tons per capita)
Per-capital use of lead in gas rose from 1941 to 1972, then dropped sharply as leaded gas was phased out.

0.36

0.13

1.0

0.5

0

1941 1964 1972 1986

Violent crimes
(per 100,000 people)

Babies born in 1972 come of age in 1995. Nevins findings suggest that violent crime rates will drop even more as children born after 1985 come of age in 2008 and beyond.

Babies born in 1941 come of age.

600

400

200

190.6

463.21

0

1964 1995 2004

Note: Data not available beyond 2004.

FIGURE 7.4 Crime Rates Rise, Fall with Lead Levels

2. For Figure 7.3, determine which part of the information is verifiable, or fact, and which part of the information is a projection, or a reasonable inference (therefore an opinion), based on already verified factual information.

_____

_____

_____

_____

_____

3. Determine the topic, structure, and most important point of Figure 7.4.

_____

_____

_____

_____

_____

4. For both Figure 7.3 and 7.4, determine which part of the information is verifiable, or fact, and which part of the information is a projection, or a reasonable inference (therefore an opinion), based on already verified factual information.

_____

_____

_____

_____

_____

5. How might Figures 7.3 and 7.4 relate to the reading "Theory Links Lead Exposure, Crime"?

_____

_____

_____

_____

_____

_____

DEVELOPING YOUR COLLEGE-LEVEL VOCABULARY

1. How would you describe the author's tone in the reading? _____

_____

2. Is the author biased? If yes, provide some examples of loaded or biased language from the concluding paragraph of the reading to support your point of view. _____

_____

_____

_____

(Continued)

3. In paragraph 9, the word *legalization* is used. What is the origin of the root *leg*? _____

_____

4. In paragraph 25, the word *substandard* is used. What is the origin of the prefix *sub*? _____

_____

5. What is the connotation of the following language from the reading?

Paragraph 9: Why does the author use quotation marks for the following: "unwanted babies"?

_____

_____

Paragraph 10: "most of the theories have been long on intuition and short on evidence."

_____

_____

THEMATIC CONNECTIONS

1. Do you think Rick Nevin's argument is convincing or not? Provide reasons to back up your opinion.
2. What other possible causes may explain the reduction of the crime rate in major American cities since 1994?
3. What type of support is used in this reading to support the theory that lead exposure leads to crime?

WRAPPING IT UP

In the following study outline, fill in the definitions and a brief explanation of the key terms in the "Your Notes" column. Use the strategy of spaced practice to review these key terms on a regular basis. Use this study guide to review this chapter's key topics.

KEY TERM OR CONCEPT	YOUR NOTES
Editorial	
Lead statement in newspaper articles	

Research Study
   Abstract
   Hypothesis
   Introduction
   Methods
   Results
   Discussion
   References	

Prescriptive writing	
Descriptive writing	
Issue	
Point of view	
Supporting argument	
Fact	
Opinion	
Reason	

KEY TERM OR CONCEPT	YOUR NOTES
Example	
Testimony	
Counterargument	
Connotation	
Denotation	
Bias	
Tone	
Loaded language	

GROUP ACTIVITY: CASE STUDY

In small groups, research a case of a person who was convicted of a crime and later exonerated of that crime. Conduct a general search using a search engine. A good site is the Innocence Project Web site. However, cases of exoneration are often reported in newspapers.

Provide the following in your report.

1. Background information about the case, answering the journalist's questions of who, what, where, when, and how

2. Information about the process of the exoneration, the type of evidence found, and a timeline of those findings

3. The outcome of the exoneration: Did the victim (the person falsely accused) receive compensation for the false conviction?

REFLECTIVE JOURNAL QUESTIONS

1. In a reading assigned for another class, choose a passage and find several examples of words that indicate an author's bias or tone. Explain your reasoning.

2. In the introduction to this chapter, you read, "One of the foundations of a 'civilized' society is a fair and equitable justice system. Your education as an informed citizen will help you assess the pros and cons of the U.S. justice system. While this system is not perfect, there is at least some concern and support for its continual improvement." What do you think ought to be our primary focus to improve our justice system? Make sure to clarify facts you use in your answer from your opinion.

THEMATIC CONNECTIONS

Respond to one of the following questions. Prepare notes for class discussion or write a polished essay of several paragraphs to support your thesis. Type your essay and check it for typing, spelling, and grammatical errors before handing it in to your instructor.

1. What do you believe is the most significant issue in crime and punishment in the United States today? What are some ways to address this issue?

2. What is your position on the death penalty? State your point of view on this issue as your thesis and support your point of view with three or more arguments.

3. What are the qualities needed in an individual who works in the justice system? Choose three qualities (behaviors or attitudes) that characterize a successful professional in criminal justice. Support your answer with specific examples.

4. What do you feel should be done about wrongful convictions? Are there ways to stop this error in justice from happening?

5. What do you think should be the process for punishing juvenile crime? Should juveniles be sentenced to life without parole?

ADDITIONAL SKILL AND STRATEGY PRACTICE

Read the following argument about the deterrent effect of the death penalty. The deterrent effect refers to whether having capital punishment in a state functions to reduce crime; if a potential criminal knows that he or she may be eligible for execution for his or her crime, he or she decides against committing that crime. After you read, map the argument and determine if each is fact or opinion and decide on what type of support each argument uses. Then find two examples of loaded language from the reading.

The author is the director of the North Carolina Coalition for a Moratorium (NCCM). He educates, organizes, and provides legal assistance to citizens with social justice problems through his nonprofit work.

The Death Penalty Has Not Been Proven to Deter Murder
By Jeremy J. Collins

1   Though most experts have long dismissed any measurable deterrent effect from the use of the death penalty, a recent AP [Associated Press] story helped spark new discussion on the topic.

2   According to the report, some academic studies have purported to find such a deterrent impact. The story cited a 2003 Emory University study which concluded that each execution deters an average of 18 murders. To read the story, one might believe that new life has been pumped into what had largely been a settled argument.

Experts Reject the Deterrence Claim

3   A closer look at the facts, however, reveals that there was very little to the story. The truth is that leading academics have roundly rejected these studies. A rigorous 2006 study conducted by John Donohue of Yale Law School and the National Bureau of Economic Research (NBER) and Justin Wolfers of the Wharton School of Business and NBER analyzed the same data used in the Emory study and like studies and debunked their conclusions in striking terms: "The view that the death penalty deters is still the product of belief, not evidence." In fact, the researchers found that, if anything, "the evidence suggests that the death penalty may increase the murder rate."

4   Jeffrey Fagan, a professor at Columbia Law School and an expert on statistics, testified before Congress that the Emory study and similar Ehrlich-inspired studies finding a deterrent effect are "fraught with numerous technical and conceptual errors."

Evidence Contradicts the Deterrence Claim

5   When touting superficially powerful arguments in favor of the state executing our fellow human beings, the media and academics have a duty to acknowledge the facts contradicting their claims. These facts include not only that respected academics have rejected claims that the death penalty deters, but also the following:

- Murder rates are lower in states without the death penalty. This holds true even when comparing neighboring states.
- While Southern states account for over 80 percent of the executions in this country, they have consistently had the highest murder rate of the nation's four regions.
- Since 1972, homicide rates in Canada and the United States have moved in lockstep, yet in that period, Canada has not executed a single person and the United States has executed over 1,000 people. When homicides go down in the United States, they go down in Canada, even though Canada does not use capital punishment.
- One of the authors of the Emory study (Joanna Shepherd) found in a separate study that while the death penalty deterred murder in six states, it actually increased murder in 13 states and had no effect on the murder rate in eight states. Other studies have found that the death penalty has a "brutalization effect," increasing the number of murders.

6   Danger lurks whenever we look at statistical claims without a skeptical eye, never more so than when the issue is life and death. We need straight information before making an informed decision on the death penalty. Statistical claims that wilt under the mildest scrutiny woefully fail to meet that test.

SOURCE: Adapted from Collins, Jeremy J. "The Death Penalty Has Not Been Proven to Deter Murder." Reprinted with permission by the author.

Issue: Whether or not . . . _____

Point of View: _____

_____

ARGUMENTS	FACT OR OPINION	TYPE OF SUPPORT
1.		
2.		

ARGUMENTS	FACT OR OPINION	TYPE OF SUPPORT
3.		
4.		
5.		

Examples of loaded language:

_____

_____

_____

POST-ASSESSMENT

Preview the following article. Then go to the end of this article and answer the questions. This assessment will help you determine your strengths and weaknesses in understanding and applying the skills and strategies discussed in this chapter

The Real Crime: 1,000 Errors in Fingerprint Matching Every Year
by the LiveScience Staff

1   Nobody knows how many people sit wrongfully convicted in prison due to errors in fingerprint matching. But a new study suggests there could be a thousand or more unknown identification errors a year in the United States.

2   Criminologist Simon Cole of the University of California at Irvine examined all 22 known cases of fingerprint mistakes made since 1920.

3   Most of the 22 cases were revealed only through "extremely fortuitous circumstances," such as a post-conviction DNA test, the intervention of foreign police, and, in one case, a deadly lab accident that led to the re-evaluation of evidence, Cole said today.

4   One highly publicized example was the case of Brandon Mayfield, a Portland lawyer held for two weeks as a suspect in the Madrid train bombings in 2004. FBI investigators matched prints at the scene to Mayfield, and an independent examiner verified the match. But Spanish National Police examiners insisted the prints did not match Mayfield and eventually identified another man who matched the prints.

5   The FBI acknowledged the error and Mayfield was released.

6   Cole thinks the high-profile cases are the <u>tip of an iceberg</u> of wrongfully accused, cases that are sometimes <u>swept under the rug</u> or lead to convictions. Other studies have shown an error rate of 0.8 percent in matching prints. Multiplied across all cases processed by U.S. crime labs in 2002, that would be 1,900 mistaken fingerprint matches.

7   Cole says the public is led to believe that fingerprint analysis is infallible.

8   "Rather than blindly insisting there is zero error in fingerprint matching, we should acknowledge the obvious, study the errors openly, and find constructive ways to prevent faulty evidence from being used to convict innocent people," Cole said.

COMPREHENSION CHECK

Circle the best answer to the following questions.

Reading Comprehension

1 What is the main idea of this passage?

A. Based on the 22 cases of know fingerprint errors, we can assume there are many more—possibly thousands—per year.

B. Fingerprint evidence is very difficult to obtain and police should find other forensic evidence to prove a crime.

C. Studies of high-profile cases, while disturbing, are not conclusive.

D. Fingerprint evidence is not admissible in courts because of high error rates.

2 How does the author of the study reach his conclusion?

A. He studies real crime casebooks to find errors.

B. The author extrapolated (drew conclusions) from studies done by experts in the field.

C. The author extrapolated from the 22 high-profile cases and deduced his estimate.

D. The author has proof of the mistakes from cases retried during appeals.

3 What is a reasonable inference you can draw about the following sentence from paragraph 1?

But a new study suggests there could be a thousand or more unknown identification errors a year in the United States.

A. Police exhaust every avenue to double-check evidence.

B. Confessions are more reliable than fingerprint evidence.

C. Evidence analysis is approaching foolproof in the modern, technological age.

D. Evidence collection is subject to error, and we ought to investigate new methods to ensure accuracy.

4 What type of support is used in the sentence in question 3?

A. Facts

B. Reasons

C. Testimony

D. Examples

5 Is the sentence in question 3 fact or opinion?

A. Fact

B. Opinion

C. Both fact and opinion

D. Neither fact nor opinion

(Continued)

6   **Is this passage from paragraph 4 fact or opinion?**

FBI investigators matched prints at the scene to Mayfield, and an independent examiner verified the match. But Spanish National Police examiners insisted the prints did not match Mayfield and eventually identified another man who matched the prints.

A. Fact
B. Opinion
C. Both fact and opinion
D. Neither fact nor opinion

7   **What type of support is used in the passage in question 6?**

A. Facts
B. Reasons
C. Testimony
D. Examples

8   **This is a summary of a real research study. Original research studies include an abstract, an introduction, a description of participants and the research method used, results of the study, and discussion of the implications of the research results. What parts of the original study are probably used in this article?**

A. Discussion or abstract
B. Subjects and method
C. Hypothesis and results
D. All parts of the original study are summarized

Vocabulary Comprehension

9   **What does the expression "tip of an iceberg" mean as used in paragraph 6?**

A. The lowest of the low
B. Absurdity
C. Implying far more than is visible or apparent
D. An eye for an eye

10   **What does the expression "swept under the rug" mean as used in paragraph 6?**

A. Kept secret
B. In need of a cleaning
C. Vindictive
D. Obvious or evident

Evaluating
ARGUMENTS

✳ Why Do You Need to Know This?

What is the goal of a critical reader? A critical reader goes beyond understanding what is written and makes a judgment about the strengths and weaknesses of a piece of writing. In Chapter 7, you learned how to map an argument and determine its different parts, using the critical thinking skill of analysis. Now you will develop skills in synthesis and evaluation. Synthesis is drawing conclusions from two or more sources in order to put them together, either in developing a clear thought about an issue, or in writing or speaking about two or more related topics. In this chapter, you will also consider how to evaluate an argument—that is, to make a critical judgment not only about the contents of a reading

IN THIS CHAPTER, YOU WILL LEARN

- To recognize deductive and inductive arguments
- To evaluate reasoning in an argument
- To determine the relevance of arguments
- To determine if arguments are complete, believable, and consistent
- To recognize common types of propaganda and errors in reasoning
- To understand graphics: recognizing propaganda in advertisements

A READING STUDY STRATEGY

- Critical thinking strategies

VOCABULARY STRATEGIES

- Recognizing intended meaning: euphemisms and doublespeak
- Increasing your discipline-specific vocabulary: medicine

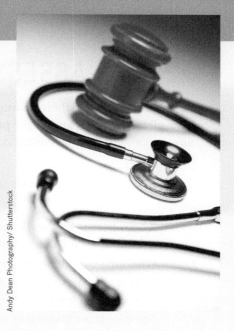

Andy Dean Photography/ Shutterstock

" **MEDICINE IS A SCIENCE OF UNCERTAINTY AND AN ART OF PROBABILITY.** "

SIR WILLIAM OSLER Canadian physician (1849–1919)

and the use of propaganda (a deliberate attempt to convince a reader of a specific agenda), but also about the relevance and soundness of the author's support for his or her point of view. You'll also learn the most common errors in reasoning.

Medical research has yielded complex and controversial ethical dilemmas that society grapples with every day. With

what we know about genetics, medical technology, and the brain, we are rapidly expanding our insight into what we *can* do medically versus what we *should* do ethically. Do some of our new medical technologies cross the ethical line? What is the ethical line? Just because we have the knowledge to launch exploration into the frontier of modern medical science, should we?

✓ **CHECK YOUR PRIOR KNOWLEDGE**

Jot down some facts you know about medical ethics. Do not edit your list—just brainstorm!

_____
_____
_____
_____
_____
_____
_____
_____
_____
_____
_____
_____

PRE-ASSESSMENT

ONLINE SCIENCE MAGAZINE

Read the passage and then answer the questions that follow. Don't worry if you do not know what all the terms mean yet. The purpose of this Pre-Assessment is to find out how much you already know about the reading skills and strategies introduced in this chapter.

Designer Babies: Ethical? Inevitable?
by Robert Roy Britt

1   A baby born in England recently was chosen in the embryonic stage to be free of a gene linked with certain types of cancer.

2   "This little girl will not face the specter of developing this genetic form of breast cancer or ovarian cancer in her adult life," said Paul Serhal, medical director of the assisted conception unit at University College hospital, London.

3   The case is not the first of its kind.

4   In the United States, a man with a 50 percent chance of passing on a gene for deadly colon cancer used the technique, too. He and his wife had embryos screened prior to implanting one in her womb, resulting in a daughter that won't get the disease.

5   The British woman, who has remained anonymous, made the decision in June to undergo screening of 11 embryos, each three days old, because her husband's female relatives suffered cancers, according to *The Guardian*. "We felt that, if there was a possibility of eliminating this for our children, then that was a route we had to go down," she said at the time.

6   The same genetic testing, called pre-implantation genetic diagnosis (PGD), has been used to test for inherited disorders such as cystic fibrosis and Huntington's disease, life-shortening diseases known to be certainly acquired by those carrying a single gene. What's new in this case is that the gene tested for, called BRCA1, does not inevitably lead to cancer in someone who carries it and if the cancers do develop they are potentially treatable.

7   Women who carry the BRCA1 gene have an 80 percent chance of developing breast cancer and a 60 percent chance of developing ovarian cancer during their lifetime. They also have a 50 percent chance of passing the gene on to each of their children.

8   The events might presage other screenings designed to create <u>designer babies</u> based on gender, IQ or athletic ability, some ethicists fear.

9   "There are many complex issues to take into account and the decision will finally come down to an individual's personal ethics," said Kath McLachlan, a clinical nurse specialist at the charity Breast Cancer Care.

10   Some fear the worst if laws are not crafted to corral the burgeoning field of "<u>reprogenetics</u>," as it is called—combining reproductive technologies with genetic screening.

11   "If misapplied, [these technologies] would exacerbate existing inequalities and reinforce existing modes of discrimination . . . the development and commercial marketing of human genetic modification would likely spark a techno-eugenic rat-race," Richard

Hayes, executive director of the Center for Genetics and Society. "Even parents opposed to manipulating their children's genes would feel compelled to participate in this race, lest their offspring be left behind."

12   The polar opposite argument is made by Dartmouth College ethics professor Ronald M. Green, who envisions a nearly disease-free future in which the information gleaned from reprogenetics allows genes to be tweaked, producing healthier humans without discarding embryos. "Why not improve our genome?" Green asks.

13   A report last year in the journal *Nature* predicted a host of changes to human fertility technology in 30 years' time: Artificial wombs and experiments on human embryos grown in the lab will be commonplace, several scientists said. With embryos grown in labs, mutations could be corrected and improvements could be engineered. The same researcher said there would be no designer babies, however, because no single gene is that predictive of a perfect child.

14   Meanwhile, the British mother and daughter are said to be doing well.

SOURCE: Robert Roy Britt, "Designer Babies: Ethical? Inevitable?", *Live Science*, July 2009 (from http://www.livescience.com/3213-designer-babies-ethical-inevitable.html). Reprinted with permission of TechMediaNetwork, Inc.

COMPREHENSION CHECK

Circle the best answer to the following questions.

Reading Comprehension

☐1☐ **What is the issue in this reading?**

A. Whether or not pre-implantation genetic diagnosis (PGD) is ethical

B. Whether or not pre-implantation genetic diagnosis (PGD) causes health concerns

C. Whether or not pre-implantation genetic diagnosis (PGD) should be legal

D. Whether or not pre-implantation genetic diagnosis (PGD) can help us improve our genome

☐2☐ **What is the author's point of view?**

A. Yes, pre-implantation genetic diagnosis (PGD) is ethical.

B. Yes, the government will endorse continued use of pre-implantation genetic diagnosis (PGD).

C. No, pre-implantation genetic diagnosis (PGD) is not ethical.

D. The author does not take a side on the issue.

☐3☐ **Which of the following arguments is *against* pre-implantation genetic diagnosis (PGD)?**

A. If misused, such technology could lead to more inequality and discrimination.

B. The technique could lead to the marketing of human genetic modification.

(Continued)

C. The technique could lead to competition between parents for "flawless" babies.

D. All of the given are answers.

4 **What type of support is used for arguments *against* pre-implantation genetic diagnosis (PGD)?**

A. Facts

B. Testimony

C. Examples

D. Reasons

5 **Which of the following arguments is used to *support* the use of pre-implantation genetic diagnosis (PGD)?**

A. PGD is unethical and may pose social hazards.

B. PGD can lead to healthier people.

C. PGD can compromise privacy.

D. PGD may pose health risks.

6 **Which of the following is a reasonable assumption underlying the argument in *favor* of pre-implantation genetic diagnosis (PGD)?**

A. Having medical intervention with PGD can save lives.

B. This treatment will not unfairly impact people or be abused.

C. Both a and b are reasonable assumptions.

D. None of the stated assumptions is reasonable.

7 **What type of support is used for the argument *in favor* of pre-implantation genetic diagnosis (PGD)?**

A. Facts

B. Testimony

C. Examples

D. Reasons

8 **What is the ethical dilemma with the specific case of the British couple and the genetic testing of their embryo?**

A. Some people feel that they should take their chances with passing on the gene called BRCA1.

B. They only wanted the perfect child.

C. The BRCA1 gene is predictive of certain cancers but not everyone who has the gene will get the cancer, and, even if they did, there are treatments.

D. The BRCA1 gene is only found in male embryos.

Vocabulary Comprehension

9 **What does the word *reprogenics* mean in paragraph 10?**

A. Combining reproductive technologies with genetic screening

B. Pre-implantation genetic diagnosis

C. Genetic testing

D. Embryonic research

10 **What does the euphemism "*designer babies*" mean?**

A. Babies who grow up to design their own futures

B. Babies who were designed by their parents

C. The medical community's word for embryonic studies

D. Genetically tested embryos selected for the absence of mutations that link to disease

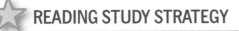 READING STUDY STRATEGY

CRITICAL THINKING STRATEGIES

Whereas high school tests often tend to involve memorization, college tests also require proficiency in **critical thinking.** Thinking critically means analyzing, evaluating, and synthesizing information. The first step in thinking critically is to **comprehend,** or understand, the material. This involves recognizing the topic, determining the main idea, seeing the relationship between ideas, and understanding how supporting details reinforce and elaborate on the main idea.

Bloom's Taxonomy

To understand the different types of thinking for college success, spend a moment considering Bloom's taxonomy, a six-level hierarchy of thinking skills that corresponds to levels of understanding in Figure 8.1. These levels of understanding are related to how you interpret and use information that you read, from simple comprehension to more complex levels of reasoning. In college, instructors expect that you can perform on the first three levels—that you comprehend and can apply what you read for class. In college, the focus, then, is thinking critically about what you read—the higher three levels.

Only after you fully understand what the author has written can you begin to take your understanding further and think about the author's ideas critically. Reading or thinking critically does not mean picking apart an idea to find fault, as the word *criticize* is often construed in everyday speech. Rather, critical thinking involves applying reasoning skills on a more sophisticated or complex level to really

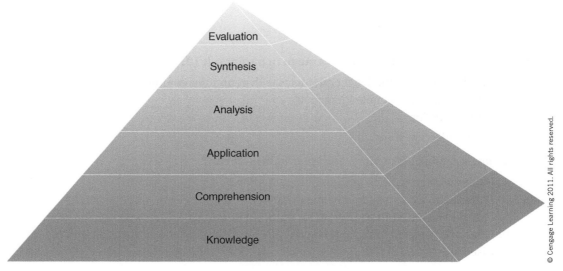

FIGURE 8.1 Bloom's Taxonomy

understand and interact with the new material, and see how it relates to your prior knowledge. Critical thinking involves analysis, synthesis, and evaluation of information.

- **Analyzing** information requires that you see the relationship between ideas and processes and understand how these parts interrelate with the topic, or the whole reading.

- **Synthesizing** information requires that you fully understand *related* concepts or ideas, or can see the relationship between ideas from more than one source and can then draw conclusions and derive judgments by integrating, or putting together, information from these different sources to come up with a conclusion on your own.

- **Evaluating** information requires that you fully understand the concept, or idea, and, furthermore, can judge strengths, weaknesses, and issues or ramifications of the concept.

So, if you do not "get" what you are reading, you cannot begin to think critically about it. In Table 8.1, the differences between the six levels of thinking are discussed as well as key words that indicate the level of question you are being asked to consider.

TABLE 8.1 Bloom's Taxonomy

BLOOM'S CATEGORY	EXAMPLE	KEY WORDS
Knowledge: Understand and recall information	Answering questions that are explicit in the text	*Define, describe, identify, state*
Comprehension: Understand a problem, interpret it, and be able to paraphrase it	Paraphrasing a passage, finding a main idea, summarizing a reading	*Comprehend, explain, restate, interpret, paraphrase, summarize, outline, discuss*

BLOOM'S CATEGORY	EXAMPLE	KEY WORDS
Application: Apply or use a new concept or idea in another context	Applying a skill to a new reading (On Your Own exercises)	*Apply, construct, demonstrate, relate*
Analysis: Separate information into parts to see how they fit together	Seeing the relationship between ideas, drawing conclusions	*Analyze, compare, contrast*
Synthesis: Put parts together to form a whole, focusing on creating something new and forming a new conclusion	Putting together two or more readings on a topic and integrating ideas	*Combine, compose, reconstruct, rewrite*
Evaluation: Make a judgment about the value of a reading or point of view	Looking at the strengths and weaknesses in an argument Applying the most useful reading strategy to the task at hand	*Compare, conclude, criticize, contrast, interpret, justify, support*

Question–Answer Relationships

Question–Answer Relationships, or **QAR,** is a strategy that helps you understand what type of question is being asked and, therefore, how to answer it. In other words, using QAR gives you insight into what level the question roughly corresponds to in Bloom's taxonomy. QAR, however, is simpler than the six levels because this strategy breaks question types into four levels. This reading and learning strategy is very helpful when you interact with written text. By identifying the particular type of question you are being asked, you can gain insight into how to answer it.

This strategy works well for reading comprehension questions as well as for answering test questions. Questions fall into one of these four categories. If you identify the category, you will be able to answer the question more accurately.

1. **Right There.** This type of question is literal. You are being asked to locate information in the text that is explicitly stated and can be found in a particular spot.

    Example: According to the passage, in what year was the author born?

2. **Think and Search.** Like Right There, this type of question compels you to find a literal or directly stated answer and locate information in the passage. However, unlike a Right There question, Think and Search requires you find the answer in at least two areas of the passage.

    Example: Describe two or more techniques the author suggests to reduce the effects of stress.

3. **Author and You.** This type of question requires you to comprehend the passage and to locate information. However, you must also use your own experience or opinion along with that of the author.

> **Example:**   Do you agree or disagree with the thesis of the article?

4. **On Your Own.** This type of question refers exclusively to your own opinion about a topic or your own experience and background knowledge.

> **Examples:**   How do you think the U.S. prison system could be improved?
>
> In your opinion, what stresses do teenagers in the United States have to confront today?

With a partner or individually, find an example of each of the four types of questions in the QAR strategy in this chapter or another college textbook chapter.

RECOGNIZING DEDUCTIVE AND INDUCTIVE REASONING

To evaluate an argument, first and foremost you need to identify the issue, point of view, and supporting arguments—you have to understand *what* an author has said. You learned how to map an argument in Chapter 7. However, to judge an author's argument, you need to understand how the author constructed the argument—you have to understand *how* an author has put the argument together. When an author tries to convince a reader of his or her point of view, he or she follows a form of reasoning to try to persuade the reader to agree. There are two types of reasoning. **Deductive reasoning** follows from the general to the specific. **Inductive reasoning,** in contrast, follows from the specific to a conclusion or generality. Recognizing deductive and inductive reasoning, in short, is another way to read critically.

Deductive Reasoning

Deductive reasoning occurs when general principles are used to reach specific conclusions. The conclusion *leads to* proof, data, or reasons. Deductive reasoning is used when the author begins with a general statement that is assumed to be true. The general point leads to determining the specifics. This would be the type of reasoning used by a lawyer who is defending a client. His or her stance is that the client is not guilty. The conclusion is stated and evidence is garnered to support the conclusion. Scientists use deductive reasoning to prove a generality by conducting different experiments. This could be called a "top-down" approach. One of the most common types of deductive reasoning is called a **syllogism.** A syllogism is a specific form of deductive argument that has three basic steps.

X is Y.

B is X.

Therefore, B is also Y.

All dogs are mammals.

Goldie is a dog.

Therefore, Goldie is a mammal.

In this example, the conclusion is that all dogs are mammals. The fact that Goldie is a mammal follows from the generality that all dogs are mammals.

Inductive Reasoning

Inductive reasoning occurs when specific information leads to a general conclusion. Proof, data, or support makes the conclusion reached logical. This would be the type of reasoning used by a jury to pass judgment on a defendant of guilt or innocence beyond a reasonable doubt. The jury has not formed a prior conclusion in hearing the case and must weigh the evidence to reach a verdict. This type of reasoning might be called a "bottom-up" approach. This is the most common form of reasoning. For example, we assume that tomorrow the sun will rise because each morning in the past it has risen. While it is not certain this will occur again tomorrow, the outcome or conclusion is likely.

The sun rose this morning.

The sun has risen for all the mornings I can remember.

Therefore, the sun will probably rise tomorrow.

The likelihood of the conclusion following from the supporting arguments, then, is what makes an argument inductive. Assume that a child has had only negative experiences with dogs in the past. It is reasonable for that child to assume that all dogs will bring negative experiences.

The neighbor's dog barked at me.

Our new friends have a dog.

Therefore, their dog will (probably) bark at me.

Look at how Frank is behaving.

He's out of control.

He must be mad.

The conclusion that Frank must be mad is arrived at from the evidence that precedes it.

Deductive or inductive reasoning does not have to do with whether the thesis of a reading is at the beginning or end of a passage. Instead, whether a passage uses deductive or inductive reasoning has to do with *how* the conclusion is reached. Just as you focus on recognizing the pattern of organization in an informative text that an author uses to construct and present his information, recognizing how an author constructs his argument—whether inductive or deductive—reveals the author's reasoning and approach in writing persuasive text. Paying attention to the author's thought process adds to your arsenal of skills in comprehending the author's point of view.

QUICK TIPS RECOGNIZING DEDUCTIVE AND INDUCTIVE REASONING

Deductive reasoning occurs when

- ☑ The conclusion *leads to* proof, evidence, or support.
- ☑ General principles are used to reach specific conclusions.

Inductive reasoning occurs when

- ☑ Proof, evidence, or support *leads to* a *probable* conclusion by a process of logic.
- ☑ The specific supporting points *lead* to the generality.

 On Your Own RECOGNIZING DEDUCTIVE AND INDUCTIVE REASONING

Below are arguments or puzzles using either deductive or inductive reasoning. Write an *I* beside examples of inductive reasoning and a *D* beside examples of deductive reasoning.

_____ 1. Justin is a man. All men are actors. Therefore, Justin is an actor.

_____ 2. Miranda used a cookie sheet for three batches of cookies that all came out burned. So, the next batch on that cookie sheet will be burned.

_____ 3. 3, 5, and 7 are prime numbers, so all prime numbers are odd numbers.

_____ 4. Our dog Etch ran away. He has run away before and has always come back. Don't worry—Etch will come back.

_____ 5. All *a* are *c,* and all *b* are *c;* therefore, all *a* are *b.*

EVALUATING ARGUMENTS

When you watch a sports match, you probably have a favorite team. However, the fact that you favor one team over the other may not influence your opinion about which team played the best game. Furthermore, if you're a serious sports fan, you could see errors in your team's game that made them the unsuccessful team by the end of the game. While you may not endorse the other team, you probably could see why they won—their strategy, moves, and teamwork resulted in the outcome that they were the best players in that game. This sports analogy can be applied to critical reading.

Just because you agree with an author's point of view doesn't mean you have to agree that his or her argument was well constructed. To think critically, it is very important that you can identify, deconstruct, and evaluate arguments. As a college student, you know not to believe everything you read. But how do you back up your judgment about whether an argument is good or bad?

One way to determine if an argument is good or bad is to think about whether you agree with the author's position on the issue. While this may influence your decision, a critical reader also has tools to help him or her make a judgment about an author's argument not based on emotion, but rather on logic and reasoning. Deconstructing an argument means analyzing it to see how the parts fit together and make an informed judgment about the strengths and weaknesses of the argument.

Evaluating Reasoning in an Argument

As you learned in Chapter 7, an author's argument is made up of two parts: the main point or point of view and the support or supporting arguments that provide evidence for the author's main point. The purpose of an argument is to persuade the reader to accept the point of view of the author. As a critical reader, you must consider who the author's intended audience is for the reading. The author's goal is to persuade the reader with a well-organized argument in which the point of view is clearly stated and the supporting evidence is relevant and sufficient to prove the point of view. The author persuades the reader with supporting evidence in the form of facts, reasons, examples, or testimony. The author can also use counterargument as a technique to persuade the reader. The first step in evaluating an argument is to identify the components of the argument, or to *map* the argument. Mapping involves identifying the

- issue;
- author's point of view on the issue;
- supporting arguments;
- type of support used to persuade the reader.

Once you have determined the components of the argument, you need to evaluate the argument as a whole. As a reader, you will have to decide if an author's point of view is sufficiently supported by the supporting arguments. To be a critical reader, you need to dissect an argument to make sure the information is logical and reasonable. A **relevant argument** is one in which the point of view is proven by the supporting arguments; in other words, the support is relevant, or directly relates to the point of view expressed. When the supporting arguments are complete, believable, and consistent with the point of view, we judge the argument to be **sound.**

However, an argument will not be sound if the supporting evidence is not complete, if it is not believable, or if it is not consistent with the author's point of view. You can have a relevant argument with relevant support, but if that support is not complete, believable, or consistent with the arguer's point of view, it will not be a sound argument. Sound arguments are strong arguments. To see errors in reasoning in an argument, you need to map the argument first, as you learned in Chapter 7. Then you need to evaluate the reasoning in the argument.

QUICK TIPS STEPS TO EVALUATING AN ARGUMENT

1. Map the argument.

2. Evaluate the reasoning.
   a. Determine if the reasoning is deductive or inductive.
   b. Determine if the supporting arguments are relevant.

3. Determine if the argument is sound.
   a. Determine if the argument is complete.
   b. Determine if the argument is believable.
   c. Determine if the argument is consistent.

DETERMINING IF SUPPORT IS RELEVANT

Evaluating an argument involves first deciding if the support is relevant to the point of view. In other words, does the support directly back up the point the author is making? Whether or not a supporting argument is relevant has to do with whether there are errors in the author's reasoning that make you question if the supporting argument directly relates to the point of view. If you are a fan of courtroom drama in novels, movies, or television, you may have read or seen how lawyers approach the judge when the other side presents evidence that is not relevant, shouting, "Irrelevant, your Honor!" Based on whether the newly submitted evidence relates directly to the issue at hand, the judge may choose to allow or not allow that evidence to be heard.

There are many types of errors in reasoning that logicians, those who study logic, have categorized; literally dozens of subcategories have been outlined by experts. These logical errors are also known as **fallacies.** A fallacy, from the Latin word meaning deceitful or false, is a flaw in reasoning that, at first glance, may appear to be reasonable or logical. Upon closer inspection, however, you will discover that the logic behind the argument is absent or confused. These errors in reasoning are not necessarily intentional, as is propaganda.

Logical Fallacies: Unintentional Errors in Reasoning

Often, the error in reasoning is that an author is operating from certain assumptions, or beliefs, that render the argument unsound. **Assumptions** are beliefs that an author holds true, often unstated, that inform his or her argument. Assumptions may take the form of bias, prejudice, and stereotyping. Assumptions may also make the author "jump to conclusions" rather than clearly and sufficiently explain the support for his or her argument. When an author's assumptions disrupt his or her argument, the result is a logical fallacy. A **logical fallacy** occurs when the premises or supporting arguments do not support the conclusion directly, which makes an argument either irrelevant, not sound, or both. An author may make an unintentional error in reasoning if she makes an error in calculation, judgment, opinion, or has insufficient knowledge.

For example, if an argument was made that teenage birth rates rose in the United States between 2009 and 2010 and that we need to reconsider education to counteract this alarming trend, the author has made a logical fallacy. The conclusion is that we need to create educational reforms to prevent this trend. The supporting argument is that teen birth rates rose within the years mentioned. This supporting argument is fallacious—it is not true. The author committed a logical fallacy, assuming the misinformation was not deliberate, since teenage birth rates in the United States, in fact, declined between 2009 and 2010 based on information provided from the Center for Disease Control.

Propaganda: Intentional Errors in Reasoning

Unlike logical fallacies, propaganda is an error in reasoning that an author makes deliberately in order to sway the opinion of the reader or to manipulate the reader. Propaganda is defined as

1. words or ideas that are used deliberately to harm a person, institution or group

2. the spreading of rumor or slander

3. doctrines or principles used by a source to manipulate or obfuscate

To help make their argument, authors may use intentional errors in reasoning to support their point of view, showing a one-sided, biased position on an issue. As you can see from the definition, propaganda is intended to harm and is deliberate.

The opposite of propaganda is impartiality. While all arguments promote one side of the issue (after all, the purpose is to persuade the reader of the author's point of view), propaganda has negative connotations because the term implies that an author deliberately manipulates the reader by confusing the issue and using deceptive tactics. While all persuasive text seeks to manipulate or convince the reader to some extent, the *purpose* of propaganda is to manipulate the reader.

An example of propaganda is literature promoting a helpline or help center for teenage pregnancies, suggesting that all options for the teenager are presented in deciding what to do about the pregnancy. In truth, the help center has a pro-life agenda and seeks to manipulate the teenager into continuing the pregnancy using inaccurate and biased information in order to manipulate the outcome. This one-sidedness, promoting a specific agenda and obscuring the alternative while posing as an impartial resource, is propaganda. This has nothing to do with the merits of pro-choice or pro-life perspectives but with deliberate obfuscation—not presenting all options while representing that the agency presents itself as offering all options but, in reality, does not.

There are eight common propaganda devices, or fallacies of relevance.

1. **Card stacking** is a device whereby the author presents information in support of one side of the argument but not the other. Card stacking is a propaganda device. The name derives from magicians appearing to present a clean deck of cards for a trick when, in reality, the deck has been rigged. This device is common in persuasion and is difficult to recognize because the purpose of an argument is to support one side of an issue and convince the reader to accept that particular point of view. An example of card stacking is when a television channel or biased print media source presents one side of political perspective without representing the other point of view. This is card stacking since the audience does not get to consider all sides of the argument.

2. **Glittering generalities** are sweeping statements that are unsupported by hard evidence. The positive support is vague and usually has to do with abstract concepts such as love, honor, freedom, and other positive, but abstract, values. No concrete argument is made.

> Smokers have rights. We have the right to freedom and the right to the pursuit of happiness like everyone else. Those who seek to take away your rights are taking away your liberty. That is un-American.

Issue: Whether or not smokers have rights

Author's Point of View: Yes, smokers have rights.

Supporting Arguments:
1. We have the right to freedom and the right to pursue happiness.
2. Opponents take away our liberty, which is un-American.

By declaring smoking laws un-American and by equating smoking with the exercise of freedom, the author is making sweeping statements using vague abstractions like "freedom" and "happiness." The argument is weak and without clear support.

3. **Personal attack,** or ***ad hominem*** (from the Latin for "argument to the person"), is a technique of attacking the opponent with name-calling rather than addressing the issue at hand.

> How can we trust the eyewitness who claims that Mr. Smith is not guilty of the crime for which he is accused? This witness is a known drug user and, therefore, her testimony is irrelevant.

Issue: Whether or not the witness can be trusted

Author's Point of View: No, the witness cannot be trusted.

Supporting Argument: She is a known drug user.

Here, the issue of the eyewitness testimony is avoided and, instead, "mud is slung" at the eyewitness. Not taken into consideration is whether the eyewitness has recovered from her problems or may be a credible witness. The content of the testimony is dismissed through name-calling. The testimony is dismissed before it is even considered.

4. **Appeal to authority,** or **testimonial** is the opposite of a personal attack. Here, an individual's testimony is considered "proof" of the point of view simply because the person is considered

an authority. However, the person's authority is questionable; he or she is not qualified to be an authority on the subject in question.

> Our Founding Fathers would never have tolerated the war over a citizen's right to bear arms. They felt and wrote that all people should have this constitutional right, and so we must listen to their sound judgment.

Issue: Whether or not citizens have a right to bear arms

Author's Point of View: Yes, citizens should have the right to bear arms.

Supporting Arguments:
1. The Founding Fathers would not approve of the opposition to bearing arms.
2. Their judgment is sound.

Here, the basis of the argument relies on the opinions of the Founding Fathers. No actual support as to why we should continue to support the constitutional right is offered. The Founding Fathers' point of view is an appeal to authority. While the right to bear arms may have been necessary at the time of the Founding Fathers, are social conditions the same today?

5. **Bandwagon** is an error in reasoning where the author claims that "everyone's doing this," so you ought to as well. This term derives from the expression "hopping on the bandwagon," which refers to joining a popular movement. Politicians used to ride on large wagons while campaigning. Bands would play atop the wagons, and people would jump on in excitement.

> Bry Carter has proven to be an excellent choice for mayor. Everyone's voting for her, and we all know she will be the best person for the job.

Issue: Whether or not Bry Carter should be mayor

Author's Point of View: Yes, Bry Carter should be elected mayor.

Supporting Argument: Everybody's voting for her.

The implication of this message is that because everyone's voting for Bry Carter for mayor, you should, too.

6. **Plain folk** is an error in reasoning in which an author tries to convince the reader that a person is trustworthy. The author wants you to trust this character because he or she is a "regular" person, just like you and me. This technique is used frequently in political campaigns.

> The secretary of state loves to go fishing and attend local meetings when he is back on his ranch in his hometown. Isn't he what America needs in the White House?

Issue: Whether or not the secretary of state is good for the position

Author's Point of View: Yes, the secretary of state is good for the position.

Supporting Argument: The secretary of state likes to go fishing and attend his hometown meetings when he can.

The fact that the secretary of state likes to attend hometown meetings and fish is not relevant to his position in the government. But the author manipulates you, the reader, by making you think the secretary of state is "just a regular guy" and, therefore, will do a good job for you.

7. A **straw man fallacy** occurs when an opponent's argument is misrepresented and then it is argued that the original point of view has been addressed. This error in reasoning oversimplifies, misconstrues, or misrepresents the original argument. Sometimes, quotations are used out of context as evidence for an opponent's position. This position is, then, counterargued. The problem is that what is counterargued is not the original position of the opponent in the first place. The name derives from the idea of attacking a straw man and claiming victory while the real opponent has not been defeated at all. Straw man is, in short, a diversion tactic to divert attention from the real issue.

> Cassandra thinks that parents should carefully monitor their children's TV viewing. That's ridiculous; you cannot place children in a vacuum their whole lives.

Issue: Whether or not children's TV should be monitored

Author's Point of View: Children's TV viewing should not be monitored.

Supporting Argument: Children cannot be kept in a vacuum, away from daily life.

You can see from this example that the position of the opponent, Cassandra, is simply to monitor children's TV watching. To prove her wrong, the author has made a straw man argument by suggesting that Cassandra's original intent was to keep children from experiencing real life. This is not at all what Cassandra intended.

8. An **appeal to emotion** is used to evoke a strong emotion in a reader in order to give power to the author's point of view. The appeal is to emotion instead of to logic. The author uses loaded and emotionally charged language and manipulates the reader. This often takes the form of **appeal to fear,** where the danger of a situation is stressed in order to convince the reader that the author's point of view is reasonable. **Appeal to pity** is a manipulative technique to convince you to support the underdog or someone in need. The support does not directly relate to the issue. Instead, the author is "tugging on your heartstrings" to convince you to go along with his or her point of view. In addition, an author may use an appeal called **the slippery slope,** which means that unless you adopt the point of view of the author, you are doomed.

> If we do not do something now about the war on terror, we will be at the mercy of those who want nothing more than to see us perish. Thousands will suffer at the hands of the terrorists. Many will be women and children—unless you take action at once.

Issue: Whether or not you should take action on the war on terror

Author's Point of View: You must take action on the war on terror.

Supporting Arguments:
1. If we don't act now, the terrorists will kill us.
2. Thousands of women and children will suffer.

In this example, notice how emotionality is the main component of the support. Rather than offer specific support as to how the war on terror should be launched, the author just appeals to our fear and our pity for potential victims.

QUICK TIPS RECOGNIZING ERRORS IN REASONING: PROPAGANDA

Question to Ask Yourself	Type of Error in Reasoning
■ Does the author make an undeliberate argument where the support does not back up the conclusion?	Logical fallacy
■ Does the author present one point of view on an issue while claiming to be unbiased?	Card stacking
■ Does the author make sweeping statements about abstract values?	Glittering generalities
■ Does the author use an authority figure as the basis of support for a point of view?	Appeal to authority
■ Does the author contend that you should agree because everyone else does?	Bandwagon
■ Does the author suggest that someone is trustworthy just because he or she acts like a "regular" person?	Plain folk
■ Does the author attack the opponent rather than address the issues?	Personal attack
■ Does the author attack an opponent's argument by distorting the original argument?	Straw man
■ Does the author manipulate the reader with emotional appeals?	Appeal to emotion

On Your Own IDENTIFYING ERRORS IN REASONING

Here are statements that have an error in reasoning related to relevance. Identify the error from the list of possibilities below. Be ready to support your reasoning.

    A. Glittering generalities
    B. Bandwagon
    C. Personal attack
    D. Appeal to authority
    E. Plain folk
    F. Straw man
    G. Appeal to emotion
    H. Card Stacking
    I. Logical Fallacy

_____ 1. You always tell me not to smoke. How can you say this when you smoke a pack of cigarettes a day?

_____ 2. I am not a doctor, but I play one in the television drama *Medical Maelstrom*. I find that Relief Tabs always work on my headache. You should try them, too. *(Continued)*

_____ 3. Sean tells his new peer group that Heat Wave is his favorite band. Everyone looks at him and smirks at his comment. "Really?" they say. "We like Smash Freak. They are by far the best band to come along in years." Sean looks embarrassed. Finally, he says, "I was just kidding; Smash Freak is way better!"

_____ 4. Travie asks her parent if she can attend a party late one Saturday night. Her parent disapproves of this idea. "You never let me do anything," Travie responds.

_____ 5. The Dove beauty campaign "Real Beauty" doesn't promise to make you look like a supermodel if you use their products. But Dove will make you look like a "regular" person who is very wholesome and attractive.

_____ 6. Bryonie, misinformed in her knowledge of literature, argues that we should read more American literature at school since *Hamlet* has so much wisdom from which students can benefit.

_____ 7. We have to stop the rising tuition costs at our school. If we don't, we will soon be paying the same amount as students at private colleges: $30,000 per year!

_____ 8. Miranda is heading a debate on the merits of the American versus Canadian health care systems—yet only provides American health care facts, while claiming to be unbiased.

_____ 9. Kristen drives by a billboard that features a picture of a car. The caption reads, "Chevrolet, an American Revolution."

_____ 10. Cassandra is asked to help her friend Jeff decide whether to get a cat or a dog as a pet; Cassandra, uninformed on the facts, tells Jeff that cats are the most popular pets in the United States.

UNDERSTANDING GRAPHICS

RECOGNIZING PROPAGANDA IN ADVERTISEMENTS

Each day, you are bombarded with images aimed to convince you to buy products. Advertisements contain propaganda in order to sway the buyer to identify with the product and be convinced to purchase the product. Like arguments, good advertisements persuade the reader to adopt the advertiser's point of view. In the case of the advertiser, the point of view you are convinced to adopt is that you want to buy the product. In the example here, which propaganda device is used to sell Nike shoes?

a. Appeal to authority

b. Appeal to emotion

c. Bandwagon

Advertising Archives

In this advertisement, Michael Jordan is winning the game and wearing Nike shoes. Isaac Newton is losing the game. To understand the impact of the advertisement, you need to understand the allusion to Isaac Newton. Newton was a famous British physicist, born in the eighteenth century, who wrote about gravity and wrote the three laws of motion. Why is Newton Michael Jordan's competition? The advertisement implies that by wearing Nike shoes, Jordan is a winner, and even the known genius of Newton (especially in the area of gravity) cannot compete with the gravity-defying power of Nike shoes! Jordan is one of the foremost professional basketball players and an authority on the game. He wears Nike shoes, and so should you. The answer is "a," appeal to authority.

DETERMINING IF AN ARGUMENT IS SOUND

An argument is sound if the support is complete, believable, and consistent.

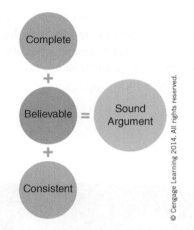

FIGURE 8.2 Factors Determining a Sound Argument

- **Complete.** Does the support prove the conclusion or substantiate the author's point of view? If the support is insufficient in supporting the point of view, then the argument is incomplete.

- **Believable.** Sometimes support for an argument is not believable, which leads the reader to question whether the foundation of the argument is credible. If it is not believable, then the point of view is in question.

- **Consistent.** Similarly, sometimes the support for an argument is not consistent. This means that support can contradict itself, other supporting points, or the point of view. If an essential piece of information is lacking, the argument is inconsistent.

The following four errors in reasoning are related to errors in completeness, believability, and consistency. They may show relevance, but they are either incomplete and do not adequately explain and substantiate the point of view, are unbelievable, or are inconsistent in supporting the point of view. These errors in reasoning stem from the faulty assumptions of an author. They are probably unintentional, unlike deliberate errors in reasoning such as propaganda.

1. **Non sequiturs,** from the Latin "does not follow," are errors in reasoning whereby the conclusion does not logically follow from the arguments. The author makes an **assertion,** or an unsupported claim, and provides evidence that does not support the claim. Alternatively, the author may simply not have thought of other explanations.

   The FDA has begun to fund preventative drug therapy for Parkinson's disease. Clearly, the FDA has found a cure.

Issue: Whether or not the FDA has found a cure for Parkinson's disease

Author's Point of View: The FDA has found a cure for Parkinson's disease.

Supporting Argument: The FDA is now funding preventative drug therapy.

In this example, the author uses the funding of preventative medication as proof that a cure has been found for Parkinson's disease, but evidence is not provided to support this claim.

2. A **false cause** is attributed when an author maintains that because two or more events occurred simultaneously, they are related by a cause-and-effect relationship. This error in reasoning is also known as **oversimplification.** In other words, all the conditions surrounding the claim are either "black or white" or "right or wrong." There is no room for "gray" areas. Of course, few issues in our world are so well defined as to allow no contingencies, or exceptions. Often, an author attributes an issue to a single cause.

> Video games must be closely monitored and even censored because of the violence they encourage. The perpetrators of the crime were both adolescents who were known to play video games frequently. Clearly, gaming unleashed their savage impulses as they became desensitized to violence.

Issue: Whether or not video games should be monitored and censored because they encourage violence

Author's Point of View: Yes, video games should be monitored and censored.

Supporting Arguments:
1. Perpetrators of the crime were adolescents who played video games.
2. Gaming made them savage and desensitized to violence.

In this example, the crime committed by the adolescents was attributed to the video games. The author jumps to a conclusion without proof.

3. A **faulty analogy** is made when an author assumes that two situations are parallel when, if fact, there are substantial differences.

> The social turmoil and decadence in today's society is the same as that of ancient Rome before the fall of the republic. Like the modern Western world, Rome had a corrupt government that did not pay attention to civil unrest. Also, in both societies, money was squandered by the rich and was in short supply by the poor. Rome fell, and so shall we.

Issue: Whether or not modern society is the same as ancient Rome before the fall of the republic

Author's Point of View: Yes, modern society is the same as ancient Rome and we, too, will "fall."

Supporting Arguments:
1. Government is corrupt.
2. No attention is paid to civil unrest.
3. Money is squandered by the rich and is in short supply to the poor.

In the arguments to support the point of view, the author does not address the substantial differences between the modern world and ancient Rome.

4. **Circular reasoning** simply restates the point of view of the argument rather than providing supporting evidence and actually addressing the argument. The author uses the point of view as one

of the arguments. This type of support is also called "begging the question." To "beg" the question means that the author is asking you to give in.

> We should ban the use of Propranolol, the memory-blocking drug. Ethically, blocking someone's memory, regardless of motivation, equals altering the person's mind. Some argue that memory-blocking pharmaceuticals are useful and humane for people who have suffered posttraumatic stress disorder or who have suffered from the aftermath of a violent crime or similar trauma. But wiping out memory takes therapy too far; it takes away memory.

Issue: Whether or not the memory drug Propranolol should be banned

Author's Point of View: Yes, the memory-blocking drug Propranolol should be banned.

Supporting Arguments:
1. Blocking memory is altering a person's mind.
2. Wiping out memory takes away memory.

In the arguments, the author merely restates the point of view without providing any evidence to support the claim that the drug should be banned.

QUICK TIPS DETERMINING IF AN ARGUMENT IS SOUND

Four Errors in Reasoning	
Non sequiturs	The point of view or conclusion does not follow from the arguments.
False cause	The cause-and-effect relationship does not necessarily make sense. There may be other explanations for the apparent cause-effect.
Faulty analogy	There is an incorrect assumption that two situations are parallel and can be compared.
Circular reasoning	The author supports the point of view with a restatement of the point of view. No genuine support is offered.

Question to ask yourself: Is the support complete, believable, and consistent?	Type of error in reasoning
▪ Does the author provide sufficient proof or evidence to support a claim that is made or implied?	Non sequitur
▪ Is the support resting on a faulty cause and effect relationship?	False cause
▪ Does the author make a comparison that is unsupported?	False analogy
▪ Is the support restating the point of view?	Circular reasoning

On Your Own IDENTIFYING IF AN ARGUMENT IS SOUND

Below are statements that contain an error in reasoning related to completeness, believability, and consistency. Identify the error from the list of possibilities. Be ready to support your reasoning.

    A. False analogy
    B. Circular reasoning
    C. Non sequitur
    D. False cause

_____ 1. Grunge music became popular at the same time things started to go wrong in our cities. Crime rates skyrocketed and drug abuse doubled. If we got rid of grunge, our cities would be better and safer.

_____ 2. Being in college is like working for a company: You have to put in the time each day, and you are expected to produce results by deadlines.

_____ 3. Ford was the best automaker for decades. Ford cars dominated the American auto market and, as a result, employees of Ford Manufacturing were paid well. Ford could afford to pay well because they made the best cars.

_____ 4. Pat is great at racing cars on his new video game. He must be a good driver on our city streets, too.

_____ 5. The problem with youth today is that they wear inappropriate fashions. If they dressed more conservatively, we would have less drug abuse.

Evaluating Author's Credentials and Intended Audience

To evaluate an argument, you need to pay attention to who the author is and whom he or she intends to read the argument. These two considerations are important because they influence your judgment about whether or not the argument is relevant, consistent, believable, and complete.

AUTHOR'S CREDENTIALS

Whether or not an author's background, experience, and expertise lend authority to his or her point of view is an important consideration. The word *credentials* comes from the Latin root, *cred,* which means "believable." As a critical reader, you want to consider if the author is qualified to render a decision on the issue. If the author has authority by virtue of his or her background, experience, or expertise, then this authority lends some weight to the author's point of view and supporting arguments. If the author does not have the background, experience, or expertise to pass judgment on the issue, then this weakens the author's argument. For example, an author with a medical degree would hold more credibility when arguing a medical issue than an author who is simply a medical correspondent for a newspaper.

INTENDED AUDIENCE

It is important to consider whom the author has in mind as his or her readers. You can determine the author's intended audience by looking at the choice of language and style of writing (level of vocabulary, tone, bias, and loaded language), as well as the type of publication in which the writing is found and typical readership of that publication (Figure 8.3). For example, if the reading is from a college-level textbook, the probable intended audience is college students. If the publication is a general U.S. newspaper, the probable audience is the general public. If the publication is an academic journal, the probable audience is those educated in that discipline.

FIGURE 8.3 Determining an Author's Credentials and Intended Audience

QUICK TIPS HOW TO EVALUATE AN ARGUMENT

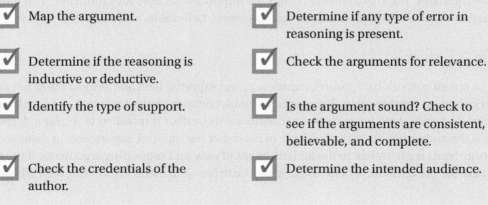

- ☑ Map the argument.
- ☑ Determine if the reasoning is inductive or deductive.
- ☑ Identify the type of support.
- ☑ Check the credentials of the author.
- ☑ Determine if any type of error in reasoning is present.
- ☑ Check the arguments for relevance.
- ☑ Is the argument sound? Check to see if the arguments are consistent, believable, and complete.
- ☑ Determine the intended audience.

Thinking It Through EVALUATING AN ARGUMENT

Preview this article, identifying the issue and the author's point of view (POV). Then read the article through, identifying the supporting arguments and noting them in the margins. Next, identify the type of support in brackets after the supporting argument. After you read the article, determine if the reasoning in the argument is inductive or deductive and whether the arguments are relevant and sound. If they are not, refer to the Quick Tips on page 561 to identify the propaganda or errors in reasoning. Make sure to consider the author's credentials and authority when you evaluate the argument. In addition, consider whom the author intends as the audience.

The "conscience clause" laws protect medical professionals who refuse to perform medical procedures or in any way engage in medical practices that are in opposition to their ethical, moral, or religious personal beliefs. The majority of the ethical debate concerns abortions, nonresuscitation issues, prescriptions for contraceptives, or opposition to stem cell research and/or procedures. While traditionally medical bodies support the conscience clause in theory, many are concerned with the issues where a pharmacist, doctor, or other medical professional may refuse service and also refuse to refer patients to appropriate bodies that may perform or fulfill a service. James O'Neill, the principal associate deputy secretary of the Department of Health and Human Services in 2008, wrote this editorial that was published in *USA Today* in 2009.

Medical Workers Deserve Robust "Conscience Clause"
by James O'Neill

1   Over three decades, Congress has passed laws (often collectively called the **"conscience clause"**) that prohibit hospitals and other institutions that accept federal funds from forcing employees to act against their moral or religious convictions—such as providing sterilization or Plan B, or coercing them to perform or refer for abortions.

Right to Object

2   As a Department of Health and Human Services official, I discovered that many doctors didn't even know that they had the right to conscience protection. How could they be expected to defend such a right? In fact, a quasi-governmental certification organization, the American Board

Issue: Whether or not medical personnel should be able to act on the conscience clause.

POV: Yes, medical personnel should be able to act on the conscience clause (refuse to perform certain medical procedures because of personal ethical or moral objections).

Argument 1: As a Department of Health and Human Services official, I discovered that many doctors didn't even know that they had the right to conscience protection. (Reason or testimony, but sources are not identified)

(Continued)

of Obstetrics and Gynecology, warned OB/GYNs in 2007 that "disqualification or diplomate revocation . . . may occur whenever" their practices conflict with the ethical code of the American College of Obstetricians and Gynecologists, which proposed to add a requirement that "health care professionals have the duty to refer patients" to abortion providers, regardless of conscience objections.

3   Many U.S. health professionals have been asked to suppress their moral objections, including a medical school applicant interrogated about abortion views, a medical student who was sent without warning to assist in a second-trimester abortion, and a nurse at a podiatry surgery center whose boss announced one day that the center would start performing abortions, and that nurses would assist or be fired.

Argument 2: Many U.S. health professionals have been asked to suppress their moral objections. (Reason or testimony, but sources are not identified)

Setting Guidelines

4   While at HHS, I led a team that designed a regulation to enforce the laws for the first time. We based it on the common-sense principle that patients and doctors have the right to agree on treatments and compensation. Neither should force the other to do something. As fellow human beings, their rights are equal.

Argument 3: Both patients and doctors have the right to agree on treatments and payment where one does not force the other to do something against their will. (Reason)

5   Critics suggest the goal of the regulation was to deny women access to abortions. But doctors and nurses at abortion clinics choose to work there.

Argument 4: This issue is not anti-abortion related but a matter of choice of participation in abortions. (Reason, but supported by fact)

6   America could use more doctors and nurses, especially OB/GYNs, so that patients can have greater access. But when 52% of doctors object to abortion for failed contraception, as The *New England Journal of Medicine* reported in 2007, a signal from the

Argument 5: Doctors who oppose abortion ought to be respected—the government should not penalize doctors for their ethics. (Reason)

president that they and medical students like them are not wanted would send the wrong signal.

7   This is not a liberal or conservative issue but individual conscience. As the president has said, "I believe in vigorous enforcement of our non-discrimination laws." Now he has a chance to back up those words with action—or in this case, inaction.

Argument 6: The right to act on the conscience clause is not political but is in accord with non-discrimination laws.

Issue: Whether or not medical personnel should be able to act on the conscience clause.

Point of View: Yes, medical personnel should be able to act on the conscience clause (refuse to perform certain medical procedures because of personal ethical or moral objections).

Supporting Argument 1: As a Department of Health and Human Services official, I discovered that many doctors didn't even know that they had the right to conscience protection.

   a. The American College of Obstetricians and Gynecologists proposed to add a requirement that "health care professionals have the duty to refer patients" to abortion providers, regardless of conscience objections.

This argument does not directly support the author's point of view. While it may be related in topic, it does not back up the author's point that medical personnel ought to be able to act according to their conscience. This argument is not relevant. While the supporting point that the American College of Obstetricians and Gynecologists proposed forcing medical professionals to adhere to an agenda that provided referrals to abortion providers does support the point of view that medical professionals are being forced into participating in medical referrals with which they don't agree, this support does not directly prove the point that many medical professionals are not aware of the conscience clause.

Supporting Argument 2: Many U.S. health professionals have been asked to suppress their moral objections.

   a. A medical school applicant was interrogated about abortion views.

   b. A medical student was sent without warning to assist in a second-trimester abortion.

   c. A podiatry surgery center nurse's boss decided that the center would start performing abortions, and that nurses would assist or be fired.

(Continued)

This argument does directly support the author's point of view. Since the author argues in support of a conscience clause, evidence that suggests that medical personnel are being compelled to engage in unethical treatment directly backs up the author's argument with examples. This argument is relevant.

Supporting Argument 3: Both patients and doctors have the right to agree on treatments and payment where one does not force the other to do something against their will.

While at first glance, this argument appears to support the author's point of view, careful thought reveals that this supporting argument, in fact, restates the author's point of view. Saying that medical professionals ought to be able to act according to their conscience is the same as saying that they ought to be able to refuse to do something against their will. The only additional information in this supporting argument is to include the will of the patient as well. This supporting argument is an example of circular reasoning.

Supporting Argument 4: This issue is not anti-abortion related but a matter of choice of participation in abortions.

The author states that physicians have a right to shun practices they judge immoral. This argument directly supports the author's point of view that the conscience clause should remain intact.

Supporting Argument 5: Doctors who oppose abortion ought to be respected—the government should not penalize doctors for their ethics.

    a. Fifty-two percent of doctors object to abortion for failed contraception, as the *New England Journal of Medicine* reported in 2007.

In this supporting argument, the author again resorts to circular reasoning to restate his position on the conscience clause. Here, however, the author also backs up this supporting argument with fact—that the majority of doctors object to abortion for failed contraception, according to the 2007 journal report. However, the author does not account for medical reaction to abortion for other reasons or due to other circumstances—how do the majority of doctors feel about abortion after rape or incest? Also, just because doctors may "object" to abortion for failed contraception, does this mean that objection is the same as refusal to perform this procedure?

Supporting Argument 6: The right to act on the conscience clause is not political but is in accord with nondiscrimination laws.

    a. The president should uphold this right.

In this last supporting argument, the author presents a new point, equating the conscience clause revocation with discrimination. While the author does not go into detail about this point, he says that the president ought to uphold the conscience clause and not rescind it.

Is the reasoning in the argument deductive or inductive? The argument involves deductive reasoning. The conclusion that "medical personnel should be able to act on the conscience clause" is supported by evidence or leads to the support.

Does each of the supporting arguments back up the point of view directly? Arguments 2, 4, and 6 support the author's point of view. Arguments 1, 3, and 5 do not substantiate the point of view.

Is each of the arguments relevant to the point of view and complete, believable, and consistent? There are three errors in reasoning out of six supporting arguments.

Is the argument sound? No, despite the fact that we may ultimately agree with the author, the argument as it stands is not sound. The author was the Principal Associate Deputy Secretary of the Department of Health and Human Services in 2008, which makes him a credible authority on this issue. However, this argument is too flawed in its reasoning to be either sound or convincing. Because the piece is an editorial for a national newspaper, the intended audience is the general public.

On Your Own EVALUATING AN ARGUMENT

Follow the outline from Thinking It Through to evaluate the following argument. Preview the article, ascertaining the issue and the author's point of view. Then read the article through, identifying the supporting arguments and noting them in the margins. Identify the type of support in brackets after the supporting argument. After you read the article, determine if the reasoning in the argument is inductive or deductive. Next, determine if the arguments are relevant and sound. If not, refer to the Quick Tips on page 561 to identify the propaganda or errors in reasoning. Make sure to consider the author's credentials and authority when you evaluate the argument. In addition, consider whom the author intends as the audience.

Doctors Who Fail Their Patients
Editor, the *New York Times*

1   It was bad enough when pharmacists who call themselves pro-life refused to fill prescriptions for morning-after pills and an emergency medical technician refused to help drive a woman to an abortion clinic. Now a new survey has revealed that a disturbing number of doctors, at the presumed pinnacle of the health professions, feel no responsibility to inform patients of treatments that the doctors deem immoral or to refer them to other physicians for care. Although the close-mouthed doctors claim a right to follow their consciences, they are grievously failing their patients and seem to have forgotten the age-old admonition to "do no harm."

(Continued)

2   The survey, by researchers at the University of Chicago, was published last week in The New England Journal of Medicine. The researchers mailed questionnaires to some 2,000 doctors asking whether they had religious or moral objections to three controversial practices. Of the 1,144 who responded, only 17 percent objected to "terminal sedation" to render dying patients unconscious, but 42 percent objected to prescribing birth control for adolescents without parental approval, and 52 percent opposed abortion for failed contraception.

3   The encouraging news is that substantial majorities thought that doctors who objected to a practice nevertheless had an obligation to present all options and refer patients to someone who did not object. But that left 8 percent who felt no obligation to present all options and an alarming 18 percent who felt no obligation to refer patients to other doctors. Tens of millions of Americans probably have such doctors and are unaware of their attitudes.

4   The researchers put the burden on patients to question their doctors upfront to learn where they stand before a crisis develops. But that lets doctors off the hook. Physicians have a right to shun practices they judge immoral, but they have no right to withhold important information from their patients. Any doctors who cannot talk to patients about legally permitted care because it conflicts with their values should give up the practice of medicine.

Issue: _____

_____

_____

Point of View: _____

_____

_____

_____

Supporting Argument 1: _____

_____

_____

_____

_____

_____

_____

_____

Supporting Argument 2: _____

_____

_____

_____

_____

_____

_____

_____

_____

Supporting Argument 3: _____

_____

_____

_____

_____

_____

_____

_____

_____

_____

Supporting Argument 4: _____

_____

_____

_____

_____

_____

Is the reasoning in the argument deductive or inductive? _____

_____

Does each of the supporting arguments back up the point of view directly? _____

_____

(Continued)

_____

_____

_____

_____

_____

_____

_____

Is each of the arguments relevant to the point of view and complete, believable, and consistent? _____

Is the argument sound? _____

_____

_____

_____

_____

_____

_____

_____

_____

 VOCABULARY STRATEGY

INTENDED MEANING: EUPHEMISMS
AND DOUBLESPEAK

In Chapter 7, you learned that loaded language reveals bias as well as tone in an author's writing. As a critical reader, you know that the connotations of words and the use of a particular writing style can reveal the author's position on an issue as well as the author's underlying attitude.
Sometimes, however, the author may say one thing in writing and mean another. This is called the
author's **intended meaning.** Euphemisms and doublespeak are specific kinds of loaded language
and exhibit further subtleties of language that can blur what an author says and what that author
really means.

Euphemisms

A **euphemism** is a "nice" way of saying something unpleasant or blunt. The root word for *euphemism* is *eu,* the ancient Greek word for "good." So a euphemism is a socially acceptable way of substituting agreeable wording for unpleasant or offensive truths. We use euphemisms all the time. For example, consider the following:

> We put a suffering or aged pet *to sleep* instead of *killing* it.
>
> We say a loved one has *passed away* instead of saying that he or she has *died.*
>
> We say that an employee has been *let go* instead of *fired.*
>
> We refer to the *ladies' room* instead of *toilet.*
>
> We use the word *incident* instead of *fight* to describe a confrontation or showdown.

All these examples use an agreeable term to "disguise" an unpleasant truth. Even though euphemisms cloak unpleasant realities with pleasant terminology, they do function to mislead the reader by manipulating the realities of the situation. Sometimes this is deliberately misleading, as with propaganda, and serves to manipulate for gain. Sometimes euphemisms serve to cushion social situations out of politeness or pleasantry. In any event, while not always sinister, euphemisms deliberately cloak reality under the guise of pleasantry.

Doublespeak

Doublespeak, a type of euphemism, is the use of language to blunt or nullify a harsh truth. This type of loaded language definitely functions to manipulate and obfuscate (or confuse) the situation. Doublespeak is deliberately constructed to disguise or distort the truth. It can take the form of euphemism or can involve deliberately ambiguous terminology. Like propaganda, doublespeak has one intent: manipulation to serve an agenda. In fact, doublespeak is a type of propaganda technique! Its purpose is to distort thought using language that has neutral or even positive connotations. Doublespeak can be distinguished from euphemisms by its use by large, powerful groups.

Sometimes this type of propaganda is exercised by corporations, governments, the military, social agencies, sports agencies, religious institutions, and other powerful bodies. It functions as a deliberate, manipulative effort to cloud negative connotations of words or phrases and make the terminology neutral. Moreover, this type of euphemism distorts the truth of what it depicts by making an upsetting reality bland and disguised as something not so bad. As the name implies, the language says one thing, but means another. Notice how these examples neutralize the strong emotions that might be evoked when what is being communicated is comprehended.

> *Collateral damage* means killing innocent civilians while attacking an enemy of war.
>
> *Friendly fire* means accidentally killing military personnel on your own side.
>
> *Downsizing* means firing employees.

Ethnic cleansing means genocide.

Person of interest means suspect.

Shock and awe means massive bombing.

Subsidized means welfare.

Outsourced means dismissing local labor to hire cheap labor in other countries.

Human intelligence means spies.

Physical persuasion or pressure means torture.

Aggressive enforcement means racial profiling or harassment.

On Your Own IDENTIFYING EUPHEMISMS AND DOUBLESPEAK

The following terminology makes a negative connotation more acceptable. Decide if the phrase is a euphemism or, if it is more manipulative, an example of doublespeak. Write an *E* next to the phrases that qualify as euphemisms and a *D* next to the phrases that qualify as doublespeak.

___ 1. *Restroom* for lavatory

___ 2. To *take out,* meaning "to assassinate"

___ 3. *Casualty* for those killed or maimed in war

___ 4. *Correctional facility* for prison

___ 5. *Incentive* for bribe

___ 6. *Capital punishment* for executing inmates

INCREASE YOUR DISCIPLINE-SPECIFIC VOCABULARY

MEDICINE

Medical terminology comes up across the media and in daily conversation as well as in medically oriented college textbooks. Familiarizing yourself with these affixes as well as with these commonly used medical words will jump-start your vocabulary (Table 8.2).

TABLE 8.2 Vocabulary Associated with Medicine

WORD PART	MEANING	VOCABULARY
ab	apart, away, down	abnormal, abstain, abstract, aberrant, absorb
anti	against, opposite	antagonist, antibiotic, antidote, anticlimax, antithesis
derma	skin	dermatology, epidermis, pachyderm, taxidermy
dia	across, through	dialogue, diagram, diagnose, diagonal
eu	good, well	eulogy, euphemism, euphoria, euthanasia
mal	bad	malicious, malignant, malevolent, maladaptive
morph	form/shape	amorphous, anthropomorphism, endomorphic, morphine, ectomorph
path	feeling	pathology, empathy, sympathy, telepathy, pathetic
ped	child/foot	pediatrics, pedal, pedigree, impediment, pedestrian
tomy	act of cutting	lobotomy, hysterectomy, vasectomy

Key Terms—Medicine

- **Chronic:** an ongoing condition or an illness of duration.
- **Etiology:** the study of the origins of disease.
- **Benign:** not deadly.
- **Malignant:** terminal, deadly or life-threatening.
- **Cardiology:** the study of the heart.
- **Gynecology:** the medical study of women.
- **Pediatrics:** the medical field of children's health.
- **Pathology:** the study of disease and the cause of disease.
- **Dermatology:** the study of the skin.
- **Hematology:** the study of blood.

APPLICATIONS

APPLICATION ①

In this application, you will read an editorial, published in the *Miami Herald* newspaper's editorial section, about whether doctors should contract with pharmaceutical companies to sell prescription medications.

Read the editorial, think critically, and use the critical reading strategies you have learned in this chapter to evaluate the arguments presented. After you read, mark the text. Then write the arguments in the margin, indicating the type of support for each supporting argument, or map the argument in the chart following the reading. Next, determine if the arguments are relevant to the author's point of view and if those arguments are consistent, believable, and complete. Be careful to determine if the writer of the article possesses the expertise to argue convincingly and with authority. In addition, consider whom the author intends as his or her audience. If you notice any euphemisms or examples of doublespeak in the readings, circle them and write them in the chart following the reading.

Cash to Doctors Can Ruin Patients' Trust
by the Editor, *Miami Herald*

1   Here's a <u>disturbing proposition.</u> What if your doctor is getting cash rebates based on the volume of drugs he or she prescribes to you and other patients? That would pretty much destroy the trust that you have in your doctor, wouldn't it?

Issue:

POV:

2   There ought to be a law against such practices and, in fact, there is. The problem, though, is that the law doesn't cover all situations. Federal law prohibits such conflicts between doctors and drug companies for medicines in pill form that are purchased by patients at pharmacies. Not covered are rebates for injected or intravenous medicines administered in clinics or doctor's offices. The Food and Drug Administration should discourage these practices immediately, and Congress should stiffen federal laws to ban them outright.

Argument 1:

Argument 2:

3   An article in *The New York Times* last week <u>shed some light</u> on the practice. The article described how two major drug companies, Amgen and Johnson & Johnson, paid millions of dollars each year to doctors who administered these companies' anemia medicines to their patients.

Argument 3:

Argument 4:

Argument 5:

Argument 6:

Argument 7:

Argument 8:

Argument 9:

4   Critics say that such large payments to doctors and kidney-dialysis centers (that also use large quantities of the drugs) create an <u>incentive</u> for doctors and the clinics to overuse the medicines. It doesn't help that the FDA released a report last week suggesting that the drugs used in cancer patients might have to be <u>curtailed.</u> The report said there was no evidence showing that the medicines improved patients' quality of life or extended their survival.

5   Nevertheless, for patients who suffer with anemia or who require kidney dialysis, the drugs are widely used in the United States and are considered <u>beneficial</u> when used appropriately. Since 1991, the average dosage given to U.S. patients has nearly tripled, *The Times* reported.

6   When patients visit a doctor or a clinic, they want to know that the doctor's advice and prescribed medications are based on what is in their best interest, not the doctor's financial interests. Rebates and payments to doctors for prescribing or administering any drug create such an obvious <u>conflict of interest.</u> These incentives should be banned outright.

7   A <u>conscientious</u> doctor will take pains to keep abreast of the latest research and medications that could help patients. A too-close relationship with a particular brand or drug company, cemented by generous financial rewards, can put doctors in the uncomfortable position of making decisions based on personal wealth rather than the health of patients.

8   Congress and the FDA should remove the temptation altogether. They should tighten the rules and strengthen the law to eliminate the potential conflict.

SOURCE: Republished with permission of McClatchy Company, from "Cash to doctors can ruin patients' trust," Editors of the *Miami Herald, Miami Herald*, May 16, 2007, p. 14; permission conveyed through Copyright Clearance Center, Inc.

COMPREHENSION CHECK

1 **Is the reasoning in the argument deductive or inductive? Does the conclusion follow from the proof or support, or does the proof or support follow from the conclusion? _____**

(Continued)

2 Does each of the supporting arguments back up the point of view directly? _____

_____

_____

_____

_____

_____

3 Is each of the arguments relevant to the point of view and complete, believable, and consistent? Justify your answers. _____

_____

_____

_____

_____

_____

_____

_____

_____

_____

_____

_____

_____

_____

_____

4 Is the argument sound? Are the arguments relevant to the author's point of view? Is the argument complete, believable, and consistent? _____

_____

_____

5 Do you think the author has proven that financial incentives from drug companies should be banned? Explain. _____

_____

_____

6 Is the author a credible source? _____

_____

_____

7 Who is the intended audience? _____

_____

_____

READING GRAPHICS

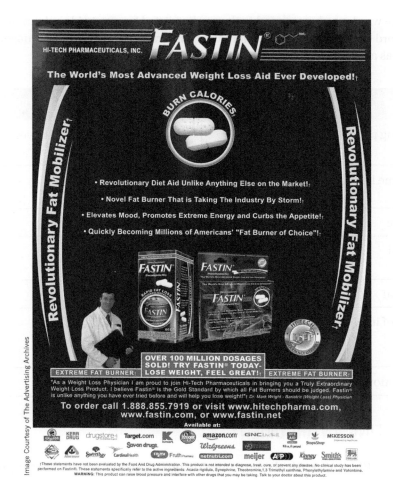

Image Courtesy of The Advertising Archives

1. What type of propaganda or error is used in this advertisement? Explain your answer.
_____
_____

2. What side of the debate does this advertisement fit best? Justify your answer. _____
_____
_____

3. How does the advertisement compel you to buy the product? _____
_____
_____

(Continued)

DEVELOPING YOUR COLLEGE-LEVEL VOCABULARY

For each of the words or phrases used in the reading listed here, provide a definition or explanation of that word from context and an alternative, preferably using loaded language. The first one is completed as an example.

VOCABULARY TERM(S)	PARAGRAPH	DEFINITION	ALTERNATIVE
1. disturbing proposition	1	a suggestion that is of concern	travesty, scam
2. shed some light	3		
3. incentive	4		
4. curtailed	4		
5. beneficial	5		
6. conflict of interest	6		
7. conscientious	7		

CONSTRUCTING AN ARGUMENT

Opposing View: Pharmaceutical companies do not influence what a doctor prescribes to patients

Construct an argument supporting the medical professionals' ethics. You will find arguments that support the point of view that these professionals prescribe drugs that are best for the patients rather than to accept bribes for using certain drugs. Next to your supporting arguments, indicate if each is a fact, reason, example, or testimony. After, analyze others' arguments and provide feedback on whether their argument is

  a. deductive or inductive;

  b. directly supports the point of view;

  c. complete, believable, and consistent;

  d. sound.

Issue: Whether or not pharmaceutical companies influence what a doctor prescribes for patients

Point of View: No, pharmaceutical companies do not control what doctors prescribe for patients.

Supporting Arguments: _____

_____

_____

_____

_____

_____

_____

_____

_____

_____

_____

_____

_____

THEMATIC CONNECTIONS

1. Do you think medical professionals are likely to accept incentives from drug companies? Why or why not?

2. If a drug company provides incentives to medical professionals and their product is in the best interests of the patient, is this morally wrong?

3. What do you think the medical establishment, government, or public can do to control financial incentives from drug companies?

APPLICATION ②

In this application, you will read two sides of a debate on whether to provide financial incentives for organ donations first published in *USA Today*. The first article is the newspaper's view that money should be used to encourage organ donations. The second editorial, written by Charles B. Fruit, chairman of the National Kidney Foundation, proposes that providing financial incentives is unethical. Read the debate, think critically, and use the critical reading strategies you have learned in this chapter to evaluate the arguments presented. After you read, mark the text. Next, determine if the arguments are relevant to the author's points of view and if they are consistent, believable, and complete. Be careful to determine if the writer of the article possesses the expertise needed to argue convincingly and with authority. In addition, consider whom the author intends as his or her audience. If you notice any euphemisms or examples of doublespeak in the reading, circle them.

READING 1

Our View: Organ Donations Fall Short; Financial Incentives Can Help
by the *USA Today* Editorial Staff

1   "Please help! My daddy needs a liver." A billboard with that stirring message greeted thousands of motorists recently on a busy Chicago expressway. It's one of many pleas from desperate families seeking organs for transplantation. Classified ads shout their need. So do Web pages.

2   In the more than 50 years since the first successful organ transplant, hundreds of thousands of patients have had their lives extended because of organ donations. Despite decades of campaigns to persuade Americans to donate organs after they die, however, the demand increasingly exceeds the supply. The waiting list for organs, mostly kidneys, has doubled over the past decade to more than 92,000 patients. Eighteen die daily before getting one.

3   The sad fact is that patients needing a transplant are more likely to die waiting than to receive organs. The wait in many locations is five years, and it could double by 2010.

4   It is a quiet crisis that argues for new approaches. Most options, though, are controversial.

5   Foremost among those are financial incentives for people to donate. The idea is an ethical minefield, conjuring visions of live donors who are young, healthy, and poor serving as organ farms for those who are old, dying, and rich, which is why people are barred from purchasing organs. But in a measure of how severe the shortage has become, the American Medical Association, which had long opposed payments to donors, now favors limited experimentation.

6 Several ideas are under consideration or already underway. Among them:

- Under a "futures" contract, the estate or family of an adult who agrees to donate organs might receive some financial remuneration, typically less than $10,000, for funeral and other expenses. Organs would go into the donor system, not be sold to individuals.
- LifeSharers is an existing network of 4,500 donors. Members agree to specify that when they die, priority in getting their organs should go to other members, also registered as donors.
- More controversial, Arkansas, Georgia, Iowa, Minnesota, New Mexico, North Dakota, Utah, and Wisconsin allow tax deductions of up to $10,000 to compensate living donors for travel, expenses, or lost income. This is legal because the money comes from the state. It also requires screening for psychological fitness.

Certainly, everything possible should be done to spur voluntary contributions, but limited financial incentives are worth trying. They should be confined for now to post-mortem donations, and organs should be distributed as they are, based on medical need and time on the waiting list—not on ability to pay. (Transplant priority is decided by the United Network for Organ Sharing, a non-profit group that works with hospitals to coordinate transplants. Directed donations are allowed within certain limits.)

7 More than 6,000 patients die each year while on waiting lists. Demanding patience, when the price of delay is death, is no answer. It's time to try new ideas.

COMPREHENSION CHECK

Issue:_____

_____

Point of View: _____

_____

Supporting Arguments:

1 _____

_____

2 _____

_____

3 _____

_____

(Continued)

4 _____

_____

5 _____

_____

_____

_____

_____

_____

_____

_____

_____

6 _____

_____

7 _____

_____

Is the reasoning in the argument deductive or inductive?_____

_____

_____

_____

_____

Does each of the supporting arguments back up the point of view directly?_____

_____

_____

_____

_____

Is each of the arguments relevant to the point of view and complete, believable, and consistent? _____

_____

_____

_____

_____

_____

_____

Is the argument sound? _____

_____

_____

_____

READING GRAPHICS

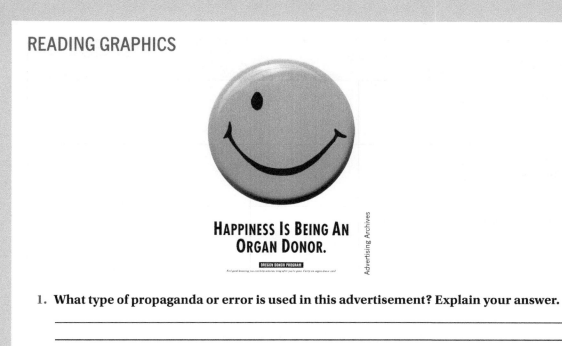

HAPPINESS IS BEING AN ORGAN DONOR.

OREGON DONOR PROGRAM

Feel good knowing you can help someone long after you're gone. Carry an organ donor card.

Advertising Archives

1. **What type of propaganda or error is used in this advertisement? Explain your answer.**

   _____

   _____

   _____

2. **What side of the debate does this advertisement fit best? Justify your answer.** _____

   _____

   _____

DEVELOPING YOUR COLLEGE-LEVEL VOCABULARY

For each of these phrases used in the reading, identify whether it is a euphemism or an example of doublespeak. Also provide a definition or explanation of the phrase.

EXAMPLE	PARAGRAPH	EUPHEMISM OR DOUBLESPEAK?	DEFINITION
organ donations			
financial incentives			
a "futures" contract			

(Continued)

EXAMPLE	PARAGRAPH	EUPHEMISM OR DOUBLESPEAK?	DEFINITION
living donors			
psychological fitness			
post-mortem donations			

READING 2

Opposing View: Organs Aren't Commodities

by Charles B. Fruit

1   Recently, a cartoon in a national magazine showed a middle-aged man standing behind a table on the sidewalk. Beneath the table was a large ice chest, and above it, hawking his wares, was a sign that read: "Lemonade and kidneys."

2   Unfortunately, this cartoon looms as a cautionary tale. That is why the National Kidney Foundation opposes any market-based incentives that financially reward donors or their families who offer life-saving organs.

3   Even on a trial basis, introducing money into such a fragile human decision-making process would set a dangerous precedent. Once we start down the road of treating organs like commodities, there's no turning back.

4   This view was underscored in a recent report by the Institute of Medicine. It emphasized that financial incentives—such as direct payments, funeral expenses, or charitable contributions—shouldn't be used to increase donation rates. Such incentives could move people to view organs as commodities, diminish altruistic donations, and lead to the potential exploitation of lower income individuals.

5   Payment stands as an affront to those families that have already donated organs of loved ones out of charity. There is evidence to suggest it might prove similarly offensive to future donors. In 2005, the National Survey of Organ Donation found that 10.8 percent of those polled would be less likely to grant consent for the organs of a deceased family member to be used for transplant if they were offered payment; 68 percent said they would be neither more nor less likely to grant consent. Thus, there is little data to show that financial incentives would increase donation rates.

6   Rather than rely on incentives, we favor practical new policies to increase organ donation. For example, by working to implement best practices, the Department of Health and Human

Services has helped to produce a steady increase in donation rates over the past 10 years—most effectively by making the option of donation available to families with loved ones who've suffered cardiac death who would not previously have been considered potential donors. As a result, many hospitals now have donation rates of 75 percent. HHS has announced a goal of doubling transplantation in a decade.

7   With this type of breakthrough, it should not be necessary to experiment with radical marketplace proposals.

COMPREHENSION CHECK

Issue: _____

_____

Point of View: _____

_____

Supporting Arguments:

1 _____

_____

2 _____

_____

3 _____

_____

_____

_____

4 _____

_____

5 _____

_____

_____

_____

_____

_____

_____

(Continued)

6 _____
_____
_____

Is the reasoning in the argument deductive or inductive? _____
_____
_____
_____
_____

Does each of the supporting arguments back up the point of view directly? _____
_____

Is each of the arguments relevant to the point of view and complete, believable, and consistent? _____
_____
_____
_____

Is the argument sound? _____
_____
_____
_____
_____

DEVELOPING YOUR COLLEGE-LEVEL VOCABULARY

Examples of loaded language:

EXAMPLE	PARAGRAPH	EUPHEMISM OR DOUBLESPEAK?	ACTUAL MEANING OF THE WORD OR PHRASE

THEMATIC CONNECTIONS

1. Which side of the debate on organ donations do you favor? Provide sound reasons for your support.
2. Do you think that the debate on organ donations will intensify in coming years? Why or why not?

WRAPPING IT UP

In the following study outline, fill in the definitions and a brief explanation of the key terms in the "Your Notes" column. Use the strategy of spaced practice to review these key terms on a regular basis. Use this study guide to review this chapter's key topics.

KEY TERM OR CONCEPT	YOUR NOTES
Deductive reasoning	
Inductive reasoning	
Relevant	
Sound	
Propaganda	
Card stacking	
Fallacy(ies)/errors in reasoning	
Glittering generalities	
Personal attack (*ad hominem*)	
Appeal to authority	
Bandwagon	
Plain folk	
Straw man	

KEY TERM OR CONCEPT	YOUR NOTES
Appeals to emotion	
Slippery slope	
Assumptions	
Non sequiturs	
False cause	
Oversimplification	
Faulty analogy	
Circular reasoning	
Author's credibility	
Intended audience	
Intended meaning	
Euphemism	
Doublespeak	

GROUP ACTIVITY: CASE STUDY ON MEDICAL ETHICS

Read the following article about the pros and cons of genetic testing. Working with a team, take a side—pro or con—on this issue: Should the individual take the test? Using what you have learned in this chapter, make sure to construct your argument clearly, avoiding errors in reasoning. A good debater is also aware of counterarguments to respond to the other side's arguments!

Testing Fate
Would You Want to Know Whether You Were Destined to Contract a Devastating Neurological Disorder?

by Alexa Shaffer

1   June 28, 2007—To test or not to test. It's a question I debate frequently. I wrestle with it because I have a parent with Huntington's Disease, a rare, degenerative neurological disorder that robs people of the ability to walk, talk, and function on their own. Like me, all children of a parent with Huntington's have a 50-50 chance of inheriting the mutated gene. I'm 16 and I have not taken the test yet, so I am still uncertain of my fate.

2   My grandfather lived with HD for 15 years; my mom is now in the early stages. I've known about the possibility that I could have the disease for several years and have learned to live with it. Although I have become somewhat comfortable with the idea of what Huntington's will do to my family, I still realize there are many uncertainties in the future: Can I live a good life with a positive test result for the mutant gene? Can my family and I cope with a positive result? How will this affect my future relationships and goals? All these questions leave me confused.

3   As I get older, I have to start making decisions for my future. I have always had my mind set on getting tested as soon as possible, but now I'm having doubts. (Testing isn't recommended for anyone under 18.) I know I still have time to make whichever decision I feel is best, but I also know that deciding is not going to get any easier. I want to continue school, marry, and have my own children. Do I pursue these dreams in spite of the possibility of HD, or do I test to determine if I carry the gene? I am, of course, afraid of causing my future children pain. I want to be responsible for my decisions and have as much information as possible.

4   On the other hand, I'm scared that I may not cope well with the test results, or lose my motivation for life. The last thing I want to happen is to lose hope. I know that whatever the result of the test, I need to stay focused on school and my goals in life. As long as I channel my energy towards causes for HD, I hope to stay on the right track.

5   I also think about my younger sister. She is 11 years old and although she has been well exposed to the world of HD, I can never be sure what she thinks about the situation. Since she is not especially open about the topic, I have trouble understanding her or gauging how much she knows. Another concern I have for her is how she will deal with mom when her symptoms worsen. My sister is so young.

6   My parents have taught my sister and me that all of the doubts, the "symptom searching," and the stresses can be successfully managed. They've demonstrated this by empowering themselves with involvement in the HD community. As they take us to Huntington's events, I've seen people go through the growth and adjustment caused by the rollercoaster of HD.

7   When I think about getting tested, I worry that it will put additional emotional stress on my family and friends. What if my parents don't want to know? All of us at risk for HD will eventually reach this fork in the road. Testing is a personal and emotional choice. Each individual has his or her own reasons for wanting or not wanting this information. Although the initial result may feel overwhelming, as I've seen, time is a major factor in the coping process—so is an optimistic outlook. There are no guarantees in life, so even with a positive test result, the world, as I know it, will not come to a halt. Embracing life and living it to its fullest potential is a choice, especially with the difficult reality of HD.

8   I keep in mind that every day researchers get a step closer to finding a cure. Through fund-
raisers we can assist the dedicated medical people who are so passionate about finding a cure.
One of my goals is to make my generation the last HD generation.

9   We need to spread awareness about the disease. I believe that more can and should be done to
help those who are suffering from HD and for those at risk. Meantime, I continue to have that inner
dialogue: To test or nor to test. I'm still not sure.

SOURCE: Testing Fate by Alexa Shaffer from *Newsweek*, June 28, 2007. Reprinted by permission of the author.

REFLECTIVE JOURNAL QUESTIONS

1. Write about a time either you or someone you know used propaganda devices to convince others to adopt a certain point of view. Were those devices effective?

2. Considering the arguments you have read, what is your position on whether or not medical
professionals should be allowed to accept incentives if the drugs are in the best interests of the
patient anyway? Why or why not?

3. Considering the arguments you have read, what is your position on whether or not we should
provide financial incentives for organ donations? In light of the reasoning techniques you have
learned in this chapter, with which point of view do you most agree? Why?

THEMATIC CONNECTIONS

Respond to one of the following questions in a polished essay of several paragraphs that support
your thesis. Type your essay and, as always, review it for any errors in grammar, spelling, or
punctuation before submitting it to your instructor. Research your topic and then argue your position
on the issue. Pay careful attention to the relevance of your argument. Make sure that your reasoning
is sound.

1. What do you think is the most pressing issue in medical ethics today?

2. Decide on another medical ethics issue currently in the news, such as abortion, stem cell
research, the use of non-FDA-approved experimental drugs, genetic testing, or animal rights in
relation to medical testing. Explain your point of view on this issue.

3. What is your position on the "conscience clause" issue discussed in the Thinking It Through
titled "Evaluating an Argument" on page 569. Do you think medical professionals should have
the right to refuse treatment based on their personal beliefs?

ADDITIONAL SKILL AND STRATEGY PRACTICE

This reading is an editorial about a new memory-blocking drug, Propranolol, and whether the news
headlines accurately represent the effects of this drug on memory, based on a recent study. Here's
is a synopsis of the study that is in question: Scientists in the Netherlands "taught" subjects to "fear"

spiders by showing them pictures of the spider and then administering electric shocks. The next time spider pictures were shown, one half of the subjects were given a placebo and the other half Propranolol. Those who got Propranolol did not show any startle response to the spider picture, but those who got the placebo did. For more information about propranolol and some background on its properties, refer to the Post-Assessment in Chapter 1 of this textbook.

Use active reading strategies to review the information in the passage. Then answer the critical thinking questions that follow the reading.

Does Propranolol Erase Memories? Still No
By John M. Grohol, PsyD

1   Cool, a new memory erasing drug!

2   At least that's what you'd think if you read the health news headlines plastered over the 'net over the past few days about propranolol's magical memory erasing abilities:

- Blood Pressure Drug May Erase Fearful Memories—*WebMD*
- Common drug eases memories of fear—*Boston Globe*
- Could a blood pressure drug dim bad memories?—*Scientific American*

3   How could so many respectable publications get the basic facts of this research so wrong? How wrong? Well, first of all, you'd think the new study studied memory. But you'd be wrong, of course. What the research actually looked at was the startle response and an artificial fear connection made to a picture.

4   When those in the placebo group were given a series of electric shocks, their fear of the spider also returned, while those in the propranolol group continued to react calmly to the spider picture, suggesting that the association may have been permanently erased, or at least negated to such a point that it has no effect.

5   What did the propranolol block? A laboratory-created fear association, which isn't quite the same thing as an actual real, vivid memory. Just so we're clear here—pictures do not equal trauma, and a startle response to a fearful stimuli does not equal a "memory."

6   *New Scientist* did the best job of putting the new research into some context, even going so far as to get the headline mostly right—"'Anti-phobia pill' breaks link between memory and fear." That's a pretty good summary of the research, but still uses the word "memory" when it's not quite clear that's what the researchers tapped into here. But I won't split hairs.

7   We noted these same sorts of problems a year and a half ago when we discussed a previous study conducted on this drug. The media went ga-ga over that study as well, and made the exact same claims—that a common hypertension drug can erase bad memories. Apparently a year and a half later, health journalism hasn't gotten any better.

8   Do the "memories" treated by the drug propranolol stay away forever? Who knows, as the current study only looked at subjects for 3 days.

9   However, Chris Brewin, a memory expert at University College London, UK, says the findings are interesting, but cautions that Kindt's group only tested the volunteers over the course of three days.

10   "The fear might come back if they tested them several weeks later," he says.

11   In other words, this is a nice study, building upon previous research. The drug propranolol's effects don't magically "erase" bad memories. They do, however, prevent a common physiological

startle response in our bodies to a phobic stimuli. Are the results long-lasting in lieu of taking the medication for life? We still don't know. Hopefully future research will answer some of these additional questions.

SOURCE: John M. Grohol, "Does Propranolol Erase Memories? Still No" (from http://psychcentral.com/blog/archives/2009/02/17/does-propranolol-erase-memories-still-no/). Reprinted with permission by the author.

Map and evaluate this argument.

1. Issue: _____

2. Point of View: _____

3. Supporting Arguments:

   ■ _____
     _____

   ■ _____
     _____

      □ _____

      □ _____

   ■ _____
     _____

4. Primary Type of Support: _____

5. Is each of the arguments relevant to the point of view and complete, believable, and consistent?
   _____

6. Is the argument sound? _____

✤ POST-ASSESSMENT

PSYCHOLOGY MAGAZINE

Preview the following article. Then, after you have read it all the way through, answer the questions that follow it. This assessment will help you determine your strengths and weaknesses in understanding, learning, and applying the skills and strategies discussed in this chapter.

Hoping for a Girl
by Jeff Grossman

1   In 2002, when Johanna, an Arkansas mom, learned she would give birth to her third baby boy, she decided to investigate high-tech help for her next child, which she hoped would be a girl. Now she's expecting what she thinks will be her first daughter, thanks to MicroSort, a new reproductive technology.

2   The technology, originally developed for farm animals, uses a laser to separate sperm cells by size (X-chromosome cells are larger). At Genetics and IVF Institute, in Fairfax, Virginia, the basic procedure costs between $2,000 and $4,000, says nursing director Mary Fusillo.

3   With about 500 cases by 2004, MicroSort had a 91 percent success rate in sorting for girls, and close to 75 percent for boys, Fusillo says. Because MicroSort is experimental, it is so far offered only as part of a controlled trial. After 750 births, the Food and Drug Administration will rule whether the technique should be widely available. Only two clinics are currently authorized by the FDA to offer MicroSort.

4   So far, only families seeking "balance" or those at risk for gender-related genetic diseases are eligible, a restriction imposed by the company. To qualify, parents must have more than one child of the same gender. A family with two boys and a girl, for example, could only sort for another girl.

5   Nearly all of the families who have used MicroSort are hoping for girls, partially because sex-linked diseases overwhelmingly affect boys. Even those families seeking balance, though, try for daughters up to twice as often as sons.

6   But is MicroSort headed for a collision with medical ethics? Sex selection for nonmedical reasons is already illegal in the United Kingdom, and earlier this year, the American College of Obstetricians and Gynecologists (ACOG) said it contradicts their code of ethics. "The very idea of preferring a child of a particular sex may be interpreted as condoning sexist values, and, hence, [could] create a climate in which sex discrimination can more easily flourish," says ACOG's ethics committee. The American Society of Reproductive Medicine cautiously endorses gender selection, but warns that gender-sorted kids may disappoint parents when the technique fails or feel pressure to conform to their gender role.

SOURCE: "Insights: Hoping for a Girl" by Jeff Grossman from *Psychology Today*, May/June 2004. Reprinted with permission from *Psychology Today Magazine*, (Copyright © 2004 Sussex Publishers, LLC.)

(Continued)

COMPREHENSION CHECK

Circle the best answer to the following questions.

Reading Comprehension

1 **What is the issue?**

A. Whether or not girls are favored over boys in the United States
B. Whether or not balancing families is ethical
C. Whether or not the government will endorse sex-selection techniques
D. Whether or not sex-selection techniques are ethical

2 **What is the author's point of view?**

A. Yes, girls are favored over boys in sex-selection procedures.
B. Yes, the government will endorse sex-selection techniques.
C. No, sex-selection techniques are not ethical.
D. The author does not take a side on the issue.

3 **Which of the following is an argument against selecting the sex of a child?**

A. Parents overwhelmingly choose to screen for girls.
B. The technique can screen to achieve "balance" in families.
C. The technique can screen to weed out sex-linked abnormalities.
D. The test is accurate up to 75 percent of the time for boys and 91 percent of the time for girls.

4 **What type of support is used to support the argument that parents should be allowed to select the sex of a child?**

A. Facts and testimony
B. Facts and reasons
C. Reasons and examples
D. Examples and testimony

5 **Which of the following is a reasonable assumption in the arguments in favor of the procedure?**

A. Gender balance in a family is good.
B. Weeding out sex-related abnormalities is ethical.
C. Both a and b are reasonable assumptions.
D. None of the stated assumptions are reasonable.

6 **What would be a strong argument against the use of this procedure that is *not* presented in the article?**

A. Gender selection is unethical.

B. Sex selection for reasons other than medical purposes is illegal in the United Kingdom.

C. Sex-selection techniques are inaccurate.

D. Sex-selection techniques violate the American College of Obstetricians and Gynecologists' code of ethics.

7 **Which of the following is a reasonable assumption in the argument against using the procedure?**

A. Sex selection is cautiously endorsed by the American Society of Reproductive Medicine.

B. Gender selection can be dangerous because of both foreseen and unforeseen reasons.

C. Gender selection will improve the gene pool.

D. Families have a right to determine the sex of their baby if they can afford it.

8 **This statement from paragraph 6 is an example of which of the following errors in reasoning?**

The very idea of preferring a child of a particular sex may be interpreted as condoning sexist values, and, hence, [could] create a climate in which sex discrimination can more easily flourish," says ACOG's ethics committee.

A. Bandwagon

B. Plain folk

C. Straw man

D. Circular reasoning

Vocabulary Comprehension

9 **The word *balance* in this article is enclosed in quotation marks. It is an example of which of the following types of biased language?**

A. Alliteration

B. Euphemism

C. Doublespeak

D. Contradictory language

10 **What does the word *balance* really mean?**

A. Parents want a girl.

B. Parents want a boy.

C. Parents don't want to determine the sex of their child.

D. Parents do not want all children to be of only one sex.

TEXTBOOK APPLICATION

Chapter 14: Law and Medicine from *Law, Politics, and Society* by Suzanne Samuels

This textbook application, a full chapter from a political science textbook, follows from the discussion in Chapters 7 and 8 on the topics of the legal system and medical ethics. The chapter concerns both topics equally, and delves into several ethical arguments concerning topics of a controversial nature, such as medical research, euthanasia, the legality of medical marijuana, and the Federal Drug Administration's regulation of pharmacogenomics (tailoring drugs for treatment based on a patient's genetic structure).

Your instructor may assign a subsection of this chapter for you to complete with a small group. Alternatively, your instructor may require you to complete activities independently during or outside of class. This chapter may also be assigned as the basis for an exam.

Apply all you have learned about reading and learning this semester. In particular, use the skills and strategies you have learned in this unit with regard to reading critically. The chapter features a pro and con argument on the issue of the FDA and pharmacogenomics. In addition, the author discusses several controversial topics that clearly contain pro and con perspectives. In examining and interacting with the chapter, also be sure to use your strategies for learning new vocabulary and decoding graphic material.

There are two major sections in this chapter: Doctors, Patients, and the Law and Medical Research and Development and the Law. Each of these major sections contains several subsections.

Survey the chapter, paying special attention to the headings of the sections. Then, depending on the assignment, preview a subsection of the chapter. In this chapter, the predominant patterns of organization will be cause and effect, sequence, and comparison and contrast. As part of your survey of the text chapter, pay close attention to the summary on page 622, and read the "Active Learning" questions on page 623. Then read and mark the text. Complete the following note-taking exercise(s) as your instructor assigns.

Answer these questions as you read.

1. Why do you think the author included the Oregon Death with Dignity Act passage (Box 14.1, page 609)?

2. What is the function of the two introductory paragraphs at the beginning of this chapter? Complete the following activities to focus on important information in each subsection of the chapter.

I. DOCTORS, PATIENTS, AND THE LAW

A. Give a general description of the American Medical Association and its prominent role in the United States.

B. Abortion
   1. Create a timeline of important dates regarding the issue of abortion.
   2. What was the role of the physician and how, if at all, has it changed?

C. Physician Aid in Dying
   1. Create a timeline of important dates regarding the issue of physician aid in dying.
   2. What was the role of the physician and how, if at all, has it changed?
   3. Explain the following landmark cases and laws and discuss how they relate to the history of this topic.
      - *Vacco v. Quill*
      - *Washington v. Glucksberg*
      - Law in Action: Oregon Death with Dignity Act
      - *Ashcroft v. Oregon*

D. Medical Marijuana
   1. Create a timeline of important dates regarding the issue of medical uses of marijuana.
   2. What was the role of the physician and how, if at all, has it changed?
   3. Explain the following landmark cases and laws and discuss how they relate to the history of this topic.
      - War on Drugs
      - Controlled Substances Act
      - Compassionate Use Act
      - *Raich et al. v. Ashcroft*

II. MEDICAL RESEARCH AND DEVELOPMENT AND THE LAW

A. What is the difference between the foundation of laws for abortion, aid in dying, and medical marijuana as compared with laws related to medical research and informed consent?

B. Medical Research and Informed Consent
   1. Create a timeline of important dates regarding the issue of medical research and informed consent.
   2. List or chart the ethical considerations these developments reflect.
   3. What was the role of the U.S. Department of Health and Human Services?
   4. Relate the following landmark studies, statutes, and concepts to the issue of medical research and informed consent.
      - Tuskegee Syphilis Study
      - National Research Act
      - Informed consent

C. Drug-Approval Process
   1. Discuss the history of the drug-approval process.
   2. Create a chart of the steps followed in drug approval.
   3. Discuss the role of the FDA and the drug companies in this process.

D. Experimental Drugs and the Drug Approval Process
   1. What are experimental drugs?
   2. What is the process for drug approval?
   3. List key points of the following terms and acts as they relate to the drug approval process.
      • ACT UP
      • Food and Drug Administration Modernization Act of 1997
E. Debate: Should the FDA Have a Central Role in Regulating Pharmocogenomics?
   1. Map the "yes" and "no" arguments, identifying the supporting arguments.
   2. Identify the type of support presented.
   3. After you read the article, determine if the arguments are relevant, consistent, believable, and complete.
   4. If not, determine the type of error in reasoning.
   5. Decide if the argument is sound.
   6. Determine if the reasoning in the argument is inductive or deductive.
F. Controversies in Medical Research
   1. What are the major areas of controversy in medical research?
   2. Discuss the Human Genome Project and the ethical concerns associated with it.
   3. What is the timeline for the Human Genome Project?
   4. Discuss genetic engineering and the ethical concerns associated with it.
   5. Discuss the timeline for this technology and the possible future of such knowledge, both positive and negative.

INCREASE YOUR DISCIPLINE-SPECIFIC VOCABULARY

LAW AND MEDICINE

Key Terms

The terms listed are used on the page indicated. Define each of these terms or references. The page references are provided.

KEY TERM	DEFINITION
social facts, p. 606	
American Medical Association, p. 607	
Roe v. Wade, p. 607	
physician aid in dying, p. 608	

KEY TERM	DEFINITION
Vacco v. Quill and *Washington v. Glucksberg*, p. 608	
Death with Dignity Act, p. 608	
Ashcroft v. Oregon, p. 610	
war on drugs, p. 610	
Controlled Substances Act, p. 610	
Compassionate Use Act, p. 611	
Raich et al. v. Ashcroft, p. 611	
Tuskegee Syphilis Study, p. 615	
National Research Act, p. 616	
informed consent, p. 616	
ACT UP, p. 619	
fast track, p. 619	
Food and Drug Administration Modernization Act of 1997, p. 619	
pharmacogenomics, p. 619	
Human Genome Project, p. 621	
genetic engineering, p. 621	

Be able to respond to the questions in the "Active Learning" section and multiple choice questions at the end of the chapter.

CHAPTER 14

Law and Medicine

Biotechnology and medicine are critical sectors in the U.S. economy. In this chapter, we examine the impact of lawmaking on medicine and biotechnology. Specifically, we look at the role of physicians in the implementation of laws, the regulation of research and development, and the drug-approval process. The law in all three areas has changed dramatically as it attempted to respond to important developments in law and medicine. Emil Durkheim believed that law is the expression of the norms of a society and that in a modern legal system, the goal of law is to compensate the individual for harm suffered and damages inflicted. According to Durkheim, laws are based on **social facts***, that is, those ways of thinking, acting and feeling that are shared by the collective and have coercive power over the individual. Social facts and norms are helpful concepts for understanding the relationship between law and medicine.*

Although lawmaking in this area has undergone an important shift over the last several decades, clear norms continue to underlie our approach to this field. Perhaps most importantly, physicians are viewed as professionals who pursue or should pursue the interest of their patients. The doctor-patient relationship has protection in both law and medical practice, and the physician's primary duty under both law and medical ethics is to act in the best interest of his or her patient. This belief in the sanctity of the doctor-patient relationship is a social fact, and it animates much of our law in this area. This is not to say that there have been no changes in how our law treats physicians or on the obligations imposed upon them. Until the 1950s, research and development were not well regulated, and physicians practiced medicine with little governmental regulation. It was assumed that doctors would police themselves as a profession. There was also far less regulation of the development process for drugs and treatments. In the last several decades, however, issues relating to medical practice and to biotechnology have moved to the forefront of public debate, and the physician's obligation, both to his or her patient and to the larger society, has moved front and center.

social facts

ways of thinking, acting, and feeling that are shared by the collective and have coercive power over the individual; Emil Durkheim argued that our laws are based on these social facts.

DOCTORS, PATIENTS, AND THE LAW

American Medical Association

national organization of physicians that has played an important role in many medical-legal debates, among these, the debate about how to regulate abortion. The AMA's role in the regulation of abortion began with its campaign in the mid- to late 1800s to institute state abortion bans

The **American Medical Association** has had a prominent role in American society for more than one hundred years. Throughout this time, lawmakers who were contemplating regulations that pertained to medicine, science, and biotechnology have turned to physicians for their expertise and have often relied heavily on groups like the AMA. In at least three currently controversial areas, physicians have played a central role in the legal debate. In the controversies over abortion, aid in dying, and the use of medicinal marijuana, the law has conferred certain responsibilities, and a certain authority, on physicians. In these areas and others, American law has made the physician the central gatekeeper; that is, it has bestowed on physicians the responsibility for determining patient access to medical treatment.

Abortion

The AMA and other physician groups played a pivotal role in the creation of abortion bans in the mid- to late 800s. In fact, many of the abortion laws in place until the 1973 *Roe v. Wade* decision allowed a medical exception. Under this exception, women whose continued pregnancy endangered their lives or health could obtain an abortion. Physicians had the responsibility for determining whether the medical exception applied and thus served as gatekeepers. Even the Roe decision envisioned that physicians would continue to play an important gatekeeping role.

Under *Roe,* physicians were expected to provide information to women about the abortion procedure, and they ultimately had to determine how pregnancy and abortion would affect women's health. Many abortion laws passed since *Roe* effectively limit the physician's discretion. For example, many laws require that physicians provide their patients with specific descriptions of fetal development and of the abortion procedure and that they obtain parental consent before performing an abortion on a minor. Laws also now regulate some aspects of the abortion procedure—for example, federal law now bans what is termed the "partial-birth abortion," and many state laws regulate the disposal of fetal remains. Even with these limitations, however, physicians continue to play an important role in providing access to abortion. Perhaps most importantly, physicians can decide to opt out completely and refuse to provide any abortion services at all. This has happened in many areas of the country, as doctors have decided against providing abortion services. As a result, some states and counties face a severe shortage of physicians who will perform abortions.

Physicians also continue to be responsible for determining whether second- and third-trimester abortions are necessary to protect the life or health of the mother. Many state legislatures who opted to regulate abortion in the wake of *Roe* have severely limited access to abortion in these two trimesters. Courts have required that these states provide an exception to their abortion bans where the women's life and health is in serious jeopardy. This exception provides physicians with significant discretion in determining whether these abortions should go forward. For physicians, the downside has been that they are liable if a court determines that their medical judgment is incorrect. In other words, if a physician permits a second-trimester abortion to proceed and a court determines that the assessment that the procedure is necessary to save the life of the woman or protect her from serious and irreversible harm is incorrect, it can find the doctor legally liable. Moreover, in many states, the physician has a responsibility to protect the life, not only of the woman, but of the viable fetus, as well. If a fetus reaches viability, which happens at about the twenty-eighth week of pregnancy, many states mandate that the physician take steps to save his or her life. The abortion law in place in Ohio is typical of these regulations, and if you want to review this law, you can view it on our webpage. In an important sense, the physician serves, not only the patient seeking the abortion, but the fetus, as well.

Physician Aid in Dying

physician aid in dying
the practice by physicians of providing death-hastening medications, usually to terminally ill patients who have significant pain and suffering; barred in most states by laws that make it a crime to assist another in committing suicide, but permitted in some states in certain narrowly defined circumstances

Vacco v. *Quill* and *Washington* v. *Glucksberg*
two cases in which the Supreme Court ruled that state laws that banned physician aid in dying did not violate the constitutional rights of those who seek this assistance

Death with Dignity Act
1997 Oregon law passed by voter initiative that allows individuals in Oregon who are terminally ill to access physician aid in dying

Physicians also play a central role in the debate about **physician aid in dying**, and in fact, the debate about euthanasia has shifted in recent years to focus on the right of terminally ill individuals to receive physician aid in dying. In two cases decided in 1997, *Vacco* v. *Quill* and *Washington* v. *Glucksberg,* the U.S. Supreme Court ruled that state laws that banned physician aid in dying did not violate the constitutional rights of those who seek this assistance. Doctors and terminally ill patients in Washington and New York had sued their states, arguing that bans against assisted suicide violated two provisions of the U.S. Constitution. First, they claimed that when terminally ill persons enduring significant pain and suffering chose to hasten their death, this choice was constitutionally protected, and states couldn't impose an "undue burden" on this choice by making it difficult or impossible to exercise the choice. Second, the doctors and patients claimed that since states allowed individuals to refuse treatment, they had to also permit aid in dying for that group of individuals who are facing imminent death. Since Washington and New York didn't permit this choice, the parties argued that they violated the constitutional equal protection guarantee. The U.S. Supreme Court rejected both challenges, arguing that the U.S. Constitution didn't forbid states from enacting assisted-suicide bans, and that states had significant leeway in regulating aid in dying.

Voters in Oregon responded to the Court's decision quickly and decisively by using a voter initiative to pass the 1997 **Death with Dignity Act**. A physician may help individuals in Oregon who are suffering from a terminal illness by prescribing medication to hasten death. To access aid in dying, the individual must initiate a written request for the medication and two physicians must attest that the individual has been informed about his or her illness and that he or she is mentally competent to make this decision. This request must be witnessed by at least two additional people. The actual form that individuals in Oregon use to trigger the request for physician aid

LAW IN ACTION

Box 14.1 **Oregon Death with Dignity Act**

Under the Oregon Death with Dignity Act, a request for a medication as authorized by ORS 127.800 to 127.897 shall be in substantially the following form as follows:

REQUEST FOR MEDICATION
TO END MY LIFE IN A HUMANE
AND DIGNIFIED MANNER

I, _____, am an adult of sound mind.

I am suffering from _____, which my attending physician has determined is a terminal disease and which has been medically confirmed by a consulting physician.

I have been fully informed of my diagnosis, prognosis, the nature of medication to be prescribed and potential associated risks, the expected result, and the feasible alternatives, including comfort care, hospice care and pain control.

I request that my attending physician prescribe medication that will end my life in a humane and dignified manner.

INITIAL ONE:

_____ I have informed my family of my decision and taken their opinions into consideration.

_____ I have decided not to inform my family of my decision.

_____ I have no family to inform of my decision.

I understand that I have the right to rescind this request at any time.

I understand the full import of this request and I expect to die when I take the medication to be prescribed. I further understand that although most deaths occur within three hours, my death may take longer and my physician has counseled me about this possibility.

I make this request voluntarily and without reservation, and I accept full moral responsibility for my actions.

Signed: _____

Dated: _____

DECLARATION OF WITNESSES

We declare that the person signing this request:
(a) Is personally known to us or has provided proof of identity;
(b) Signed this request in our presence;
(c) Appears to be of sound mind and not under duress, fraud or undue influence;
(d) Is not a patient for whom either of us is attending physician.

_____ Witness 1/Date

_____ Witness 2/Date

NOTE: One witness shall not be a relative (by blood, marriage or adoption) of the person signing this request, shall not be entitled to any portion of the person's estate on death and shall not own, operate or be employed at a health care facility where the person is a patient or resident. If the patient is an inpatient at a health care facility, one of the witnesses shall be an individual designated by the facility.

[1995 c.3 s.6.01; 1999 c.423 s.11]

in dying is shown in Box 14.1. Under the Oregon law, the doctor's responsibility is extensive: she or he must ensure that the person who seeks aid in dying has given informed consent after having been informed about a wide range of issues, including his or her diagnosis, prognosis, and alternatives like hospice and palliative care. The physician must also meet extensive record-keeping and reporting requirements and may be liable for any failure to do so. Between 1998 and 2004, 171 people were reported to have used medication to hasten their deaths. Physicians have a central role in the implementation of the Oregon law—they not only serve as gatekeepers, limiting access to only those terminally patients whom they consider competent, but they are also the primary source of information about how the law is being implemented. While individual patients must swallow the medicine on their own, the physicians are on the frontlines providing access to it.

Perhaps recognizing the centrality of physicians to the Death with Dignity Act, U.S. Attorney General John Ashcroft issued a policy directive that interpreted the federal Controlled Substances Act (CSA) as banning use of prescription medicines to hasten death. The CSA requires that medicines be used for a "legitimate medical purpose," and Attorney General Ashcroft claimed that hastening death did not meet this requirement. He threatened that physicians who continued to use medicines to hasten death would not be allowed to prescribe any controlled substances. He also warned that physicians would be held criminally liable for providing aid in dying. An Oregon federal district court blocked the enforcement of this order, and the lawsuit is now pending in the Court of Appeals for the Ninth Circuit. In the 2004 case *Ashcroft* v. *Oregon,* the Ninth Circuit Court of Appeals upheld the law, finding that Attorney General Ashcroft had overstepped his authority in trying to block physician aid in dying in Oregon. The court held that states, not the federal government, have the principal authority to regulate medicine and that if Congress wanted to regulate aid in dying, it would need to pass legislation.

Ashcroft v. Oregon
case decided by a federal appeals court that upheld the Oregon Death with Dignity Act and struck down a policy directive issued by U.S. Attorney General John Ashcroft that would have barred doctors from using prescriptions to assist individuals in hastening their deaths under the federal Controlled Substances Act

Medical Marijuana

For nearly five thousand years, cannabis, the plant from which marijuana is derived, has been used to ease suffering and to facilitate recovery in cultures worldwide. There is evidence of medical use dating back to 2737 BCE, when Chinese emperor Shen Neng began prescribing the drug to treat a variety of ailments, including gout, rheumatism, and malaria. It was also widely used to treat pain and protect against and treat infections. As other drugs were developed, cannabis was used less, and in 1937, Congress joined a number of states in banning the use of marijuana. The **war on drugs**, which began in earnest in the early 1970s, targeted all drugs but focused especially on marijuana because many drug warriors claimed that use of this drug inevitably spiraled into use of more serious and addictive drugs. One of the laws that initiated this war was the 1970 **Controlled Substances Act**, which prohibits the sale and distribution of marijuana across state lines. This law and its state counterparts have lately been under intense fire, as advocates have fought to be able to use marijuana for medical purposes. These advocates, many of them physicians and individuals with medical illnesses, argue that marijuana is an effective drug for treating many illnesses, including multiple sclerosis. They also argue that marijuana alleviates pain and nausea, which are often associated with cancer and cancer

war on drugs
program initiated in the early 1970s that targets all aspects of the production, distribution, and use of illegal drugs

Controlled Substances Act
federal law that prohibits the sale and distribution of marijuana across state lines

treatments. Despite these arguments, the federal Drug Enforcement Agency continues to classify marijuana as a Schedule I drug, meaning that it has no medical use.

Advocates of medical marijuana have recently brought their case to the states, and in particular, to voters, and in 1996, California voters approved the **Compassionate Use Act,** which established that state drug laws would not "apply to a patient, or to a patient's primary caregiver, who possesses or cultivates marijuana . . . upon the written or oral recommendation or approval of a physician." Eleven other states and many municipalities have joined California in allowing physicians to prescribe marijuana for certain medical conditions or treatments. In many other states, researchers are permitted to study the therapeutic effects of the drug. Perhaps ironically, the drug Marinol, a cannabis-derived medicine that is administered in tablet form, rather than being smoked, is widely available to physicians, who use it to treat nausea and stimulate appetite, especially for patients with chronic illness. Like the debates about abortion and aid in dying, physicians and medical personnel play an important role in the medicinal marijuana controversy. In all states and municipalities, there must be some assessment by a member of the medical community that use of the drug is therapeutic and aimed at treatment of a specific illness.

A case currently before the U.S. Supreme Court, *Raich et al.* **v.** *Ashcroft,* tests the limits of existing drug laws. At issue in this case is the conviction of a California woman under the federal Controlled Substance Act for cultivation of medical marijuana. She claims that the Controlled Substances Act only applies to drugs that enter interstate commerce and that her home-grown farm only cultivates the drug for local distribution. The Ninth Circuit Court of Appeals agreed with her, finding that the cultivation, use, and distribution of marijuana for medical purposes was a state activity and governed by state law alone.

Physicians are granted a prominent role and wide latitude in making treatment decisions in all three of the areas we have discussed: abortion, physician aid in dying, and medicinal marijuana. The norm that permits this latitude has animated lawmaking. While many pro-life advocates argue that abortion involves a woman's self-interested choice about whether to continue her pregnancy, laws are framed less in terms of women's liberty rights and much more in terms of medical practice. *Roe* v. *Wade* is still good law, and because of this, states and the federal government must recognize that there is some liberty or privacy interest in the abortion right. Perhaps because of this, lawmakers have turned their attention to the medical procedure itself. These laws regulate the abortion procedure but continue to recognize the rights and obligations of the physician. In fact, the only federal law that has regulated the abortion procedure itself, the so-called partial-birth-abortion ban, has been struck down by federal courts because it does not sufficiently protect women when their lives are endangered by continuing a pregnancy, a judgment that has historically been left to her physician. In 2004, federal district courts in New York, San Francisco, and Nebraska struck down the 2003 federal Partial Birth Abortion Ban. Similarly, the issue of euthanasia

Compassionate Use Act

initiative approved by California voters in 1996 that allowed patients and their primary caregivers to possess or cultivate marijuana without being penalized under state drug laws

Raich et al. v. Ashcroft

case currently before the U.S. Supreme Court that raises the question of whether the federal Controlled Substances Act prohibits the cultivation of medical marijuana in California

LAW IN ACTION

The Regulation of Medical Marijuana

RAICH ET AL. V. *ASHCROFT* U.S. SUPREME COURT, 2005

Alberto R. Gonzales, Attorney General, *et al.,* **Petitioners** *v.* **Angel McClary Raich** *et al.*
June 6, 2005

Justice Stevens **delivered the opinion of the Court.**

California is one of at least nine States that authorize the use of marijuana for medicinal purposes. The question presented in this case is whether the power vested in Congress by Article I, §8, of the Constitution "[t]o make all Laws which shall be necessary and proper for carrying into Execution" its authority to "regulate Commerce with foreign Nations, and among the several States" includes the power to prohibit the local cultivation and use of marijuana in compliance with California law.

California has been a pioneer in the regulation of marijuana. In 1913, California was one of the first States to prohibit the sale and possession of marijuana, and at the end of the century, California became the first State to authorize limited use of the drug for medicinal purposes. In 1996, California voters passed Proposition 215, now codified as the Compassionate Use Act of 1996. The proposition was designed to ensure that "seriously ill" residents of the State have access to marijuana for medical purposes, and to encourage Federal and State Governments to take steps towards ensuring the safe and affordable distribution of the drug to patients in need. The Act creates an exemption from criminal prosecution for physicians, as well as for patients and primary caregivers who possess or cultivate marijuana for medicinal purposes with the recommendation or approval of a physician. A "primary caregiver" is a person who

has consistently assumed responsibility for the housing, health, or safety of the patient.

Respondents Angel Raich and Diane Monson are California residents who suffer from a variety of serious medical conditions and have sought to avail themselves of medical marijuana pursuant to the terms of the Compassionate Use Act. They are being treated by licensed, board-certified family practitioners, who have concluded, after prescribing a host of conventional medicines to treat respondents' conditions and to alleviate their associated symptoms, that marijuana is the only drug available that provides effective treatment. Both women have been using marijuana as a medication for several years pursuant to their doctors' recommendation, and both rely heavily on cannabis to function on a daily basis. Indeed, Raich's physician believes that forgoing cannabis treatments would certainly cause Raich excruciating pain and could very well prove fatal.

Respondent Monson cultivates her own marijuana, and ingests the drug in a variety of ways including smoking and using a vaporizer. Respondent Raich, by contrast, is unable to cultivate her own, and thus relies on two caregivers, litigating as "John Does," to provide her with locally grown marijuana at no charge. . . .

On August 15, 2002, county deputy sheriffs and agents from the federal Drug Enforcement Administration (DEA) came to Monson's home. After a thorough investigation, the county officials concluded that her use of marijuana was

LAW IN ACTION-(CONT'D)

entirely lawful as a matter of California law. Nevertheless, after a 3-hour standoff, the federal agents seized and destroyed all six of her cannabis plants.

Respondents thereafter brought this action against the Attorney General of the United States and the head of the DEA seeking injunctive and declaratory relief prohibiting the enforcement of the federal Controlled Substances Act (CSA) to the extent it prevents them from possessing, obtaining, or manufacturing cannabis for their personal medical use. . . . Respondents claimed that enforcing the CSA against them would violate the Commerce Clause, the Due Process Clause of the Fifth Amendment, the Ninth and Tenth Amendments of the Constitution, and the doctrine of medical necessity. . . .

The question before us . . . is not whether it is wise to enforce the statute in these circumstances; rather, it is whether Congress' power to regulate interstate markets for medicinal substances encompasses the portions of those markets that are supplied with drugs produced and consumed locally. Well-settled law controls our answer. The CSA is a valid exercise of federal power, even as applied to the troubling facts of this case. . . .

Marijuana itself was not significantly regulated by the Federal Government until 1937 when accounts of marijuana's addictive qualities and physiological effects, paired with dissatisfaction with enforcement efforts at state and local levels, prompted Congress to pass the Marihuana Tax Act. . . . Then in 1970, after declaration of the national "war on drugs," federal drug policy underwent a significant transformation . . . [P]rompted by a perceived need to consolidate the growing number of piecemeal drug laws and to enhance federal drug enforcement powers, Congress enacted the Comprehensive Drug Abuse Prevention and Control Act.

Title II of that Act, the CSA repealed most of the earlier antidrug laws in favor of a comprehensive regime to combat the international and interstate traffic in illicit drugs. The main objectives of the CSA were to conquer drug abuse and to control the legitimate and illegitimate traffic in controlled substances. . . . In enacting the CSA, Congress classified marijuana as a Schedule I drug. . . . Schedule I drugs are categorized as such because of their high potential for abuse, lack of any accepted medical use, and absence of any accepted safety for use in medically supervised treatment. By classifying marijuana as a Schedule I drug, as opposed to listing it on a lesser schedule, the manufacture, distribution, or possession of marijuana became a criminal offense. . . . Despite considerable efforts to reschedule marijuana, it remains a Schedule I drug.

. . . [R]espondents' challenge is actually quite limited; they argue that the CSA's categorical prohibition of the manufacture and possession of marijuana as applied to the intrastate manufacture and possession of marijuana for medical purposes pursuant to California law exceeds Congress' authority under the Commerce Clause.

In assessing the validity of congressional regulation, none of our Commerce Clause cases can be viewed in isolation. [There are] . . . three general categories of regulation in which Congress is authorized to engage under its commerce power. First, Congress can regulate the channels of interstate commerce. Second, Congress has authority to regulate and protect the instrumentalities of interstate commerce, and persons or things in interstate commerce. Third, Congress has the power to regulate activities that substantially affect interstate commerce. Only the third category is implicated in the case at hand.

LAW IN ACTION–(CONT'D)

Our case law firmly establishes Congress' power to regulate purely local activities that are part of an economic "class of activities" that have a substantial effect on interstate commerce . . . (*Wickard* v. *Filburn*, 317 U. S. 111, 128-129 [1942]). As we stated in *Wickard*, "even if appellee's activity be local and though it may not be regarded as commerce, it may still, whatever its nature, be reached by Congress if it exerts a substantial economic effect on interstate commerce." *Id.*, at 125. . . . *Wickard* thus establishes that Congress can regulate purely intrastate activity that is not itself "commercial," in that it is not produced for sale, if it concludes that failure to regulate that class of activity would undercut the regulation of the interstate market in that commodity.

The similarities between this case and *Wickard* are striking. Like the farmer in *Wickard*, respondents are cultivating, for home consumption, a fungible commodity for which there is an established, albeit illegal, interstate market. . . . In *Wickard*, we had no difficulty concluding that Congress had a rational basis for believing that, when viewed in the aggregate, leaving home-consumed wheat outside the regulatory scheme would have a substantial influence on price and market conditions. Here too, Congress had a rational basis for concluding that leaving home-consumed marijuana outside federal control would similarly affect price and market conditions. . . . In both cases, the regulation is squarely within Congress' commerce power because production of the commodity meant for home consumption, be it wheat or marijuana, has a substantial effect on supply and demand in the national market for that commodity . . . That the regulation ensnares some purely intrastate activity is of no moment . . .

The exemption for cultivation by patients and caregivers can only increase the supply of marijuana in the California market. The likelihood that all such production will promptly terminate when patients recover or will precisely match the patients' medical needs during their convalescence seems remote; whereas the danger that excesses will satisfy some of the admittedly enormous demand for recreational use seems obvious. Moreover, that the national and international narcotics trade has thrived in the face of vigorous criminal enforcement efforts suggests that no small number of unscrupulous people will make use of the California exemptions to serve their commercial ends whenever it is feasible to do so. Taking into account the fact that California is only one of at least nine States to have authorized the medical use of marijuana . . . Congress could have rationally concluded that the aggregate impact on the national market of all the transactions exempted from federal supervision is unquestionably substantial. . . .

Under the present state of the law . . . the judgment of the Court of Appeals must be vacated. The case is remanded for further proceedings consistent with this opinion.

It is so ordered.

or aid in dying, which burst on the public scene in the early 1980s and has remained there since, has morphed into a debate about whether physicians can aid in hastening the death of their patients. While lawmakers are very reluctant to say that terminally ill persons have a constitutional right to die, they have been more willing to consider the rights and obligations that a physician may have to aid a patient who is suffering and in great pain. And finally, the larger debate about legalizing marijuana, on the fringe of American politics since the Controlled Substances Act of 1970 utilized its ban against marijuana use and distribution to kick off its war on drugs, has become a much narrower debate about the compassionate use of the drug to treat suffering. We believe that physicians have an important role in our society and that they act primarily out of concern about their patients. This social fact, as Durkheim would have noted, is very much a part of our social order and at the core of our laws.

MEDICAL RESEARCH AND DEVELOPMENT AND THE LAW

Abortion, aid in dying, and medicinal marijuana are all good examples of policy areas where laws privilege the practice of medicine and where physicians are assumed to be acting primarily out of concern for their patients' best interests. In the areas of medical research and informed consent, however, laws reflect our concerns or fears that physicians and researchers are motivated by more self-interested motives. Perhaps because of this, medical research and development is an area that has been subject to much greater scrutiny by governmental bodies, especially since the 1970s. Extensive regulations govern the development of new research protocols and the investigation and approval of new drugs, and governmental control over these sectors is fairly intense. The public, or at least certain interest groups, have played an increasingly important role in the development of new drugs, and it is likely that this will continue well into the future. If law is an index of the moral conditions in a society, as Durkheim claimed, then our increasing regulation of this field reflects real concern about the conduct of research and development in the field of medicine.

Medical Research and Informed Consent

Tuskegee Syphilis Study

a study of untreated syphilis, conducted between 1932 and 1972, in which poor black men were not informed that they were test subjects and were not receiving treatment of their disease; public outcry against this study resulted in more protective regulations governing research on human subjects

Many regulations affecting medical research were adopted in the last fifty to sixty years, as regulators and the public learned of egregious practices involving research subjects. The Nuremberg Trials conducted after World War II brought to light horrific abuses by Nazi doctors who conducted medical research on human subjects. Much closer to home, a federally funded program studied the effects of syphilis on black men but withheld treatment. During the course of this study, which was known as the **Tuskegee Syphilis Study** and lasted from 1932 to 1972, poor black men believed that they were receiving effective treatment for their disease. In reality, however, treatment was deliberately withheld, so that researchers could study the disease's progression in those who were untreated. These men were never informed that they were actually research subjects and not patients, and many of these men suffered and died from the disease, despite the fact that penicillin was a widely available and effective treatment for syphilis.

National Research Act

federal statute passed in the wake of the outcry over the Tuskegee Syphilis Study that required all federally funded research projects involving human subjects to be approved by an institutional review board

informed consent

a central tenet of medical research; requires that a person consent to participate in clinical research, meaning that they be fully informed of the risks and benefits of clinical research

In the wake of the Nuremberg Trials and the Tuskegee Syphilis Study, the U.S. Congress passed the **National Research Act,** which mandates that all federally funded trials involving human subjects be approved by an institutional review board or IRB. The National Commission for the Protection of Human Subjects of Biomedical and Behavioral Research issued the Belmont Report, which stated that all human research should be guided by the principles of justice, beneficence, and respect for all persons. Before someone can participate in clinical research, they must give **informed consent;** that is, they must be informed of the risks and possible benefits of treatment; in addition, the benefits of not receiving treatment must be described. Researchers must assess whether study participants understand these risks and benefits and whether they are capable of giving consent. The Food and Drug Administration's website lists the requirements for informed consent in experiments involving human subjects. The U.S. Department of Health and Human Services recognizes that some groups of people may be less able to consent to a

THE LAW IN POPULAR CULTURE

Miss Evers' Boys

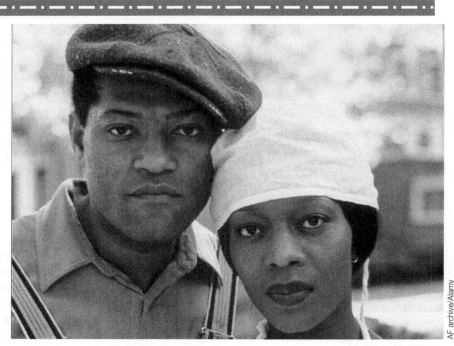

AF archive/Alamy

This film depicts the relationship between black men who are subjects of the Tuskegee Syphilis Study and their nurse. The men, who are mostly poor and illiterate, are told that they are being treated for the disease, but they are receiving only placebos so that the medical establishment can study the effects of untreated syphilis on this group. Their nurse, Eunice Evers, shown with a patient above, knows that the men are not being treated and must provide comfort without revealing that they are being denied an effective cure.

research protocol and more susceptible to coercion or undue influence. Among these groups are children, prisoners, pregnant women, the mentally disabled, or those who are "economically or educationally disadvantaged." For some of these groups, there are specific rules that researchers must follow before enrolling participants. For prisoners, the federal rules require that the research involve questions that relate to the effects of incarceration; for children, the research must either involve only minimal risk or provide some direct benefit or benefit to other children with the same or similar illnesses. It is notable, however, that there are no additional rules for informed consent of those who are poor or uneducated.

Drug-Approval Process

Informed consent is of central importance in medical research, in large part because the development of new drugs and medical devices depends on human testing. The Food and Drug Administration was created to administer the 1938 Food, Drug and Cosmetic Act. Early on, the FDA focused on ensuring that misbranded, dangerous, or adulterated goods were not sold in interstate commerce. Over time, much of the FDA's work has become focused on the approval of new drugs and medical devices.

The process for approval of new prescription drugs and medical devices is cumbersome, time-consuming, and extremely costly. It is estimated that it takes between ten and fifteen years and costs upwards of $800 million to have a new drug approved, and more than 80 percent of the costs of this process are shouldered by pharmaceutical companies. To garner FDA approval, a new drug must survive three rounds of study—Phase I, which tests a relatively small group of volunteers in an attempt to determine whether a drug or device is safe; Phase II, which employs a larger group of patients to study not only safety but how effective the drug or device is; and Phase III, which uses a much larger group of patients, usually in multisite trials. The FDA may, and often does, reject a drug or medical device at any stage of the approval process.

In addition, even after the FDA has given approval, it may still exercise control over the medication, as the FDA did with the antipsychotic drug Zyprexa. In March 2004, the FDA asked Eli Lilly and Company, which manufactures the drug, to send a letter to physicians notifying them that labeling information for the drug would be changed to inform patients using this drug of the increased risk of hyperglycemia and diabetes. The FDA sometimes recalls drugs that it has approved. This often happens in cases where the label for a lifesaving drug is either misleading or wrong or where a drug is not being prescribed at a strength adequate to treat a medical condition. Recently, two very popular anti-arthritis drugs, Vioxx and Bextra, were linked to an increased risk of heart attack, and Vioxx was recalled. Drug companies almost always comply with the rules for drug approval and recalls, but when they fail to comply, they can be subject to both civil and criminal penalties. Where a controlled substance is involved, the Drug Enforcement Agency also has enforcement powers, and the DEA has targeted physicians for not complying with its regulations.

Experimental Drugs and the Drug-Approval Process

For a drug to be approved by the FDA, the researchers must prove that it provides a clear therapeutic benefit without exposing the patient to undue risk. Critics claim that the FDA has stifled innovation by imposing a lengthy and very costly drug-approval process. Especially fierce criticisms have been aimed at development of treatments or vaccines for diseases that are fatal. For example, by the mid-1980s, Acquired Immune Deficiency Syndrome, or AIDS, had killed tens of thousands of people and there was no effective treatment for the disease. AIDS activists condemned the FDA for its business-as-usual approach, and urged the agency to relax its approval process and allow for an expedited review of medications.

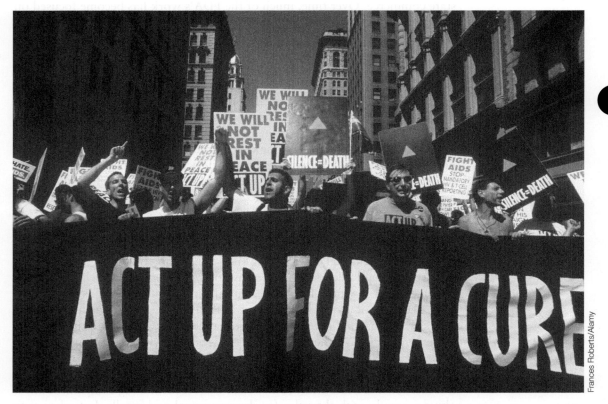

Frances Roberts/Alamy

Throughout the late 1980s and 1990s, ACT UP was very effective in using protest and civil disobedience to lobby aggressively for increased funding and support for AIDS research.

ACT UP

an activist group that staged protests to bring pressure on governmental officials to increase funding for AIDS research and to expedite the FDA's drug-review process; often outside the mainstream

fast track

streamlined procedures created by the FDA in the wake of the AIDS epidemic to expedite delivery of some experimental drugs to patients with Human Immunodeficiency Virus (HIV)

Food and Drug Administration Modernization Act of 1997

act that institutionalized the fast-track procedure for experimental drugs being studied for possible treatment of serious or life-threatening illness

AIDS activists like the AIDS Coalition to Unleash Power, or **ACT UP**, staged protests, which they called acts of civil disobedience, to bring pressure to bear on governmental officials and to expedite the drug review process. ACT UP used tactics that were outside the mainstream, engaging in protest activities that were intended to maximize media exposure. For example, members staged "die ins," shut down the offices of the FDA by blocking access to the building, and delivered empty coffins to federal, state, and local officials. ACT UP politicized the drug-approval process and argued that those with life-threatening or serious illnesses had a right to access to drugs, even if these drugs were experimental. See the website for more information about ACT UP's activities in the early years of the AIDS epidemic.

In large part because of the protest activities of groups like ACT UP, the FDA created a **fast track** for AIDS drugs, allowing a number of medications to be distributed to patients before they had actually been approved. In 1994, the National Task Force on AIDS Drug Development was created to expedite the development of drugs. This expanded access is credited with stemming the tide of AIDS-related disease and death. Interestingly, a number of other activists have looked to the work of AIDS advocates to try to convince the FDA to expedite the approval process for other drugs. Breast cancer activists used some of the same kinds of tactics to try to convince the FDA to expedite cancer-fighting drugs. The **Food and Drug Administration Modernization Act of 1997** institutionalized the fast-track procedure for serious or life-threatening diseases. Under this law, researchers who are working on the development of drugs that address "unmet medical needs" may be eligible for a number of important benefits, among these, regular and frequent meetings with FDA officials and expedited clinical trials.

The FDA will probably be receptive to the use of fast-track approval in the future. In fact, in 2004, FDA commissioner Mark McClellan announced that the agency would try to encourage drug innovation by shortening Phase III and that it would decrease the number of review cycles for generic drugs. In addition, both the public and government officials are placing significant pressure on the FDA to encourage them to expedite research into treatments for bioterrorism. The mapping of the human genome has also intensified efforts to reform the FDA's drug-approval process. In particular, researchers and pharmaceutical companies are rushing to develop therapies to "fix" defective genes and to treat genetically influenced illness. Any such medical products, devices, or treatments would have to be FDA-approved. In addition, the field of **pharmacogenomics** is booming as researchers try to figure out how to use an individual's genetic blueprint to ensure that medical treatments—in particular, drug therapies—will deliver the maximum therapeutic impact. For the lucky researchers who unlock these fields, the financial reward will be tremendous, which only increases the huge incentive to try to accelerate the FDA approval process.

In addition, recent controversies involving several drugs, including hormone replacement therapies and the diet drug Fen Phen, which were recalled after concerns about safety began to mount, will likely increase pressure on drug companies to ensure further testing both before and after the approval process.

DEBATE

Should the FDA have a central role in regulating pharmacogenomics?

Yes: The FDA must have a central role in the debate about pharmacogenomics. The Human Genome Project makes it possible for us to specifically tailor drugs for treatment or prevention of disease according to an individual's genetic structure. Genetic engineering could revolutionize medicine by allowing for the replacement or repair of genetic material, as opposed to treating the manifestations of disease. In the absence of legal or regulatory safeguards, the use of genetic material could be commercialized and exploited for profit. If this happened, access to these new treatments could be limited to those who could pay, and those without the means would be denied access to cutting-edge technology. The U.S. health care system would truly become a two-tiered system, where those with money might have vastly different treatment outcomes than those with fewer resources. In addition, genetic medicine is in its earliest stages and continues to be fairly dangerous—in fact, in several trials, subjects have died after gene therapy compromised their immune systems. Without regulation, genetic engineering may spawn designer babies or designer medicine, where people seek treatment to achieve the "perfect" child or sculpt the "perfect" body. This area of medicine is at a very vulnerable and dangerous stage and FDA involvement is clearly needed to safeguard against abuse.

No: Unfortunately, in a number of areas, including AIDS research, the FDA has shown itself to be unable to respond effectively to the need for testing of experimental and cutting-edge therapies. This agency is incredibly risk-averse and is unwilling to take the chances necessary to develop innovative genetic testing and treatment plans. Ultimately, the agency fast-tracked AIDS drugs only in response to immense public pressure. We are hoping that the agency has learned its lesson and that it will look to develop cooperative relationships with pharmaceutical companies instead of trying to order them to take certain actions. We are not hopeful, however, about the prospects for a new agency approach. There is some evidence that gene therapy could be successful in treating a number of diseases, but there has been little movement by the FDA toward testing genetic therapies, and the agency continues to be immobilized by its concerns about the risks attendant on these therapies. At this point, testing on mice has already provided great insight into the testing and treatment of sickle cell anemia. Research in other areas, including diabetes and breast cancer research, is just as promising. The FDA needs to allow pharmaceutical companies to continue to develop these therapies. It needs to adopt a cooperative rather than a combative stance. The agency should not have a central role; instead, it should share its place with those who are already engaged in research and development in this important area.

The activities of large, transnational pharmaceutical companies also raise questions about drug testing and approval. Recently, the drug manufacturer Pfizer, Inc. was sued by thirty Nigerian families who claimed that the company conducted drug experiments on their children without their approval and that six children died as a result of these experiments. These families claim that Pfizer was testing an experimental drug, Trovan, to be used against meningitis. Pfizer researchers chose to use Trovan despite the availability of alternative medicines that had been tested and approved for the treatment of this fatal disease. Major pharmaceutical companies have also been accused of paying doctors in other countries to recruit patients and failing to provide any real guidance about informed consent requirements. As a result, many third-world citizens have been induced to participate in drug trials without giving informed consent. In some cases, the information given to them was misleading and inaccurate or participation was coerced. Some commentators have starkly criticized what they term the globalization of drug testing, claiming that pharmaceutical companies are avoiding the cumbersome drug-approval process in place in countries like the United States by shifting their attention to the third world, where there are few requirements for drug testing and little governmental oversight of pharmaceutical companies.

Controversies in Medical Research

Human Genome Project

an international collaboration of scientists who created a blueprint or map of all human genes, the entities that establish the basic structure and function of the human body that may ultimately be used to identify an individual's predisposition to certain medical diseases

In the last two decades, the drug-approval process has become more sensitized to politics and public opinion in the United States. Other areas of medical research have also become more controversial and susceptible to political decisions, as opposed to policy choices. Among these are the areas of stem cell research, fetal cell research, and cloning. All of these research avenues raise serious questions about the rights of embryos and fetuses. Researchers believe that fetal and embryonic tissue and cells may be very helpful in developing treatments for Parkinson's disease, Alzheimer's, strokes, spinal cord injuries, and other diseases or conditions. We now know much more about how the human body functions than we have ever known, and very recently, scientific research has yielded important insight about the very structure and composition of our genetic makeup. The **Human Genome Project**, which was completed in 2003, provides a complete blueprint of the basic building blocks of human life. The project, a work of international collaboration, has established the location and function of all of the genes in the human genome. If you recall from your basic biology courses, our genes are responsible for much of our physical makeup and perhaps even our behavioral predisposition, as well. Using this map, we may ultimately be able to identify each individual's predisposition to medical issues or diseases. **Genetic engineering**, which is only in its earliest stages, will use the map to expand its applications, and we may one day be able to alter the genetic structure of individuals or groups to lessen their risk of disease.

genetic engineering

using genetic information to treat disease or possibly to alter a person's predisposition to certain illnesses

While genetic testing and engineering have the potential to ease human suffering and ameliorate or eliminate certain diseases, many people worry about how it might be used to undermine individual rights. In the wake of 9/11, commentators have become increasingly concerned about the use of DNA profiling and testing—and about the impact of these practices on the right to privacy. There are serious concerns that genetic testing and screening might be used by employers, insurance companies, and even governmental institutions to identify individuals who might have a disposition toward certain diseases or even behavioral traits. While some analysts argue that our existing laws protect against such abuses, it remains to be seen how this information will ultimately be used. It is very likely that this striking advance in medical technology will place pressure on legislators and regulators to pass laws that protect individual rights, but serious questions remain about the shape that these laws will ultimately take.

SUMMARY

In this chapter, we have been discussing how law affects the practice of medicine and scientific research in the United States and the different social facts or norms that help us understand why these laws look the way they do. Throughout much of the last one hundred years, our laws reflected the assumption that the doctor-patient relationship was privileged and that physicians should be permitted to exercise significant autonomy in treating their patients. We discussed one area of the law, abortion, where the law continues to afford physicians considerable leeway and two other emerging areas, aid in dying and medicinal marijuana, where the law recognizes a special role for physicians. In all three areas, doctors argue that the needs of their patients should trump broad and amorphous arguments about public morality. Like doctors who fight to keep abortion safe and legal, doctors who administer aid in dying or prescribe medicinal marijuana are asserting that they should be permitted substantial latitude in making treatment decisions. Many of our laws reflect an acceptance of this argument. Somewhat paradoxically, while the law in many ways privileges the doctor-patient relationship, the increasingly complex regulations governing medical research seem to be based on the assumption that patients and research subjects should be protected from overzealous doctors and researchers. Our laws aim at ensuring that patients are autonomous and that they fully consent to taking part in research protocols.

This chapter also examined changes in the law governing the testing and approval process for new medications. We talked about how interest-group politics—especially the activities of AIDS activists—have had a powerful effect on the FDA's drug-approval process and have created a fast-track approval process for certain medicines. Finally, in this chapter, we examined developments in mapping the human genome and talked about how the use of genetic testing and profiling will inevitably create pressure for the passage of new laws in this area.

Where law regulates specific practices, like abortion, aid in dying, and medicinal marijuana, we are more likely to allow physicians leeway in providing care. This reflects the norm that the physician's primary responsibility is to the patient. Our experiences with medical research and development, however, lead us to question whether physicians or researchers act as selflessly in these areas. Specifically, the Tuskegee Syphilis Study and the slow federal response to the AIDS crisis lead many to believe that physicians and researchers may sometimes act in their own self-interest. Perhaps not surprisingly, this concern about professional ethics has opened the door to much greater regulation in these areas.

The public debate surrounding these public health issues has grown increasingly fierce, especially in the last decade. Even a cursory glance at the laws governing biomedicine reveals that law has lagged far behind scientific research. There are a number of serious challenges in the near future: among them crafting laws that readily adapt to the rapidly changing biomedical frontier and creating laws that respect the time-honored doctor-patient relationship. It remains to be seen how lawmakers will ultimately address these challenges, but it seems clear that medical and scientific technology will be the subject of an ever-expanding and varied array of federal, state, and municipal laws.

ACTIVE LEARNING

1. Consider the model act on physician aid in dying that was recently created by lawyers, physicians, academics, and Hemlock Society members in Boston to help guide state legislatures that are considering adopting aid-in-dying laws. What are the responsibilities of physicians under this law? What do you think of this law—does it address the needs of those with terminal illnesses while still ensuring that states protect all human life? You can find the act at http://www.pbs.org/newshour/bb/health/die.html.

2. Consider the fast-track provision of the FDA Modernization Act of 1997. What goals do you think it advances? Why do you think this provision is included under the subheading "Improvements"? Note the inclusion of the "information program on clinical trials for serious or life-threatening diseases." Why do you think that Congress established this program? What's the relationship between these two aspects of the statute?

SOURCE: From SAMUELS, *Law, Politics, and Society*, 1E. © 2006 Cengage Learning.

REVIEW QUESTIONS

Multiple-Choice Questions

1 **The law in three areas has changed dramatically as it attempted to respond to important developments in law and medicine. Which of the following is not an area of change?**

A. The role of physicians in the implementation of laws
B. The regulation of research and development
C. The drug approval process
D. The pharmaceutical process

2 **According to Durkheim, laws are based on social facts, which are helpful for**

A. understanding the relationship between law and medicine.
B. understanding political activism specifically.
C. understanding figures of speech.
D. understanding feeling and thinking.

3 **The 1973 *Roe v. Wade* decision allowed a medical exception. Under this exception,**

A. physician groups played a pivotal role in the creation of abortion bans.
B. women whose continued pregnancy endangered their lives or health could obtain an abortion.
C. physicians were expected to provide information to women.
D. physicians would continue to play an important gatekeeping role.

4 **In two cases decided in 1997, *Vacco v. Quill* and *Washington v. Glucksberg,* the U.S. Supreme Court ruled that state laws that banned physician aid in dying**

A. were not unconstitutional.
B. were egregious.
C. did violate the constitutional rights of those who seek this assistance.
D. did not violate the constitutional rights of those who seek this assistance.

5 **One of the laws that initiated the "war on drugs" was**

A. The 1970 Controlled Substances Act.
B. *Vacco v. Quill.*
C. *Washington v. Glucksberg.*
D. *Roe v. Wade.*

6 **The Controlled Substances Act**

A. prohibits the transport of minors across state lines.

B. is a decision that allowed a medical exception.

C. prohibits the sale and distribution of marijuana across state lines.

D. is a decision that allowed physicians to continue to place an important gatekeeping role.

7 **Which of the following is a good example of a policy area where laws privilege the practice of medicine and where physicians are assumed to be acting primarily out of concern for their patients' best interests?**

A. Abortion

B. Aid in dying

C. Medicinal marijuana

D. All of the given answers

8 **What was unethical about the Tuskegee Syphilis Study and lasted from 1932 to 1972?**

A. The treatment was deliberately withheld, so that researchers could study the disease's progression in those who were untreated.

B. The afflicted were all men.

C. The state did not pay the participants in the study.

D. The results were inaccurate.

9 *Informed consent* **means**

A. participants must be informed of the risks and possible benefits of treatment.

B. the benefits of not receiving treatment must be described.

C. both a and b.

D. neither a nor b.

10 **Among current controversies in medical ethics are**

A. stem and fetal cell research.

B. the activities of large, transnational pharmaceutical companies.

C. cloning.

D. all of the given answers.

APPENDIX

World Map

United States Map

INDEX

b after page numbers indicates box; f indicates figure; t indicates table

CHAPTER STRUCTURE AT A GLANCE

	CHAPTER	THEME	READING COMPREHENSION	VOCABULARY COVERAGE	READING STUDY STRATEGY
UNIT 1 READING FOR STRUCTURE THEME *The Brain: Memory, Learning, and Substance Use* Textbook Application Chapter 3: "Caring for Your Mind" from *An Invitation to Health*	1	The Brain and Learning	**Understanding Active Reading** How the Brain Learns Reading Strategies Identifying Topic	Using Context Clues	Surveying and Previewing a Reading
	2	The Brain and Substance Use	**Understanding Patterns of Organization and Supporting Details** Patterns That List Patterns That Explain Patterns That Analyze	Identifying Prefixes and Suffixes	Paraphrase to Aid Comprehension
UNIT 2 READING FOR MAIN IDEAS THEME *Communication and Conflict Across Cultures* Textbook Application Chapter 27: "The Limits of Liberalism: The 1970s" from *HIST*	3	Communication Across Gender and Culture	**Understanding Explicit Main Ideas** Author's Purpose Explicit Main Idea	Recognizing Root Words	Summarizing to Express Main Idea and Supporting Details
	4	Group Behavior	**Understanding Implied Main Ideas** Making Inferences Implied Main Idea	Understanding Figurative Language	Reading and Understanding Literature
UNIT 3 READING FOR STUDY THEME *Education and Responsibility* Textbook Application Chapter 4: "Equity and Education Practice" from *Diverse Histories, Diverse Perspectives*	5	Education and Motivation	**Understanding Text Marking and Annotation**	Improving Your College-Level Vocabulary	Monitoring Your Reading Rate and Comprehension
	6	Social Issues and Social Responsibility	**Understanding Text Note Taking** Types of Notes Note Taking from Reading	Studying Vocabulary	College Reading in the Disciplines
UNIT 4 READING CRITICALLY THEME *Crime, Medicine, and Ethics* Textbook Application Chapter 14: "Law and Medicine" from *Law, Politics, and Society*	7	Crime and Punishment	**Understanding Arguments** Mapping Arguments Fact and Opinion	Recognizing Bias and Tone: Denotation, Connotation, and Loaded Language	How to Read a Variety of Sources
	8	Medical Ethics	**Evaluating Arguments** Evaluating Support Logical Fallacies and Propaganda	Intended Meaning: Euphemisms and Doublespeak	Critical Thinking Strategies